The **Rough Guide** to

Languedoc
and Roussillon

written and researched by

Brian Catlos

**ROUGH
GUIDES**

NEW YORK • LONDON • DELHI

www.roughguides.com

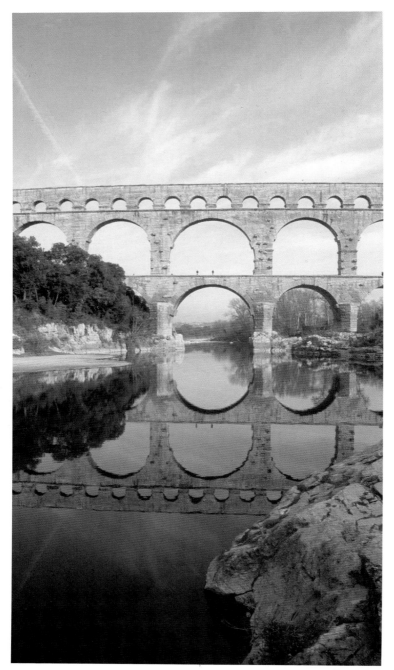

▲ Pont du Gard

Introduction to

Languedoc and Roussillon

The Languedoc and Roussillon region is one of France's best-kept secrets. While Provence and the Côte d'Azur just across the Rhône have been living it up, attracting movie stars and the masses, its less pretentious neighbour has remained in comfortable obscurity. And so much the better for those in the know. Dramatically varied landscapes, two distinct, proud cultures – Occitan and Catalan – a tradition of heresy and steadfast rebellion and age-old customs all combine to make this a great region unmatched in its romantic associations, at once epitomizing and defying everything that is France. Now shaking off centuries of sleepy neglect, Languedoc and Roussillon are emerging as one of the most enticing parts of the country, its remote villages and little-travelled byways affording a window onto a vanishing European rural culture, and its beaches and cities offering a thrilling diversity of activity.

The boundaries of Languedoc have never been easy to fix. In its broadest – and original – sense, Languedoc includes the lands where the Occitan language (the *langue d'Oc*) was spoken in the Middle Ages, an area stretching along the north towards Savoy, through the Massif Central and west along the Atlantic coast, taking in even Bordeaux. Nowadays, for administrative purposes, it has been lumped in together with its neighbour as the modern *région* of Languedoc-Roussillon, and

trimmed down to the strip of coast running from Montpellier west to the
border of Spain. But this latter, narrow definition of Languedoc is as
inappropriate as the traditional one is vague. In defining Languedoc in this
guide we've avoided artificial boundaries in favour of cultural and historical cohesion and the logistics of travel, so that the region butts up to neigh-

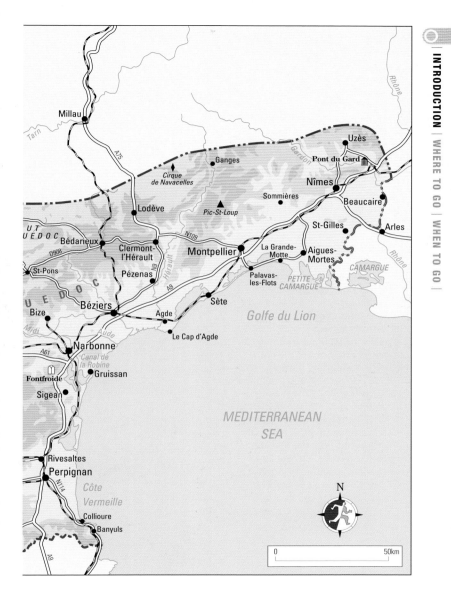

bouring Provence at the Rhône, and stretches west and inland to include the medieval capital of Toulouse, as well as the lands of Foix and Albi. Roussillon, Languedoc's accidental partner, squashed in between the eastern Pyrenees and the Corbières hills, is also characterized by a particular linguistic heritage, derived in this case from a long history as part of the

Fact file

• The area covered by this guide includes most of the modern *région* of Languedoc-Roussillon and the some of the most populated parts of the Midi-Pyrénées. The population of this area is approximately 3,400,000, concentrated in a handful of **urban centres**, including Toulouse, Montpellier, Nîmes and Perpignan. Mid-sized towns include Albi, Béziers, Narbonne, Sète and Carcassonne. Away from the coast, the broad plains of the Lauragais are lightly populated, and many areas of the hilly uplands are all but deserted.

• Languedoc's **terrain** is highly varied. The windswept coast, although rocky in the shadow of the Pyrenees, is generally a flat and sandy expanse, punctuated by salty inlets. Scrubby *garrigues*, rocky hills, rise out of the sun-baked littoral plain, providing shelter for vineyards. Further from the sea, the highlands of Haut Languedoc and the cordillera of the Pyrenees are covered by cooler and damper forests, and mark the transition from the Mediterranean to Atlantic climate zone. On their far side, broad expanses of grain-lands are cut across by the occasional river-valley or ridge.

• Gone are the glory days of woad and silk; today, aside from the industry of Toulouse – and on a smaller scale, that of Carcassonne, Perpignan, Sète and Montpellier – the region's economy depends for the most part on wine and, increasingly, **tourism**. On the coast, mollusc farming supplements the still functioning but declining fishing industry.

Catalan confederacy centred in Barcelona. Both regimes have distinct cultures but, in addition to their border, share a common history of occupation and of resistance and eventual submission to the modern France of Paris and the North.

Where to go

With the tremendous range of sights and activities on offer in Languedoc and Roussillon, where you go will be determined by your interests and inclinations. **Toulouse** is the region's largest city and its most important cultural hub. Here you'll find a thriving nightlife and a collection of world-class museums and monuments, including the Les Abattoirs contemporary art museum and the basilica of St-Sernin. North of the city, the famous vineyards of Gaillac stretch up towards **Albi**, home to the Toulouse-Lautrec museum and an obligatory stop for anyone interested in modern painting. Nearby, the hills and forests of the **Parc du Haut Languedoc,** once the refuge of Protestant Huguenots, are now presided over by the herds of Brébais goats which give Roquefort cheese its famous flavour. To the south, the Ariège river, excellent for rafting in the summer, can

Food and drink

Languedoc and Roussillon present a culinary terrain as varied as their landscape. The coastal towns brim with fresh catch and the cultivated shellfish of the saltwater *étangs*. In the east, the marshy Camargue is home to some of continental Europe's best beef. The rough hills which rise above the plain provide a range of fresh herbs and, in a brief season of glory, truffles. In the broad plains of the Lauragais, duck, the Frenchman's steak, is ubiquitous, along with its fellow fowl, goose, usually in the shape of rich foie gras. This is also the home of Languedoc's "national" dish, cassoulet – a baked-bean stew. In the desolate uplands, pork dominates in the form of chops, feet and a range of regional sausages, while sheep and goats provide the milk for cheeses, both pungent and sweet, and a series of micro-climate valleys produce a bounty of fruit. Aside from Catalan, Spanish and North African food, there is little "ethnic" element in culinary Languedoc, although you will find other French cuisines well represented. The best respite from what can be delicious but eventually monotonous *terroir* fare, is *gastronomique* – adventurous cuisine blending regional elements with diverse ingredients and creative culinary techniques. Wherever you are, wash your meal down with the local wine. Languedoc has a wide selection of traditionally underrated vintages, while along the Tarn, at Gaillac, the interface between Atlantic and Mediterranean climate zones provides conditions for one of the most venerable of appellations.

be followed up into the Pyrenees. Here, south of medieval **Foix**, you'll find some of Europe's oldest and most enigmatic prehistoric caves. The mountains themselves have trails and pistes which make for spectacular hiking or skiing, depending on the season. The **Canal du Midi**, a placid tree-lined waterway and the largest UNESCO World Heritage site on earth, leads east from Toulouse towards the Mediterranean, passing under the walls of **Carcassonne**, the greatest of the heretic fortresses and France's most recognizable medieval monument. Southeast of here, **Montségur** lies deep in Cathar country, at the upper end of the Aude and its stunning array of castle ruins, romantically perched on isolated cliff-tops.

Nothing could contrast with this more than the **Camargue**, the swampy delta of the Rhône, which forms Languedoc's northern frontier – home to the bull ranches which fuel the region's passion for the *corrida*. The beauty of the sun-baked *garrigues* just inland

Cathars

It's hard to imagine a more romantic episode of the Middle Ages. A peaceful people, living in a land of troubadours and poets, following the religion of their choosing, are declared heretics by a grasping and imperious papacy. This unleashes a series of brutal and drawn-out military campaigns, sanctified as Crusades, but in fact wars of aggressive colonialism waged by northern French nobles and churchmen on the unsuspecting locals.

▼ Foix Castle

It's a story of knights and lords, martyrdoms, Inquisition, lost treasures, a proud but beleaguered nation and castles perched on rocky spurs, ending in the destruction of the Cathar faith, the suppression of Occitan culture and the subjugation of the people of Languedoc. The truth was far more complex than this popular and exaggerated Sir Walter Scott-ish version of the events, but the story of the Cathars is a fascinating and exciting introduction to the region's history, long buried by the modern French state.

was well known to the Romans, whose monuments in and around **Nîmes**, including the famous **Pont du Gard** aqueduct, bear witness to the area's ancient glory. From here, you can either follow the path of the Roman super-highway, the **Via Domitia**, or the medieval Santiago pilgrim route past a series of atmospheric fortress-towns, like **Aigues-Mortes** and **Sommières**, or you can dip down to the coast, a long swathe of sandy beach broken only by the salty inlets which are home to shellfish and windsurfers. Just south, **Montpellier** is a thriving multicultural city, close to the sea and with a lively street-life sustained by the student population of its famous university, which has been turning out graduates for eight hundreed years. From here, the Hérault valley provides access to a rocky hinterland where you can visit the ancient monastery of **St-Guilhem-le-Désert** or hike through the spectacular **Cirque de Navcelles**.

At **Pézenas**, a town whose cobbled streets are girded by seventeenth-century palaces, the sun-baked Languedocian plain opens out. Medieval **Béziers** and Roman **Narbonne** preside over an expanse of archetypal Midi landscape. Blue skies are set off against the red soil and the iridescent green of seemingly endless vineyards. Only the ports, **Agde** and **Sète**, justly famed for their seafood and maritime traditions, manage to shake off the pleasant torpor of the plains.

Further south, Roussillon (French Catalonia), snuggles in the foothills of the Pyrenees, a region whose vivid contrasts have inspired artists including the Fauvists and Picasso. The capital, **Perpignan**, makes an ideal jumping-off point for visiting the rocky coves of the Côte Vermeille, or ascending the river valleys into the heart of the *département*. On the coast, **Collioure** and **Banyuls** are beautifully set beach towns, lacking the crass commercialism which characterizes the worst of the coastal resorts. Inland, the narrow-gauge Train

The Camargue forms Languedoc's northern frontier – home to the bull ranches which fuel the region's passion for the *corrida*

Jaune winds upwards past **Le Canigou**, the mountain-symbol of the Catalan people, and the evocative old garrison towns of **Villefranche** and **Mont–Louis**, while the festivals at **Prades** and **Céret** make a great introduction to the lively Catalan folk traditions.

▲ Collioure market

▲ St-Guilhem-le-Désert

When to go

Whenever you visit, Languedoc and Roussillon offer a rich range of sights and activities to enjoy. The **summer season**, the time when most people come, offers a range of advantages but also some short-comings. In July and August you can count on long **museum and monument hours**, as well as the widest selection of hotels and restaurants, many of which are seasonal. The weather is generally **warm** and **sunny** enough that you can swim throughout the region, be it in the Mediterranean or in the nearest lake or river. Many of the region's village festivals take place in the summer, along with an array of special concert series. On the other hand, queues lengthen along with the opening hours. In summer months competition for accommodation is often fierce; you'll be forced to book ahead for hotels, particularly on the coast, and this can detract from the spontaneous aspect of your travels. Traffic is also increasingly problematic in summer; the coastal highways and byways are chock-a-block with frenzied drivers rushing to get either to the beach or back home. If you're thinking of a cycling holiday, you'll probably want to confine yourself to the quieter (and hillier) upland roads.

On the other hand, the long **off-season**, from November through to Easter, sees many services shut down and museum and monument hours reduced. Many of the villages, along with a lot of hotels and restaurants, all but shut down, with the exception of the Pyrenean **ski resorts** which, of course, are at their busiest. The weather is unreliable; it is frequently cold and grey, and a light layer of snow makes the Cathar ruins more **romantic** but less comfortable to explore. This is, however, arguably the best time

Canal du Midi

In the 1660s, a local tax-collector, Paul Riquet, dreamed of bringing prosperity back to Languedoc by building a canal to link it to the Mediterranean and the Atlantic. This mammoth civic engineering project was the most complex and greatest such undertaking since the time of the Romans. Although it bankrupted the visionary Riquet, who did not live to see its inauguration, by 1856 the canal was carrying one million passengers and over 100,000 tonnes of freight per year. Struck down into sudden obsolescence by the invention of the steam engine, the canal system languished in over a century of disrepair, before being resurrected in the last few decades as a tourist attraction. The quintessential Languedoc experience is to boat, walk or cycle along Riquet's canal, travelling at an easy pace, the tree-lined hedges providing shelter from the same sun which coaxes up the region's famous grapes.

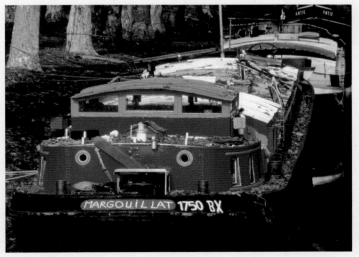

▲ Barge on the Canal du Midi

▲ Camargue festival

to visit urban centres like Toulouse and Montpellier; with their student populations in residence, these cities spring to life. Not only do theatre and opera seasons get under way, but the **bars and clubs** pack out with throngs of young folk. Christmas and Lent breathe additional life into the countryside in the form of an array of colourful and unique festivities.

> The beauty of the sun-baked garrigues was well known to the Romans, whose monuments bear witness to the area's ancient glory

The best time to go is probably the **shoulder seasons**, May and June, and September, which offer a good balance between tranquillity and action. In early June you can visit a town like Cordes and find it quiet and not yet overrun. The cities will be winding down their university seasons and the cultural programmes are preparing their finales. With a bit of luck, you'll get good weather, although you may find swimming only suits the

▲ Carré d'Art, Nîmes

brave. The **grape harvest** and **bull-fighting** festivals are in full swing, and even the coastal roads are still relatively safe for two-wheelers. You'll also more or less have your pick of the hotels and restaurants and will generally still be charged low-season prices.

Average temperatures and rainfall

		Jan	Apr	Jul	Oct
Toulouse	precipitation mm/in	50/2	60/2.4	38/1.5	58/2.3
	av high temp °C/F	7/45	17/62	27/81	17/63
	av low temp °C/F	3/38	6/43	15/59	9/48
Montpellier	precipitation mm/in	50/2	60/2.4	38/1.5	58/2.3
	av high temp °C/F	10/50	17/63	28/82	19/67
	av low temp °C/F	2/36	6/43	16/60	9/48
Foix	precipitation mm/in	68/2.7	54/2.6	22/0.88	61/2.4
	av high temp °C/F	10/50	17/62	27/81	19/66
	av low temp °C/F	2/36	9/48	17/63	10/50
Perpignan	precipitation mm/in	51/2	56/2.4	18/0.7	89/3.6
	av high temp °C/F	12/53	17/62	28/82	20/68
	av low temp °C/F	4/40	9/48	19/67	12/54

things not to miss

It's not possible to see everything that Languedoc and Roussillon have to offer in one trip – and we don't suggest you try. What follows is a selective and subjective taste of the region's highlights: outstanding natural features, spectacular cities, history, culture and beautiful architecture. They're arranged in five colour-coded categories to help you find the very best things to see, do and experience. All entries have a page reference to take you straight into the Guide, where you can find out more.

01 **La Grotte de Niaux** Page **164** • Enigmatic prehistoric cave-paintings in the remote Pyrenees.

02 **Train Jaune** Page **364** • Twisting up into the high valleys of the Pyrenees, this revived narrow-gauge line is a worthy excursion in itself and perfect for hikers.

04 **The Orb valley** Page **333** • Follow this mountain river valley through near-forgotten hamlets.

03 **La Petite Camargue** Page **253** • Ride on horseback or cruise the canals and saltpans of Durrell's "Little Argentina."

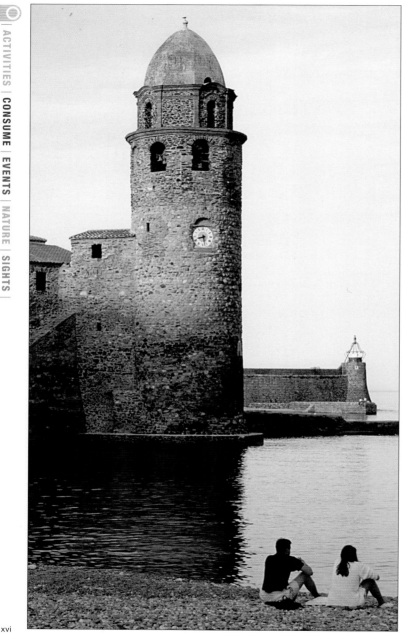

05 Collioure Page **380** • Roussillon at its most Catalan: a picturesque beach town presided over by a medieval castle.

06 **Tauromachie** Page **226** • Get swept up in the excitement and drama of the "art of the bull".

07 **Rabastens** Page **190** • Get a rare glimpse of a medieval church in all of its painted glory.

08 **Le Canigou** Page **362** • Bonfires and a torch-light pilgrimage illuminate Catalonia's sacred mountain in mid-summer.

10 Seafood Page **44** • Whether cultivated in the Bassin de Thau or fished from the sea, the area's seafood is a must.

11 Montségur Page **145** • The romantic and mysterious last redoubt of the Cathars.

09 The monastery of St-Roman Page **243** • Medieval monks hewed out this underground monastic complex on the banks of the Rhône.

12 Nîmes amphitheatre Page **226** • The gladiators have been replaced by bullfighters but, 2000 years on, this 20,000-seat stadium is still packing in the crowds.

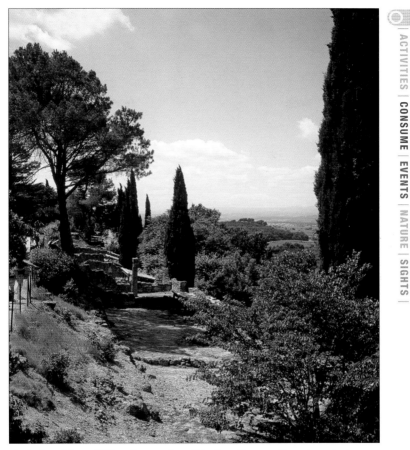

13 **Oppidum D'Ensérune** Page **324** • A pre-Roman settlement, perched on a ridge above the vineyards of Béziers.

xix

14 **Beaches** Page **261** • From naked hedonism to romantic solitude, Languedoc's Mediterranean beaches offer it all.

15 **Cordes-sur-Ciel** Page **186** • Cruise the boutiques, or enjoy the evocative atmosphere in this hill-top Cathar town.

16 **Swimming at the Pont Du Gard** Page **237** • Take a dip under the lofty arches of this extraordinary Roman Aqueduct.

17 **Water jousting** Page 282 • Originating centuries ago in Sète, this sport is now a passionate fixture of Languedoc traditional culture.

18 **Cirque de Navacelles** Page 293 • A dramatic ox-bow canyon, which cuts through the causse of the upper Hérault.

19 **Christmas traditions** Page **349** • Pessebres, caganers and cagatiós set Roussillon's Christmas festivities apart from the rest of France.

20 **Outdoor activities** Page **55** • The regions' rivers and hills offer a full range of hiking, trekking and winter-sports activities.

21 Pézenas Page **260** • Languedoc's former capital and the stomping ground of Molière still evokes the glory of the Age of Absolutism.

22 Carcassonne Page **121** • France's most famous and evocative medieval citadel.

24 Aigues Mortes Page **243** •
Visit this "perfectly embalmed" medieval walled town, romantically set among swamps and dunes.

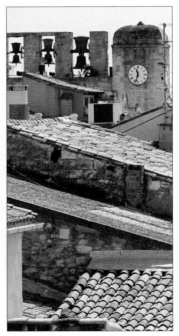

23 Toulouse Lautrec Page **178** •
This Languedoc native revolutionized nineteenth-century art; enjoy the largest collection of his work and visit his childhood estate.

Contents

Using this Rough Guide

We've tried to make this Rough Guide a good read and easy to use. The book is divided into six main sections, and you should be able to find whatever you want in one of them.

Colour section

The front colour section offers a quick tour of Languedoc and Roussillon. The **introduction** aims to give you a feel for the place, with suggestions on where to go – we also tell you what the weather is like. Next, our authors round up their favourite aspects of Languedoc and Roussillon in the **things not to miss** section – whether it's great food, amazing sights or a special hotel. Right after this comes a full **contents** list.

Basics

The Basics section covers all the **pre–departure** nitty-gritty to help you plan your trip. This is where to find out which airlines fly to your destination, what paperwork you'll need, what to do about money and insurance, about Internet access, food, security, public transport, car rental – in fact just about every piece of **general practical information** you might need.

Guide

This is the heart of the Rough Guide, divided into user-friendly chapters, each of which covers a specific region. Every chapter starts with a list of **highlights** and an **introduction** that helps you to decide where to go, depending on your time and budget. Likewise, introductions to the various towns and smaller regions within each chapter should help you plan your

itinerary. We start most town accounts with information on arrival and accommodation, followed by a tour of the sights, and finally reviews of places to eat and drink, and details of nightlife. Longer accounts also have a directory of practical listings. Each chapter concludes with **public transport** details for that region.

Contexts

Read Contexts to get a deeper understanding of what makes Languedoc and Roussillon tick. We include a brief history, and a detailed further reading section that reviews dozens of **books** relating to the country.

Language

The **language** section gives useful guidance for speaking French and Occitan and pulls together all the vocabulary you might need on your trip, including a comprehensive menu reader. Here you'll also find a glossary of words and terms peculiar to the area.

Index + small print

Apart from a **full index**, which includes maps as well as places, this section covers publishing information, credits and acknowledgements, and also has our contact details in case you want to send in updates and corrections to the book – or suggestions as to how we might improve it.

Map and chapter list

- Colour section
- Contents
- **B** Basics
- **1** Toulouse and around
- **2** Carcassonne, the Upper Aude and Ariège
- **3** Albi and Haut Languedoc
- **4** Nîmes and around
- **5** Montpellier and around
- **6** Narbonne, Béziers and around
- **7** Roussillon
- **C** Contexts
- **L** Language
- **I** Index + small print

3

Contents

Colour section   i–xxiv

Introduction iii
Colour map iv
Where to go vi

When to go x
Things not to miss xiv

Basics   7–67

Getting there 9
Red tape and visas 18
Information, websites and maps 19
Insurance 23
Costs, money and banks 24
Getting around 28
Accommodation 36
Eating and drinking 41
Communications 47
The media ....:......................................51

Opening hours, public
    holidays and festivals 52
Sports and outdoor activities 53
Crime and personal safety 56
Living and working in France 58
Travellers with disabilities 61
Senior travellers 64
Travelling with children 64
Gay and lesbian travellers 65
Directory 66

Guide   69–384

**❶ Toulouse and
    around**............................71–115
Toulouse 73
Lavaur and around 100
Revel and around 105
Sorèze and Dourgne 106
Castelnaudary 107
Canal du Midi: Toulouse
to Carcassonne 111

**❷ Carcassonne, the Upper
    Aude and Ariège** 117–168

Carcassonne 121
The upper Aude valley 132
The Pays de Sault 141
Mirepoix and the lower
    Ariège valley 147
The Couserans 157
The upper Ariège valley 161

**❸ Albi and Haut
    Languedoc** 169–211
Albi and around 174
Ambialet 182

4
■

Carmaux and around 183
Cordes-sur-Ciel 186
Gaillac and around 188
Graulhet, Réalmont and Lautrec 191
Castres and around 193
The Parc du Haut Languedoc 198
Mazamet and the Montagne Noire .. 207

❹ **Nîmes and around** 213–258
Nîmes 219
Uzès 233
The Pont du Gard and around 237
Beaucaire and around 240
St-Gilles and around 244
The Camarguaise coast 249
The Vidourle valley 254

❺ **Montpellier and
   around** 259–298
Montpellier 262
La Grande-Motte and around 277
Palavas and Maguelone 278
Sète 280
The Bassin de Thau and Mèze 283
Pézenas and around 285
Clermont-l'Hérault, Lac
   Salagou and around 289

Lodève and around 291
North to Ganges via the
   Cirque de Navacelles 293
Ganges and around 294
South to Montpellier 295

❻ **Narbonne, Béziers
   and around** 299–336
Narbonne and around 303
The Corbières 315
Canal du Midi: east
   from Carcassonne 318
Béziers and around 325
The Orb valley 333

❼ **Roussillon** 337–384
Perpignan and around 341
The Fenouillèdes 354
The lower Têt valley 357
The Pic du Canigou and around 362
The upper Têt and the Capcir 365
The Cerdagne and the
   Carlit Massif 368
The Tech valley and the Albères 371
The Côte Vermeille 376

Contexts   385–410

History 387

Books 405

Language   411–432

Occitan 413
Catalan 415

French 417
Glossary 430

Index + small print   453–464

Credits...455
Acknowledgements 456
Readers' letters..................................456

Photo credits.......................................457
Index 458
map symbols 464

Basics

Basics

Getting there 9

Red tape and visas 18

Information, websites and maps 19

Insurance...23

Costs, money and banks..24

Getting around 28

Accommodation..36

Eating and drinking..41

Communications 47

The media 51

Opening hours, public holidays and festivals............52

Sports and outdoor pursuits......................................53

Crime and personal safety...56

Living and working in France......................................58

Travellers with disabilities 61

Senior travellers 64

Travelling with children...64

Gay and lesbian travellers..65

Directory...66

Getting there

The quickest and most cost-effective way of reaching Languedoc and Roussillon from most parts of Britain is by air, though in the southeast of England this is now rivalled closely by the Channel Tunnel rail link, from where you can connect to the fast and efficient TGV services south from Lille and Paris. The standard rail- or road-and-sea routes are more affordable, but can be uncomfortable and tiring – and if you're just going for a short break, the journey time can significantly eat into your holiday. This is doubly so for Ireland, from where the least troublesome option is a flight to Languedoc, usually via a London hub.

Getting to Languedoc and Roussillon from North America is straightforward; there are direct flights from over thirty major cities to Paris, from where you can either take an internal flight to the region or transfer to France's excellent train network. Many people travelling to France from Australia and New Zealand will choose to travel via London although there are scheduled flights to Paris from Sydney, Melbourne, Brisbane, Cairns, Perth and Auckland.

Airfares always depend on the season, with the highest being around mid-June to mid-September, when the weather is best; fares drop during the "shoulder" seasons – Easter to mid-June and mid-September through October – and you'll get the best prices during the low season, November to Easter (excluding Christmas and New Year when prices are hiked up and seats are at a premium). Note also that flying on weekends ordinarily adds to the round-trip fare; price ranges quoted below assume midweek travel.

You can often cut costs by going through a specialist flight agent – either a consolidator, who buys up blocks of tickets from the airlines and sells them at a discount, or a discount agent, who in addition to dealing with discounted flights may also offer special student and youth fares and a range of other travel-related services such as travel insurance, rail passes, car rentals, tours and the like. Some agents specialize in charter flights, which may be cheaper than anything available on a scheduled flight, but again departure dates are fixed and withdrawal penalties are high.

Booking flights online

Many airlines and discount travel websites offer you the opportunity to book your tickets **online**, cutting out the costs of agents and middlemen. Good deals can often be found through discount or auction sites, as well as through the airlines' own websites.

Online booking agents and general travel sites

Ⓦ **travel.yahoo.com** Incorporates a lot of Rough Guide material in its coverage of destination countries and cities across the world, with information about places to eat, sleep and so on.
Ⓦ **www.cheapflights.com** Bookings from the UK and Ireland only (for US, wwww.cheapflight.com; for Canada, Ⓦ www.cheapflights.ca; for Australia, Ⓦ www.cheapflights.com.au). Flight deals, travel agents, plus links to other travel sites.
Ⓦ **www.cheaptickets.com** Discount flight specialists (US only).
Ⓦ **www.etn.nl/discount.htm** A hub of consolidator and discount agent Web links, maintained by the nonprofit European Travel Network.
Ⓦ **www.expedia.com** Discount airfares, all-airline search engine and daily deals (US only; for the UK, Ⓦ www.expedia.co.uk; for Canada, Ⓦ www.expedia.ca).
Ⓦ **www.flyaow.com** Online air travel info and reservations site.
Ⓦ **www.gaytravel.com** Gay online travel agent, offering accommodation, cruises, tours and more.
Ⓦ **www.geocities.com/thavery2000** Has an extensive list of airline toll-free numbers (from the US) and websites.
Ⓦ **www.hotwire.com** Bookings from the US only. Last-minute savings of up to forty percent on regular

9
▪

published fares. Travellers must be at least 18 and there are no refunds, transfers or changes allowed. Log-in required.

Ⓦ **www.lastminute.com** Offers good last-minute holiday package and flight-only deals (UK only; for Australia, Ⓦ www.lastminute.com.au).

Ⓦ **www.opodo.co.uk** User-friendly, UK-only booking site – owned by major airlines such as BA and Air France – with good deals on flights and packages.

Ⓦ **www.priceline.com** Name-your-own-price website that has deals at around forty percent off standard fares. You cannot specify flight times (although you do specify dates) and the tickets are non-refundable, non-transferable and non-changeable (US only; for the UK, Ⓦ www.priceline.co.uk).

Ⓦ **www.skyauction.com** Bookings from the US only. Auctions tickets and travel packages using a "second bid" scheme. The best strategy is to bid the maximum you're willing to pay, since if you win you'll pay just enough to beat the runner-up regardless of your maximum bid.

Ⓦ **www.smilinjack.com/airlines.htm** Lists an up-to-date compilation of airline website addresses.

Ⓦ **www.travelocity.com** Destination guides, hot Web fares and best deals for car hire, accommodation and lodging as well as fares. Provides access to the travel agent system SABRE, the most comprehensive central reservations system in the US.

Ⓦ **www.travelshop.com.au** Australian website offering discounted flights, packages, insurance and online bookings.

Organized tours

Many tour operators are discovering the walking, biking and boating possibilities of Languedoc and Roussillon. Listed below are some of the better companies which offer tours in the region. Flight arrangements from home may or may not come as part of the packages.

Tour operators

Abercrombie & Kent UK ☎020/7730 9600, Ⓦ www.abercrombiekent.co.uk; US & Canada ☎1-800/323-7308 or 630/954-2944, Ⓦ www.abercrombiekent.com; Australia ☎03/9536 1800 or 1300/851 800, New Zealand ☎0800/441 638,

Ⓦ www.abercrombiekent.com.au. Upmarket biking and walking tours.

In France

Château de Quarante ☎04.67.89.40.41, Ⓦ chateaudequarante.com. For the upper-crust. Gourmet living in a private castle by night, chauffeur-driven custom touring by day.

France OK France Ⓦ www.franceok.com. Based in Argèles-sur-Mer; arranges walking and gourmet tours in Roussillon.

Rosé Exposé Events ☎04.68.43.99.70 Ⓦ www.drink-pink.com. Wine get-away weekends in the Aude.

In the UK

ACE Study Tours ☎012/23 835055, Ⓦ www.study-tours.org. Sophisticated educational tours including Romanesque art itineraries.

Susie Madron's Cycling for Softies 2 & 4 Birch Polygon, Manchester M14 5HX ☎0161/248 8282, Ⓦ www.cycling-for-softies.co.uk. An easy-going cycle holiday operator. Although luggage transfer is not included in the deals, this can be arranged for an additional fee.

Thomas Cook ☎0870/5666 222, Ⓦ www.thomascook.co.uk. Long established one-stop 24-hour travel agency for package holidays or scheduled flights, with bureau de change issuing Thomas Cook travellers' cheques, travel insurance and car rental.

In the US and Canada

Adventure Center ☎1-800/228-8747 or 510/654-1879, Ⓦ www.adventurecenter.com. Hiking and "soft adventure" specialists.

Caprice Tours ☎1-866-2FRANCE, Ⓦ www.caprice-tours.com. Cultural and linguistic tours.

Discover France ☎1-800/960-2221 or 480/905-1325, Ⓦ www.discoverfrance.com. Bike tours in Languedoc.

Europe Through the Back Door ☎425/771-8303 ext. 298, Ⓦ www.ricksteves.com. Small-group and tailor-made tours.

Globus ☎1-866/755-8581, Ⓦ www.globusjourneys.com. Planned vacation packages.

In Australia and New Zealand

Explore Holidays ☎02/9423 8080, Ⓦ www.exploreholidays.com.au. Accommodation, boat rental and package tours.

Walkabout Gourmet Adventures ☎03/5159 6556, Ⓦ www.walkaboutgourmet.com. Classy food, wine and walking tours, including a Pyrenees itinerary.

Flights from the UK and Ireland

Flying is the quickest way of getting to Languedoc and Roussillon: you can fly into Toulouse in less than two hours from London, for example. Direct flights from British regional airports also exist, and prices are not unfavourable compared with London fares. However, as often as not, if you live outside London, you'll find it pays to go to the capital and fly on to France from there: scheduled flights from London to Toulouse are available for as little as £120 and to Montpellier for around £140. To find the best deals you should shop around, ideally a month or so before you plan to leave.

Predictably, Air France and British Airways are the main carriers to France from Britain, offering **scheduled flights** and Apex fares which must be reserved one or two weeks in advance (depending on the route taken), and must include one Saturday night. Your return date must be fixed when purchasing, and no subsequent changes are allowed. **Air France** fly from Heathrow at least once daily direct to Toulouse, and to Paris Charles de Gaulle (from where you can make onward connections to Montpellier and Toulouse) around ten times daily; they also fly four times daily from London City (Mon–Fri) to Paris CDG, and daily from Manchester, Birmingham, Edinburgh and Glasgow. **British Airways** fly three times daily from Gatwick to Marseille, and once daily to Montpellier; they also fly to Paris CDG three times daily from Gatwick, eight times daily from Heathrow and at least once daily from Birmingham, Manchester, Newcastle, Aberdeen, Edinburgh and Glasgow.

A couple of **low-cost airlines** – Ryanair and EasyJet – also offer scheduled flights into the region – or hubs within easy striking distance of it. There are no advance purchase conditions with these airlines, but obviously the earlier you book your seat the greater chance you have of taking advantage of special offers and availability. **Ryanair** fly once daily out of Stansted to Montpellier, Nîmes and Perpignan and Carcassonne; return fares can drop as low as £20, but generally they range, depending on season, from £60–150 for Carcassonne, and £45–125 for other destinations, all exclusive of tax and subject to restrictions. **EasyJet** flies daily from Stansted to Toulouse, for as little as £60 each way. Both airlines service Scottish and Irish regional airports. **BMIBaby** connects Toulouse to the East Midlands and Cardiff (several weekly).

By far the most convenient way to fly from the **Irish Republic** to Languedoc and Roussillon is with Go Holidays, who arrange charter flights in high season (April–Sept) from Shannon, Cork and Dublin to Toulouse, Montpellier and Marseille (from about £300), and also do fly-and-drive rental deals. Other options include flying with Aer Lingus, direct from Dublin to Toulouse, or to Paris CDG, and continuing by air or overland from there; or with Ryanair, who have two flights daily from Dublin to Beauvais Tillé airport outside Paris.

From **Northern Ireland**, British Airways fly directly from Belfast City Airport to Paris CDG, but prices are generally much higher than taking a routing through London or Amsterdam – for example, Ryanair fly out of Derry Airport to London Stansted for around £75, from where you can pick up their onward flight to their various Languedoc destinations.

A good place to look for **discount fares** from London to France is the classified travel sections of papers such as the *Independent* and the *Daily Telegraph* (Saturday editions), the *Observer*, *Sunday Times* and *Independent on Sunday*, where agents advertise special deals; if you're in London, check the back pages of the listings magazine *Time Out*, the *Evening Standard* or the free travel mag *TNT*, found outside mainline train stations. Independent travel specialists such as STA Travel and Campus Travel do deals for students and anyone under 26, or can simply sell a scheduled ticket at a discount price. Bear in mind that any travel agent can sell you a **package deal** with a tour operator (see p.10) and these can often offer exceptional bargain travel; sometimes it's possible to just buy the ticket for the **charter flight** – in theory supposed to be sold in conjunction with accommodation – at a discount.

Airlines

Aer Lingus UK ☎0845/084 4444, Republic of Ireland ☎0818/365 000, ⓦwww.aerlingus.ie
Air France UK ☎0845/0845 111, ⓦwww.airfrance.co.uk, Republic of Ireland ☎01/605 0383, ⓦwww.airfrance.com/ie
bmibaby UK ☎0870/264 2229, Republic of Ireland ☎01/236 6130 ⓦwww.bmibaby.com
British Airways UK ☎0845/77 333 77, Republic of Ireland ☎1800/626 747, ⓦwww.ba.com
British European UK ☎0870/5676 676, Republic of Ireland ☎1890/925 532, ⓦwww.flybe.com
British Midland UK ☎0870/607 0555, Republic of Ireland ☎01/407 3036, ⓦwww.flybmi.com
CityJet Republic of Ireland ☎01/844 5566 for reservations via Air France
easyJet UK ☎0870/600 0000, ⓦwww.easyjet.com
Ryanair UK ☎0871/246 0000, Republic of Ireland ☎0818/303 030, ⓦwww.ryanair.com

Flight and travel agents

Aran Travel International Republic of Ireland ☎091/562 595, ⓦhomepages.iol.ie/~arantvl/aranmain.htm. Good-value flights to all parts of the world.
CIE Tours International Republic of Ireland ☎01/703 1888, ⓦwww.cietours.ie. General flight and tour agent.
Flightbookers UK ☎0870/010 7000, ⓦwww.ebookers.com. Low fares on an extensive selection of scheduled flights.
Flynow UK ☎0870/444 0045, ⓦwww.flynow.com. Large range of discounted tickets; official South African Airways agent.
Go Holidays Republic of Ireland ☎01/874 4126, ⓦwww.goholidays.ie. Package tour specialists.
Joe Walsh Tours Republic of Ireland ☎01/676 0991, ⓦwww.joewalshtours.ie. General budget fares agent.
McCarthy's Travel Republic of Ireland ☎021/427 0127, ⓦwww.mccarthystravel.ie. General flight agent.
Neenan Travel Republic of Ireland ☎01/607 9900, ⓦwww.neenantrav.ie. Specialists in European city breaks.
Premier Travel Northern Ireland ☎028/7126 3333, ⓦwww.premiertravel.uk.com. Discount flight specialists.
STA Travel UK ☎0870/1600 599, ⓦwww.statravel.co.uk. Worldwide specialists in low-cost flights and tours for students and under-26s, though other customers welcome.
Student & Group Travel Republic of Ireland

☎01/677 7834. Student and group specialists, mostly to Europe.
Top Deck UK ☎020/7244 8000, ⓦwww.topdecktravel.co.uk. Long-established agent dealing in discount flights.
Travel Cuts UK ☎020/7255 2082 or 7255 1944, ⓦwww.travelcuts.co.uk. Canadian company specializing in budget, student and youth travel and round-the-world tickets.
usit NOW Republic of Ireland ☎01/602 1600, Northern Ireland ☎028/9032 7111, ⓦwww.usitnow.ie. Student and youth specialists for flights and trains.

Flights from the US and Canada

Transatlantic fares to France from the US are very reasonable, thanks to intense competition. Any local travel agent should be able to access airlines' up-to-the-minute fares, although they may not have time to research all the possibilities, and you could call the airlines direct. The lowest discounted scheduled fares you're likely to get in low and high season flying midweek to Paris are in the $500/1000 range (low/high season) from Chicago or Houston, slightly higher from Los Angeles, and cheapest from New York and Washington DC. From Canada, the lowest discounted scheduled **fares** for mid-week travel to Paris in low/high season will be around Can$700/1200 from Montréal or Toronto and Can$1000/1500 from Vancouver. In both Canada and the US, regular carriers often have trans-Atlantic seat-sales and specials in shoulder- and off-season. It is sometimes possible to get to Paris for as little as US$300/Can$450.

Most airlines use Paris as the transatlantic gateway to France, though some charter carriers offer direct flights to Marseille in late spring to early autumn. Nearly a dozen different **scheduled airlines** operate flights to Paris. Air France has the most frequent and convenient service, but their fares tend to be on the expensive side. Other airlines offering non-stop services to Paris from a variety of US cities are United, daily from Chicago, San Francisco and Washington DC; Delta, daily from Cincinnati, Atlanta and New York; and TWA, daily from New York and St Louis. For the best fares, check the ads in Sunday newspaper travel sections and book with a discount agent or consolidator. It's also worth considering **charter flights**, which operate from late spring to early autumn. Barring special offers, the cheapest fare is usually an **Apex** ticket, although this will carry certain restrictions: you have to book – and pay – at least 21 days before departure, spend at least seven days abroad (maximum stay three months), and you tend to get penalized if you change your schedule. On transatlantic routes there are also winter **Super Apex** tickets, sometimes known as "Eurosavers" – slightly cheaper than an ordinary Apex, but limiting your stay to between seven and 21 days. Some airlines also issue **Special Apex** tickets to people younger than 24, often extending the maximum stay to a year. Many airlines offer youth or student fares to **under-25s**; a passport or driving licence is sufficient proof of age, though these tickets are subject to availability and can have eccentric booking conditions. It's worth remembering that most cheap return fares involve spending at least one Saturday night away and that many will only give a percentage refund if you need to cancel or alter your journey, so make sure you check the restrictions carefully before buying a ticket.

A further possibility is to see if you can arrange a **courier flight**, although the hit-or-miss nature of these makes them most suitable for a single traveller who travels light and has a very flexible schedule. In return for shepherding a parcel through customs and possibly giving up your baggage allowance, you can expect to get a deeply discounted ticket. For more options, consult *Courier Bargains: How to Travel Worldwide for Next to Nothing* by Kelly Monaghan (US$14.95) or read *The Intrepid Traveler* (ⓦwww.intrepid-traveler.com), now out of print and slightly out-dated (1998) but still useful for ideas. Flights are issued on a first-come, first-served basis, and there's no guarantee that the Paris route will be available at the time you want. Round-trip fares cost from around US$375, with last-minute specials as low as US$175 for flights booked within three days of departure.

Airlines

Air Canada ☎1-888/247-2262, ⓦwww.aircanada.ca

Air France US ☎1-800/237-2747, ⓦwww.airfrance.com, Canada ☎1-800/667-2747, ⓦwww.airfrance.ca
American Airlines ☎1-800/433-7300, ⓦwww.aa.com
British Airways ☎1-800/247-9297, ⓦwww.british-airways.com
Continental Airlines domestic ☎1-800/523-3273, international ☎1-800/231-0856, ⓦwww.continental.com
Delta Air Lines domestic ☎1-800/221-1212, international ☎1-800/241-4141, ⓦwww.delta.com
Iberia ☎1-800/772-4642, ⓦwww.iberia.com
Lufthansa US ☎1-800/645-3880, Canada ☎1-800/563-5954, ⓦwww.lufthansa-usa.com
Northwest/KLM Airlines domestic ☎1-800/225-2525, international ☎1-800/447-4747, ⓦwww.nwa.com, ⓦwww.klm.com
United Airlines domestic ☎1-800/241-6522, international ☎1-800/538-2929, ⓦwww.ual.com
US Airways domestic ☎1-800/428-4322, international ☎1-800/622-1015, ⓦwww.usair.com
Virgin Atlantic Airways ☎1-800/862-8621, ⓦwww.virgin-atlantic.com

Courier flights

Air Courier Association ☎1-800/282-1202, ⓦwww.aircourier.org. Courier flight broker. Membership (3 months/$19, 1yr/$29, 3yr/$58, 5yr/$87) also entitles you to twenty percent discount on travel insurance and name-your-own-price non-courier flights.
International Association of Air Travel Couriers ☎308/632-3273, ⓦwww.courier.org. Courier flight broker with membership fee of $45/yr or $80 for two years.

Discount travel companies

Air Brokers International ☎1-800/883-3273, ⓦwww.airbrokers.com. Consolidator and specialist in round-the-world and Circle Pacific tickets.
Airtech ☎212/219-7000, ⓦwww.airtech.com. Standby seat broker; also deals in consolidator fares and courier flights.
Council Travel ☎1-800/2COUNCIL, ⓦwww.counciltravel.com. Nationwide organization that mostly specializes in student/budget travel. Flights from the US only. Owned by STA Travel.
Educational Travel Center ☎1-800/747-5551 or 608/256-5551, ⓦwww.edtrav.com. Student/youth discount agent.
New Frontiers ☎1-800/677-0720 or 310/670-

7318, ⓦ www.newfrontiers.com. French discount travel firm based in Los Angeles.

SkyLink US ☎ 1-800/AIR-ONLY or 212/573-8980, Canada ☎ 1-800/SKY-LINK, ⓦ www.skylinkus.com. Consolidator.

STA Travel US ☎ 1-800/781-4040, Canada 1-888/427-5639, ⓦ www.sta-travel.com. Worldwide specialists in independent travel; also student IDs, travel insurance, car rental, rail passes, etc.

Student Flights ☎ 1-800/255-8000 or 480/951-1177, ⓦ www.isecard.com. Student/youth fares, student IDs.

TFI Tours ☎ 1-800/745-8000 or 212/736-1140, ⓦ www.lowestairprice.com. Consolidator.

Travac ☎ 1-800/TRAV-800, ⓦ www.thetravelsite.com. Consolidator and charter broker with offices in New York City and Orlando.

Travel Avenue ☎ 1-800/333-3335, ⓦ www.travelavenue.com. Full-service travel agent that offers discounts in the form of rebates.

Travel Cuts Canada ☎ 1-800/667-2887, US ☎ 1-866/246-9762, ⓦ www.travelcuts.com. Canadian student travel organization.

Worldtek Travel ☎ 1-800/243-1723, ⓦ www.worldtek.com. Discount travel agency for worldwide travel.

Flights from Australia and New Zealand

Airfares **from east-coast gateways** are common rated, with Ansett and Qantas providing a shuttle service to the point of international departure. **From Perth and Darwin** they're around Aus$100–300 less via Asia, and Aus$400 more via the US. There's a host of airlines operating a service between major cities in Australia – with either a transfer or overnight stop in their home ports – to Paris.

The airlines listed below all have service from Australia to Paris CDG, and most also connect to New Zealand. Regularly priced tourist class fares should be upwards of Aus$2000 and NZ$3500. Be sure to check **discount brokers** and specialist agents (listed below) before settling on a fare. You also may want to investigate **Round-the-World** fares as a possible alternative to a return flight.

Airlines

Air Canada Australia ☎ 1300/655 747 or 02/9286 8900, New Zealand ☎ 09/379 3371, ⓦ www.aircanada.com

Air France Australia ☎ 02/9244 2100, New Zealand ☎ 09/308 3352, ⓦ www.airfrance.com.au

Air New Zealand Australia ☎ 13 24 76, ⓦ www.airnz.com.au, New Zealand ☎ 0800/737 000, ⓦ www.airnz.co.nz

American Airlines Australia ☎ 1300/130 757, New Zealand ☎ 09/309 9159, ⓦ www.aa.com

British Airways Australia ☎ 1300/767 177, New Zealand ☎ 0800/274 847 or 09/356 8690, ⓦ www.britishairways.com

Cathay Pacific Australia ☎ 13 17 47, ⓦ www.cathaypacific.com/au, New Zealand ☎ 09/379 0861 or 0508/800 454, ⓦ www.cathaypacific.com/nz

Delta Air Lines Australia ☎ 02/9251 3211, New Zealand ☎ 09/379 3370, ⓦ www.delta.com

KLM/Northwest Airlines Australia ☎ 1300/303 747, ⓦ www.klm.com/au_en, New Zealand ☎ 09/309 1782, ⓦ www.klm.com/nz_en

Lufthansa Australia ☎ 1300/655 727, ⓦ www.lufthansa-australia.com, New Zealand ☎ 09/303 1529, ⓦ www.lufthansa.com/index_en.html

Qantas Australia ☎ 13 13 13, ⓦ www.qantas.com.au, New Zealand ☎ 0800/808 767, ⓦ www.qantas.co.nz

Scandinavian Airlines (SAS) Australia ☎ 1300/727 707, New Zealand agent: Air New Zealand ☎ 09/357 3000, ⓦ www.scandinavian.net

Singapore Airlines Australia ☎ 13 10 11, New Zealand ☎ 0800/808 909, ⓦ www.singaporeair.com

Swiss Australia ☎ 1300/724 666, ⓦ www.swiss.com

Thai Airways Australia ☎ 1300/651 960, New Zealand ☎ 09/377 0268, ⓦ www.thaiair.com

United Airlines Australia ☎ 13 17 77, ⓦ www.unitedairlines.com.au, New Zealand ☎ 09/379 3800 or 0800/508 648, ⓦ www.unitedairlines.co.nz

Virgin Atlantic Airways Australia ☎ 02/9244 2747, New Zealand ☎ 09/308 3377, ⓦ www.virgin-atlantic.com

Travel agents

Flight Centre Australia ☎ 13 31 33 or 02/9235 3522, ⓦ www.flightcentre.com.au, New Zealand ☎ 0800 243 544 or 09/358 4310, ⓦ www.flightcentre.co.nz

New Zealand Destinations Unlimited New Zealand ☎ 09/414 1685 ⓦ www.holiday.co.nz

Northern Gateway Australia ☎ 1800/174 800, ⓦ www.northerngateway.com.au

STA Travel Australia ☎ 1300/733 035, ⓦ www.statravel.com.au, New Zealand ☎ 0508/782 872, ⓦ www.statravel.co.nz

Student Uni Travel Australia ☎02/9232 8444,
🖥www.sut.com.au, New Zealand ☎09/379 4224,
🖥www.sut.co.nz
Trailfinders Australia ☎02/9247 7666,
🖥www.trailfinders.com.au

Specialist agents

Adventure World Australia ☎02/8913 0755,
🖥www.adventureworld.com.au, New Zealand
☎09/524 5118, 🖥www.adventureworld.co.nz.
Agents for a vast array of international adventure
travel companies.
Australian Pacific Touring Australia
☎1800/675 222 or 03/9277 8555, New Zealand
☎09/279 6077, 🖥ww.aptours.com. Package tours
and independent travel to Europe.
France Unlimited Australia ☎03/9531 8787. All
French travel arrangements, including châteaux
stays, Alpine hiking and cycling tours.
French Travel Connection Australia ☎02/9966
1177, 🖥www.frenchtravel.com.au. Everything to
do with travel to and around France.
Silke's Travel Australia ☎1800 807 860, or
02/8347 2000, 🖥www.silkes.com.au. Gay and
lesbian specialist travel agent.
Snow Bookings Only ☎1800/623 266,
🖥www.snowbookingsonly.com.au. Skiing holidays,
including in France.
travel.com.au and **travel.co.nz** Australia
☎1300/130 482 or 02/9249 5444,
🖥www.travel.com.au, New Zealand ☎0800/468
332, 🖥www.travel.co.nz. Comprehensive online
travel company.
Travel Notions Australia ☎02/9552 3355,
🖥www.unitednotions.com.au/travelnotions. France
specialists, and agents for leisurely "Cycling for
Softies" tours.
Travelplan Australia ☎02/9958 1888 or
1300/130 754, 🖥www.travelplan.com.au. Skiing in
Europe.

By rail from the UK and Ireland

The Channel Tunnel has slashed travelling
time by **train** to France and has also led to a
multitude of cut-rate deals on regular train
and ferry or hovercraft fares via Calais,
Boulogne and Dieppe. Crossing the Channel
by sea and making onward connections to
Languedoc and Roussillon by train can work
out to be slightly cheaper than using the
Channel Tunnel, but you should note that it
does take considerably longer, and is generally less convenient.

See "Getting Around", p.29 for details of
the various rail passes available for travel
within Europe.

Rail contacts

Eurostar UK ☎0870/160 6600,
🖥www.eurostar.com.
Passenger train which goes from Waterloo
International in London to the Continent via Ashford
in Kent (itself 1hr from London) and the Channel
Tunnel. The cheapest return ticket to Paris is
currently £60, though restrictions apply. You can get
through-ticketing – including the tube journey to
Waterloo International – from Eurostar (see above),
from most travel agents or from mainline train
stations in Britain; typical add-on prices for a return
ticket to Paris from Edinburgh or Glasgow is £35,
from Manchester £25 and Birmingham £15. Note
that Inter-Rail passes give discounts on the Eurostar
service.
International Rail UK ☎0870/120 1606 or
01962/773 646, 🖥www.international-rail.com.
Formerly known as Holland Rail; offers a wide variety
of rail options.
Northern Ireland Railways UK ☎028/9089
9411, 🖥www.nirailways.co.uk. Also sells Inter-Rail
passes.
Rail Europe UK ☎0870/584 8848,
🖥www.raileurope.co.uk. SNCF French Railways.
Trainseurope UK ☎0900/195 0101,
🖥www.trainseurope.co.uk

By ferry from the UK and Ireland

Though undoubtedly less convenient than
travelling by plane or via the Channel Tunnel
by train, **ferry**, **hovercraft and catamaran
services** can work out to be much the
cheapest way of getting to Languedoc and
Roussillon, especially if you are travelling in a
group, or are planning on hitching your way
south through France. The most frequent
crossings are between Dover and Calais,
and Folkestone and Boulogne, while the
services out of Portsmouth to St-Malo,
Cherbourg, Caen and Le Havre are amongst
the most competitively priced. If you're coming from the north of England or Scotland,
you should consider an overnight ferry to
Zeebrugge (Belgium), either from Hull (with
P&O North Sea Ferries) or from Rosyth (with
Rosyth Zeebrugge ferries, 🖥www.rosythfer-
ry.co.uk). From Ireland you can take a ferry

direct from Rosslaire (near Wexford) to either Cherbourg or Roscoff.

Ferry **prices** are seasonal and, for motorists, depend on the size of your vehicle. The popular Dover–Calais routing costs from £120 one-way for a car and two adults. Note that return prices are substantially cheaper than one-way fares, but generally need to be booked in advance – details of routes and companies are listed below. You can either contact the companies direct to reserve space in advance – essential in peak season if you're intending to drive – or any travel agent in the UK or France will do it for you. All ferry companies also offer foot passenger fares only, from £20 one-way; accompanying bicycles can usually be carried free, at least in the low season, and for a charge of around £5 one-way in mid- and high seasons.

The ferry companies will often offer **special deals** on three-, five- and ten-day returns, or discounts for regular users who own a property abroad. The tour operator **Eurodrive** (☎020/8324 4009, ⓦwww.eurodrive.co.uk) can also arrange discounts on ferry crossings for people taking their cars across the Channel. The cheapest way of getting to France from Ireland – though far from the quickest – is by **ferry** from Cork or

Rosslare outside Wexford to Cherbourg or Roscoff, in Brittany. From here you can head south by car or continue your journey by train – any of the ferry operators detailed below should be able to arrange an **onward train ticket** when you book your ferry crossing direct with them.

Ferry contacts

Brittany Ferries UK ☎0870/901 2400, Republic of Ireland ☎021/4277 801, ⓦwww.brittanyferries.co.uk. Poole to Cherbourg; Portsmouth to Caen and St Malo; Plymouth to Roscoff and to Santander (March–Nov/Dec); Cork to Roscoff (March–Oct only).

Hoverspeed UK ☎0870/240 8070, ⓦwww.hoverspeed.co.uk. Twenty-four daily departures. Dover to Calais and Ostend; Newhaven to Dieppe.

Irish Ferries UK ☎0870/517 1717, Northern Ireland ☎0800/0182 211, Republic of Ireland ☎1890/313 131, ⓦwww.irishferries.com. Dublin to Holyhead; Rosslare to Pembroke, Cherbourg and Roscoff. Continental services March to end Sept.

P&O North Sea Ferries UK ☎0870/129 6002, ⓦwww.ponorthseaferries.com. Hull to Rotterdam and Zeebrugge.

P&O Portsmouth UK ☎0870/242 4999, ⓦwww.poportsmouth.com. Portsmouth to

CHANNEL PORTS & ROUTES TO PARIS

Cherbourg, Le Havre and Bilbao.

P&O Stena Line UK ☎ 0870/600 0600 or 01304/864 003, ⓦ www.posl.com. Dover to Calais.

Sea Cat UK ☎ 0870/5523 523, Republic of Ireland ☎ 1800/805055, ⓦ www.seacat.co.uk. Belfast to Stranraer, to Heysham, to Troon, and to Isle of Man; Dublin to Liverpool and to Isle of Man.

Sea France ☎ 0870/571 1711, ⓦ www.seafrance.com. Dover to Calais.

By car from the UK and Ireland

It's a long drive south to Languedoc and Roussillon from the north coast of France, but if you do want to take your **car** with you, the most convenient way is to drive down to the **Channel Tunnel**, load your car on the train shuttle, and be whisked under the Channel in 35 minutes, arriving at Coquelles on the French side, near Calais. The Channel Tunnel entrance is off the M20 at junction 11A, just outside Folkestone, and the sole operator, **Eurotunnel** (☎ 0870/535 3535, ⓦ www3.eurotunnel.com), offers a frequent, daily service. Because of the frequency of the service, you don't have to buy a ticket in advance (though this might be advisable in mid-summer and during other school holidays), but you must arrive at least thirty minutes before departure; the target loading time is just ten minutes.

Inside the carriages, you can get out of your car to stretch your legs during the crossing. Tickets are available through Eurotunnel's Customer Service Centre, on the Internet or from your local travel agent. Fares are calculated per car, regardless of the number of passengers, and rates depend on the time of year, time of day and length of stay (the cheapest ticket is for a day-trip, followed by a five-day return); it's cheaper to travel between 10pm and 6am, while the highest fares are reserved for

weekend departures and returns in July and August. As an example, a five-day trip at an off-peak time starts at £99 (passengers included) in the low season and goes up to £163 in the peak period.

If you don't want to drive far when you've reached France, you can take advantage of SNCF's **motorail**, which you can book through Rail Europe, putting your car on the train in either Calais or Paris for Narbonne or Toulouse. This is a relatively expensive option though: for four people travelling from Calais to Toulouse, for example, the regular one-way price ranges from £269, dependent on the time of year.

By bus

Eurolines run regular bus-ferry services from London Victoria to over sixty French cities. Prices are very much lower than for the same journey by train, with adult return fares at the time of writing £49 (£29 if booked 30 days in advance) to Toulouse, the journey time being roughly nineteen hours. Regional return fares from the rest of England and from Wales are available as are student and youth discounts. Again, prices are very much lower than for the same journey by train. **Tickets** are available directly from the company, from National Express agents and from most high-street travel agents.

Bus contacts

Busabout UK ☎ 020/7950 1661, ⓦ www.busabout.com. Sells European bus passes of varying duration (available via STA in the US). **Eurolines** UK ☎ 0870/514 3219, Republic of Ireland ☎ 01/836 6111, ⓦ www.eurolines.co.uk. Tickets can also be purchased from any Eurolines or National Express agent (☎ 0870/580 8080, ⓦ www.nationalexpress.co.uk or ⓦ www.gobycoach.com).

Red tape and visas

Citizens of EU (European Union) countries can travel freely in France; and citizens of Australia, Canada, the United States and New Zealand, among other countries, do not need any sort of visa to enter France, and can stay for up to ninety days. However, the situation can change and it is advisable to check with your embassy or consulate before departure. Note that the British Visitor's Passport is no longer available.

EU citizens (or other non-visa citizens) who **stay longer than three months** are officially supposed to apply for a **carte de séjour**, for which you'll have to show proof of income at least equal to the minimum wage (at least €1050 per month). However, EU passports are rarely stamped, so there is no evidence of how long you've been in the country. If your passport does get stamped, you can cross the border – to Spain, for example – and re-enter for another ninety days legitimately.

French embassies and consulates overseas

Britain

Embassy 58 Knightsbridge, London SW1X 7JT ☎020/7201 1004

Ireland

Embassy 36 Ailesbury Rd, Ballsbridge, Dublin 4 ☎01/260 1666

US

Embassy 4101 Reservoir Rd NW, Washington DC 20007 ☎202/944 6195, Ⓦwww.info-france-usa.org
Consulates Prominence in Buckhead, Suite 1840, 3475 Piedmont Rd NE, Atlanta, GA 30305 ☎404/495 1660, Ⓦwww.consulatfrance-atlanta.org; 31 St James Ave, Park Square Building, Suite 750, Boston, MA 02116 ☎617/542 7374, Ⓦwww.consulatfrance-boston.org; 737 North Michigan Ave, Suite 2020, Chicago, IL 60611 ☎312/787 5360, Ⓦwww.consulatfrance-chicago.org; 777 Post Oak Blvd, Suite 600, Houston, TX 77056 ☎713/572 2799, Ⓦwww.consulatfrance-houston.org; 10990 Wilshire Blvd, Suite 300, Los Angeles, CA 90024 ☎310/235 3200, Ⓦwww.consulatfrance-losangeles.org; One Biscayne Tower, 17th floor, South Biscayne Blvd, Miami, FL 33131 ☎305/372 9799, Ⓦwww.consulatfrance-miami.org; 1340 Poydras St, Amoco Building, Suite 1710, New Orleans, LA 70112 ☎504/523 5772, Ⓦwww.consulfrance-nouvelleorleans.org; 934 Fifth Ave, New York, NY 10021 ☎212/606 3689, Ⓦwww.consulatfrance-newyork.org; 540 Bush St, San Francisco, CA 94108 ☎415/397 4330, Ⓦwww.consulatfrance-sanfrancisco.org

Canada

Embassy 42 Sussex Drive, Ottawa, ON K1M 2C9 ☎613/789 1795, Ⓦwww.amba-ottawa.fr
Consulates 777 Main St, Suite 800, Moncton, NB E1C 1E9 ☎506/857 4191, Ⓦwww.moncton.consulfrance.org; 1 place Ville Marie Bureau 2601, Montréal, QC H3B 4S3 ☎514/878 4385, Ⓦwww.montreal.consulfrance.org; 25 rue St-Louis, Québec, QC G1R 3Y8 ☎418/694 2294, Ⓦwww.quebec.consulatfrance.org; 130 Bloor St West, Suite 400, Toronto, ON M5S 1N5 ☎416/925 8044, Ⓦwhttp://www.consulfrance-toronto.org/; 1100–1130 West Pender St, Vancouver, BC V6E 4A4 ☎604/681 4345, Ⓦwhttp://www.consulfrance-vancouver.org/

Australia

Consulates Ⓦwww.ambafrance-au.org: 492 St Kilda Rd, Melbourne, VIC 3001 ☎03/9820 0921; 31 Market St, Sydney, NSW 2000 ☎02/9261 5779.

Information, websites and maps

The French Government Tourist Office gives away large quantities of maps and glossy brochures for Languedoc and Roussillon, including lists of hotels and campsites. Some of these – like the maps of the inland waterways or footpaths, lists of festivals and so on – can be useful; others are just so much dead wood. For reviews of useful websites in France, see p.20.

In Languedoc and Roussillon itself you'll find a **tourist office** – usually an Office du Tourisme (OT) but sometimes a Syndicat d'Initiative (SI) – in practically every town and many villages (addresses, contact details and opening hours are detailed in the Guide). For the practical purposes of visitors, there is little difference between them: SIs have wider responsibilities for encouraging business, while Offices du Tourisme deal exclusively with tourism; sometimes they share premises and call themselves an OTSI. In small villages where there is no OT or SI, the *mairie* (mayoral office), frequently located in the Hôtel de Ville (town hall), will offer a similar service.

From all these offices you can get specific local information, including listings of hotels and restaurants, leisure activities, car and bike rental, bus timetables, laundries and countless other things; many can also book accommodation for you. Most offices will provide a free town plan (though some places charge a nominal €0.75–1.50), if asked, and will have maps and local walking guides on sale. In mountain regions they display daily meteorological information and often share premises with the local hiking and climbing organizations. In the larger cities you can usually also pick up free *What's On* guides. The regional or departmental tourist offices also offer useful practical information (see below).

French government tourist offices

The official French Government Tourist Office, La Maison de France, is on the Web at ⓦ www.franceguide.com.

UK

178 Piccadilly, London W1V 0AL ☎ 0891/244 123, 50p/min, ⓕ 020/7493 6594

Ireland

10 Suffolk St, Dublin 2 ☎ 01/679 0813, ⓕ 679 0814

US

444 Madison Avenue, 16th floor, New York, NY 10022 ☎ 212/838 7800, ⓕ 838 7855, ⓦ www.francetourisme.com; 676 North Michigan Avenue, Suite 3360, Chicago, IL 60611-2819 ☎ 312/751 7800, ⓕ 337 6339; 9454 Wilshire Blvd, Suite 715, Beverly Hills, CA 90212-2967 ☎ 310/271 6665 or 310/272 2661, ⓕ 276 2835

Canada

1981 Avenue McGill College, Suite 490, Montréal, QUE H3A 2W9 ☎ 514/288 4264, ⓕ 845 4868

Australia

25 Bligh St, Level 22, Sydney, NSW 2000 ☎ 02/9231 5244, ⓕ 9221 8682.
Note that New Zealand does not have a French Government Tourist Office.

Regional and departmental tourist offices

Comité Régional du Tourisme Languedoc-Roussillon: 20 rue de la République, 34000 Montpellier ☎ 04.67.22.81.00, ⓕ 04.67.58.06.10, ⓦ www.cr-languedocroussillon.fr/tourisme
Comité Départemental du Tourisme Ariège-Pyrénées: 31bis av de Général-de-Gaulle, BP 143, 09004 Foix ☎ 04.61.02.30.70, ⓕ 04.61.65.17.34, ⓦ www.ariege.pyrenees.com
Comité Départemental du Tourisme Aude: Conseil General, 11855 Carcassonne ☎ 04.68.11.66.00, ⓕ 04.68.11.66.01, ⓦ www.audetourisme.com
Comité Départemental du Tourisme Gard: 3 pl des Arènes, 30010 Nîmes ☎ 04.66.36.96.30, ⓕ 04.66.36.13.14
Comité Départemental du Tourisme Hérault

en Languedoc: Maison du Tourisme, av des Moulins, BP 3067, 34043 Montpellier ☎04.67.67.71.71, ⓕ04.67.67.71.77, ⓦwww.herault-en-languedoc.com
Comité Régional du Tourisme du Midi-Pyrénées: 54 bd de l'Embouchure, BP 2166, 31022 Toulouse ☎05.61.13.55.55, ⓕ05.61.47.17.16, ⓔcrt.midi-pyrenees@wanadoo.fr
Comité Départemental du Tourisme Pyrénées-Orientales: 7 quai de Lattre-de-Tassigny, BP 540, 66005 Perpignan ☎04.68.66.61.11, ⓕ04.68.67.06.10, ⓦwww.pyrenees-orientales.com
Comité Départemental du Tourisme Tarn: BP 225, 81006 Albi ☎05.63.77.32.10, ⓕ05.63.77. 32.32, ⓦwww.resinfrance.com

Websites

The existence of Minitel and the relatively low level of personal computer ownership in France contributed to the rather slow adoption of the **Internet** here, but in recent years the situation has changed and France as a nation has come fully online. You'll find websites which deal with practically every aspect of life in Languedoc and Roussillon, from Cathars to cookery. On the down side, many of these pages do not have working **English-language** versions, although they are gradually coming to be seen as indispensable in all but the most locally focused sites. As anywhere on the Net, persistent combing of links pages and use of search engines (among the best are ⓦwww.google.com and ⓦwww .dogpile.com, and the France-based ⓦwww.enfin.com) will almost certainly get you the information you are looking for.

Websites or, in the case of accommodation and tourist offices email addresses (if there's no website available), are given throughout the Guide, and as a supplement to this see below for a list of some of the most useful and important French websites. See ⓦwww .kropla.com for details of how to plug your laptop in when abroad, phone country codes around the world and information about electrical systems in different countries.

France on the Net

Tourism and recreation sites

ⓦ**www.tourist-office.org** Handy database of

France's municipal and local tourist offices arranged by région and département. Town listings have practical and cultural information and links to local websites.

ⓦ**www.pagesjaunes.fr** The complete French Yellow pages, unbeatable for hunting down goods and services. If your French is weak use inc onjunction with a dictionary/translation site like ⓦwww.babelfish.com.

ⓦ**www.viamichelin.com** The Euro-version of MapQuest allows you to map out detailed point-to-point driving itineraries around France and Europe, and gives you complete trip information and driving directions, free.

ⓦ**www.franceguide.com** The official site of the French Government Tourist Office, with news, information on local festivals and useful links. Has a good English-language version.

ⓦ**www.cr-languedocroussillon.fr** Languedoc-Roussillon's official website, with links to activities, accommodation, gastronomy and culture. One of the best starting points, but limited to the boundaries of the modern administrative région.

ⓦ**www.monuments-france.fr** and ⓦ**www.monum.fr** Information on over 200 national monuments and museums – many in Languedoc and Roussillon – including news on special events.

ⓦ**www.fr-holidaystore.co.uk** France Holiday Store is a useful site for planning with tour operators – everything from cycling to canal cruising, fly-drive and short breaks and skiing. Property search with over 1000 places listed with photos-plus-brochure searches and regional and tourist info.

ⓦ**www.little-france.com** Roussillonaise weekly webzine with information on culture, tourism, art, politics and economy.

ⓦ**www.pyrenees-online.fr** The homepage of Pyrénées-Online, with information on accommodation, sights, recreational activities and regional specialities.

ⓦ**www.cr-mip.fr** Guide to festivals in the Midi-Pyrénées région, with information dates, venues and admission prices as well as links to web pages of participating cultural and arts groups.

ⓦ**www.europe-today.com/france** English-language master-site for outdoor activities in Languedoc and Roussillon. Features contact details for a variety of sports and pursuits, from canyoning to parachuting.

News and information sites

ⓦ**www.gksoft.com/govt** Gateway to English-language listings of all French government websites, including embassies, departmental and regional tourist boards, political parties, municipalities and media.

@ **www.radio-france.fr** Radio France's official
page has national and international news coverage,
current affairs, as well as music, culture and the
latest in French sports. French language only.
@ **www.lemonde.fr** The French-language Web
version of one of France's most reputable daily
newspapers. Includes national and international
news, culture and sports.
@ **www.france2.fr** France TV 2's daily Web page
has the latest on news, weather and road conditions,
as well as listings and reviews of cultural events.
Also has a youth section.
@ **www.humanite.presse.fr** France's oldest daily,
the official Communist paper, co-founded by Jean
Jaurès.
@ **www.francedaily.com** English language Web
newspaper with French, European and world news.

Arts and culture sites

@ **web.culture.fr** French Ministry of Culture's
page, with information on everything from
monuments to exhibitions and also comprehensive
lists of links to organizations related to the whole
gamut of artistic media.
@ **www.bpi.fr** Home page of the Bibliothèque
Pompidou, with good links to media and a very
comprehensive list of arts and humanities pages for
France.
@ **www.revue-spectacle.com** Arts page, set up
by a group of newspapers and radio stations in
cooperation with the Ministry of Culture. Covers
theatre, dance and mime events and is updated
monthly. No English version presently, but a link to
the Babelfish translation page.
@ **www.ladanse.com** Multilingual site with
comprehensive information on French and
international dance including news, links and a
database of artists and companies.
@ **www.cathares.org** Everything you wanted to
know about Cathars but were afraid to ask. A
French-only site featuring information on culture,
history and historical sites, as well as regular
updates on related events and exhibitions.
@ **wwwoccitanet.free.fr** A French-only site
dedicated to the cuisine of Languedoc, and featuring
weekly recipes, information regarding food-oriented
events and festivals, and links to other culinary sites.
@ **www.multimania.com/simorre/oc/presoc.htm**
English-language website ideal if you want to learn
more about Occitan langauge. Links to the history
and literature (including works in translation), as well
information on grammar and a short tutorial.
@ **perso.wanadoo.fr/joseph.riera/menu.htm**
French-language page dedicated to the history and
culture of "French Catalonia" – Roussillon – with
detailed explanations of history, customs and language.

Maps

In addition to the various free leaflets – and
the maps in this guide – the one extra map
you'll probably want is a reasonable **road
map** of Languedoc and Roussillon. The
Michelin (@ www.michelin-travel.com) yellow
series (1:200,000 scale) is best for the
motorist; maps 235 and 240 cover the entire
area of the Guide. You can get the whole
series in one large spiral-bound *Atlas Routier*.
For a single map of Languedoc and
Roussillon (except for the St-Girons area) try
Euromap's Languedoc (1:300,000). A useful
free map for car drivers, obtainable from filling stations and traffic information kiosks in
France, is the Bison Futé map, showing alternative back routes to the congested main
roads, clearly signposted on the ground by
special green Bison Futé road signs.

If you're planning to **walk or cycle**, check
the IGN (Institut Géographique National)
maps – either green (1:100,000 and
1:50,000), or the more detailed blue
(1:25,000) series. The IGN 1:100,000 series
is the smallest scale available that has the
contours marked – essential for cyclists,
who tend to cycle off 1:25,000 maps in a
couple of hours. Routes in the French
Pyrenees are well covered by the twelve
maps in the *Randonnées Pyrénées* series
(1:50,000). Route planning can be done
online at @ www.viamichelin.com.

Map outlets

In the UK and Ireland

Blackwell's Map and Travel Shop 50 Broad St,
Oxford OX1 3BQ ☎01865/793 550,
@ maps.blackwell.co.uk
Easons Bookshop 40 O'Connell St, Dublin 1
☎01/858 3881, @ www.eason.ie
Heffers Map and Travel 20 Trinity St, Cambridge
CB2 1TJ ☎01865/333 536, @ www.heffers.co.uk
Hodges Figgis Bookshop 56–58 Dawson St,
Dublin 2 ☎01/677 4754
The Map Shop 30a Belvoir St, Leicester LE1 6QH
☎0116/247 1400,
@ www.mapshopleicester.co.uk
National Map Centre 22–24 Caxton St, London
SW1H 0QU ☎020/7222 2466,
@ www.mapsnmc.co.uk, @ info@mapsnmc.co.uk
Newcastle Map Centre 55 Grey St, Newcastle-
upon-Tyne, NE1 6EF ☎0191/261 5622

Ordnance Survey Ireland Phoenix Park, Dublin 8 ☎ 01/802 5300, ⓦ www.osi.ie

Ordnance Survey of Northern Ireland Colby House, Stranmillis Ct, Belfast BT9 5BJ ☎ 028/9025 5755, ⓦ www.osni.gov.uk

Stanfords 12–14 Long Acre, London WC2E 9LP ☎ 020/7836 1321, ⓦ www.stanfords.co.uk, ⓔ sales@stanfords.co.uk

The Travel Bookshop 13–15 Blenheim Crescent, London W11 2EE ☎ 020/7229 5260, ⓦ www.thetravelbookshop.co.uk

In the US and Canada

Adventurous Traveler.com US ☎ 1-800/282-3963, ⓦ adventuroustraveler.com

Book Passage 51 Tamal Vista Blvd, Corte Madera, CA 94925 ☎ 1-800/999-7909, ⓦ www.bookpassage.com

Distant Lands 56 S Raymond Ave, Pasadena, CA 91105 ☎ 1-800/310-3220, ⓦ www.distantlands.com

Elliot Bay Book Company 101 S Main St, Seattle, WA 98104 ☎ 1-800/962-5311, ⓦ www.elliotbaybook.com

Globe Corner Bookstore 28 Church St,

Cambridge, MA 02138 ☎ 1-800/358-6013, ⓦ www.globercorner.com

Map Link 30 S La Patera Lane, Unit 5, Santa Barbara, CA 93117 ☎ 1-800/962-1394, ⓦ www.maplink.com

Rand McNally US ☎ 1-800/333-0136, ⓦ www.randmcnally.com

The Travel Bug Bookstore 2667 W Broadway, Vancouver V6K 2G2 ☎ 604/737-1122, ⓦ www.swifty.com/tbug

World of Maps 1235 Wellington St, Ottawa, Ontario K1Y 3A3 ☎ 1-800/214-8524, ⓦ www.worldofmaps.com

In Australia and New Zealand

The Map Shop 6–10 Peel St, Adelaide, SA 5000 ☎ 08/8231 2033, ⓦ www.mapshop.net.au

Specialty Maps 46 Albert St, Auckland 1001 ☎ 09/307 2217, ⓦ www.specialtymaps.co.nz

MapWorld 173 Gloucester St, Christchurch ☎ 0800/627 967 or 03/374 5399, ⓦ www.mapworld.co.nz

Mapland 372 Little Bourke St, Melbourne, Victoria 3000 ☎ 03/9670 4383, ⓦ www.mapland.com.au

Perth Map Centre 900 Hay St, Perth, WA 6000 ☎ 08/9322 5733, ⓦ www.perthmap.com.au

Insurance

Even though EU health care privileges apply in France, you'd do well to take out an insurance policy before travelling to cover against theft, loss and illness or injury. Before paying for a new policy, however, it's worth checking whether you are already covered: some all-risks home insurance policies may cover your possessions when overseas, and many private medical schemes include cover when abroad. In Canada, provincial health plans usually provide partial cover for medical mishaps overseas, while holders of official student/teacher/youth cards in Canada and the US are entitled to meagre accident coverage and hospital in-patient benefits. Students will often find that their student health coverage extends during the vacations and for one term beyond the date of last enrolment.

After exhausting the possibilities above, you might want to contact a specialist travel insurance company, or consider the travel insurance deal we offer (see box below). A typical travel insurance policy usually provides cover for the loss of baggage, tickets and – up to a certain limit – cash or cheques, as well as cancellation or curtailment of your journey. Most of them exclude so-called dangerous sports unless an extra premium is paid: in France this can mean scuba-diving, whitewater rafting, windsurfing and trekking, though probably not kayaking or jeep safaris. Many policies can be chopped and changed to exclude coverage you don't need – for example, sickness and accident benefits can often be excluded or included at will. If you do take medical coverage, ascertain whether benefits will be paid as treatment proceeds or only after you return home, and whether there is a 24-hour medical emergency number. When securing baggage cover, make sure that the per-article limit – typically under £500 – will cover your most valuable possession. If you need to make a claim, you should keep receipts for medicines and medical treatment, and in the event you have anything stolen, you must obtain an official statement from the police (called a *constat de vol*).

Rough Guide travel insurance

Rough Guides Ltd offers a low-cost travel insurance policy, especially customized for our statistically low-risk readers by a leading British broker, provided by the American International Group (AIG) and registered with the British regulatory body, GISC (the General Insurance Standards Council). There are five main Rough Guides insurance plans: **No Frills** for the bare minimum for secure travel; **Essential**, which provides decent all-round cover; **Premier** for comprehensive cover with a wide range of benefits; **Extended Stay** for cover lasting four months to a year; and **Annual Multi-Trip**, a cost-effective way of getting Premier cover if you travel more than once a year. Premier, Annual Multi-Trip and Extended Stay policies can be supplemented by a "Hazardous Pursuits Extension" if you plan to indulge in sports considered dangerous, such as scuba-diving or trekking. For a policy quote, call the Rough Guide Insurance Line: toll-free in the UK ☏0800/015 09 06 or ☏+44 1392 314 665 from elsewhere. Alternatively, get an online quote at ⊕www.roughguides.com/insurance.

Costs, money and banks

Because of the relatively low cost of accommodation and eating out, at least by northern European standards, Languedoc and Roussillon are not expensive places to visit, though this will depend on the relative strength of your own country's currency against the euro. When and where you go also makes a difference: hotel rates rise throughout the region in July and August, most dramatically in coastal resorts, but also in places which are major tourist attractions, like Carcassonne. More economical accommodation can sometimes be found in less visited areas, but increasing regulation has led many small-town hotels to close down, with those remaining deliberately aimed at tourists.

Standard **banking hours** are Monday to Friday 9am to 4pm or 5pm. Some close at midday (noon/12.30pm–2/2.30pm); some are open on Saturday 9am to noon. All are closed on Sunday and public holidays. They will have a notice on the door if they do currency exchange. **Rates and commission** vary from bank to bank, so it's worth shopping around; the usual procedure is a 1–2 percent commission on travellers' cheques and a flatrate charge on cash. Be wary of banks claiming to charge no commission at all; often they are merely adjusting the exchange rate to their own advantage.

There are **money exchange counters** (*bureaux de change*) at all the airports in the region and at the train stations of Toulouse and Montpellier, with usually one or two in town centres as well, often keeping much longer hours than the high-street banks. You'll also find **automatic exchange machines** at airports and train stations and outside many money exchange bureaux. They accept £10 and £20 notes as well as dollars and other European currency notes, but offer a very poor rate of exchange.

Average costs

For a reasonably comfortable existence, including a hotel room for two, a light restaurant lunch and a proper restaurant dinner plus moving around, café stops and museum visits, you need to allow at least €90 a day per person. But by counting the pennies, staying at cheap **hostels** (around €18 for bed and breakfast) or **camping** (from €6), and being strong-willed about extra cups of coffee and doses of culture, you could manage on €45 a day, to include a cheap restaurant meal – less if your eating is limited to street snacks or market food.

For two or more people, **hotel accommodation** is nearly always cheaper and better value than hostels, which are only worth staying at if you're by yourself and want to meet other travellers. A sensible average estimate for a double room would be around €45, though perfectly adequate but simple doubles can be had from €30. Single-rated and -sized rooms are often available, beginning from €25 in a cheap hotel. **Breakfast** at hotels is normally an extra €4.50–6, for coffee, croissant and orange juice – about the same as you'd pay in a bar (where you'll normally find the coffee and ambience more agreeable). As for other **food**, you can spend as much or as little as you like. There are large numbers of reasonable **restaurants** with three- or four-course menus for between €12 and €25; the lunch-time or *midi* menu is nearly always cheaper. **Picnic fare**, obviously, is much less costly, especially when you buy in the markets and cheap supermarket chains, and takeaway baguette sandwiches from cafés are not extortionate. **Wine** and **beer** are both very cheap in supermarkets; buying wine from the barrel at village co-op cellars will give you the best value for money. The mark-up on wine in restaurants is high, though the house wine in cheaper establishments is still very good value. **Drinks** in cafés and bars are what really make a hole in your pocket: black coffee, wine and draught lager are the cheapest drinks to order; glasses of tap water are free; and remember that it's cheaper to be at the bar than at a table. Also, given that a small bottled water typically costs €2.50–4, you can save considerably by ordering tap water – *un carafe d'eau* – instead.

Transport will inevitably be a large item of expenditure if you move around a lot. However French trains are good value, with many discounts available – two sample long-distance one-way fares are Paris to Toulouse, €59.90, and Paris to Montpellier, €83.30. Rising petrol prices and aggressive marketing by the SNCF has been closing the gap on train and bus prices, though buses remain marginally cheaper: a one-way bus ticket from Toulouse to Carcassonne for instance costs €12, compared with €13.50 for the same journey by train. Bicycles cost about €15–20 per day to rent. Petrol prices at the time of writing were around €1.04 a litre for unleaded (*sans plomb*), around €1.16 a litre for Super, and around €0.82 a litre for diesel; there are 3.8 litres to the US gallon. Most *autoroutes* have tolls: rates vary, but to give you an idea, travelling only by motorway the 1055km from Calais to Montpellier would cost you around €63.40, plus €94 in fuel (based on a mid-sized car), taking you approximately 10 hours.

Museums and monuments can also prove a big wallet-basher. Reduced admission is often available for those over 60 and under 18 (for which you'll need your passport as proof of age) and for students under 26 (for which you'll need an International Student Identity Card, or ISIC). Many museums and monuments are free for children (the age bar for which may range from 12 to 18), and nearly always for kids under 4. Under-26s can also get a free **youth card**, or *Carte Jeune*, available in France from youth travel agencies like USIT and from main tourist offices for under €20 (valid for a year), which entitles you to reductions in France and throughout Europe. Several towns operate a discount pass for their museums and monuments (detailed throughout the Guide).

Youth and student discounts

Once obtained, various official and quasi-official **youth/student ID cards** soon pay for themselves in savings. Full-time students are eligible for the International Student ID Card (ISIC, Ⓦ www.isiccard.com), which entitles the bearer to special air, rail and bus fares and discounts at museums, theatres and other attractions. For Americans there's also a health benefit, providing up to $3000 in emergency medical coverage and $100 a day for 60 days in the hospital, plus a 24-hour hotline to call in the event of a medical, legal or financial emergency. The card costs $22 in the US; Can$16 in Canada; A$16.50 in Australia; NZ$21 in New Zealand; £6 in the UK; and €12.70 in the Republic of Ireland.

You have to be 26 or younger to qualify for the **International Youth Travel** Card, which costs US$22/£7 and carries the same benefits. Teachers qualify for the **International Teacher Card**, offering similar discounts and costing US$22, Can$16, Aus$16.50, NZ$21 or £7 in the UK. All these cards are available in the US from Council Travel, STA, Travel CUTS and, in Canada, Hostelling International (see p.13–14, 40 for addresses); in Australia and New Zealand from STA or Campus Travel; and in the UK from STA.

Several other travel organizations and accommodation groups also sell their own cards, good for various discounts. A university photo ID might open some doors, but is not easily recognizable as an ISIC card. However, the latter are often not accepted as valid proof of age, for example in bars or liquor stores.

Currency

France is one of twelve European Union countries who have changed over to a single currency, the **euro** (*eh-oo-ro*; €), which has now replaced the former national currency, the *franc* (6.5 of which equalled one euro). Bank notes have been issued in denominations of 5, 10, 20, 50, 100, 200 and 500 euros, as well as coins of 1, 2, 5, 10, 20 and 50 cents and 1 and 2 euros. Typical **exchange rates** are: €1.45 to the pound sterling (€1=0.70), €0.84 to the US dollar (€1=$1.20), €0.64 to the Canadian dollar

(€1=$1.55), €0.58 to the Australian dollar (€1=$1.70), and €0.51 to the New Zealand dollar (€1=1.94). For the most up-to-date exchange rates, consult the Currency Converter Website ⓦ www.oanda.com. Return visitors who have not been back to France since the introduction of the euro may be shocked at the jump in prices, which contrary to promises and predictions has been dramatic.

Cash and travellers' cheques

Travellers' cheques are one of the safest ways of carrying your money. Worldwide, they're available from almost any major bank (in most cases whether you have an account there or not), and from special American Express or Thomas Cook offices, usually for a service charge of 1 or 2 percent on the amount purchased. Banks may charge more to purchase, but check first with your own establishment as some offer cheques free of charge to customers meeting certain criteria. The most widely recognized brands of travellers' cheques are Visa, Thomas Cook and American Express, which most banks will change, and there are American Express and Thomas Cook offices in France; American Express travellers' cheques can also be cashed at post offices.

Euro travellers' cheques can be worthwhile: they may often be used as cash, and you should get the face value of the cheques when you change them, so commission is only paid on purchase. Banks being banks, however, this is not always the case.

Credit and debit cards

Credit cards are widely accepted; just watch for the window stickers. Visa – known as the *Carte Bleue* in France – is almost universally recognized; Access, Mastercard – sometimes called Eurocard – and American Express rank a bit lower. It's always worth checking, however, that restaurants and hotels will accept your card; some smaller ones don't. Be aware, also, that French cards have a smart chip, and machines may reject cards with a magnetic strip even if they are valid. If your card is refused because of this, you may be able to get them to confirm it by explaining the problem

to the cashier or waiter in question: "Les cartes britanniques/américaines/canadiennes/australiennes/de Nouvelle Zealand ne sont pas cartes à puce, mais à piste magnétique. Ma carte est valable et je vous serais très reconnaissant(e) de demander la confirmation auprès de votre banque ou de votre centre de traitement."

You can also use credit cards for **cash advances** at banks and in ATMs. The charge tends to be higher – for example 4.1 percent instead of the 1.5 percent at home for Visa cards. The PIN number should be the same as you use at home but check with your credit-card company before you leave. Also, because French credit cards are smart cards, some ATMs baulk at foreign plastic and tell you that your request for money has been denied. If that happens, just try another machine. All ATMs give you the choice of instructions in French or English. Post offices will give cash advances on Visa credit cards if you are having a problem using them in ATMs.

Debit cards can also be used in ATMs or to pay for goods and services if they carry the appropriate Visa symbol or there's an "edc" (European acceptance) sign. British cards are charged around 1 percent or a minimum of £1.50 when used in an ATM, so it makes sense not to take small sums out constantly. You should verify your banks rates, as some institutions charge up to €7 per transaction. North American cards tend to charge a flat rate of $2–3, making it the most economical and convenient method for travellers from that area but, again, double-check with your bank before leaving home. You would not want the use of ATMs to be your sole source of money on a long trip far from home as a lost, stolen or malfunctioning card would leave you with nothing, so always have some spare currency or travellers' cheques as a backup. When travelling you should be especially careful of credit and ATM-card scam. Never let your credit card out of sight when it is being charged (to avoid double-charging), avoid using ATMs that require a card swipe to enter (fake swipers copy card details), and if your card appears to jam in the machine, make sure no one is watching you punch in your pin (the card is retrieved later). Scams have even included mounting fake bank machines over existing ones

A compromise between travellers' cheques and plastic is **Visa TravelMoney**, a disposable pre-paid debit card with a PIN which works in all ATMs that take Visa cards. You load up your account with funds before leaving home, and when they run out, you simply throw the card away. You can buy up to nine cards to access the same funds – useful for couples or families travelling together – and it's a good idea to buy at least one extra as a backup in case of loss or theft. There is also a 24-hour toll-free customer assistance number ☏ 08.00.90.12.35. The card is available in most countries from branches of Thomas Cook and Citicorp. For more information, check the Visa TravelMoney website at ⓦ wusa.visa.com /personal/cards/visa_travel_money.html.

Loss or theft of credit cards

If your credit card is **lost or stolen** you should ring your credit card company to cancel it. Some companies, like Diners' Club in the UK, allow you to reverse the charges; others will pay for the call if you're absolutely desperate. It is very important to cancel cards straight away as purchases can be made without the signature even being glanced at. If you don't have the relevant number to call, contact the French 24-hour lines below; they will speak English.

Access, Mastercard, Eurocard
☏ 08.36.69.08.80, ⓦ www.euromastercard.com
American Express lost or stolen cards or travellers' cheques ☏ 08.00.83.28.20, ⓦ www.americanexpress.com

Diners' Club ☏ 0810 314 159, ⓦ www.dinersclub.fr
Visa ☏ 08.00.90.11.79, ⓦ www.visa.com

Wiring money

Having money wired from home using one of the companies listed below is never convenient or cheap, and should be considered a last resort. It's also possible to have money wired directly from a bank in your home country to a bank in France, although this is somewhat less reliable because it involves two separate institutions. If you go this route, your home bank will need the address of the branch bank where you want to pick up the money and the address and telex number of the capital city head office, which will act as the clearing house; money wired this way normally takes two working days to arrive, and costs around £25/$40 per transaction.

Money-wiring companies

Thomas Cook US ☏ 1-800/287-7362, Canada ☏ 1-888/823-4732, Great Britain ☏ 01733/318 922, Northern Ireland ☏ 028/9055 0030, Republic of Ireland ☏ 01/677 1721, ⓦ www.thomascook.com
Travelers Express MoneyGram US ☏ 1-800/955-7777, Canada ☏ 1-800/933-3278, UK ☏ 0800/018 0104, Republic of Ireland ☏ 1850/205 800, Australia ☏ 1800/230 100, New Zealand ☏ 0800/262 263, ⓦ www.moneygram.com
Western Union US and Canada ☏ 1-800/325-6000, Australia ☏ 1800/501 500, New Zealand ☏ 0800/270 000, UK ☏ 0800/833 833, Republic of Ireland ☏ 1800/395 395, ⓦ www.westernunion.com

Getting around

France has the most extensive train network in western Europe, and rail is the best way of moving between almost all of the major towns within Languedoc and Roussillon. The nationally owned French train company, the SNCF (Société Nationale des Chemins de Fer), runs fast, modern trains. In rural areas where branch lines have been closed, routes (such as Castres–Montpellier) are covered by buses operated solely by SNCF or in partnership with independent lines. It's an integrated service, with buses timetabled to meet trains and the same ticket covering both.

The private **bus** services that supplement the SNCF services are confusing and uncoordinated. Some areas, such as the coast or around larger centres like Toulouse, Albi and Castres, are quite well served, while the service in less populated regions, like the Corbières and parts of the Pyrenees and Haut Languedoc, is barely existent – often designed to carry the inhabitants of hamlets to and from weekly markets, and thus not very useful for travellers. Approximate journey times and frequencies can be found in the "Travel details" at the end of each chapter. Bus schedules are highly idiosyncratic in rural regions; some lines operate only on school days, others coincide with town markets, and still others only run in tourist season. Weekends and holidays frequently have no service. If you are travelling by bus check the schedule ahead of time to avoid getting stranded.

For a more private kind of independent transport, by **car** or **bicycle**, you'll need to be aware of a number of French road rules and peculiarities. **Hitching** is also an option, but is not easy and is becoming less and less popular. **Walking** (see p.35), on the extensive network of "GR" footpaths, is recommended, as are the more specialist realms of inland **boating** and **cross-country skiing** (see pp.35, 55), both of which have a high profile in Languedoc and Roussillon.

By rail

The SNCF has pioneered one of the most efficient, comfortable and user-friendly **railway systems** in the world. Its staff are, with a few exceptions, courteous and helpful, and its trains – for the most part, fast, clean and frequent – continue, in spite of the closure of some rural lines, to cover much of Languedoc and Roussillon; a main rail corridor runs from Toulouse to Narbonne, where it joins the coastal line, linking Cerbère on the French border and Beaucaire (Tarascon) at the Rhône, while spur lines run up major river valleys – including the Tarn, Ariège and Conflent. For national train **information**, you can either phone ☎08.36.35.35.35 (€0.34 per minute) or check and make reservations on the Internet at ⊛www.sncf.com.

Pride and joy of the system are the high-speed **TGVs** (*trains à grande vitesse*), capable of 300kph, and their offspring Eurostar. There are several stations connected to the TGV in Languedoc and Roussillon, among them Nîmes (journey time from Paris 4hr), Montpellier (4hr 30min), Narbonne (5hr), Béziers (4hr 45min), Perpignan (6hr) and Toulouse (4hr 30min). The only difference between TGV and other train fares is that you pay a compulsory reservation charge (from €3), plus a supplement on certain peak-hour trains. It is easiest to use the counter service for buying tickets, though if there are language problems or long queues the touch-screen computerized system available in most stations can be read in English and is a good way to check various fares and times – if need be, you can always press the red annulment button to cancel the transaction before committing yourself.

All tickets – but not passes (see below) – must be validated in the orange machines at station platform entrances, and it is an offence not to follow the instruction

Compostez votre billet ("Validate your ticket"). Train journeys may be broken any time, anywhere, for as long as the ticket is valid (usually two months), but after a break of 24 hours you must validate your ticket again when you resume your journey.

After a spate of terrorist bombings in the late 1990s, most train stations closed their **luggage lockers** (*consignes automatiques*); these days a few have reopened, and larger stations have a staffed luggage check-in, usually with limited hours (*consignes* are noted in the Guide). Many stations also rent out **bicycles**, sometimes of rather doubtful reliability.

Regional rail **maps** and complete **time tables** are on sale at tobacconist shops (*tabacs*). Leaflet timetables for particular lines are available free at stations. *Autocar* or a bullet symbol at the top of a column means it's an SNCF bus service, on which rail tickets and passes are valid.

Aside from the regular lines there are a number of special tourist-oriented railways, including the spectaular **Train Jaune** which winds its way through the Pyrenees, and the ATM train, which heads up into the hinterland of Narbonne. These are detailed in the Guide.

Rail passes

There's a huge array of **rail passes** available, covering regions as well as individual countries. Some have to be bought before leaving home while some can only be bought in the country itself. The national rail companies of many European countries also offer their own passes, most of which can be bought in advance through Rail Europe or direct from the national rail company or tourist office. Rail Europe is the umbrella company for all national and international rail purchases, and its comprehensive website (ⓦ www.raileurope.com) is the most useful source of information on which rail passes are available; it also gives all current prices.

Eurailpasses

A **Eurailpass** is not likely to pay for itself if you're planning to stick to Languedoc or even to France. The pass, which must be purchased before arrival in Europe (and cannot be purchased by European residents), allows unlimited free first-class train travel in France and seventeen other countries, and is available in increments of fifteen days, 21 days, one month, two months and three months. If you're under 26, you can save money with a **Eurailpass Youth**, which is valid for second-class travel or, if you're travelling with one to five other companions, a joint **Eurailpass Saver**, both of which are available in the same increments as the Eurailpass. You stand a better chance of getting your money's worth out of a **Eurailpass Flexi**, which is good for ten or fifteen days' first-class travel within a two-month period. This, too, comes in under-26/second-class (**Eurailpass Youth Flexi**) and group (**Eurailpass Saver Flexi**) versions.

In addition, a scaled-down version of the Eurailpass Flexi, the **Eurail Selectpass**, is available which allows travel in your choice of three, four or five of the seventeen countries Eurail covers (they must be adjoining, by either rail or ship) for any five days, six days, eight days, ten days or fifteen days (five-country option only) within a two-month period. In this plan, Belgium, the Netherlands and Luxembourg are taken as one "country". Like the Eurailpass, the Selectpass is also available in first-class, second-class youth, or first-class saver options.

Deatails of prices for all these passes can be found on ⓦ www.eurail.com, and the passes can be purchased from one of the agents listed on p.30.

Inter-Rail pass

Inter-Rail passes are only available to European residents, and you will be asked to provide proof of residency before being allowed to purchase one. They come in over-26 and (cheaper) under-26 versions, and cover 28 European countries (including Turkey and Morocco) grouped together in zones. The Zone E Pass includes France, Belgium, the Netherlands and Luxembourg. The passes are available for 22 days (one zone only), or one month and you can purchase up to three zones or a global pass covering all zones. You can save £5 by booking via the Inter-Rail website (ⓦ www.inter-rail.co.uk). Inter-Rail passes do not include travel between Britain and the continent, although Inter-Rail Pass holders are eligible for discounts on rail travel in

Britain and Northern Ireland and cross-Channel ferries, plus discounts on other shipping services around the Mediterranean, Scandinavia and the Balearics. The Inter-Rail Pass also gives a discount on the London–Paris Eurostar service.

Euro Domino pass

The **Euro Domino** pass is only available to European residents. Individual country passes provide unlimited travel in 28 European and North African countries. The passes are available for between three and eight days' travel within a one-month period; prices vary depending on the country, but include most high-speed train supplements. You can buy as many separate country passes as you want. There is a discounted youth price for those under 26, and a half-price child (age 4–11) fare.

French rail discounts and passes

In addition, the SNCF itself offers a whole range of **discounted fares** within France on standard rail prices on *période bleue* (blue period) and *période blanche* (white period) days, depending on exactly when you want to travel. A leaflet showing the blue, white (smaller discount) and red (peak) periods is given out at *gares SNCF*. In addition, there are various of **reductions** for which no pass is required. Any two people travelling together (*à deux*), or a small group of up to five people – whether a married couple, friends, family, whatever – are entitled to a 25 percent discount on return tickets on TGVs, subject to availability, or on other trains if they start their journey on a blue period day; the same reduction applies to a group of up to four people travelling with a child under 12, to under 26-year-olds, over-60s, and for anyone who books a return journey of at least 200km in distance, including a Saturday night away (this latter is called the *séjour*).

Finally, there is a range of other train passes, which can be purchased through most travel agents in France or from main *gares* SNCF and are valid for one year. Over-60s can get the **Carte Senior**, which costs €49 for unlimited travel. It offers up to 50 percent off tickets on TGVs, subject to availability, or other journeys starting in blue periods, a 25

percent reduction on white period journeys, as well as a 30 percent reduction on through international journeys involving most countries in western and central Europe. The same percentage reductions are available for under-26s with a **Carte 12–25** pass, which costs €48. Under-12s can obtain the same advantages for themselves and up to four travelling companions of any age by purchasing the **Enfant Plus Carte** (€63).

Rail contacts

In the UK and Ireland

Rail Europe (SNCF French Railways) UK ☎ 0870/5848 848, 🖳 www.raileurope.co.uk

In North America

DER Travel US ☎ 1-888/337-7350, 🖳 www.dertravel.com/rail. Eurail, Europass and many individual country passes.
Europrail International Canada ☎ 1-888/667-9734, 🖳 www.europrail.net. Eurail, Europass and many individual country passes.
Rail Europe US ☎ 1-877/257-2887, Canada ☎ 1-800/361-RAIL, 🖳 www.raileurope.com/us. Official North American Eurail Pass agent; also sells Europass, multinational passes and most single-country passes.
ScanTours US ☎ 1-800/223-7226 or 310/636-4656, 🖳 www.scantours.com. Eurail, Scandinavian, and many other European country passes.

In Australia and New Zealand

Busabout Europe Australia ☎ 1300/301 776, 🖳 www.busabout.com. Hop-on/hop-off bus passes.
CIT World Travel Australia ☎ 02/9267 1255 or 03/9650 5510, 🖳 www.cittravel.com.au. Eurail, Europass and Italian rail passes.
Rail Plus Australia ☎ 1300/555 003 or 03/9642 8644, 🖳 www.railplus.com.au. Sells Eurail, Europass, Britrail and Amtrak passes.
Trailfinders Australia ☎ 02/9247 7666, 🖳 www.trailfinder.com.au. All Europe passes.

By bus

The most convenient **bus services** are those run as an extension of rail links by SNCF, which always run to and from the SNCF station and access areas formerly served by rail. In addition to SNCF buses, private, municipal and *départemental* buses can be useful for mid- to long-distance journeys. The most frustrating thing about them is the multiplicity of services and the difficulty in obtaining departure information other than at bus stops and stations. In Toulouse, city buses can be used to access outlying villages, and in Montpellier the network goes as far out as the coast. Some *départements*, like the Hérault and the Tarn, have rural bus networks; their roadside stops usually have a copy of the schedule attached to the sign or shelter. Private operators cover much of rural Languedoc and Roussillon too – unfortunately, their routes miss some of the more interesting and less inhabited areas, and the **timetable** is constructed to suit working, market and school hours – all often dauntingly early. All buses are, generally speaking, cheaper and slower than trains.

Larger towns usually have a **gare routière** (bus station), often next to the gare SNCF. However, the private bus companies don't always work together and you'll frequently find them leaving from an array of different points (the local tourist office will usually help locate them).

By car

Driving in Languedoc and Roussillon can be a real pleasure. **Autoroutes** in the region run through the same corridors as the main rail lines: connecting Toulouse and Narbonne, and from here, running north and south along the Mediterranean coast. If you are in a hurry, it is well worth paying the toll (see below) for their use, as the free national routes, which also follow this corridor, tend to be heavily travelled by both local drivers and long-distance truckers. By *autoroute*, in good traffic conditions, you can reach Nîmes from Toulouse in a matter of hours. Away from the main arteries, the older main roads or **routes nationales** (marked N9 or RN230, for example, on signs and maps) are generally uncongested and, passing through the centres of the towns along the way, make for a more scenic, if slower, drive than the *autoroutes*. Smaller **routes départementales** (marked with a D) should not be shunned. Although they are occasionally in relatively poor condition, you can often travel for kilometres across country, seeing few other cars, on broad and well-maintained roads.

The most challenging part of driving in Languedoc and Roussillon is likely to be entering large cities for the first time. Specific directions are given for each city in the Guide, but as a general rule of thumb you can usually reach the centre by following signs for the tourist office. That said, parking is likely to be problematic, so you may instead want to follow the indications for the gare SNCF, which will have some pay parking and most likely be in walking distance of the centre.

Of course, there are times when it is wiser not to drive: **congestion** is a major problem on the *Autoroute Méditerranéen* in summer, particularly in the first and last few days of July and August, when holiday periods tend to begin or end, and the same goes for roads of all categories along the coast on summer weekends, when the going is frustratingly slow. The high cost of **fuel** can also be a discouraging factor; you'll find the cheapest gas (*essence*) or diesel fuel (*gasoil*) at out-of-town superstores. Four-star is *super*; unleaded is *sans plomb*. Leaded is, in fact, becoming hard to find, so if you are travelling with an older vehicle, top up when you can. Also note that the automated *hypermarché* gas stations, which are by far the cheapest, do not recognize most non-French credit cards.

In addition, there is a charge (*péage*) for the use of most of the *autoroutes* themselves. To give you an idea of the costs involved, the toll from Calais to Montpellier, taking in three different toll gates, would cost you €63.40 for a car without trailer, while the trip from Montpellier to Toulouse would come to €17.

The costs of driving can, however, be reduced if your car carries a full complement of passengers, and the extra mobility and carrying capacity make it much easier to camp. But, practical considerations aside, the great gain is the freedom to explore places that would otherwise remain inaccessible, in particular the sparsely populated upland of Haut Languedoc, the Hérault and the Pyrenees. Most cities have sufficient underground **parking** garages (typical clearance 1.70–2m), where you may pay up to €20 over night. Outside of the city cores, street parking is usually free, although it may mean spending a considerable time hunting around. Many hotels have garages for which they typically charge €5 and up per night.

All the major car manufacturers have garages and service stations in Languedoc and Roussillon, which can help if you run into **mechanical difficulties**. You can find them in the Yellow Pages (Ⓦwww.pages-jaunes.fr) under "Garages d'automobiles". For breakdowns, look under "Dépannages". If you have an accident or break-in, you should make a report to the local police (and keep a copy) in order to make an insurance claim. Many car insurance policies cover taking your car to Europe; check with your insurer while planning your trip. However, you're advised to take out extra cover for motoring assistance in case your car breaks down, costing around £45 for seven days. Check with your home country's automobile association.

Motoring organizations

In North America

AAA ☎1-800/AAA-HELP, Ⓦwww.aaa.com. Each state has its own club – check the phone book for local address and phone number.
CAA ☎613/247-0117, Ⓦwww.caa.ca. Each region has its own club – check the phone book for local address and phone number.

In the UK and Ireland

AA UK ☎0870/600 0371, Ⓦwww.theaa.com
AA Ireland Dublin ☎01/617 9988,
Ⓦwww.aaireland.ie
RAC UK ☎0800/550 055, Ⓦwww.rac.co.uk

In Australia and New Zealand

AAA Australia ☎02/6247 7311,
Ⓦwww.aaa.asn.au
New Zealand AA New Zealand ☎09/377 4660,
Ⓦwww.nzaa.co.nz

Road information

For information on **traffic** and road conditions on *autoroutes* throughout France, ring the multilingual service, Autoroutel (☎08.36.68.10.77) or consult Ⓦwww.autoroutes.fr. Traffic information for non-motorway routes can be obtained 24 hours a day at ☎01.56.96.33.33.

For **route planning**, Ⓦwww.via michelin.com can provide you with point-to-point driving directions for custom itineraries throughout France (it is modelled on the popular North American page, MapQuest).

Rules of the road

British, Irish, Australian, Canadian, New Zealand and US **driving licences** are valid in France, though an International Driver's Licence makes life easier if you get a police officer unwilling to peruse a document in English. If the vehicle is rented, its registration document (*carte grise*) and the insurance papers must be carried. GB stickers are, by law, meant to be displayed, and a Green Card, though not a legal requirement, might save some hassle. If your car is right-hand drive, you must have your headlight dip adjusted to the right before you go – it's a legal requirement – and as a courtesy change or paint them to yellow or stick on black glare deflectors. Remember also that you have to be 18 years of age to drive in France, regardless of whether you hold a licence in your own country.

The law of *priorité à droite* – **giving way** to traffic coming from your right, even when it is coming from a minor road – is being phased out as it is a major cause of accidents. It still applies in built-up areas, so you still have to be vigilant in towns, keeping a lookout along the roadside for the yellow diamond on a white background that gives you right of way – until you see the same sign with an oblique black slash, which indicates vehicles emerging from the right have right of way. At roundabouts the *priorité à droite* law no longer applies. *Stop* signs mean stop completely; *Cédez le passage* means "Give way". Other signs warning of potential dangers include *déviation* (diversion), *gravillons* (loose chippings), *nids de poules* (potholes) and *chaussée déformée* (uneven surface).

Fines of up to €400 for driving violations are exacted on the spot on non-residents, and only cash is accepted. The fines for exceeding the speed limit by 1–30kph (1–18mph) range from €150 to €800. Speed limits are: 130kph (80mph) on *autoroutes*; 110kph (68mph) on dual carriageways; 90kph (56mph) on other roads; and 50kph (37mph) in towns. The town limit is constant, but in wet weather, and for drivers with less than two years' experience, the three road limits are 110kph (68mph), 100kph (62mph) and 80kph (50mph) respectively. Random breath tests are common, and the legal blood alcohol limit (0.05 percent alcohol) is lower than in the UK and North America; your driving privileges may be immediately suspended.

Car rental

Car rental in France costs upwards of €300 a week (from around €45 a day), but can be cheaper if arranged before you leave home. You'll find the big firms – Hertz, Avis, Europcar and Budget – at airports and in most big cities, with addresses detailed throughout the Guide. Rental from airports normally includes a surcharge. Local firms can be cheaper but you need to check the small print and be sure of where the car can be returned to. It's normal to pay an indemnity of €150–300 against any damage to the car – they will take your credit card number rather than cash. You should return the car with a full tank of fuel. Extras are often pressed on you, like medical cover, which you may already have from travel insurance. The cost of car rental includes the basic legally necessary car insurance. North Americans and Australians in particular should be forewarned that it is very difficult to arrange the hire of a car with **automatic** transmission; if you can't drive a manual you should try to book an automatic well in advance, possibly before you leave home, and be prepared to pay a much higher price for it.

Most rental companies will only deal with people over 25 unless an extra insurance premium, typically around €20–25 per day, is paid (but you still must be over 21 and have driven for at least one year). OTU Voyage (Paris office ☎01.40.29.12.12, ⓦwww.out.fr), the student travel agency, can arrange car rental for young drivers.

Car rental agencies

Autos Abroad In the UK ☎020/7287 6000, ⓦwww.autosabroad.co.uk
Auto Europe US & Canada ☎1-800/223 5555, ⓦwww.autoeurope.com

Avis In Britain ☎0870/606 0100; Northern Ireland ☎0870/5900 500; Irish Republic ☎01/874 5844; US & Canada ☎1-800/331 1084; Australia ☎13/6333; New Zealand ☎09/526 5231 or 0800/655 111; ⓦwww.avis.com
Budget In the UK ☎0800/181181; Irish Republic ☎0800/973159; US & Canada ☎1-800/527 0700; Australia ☎1300/362 848; New Zealand ☎0800/ 652 227 or 09/375 2270; ⓦwww.budgetrentacar.com
Europcar In the UK ☎0845/7222 525; Irish Republic ☎01/874 5844; ⓦwww.europcar.com
Hertz In Britain ☎0870/844 8844; Northern Ireland ☎0870/5996 699; Irish Republic ☎01/676 7476; US ☎1-800/654 3001; Canada ☎1-800/263 0600; Australia ☎1800/550 067; New Zealand ☎09/309 0989 or 0800/655 955; ⓦwww.hertz.com
Holiday Autos In Britain ☎0870/400 0011; Northern Ireland ☎0870/5300 400; Irish Republic ☎01/872 9366; US & Canada ☎1-800/422 7737; ⓦwww.kemwel.com
National Car Rental In the UK ☎01895/233 300; US & Canada ☎1-800/CAR RENT; ⓦwww.nationalcar.com
Thrifty In the UK ☎01494/442 110; US & Canada ☎1-800/367 2277; ⓦwww.thrifty.com

Moped and motorbike rental

Mopeds and scooters are relatively easy to find; outside the mountainous areas everyone from young kids to grandmas seems to ride them, and although they're not built for any kind of long-distance travel, they're ideal for shooting around town and nearby. Places that rent out bicycles will often also rent out mopeds; you can expect to pay €25–30 a day for a 50cc Suzuki. No licence is needed for 50cc and under bikes, but for anything larger you'll need a valid **motorbike** licence. Rental prices are around €35 a day for an 80cc motorbike, €40 and up for a 125cc; also expect to leave a hefty deposit by cash or credit card – €1000 is not unusual – which you may lose in the event of damage or theft. Crash helmets are now compulsory on all mopeds and motorbikes.

Hitching

If you're intent on **hitching**, you'll have to rely almost exclusively on car drivers, as lorries very rarely give lifts. Even so, it won't be easy. Looking as clean and respectable as possible makes a very big difference, as conversations with French drivers soon make clear. Experience also suggests that hitching the less frequented D roads is much quicker. In mountain areas a rucksack and hiking gear will help procure a lift from fellow aficionados.

Autoroutes are a special case. Hitching on the *autoroute* itself is strictly illegal, but you can make excellent time going from one service station to another and, if you get stuck, at least there's food, drink, shelter and washing facilities at most service stations. It helps to have the *Guide des Autoroutes*, published by Michelin, which shows all the rest stops, service stations, tollbooths (*péages*), exits and so on. Remember to get out at the service station before your driver leaves the *autoroute*. The tollbooths are a second best (and legal) option; ordinary approach roads tend to be difficult and can easily lead to a fine.

For long-distance rides, or for a greater sense of safety, you might consider using the national **hitching organization**, Allostop Provoya, 8 rue Rochambeau (on square Montholon), 17009 Paris (Mon–Fri 9am–7.30pm, Sat 9am–1pm & 2–6pm; ☎01.53.20.42.43; Mº Cadet/Poissonnière); reservations are normally made through the Paris number, but there is also a local branch in Montpellier, detailed in the Guide. Similar net-based services include Covoiture (☻www.covoiturage.com) and Gnafou (☻www.gnafou.net). Generally the cost of using these services amounts to 20–40 percent of the price of normal public transport.

By bike

Bicycles (*vélos*) have high status in France. All the car ferries carry them for nothing; the SNCF makes minimal charges; and the French respect cyclists – both as traffic and, when you stop off at a restaurant or hotel, as customers. In addition, municipalities like Toulouse and Montpellier, and their respective *départements* – Haute Garonne and Hérault – are actively promoting cycling, not only with city paths, but comprehensive networks linking rural areas (frequently utilizing disused roadways and rail rights of way). These days more and more cyclists are using **mountain bikes**, which the French call

VTTs (*vélos tout terrain*), even for touring holidays, although it's much less effort, and much quicker, to cycle long distances and carry luggage on a traditionally styled touring or racing bike. Your primary concern using bicycle transport in this region will likely be the traffic, which on the narrow two-lane *routes nationales* is frequently heavy and extremely fast. Dedicated and well-practised cyclists may want to prove themselves doing all or part of the ten-day *Raid Pyrénéen*, which goes a mountainous 879km from Cerbère on the Med to Hendaye on the Atlantic. For more information or to get official recognition for having completed the *Raid*, contact Cyclo Club Béarnais (59 av L-Sallenave, 64000 Pau; ☎05.59.84.32.64 Fri only 6–7.30pm). The Féderation Française de Cyclotourisme (☻www.ffct.org) offers a whole range of resources.

Restaurants and hotels along the way are nearly always obliging about looking after your bike, even to the point of allowing it into your room. Most large towns have well-stocked retail and **repair shops**, where parts are normally cheaper than in Britain or the US. However, if you're using a foreign-made bike which doesn't have standard metric wheels, it's a good idea to carry spare tyres. Inner tubes are not a problem, as they adapt to either size, though make sure you get the right valves.

The **train** network runs various schemes for cyclists, all of them covered by the free leaflet *Guide du Train et du Vélo*, available from most stations. Trains marked with a bicycle in the timetable allow you to take a bike as free accompanied luggage. Otherwise, you have to send your bike parcelled up as registered luggage for a fee of €25. Although it may well arrive in less time, the SNCF won't guarantee delivery in under five days, and you do hear stories of bicycles disappearing altogether.

Ferries either take bikes free or charge a maximum of £5 one-way. British Airways and Air France both take bikes free – you may have to box them though, and you should contact the airlines first. **Eurostar** allow you to take your bicycle as part of your baggage allowance provided it is dismantled and stored in a special bike bag, and the dimensions don't exceed 120cm by 90cm.

Otherwise it needs to be sent on unaccompanied, with a guaranteed arrival of 24 hours (you can register it up to ten days in advance; book through Esprit Europe ☏0800/186 186, ⓦwww.espriteurope .co.uk); the fee is £20 one-way.

Bikes – usually mountain bikes – are often available to **rent** from campsites, hostels and *gîtes d'étapes*, as well as from specialist cycle shops and some tourist offices for around €15–20 per day; these machines are likely to be more reliable, though more expensive, than those of the SNCF. The bikes are often not insured, however, and you will be presented with the bill for their replacement if they're stolen or damaged. Check whether your travel insurance policy covers you for this if you intend to rent a bike.

As for **maps**, a minimum requirement is the IGN 1:100,000 series – the smallest scale that carries contours, although for route planning their *France: VTT & Randonnées Cycles* (no. 906; 1:1,000,000) is a good choice. In the UK, the Cyclists' Touring Club, Cotterell House, 68 Meadrow, Godalming, Surrey GU7 3HS (☏01483/417 217, ⓦwww.ctc.org.uk/), will suggest routes and supply advice for members (£25 p.a. or £12.50 for unemployed). They run a particularly good insurance scheme. Companies running specialist bike touring holidays are listed on pp.10 and 15.

Useful **vocabulary** for cyclists is given on p.421.

Walking

Long-distance **walkers** are well served in Languedoc and Roussillon by an extensive network of marked footpaths, including long-distance routes, known as *sentiers de grande randonnée* or, more commonly, **GRs** (see also p.55). They're fully signposted and equipped with campsites and rest huts along the way. Some of the main routes in the region are the GR10, which runs the length of the Pyrenees, the GRs 7 and 36, which wind their way down from Haut Languedoc through the Corbières, and GR653 which follows the medieval Arles–Jaca pilgrimage route (*le chemin de St-Jacques*) to Santiago in Spain. Other routes are composites, like the "Sentier Cathar", which utilizes various GRs and ARs

(local paths) to link Cathar sites between Perpignan and Foix.

Each path is described in a *Topoguide* (available in Britain from Stanfords, see p.22), which gives a detailed account of the route (in French), including maps, campsites, refuge huts and sources of provisions. In addition, many tourist offices can provide guides to their local footpaths, especially in popular hiking areas, where they often share premises with professional mountain guides and hike leaders. The latter organize climbing and walking expeditions for all levels of experience. *Topoguides* are produced by the principal French walkers' organization, the Fédération Française de la Randonnée Pédestre, 14 rue Riquet, 75019 Paris (☏01.44.89.93.93, ⓦwww.ffrp.asso.fr). The main climbing organization is the Club Alpin Français, 24 av de Laumière, 75019 Paris (☏01.53.72.87.00, ⓦwww.clubalpin.com); most of the major towns in the Guide have a branch office, the most useful being the CAF de TOULOUSE, 3 rue de l'Orient, 31000 Toulouse (Mon 2–5pm, Tues–Fri 9am–noon & 2–7pm; ☏05.61.63.74.42, ⓦperso .wanadoo.fr/clubalpintoulouse). In the Pyrenees, CIMES offers similar services and has its own network of refuges. Contact CIMES-Pyrenees at 1 rue Maye-Lane, BP 2, 65420 Ibos (☏05.62.90.09.92, ⓦwww .cimes-pyrenees.net).

Inland waterways

Languedoc is home to one of France's most famous inland waterways, the **Canal du Midi**, which leads from Toulouse (where it hooks up with the River Garonne) to Agde and Sète, passing Carcassonne and Béziers en route. A spur, the **Canal de la Robine** passes Narbonne before reaching the sea at Gruissan and Port-Nouvelle. From Sète, you can enter the **Canal de Rhône à Sète**, which heads east, passing St-Gilles and Beaucaire, until it reaches the Rhône. Subsidiary canals branch out through the flatlands of the Petit Camargue, and penetrate the extensive Rhône delta. For information on maximum dimensions, documentation, regulations and so forth, ask at a French Government Tourist Office for their booklet *Boating on the Waterways*, or contact Voies Navigables de France, 175 rue

Ludovic Boutleux, 62408 Bethune (☎03.21.63.24.24, ⓦwww.vnf.fr), which has information on boating in Languedoc and Roussillon, and lists of French firms that rent out boats (we've recommended various places in the Guide).

Accommodation

At most times of the year, you can turn up in any town in Languedoc and Roussillon and find a room, or a place in a campsite. Booking a couple of nights in advance can be reassuring, however, as it saves you the effort of trudging round and ensures that you know what you'll be paying. In most towns you'll be able to get a double for around €35–50, or a single for €32–45. We've detailed a selection of hotels in most of the destinations listed in the Guide, and given a price code for each (see box); as a general rule the areas around train stations have the highest density of cheap hotels. Phone numbers as well as addresses are given in the Guide, and the "Language" section at the back (see p.421) should help you make a reservation call, though many hoteliers and campsite managers – and almost all hostel managers – speak some English. We've also included websites or email addresses or, when these are not available, fax   numbers. Note that many municipalities charge a hotel tax, calculated on top of the posted rate, ranging from €0.20–€3.

Problems arise mainly between mid-July and the end of August, when the French take their own vacations en masse. The first weekend of August is the busiest time of all. During this period, hotel and hostel accommodation can be hard to come by, particularly in the coastal resorts, and you may find yourself falling back on local tourist offices for help and ideas. Some tourist offices offer a **booking service** but they cannot guarantee rooms at a particular price. All tourist offices can provide lists of hotels, the various hostels or the organizations such as CROUS (see p.39) to contact, details of campsites and bed-and-breakfast possibilities. With **campsites**, you can be more relaxed about finding an empty space, unless you're touring with a caravan or camper van or looking for a place on the Mediterranean coast or upper Ariège valley.

Most French **hotels** are **graded** from zero to five stars. The price more or less corresponds to the number of stars, though the system is a little haphazard, having more to

Accommodation price codes

All the hotels and guesthouses listed in this book have been price-coded according to the following scale. The prices quoted are for the cheapest available double room in high season.

❶ Under €30
❷ €30–40
❸ €40–55
❹ €55–70
❺ €70–85
❻ €85–100
❼ €100–125
❽ €125–150
❾ Over €150

do with ratios of bathrooms-per-guest than genuine quality, and non-classified and single-star hotels are often very good. What you get for your money varies enormously between establishments. For under €30, the bed is likely to be old and floppy, there won't be soundproofing, and showers will be communal. However, you should have your own toilet, bidet and washbasin (*lavabo*), partitioned off from the rest of the room in an area referred to as a *cabinet de toilette*: this allows some privacy if you're travelling with a friend and means that you can wash in the sink to save money. The shared showers down the hall are not usually free – they cost between €3 and €5 per shower (*douche*). If you plan to shower every day and there is more than one of you, it's worth adding up what the ultimate cost will be – you might be better off moving to a more expensive room with its own shower. Over €40 will get you a room with its own bath or shower though not necessarily a toilet (*WC*), and, though the decor may not be anything to write home about, comfortable furniture. If wandering dark halls late at night in search of a toilet is not your idea of fun, ask for a bathroom (*salle de bain*) which will get you both a toilet and a shower in a separate room; these occasionally have bath tubs (*bain*) too. This type of room will be had for around €48, and may also come with a TV. At more than €65, you should expect a higher standard of fittings and something approaching luxury. Hotels with one star or above have a telephone in the rooms, though some phones can only receive calls.

Big cities have a good variety of cheap establishments; in small towns or villages where the choice is limited, you may not be so lucky. The modern and cheesy resorts which have sprung up along the Languedoc coast have inordinately high July and August prices. If you are staying more than three days in a hotel it's often possible to negotiate a lower price, particularly out of season.

Breakfast is not normally included and can add €5–8 per person to a bill – though there is no obligation to take it and you will nearly always do better at a café. The cost of eating **dinner** in a hotel's restaurant can be a more important factor to bear in mind when picking a place to stay. Officially, it is illegal for hotels to insist on your taking meals, but they often do in places heavily dependent on seasonal tourism. But this is not always such a bad thing, especially in times of economic recession, and you can get a real bargain. **Single rooms** are only marginally cheaper than doubles, so sharing always slashes costs. Most hotels willingly provide rooms with **extra beds**, for three or more people, at good discounts.

Note that many family-run hotels are closed every year for two or three weeks sometime between May and September – where possible we've detailed this in the text. In addition, some hotels in smaller towns and villages close for one or two nights a week, usually Sunday or Monday – if in doubt, ring first to check.

A very useful option, especially if it's late at night, are the **motel chains**. In contrast to the downtown hotels which often offer doubtful value (worn-out mattresses, dust, noise, etc) you can count on a decent and reliable standard in the chains even if they are without much charm. Among the cheapest is the one-star **Formule 1** chain, well signposted on the outskirts of most big towns. They are characterless, but provide rooms for up to three people from €27. With a Visa, Mastercard, Eurocard or American Express credit card, you can let yourself into a room at any hour of the day or night. Addresses are most easily available on Minitel – 3615 or 3616 Formule 1 – but the hotels are not difficult to find as long as you're travelling by car, and a brochure with full details can be picked up at any of them. Other cheap chains include 1er Classe, Etap Hôtel and Balladins; they tend to be grouped together near *autoroute* exits. More comfortable but still affordable chain hotels are **Campanile** (🌐 www.campanile.fr), **Ibis** (🌐 www.ibis.fr) and **Clarine** (🌐 www.clarine.fr), which all have en-suite rooms with cable TV and direct-dial phones from €40–55. All three of these hotel chains can be reached by Internet and will accept reservations by email. They will also send a complete list of their locations in France by email request within a few days. If you are staying put in a town for three days or more, you might also look into local **Residences de Tourisme**, which are slightly more economical than hotels and sometimes offer self-catering. Aside from the chains, there a number of **hotel federations** in France. The biggest of these is **Logis de France**, an association of over three thousand hotels nationwide. They have a central reservation number (☎01.45.84.83.84) and Website (🌐www.logis-de-france.fr), which you can contact to obtain their free yearly guide. Other good resources include 🌐www.resin-france.fr, an official central reservation service, or 🌐www.francehotelreservation.com.

Several cities in Languedoc and Roussillon participate in the "**Bonne Weekend en Ville**" programme, whereby you book through the local tourist office and get two nights for the price of one (Oct–May only) at participating hotels, as well as an array of discount coupons and special deals. Participating towns include Albi, Carcassonne, Nîmes and Toulouse, but the list is growing, so it's worth enquiring about when you are making arrangements to stay in larger towns. If you are planning your trip ahead, take the time to contact local tourist offices ahead of arrival; there are very often special accommodation deals on offer, especially outside of high season.

Bed-and-breakfast accommodation

In country areas, in addition to standard hotels, you will come across *chambres d'hôtes* and *fermes auberges*, **bed-and-breakfast accommodation** in someone's house or farm. These vary in standard and are rarely a cheap option, usually costing the equivalent of a two-star hotel. However, if you're lucky, they may be good sources of traditional home cooking and French company. The brown leaflets available in tourist offices list most of them.

If you are planning to stay a week or more in any one place it might be worth considering **renting a house**. You can do this by checking adverts from the innumerable private owners in, for example, British Sunday newspapers (*Observer* and *Sunday Times*, mainly), or trying one of the numerous holiday firms that market accommodation/travel packages (see pp.10 and 15 for a brief selection of these). Otherwise, economical longer-term, self-catering options include the

gîtes rurales (rural homes renting for €300 and up per week, administered by Gîtes de France) and the Clévancances programme, which has mainly town properties for rent. Contact the Fédération Nationale des Locations de France Clévacaces (54 bd de l'Embouchure BP2166, 31022 Toulouse Cedex 2; ☎05.61.13.55.66, 🌐www.cleva-cances.fr). Alternatively check local tourist office listings for **appartements** or **meublés**.

Gîtes de France, 59 rue St-Lazare, Paris 75009 (Mon–Sat 10am–6.30pm; ☎01.49.70.75.75, 🌐www.gites-de-france.fr), a government-funded agency which promotes and manages a range of bed-and-breakfast and self-catering accommodation in France, the latter usually consisting of a self-contained country cottage, known as a **gîte rural** or **gîte de séjour**. Further details can be found in their two very useful national guides – *Chambres et Tables d'Hôtes* and *Chambres d'Hôtes de Prestige et Gîtes de Charme* – which are also sometimes on sale in bookshops and tourist offices. The national guides, however, are not exhaustive; complete listings (with photos) are available in the guides distributed by departmental Gîtes de France offices – you can either contact the main office for a complete list, or pick up copies from local and departmental tourist offices. If you're planning from home, the simplest way to make reservations is through their website. Rural bed-and-breakfast and dining accommodation can also be arranged through Bienvenue à la Ferme (9 av Georges V, 75008 Paris, ☎01.53.57.11.44, 🌐www.bienvenue-a-la-ferme.com) which also publishes regional and departmental guides.

Gîtes d'etapes and refuges

In the countryside, another hostel-style alternative exists: **gîtes d'étape**. *Gîtes d'étape* are often run by the local village or municipality (whose mayor will probably be in charge of the key) and are less formal than hostels. They provide bunk beds and primitive kitchen and washing facilities from around €8, and they are marked on the large-scale IGN walkers' maps and listed in the individual GR *Topoguides*. In addition, mountain areas are well supplied with

refuge huts, mostly run by the Club Alpin Français (CAF), but also by CIMES (in the Pyrenees). Many are open in summer only. They are the only available shelter once you are above the villages. Costs are from around €10 for the night, less if you're a member of a climbing organization affiliated to the CAF. Meals – invariably four courses – cost around €14, which is not unreasonable when you consider that all supplies have to be brought up by mule or helicopter.

More information can be found in the guides *Gîtes d'Étapes et Séjours* published by Gîtes de France (see above), and *Gîtes d'Étape et Refuges*, published by Guides La Cadole (which also has the handy webpage ⓦ www.gites-refuges.com), available in French bookshops for €18.30.

Departmental offices of Gîtes de France

Ariège 31bis av Général-de-Gaulle, BP 143, 09004 Foix ☎05.61.02.30.89, Ⓕ05.61.65.17.34, Ⓔgites-de-france.ariege@wanadoo.fr
Aude 78 rue Barbacane, 11000 Carcassonne ☎04.68.11.40.70, Ⓕ04.68.11.40.72
Gard CDT 3 pl des Arènes, BP 59, 30007 Nîmes ☎04.66.27.94.94, Ⓕ04.66.27.94.95
Haute-Garonne 14 rue Bayard, BP 845, 31015 Toulouse ☎05.61.99.70.60, Ⓕ05.61.99.41.22
Hérault Maison de Tourisme, 1977 av des Moulins, BP 3070, 34034 Montpellier ☎04.67.67.62.62, Ⓕ04.67.67.71.69, ⓦwww.gites-de-france-herault.asso.fr
Pyrénées-Orientales 30 rue Pierre-Bretonneau, 66017 Perpignan ☎04.68.55.60.95, Ⓕ04.68.50.68.44
Tarn Maison des Agriculteurs, La Milliasolle, BP 89, 81003 Albi ☎05.63.48.83.01, Ⓕ05.63.48.83.12

Hostels

At between €10 and €20 per night for a dormitory bed, and generally breakfast thrown in, **hostels** – *auberges de jeunesse* – are invaluable for single travellers on a budget. For hostels, **per-person prices** of dorm beds are given throughout the Guide. Many of the modern hostels now also offer rooms for couples, with en-suite showers, but they don't necessarily work out cheaper than hotels – particularly if you've had to pay a bus fare out to the edge of town to reach

them. However, many hostels are beautifully sited, and they allow you to cut costs by preparing your own food in their kitchens, or eating in their cheap canteens. Normally, to stay at FUAJ or LFAJ hostels (see below) you must be a member of Hostelling International (HI) or the International Youth Hostel Federation (IYHF). Head offices and membership fees, which differ from country to country, are listed on p.40. If you don't join up before you leave home, you can purchase a **membership card** in relevant French hostels for €17.40.

Slightly confusingly, there are three rival French **hostelling associations** (see below): the main two being the Fédération Unie des Auberges de Jeunesse (FUAJ; 180 hostels), which has its hostels detailed in the *International Handbook*, and the Ligue Française pour les Auberges de Jeunesse (LFAJ; 100 hostels). The third organization is the Union des Centres de Recontres Internationales de France (UCRIF), with 60 hostels in France; membership is not required.

A few large towns provide a more luxurious standard of hostel accommodation in Foyers des Jeunes Travailleurs/Travailleuses, **residential hostels** for young workers and students, where you can usually get a private room for around €10. They normally have a good cafeteria or canteen.

At the height of summer (usually July and Aug only), there's also the possibility of staying in **student accommodation** in university towns and cities. The main organization to contact for this is CROUS, Académie de Paris, 39 av Georges-Bernanos, Paris 75005 (☎01.40.51.55.90, ⓦwww.crous-paris.fr). Prices are similar to the official hostels, from around €12 per person, and you don't need membership.

Youth hostel associations

In France

Fédération Unie des Auberges de Jeunesse (FUAJ), 27 rue Pajol, 75018 Paris ☎01.44.89.87.27, ⓦwww.fuaj.org
Ligue Française pour les Auberges de Jeunesse (LFAJ), 38 bd Raspail, 75007 Paris ☎01.45.48.69.84, ⓦwww.auberges-de -jeunesse.com

Union des Centres de Rencontres Internationales de France (UCRIF), 27 rue Turbigo, 75002 Paris ☎01.40.26.57.64, ⓔinfo@ucrif.asso.fr
Fédération des Maisons des Jeunes et de la Culture de France 168 bis, rue Cardinet, 75017 Paris ☎ 01.44.85.29.50, ⓕ01.42.29.01.44

In England and Wales

Youth Hostel Association (YHA) ☎0870/770 8868, ⓦwww.yha.org.uk. Annual membership £13; under-18s £6.50; lifetime £190 (or five annual payments of £40).

In Scotland

Scottish Youth Hostel Association ☎0870/155 3255, ⓦwww.syha.org.uk. Annual membership £6, for under-18s £2.50.

In Ireland

Irish Youth Hostel Association ☎01/830 4555, ⓦwww.irelandyha.org.
Annual membership €15; under-18s €7.50; family €31.50; lifetime €75.
Hostelling International Northern Ireland ☎028/9032 4733, ⓦwww.hini.org.uk. Adult membership £10; under-18s £6; family £20; lifetime £75.

In the US

Hostelling International-American Youth Hostels ☎202/783-6161, ⓦwww.hiayh.org. Annual membership for adults (18–55) is $25, for seniors (55 or over) is $15, and for under-18s and groups of ten or more, is free. Lifetime memberships are $250.

In Canada

Hostelling International Canada ☎1-800/663 5777 or 613/237 7884, ⓦwww.hostellingintl.ca. Rather than sell the traditional one- or two-year memberships, the association now sells one Individual Adult membership with a 28- to 16-month term. The length of the term depends on when the membership is sold, but a member can receive up to 28 months of membership for just $35. Membership is free for under-18s and you can become a lifetime member for $175.

In Australia

Australia Youth Hostels Association ☎02/9261 1111, ⓦwww.yha.com.au. Adult membership rate A$52 (under-18s, A$16) for the first twelve months and then AUS$32 each year after.

In New Zealand

Youth Hostelling Association New Zealand ☎0800/278 299 or 03/379 9970, ⓦwww.yha.co.nz. Adult membership NZ$40 for one year, NZ$60 for two and NZ$80 for three; under-18s free; lifetime NZ$300.

Camping

Practically every village and town in France has at least one **campsite** to cater for the thousands of people who spend their holiday under canvas – camping is a very big deal in France. The cheapest – at around €5–8 per person per night – is usually the *camping municipal*, run by the local municipality. In season or whenever they're officially open, they are always clean and have plenty of hot water; often they are situated in prime local positions. Out of season, those that stay open often don't bother to collect the overnight charge.

If you're planning to do a lot of camping, an **international camping carnet** is a good investment. The carnet serves as useful identification, covers you for third party insurance when camping and helps you get ten-percent reductions at campsites listed in the CCI information booklet that comes with your carnet. It is available in the UK from the AA, the RAC or the Carefree Travel Service (☎0247/642 2024), who also book inspected camping sites in Europe and arrange ferry crossings; in the US go to Family Campers and RVers (FCRV), 4804 Transit Rd, Building 2, Depew, NY 14043 (☎1-800/245 9755, ⓦwww.fcrv.org), which also has members and services in Canada.

On the coast around the beach towns, there are **superior categories** of campsite where you'll pay prices similar to those of a hotel for the facilities – bars, restaurants and sometimes swimming pools. These have rather more permanent status than the *campings municipaux*, with people often spending a whole holiday in the one base. If you plan to do the same, and particularly if you have a caravan, camper or a big tent, it's wise to book ahead – reckon on paying at least €8 a head with a tent or a camper van. Inland, *camping à la ferme* – on somebody's farm – is another possibility (generally without facilities). Lists of sites are detailed in the Tourist Board's *Accueil à la Campagne* booklet.

A number of companies in the UK also specialize in selling **camping holidays**, including Canvas Holidays (☎08709/022 022, ◉www.canvasholidays.com) and Sunsites (☎01606/787 555, ◉www.sun-sites.co.uk). Twelve nights' camping at Argelès, near Perpignan, with Sunsites, for example, costs from £862 for two adults, with up to four children under 18 free, which includes the price of the Channel ferry.

Lastly, a word of **caution**: never camp rough (*camping sauvage*, as the French call it) on anyone's land without first asking permission, as you may well have to deal with an irate farmer and his dogs. On the other hand, a politely phrased request for permission will often as not get positive results. Camping on public land is not officially permitted, but is widely practised by the French, and if you are discreet you will likely not meet with problems. On beaches, it's best to camp out only where other people are doing so.

Eating and drinking

Languedoc and Roussillon – a traditionally poor and marginalized area – are not famed for the elaborate haute cuisine which typifies French cookery in the popular imagination. The food of this overwhelmingly rural region tends to be simple, and little family restaurants serving classic peasant (terroir) dishes based on local produce – and where the bill is less than €18 – are still common enough here; your chief challenge, should you stay in a single locale for any length of time, will be fighting culinary ennui. That said, as you cross the region you'll find that the huge diversity of the landscape has contributed to a correspondingly wide range in local specialities – immediately obvious when you visit town and village produce markets – and in all but the most out-of-the-way hamlet you'll be able to find relief in a more adventurous (and expensive) gastronomique restaurant. Due to its relative isolation Languedoc and Roussillon have thankfully also fared better than many regions in escaping the processed, boil-in-the-bag and ready-to-microwave productions – known in France as mal-bouffe ("bad grub") – of the global food industry.

In the rarefied world of **haute cuisine**, where the top chefs are national celebrities, a battle is currently raging between traditionalists, determined to preserve the purity of French cuisine, and those who experiment with different flavours from around the world to create novel combinations. At this level, French food is still brilliant – in both camps – and the good news is that prices are continuing to come down. Many gourmet palaces offer weekday lunch-time menus where you can sample culinary genius for around €50.

Languedoc and Roussillon are also great places for **foreign cuisine**, in particular North African, Caribbean (known as *Antillais*) and Asiatic. Moroccan, Thai or Vietnamese restaurants are not necessarily cheap options but they are usually good value for money. Chinese restaurants tend, on the other hand, to be inexpensive but disappointing.

On the whole, **vegetarians** can expect a somewhat lean time in Languedoc and Roussillon; *cuisine rurale* is relentlessly meat-based, and in some traditional farming villages even understanding the concept of vegetarianism can be a stretch. A few cities have specifically vegetarian restaurants (detailed in the text), but elsewhere you'll have to hope you find a sympathetic restaurant (crêperies and pizzerias can be good standbys). Sometimes they're willing to replace a meat dish on the *menu fixe* with an omelette; other times you'll have to pick your way through the *carte*. Remember the phrase "Je suis végétarien(ne); il y a quelques plats sans viande?" (I'm a vegetarian; are there any non-meat dishes?). **Vegans**, however, should probably forget all about eating in French restaurants and stick to self-catering.

For a **food glossary**, see pp.422–429.

Breakfast and snacks

A croissant, *pain au chocolat* (a square-shaped chocolate-filled light pastry) or a sandwich in a bar or café, with hot chocolate or coffee, is generally the best **breakfast** you'll get – at a fraction of the cost charged by most hotels. (The days when hotels gave you mounds of croissants or brioches for breakfast seem to be long gone; now it's virtually always bread, jam and a jug of coffee or tea for about €5.) Croissants and sometimes hard-boiled eggs are displayed on bar counters until around 9.30am or 10am. If you stand – cheaper than sitting down – you just help yourself to these with your coffee; the waiter keeps an eye on how many you've eaten and bills you accordingly.

At **lunch time**, and sometimes in the evening, you may find cafés offering a *plat du jour* (chef's daily special) at between €9 and €14, or *formules*, a limited or no-choice menu. *Croques-monsieur* or *croques-madame* (variations on the toasted-cheese sandwich) are on sale at cafés, brasseries and many street stands, along with *frites* (potato fries), crêpes, *galettes* (wholewheat pancakes), *gauffres* (waffles), *glaces* (ice creams) and all kinds of fresh-filled baguettes (these very filling sandwiches usually cost €3–5 to take away). For variety, there are Tunisian snacks like *brik à l'œuf* (a fried pastry with an egg inside), *merguez* (spicy North African sausage), Greek souvlaki (kebabs) and Middle Eastern falafel (deep-fried chickpea balls in flat bread with salad). Wine bars are good for regional sausages and cheese, usually served with brown bread (*pain de campagne*).

Crêpes, or pancakes with fillings, served up at ubiquitous crêperies, are popular lunch-time food. The savoury buckwheat variety (often called *galettes*) provide the main course; the sweet white-flour ones are dessert. They taste nice enough, but are usually poor value in comparison with a restaurant meal; you need at least three, normally at over €5 each, to feel full. **Pizzerias**, usually *au feu du bois* (wood-fire-baked), are also very common. They are somewhat better value than crêperies, but quality and quantity vary greatly – look before you leap into the nearest empty seats.

For **picnics**, the local outdoor market or supermarket will provide you with almost everything you need from tomatoes and avocados to cheese and pâté. Cooked meat, prepared snacks, ready-made dishes and assorted salads can be bought at *charcuteries* (delicatessens), which you'll find everywhere – even in small villages, though the same things are cheaper at supermarket counters. You purchase by weight, or you can ask for *une tranche* (a slice), *une barquette* (a carton) or *une part* (a portion).

Salons de thé, which open from mid-morning to late evening, serve brunches, salads, quiches and so on, as well as gateaux, ice cream and a wide selection of teas. They tend to be a good deal pricier than cafés or brasseries – you're paying for the posh surroundings. As bars are to men in France, *salons de thé* are to women, and they generally have a more female ambience and clientele. For cakes and pastries to take away, you'll find impressive arrays at every *boulangerie-pâtisserie*.

Meals

There's no difference between **restaurants** (or *auberges* or *relais* as they sometimes call themselves) and **brasseries** in terms of quality or price range. The distinction is that brasseries, which resemble cafés, serve quicker meals at most hours of the day, while restaurants tend to stick to the traditional meal times of noon to 2pm, and 7pm to 9.30pm or 10.30pm. After 9pm or so, restaurants often serve only à la carte meals (single dishes chosen from the menu) – invariably more expensive than eating the set *menu fixe*. In touristy areas in high season, and for all the more upmarket places, it's wise to make reservations – easily done on the same day. In small towns it may be impossible to get anything other than a bar sandwich after 10pm or even earlier; in major cities, town centre brasseries will serve until 11pm or midnight and one or two may stay open all night.

When hunting for places to eat, avoid those that are half empty at peak time, use your nose and regard long menus with suspicion. Don't forget that **hotel restaurants** are open to non-residents, and are often very good value. In many small towns and villages, you'll find the only restaurants are in hotels. Since restaurants change hands frequently and have their ups and downs, it's also worth asking people you meet (locals, not fellow tourists) for recommendations. This is the conversational equivalent of commenting on the weather in Britain and will usually elicit strong views and sound advice.

Prices, and what you get for them, are posted outside. Normally there's a choice between one or more *menus fixes*, where the number of courses has already been determined and the choice is limited, and choosing individually from the *carte* (menu). **Menus fixes** are normally the cheapest option. At the bottom end of the price range, they revolve around standard dishes such as steak and chips (*steak frites*), chicken and chips (*poulet frites*) and various concoctions involving innards. But further up the scale they can be much the best-value way of sampling regional specialities, sometimes running to five or more courses. If you're simply not that hungry, just go for the *plat du jour*.

Going **à la carte** offers greater choice and, in the better restaurants, unlimited access to the chef's specialities – though you'll pay for the privilege. A simple and perfectly legitimate tactic is to have just one course instead of the expected three or four. You can share dishes or go for several starters – a useful strategy for vegetarians. There's no minimum charge.

In the French **sequence of courses**, any salad (sometimes vegetables, too) comes separate from the main dish, and cheese precedes a dessert. You will be offered coffee, which is always extra, to finish off the meal.

Service compris or s.c. means the **service charge** is included. *Service non compris*, s.n.c. or *servis en sus* means that it isn't and you need to calculate an additional 15 percent. **Wine** (vin) or a **drink** (boisson) is occasionally included (*compris*) in the cost of a menu fixe. When ordering house wine, the cheapest option, ask for *un quart* (0.25 litre); *un demi-litre* (0.5 litre) or *une carafe* (1 litre). If you're worried about the cost ask for vin ordinaire or the vin de table. In the Guide the lowest price menu or the range of menus is given; where average à la carte prices are given it assumes you'll have three courses and half a bottle of wine.

The French are much better disposed towards **children** in restaurants than other nationalities, not simply by offering reduced-price children's menus but in creating an atmosphere – even in otherwise fairly snooty establishments – that positively welcomes kids; some even have in-house games and toys for them to occupy themselves with. It is regarded as self-evident that large family groups should be able to eat out together.

A rather murkier area is that of **dogs** in the dining room; it can be quite a shock in a provincial hotel to realize that the majority of your fellow diners are attempting to keep dogs concealed beneath their tables.

The most economical and arguably the most pleasant way to dine in France is to **picnic**. Shopping at local markets is the best way to get cheap, fresh produce and cooking it up yourself means you know what's going into it. Gallic culture is also incredibly picnic-tolerant – almost no one will fault you for pulling off the road and spreading your blanket wherever you are. If you are going by car, bringing a small barbecue and a cooler will put you in the outdoor gourmet category.

Regional specialities

Languedoc and Roussillon are extremely varied and exciting areas for cuisine. In the east, around Nîmes and in the **Gard**, the influence of Provençal cuisine is strongly felt – especially in the use of the herbs that spring up throughout the *garrigues* – while the *manades* (ranches) of the **Camargue** ensure that beef plays a notable role, especially in sausage and in the wine-marinated *brandade de la Gardienne*. Other prominent ingredients include truffles, gathered in the scrubby woodland of the northern fringe around **Uzès**, olives, cultivated in low hills rising up from the coastal plains and yielding reasonable oil, and rice, which is grown locally in the Camargue. The fair sunny climate also favours vegetables and fruit, including asparagus, but more notably peaches and apricots (especially around St-Gilles).

As can be expected, fish and seafood abound in the **coastal cuisine** of Languedoc, whether in brothy *coquillages*, the garlicky *bourride* of Sète, or baked or barbecued. Tuna, anchovy and sardine dominate, but the range of fish used is very broad. The shallow *étangs* are home to large-scale mussel and oyster farming, of which Mèze and Leucate are the main centres. In the uplands of the **Hérault**, the transition to cooler higher terrain is marked by an increase in sheep-based dishes (using both meat and cheese), although fruits such as figs also mark local cookery. Tripe (*tripoux*) is another staple along the whole inland strip of Languedoc.

The highland and forest ingredients are all the more accentuated in **Haut Languedoc**, where seasonal delicacies such as the ubiquitous mushrooms of late summer add variety. Some of the finest mutton comes from the Cabardés district, on the southern slopes of the Montagne Noire. Further northeast, the cereal lands of **Tarn** are notable for high-quality foie gras and land snails (*escargots*), while Lautrec is an undisputed garlic capital, famed for its pink version. Duck (*canard*), popular throughout France, is also a staple in the zone stretching from Toulouse to Albi, and you are likely to encounter it in the form of a *confit* (a jellied conserve). Tarn also falls heavily under the culinary influence of **Aude**, whose staple, cassoulet, a bean stew originating in Castelnaudary, has colonized the whole of Languedoc. Carcassonne marks something of a midpoint, between the wheat and bean fields which spread west to Toulouse, and the east, which is known for its olives. The city, and the lands along the Aude, are home to some of the region's most interesting sweets, ranging from the rosemary-tinged honey of the Corbières hills, to the nougat of Limoux and candied chest-

nuts, a traditional late-autumn treat. The cuisine of Aude, and its neighbour, **Ariège**, are transformed as the landscape rises towards the Pyrenees. While the foothills produce excellent beef, sheep and goats come to play an increasing role as the terrain climbs, appearing in well-reputed cheeses and supplementing or replacing pork in the ubiquitous sausage (*saucisson*).

Roussillon represents something of a shift, with its marked Catalan base and Spanish influence – immediately noticeable in the strong influence of olive oil. The region's dry and grilled pork sausages (in Catalan *embutits* and *botifares*) are particularly worth trying, and a countryside staple is the hearty pork-based *ollada* soup. Special occasions are celebrated with a *cargolada* – an elaborate dish of grilled land snails. Moving towards the milder climes of the coast, fruit makes a dramatic reappearance, in the cherries of Cèret, as well as almonds, peaches and pears. The coastal hills are swathed in olive trees, while seaside villages like Collioure and Port-Vendres have long survived from fishing. Spanish influence in the twentieth century has also helped to popularize southern Spanish dishes such as paella and tapas.

Cheeses of Languedoc and Roussillon

You can find the great **cheeses** from all over France in Languedoc and Roussillon, but it is still worth hunting out local specialities. Many cheese-makers have successfully protected their products by AOC (*appellation d'origine controlée*) laws similar to those for wines, which means that the subtle differences between French local cheeses have not been overwhelmed by the industrialized uniformity that has plagued other countries. Although just about everything is available in supermarkets, farm-produced cheese will have to be hunted down in speciality shops (a *fromagerie*, or a regional produce outlet) and country markets.

Throughout the sheep-producing areas of the region, local cheeses can be picked up at country markets, or at times directly from the farms themselves. The milk which produces the famous Roquefort cheese comes exclusively from Haut Languedoc's sheep (specifically, an ancient breed of Lacaune), while a few noteworthy cheese varieties in Languedoc and Roussillon itself include **Pélardon des Cévennes**, a flavourful goats' (*chèvre*) milk cheese recently developed at St Hippolyte-du-Fort; the creamy but acidic **Pélardon des Corbières**, an older variant of the Cévennes version, round in shape and coated in natural mould, best served after about a week; and **Le Pérail**, a white *fromage de brébis* (sheep) from Gard, whose taste transforms as it ages – from a subtle freshness when first produced to a sharp tanginess when aged a fortnight.

Drink

Wherever you can eat you can invariably drink, and vice versa. **Drinking** is done at a leisurely pace whether it's a prelude to food (*apéritif*), a sequel (*digestif*), or the accompaniment, and cafés are the standard places to do it. Every bar or café has to display its full price list, usually without the fifteen-percent service charge added, with the cheapest drinks at the bar (*au comptoir*), and progressively increasing prices for sitting at a table inside (*la salle*), or outside (*la terrasse*). If you are sitting outside, particularly in a touristy area, unpleasantness can be avoided by checking the price with the waiter when you put in your order. You pay when you leave, and it's perfectly acceptable to sit for hours over just one cup of coffee.

Wine (*vin*) is drunk at just about every meal or social occasion. Red is *rouge*, white *blanc*, and rosé *rosé*. *Vin de table* or *vin ordinaire* – table wine – is generally drinkable and always cheap, although it may be disguised and priced up as the house wine, or *cuvée*. The price of AOC (*appellation d'origine contrôlée*) wines can vary from €1.80 to €15 and over, and that's the vineyard price. You can buy a very decent bottle of wine for €3 to €5, and €10 and over will buy you something really nice. By the time restaurants have added their considerable mark-up, however, wine can constitute an alarming proportion of the bill.

The basic **wine terms** are: *brut*, very dry; *sec*, dry; *demi-sec*, sweet; *doux*, very sweet; *mousseux*, sparkling; *méthode champenoise*, mature and sparkling. There are grape varieties as well, but the complexities of the subject take up volumes. A glass of wine is simply *un rouge*, *un rosé* or *un blanc*. You may have the choice of *un ballon* (round glass) or a smaller glass (*un verre*). *Un pichet* (a pitcher) is normally a quarter-litre. A glass of wine in a bar will cost around €3.

The best way to **buy bottles** of wine is directly from the producers (*vignerons*), either at vineyards, at Maisons or Syndicats du Vin (representing a group of wine-producers), or at Coopératifs Vinicoles (wine-producer co-ops). At all these places you can sample the wines first. It's best to make clear at the start how much you want to buy (if it's only one or two bottles) and you will not be popular if you drink several glasses and then leave without making a purchase. The most economical option is to buy *en vrac*, which you can also do at some wine shops (*caves*), taking an easily obtainable plastic five- or ten-litre container (usually sold on the premises) and getting it filled straight from the barrel. In cities, supermarkets are the best places to buy your wine, and their prices often beat those of the *vignerons*.

Familiar light Belgian and German brands, plus French brands from Alsace, account for most of the **beer** you'll find. Draught beer (*à la pression*) – usually Kronenbourg – is the cheapest drink you can have next to coffee and wine; ask for *un pression* or *un demi* (0.33 litre). A *demi* costs around €2.80. For a wider choice of draught and bottled beer you need to go to the special beer-drinking establishments or English-style pubs found in most city centres and resorts. A small bottle at one of these places will cost at least twice as much as a *demi* in a café. In supermarkets, however, bottled or canned beer is exceptionally cheap.

Strong alcohol is consumed from as early as 5am as a pre-work fortifier, and then at any time through the day according to circumstance, though the national reputation for drunkenness has lost much of its truth. Brandies and the dozens of *eaux de vie* (spirits) and liqueurs are always available. *Pastis* – the generic name of aniseed drinks such as Pernod or Ricard and a favourite throughout Languedoc – is served diluted with water and ice (*glaçons*). It's very refreshing and not expensive. Mixed with *crème de menthe* it's known as a *perrouquet*. Among less familiar names, try Poire William (pear brandy), or Marc (a spirit distilled from grape pulp). Measures are generous, but they don't come cheap: the same applies for imported spirits like whisky (*Scotch*). Two drinks designed to stimulate the appetite – *un apéritif* – are Pineau (cognac and grape juice) and Kir (white wine with a dash of Cassis – blackcurrant liquor – or with champagne instead of wine for a Kir Royal). **Cocktails** are served at most late-night bars, discos and music places, as well as at upmarket hotel bars and at every seaside promenade café; they usually cost at least €7.

On the **soft drink** front, you can buy cartons of unsweetened fruit juice in supermarkets, although in the cafés the bottled (sweetened) nectars such as apricot (*jus d'abricot*) and blackcurrant (*cassis*) still hold sway. You can also get fresh orange or lemon juice (*orange/citron pressé*), at a price. A *citron pressé* is a refreshing choice for the extremely thirsty on a hot day – the lemon juice is served in the bottom of a long ice-filled glass, with a jug of water and a sugar bowl to sweeten it to your taste. Other drinks to try are syrups (*sirops*) of mint, grenadine or other flavours mixed with water. The standard fizzy drinks of lemonade (*limonade*), Coke (*coca*) and so forth are all available. Bottles of **mineral water** (*eau minérale*) and spring water (*eau de source*) – either sparkling (*gazeuse*) or still (*eau plate*) – abound, from the big brand names to the most obscure spa product. But there's not much wrong with the tap water (*l'eau de robinet* or *un carafe d'eau*), which will always be brought free to your table if you ask for it.

Coffee is invariably espresso – small, black and very strong. *Un café* or *un express* is the regular; *un crème* is with milk; *un grand café* or *un grand crème* are large cups. In the morning you could also ask for *un café au lait* – espresso in a large cup or bowl filled up with hot milk. *Un déca* is decaffeinated, now widely available. Ordinary **tea** (*thé*) is Lipton's nine times out of ten and is normally served black, and you can usually have a slice of lemon (*limon*) with it if you want; to have milk with it, ask for *un peu de lait frais* (some fresh milk). *Chocolat chaud* – **hot chocolate** – unlike tea, lives up to the high standards of French food and drink and

can be had in any café. After eating, **herb teas** (*infusions* or *tisanes*), served in every *salon de thé*, can be soothing. The more common ones are *verveine* (verbena), *tilleul* (lime blossom), *menthe* (mint) and *camomille* (camomile).

Wines of Languedoc and Roussillon

In Languedoc and Roussillon good economical **wines** can be found in the *vins de pays* category (also known as *vins d'Oc* in these parts). Quality wines are denoted by the *appellation d'origine contrôlée* (AOC), which strictly controls quality and the amount of wine that a particular area, whether several hundred square kilometres or just two, may produce. Within each *appellation* there is enormous diversity generated by the different types of soil, the lie of the land, the type of grape grown – there are over forty varieties grown in Languedoc and Roussillon – the ability of the wine to age and the individual skills of the wine-grower.

Aside from the uplands of the Pyrenees and Haut Languedoc, the grape is grown more or less throughout the region, with cultivation most concentrated along the windswept coast. The southernmost wines are those of the **Côtes de Roussillon**, classified in three distinct AOCs which produce fruity and exciting reds – reminiscent of the Catalan vintages grown on the far side of the Pyrenees. Some of the best **Muscat**, which is not a regional *appellation* but a type of sweet wine, obtained by adding alcohol during the fermentation process (thus preventing the yeast from consuming all of the sugar), also comes from Roussillon, of which the most famous is the **Byrrh of Thuir**. Just north of Perpignan lie the *domaines* of **Fitou**, a recent AOC (1948) which combines characteristics of the heavy, robust vintages yielded by the neighbouring Corbières region's hill and littoral; **Corbières** wines are one of the great AOCs of Languedoc, as varied as the terrain which stretches along the Aude and the hillsides on its southern bank.

Closer to the water, but sheltered from the strong coastal winds by the mountain which separates Narbonne and Gruissan, the **Clape** AOC produces robust and flavourful reds. The vineyards of the coastal plain stretching from Bézier to near Nîmes and inland along the Hérault valley were grouped together some twenty years ago as the AOC **Côteaux de Languedoc**, which produces a solid if unexceptional range of reds, whites and rosés. On the other hand, the vintages of the **Costières de Nîmes**, which spread south and east of the city to the marshes of the Camargue, produce well-regarded reds, known for their strength and subtlety. Lastly, **Listel**, a rosé, is one of the best of the *vins du sable*, the "sand wines" of the Camarguais coast, which originated around Aigues-Mortes and Grau-du-Roi.

But the coast does not exercise a monopoly on fine wines in Languedoc and Roussillon. The foothills of Haut Languedoc, stretching west from Narbonne as far as the Montagne Noire, are home to the full-bodied reds of the **Cabardès**, and the honey-tinted whites and fruity reds of the **Minervois**.

South of Carcassonne, you'll find **Blanquette de Limoux**, Aude's most famous *appellation*: a sweetish sparkling white produced since at least the mid-sixteenth century. Curiously, one of Languedoc's most venerable and well-reputed vintages comes from far inland, in the district around **Gaillac**, the transitional zone between the Atlantic and Mediterranean climatic systems where cool ocean-borne winds take the edge off the harsh southern weather. First established as an AOC over a thousand years ago, it is best known for its whites, but also produces excellent reds and rosés. Virtually every tourist office has a brochure on local vintages and a list of *domaines* which can be visited for tasting. For a general orientation on the wines of the region, consult ⓦwww.vins-du-roussillon.com.

Communications

You should have no problem keeping in contact with people at home while you are in France. The country has an efficient postal system and you can have letters and packages sent general delivery to any of the official branches. The Internet is widely accessible, and is gradually displacing the now-primitive Minitel telnet system which France pioneered. Should you need to use the phone, you can use cheap pre-paid phone cards or access home-country operators via free numbers.

Mail

French **post offices** (*bureaux de poste* or *PTT*s) – look for bright yellow La Poste signs – are generally open 9am to 7pm Monday to Friday, and 9am to noon on Saturday. However, don't depend on these hours: in smaller towns and villages offices may close earlier and for lunch.

You can receive mail at the central post offices of most towns. It should be addressed (preferably with the surname first and in capitals) "**Poste Restante**, Poste Centrale", followed by the name of the town

and its postcode, detailed in the Guide for all the main cities. To collect your mail you need a passport or other convincing ID and there may be a charge of a couple of euros. You should ask for all your names to be checked, as filing systems are not brilliant.

For sending letters, remember that you can buy **stamps** (*timbres*) with less queuing from *tabacs*. Standard letters (20g or less) and postcards within France and to European Union countries cost €0.46, to North America €0.67 and to Australia and New Zealand €0.79. Inside many post offices you will find a row of yellow-coloured guichet automatiques – automatic ticket machines with instructions available in English with which you can weigh packages and buy the appropriate stamps; sticky labels and tape are also dispensed. A machine can change notes into change, so there is no need to queue for counter service. If you're sending parcels abroad, you can try to check prices on the guichet if available or in various leaflets: small post offices don't often send foreign mail and may need reminding, for example, of the reductions for printed papers and books. See Ⓦ www.laposte.fr for details on rates and services.

You can also use Minitel (see p.50) at post offices, change money, make photocopies, send faxes and make phone calls. To post your letter on the street, look for the bright yellow **postboxes**.

Telephones

You can make domestic and international **phone calls** from any telephone box (cabine) and can receive calls where there's a blue logo of a ringing bell. **Phone cards** (called télécartes) – available in €5 and €10 increments – are essential, since coin boxes are now only found in the most remote villages. The cards are available from tabacs and newsagents as well as post offices, tourist offices and some train station ticket offices. You can also use **credit cards** in many call boxes. Coin-only boxes still exist in cafés, bars, hotel foyers and rural areas; they take 10, 20 and 50 centimes and €1 pieces; put the money in

after lifting up the receiver and before dialling. You can keep adding more coins once you are connected. Local calls are costed in France at €0.30 for four minutes; long-distance calls within France cost up to €1.20 for three minutes depending on the distance. **Off-peak charges** apply on weekdays between 7pm and 8am and after noon on Saturday until 8am Monday.

For calls within France – local or long-distance – simply dial all ten digits of the number. Numbers beginning with ☎08.00 are free numbers; those beginning with ☎08.36 are premium rate (from €0.34 per minute), and those beginning with ☎06 are mobile and therefore also expensive to call. The major international calling codes are given in the box below; remember to omit the initial zero of the local area code from the subscriber's number.

A call to the UK (Royaume-Uni), the US (Les États Unis) or Canada will cost roughly €0.22 per minute, whereas Australia and New Zealand (Nouveau Zealand) start at €0.48; check Ⓦ www.francetelecom.com for detailed rates. By far the most convenient way of making international calls is to use a **calling card**, opening an account before you leave home; calls will be billed monthly to your credit card, to your phone bill if you are already a customer or to your home address. However, the rates per minute of these cards are many times higher than the cost of calling from a public phone in France, with flat rates only. Since these cards are free to obtain, it's certainly worth getting one at least for emergencies. You dial a free number (make sure you have

---

Useful numbers within Languedoc and Roussillon

Weather ☎08.36.68.02 + the number of the department: Ariège, 09; Aude, 11; Haute-Garonne, 31; Hérault, 34; Pyrénées-Orientales, 66; Tarn, 81.
Traffic and road conditions ☎08.36.68.20.00.
Telegrams by phone Internal ☎36.55; external ☎08.00.33.44.11 – all languages.
Time ☎36.99.
International operator For Canada and the US ☎00 33 11; for all other countries ☎00 33 followed by the country code.
International directory assistance For Canada and the US ☎00 33 12 11; for all other countries ☎00 33 12 followed by the country code.
French operator ☎13 to signal a fault.
French directory assistance ☎12.

with you the relevant number for France), your account number and then the number you wish to call. The drawback is that the free number is often engaged and you have to dial a great many digits. If you need to make many foreign calls from France, several companies offer cheap-rated phone cards on sale at tobacconists and newsagents; competition is fierce and a great many companies offer these services, so compare the calling times for your destination before choosing which one to buy (and beware hidden activation and connection charges).

To avoid payment altogether, you can, of course, make a reverse charge or **collect call** – known in French as *téléphoner en PCV* – by contacting the international operator (see box opposite). You can also do this through the operator in the UK, by dialling the Home Direct number ☎08.00.89.00.33; to get an English-speaking operator for North America, dial ☎00.00.11.

Calling home from abroad

One of the most convenient ways of phoning home from abroad is via a **telephone charge card** from your phone company back home. Using a PIN number, you can make calls from most hotel, public and private phones that will be charged to your account. Since most major charge cards are free to obtain, it's certainly worth getting one at least for emergencies; enquire first though whether your destination is covered, and bear in mind that rates aren't necessarily cheaper than calling from a public phone.

In the **US and Canada**, AT&T, MCI, Sprint, Canada Direct and other North American long-distance companies all enable their customers to make credit card calls while overseas, billed to your home number. Call your company's customer service line to find out if they provide service from France, and if so, what the toll-free access code is.

In **the UK and Ireland**, British Telecom (☎0800/345 144, ◉www.chargecard .bt.com) will issue free to all BT customers the BT Charge Card, which can be used in 116 countries; AT&T (dial ☎0800/890 011, then

888/641-6123 when you hear the AT&T prompt to be transferred to the Florida Call Centre, free 24 hours) has the Global Calling Card; while NTL (☎0500/100 505) issues its own Global Calling Card, which can be used in more than sixty countries abroad, though the fees cannot be charged to a normal phone bill.

To call **Australia and New Zealand** from overseas, telephone charge cards such as Telstra Telecard or Optus Calling Card in Australia, and Telecom NZ's Calling Card can be used to make calls abroad, which are charged back to a domestic account or credit card. Apply to Telstra ☎1800/038 000; Optus ☎1300/300 937; or Telecom NZ ☎04/801 9000.

Calling home from overseas

Note that the initial zero is omitted from the area code when dialing the UK, Ireland, Australia and New Zealand from abroad.

US and Canada international access code + 1 + area code.

Australia international access code + 61 + city code.

New Zealand international access code + 64 + city code.

UK international access code + 44 + city code.

Republic of Ireland international access code + 353 + city code.

Mobile phones

If you want to use your **mobile phone** abroad, you'll need to check with your phone provider whether it is will work and what the call charges are.

In the **UK**, for all but the very top-of-the-range packages, you'll have to inform your phone provider before going abroad to get international access switched on. You may get charged extra for this depending on your existing package and where you are travelling to. You are also likely to be charged extra for incoming calls when abroad, as the people calling you will be paying the usual rate. If you want to retrieve messages while you're away, you'll have to ask your provider for a new access code, as your home one is unlikely to work abroad. For further information about using your phone abroad, check out ◉www.telecomsadvice.org.uk/features /using_your_mobile_abroad.htm.

Unless you have a tri-band phone, it is unlikely that a mobile bought for use outside the **US** will work inside the States and vice versa, with many only working within the region designated by the area code in the phone number, ie 212, 415 etc. They tend to be very expensive to own in the US, too, as users are billed for both incoming and outgoing calls. Calling a US mobile, however, costs no more than making a call to a landline in that area code. For details of which mobiles will work outside the US, contact your mobile service provider.

Most mobiles in **Australia** and **New Zealand** use GSM, which works well in Europe – check with your provider.

Getting a mobile phone **in France** is – in principle – simply a matter of visiting a phone boutique (for instance, a France Telecom store) with identification, proof of address and proof of ability to pay. This involves setting up a French bank account, which will entitle you to the *bona fide* certificate known as an RIB (*Relève d'Identité Bancaire*); to obtain this you will need to provide a copy of a utility bill with your name on it, not necessarily a problem since banks are prepared to accept foreign utility bills.

Minitel

Many French phone subscribers have **Minitel**, a dinosaurial online computer that's been around since the early 1980s, which allows access through the phone lines to directories, databases, chat lines and so on. You will also find it in post offices. Most organizations, from sports federations to government institutions to gay groups, have a code consisting of numbers and letters, which you can call up for information, to leave messages and make reservations. You dial the number on the phone, wait for a fax-type tone, then type the letters on the keyboard, and finally press *Connexion Fin* (the same key ends the connection). If you're at all computer-literate and can understand basic keyboard terms in French (*retour* – return, *envoi* – enter, etc), you shouldn't find them hard to use. Be warned that most services cost more than phone rates. Directory enquiries (☎ 12) are free.

Email

Email is the cheapest and most hassle-free way of staying in touch with home while in France. Practically every reasonable-sized town has a **cybercafé** or connection point of some sort, and in less populated areas, the need is being filled by post offices, many of which now have rather expensive public Internet terminals, which are operated with a prepaid card (€7 for the first hour). In addition, France Telecom has street-side Internet kiosks in major cities. We have given details of cybercafés and other **Internet access** points in the Guide so you can stay online while travelling. Prices range from €3 to €8 per hour, so it can be worth shopping around. It's easy to open a free email account to use while you're away with Hotmail or Yahoo: go to ⓦ www.hotmail.com or ⓦ www.yahoo.com to find out how.

The media

English-language newspapers, such as *The Times*, the *Washington Post*, *New York Times* and the *International Herald Tribune*, are on sale the same day in some of the region's larger cities, including Toulouse, Montpellier and Nîmes, and the day after publication at resorts. Of the French daily papers, *Le Monde* is the most intellectual; it is widely respected, but somewhat austere, making no concessions to such frivolities as photographs. *Libération*, founded by Jean-Paul Sartre in the 1960s, is moderately left-wing, independent and more colloquial, with good, if choosy, coverage, while rigorous left-wing criticism of the French government comes from *L'Humanité*, the Communist Party paper. The other nationals are all firmly right-wing in their politics: *Le Figaro* is the most respected. The top-selling national is *L'Équipe*, which is dedicated to sports coverage, while *Paris-Turf* focuses on horse-racing. The widest circulations are enjoyed by the regional dailies: in Languedoc-Roussillon this is the *Midi-Libre* – though for travellers, this, like the rest of the regionals, is mainly of interest for its listings. See pp.20–21 for a list of online newspapers.

Weeklies of the *Newsweek/Time* model include the wide-ranging and socialist-inclined *Le Nouvel Observateur*, its right-wing counterpoint *L'Express,* the boringly centrist *L'Évenement de Jeudi* and the newcomer with a bite, *Marianne*. The best investigative journalism is to be found in the weekly satirical paper *Le Canard Enchaîné*. *Charlie Hebdo* is a sort of *Private Eye* or *Frank Magazine* equivalent. There is also *Paris-Match* for gossip about stars and royal families. **Monthlies** include the young, trendy and cheap *Nova*, which has excellent listings of cultural events, and *Actuel*, which is good for current events. There are, of course, the French versions of *Vogue*, *Elle* (weekly) and *Marie-Claire*, and the relentlessly urban *Biba*, for women's fashion and lifestyle.

Moral **censorship** of the press is rare. On the news-stands you'll find pornography of every shade, as well as covers featuring drugs, sex, blasphemy and bizarre forms of grossness alongside knitting patterns and DIY. You'll also find French **comics** (*bandes dessinées*), which often indulge such adult interests: wildly and wonderfully illustrated, they are considered to be quite an artform and whole museums are devoted to them.

Some of the huge numbers of homeless people in France (*les sans-logement*) make a bit of money by selling magazines on the streets which combine culture, humour and self-help with social and political issues. Costing €1.50, the best known of these is *L'Itinerant*.

French TV has six channels: three public (France 2, Arte/La Cinquième and FR3); some subscription (Canal Plus – with some unencrypted programmes); and two commercial open broadcasts (TF1 and M6). In addition there are the **cable** networks, which include France Infos, CNN, the BBC World Service, BBC Prime, MTV, Planète, which specializes in documentaries, Paris Première (lots of French-dubbed films) and Canal Jimmy (*Friends* and the like in French). There are two music channels: the American MTV and the French-run MCM, where you can get a real education in French rap. Parents travelling with children should be aware that most hotels which offer cable or satellite TV have at least one channel which shows hard-core pornography, usually from 11pm through the wee hours.

Arte/La Cinquième is a joint Franco-German cultural venture that transmits simultaneously in French and German: offerings include highbrow programmes, daily documentaries, art criticism, serious French and German movies and complete operas. During the day (6am–7pm), La Cinquième uses the frequency to broadcast educational programmes. **Canal Plus** is the main **movie channel** (and funder of the French film industry), with repeats of foreign films usually shown at least once in the original language. **FR3** screens a fair selection of serious movies, with its *Cinéma de Minuit* slot late on Sunday nights good for foreign, undubbed films. The main French **news broadcasts** are at 8.30pm on Arte and at 8pm on F2 and TF1.

If you've got a **radio**, you can tune in to English-language news on the BBC World Service on 648kHz AM or 198kHz long wave from midnight to 5am (and Radio 4 during the day). The Voice of America transmits on 90.5, 98.8 and 102.4 FM. For radio **news in French**, there's the state-run France Inter (87.8 FM), Europe 1 (104.7 FM) and round-the-clock news on France Infos (105.5 FM).

BBC (ⓦwww.bbc.co.uk/worldservice), **Radio Canada** (ⓦwww.rcinet.ca) and **Voice of America** (ⓦwww.voa.gov) list all the world service frequencies around the globe.

Opening hours, public holidays and festivals

Basic hours of business are 8am or 9am to noon or 1pm, and 2pm or 3pm to 6pm or 7pm. In big city centres, shops and other businesses stay open throughout the day, and in July and August most tourist offices and museums are open without interruption. Otherwise almost everything closes for a couple of hours at midday, or even longer in the south. Small food shops often don't reopen till halfway through the afternoon, closing around 7.30pm or 8pm just before the evening meal. Supermarkets tend to stay open 9am to 9pm Monday to Saturday.

The standard **closing days** are Sunday and/or Monday, with shops taking turns to close with their neighbours; many food shops such as *boulangeries* (bakeries) that open on Sunday will do so in the morning only. In small towns you'll find everything except the odd *boulangerie* shut on both days. This includes **banks**, which in cities are usually open Monday to Friday or Tuesday to Saturday (often Tuesday to Friday in small towns) from 8.30am to noon and 2 to 5pm, making it all too easy to find yourself dependent on hotels for money-changing at poor rates and high commission. Restaurants and cafés also often close on a Sunday or Monday.

Museums tend to open between 9am and 10am, close for lunch at noon until 2pm or 3pm, and then run through to 5pm or 6pm, although in the big cities they will stay open all day. **Closing days** are usually Tuesday or Monday, sometimes both. **Admission** charges can be very off-putting, though many state-owned museums have one day of the week (often Sun) when they're free or half-price, and you can often get reductions if you're a full-time student (with ISIC card), under 26 or over 60. **Cathedrals** are almost always open all day every day, with charges only for the crypt, treasuries or cloister and little fuss about how you're dressed. **Church** opening hours are often more restricted; on Sunday mornings (or at other times which you'll see posted up on the door) you may have to attend Mass to take a look. In small towns and villages, however, getting the key is not difficult – ask anyone nearby or seek out the priest, whose house is known as the *presbytère*.

It's hard to beat the experience of arriving in some small French village, expecting no more than a bed for the night, to discover the streets decked out with flags and streamers, a band playing in the square and the entire population out celebrating the feast of their patron saint. Apart from Bastille Day (July 14) and the Assumption of the Virgin Mary (August 15), there are many traditional folk **festivals** still thriving in Languedoc and Roussillon. Moreover, local and municipal governments have invested heavily in summer *fêtes* and free concert series, designed to bring visitors into the region's villages.

Celebrations of local patron saints are concentrated in summer months and are the occasion for fireworks, dancing and *pétanque* competitions. These are particularly colourful in the fishing ports of the Languedoc coast, where saints' effigies are paraded down to the sea and events include water-borne **jousting** competitions. In wine country, there are inevitably festivals coinciding with the grape harvest, and in other regions with that of the dominant local product. Throughout the Languedocian plain – notably from Béziers and east and in certain towns of the Pyrenees – *tauromachie* (see p.54), which involves Spanish-style *corridas* (bullfights) or indigenous *courses camarguaises*, occurs regularly throughout the summer, and at other big holidays, such as

Pentecost and the pre-Lenten carnival. The most important and interesting festivals are outlined at the beginning of each chapter of the Guide.

Public holidays

There are thirteen **national holidays** (*jours fériés*), when most shops and businesses (though not necessarily restaurants), and some museums, are closed. May in particular is a big month for holidays: as well as May Day and Victory Day, Ascension Day normally falls then, as sometimes does Pentecost.

January 1 New Year's Day
Easter Sunday
Easter Monday
Ascension Day (forty days after Easter)
Pentecost or Whitsun (seventh Sunday after Easter, plus the Monday)
May 1 May Day/Labour Day
May 8 Victory in Europe Day
July 14 Bastille Day
August 15 Assumption of the Virgin Mary
November 1 All Saints' Day
November 11 1918 Armistice Day
December 25 Christmas Day

Sports and outdoor pursuits

Languedoc and Roussillon offer a wide range of sports – both spectator and participatory. Although you can watch local teams play big league sports such as football, you'll find that locally popular games like rugby are more worthwhile to seek out. You also have the choice of a variety of outdoor activities, including hiking, cycling and skiing, and water-borne diversions such as rafting and sailing.

As well as rugby, the outdoor spectacle of **bullfighting**, or more properly, *tauromachie*, is incredibly popular across the region, both in Spanish and indigenous styles. **Water-jousting** (see box on p.282), a coastal tradition which pits boat-borne jousting teams against each other in an effort to unseat their opponents, has its home at Sète, but is practised along the length of the coast. **Pétanque**, or *boules*, is a game which you will see played in towns and villages

throughout the region, and which you can play yourself if you purchase a set (available at sports shops and large department stores).

Football and rugby

Languedoc and Roussillon are not the best places in France for **football**, and the only cities in the region which have a team in the First Division are Toulouse, whose club was clinging tenuously to the bottom, eighteenth place, at the time of writing, and Montpellier, who were faring better (although their finest moment was when they took the French Cup in 1990).

Rugby is the field game of choice in the region, and virtually every town of any size boasts a team. Top teams in the region include Toulouse, Narbonne, Perpignan, Nîmes and Castres; these have traditionally provided the core of the French national side.

Rugby originated in 1832, in England, and although it arrived in France not long after, it only really caught on in the Occitan south – perhaps as an unconscious means of marking a difference from the northern French. Post-game camaraderie is a big part of the whole experience, and you'll find yourself caught up in the cheerful spirit of things whether you see a major team like Stade Toulousain in action, or a small-town match with teams of the level of Albi or Pamiers.

Tauromachie

Bulls have been raised in eastern Languedoc since time immemorial, and in the last centuries **tauromachie** – "the art of the bull" (see box on p.226) – has come to play an important role in the culture of the whole region. While the people of the Petite Carmargue ranchlands see it as a measure of virility, Occitan patriots are attracted to it as a custom which has no equivalent in the north of France.

Two distinct types of *tauromachie* are practised in Languedoc and Roussillon, the better known of which is the Iberian-style **corrida**. This event, which can be seen at the *ferias* of Nîmes, St-Gilles and Béziers as well as smaller towns across Languedoc, and in Céret in Roussillon is a highly ritualized ceremony. In a typical afternoon, three matadors dispose of six bulls, each of which will face a number of torments, including being poked by horseback *picadores*, and pricked with spears by running *banderilleros*, before a series of choreographed passes is executed by the matador and the bull is killed. Crowds are extremely vocal; poor matadors are subjected to catcalls and shouts, while a successful performance is awarded with loud ovations.

The French **course**, which has its origin in the medieval *jeu taurin* ("bull-baiting") is quite distinct from the *corrida*. Less expensive and elaborate, it is more common in village *fêtes*, such as at Uzès or Aigues-Morte, and usually involves the bulls (or cows) being led into a ring and fitted with a rosette of ribbon and colourful tassels suspended between their horns. For fifteen minutes *raseteurs* provoke the bull into charging and attempt to snatch the rosette or tassels without getting trampled or gored. When all is complete, the bulls are herded out nervous, but otherwise unharmed, back to their pen. Unlike the ceremonial Spanish version, the *course* is more of a sport, with a stronger element of competition among the human participants.

Today *tauromachie* is more popular than ever; the **ferias** of Nîmes draw thousands of enthusiasts from all over France and the rest of Europe and are universally acknowledged as southern France's liveliest and most colourful festivities. But *tauromachie* has taken firm root even in the smallest of villages far from the *manades* of the plains. Even if they can afford no more than an *encierro*, villagers pool their money in order to pay for some sort of taurine display, without which no *fête* would be seen as complete. On the other hand, urban culture has prompted a low-level reaction against these activities, and has resulted, for instance, in the disappearance of *tauromachie* in Toulouse.

Pétanque

Once the preserve of sweatered old men in berets, recently **pétanque**, or *boules*, has seen a surge in popularity and a broadening of appeal to include more young people and women. The game is similar to English bowls. Two equally numbered teams (from one to three persons) find a space of hard, compact ground and throw a *cochonnet* (jack) a few metres (technically 6 to 10). A small circle is then marked on the ground to show the limit of the area in which the throwers must stand (hence *pétanque* from the Provençal "pied tanqués" or "feet together"). They then proceed in turns to launch a total of three balls (two in a 6-person match), each with the object of having their metal *boules* closest to the *cochonnet* at the end of the exchange. A point is gained for each ball that is closer than the nearest ball of the opposing team. The jack is then thrown again and play continues until one side scores 13. *Pétanque* matches invariably draw a crowd of onlookers, and you will not be considered rude if you stop to observe. The best times to watch are during village *fêtes*, which invariably include a tournament, drawing out the best players in the village.

Hiking, biking and riding

Walking is undoubtedly the way to get the most out of a visit to the region. Well-marked and maintained GR paths, signposted with their distinctive yellow and red bars, span the region, punctuated by *gîtes*, refuges and campsites along the way. The highest concentration of paths (and the best hiking scenery) is found in the Pyrenees, and its foothills, where you will find an extensive network of yellow- and- red-marked GRP (*grand randonnées du pays*) paths as well as HRP (*haute route des Pyrénées*) routes. In addition local AR footpaths abound, and in virtually every village you'll find an information board with a map outlining local itineraries of varying length and difficulty. Even if you're spending only a few hours in a village, it's worth enquiring at the tourist office which will almost certainly have a pamphlet outlining local walks.

Recently a series of excellent *Topoguides* has been published by the Federation Française de la Randonnée Pédestre (14 rue Riquet 75019, Paris ⓦ www.ffrp.asso.fr). Guides are published for each *région* and *département*. Regional guides detail eighty walks and VTT routes (€13.95) and departmental guides have forty (€11.95); the series is widely available in bookshops. Most tourist offices also give away free or low-priced (under €5) guides to local walks and bike trails. If you're travelling with children or are looking for less challenging routes, try the FFRP's *Les Sentiers d'Emilie*, which details thirty easy walks in the Pyrenees-Orientales. All of these guides are in French, but even non-French speakers will be able to use them with the help of a pocket dictionary. For mountain refuges, the Club Alpin Français (ⓦ www.clubalpin.com) has online information and publishes an annual guide.

Biking is the next best option, and the cities of the south have been remarkably quick to adapt to two-wheeled transport, particularly Toulouse and Montpellier. Around Montpellier, Agde and Narbonne, extensive networks of bike paths, often using decommissioned roads, link the coastal villages and the cities. In the countryside disused rail lines, such as the Gijou Valley Trail (see p.201), have been set up as bicycle (VTT) routes, and canal towpaths make it possible to cross the region with ease. Traffic off the main roads is surprisingly light, and with the exception of the coastal plain you will find the biggest challenge to be the hilliness of the terrain.

While **horse-riding** is not practical as a means of transport, it is an excellent way of enjoying the countryside. Practically every town and many farms have equestrian centres where you can ride unaccompanied or with a guide on local trails. In the Pyrenees **mules** provide a more practical alternative. Local tourist offices can give you information on riding centres or you can contact the regional equestrian tourism organization ATECREL, 14 rue des Logis, 34140 Loupian (☏04.67.43.82.50), or the Fédération Française d'Équitation (DNTE), 30 av d'Iéna, 75116 Paris (☏01.53.67.44.44, ⓦ www .ffe.com). For mule-trekking, contact the Fédération Nationale Ânes et Randonnées, Broissieux, 73340 Bellecombe-en-Bauges, (☏04.79.63.84.01, ⓦ wasin.free.fr/fnar.htm).

Skiing, rafting and watersports

There are a number of **ski stations** in the eastern Pyrenees, and although they cannot offer anything to compare to the great resorts of the French Alps, you will be able to find some decent downhill skiing if you visit between November and April. Cross-country skiing, or *ski de fond*, is also a possibility, and the broad massifs of the Cerdagne and Ariège are particularly well suited to it. The relatively low altitude of some resorts is partially off-set by the extensive use of snow-making machines. The most important and better-known resorts, among them Font-Romeu, Formiguères and Porté-Puymorens, are detailed in the Guide, and regional and departmental tourist offices – in this case Ariège and Pyrénées-Orientales (see pp.19 and 20) – will also have information. In fact, the CDT Ariège web page, ⓦ www.ariegepyrenees.com, often has special accommodation and lift-ticket deals on offer. Otherwise, for wintersports (including snowshoeing) you might also contact the Pyrénées Club de France, 8 rue de la Colombette 3100 Toulouse (☎ 05.62.73 .56.35, ⓦ www.pyrenees-club.asso.fr).

While you are exploring the hilly uplands of the Languedoc and Roussillon, you ought to sample also the thrill of **rafting** down one of the region's many dramatic rivers. This sport has exploded in recent years, and you will scarcely pass a gorge which is not capped by a rafting outfit at its upper end. The biggest concentration is in the upper Hérault south of Ganges, but good opportunities can be found on the Orbiel, west of Lamalou, and on the Ariège around

Tarascon. More placid paddling can by done by **canoe**, notably on the calmer stretches of water of the Aude and Gardon, and at the Pont du Gard. **Pot-holing** and **climbing** are also popular throughout Languedoc and Roussillon – tourist offices can hook you up with local guides and operators.

Most of the seaside towns have been fully developed as resorts, and have facilities for the whole gamut of **watersports**: in summer months you'll find everything from jet-skis and sail-boards to houseboats and yachts for rent. If you are specifically looking for beachside activities, Le-Grau-du-Roi has the best range of facilities, while La Grande-Motte runs a close second. There are a number of SCUBA clubs in the beach towns of Roussillon which arrange outings and run certified basic diving courses.

Crime and personal safety

Petty theft is endemic in all the major cities and along the coast. Drivers, particularly with foreign number plates or in rental cars with Parisian registration, face a high risk of break-ins. Vehicles are rarely stolen, but car radios and luggage make tempting targets.

It obviously makes sense to take the normal **precautions**: not flashing wads of notes or travellers' cheques around; carrying your bag or wallet securely; never letting cameras and other valuables out of your sight; and parking your car overnight in an attended garage or within sight of a police station. But the best security is having a good insurance policy, keeping a separate record of cheque numbers, credit card numbers and the phone numbers for cancelling them (see p.27), and the relevant details of all your valuables.

If you need to **report a theft**, go along to the *commissariat de police* (addresses are given in the Guide for the major cities), where they will fill out a *constat de vol*. The first thing they'll ask for is your passport, and vehicle documents if relevant. Although the

police are not always as co-operative as they might be, it is their duty to assist you if you've lost your passport or all your money.

If you have an **accident** while driving, you have officially to fill in and sign a *constat à l'aimable* (jointly agreed statement); car insurers are supposed to give you this with the policy, though in practice few seem to have heard of it. For **non-criminal driving offences** such as speeding, the police can impose an on-the-spot fine.

People caught smuggling or possessing **drugs**, even a few grams of marijuana, are liable to find themselves in jail, and consulates will not be sympathetic. This is not to say that hard-drug consumption isn't a visible activity: there are scores of kids dealing in *poudre* (heroin) in the big French cities and the authorities seem unable to do much about it. As a rule, people are no more nor less paranoid about cannabis busts than they are in the UK or North America.

Should you be **arrested** on any charge, you have the right to contact your consulate (addresses are given on p.18).

The two main types of **police** – the Police Nationale and the Gendarmerie Nationale – are for all practical purposes indistinguishable. The CRS (Compagnies Républicaines de Sécurité), on the other hand, are an entirely different proposition. They are a mobile force of paramilitary heavies, used to guard sensitive embassies, "control" demonstrations and generally intimidate the populace on those occasions when the public authorities judge that it is stepping out of line. Armed with guns, CS gas and truncheons, they have earned themselves a reputation for brutality over the years, particularly at those moments when the tensions inherent in the long civil war of French politics have reached boiling point. You can be stopped anywhere in France and asked to produce ID. If it happens to you, it's not worth being difficult or facetious. Lastly, in the Pyrenees, you may come across specialized **mountaineering sections** of the police force. They are unfailingly helpful, friendly and approachable, providing rescue services and guidance.

Emergency numbers

All these numbers are free
Fire brigade (*pompiers*) ☎18
Medical emergencies ☎15
Police ☎17
Rape crisis (*SOS Viol*) ☎08.00.05.95.95
AIDS information (SIDA Info Service) ☎08.00.84.08.00

Racism

Racist attitudes in the populace and the police are rife. A survey on French attitudes to race, commissioned by the French government and published in June 1998, resulted in 38 percent of the population declaring themselves racist, double the figures for similar surveys in Britain and Germany, and the

Front National, a neo-fascist, racist party, headed by **Jean-Marie Le Pen**, won fifteen percent of the vote in the last parliamentary elections. Support for the party was highest in Provence and the Côte d'Azur although in Languedoc and Roussillon Perpignan's *mairie* and several seats in the Hérault *département*'s council also went to the far right. The Front National's alliance with conservatives led to changes in educational, cultural and sporting programmes to suit its policies, the party's fundamental priority being the withdrawal of benefits to immigrants who have not yet been granted French citizenship.

Although the 1998 World Cup win by France's multicultural team raised a wave of popular enthusiasm for France's immigrants, the 2002 elections which saw the reactionary right of Le Pen and company sweep aside the Socialists and spring to second place showed that xenophobia is deep-rooted and durable. Travellers of non-European origin, particularly those of African or Middle Eastern extraction, may encounter racism: hotels claiming to be booked up, police demanding to see papers and abuse. In addition, even entering the country can be difficult. Changes in passport regulations have put an end to outright refusal to let some British holiday-makers in, but customs and immigration officers can still be obstructive and malicious. In North African-dominated areas of cities, identity checks by the police are very common and not pleasant. The clampdown on illegal immigration and much tougher laws have resulted in a significant increase in police stop-and-search operations. Carrying your passport at all times is a good idea.

If you suffer a **racial assault**, you're likely to get a much more sympathetic hearing from your consulate than from the police. There are many anti-racism organizations which will offer support (though they may not have English-speakers): Mouvement contre le Racisme et pour l'Amitié entre les Peuples (MRAP; ❻www.mrap.asso.fr) and SOS Racism have offices in most big cities.

Living and working in France

Specialists aside, most Britons, North Americans, Australians and Kiwis who manage to survive for long periods of time in France do it on luck, brazenness and willingness to live in pretty basic conditions. In the cities, bar work, club work, freelance translating or teaching English, software fixing, data processing and typing or working as an au pair are some of the ways people scrape by; in the countryside, the options come down to seasonal fruit- or grape-picking (*vendange*), teaching English, busking or DIY oddjobbing. Remember that unemployment in France is very high, and particularly so in traditionally depressed Languedoc and Roussillon, where it hovers around 23 percent. Obviously, the better your French, the better your chances are of finding work.

Anyone staying in France for over three months must have a *carte de séjour* (see p.18), or residency permit – citizens of the EU are entitled to one automatically. France has a **minimum wage** (the SMIC – Salaire Minimum Interprofessional de Croissance), indexed to the cost of living; it's currently around €6.85 an hour (for a maximum 169-hour month). Employers, though, are likely to pay lower wages to temporary foreign workers who don't have easy legal resources, and make them work longer hours. By law, however, all EU nationals are entitled to exactly the same pay, conditions and trade union rights as French nationals.

If you're looking for something secure, it's important to plan well in advance. A few books which might be worth consulting are *Work Your Way Around the World* by Susan Griffiths (Vacation Work), *A Year Between* and *Working Holidays* (both Central Bureau) and *Living and Working in France* by Victoria Pybus, published by Vacation Work 1998. **In France**, check out the "Offres d'Emploi" (Job Offers) in *Le Monde*, *Le Figaro* and the *International Herald Tribune*, and try the youth information agency CIDJ (Centre d'Information et de Documentation Jeunesse), 101 quai Branly, 17015 Paris, or CIJ (Centre d'Information Jeunesse) offices in other main cities, which sometimes have temporary jobs for foreigners. The national employment agency, ANPE (Agence Nationale pour l'Emploi), with offices all over France, advertises temporary jobs in all fields and, in theory, offers a whole range of servic-

es to job-seekers open to all EU citizens, but it is not renowned for its helpfulness to foreigners. Non-EU citizens will have to show a work permit to apply for any of their jobs. Vac-Job, 46 av Réné-Coty, 17014 Paris (☎01.43.20.70.51), publishes the annual *Emplois d'Été en France* (*Summer Jobs in France*), which may be useful.

Some people find jobs **selling magazines** on the street and **leafleting** by asking other vendors for the agency address. The American/Irish/British **bars** and **restaurants** in the main cities and resorts sometimes have vacancies. You'll need to speak French, look smart and be prepared to work very long hours.

Temporary jobs in the **travel industry** revolve around courier work – supervising and working on bus tours or summer campsites. You'll need good French (and maybe even another language) and should write to as many tour operators as you can, preferably in early spring. In Britain, ads occasionally appear in the *Guardian*'s "Media" section (every Mon). Getting work as a courier on a campsite is slightly easier. It usually involves putting up tents at the beginning of the season, taking them down again at the end, and general maintenance and troubleshooting work in the months between; Canvas Holidays (☎01383/644 018) are worth approaching. The British company PGL Young Adventure Ltd, Alton Court, Penyard Lane, Ross-on-Wye HR9 (☎01989/764 211, ⓦwww.pgl.co.uk) runs several children's activity centres in France, employing

French bureaucracy: a warning

French officialdom and **bureaucracy** can damage your health. That Gallic shrug and "Ce n'est pas possible" is not the result of training programmes in making life difficult for foreigners: it drives most French citizens mad as well. Sorting out social security, long-stay visas, job contracts, bank accounts, tenancy agreements, university enrolment or any other financial, legal or state matter requires serious commitment. Your reserves of patience, diligence, energy (both physical and mental) and equanimity in the face of bloody-mindedness and Catch-22s, will be tested to the full. Expect to spend days repeatedly visiting the same office and considerable sums on official translations of every imaginable document.

people proficient in watersports or with youth-work experience, and offers general catering, domestic and driving work, between May and September every year; you should apply before April.

An offbeat possibility if you want to discover rural life is being a **working guest** on an organic farm. The period can be anything from a week to a couple of months and the work may involve cheese-making, market gardening, bee-keeping, wine-producing and building. For details of the scheme and a list of French addresses, you can write to Willing Workers on Organic Farms (WWOOF), 19 Bradford Rd, Lewes BN7 1RB, in the UK; WWOOF W Tree, Buchan, VIC 3885 (⩊www.earthlink.com.au/wwoof) in Australia; or WWOOF RR2, Carlson Rd, S18 C9, Nelson, British Columbia VIL 5P5 in Canada, enclosing an self-addressed envelope.

Teaching English

There are two options: find or prepare for finding work before you go, or just wing it and see what you come up with while you're out there, particularly if you already have a degree and/or teaching experience. **Teaching English** – often abbreviated as ELT (English Language Teaching) or TEFL (Teaching English as a Foreign Language) – is the way many people finance their way around the greater part of the world; you can get a CELTA (Certificate in English Language Teaching to Adults) qualification before you leave home or even while you're abroad. International House has several branches in France (though none in Languedoc-Roussillon) which offer the course, and you could even turn it into a proper career. Strictly speaking, you don't need a degree to

do the course, but you'll certainly find it easier to get a job with the degree/certificate combination. Certified by the RSA, the course is very demanding and costs about £944 for the month's full-time tuition; you'll be thrown in at the deep end and expected to teach right away. The British Council's website, ⩊www.britishcouncil.org/work/jobs.htm, has a list of English-teaching vacancies.

Useful publications and websites

Another pre-planning strategy for working abroad, whether teaching English or otherwise, is to get hold of Overseas Jobs Express (☎01273/699 611, ⩊www.overseasjobs.com), a fortnightly publication with a range of job vacancies, available by subscription only. Vacation Work also publishes books on summer jobs abroad and how to work your way around the world; call ☎01865/241 978 or visit ⩊www.vacation-work.co.uk for their catalogue. Travel magazines like *Wanderlust* (every two months; £3.60) have a Job Shop section which often advertises job opportunities with tour companies. Check ⩊www.studyabroad.com for listings and links to study and work programmes worldwide.

Study and work programmes

From the UK and Ireland

British Council ☎020/7930 8466. Produces a free leaflet which details study opportunities abroad. The Council's Central Management Direct Teaching

(☎020/7389 4931) recruits TEFL teachers for posts worldwide (check ⊛ www.britishcouncil.org/work /jobs.htm for a current list of vacancies), and its Central Bureau for International Educational and Training (☎020/7389 4004, ⊛ www.centralbureau .org.uk) enables those who already work as educators to find out about teacher development programmes abroad. It also publishes a book, *Year Between*, aimed principally at gap-year students detailing volunteer programmes and schemes abroad.

Council Exchange ☎020/7478 2000, ⊛ www.councilexchanges.org.uk. International study and work programmes for students and recent graduates in Europe, and around the world.

Erasmus EU-run student exchange programme enabling students at participating universities in Britain and Ireland to study in one of 26 European countries (including France). Mobility grants available for three months to a full academic year. Anyone interested should contact their university's international relations office, or check the Erasmus website ⊛ europa.eu.int/comm/education/erasmus .html.

International House ☎020/7518 6999, ⊛ www.ihlondon.com. Head office for reputable English-teaching organization which offers TEFL training leading to the award of a Certificate in English Language Teaching to Adults (CELTA), and recruits for teaching positions in Britain and abroad.

From the US

Most universities have semester- or year-abroad programmes to certain countries; the following are independent organizations that run programmes in lots of countries.

AFS Intercultural Programs 10016 ☎1-800/876-2377 or 212/299 9000, ⊛ usa.afs.org. Runs summer experiential programmes aimed at fostering international understanding for teenagers and adults.

American Institute for Foreign Study ☎1-800/727-2437, ⊛ www.aifs.com. Language study and cultural immersion for the summer or school year, as well as au pair programmes.

Association for International Practical Training ☎1-800/994-2443 or 410/997-2200, ⊛ www.aipt.org. Summer internships for students who have completed at least two years of college in science, agriculture, engineering or architecture.

Bernan Associates ☎1-800/274-4888, ⊛ www.bernan.com. Distributes UNESCO's encyclopedic *Study Abroad*.

Council on International Educational Exchange (CIEE) ☎1-800/2COUNCIL, ⊛ www.ciee.org. The non-profit parent organization of Council Travel, CIEE arrange six-month work permits for currently enrolled or recently graduated students in France, and publishes *Work, Study, Travel Abroad and Volunteer! The Comprehensive Guide to Voluntary Service in the US and Abroad*.

Experiment in International Living ☎1-800/345-2929 or 802/257-7751, ⊛ www.usexperiment.org. Summer programme for high-school students.

Harper Collins Perseus Division ☎1-800/242-7737, ⊛ www.harpercollins.com. Publishes *International Jobs: Where They Are, How to Get Them*.

From Australia

Australians Studying Abroad ☎03/9509 1955, ⊛ www.asatravinfo.com.au. Study tours focusing on art and culture.

Travellers with disabilities

France has no special reputation for providing facilities for disabled travellers. For people in wheelchairs, the haphazard parking habits and stepped village streets are serious obstacles, and public toilets with disabled access are rare. In the major cities and coastal resorts, however, ramps or other forms of access are gradually being added to hotels, museums and some theatres and concert halls. APF, the French paraplegic organization, which has an office in each département (we've given details of those in Toulouse and Montpellier, see below) will be the most reliable source of information on accommodation with disabled access and other facilities. In general, watch for the Label National Tourisme Handicap (an APF initiative) affixed to disabled-friendly services and businesses.

Public **transport** is certainly not wheelchair-friendly, and although many train stations now have ramps to enable wheelchair-users to board and descend from carriages, at others it is still up to the guards to carry the chair. The high-speed **TGVs** (including Eurostar) all have places for wheelchairs in the first-class saloon coach, which you must book in advance, though no higher fee is charged; on other trains, a wheelchair symbol within the timetable denotes whether that service offers special features, and you and your companion will again be upgraded to first class with no extra charge. The *Guide du Voyageur à Mobilité Réduite*, available free at main train stations, details all facilities. **Taxis** are obliged by law to carry you and to help you into the vehicle, also to carry your guide dog if you are blind. Specialist taxi services are available in some towns: these are detailed in the Ministry of Transport and Tourism's pamphlet *Guide des Transports à l'Usage des Personnes à Mobilité Réduite*, available at airports, main train stations and some tourist offices. The guide also gives some indication of the accessibility of urban public transport systems, and the availability of cars for rent with hand controls.

Up-to-date information about handicap accessibility, special programmes and discounts is best obtained from organizations at home before you leave or from the French disability organizations. The publication *Touristes Quand Même!*, produced by the CNRH (see p.62), lists facilities throughout France but is not updated regularly. Some

tourist offices have information but, again, it is not always very reliable. The Holiday Care Service has an information sheet on accessible **accommodation** in France.

Most of the cross-Channel **ferry companies** offer good facilities, though up-to-date information about access is difficult to get hold of. **Eurostar**, having been established in the 1990s, offers an excellent deal for wheelchair users. There are two special spaces in the first-class carriages for wheelchairs, with an accompanying seat for a companion. No advance bookings are necessary, though the limited spaces might make it wise to reserve ahead of time and also to arrange the special assistance which Eurostar offers at either end. As far as **airlines** go, British Airways has a better-than-average record for treatment of disabled passengers, and from North America, Virgin and Air Canada come out tops in terms of disability awareness (and seating arrangements) and might be worth contacting first for any information they can provide.

Contacts for travellers with disabilities

In France

APF (Association des Paralysés de France), Head office, 17 bd Auguste-Blanqui, 75013 Paris ☎01.40.78.69.00, ⊛www.apf.asso.fr; 116bis, rue des Amidonniers, Toulouse ☎ 05.62.30.64.00; 1620, rue St Priest, Parc Euromédecine, 34097 Montpellier ☎04.67.10.03.25. National organization providing useful information and lists of new and accessible accommodation. Their guide *Où Ferons-Nous Étape* is available at the office or by post to a French address.

CNRH (Comité National Français de Liaison pour la Réadaptation des Handicapés), 236bis rue de Tolbiac, 75013 Paris ☎01.53.80.66.66; 91 rue de Fenouillet, 31200 Toulouse ☎05.61.13.48.00. Information service with various useful guides.

In the UK and Ireland

Access Travel 6 The Hillock, Astley, Lancashire M29 7GW ☎01942/888 844, ⊛www.access-travel.co.uk. Tour operator that can arrange flights, transfer and accommodation. This is a small business, personally checking out places before recommendation. ATOL bonded, established seven years.

Holiday Care 2nd floor, Imperial Building, Victoria Rd, Horley, Surrey RH6 7PZ ☎0845/124 9971, minicom ☎0845/124 9976, ⊛www.holidaycare.org.uk. Provides free lists of accessible accommodation abroad. Information on financial help for holidays available.

Irish Wheelchair Association Blackheath Drive, Clontarf, Dublin 3 ☎01/818 6400, ⊛www.iwa.ie. Useful information provided about travelling abroad with a wheelchair.

RADAR (Royal Association for Disability and Rehabilitation) 12 City Forum, 250 City Rd, London EC1V 8AF ☎020/7250 3222, minicom ☎020/7250 4119, ⊛www.radar.org.uk. A good source of advice on holidays and travel.

Tripscope Alexandra House, Albany Rd, Brentford, Middlesex TW8 0NE ☎0845/7585 641, ⊛www.tripscope.org.uk. This registered charity provides a national telephone information service offering free advice on UK and international transport for those with a mobility problem.

In the US and Canada

Access-Able ⊛www.access-able.com. Online resource for travellers with disabilities.

Directions Unlimited 123 Green Lane, Bedford Hills, NY 10507 ☎1-800/533-5343 or 914/241-1700. Travel agency specializing in bookings for people with disabilities.

Mobility International USA 451 Broadway, Eugene, OR 97401 ☎541/343-1284, ⊛www.miusa.org. Information and referral services, access guides, tours and exchange programmes. Annual membership $35 (includes quarterly newsletter).

Society for the Advancement of Travelers with Handicaps (SATH) 347 5th Ave, New York, NY 10016 ☎212/447-7284, ⊛www.sath.org. Non-profit educational organization that has actively represented travellers with disabilities since 1976.

Wheels Up! ☎1-888/38-WHEELS, ⊛www.wheelsup.com. Provides discounted airfare, tour and cruise prices for disabled travellers, also publishes a free monthly newsletter and has a comprehensive website.

In Australia and New Zealand

ACROD (Australian Council for Rehabilitation of the Disabled) PO Box 60, Curtin ACT 2605; Suite 103, 1st floor, 1–5 Commercial Rd, Kings Grove 2208, ☎02/6282 4333, TTY ☎02/6282 4333, ⊛www.acrod.org.au. Provides lists of travel agencies and tour operators for people with disabilities.

Disabled Persons Assembly 4/173–175 Victoria St, Wellington, New Zealand ☎04/801 9100 (also TTY), ⊛www.dpa.org.nz. Resource centre with lists of travel agencies and tour operators for people with disabilities.

▲ Boules player

Senior travellers

Languedoc and Roussillon are very senior-friendly travel regions, with a good range of services, an amenable climate and a range of activities which allows you to chose your own pace. Moreover, the demography of the region means that there will be plenty of opportunity to meet similarly aged locals, especially during the autumn "shoulder" travel season, when French retirees take advantage of lower prices to see their own country.

Contacts for senior travellers

American Association of Retired Persons ☏1-800/424-3410 or 202/434-2277, ⓦwww.aarp.org. Can provide discounts on accommodation and vehicle rental. Membership open to US and Canadian residents aged 50 or over for an annual fee of US $12.50.

Elderhostel ☏1/877-426-8056, ⓦwww.elderhostel.org. Runs an extensive worldwide network of educational and activity programmes, cruises and homestays for people over 60 (companions may be younger). Programmes generally last a week or more and costs are in line with those of commercial tours.

Travelling with children

Kids are generally welcome everywhere, and in most bars and restaurants, though French children seem to be much better trained at a younger age in restaurant etiquette. Hotels charge by the room, with a small supplement for an additional bed or cot, and family-run places will usually babysit or offer a listening service while you eat or go out. Especially in the seaside towns, most restaurants have children's menus or will cook simpler food on request.

You'll have no difficulty finding disposable nappies (*couches à jeter*), but nearly all baby foods have added sugar and salt, and French milk powders are very rich indeed. SNCF charge nothing on trains and buses for under-4s, and half-fare for 4–11s (see p.30 for other reductions). In most museums children under 4 are free and it's usually half-price or more off for under-18s, while entry to many monuments is free for under-12s. Most local tourist offices have details of specific **activities** for children – in particular, many resorts supervise "clubs" for children on the beach. And almost every town down to small ones has a children's playground with a good selection of activities. Most

parks have a children's play area; unfortunately the majority of parks are gravelled rather than grassed and when there are lawns they are often out of bounds (*pelouse interdite*), so sprawling horizontally with toddlers and napping babies is usually not an option. Something to beware of – not that you can do much about it – is the difficulty of negotiating a child's buggy over the large cobbles that cover many of the older streets in town centres. Finally, a considerable portion of French restaurants now feature reduced-price children's menus. If you're looking for general advice on travelling with children, try the online *Family Travel Times* (ⓦwww.familytraveltimes.com).

Gay and lesbian travellers

France is more liberal on homosexuality than most other European countries. The legal age of consent is 16. In Languedoc gay communities thrive in larger centres, such as Toulouse and Montpellier, and some beach towns, like Palavas, though lesbian life is rather less upfront. Addresses are listed in the Guide, and you'll find details of groups and publications for the whole region listed below.

In general, the French consider sexuality to be a private matter and homophobic assaults are very rare. On the whole, gays tend to be discreet outside specific gay venues, parades and certain coastal resorts. Toulouse has the reputation for being a city with a vibrant gay and lesbian culture, although there is no notable gay "ghetto" as such. Montpellier, traditionally politically left-wing and socially liberal, officially embraces gay culture, supporting many events in the city.

Contacts for gay and lesbian travellers

In France

ARCL (Les Archives, Recherches et Cultures Lesbiennes), based at the Maison des Femmes ☎01.46.28.54.94, ⓔarchives.lesbiennes@wanadoo.fr. ARCL publish a biannual directory of lesbian, gay and feminist addresses in France, *L'Annuaire*, and organize frequent meetings around campaigning, artistic and intellectual issues.
Centre Gai et Lesbienne Toulouse, 4 rue de Belfort ☎05.61.62.30.62. Open for phone calls and visits Mon–Fri 5–8pm, Sat 3–8pm, and on Sunday the *Café Positif*, a great place for meeting people, is open from 3 to 7pm.
Minitel 36.15 GAY is the Minitel number to dial for information on groups, contacts, messages, etc.

Gay and lesbian media in France

Fréquence Gaie (FG) 98.2 FM. 24-hour gay and lesbian radio station with music, news, chats, information on groups and events, etc.
Guide Gai Pied The most comprehensive gay guide to France, published annually and carrying a good selection of lesbian and gay addresses online at ⓦwww.gaipied.fr.
Lesbia The most widely available lesbian

publication, available from most newsagents. Each monthly issue features a wide range of articles, listings, reviews, lonely hearts and contacts.
Spartacus International Gay Guide Guidebook in English focusing mainly on gay travel in Europe with an extensive section on France. Geared mostly towards males but with some info for lesbians. Available around the world at travel and gay bookshops.

In the UK

In addition to the following information, also check out adverts in the weekly papers *Boyz* and *Pink Paper*, handed out free in gay venues.
ⓦ**www.gaytravel.co.uk** Online gay and lesbian travel agent, offering good deals on all types of holiday. Also lists gay- and lesbian-friendly hotels around the world.
Dreamwaves Holidays ☎0870/042 2475, ⓦwww.gayholidaysdirect.com. Specializes in exclusively gay holidays, including skiing trips and summer sun packages.
Madison Travel ☎01273/202 532, ⓦwww.madisontravel.co.uk. Established travel agents specializing in packages to gay- and lesbian-friendly mainstream destinations, and also to gay/lesbian destinations.
Respect Holidays ☎0870/770 0169, ⓦwww.respect-holidays.co.uk. Offers exclusively gay packages to all popular Europan resorts.

In the US and Canada

Damron ☎1-800/462-6654 or 415/255-0404, ⓦwww.damron.com. Publisher of the *Men's Travel Guide*, a pocket-sized yearbook full of listings of hotels, bars, clubs and resources for gay men; the *Women's Traveler*, which provides similar listings for lesbians; the *Road Atlas*, which shows lodging and entertainment in major US cities; and *Damron Accommodations*, which provides detailed listings of over 1000 accommodations for gays and lesbians worldwide. All of these titles are offered at a discount on the website. No specific city guides – everything

is incorporated in the yearbooks.
gaytravel.com ☎ 1-800/GAY-TRAVEL,
ⓦ www.gaytravel.com. The premier site for trip planning, bookings and general information about international gay and lesbian travel.
International Gay & Lesbian Travel Association ☎ 1-800/448-8550 or 954/776-2626, ⓦ www.iglta.org. Trade group that can provide a list of gay- and lesbian-owned or -friendly travel agents, accommodation and other travel businesses.

In Australia and New Zealand

Gay and Lesbian Tourism Australia
ⓦ www.galta.com.au. Directory and links for gay and lesbian travel in Australia and worldwide.

New Zealand Gay and Lesbian Tourism Association ⓦ www.nzglta.org.nz. Organization devoted to enhancing the New Zealand travel experience for gay, lesbian and bisexual visitors.
Parkside Travel ☎ 08/8274 1222,
ⓔ parkside@herveyworld.com.au. Gay travel agent associated with local branch of Hervey World Travel; all aspects of gay and lesbian travel worldwide.
Silke's Travel ☎ 1800/807 860 or 02/8347 2000,
ⓦ www.silkes.com.au. Long-established gay and lesbian specialist, with the emphasis on women's travel.
Tearaway Travel ☎ 1800/664 440 or 03/9510 6644, ⓦ www.tearaway.com. Gay-specific business dealing with international and domestic travel.

Directory

BEACHES Beaches are public property within 5m of the high-tide mark, so you can kick sand past private villas. Under a different law, however, you can't camp.
CAMERAS AND FILM Film is considerably cheaper in North America than France – or Britain – so stock up before travelling. If you're bringing a video camcorder, make sure any tapes you purchase in France will be compatible. Again, American videotape prices are way below French prices.
CONTRACEPTIVES Condoms (*préservatifs* or *capotes*) are available at all pharmacies, as well as from many clubs and street dispensers (€2 for 4 condoms) in larger cities. You can also get spermicidal cream and jelly (*dose contraceptive*), plus suppositories (*ovules, suppositoires*) and (with a prescription) the Pill (*la pillule*), a diaphragm (*le diaphragme*) or IUD (*le sterilet*).
ELECTRICITY This is almost always 220V, using plugs with two round pins. If you haven't bought the appropriate transformer before leaving home, the best place in France to find the right one is the electrical section of a department store, where someone is also more likely to speak English; cost is around €10. Before you plug in, check that the transformer is of sufficient voltage and amperage for the appliance that you plan on plugging in.
FISHING You get fishing rights by becoming a member of an authorized fishing club – tourist

offices have details.
LAUNDRY Laundries are common in French towns, and some are listed in the Guide – elsewhere look in the phone book under "Laveries Automatiques". They are often unattended, so come pre-armed with small change. Machines are normally graded into 5kg, 8kg or 10kg wash sizes, and the smallest costs around €2.50 for a load, though some laundries only have bigger machines and charge around €4. If you're doing your own washing in hotels, keep quantities small as most forbid doing any laundry in your room.
PEDESTRIANS French drivers pay no heed to pedestrian/zebra crossings marked with horizontal white stripes on roads. It is very dangerous to step out onto one and assume drivers will stop as in Britain and Australia. Take just as great care as you would crossing at any other point. Also be careful at traffic lights: check cars are not still speeding towards you even when the green man is showing.
SWIMMING POOLS Swimming pools (*piscines*) are well signposted in most French towns and reasonably priced, usually around €4 for a swim. Tourist offices have their addresses. You may be requested to wear a bathing cap, whether you are male or female, so come prepared.
TIME France is one hour ahead of the UK, six hours ahead of Eastern Standard Time, and nine

hours ahead of Pacific Standard Time. This also applies during daylight savings seasons, which are observed in France (as in most of Europe) from the end of March through to the end of September.

TOILETS Ask for *les toilettes* or look for signs for the WC (pronounced "vay say"); when reading the details of facilities outside hotels, don't confuse *lavabo*, which means wash-basin, with lavatory. Usually found downstairs along with the phone, French toilets in bars are still often of the hole-in-the-ground squatting variety, and tend to lack toilet paper. Standards of cleanliness are often not high, and men shouldn't expect much privacy in the urinal, which often won't have a door. Both bar and restaurant toilets are usually free, as are toilets in museums, though toilets in railway stations and department stores are commonly staffed by attendants who will expect a bit of spare change. Some have coin-operated locks, so always keep change handy for these and for the frequent Tardis-like public toilets found on the streets. These beige-coloured boxes have automatic doors which open when you insert coins and are cleaned automatically once you exit. Children under 10 aren't allowed in on their own.

Guide

Guide

1 Toulouse and around 71–115

2 Carcassonne, Upper Aude and Ariège 117–168

3 Albi and Haut Languedoc 169–211

4 Nîmes and around 213–258

5 Montpellier and around 259–298

6 Narbonne, Bezier 299–336

7 Roussillon 337–384

Toulouse and around

CHAPTER 1 # Highlights

✳ **Place du Capitole** The
square at the heart of
Toulouse, a bustling
weekend market-place.
See p.82

✳ **St-Sernin Basilica**
Romanesque Toulouse's
finest monument, a crypt
full of saints.
See p.83

✳ **Hôtels Particuliers** The
ancient mansions of the
city's woad lords.
See p.85

✳ **Les Abattoirs** Cutting-
edge modern art gallery
in a converted slaughter-
house. See p.91

✳ **La Montagne Noire** The
northern slopes provide
a scenic introduction to
Languedoc's least popu-
lated area.
See p.105

✳ **Cassoulet** Languedoc's
emblematic dish; try it at
Castelnaudary, where it
was invented. See p.108

▲ St-Sernin Basilica

1

Toulouse and around

Set midway between the cool shores of the Atlantic and the sun-baked Mediterranean coast, **Toulouse** and its surrounding area form the gateway to Languedoc. The city itself is a dynamo, undoubtedly the liveliest and most interesting on the west side of the Rhône; in addition to several notable museums, including the Musée des Augustins and Les Abatoirs, it has a vibrant cultural life and café and art scene and its medieval streets make for some of the most satisfying strolling in the South of France. The neighbouring countryside, though not especially dramatic, is a land of distinctive culture and cuisine.

Among the gently undulating wheat fields – the **Lauragais**, heartland of Toulouse's traditional agricultural prosperity – are little-known but colourful medieval towns like **Lavaur** and **Revel**. Scattered between these is an array of villages and castles whose ancient stones have witnessed both the success of the region's famous dye trade, and the violence and terror of Crusades and Wars of Religion. South of Revel is **Castelnaudary**, birthplace of the famous Languedocian staple, cassoulet, and the largest town in Toulouse's environs; it not only contains a number of unique historical buildings, but is also the main inland port of the **Canal du Midi**, an engineering marvel which stretches from Toulouse to the sea and is one of the emblems of the Southwest.

Toulouse is a major rail centre, with regular **trains** in all directions; these are complemented by SNCF and local buses, the former following several east–west routes across the Lauragais and the latter fanning out from Toulouse. Moving north to south across the area is more difficult, although the quiet roads make for good, if hilly, **biking**.

Toulouse

Although it falls into the modern administrative *région* of Midi-Pyrénées, **TOULOUSE** has a long tradition as the capital of Languedoc, while a solid industrial base, notably as the centre for French aeronautics, helps maintain it as the sixth largest city in the nation. It's a lively, cheerful place, with a vibrant arts community and a distinct Mediterranean look – as the sun edges towards the horizon, the hallmark pink brick buildings soak up the soft light and glow with a muted luminescence (hence its traditional nickname, *La Ville Rose*). For the traveller, the city has a lot to offer: aside from fine medieval churches and mansions, and first-rate galleries, there's an almost constant succession of **festivals** (see box on pp.76–77); in addition, it's the most cosmopolitan city in the Southwest, with a vigorous nightlife fuelled by the massive student population of its famous university, and a range of immigrant cultures reflected in a variety of restaurants.

It's hard not to enjoy Toulouse, whether you are sitting in one of its multitude of outdoor cafés, strolling through its ancient streets or taking in some of the best museums west of the Rhône. A stay here is the easiest way to introduce yourself to southwest France, and you could easily spend a week exploring, but if you're short of time, the two sights which should not be missed are the Romanesque **Basilique de St-Sernin** and the modern art gallery, **Les Abattoirs**.

Some history

Originally located a bit further upstream on the Garonne from the present city centre, Toulouse (then called Tolosa) was moved to the plain which it

TOULOUSE

N20 & Camping de Rupé
Albi

Gare Routière
Gare Matabiau

BD. D'ARCOLE

BD. LASCROSSES

Aérospatiale, Auch, Airport &

EDF Bazacle, Canal de Brienne &

Les Abattoirs, St-Cyprien & Amphitheatre &

Foix

Musée St-Raymond
Basilique de St-Sernin
Université des Sciences Sociales
Palace d'Esquiral
Les Cordeliers
Notre-Dame du Taur
Covered Market
St Pierre-des Cuisines
Les Jacobins
Capitole
Hôtel du Burnuy
Musée du Vieux Toulouse
Tour de Sarta
Notre-Dame de la Daurade
Hôtel L'Assézat
Palais des Artes
Musée des Augustins
Hôpital de St-Jacques & Musée de Médécin
Cathédrale St-Etienne
Château d'Eau
Théâtre de la Cité
Notre-Dame-de-la-Dalbade
Hôtel du Vieux Raisin
Hôtel de Clary
Musée Dupuy
Grand Rond
Jardin des Plantes

River Garonne

PONT NEUF
RUE DE METZ
PONT ST-MICHEL

Cité de l'Espace & Castres
George-Labit Museum

Musée de la Résistance & Montpellier

0   200 m

ACCOMMODATION					
Albert 1er	L	Grand Balcon	S		
des Ambassadeurs	C	Grand Hôtel de l'Opéra	U		
Anatole France	G	Holiday Inn Toulouse			
des Arts	V	Centre	T		
Athénée	E	Mermoz	A		
Beausejour	J	Ours Blanc	P		
des Beaux-Arts	W	Park Hotel	M		
Castellane		Phoenicia	D		
Le Chartreuse	F	St-Sernin	H		
Le Clochez de Rodez	I	Splendid	K		
France Belossi	Q	Terminus	B		
François 1er	R	Wilson Square	N		

RESTAURANTS			
Les Abbatoirs	22	Faim des Haricots	17
Asia Fast Food	2	Chez Fazoul	23
Chez Atilla	6	Les Jardins de l'Opéra	13
La Bascule	26	Kaviar Rouge	8
Benjamin	14	Michel Sarran	11
Cantine du Curé	25	Brasserie de l'Opéra	U
Au Chat Deng	18	Au Petit Paradoux	21
Le Chateaubriand	9	Au Pois Gourmand	1
Le Colombier	3	Saveurs Bio	12
Cosi Fan Tutte	24	Semiramis	19
La Côte de Boeuf	15	Le Sept place St-Sernin	5
La Embarcadère	20	Shun	7
Chez Émile	16	Taverna Casa Manolo	4
		Le Ver Luisant	10

Festivals in and around Toulouse

Toulouse and the surrounding area aren't the best places to look for folk or traditional festivals – for these you're better off heading for the uplands of Languedoc or the Pyrenees to the south. Toulouse's strength is the arts – its splendid galleries and museums are complemented by a series of **music**, **dance** and **art festivals** which bring in top-notch names from around the world. Where we haven't given contact details, enquire at the tourist office (see p.79).

Second weekend in Jan Toulouse: DJ's Attack ☏05.34.31.26.50, ⓦwww.avant -mardi.com. Four days and three nights of non-stop electronic music: house, trance, techno and drum'n'bass.

Feb 17 Dourgne: Fête Médiéval du Romarin. A one-day medieval pageant ostensibly to celebrate the herb rosemary, the symbol of the village, but in reality a typical but entertaining *terroir fête*, including music, dancing, sports competitions and, of course, a market of crafts and local produce.

First or second Saturday in Feb Toulouse: Fête de la Violette. The city's massive violet market features exhibitions relating to flower production, as well as a market and events.

Feb & March Toulouse: Festival Toulouse Bahia Danse. Acclaimed dance festival held annually since 1989, which in recent years has placed heavy emphasis on its international flavour, drawing groups from as far afield as South America and Asia. For programme information and list of venues contact Collectif Chorégraphes Midi-Pyrénées (CHOC; ☏05.61.39.17.39), or the tourist office.

Mid-March Toulouse: Festival Irlandais. A festival of Irish music, theatre and dance leading up to the St Patrick's Day festivities and featuring highly rated Irish performers. For information contact TILT, 27 rue Ste-Blanche, 31200 Toulouse ☏05.61.13.20.08.

Mid-March Toulouse: Rencontres Cinémas d'Amérique Latine ☏05.62.30.25.35, ⓔarcalt@easynet.fr. Long-running Toulousain eight-day film festival, with both feature-length and short productions ranging from documentary and drama to the experimental. Also talks and exhibitions. Held in various venues around town.

Late March Toulouse: Printemps du Rire ☏05.62.21.23.24, ⓦwww.printemps-du-rire.com. A festival featuring France's most renowned comedians as well as local talent. Performed at various venues.

May Toulouse: Hep, un Livre! A month-long book exhibition put on by seventy publishing houses from the Midi-Pyrénées region. Held in the place du Capitole.

First week in mid-June Toulouse: Festival International de Théatre d'Enfants ☏05.62.16.00.78. Works of children's theatre performed by troupes from France and the world over in the city's smaller theatres.

Last week of June to start of July Toulouse: Garonne! Le Festival ☏05.61.25.96.93, ⓦwww.festival.garonne.org. Massive festival of theatre, art, film and dance, attracting international artists. It has a different theme each year, and many exhibitions continue on into September.

Throughout June & July Toulouse & St-Félix: Festival Déodat-de-Séverac ☏05.61.83.01.83, ⓔjjcubaynes@netscape.net. Wednesday- and Thursday-night

currently occupies when the Romans took it over in 120 BC. With the disintegration of the empire the city briefly became the capital of the Visigoths in 414 AD, but when their centre of power shifted to Spain, the Franks moved in and gained control in 628. Under their feudal agrarian regime the town stagnated until the eleventh century, when the local **counts** (who were almost without exception named Raymond) began to encourage the nascent carpentry and leather industries. A century later a city council, or **Capitolo**, was set up to handle administration and justice and the wealthiest townsfolk – mer-concert series at the church of St-Pierre-des-Cuisines and various venues in St-Félix, featuring works of or inspired by the celebrated nineteenth-century St-Félix-born composer.

Throughout July Toulouse: Musique d'Été. Eclectic programme of concerts held in the Couvent des Jacobins, Notre-Dame-de-la-Daurade and Zénith on Tuesday and Thursday nights, featuring a diversity of styles, from classical to gospel and flamenco.

July Toulouse: "Festiu" Aiga Nativa ℡05.61.20.85.37. A two-week festival of Occitan music and culture, with a variety of events including free shows in and around the place St-Georges and ticketed concerts in the city's churches. Reservations through the tourist office.

Throughout July Toulouse: Les Siestes Electroniques ⓦwww.les-siestes-electron-iques.com). The city's newest festival (since 2001); a international celebration of electronic and ambient music, showcasing performers from the world over. Free afternoon concerts (Sat & Sun 4pm) are held in the Jardin Raymond VI, behind Les Abattoirs on the left bank of the Garonne.

Late July/early Aug Sorèze: Musique des Lumières ℡05.63.50.86.38. Festival of music and theatre, held at the old abbey-church, featuring Baroque and chamber music, dance and plays (performances 9pm; €8–20).

Throughout Sept Toulouse: Piano aux Jacobins ℡05.61.22.40.05. Nightly piano recitals in the cloister of the Jacobins. For programme details, contact the Piano aux Jacobins, 61 rue de la Pomme, 31000 Toulouse.

One weekend in Sept Toulouse: Estrambord Garonnes ℡05.61.29.80.01. Traditional Occitan water-jousting matches are held on the Garonne, amidst a lively street festival; see p.282 for more on water-jousting.

Throughout Oct Toulouse: les Orgues ℡05.61.53.81.16, ⓦwww.toulouse-les-orgues.org. Using some of the city's finest antique organs, this music and choral series features Saturday and Sunday night concerts in the city's famous churches.

Mid-Oct Toulouse: Cinespaña ℡05.61.12.12.20, ⓦwww.cine-espagne.com. This event brings in Spanish directors and actors for twelve days of screenings and awards.

End Oct Toulouse: Jazz sur Son 31 ℡05.24.45.05.92. The world-class jazz, blues and salsa festival of the Haute-Garonne *département* brings in the biggest and best names in jazz, blues and salsa. Past performers have included Miles Davis, Campay Segundo and Carlos Santana. Programme available early Sept.

Two weeks in Nov Toulouse: Marionettissimo ℡05.61.49.63.41. Sixteen marionette companies from around the world are invited to the city to put on various puppet shows, not all of which are composed with children in mind.

Second week in Nov Toulouse: Salon des Antiquaires ℡05.61.21.93.25. Internationally renowned antiques fair, featuring 300 antiques dealers from around Europe. Held at the Parc de Expositions (ⓦwww.toulouseexpo.com).

Dec 1–10 Toulouse: Sequence Court-Métrage ℡05.62.49.37.48. Ten-day programme and competition of short films. Screenings at various venues.

One week in Dec Toulouse: 1,2,3 En scène ℡05.61.22.27.77. A children's festival featuring drama, marionettes and magic acts, held at various small theatre venues.

chants and landholders – served as its members (the *capitouls*); the resulting convergence between their economic interests and political power allowed the city to flourish. Meanwhile, the counts – for all intents and purposes independent sovereigns – began to extend their influence over the other major families of the south, including the Trencavels (see p.121). By the late twelfth century they effectively controlled all of Languedoc, and adopted the surname of "St-Gilles", in honour of one of their favourite fiefs.

Both the counts and the city prospered until the reign of Raymond VI, by which time Cathar beliefs, considered heretical by the Church, had taken firm root in the region (see p.149). Raymond may or may not have been a Cathar himself, but was content to let his subjects choose their religious beliefs, thus provoking the ire of the papacy and providing the northern French aristocracy with a justification for war against him. When their knights stormed into Languedoc on a campaign of religious and political conquest – the **Albigensian Crusade** – Toulouse fell to forces led by the cruel Simon de Montfort. Raymond, with the help of Catalan allies, recovered it in 1217, but it fell definitively under the power of the French Crown in 1271. One of the consequences of the Catholic takeover was the foundation, early in the thirteenth century, of Toulouse's **university**, which the strong presence of the Dominican Order helped make into the second most important theological centre in France after Paris.

Despite suffering grievously from a series of plagues, the city's prosperity soared with the booming woad **dye** industry in the 1400s (see box on p.100), and in the sixteenth century it became the official capital of Languedoc, although it later suffered – along with the whole of the South – as a result of the Wars of Religion, and as a consequence of the failed **revolt** against Cardinal Richelieu led by Henri de Montmorency (1595–1632), Governor of Languedoc. The Revolution of 1789, which the city fervently supported, heralded a new age of affluence as industry recovered and the Canal du Midi provided better market access for the agricultural hinterland. The good times were interrupted only by the Napoleonic Wars, during which the English general, Wellington, pursued the retreating Soult to the city in 1814; the French field marshal broke through the near encirclement, dealing the English a minor defeat before escaping towards the Montagne Noire.

Occupied by the Germans during World War II, Toulouse passed through the war more or less unscathed, and today the city is best known for its thriving **aerospace** industry, along with electronics and related hi-tech manufacturing. Home to Airbus Industries, the principal manufacturer of commercial airliners in Europe, this is where the successful A340 and A440 crafts, the first "fly-by-wire" (entirely electronically controlled) planes are assembled, and where plans are being made to launch a new two-level super-liner, bigger even than Boeing's largest Jumbo. On September 21, 2001, Toulouse made the world news when a massive **explosion** ripped through a petrochemical plant in the south of the city, devastating the surrounding industrial suburbs, leaving 90 acres of city razed, 29 dead and almost 2500 wounded. Despite early speculation that the tragedy was terrorist-related, investigations revealed it was the result of industrial malpractice. On a brighter note, since 1985 the city's **violet** cultivation industry – once a major concern, but dormant for nearly a century – was revived thanks to "test tube" technology. The annual flower fair (see box on p.76) is once again a major event.

Arrival, information and city transport

Toulouse's **airport** (℡05.34.61.80.00, Ⓦwww.toulouse.aeroport.fr) is located 6km northwest of the centre in the suburb of Blagnac. As you'd expect, it has better services than many regional airports, with banking and exchange facilities including an automatic exchange dispenser, car rental offices (all the major companies) and a small selection of shops and travel agencies, although it lacks a left-luggage facility. A **shuttle bus** runs to the centre (from 5am–8.20pm every 20min, returning 7.35am–12.15am; 20min; €3.70; ticket can be bought from driver), making various stops in town, including the Compan-Caffarelli, place Jeanne d'Arc (near St-Sernin), place Jean-Jaurès (near place Wilson) and the *gare routière*. A taxi (☎05.61.30.02.54) to the centre will normally cost around €17.

Trains arrive at the grand old **Gare Matabiau** on boulevard Pierre-Sémard along the banks of the Canal du Midi – a twenty-minute walk northeast of the old town. The large station has a good café, but the left-luggage facility is still closed for security reasons. Any of the city buses which stop here will take you down to the boulevard Strasbourg (the ring road around the old town), while bus #2 carries on through old Toulouse, passing rue de Metz and the Grand Rond; the place du Capitole is just two stops away from Matabiau on the *metro*. **Buses** pull in at the modern **gare routière** right beside the gare SNCF, which has an excellent information desk (Mon–Sat 7am–8pm). **Driving** into town, follow directions for the "Centre" and you will wind up on the A61 ring road – from this take any one of exits 14–17 or 21–30. There are plenty of car parks, as well as metered street parking and free parking in place St-Sernin in the centre, place St-Auban east of the centre and les allées Jules-Guesde south of the centre. For contact details regarding departures from Toulouse see "Listings", p.98.

The main **tourist office** (June–Sept Mon–Sat 9am–7pm, Sun 10am–1pm & 2–6.15pm; Oct–May Mon–Fri 9am–6pm, Sat 9am–12.30pm & 2–6pm, Sun 10am–12.30pm & 2–5pm; ☎05.61.11.02.22, ⊛www.ot-toulouse.fr) is housed in a restored tower in place Charles-de-Gaulle, directly behind the Capitol building (*metro* Capitole). This large and efficient office can help make hotel reservations, sells tickets to many festivals and events and organizes walking tours of the city (in English, June–Sept Sat 2pm; €7.80). If you don't feel like going with a group, you can purchase a booklet of self-guided tours for €1.50.

The narrow streets of the old town necessarily make **walking** the best way to see Toulouse; the account below has been written with this in mind. **Cycling** is also an option – you can rent bikes at Movimento, 36 rue Bernard Mulé (☎05.61.80.27.82, ⊛www.moviemnto.coop), while Holiday Bikes, 9 bd des Minimes (☎05.34.25.79.62, ✉toulouse@holiday-bikes.com) also has scooters and motorcycles. The tourist office distributes a map of bike paths, although these are generally confined to the new part of the city. Additionally, there's a comprehensive bus and *metro* network, which covers Toulouse and outlying villages. Although more are planned, for the time being there is just one **metro** line, running from the northeast (via Gare Matabiau) to the new university campus in the southwest; for visitors it comes in handy for getting from the *gares* to the main hotel districts (*metro* Jean-Jaurès or Capitole), or over the river to see the Les Abattoirs (*metro* Cyprien-République). With the exception of getting to outlying sights, like the Cité de l'Espace or the campsite, Toulouse's **bus** network won't be of much use – it's also quite elaborate, so you'd do well to pick up a transport map, available at the SEMVAT **information office**, 7 place Esquirol (☎05.61.41.70.70, ⊛www.semvat.com; *metro* Esquirol), or at the tourist office and *metro* stations. **Tickets** serving both bus and metro are available from bus drivers, as well as at metro stations and tobacconists; a single costs €1.20, a return €2.30, and you can also buy a day-pass for €5.20 or a ten-trip ticket for €9.80. The only problem with the city's public transport network is that it shuts down very early (by 9pm), and even the nightbus network, whose hub is the *gare*, winds up around midnight. If time is short and you want to see the highlights, **taxis** offer a special "taxi touristique" tariff: €31 for a one-hour circuit and €46 for a two-hour circuit of the town, for up to three people (see "Listings", p.99).

Accommodation

Unless you are planning on staying in Toulouse for a lengthy period you will be more or less confined to **hotels** – and there's no shortage of them, in every bracket of price and comfort. You'll find a whole cluster of establishments right around the station, which range from inexpensive to moderate, but have the disadvantage of being in a zone which is rather nondescript and far from the centre. Closer in, there are cheap options around place de Belfort, which is also a sort of red-light district. In the old town, the hotels concentrated around place Victor Hugo (just up from the Capitole and place Wilson) are an easy bet, with a wide selection of two-star options in the ❸ bracket. One of the best options for a short visit is the "Week-end en liberté". Booked through the tourist office, it includes a **pass** to the city's main museums plus hotel accommodation (two-star €25 per person, three-star €40, four-star €55). Rooms in the city can also be booked through the **free reservation service** (☎05.34.31.71.40, ⓦwww.toulousehotel.com).

There is no youth hostel as such, but there are a number of **accommodation centres**, primarily designed for students but also useful for visitors who plan on staying for more than a few days. Their facilities vary considerably: some provide dorm accommodation, others private rooms or self-catered shared suites. The local youth information centre, the CRIJ (Centre Régional d'Information de Jeunesse), 17 rue de Metz (Mon–Sat 10am–1pm & 2–7pm; ☎05.61.21.20.20) can inform you about current availability. The only **campsite** close enough in to be of use is the well-outfitted *Camping de Rupé*, just a few kilometres north from the centre on chemin du Pont du Rupé (☎05.61.70.07.35; bus #59 from place Jeanne-d'Arc to "Rupé").

Cheap hotels

Albert 1er 8 rue Rivals ☎05.61.21.17.91, ⓦwww.hotel-albert1.com. Set in a quiet side street just off the Capitole and close to the central market in pl Victor-Hugo. A small, comfortable and good-value establishment. ❷

des Ambassadeurs 68 rue Bayard ☎05.61.62.65.84, ⓕ05.61.62.97.38. Very friendly little hotel run by a young couple, just down from the station. Its rooms all have TV, en-suite bath and phone – a surprisingly good deal given the price. ❶

Anatole France 46 pl Anatole-France ☎05.61.23.19.96, ⓕ05.61.21.47.66. Another acceptable low-price-bracket option, the *Anatole France* boasts a TV in each room, and is located in a quieter section of the old city. ❶

des Arts 1bis rue Cantegril ☎05.61.23.36.21, ⓕ05.61.12.22.37. On a corner diagonally opposite the Augustins museum, this is a top choice in the lower price range, with large, quirky rooms (some with fireplace) in a superb old building. ❶

Beausejour 4 rue Caffarelli ☎ & ⓕ05.61.62 .77.59. Basic, but dirt cheap and with a great copper-balconied facade and sound-proofed rooms. This is the best of the hotels in this slightly dodgy but engagingly gritty neighbourhood around pl de Belfort. ❶

Le Chartreuse 4bis bd Bonrepos ☎05.61.62.93.39, ⓔla.chartreuse@wanadoo.fr. Efficiently modern if soulless choice, right by the station. Great value, considering the amenities: each room has a private shower, toilet and TV. ❶

François 1er 4 rue d'Austerlitz ☎05.61.21.54.52, ⓕ05.61.22.88.25. Small and basic hotel near the main market. Clean and very friendly, but rather desperately in need of remodelling – a good fall-back if the neighbouring hotels are full. Rooms have TV. Closed part Aug. ❷

Grand Balcon 8 rue Romiguières ☎05.61.21.48.08, ⓕ05.61.21.59.98. Just off place du Capitole, this ageing classic was frequented by aviation pioneers, such as St-Exupéry, who first established Toulouse as a capital of manned flight. It's now rather run-down, but definitely a good bargain, and smack in the centre of things. Closed most of Aug. ❷

Splendid 13 rue Caffarelli ☎05.61.62.43.02, ⓕ05.61.62.43.02. Another reasonable cheapie in the pl de Belfort area. Very basic (no TV), clean and very cheap. Reception closed Sun pm. ❶

Wilson Square 12 rue d'Austerlitz ☎05.61.21.67.57, ⓦwww.hotel-wilson.com. Clean and well-kept place at the top end of Austerlitz, with TV, AC and a lift. Also has a great *pâtisserie* on street level. ❷

Moderate hotels

Athénée 13bis rue de Matabiau
℡05.61.63.10.63, ⓦwww.athenee-hotel.com.
This well-renovated hotel offers all mod cons,
including TV, garage parking and a cocktail bar,
and features carefully chosen contemporary decor.
Quiet, despite its location between the station and
the old town. Wheelchair accessible. ❹

des Beaux-Arts 1 pl du Pont-Neuf
℡05.34.45.42.42, ⓦwww.hotel
desbeauxarts.com. Located in a 150-year-old
building, this hotel's contemporary but refined
interior contrasts well with its ageing facade, making for solid, old-world elegance. Each room is
individually decorated, and some have views of the
Garonne. ❺

Castellane 17 rue Castellane ℡05.61.62.18.82,
ⓦwww.castellanehotel.com. A cheerful hotel with
a wide selection of room types and sizes, most of
which are bright and quiet. One of the few wheel-
chair-accessible hotels in this price range. ❸

Le Clochez de Rodez 14 pl de Jeanne-d'Arc
℡05.61.62.42.92, ⓦwww.couleursud.com.
Comfortable and central, with secure parking and
all mod cons. Despite its size, it exudes a very personal hospitality. Wheelchair accessible. ❺

France Belossi 5 rue d'Austerlitz
℡05.61.21.88.24, ⓦwww.hotel-france-
toulouse.com. One of the better options in the rue
d'Austerlitz/pl Wilson area. Clean rooms with cable
television and AC. ❸

Ours Blanc 25 pl de Victor-Hugo
℡05.61.21.62.40, ⓦwww.hotel-ours-blanc.fr.
Right by the covered market and steps from the
Capitole, this welcoming hotel is one of the city's
better bargains. The entire building has recently
been renovated and each room has TV, AC and
telephone, as well as a private bath. ❸

Park Hotel 2 rue Porte Sardane
℡05.61.21.25.97, ⓦwww.au-park-hotel.com.
Another solid two-star establishment, sandwiched
between rue d'Austerlitz and the central market,
with AC and elevator, cable TV and a small bar. ❸

Phoenicia 7 bd Bonrepos ℡05.61.63.81.63,
ⓔhotelphoenicia@gofornet.com. Weird retro decor
but good service and facilities in this three-star
place just down from the *gares*. The staff are
friendly, and it has a small cocktail bar on the
main floor. ❸

St-Sernin 2 rue St-Bernard ℡05.61.21.73.08,
ⓕ05.61.22.49.61. Well-renovated old hotel in one
of the best districts of the old town, around the
basilica – close to all the action, but far enough
away to provide peace in the evening. ❸

Terminus 13 bd Bonrepos ℡05.61.62.44.78,
ⓦwww.terminus31.com. This old three-star
station-side hotel has large, renovated rooms that
make it worth the price, and there are special
room prices for off-season weekends. Parking
and buffet breakfast (€7) available, the only
drawback being that the hotel is rather far from
the sights. ❸

Expensive hotels

Grand Hôtel de l'Opéra 1 pl du Capitole
℡05.61.21.82.66, ⓦwww.grand-hotel-
opera.com. The *grand dame* of Toulouse's hotels
presides over the pl du Capitole in the guise of a
seventeenth-century convent. Rich decor, peppered with antiques and artwork, and a sophisticated atmosphere. Also has a fitness centre for
working off that second helping of foie gras. ❾

Holiday Inn Toulouse Centre 13 pl Wilson
℡05.61.10.70.70, ⓦwww.hotel-capoul.com. The
best of the hotels on pl Wilson, combining elegance with warmth and contemporary design; it
has all of the conveniences and amenities you'd
expect and the staff are attentive, professional and
friendly. ❼

Mermoz 50 rue de Matabiau ℡05.61.63.04.04,
ⓦwww.hotel-mermoz.com. Immaculate, comfortable rooms in this 1930s Art Deco-style hotel close
to the station. Also has wheelchair access and a
garage. ❻

The City

Toulouse's **old town**, straddling a curve in the River Garonne and hedged by
a busy, roughly hexagon-shaped ring road (which marks the course of its former defensive walls), is where you'll find most of the city's points of interest.
Its heart is the majestically broad **place du Capitole**, the town hall square near
the northeastern edge, from which crooked streets radiate out, web-like, to a
series of *places*. East from the place du Capitole is primarily a business district,
where you'll find a great deal of the city's offices, hotels and restaurants. To the
north, the area around the wonderful **Basilique de St-Sernin**, with the nearby archeological museum, forms the university quarter, while west of the
Capitole towards the river lies the bulk of medieval Toulouse – major sights

Toulouse museums

The normal entrance fee for Toulouse's historical museums is €2.20, except for the first Sunday of each month, when they're free. You can also buy museum **passeports** for three or six visits (€4.60 or €7.60 respectively) to the following museums: the Augustins, the Musée St-Raymond, the Musée Paul-Dupuy, the Musée Georges-Labit and the Jacobins.

here include the Dominicans' **Les Jacobins** complex, plus a number of noteworthy churches: St-Pierre-des-Cuisines, Notre-Dame-de-la-Dalbade and Notre-Dame-de-la-Daurade. It is also home to most of the city's majestic Renaissance-era **hôtels particuliers** (private mansions), some of which, like the magnificent **Hôtel d'Assézat**, are now open as museums; most though are simply worth seeing for their striking and varied facades. The city's shopping district, focused on rue d'Alsace-Lorraine and rue St-Rome, stretches south to intersect with rue de Metz, south of which again, after the **cathedral**, a further series of *places* leads down to the formal gardens, the **Grand Rond** and **Jardin des Plantes** at the southeast corner of the old town. Beyond this, you'll find the town's canal port and a couple of small museums. Across the Garonne to the west, the neighbourhood of **St-Cyprien** is of interest for its stunningly renovated cutting-edge modern art gallery, **Les Abattoirs**, while the only reason to visit the **suburbs** is to see two modern exhibitions revolving around the city's aeronautical tradition.

Place du Capitole and place Wilson

Place du Capitole, the sweeping plaza containing Toulouse's historical seat of government, the **Capitole**, forms the administrative and civic hub of the city. Apart from when it fills up with market stalls on Wednesday and Sunday mornings, the *place* is a magnet for rollerbladers and host to a constant surge of pedestrian traffic – great for people-watching. Prettiest at sunset, when permeated by a pink glow reflected off the huge Capitole's brickwork, the square is best appreciated from one of the bank of cafés which line its western side – the perfect spot from which to contemplate the Neoclassical symmetry and elegance of the building's 130-metre-long facade. Deriving its name from the twelfth-century administration of the city (see p.76), the palace dates back to the sixteenth century, although the frontage you see today was raised in the mid-eighteenth. In addition to its function as the centre of municipal government, it serves as home to the city's most prestigious opera and ballet venue (see p.98). There's not much to see in the cavernous seventeenth-century **foyer** (daily 9am–7pm; free), aside from a gallery of paintings extolling the glories of France and celebrating the execution of revolt-leader Montmorency, which took place in the square, but you can stroll through to place Charles-de-Gaulle on the other side of the palace. Sadly, this small patch of green, presided over by Viollet-le-Duc's (see box on p.128) restored 1529 pseudo-medieval *donjon* – the only remnant of the original Capitole and now the tourist office – has become a haven for local junkies.

East of here along rue la-Fayette is the oblong **place Wilson**, which, edged by modern, expensive hotels, retains a certain grandeur despite the traffic. Directly north of place Wilson is the lively triangle of streets centred on the town's main **indoor market** (Tues–Sun 6am–noon) in place Victor-Hugo. The market sells local agricultural produce, meat and fish, and the surrounding area is home to an array of cheapie hotels and restaurants, as well as some great places to pick up regional culinary goodies – look out for the Ducs de Gascogne delicatessen at 1 rue du Remparts Villeneuve, and the Chocolatier de Bayonne, next door. **Rue d'Alsace Lorraine**, the western boundary of the triangle, is Toulouse's principal shopping street, its towering nineteenth-century apartments for the most part converted into shops and office space. Nevertheless, the magnificent facades, with their monumental doorways, elaborately carved cornices and wrought-iron balconies, still exude *fin-de-siècle* elegance.

North to the Basilique de St-Sernin and beyond

Leading north out of place du Capitole, rue de Taur is a street full of lively studenty cafés and shops, a reminder that Toulouse has long been a university city. Just along from the *place* is the church of **Notre-Dame du Taur**, the original resting place of St-Sernin, boasting a turreted facade; further up the street, you'll pass the sprawling sixteenth-century Palace d'Esquiral, now home to the city's main cinema and a meeting place for student literary groups.

This is just steps from the **Basilique de St-Sernin** (daily 8.30am–6.15pm; free), which, with its wedding-cake bell tower – an emblem of Toulouse – is arguably southern France's greatest Romanesque church and the largest of its style in Western Europe. Begun in 1080 to hold the remains of the city's first bishop, who was killed by the Romans in 250 AD – dragged to death by a bull (hence the name of the street) – the church was an important stop on the pilgrimage to Santiago de Compostela. Despite the fact that the present building was not completed until the fourteenth century, it has almost no Gothic elements: it's this stylistic purity, combined with the sheer size of the construction, that makes it such a singular monument. The most striking feature of its exterior is the early twelfth-century **Miégeville door**, whose restrained but expressive biblical sculptures mark it as a product of the pivotal era in the evolution of medieval art. Inside, the uniform simplicity of the cavernous nave is impressive; the plain marble altar, which is still used today, was consecrated by Urban II in 1096. But the real attraction is the church's incredible collection of **reliquaries** (daily 10am–6pm; €2), which it amassed over the years under the patronage of kings and with the financial help of donations from Santiago-bound pilgrims. Body parts of all of the major saints can be found here reposing in carved and gilded boxes set into the walls and chapels of the ambulatory and stored in the crypt below the altar, including a spectacular bust of James the Greater, whose thirteenth-century painted effigy is decked out in pilgrim's garb. The crypt also contains some very good examples of fourteenth-century polychrome saints' **statues**.

On the other side of place St-Sernin, which is unfortunately used as a car park, is the small **Musée St-Raymond** (daily: June–Aug 10am–7pm, Sept–May 10am–6pm; €2.20, €3 for special exhibits), which holds the city's archeological finds. The best part of this collection is the prehistoric and Bronze Age section on the first floor, which includes not only the usual arrowheads and brooches, but a decent range of pre-Roman jewellery, weapons and even chariot wheels. The Roman religious sculpture and third-century portraiture is also worth seeking out. In the basement you'll find the remains of part of the city wall as well as the excavations of Roman and medieval cemeteries.

North from the *place*, up rue Gatien-Arnoult, there's a small but lively **African quarter**, populated by immigrants from the Maghreb, in particular and the shops and restaurants of rue Trois Pilliers exude wafts of mint and parsley. Narrow rue Gramat, just before Trois Pilliers, is also worth a look – after a long campaign to convince the city, local artists were permitted in July 2000 to decorate the walls, cheering up the previously decrepit street with a series of colourful murals. From here, the concrete blight of place Bernard marks the end of the old town and a dull zone of low-rent apartments and university buildings. It's better to turn back and follow a series of quiet neighbourhood squares – des Tiercerettes, St-Julien and Peyrou – each of which has a couple of small café-restaurants. From place du Peyrou, rue des Lois will take you back to the Capitole.

Les Jacobins and west

The most colourful part of Toulouse's old town is found in the labyrinth of streets radiating west and south from the place du Capitole, and dominated by the former Dominican headquarters, known as **Les Jacobins** (daily 10am–7pm; €5, cloister only €2.50), tucked away off rue Lakanal. Built in 1230, this was the first-ever permanent convent of St Dominic's Order of Preachers (the Dominicans), founded in the city in 1215 to combat the Cathar heresy. From its humble beginnings the Order quickly grew in power, soon taking charge of the Church's Holy Inquisition and exercising, for a time, a near monopoly over the bishoprics and universities of the medieval Latin West. This building is, in fact, Toulouse's original university, home of the theology Faculty which the Dominicans established in order to strengthen Catholic orthodoxy. The cavernous fourteenth-century **interior** (free entry), through which you enter the complex, contains a single file of seven enormous supporting columns, from which a web of delicate interlacing ribs fan out across the vaulted ceiling. These ribs, still bearing their original painted pattern of red and black bands, contrast beautifully with the cream-coloured brick they support. In a modest gilt box under the grey marble altar in the centre of the nave rest the remains of **St Thomas Aquinas** (1225–74), the great Dominican philosopher who strove to introduce the thought of Aristotle into Catholic theology – there's still a pilgrimage here on his feast day (Jan 28). Leaving the church, you enter a low Gothic **cloister**, which, with its stubby and unadorned columns, is as sober in style as the Order that built it. In fact, the cloister isn't original, but the structures along its north side are, including the large **chapterhouse**, which also preserves its wall decoration, and the fourteenth-century **chapel of St-Antonin**, whose walls are graced by richly detailed period paintings. The old **refectory**, also accessed from the cloister, now houses high-quality temporary art exhibitions of a decidedly secular character.

From the north end of rue Lakanal, rue Pargaminières leads to the placid little **place St-Pierre** on the banks of the Garonne. There are a couple of small pubs here and, on its northern side, **St-Pierre-des-Cuisines** (June Mon 9am–12.30pm, July daily 2–7pm; €1.50), an ancient church reputed to be the oldest ecclesiastical building in Southwest France, constructed over a substantial Gallo-Roman necropolis, accessed via the church's **crypt** (guided tour June Mon 11am, July daily 4pm; €2.30). The present edifice goes back to the twelfth century, but it was undoubtedly the site of late Roman church. Recently it was converted into a four-hundred-seat concert hall.

Just west of the *place*, the languid **Canal de Brienne** angles away from the river through a nineteenth-century industrial area, where newly erected student apartment buildings abut old warehouses and cigarette factories. The River Garonne has been exploited for industrial purposes since grain mills were first set up here in the twelfth century. They became a symbol of the city's prosperity, which was at that time based on local wheat production, and achieved such renown that the sixteenth-century satirist Rabelais cited them as the most powerful in the world. In 1890 the **EDF Bazacle** (Mon–Fri 10am–noon & 2–6pm, Sat & Sun 2–7pm; free), a generating plant that powers up Toulouse to this day, was built on the banks at the former site of the mills, about a ten-minute walk from St-Pierre. Here you can see both the modern and the original turbines churning away, have a look at the cascading fish ladder and take in local and international art exhibits, displayed in the station's main foyer (free).

Back at place St-Pierre, an old ironwork bridge still decked out with gaslight fixtures leads south over the Garonne. This is the most direct route to the Les Abattoirs art gallery in St-Cyprien (see p.91) – you can see the mammoth cupola of the St-Joseph hospital ahead. If you prefer to stay on this side of the river, your best bet is to climb down to the riverside promenade Henri-Martin, whose grassy verge will take you down towards the place de la Daurade.

Place de la Daurade and around

A rare green space in the old town, **place de la Daurade** makes a great spot to take a break and loll by the riverside, or, should you wish to get on the river, is also the point from where boats depart on cruises (see "Listings", p.98). Across the Garonne you can see Toulouse's medieval hospital, the Hôtel-Dieu St-Jacques, with the stub of the old bridge still poking out from its walls, while on the flood banks above the square you'll find the city's oddest church, **Notre-Dame-de-la-Daurade** (opening times vary), a curious compound of disparate architectural styles. The church started out as a pagan temple and was then converted to Christian worship in the fifth century, but today's building, with its weighty Neoclassical facade, dates from the eighteenth. Entering the church through the modern parish hall tacked incongruously on the north side, you'll be met by a hive of painted Baroque busyness, with fields of trompe l'oeil held back by armies of cherubs, all presided over by a massive array of organ pipes. At the centre of it all sits the *Vierge noire*, a black Madonna reputedly empowered to cure ailments and bring good fortune to the unborn child.

Toulouse's hôtels particuliers

One of the hallmarks of Toulouse is its multitude of luxurious private mansions, or **hôtels particuliers**, scattered throughout the old town. Built for the most part in the fifteenth and sixteenth centuries, they are testament to the tremendous prosperity which the town enjoyed at that time as a result of the *pastel* dye industry, which turned the local merchants and bankers into veritable princes (see box on p.100). The earliest mansions have some sections of timber and daub, but the majority are constructed from local brick, which – ageing badly – detracts somewhat from their majesty. There is often, however, wonderful **masonry**; the mansions' splendour tends to reside in their stone doorways and window frames, which were embellished with carved figures, statues, coats of arms and floral designs. Stone was relatively expensive here, so more masonry was a sign of greater wealth; the most opulent buildings have facades constructed entirely from stone. In later examples, you'll find Renaissance flourishes, imported from Italy to lighten the solid, but rather plain and chunky, medieval building style, and which can be distinguished by a movement towards greater symmetry and complexity of carving. Some of these "mature" *hôtels* have graceful **turrets**, built to reflect the status of the owner; only the chartered elite – those who were wealthy enough to serve as *capitouls* – could add a tower. The heady times of mansion-building, however, were not to last, and in the late sixteenth century declining *pastel* production precipitated the end of the woad lords, leaving their magnificent homes to fall into gradual decay. Today they serve a variety of functions, including apartments, offices, schools and museums.

It's still the object of popular pilgrimage even today, with many devotional plaques fixed around the entrance. Next door, on quai de la Daurade, you'll find the **Palais des Artes**, now sadly abandoned except when used for temporary exhibitions (free), but possessing a typically nineteenth-century facade, which attempts in vain to immortalize a series of forgotten French artists.

Back in place de la Daurade, the *Café des Artistes* (see p.96) makes a handy refreshment stop. If you head up back to the Capitole keep an eye out for the sixteenth-century **Hôtel de Burnuy**, one of Toulouse's famed *hôtels particuliers* (see box on p.85), at the beginning of rue Gambetta. Although it has been incorporated into a school, you can still poke your head inside to have a look at the two luxurious courtyards. This was the home of Jean de Burnuy, the town's wealthiest woad merchant, who was rich enough to literally afford a king's ransom. In fact, he stood his fortune as security to pay for François I's release from captivity at the hands of the Hapsburgs, against whom the king had fought in vain for the title of Holy Roman Emperor. Even when the palace is closed, its 1504 **facade** will draw your attention – the square windows are complemented by delicate Gothic details, while its cherub-topped main entrance completes the strange stylistic mix. Stepping back from the building, you'll see its slender tower rising high above the street.

Rue St-Rome and the Hôtel d'Assézat

A number of less grand but still intriguing sights can be found along the pedestrian promenade which heads straight south from the place du Capitole. This route starts with **rue St-Rome**, a busy shopping street lined with clothing stores and sandwich stands. The second street on the right after the *place* leads to the sixteenth-century **Hôtel du May**, built by a regent dean of the university's medical faculty, and now home to the **Musée du Vieux Toulouse** (midMay to mid-Oct Mon–Sat 2–6pm; €2.20). One of the town's least ornate *hôtels* – with only a simple door decoration to boast – it is proof that even then academics were underpaid. Nor is the museum itself particularly stimulating, as its collection consists of items of purely local interest: ceramics, paintings of local grandees and nineteenth-century knick-knacks.

Back on rue St-Rome, opposite rue de Muy, is an old Neoclassical bank building, dating from 1734, and behind it, at no. 4 rue Jules-Chalande, you'll find another courtyard, whose small tower marks it as the home of a former *capitoul*. Rue Chalande itself leads into an eminently explorable warren of narrow streets punctuated by tiny, and wonderfully serene, *places* – most of which have some sort of bar and a number of shops. Back on St-Rome, you can look down rue Tripière, where an old timber-and-brick **mansion** is studded with stone decorations in the form of rabbits. Its period interior can be seen on a guided tour (every 30min Wed 2.30–6pm; free). A little further south, rue StRome turns into rue des Changes, dominated by the three-storey **Tour de Sarta**, another former palace. The length of this old street is lined by overhanging sixteenth-century homes, until it opens up abruptly at the nineteenthcentury place Esquirol.

To the west of rue des Changes is a little commercial area of wholesalers and workshops, centred around the place de Bourse. The main reason for venturing into this neighbourhood is to find the **Hôtel d'Assézat**, which you enter from rue de l'Écharpe. This is Toulouse's most famous and possibly most luxurious *hôtel particulier*, home to a hugely successful woad merchant, Pierre d'Assézat, and which for a time hosted the *jocs florals* (see p.414). The former owner's wealth is evident in the predominance of stone over brick in its construction, endowing it with a sense of majesty which many of the town's best

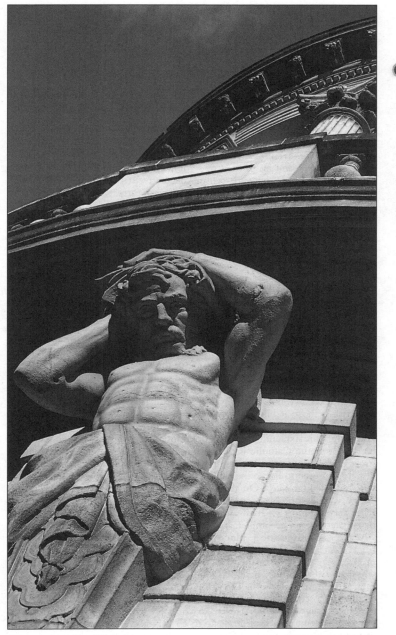

▲ Balcony support, Toulouse

buildings lack. Assézat commissioned Nicholas Bachelier, a renowned local architect, to build the mansion in 1555 in cutting-edge style – its weighty, columned stone facade anticipates the Neoclassicism which would soon dominate European architecture. Inside, the patio is no less splendid, with a magnificent covered porch and columns. Despite his riches, d'Assézat suffered a tragic fate: having taken up Protestantism, he was deprived of his fortune, and Catholic repression forced him into exile.

Today the building is home to an impressive art gallery, the **Foundation Bemberg** (Tues–Sun 10am–6pm, Thurs until 9pm; €4.60, plus €3 for temporary exhibits). On the first floor up you'll pass through a collection of Renaissance furniture, including painted leather chairs and cabinets, before reaching a gallery displaying fifteenth- and sixteenth-century Flemish art, dominated by portraiture. Works by Lucas Cranach the Elder, in particular *Venus and Cupid*, and his portrait of a young woman, stand out. Further along there's a collection of sixteenth-century decorative statuary, whose kinetic realism bears an odd but striking resemblance to early twentieth-century Art Nouveau. Upstairs you'll find a worthy collection of more recent art, with the Impressionists and their successors well represented, among them Monet, Gauguin, Matisse and Bonnard, who has a whole roomful of works here, including *Still Life with Lemons*. On the museum's covered porch you can enjoy a coffee or light snack from the in-house café and soak up the atmosphere of the courtyard.

Place Esquirol to place du Salin

South of **place Esquirol** the street opens almost immediately into **place de la Trinité** – one of the many squares which punctuate the old town south of rue de Metz. Like the others, Trinité is dominated by a pleasant fountain, and there are several lively bars and brasseries where you can stop for a drink or a meal. While on the square, look out for the high-relief allegorical statues on the facade of the Maison Lamothe, one of the city's finest nineteenth-century buildings. From here, rue des Filatiers, the continuation of the shopping area, heads south to the place de Carmes. This is the site of the city's other big **covered market** (Mon–Sat 6am–noon); unfortunately, the several storeys of car park rising above it blight the square. Heading west on either of the streets leading off the *place* you come to the church of **Notre-Dame-de-la-Dalbade**. This sixteenth-century brick monster, scrubbed white inside in the best spirit of the Catholic Reformation, is itself hardly worth a stop, but the street of the same name, leading south, takes you through the heart of the old district that used to house the faculty of theology, an evocative neighbourhood with several fine *hôtels*. On the right you'll pass the magnificent **Hôtel de Clary**, whose stone Neoclassical facade of 1613 is very flamboyant, with high-relief *faux* columns separating the window casings, which in turn are capped by ornate lintels. The simpler, and grimy, courtyard is also worth a look.

At the end of the street, **place du Salin** opens up in front of the massive brick Palais de Justice, built on the site of Toulouse's medieval castle, and its predecessor, the Roman fort. On the adjacent place du Parlement, at no. 7, you'll find the house where St Dominic and his early disciples stayed when they arrived in Toulouse in 1215 to preach against Catharism. The building is abutted by a scrap of the city's ancient Gallo-Roman wall. From the place du Parlement, rue du Renfort will take you over to the bank of the Garonne, where a pleasant path leads back up to La Daurade. Alternatively, head northeast out of place du Salin on Grande Rue Nazareth towards the cathedral and another cluster of fine squares and mansions.

The cathedral and around

Although it holds ecclesiastical priority, Toulouse's **cathedral** (Mon–Sat 8am–7pm, Sun 9am–7pm; free) has always played second fiddle to its rival St-Sernin. The discord between its average-sized brick entrance, which dates from the beginning of the thirteenth century, and the incongruously massive choir plonked on the back some seventy years later is obvious, and continues when, on entering, you discover that the huge ambulatory isn't even lined up squarely with the older church. The reason for this lack of harmony is that the cathedral was slated to be rebuilt on a much grander scale – the original nave demolished and a new one of the same proportions as the entrance added on – but money ran out, and the church was left as it is today. The **interior** of the cathedral holds few surprises, but is worth a quick look, if only for the Renaissance tapestries which line the walls of the nave, the sixteenth-century carved walnut choir, and the details of some the chapels behind the main altar: there are several good **stained-glass windows**, going back as early as the fifteenth century, and some carved ceiling medallions date from the 1200s.

Place St-Étienne itself, which boasts the city's oldest fountain – the Griffoul, dating from 1546 – is surprisingly dead, with hardly a café to detain you. But if you head west, a short walk down rue Croix-Baragnon will take you past the city's oldest house (at no. 15) before leading you into the livelier place Rouaix, bounded to the northeast by the town's impressive eighteenth-century Chamber of Commerce building. On the far side of this, you'll be back in place Esquirol, right at the Musée des Augustins.

South from the cathedral you'll find a quiet neighbourhood of old houses and narrow streets. There are fewer shops and restaurants here, although each of the small **places** – and there seems to be one at every intersection – has somewhere to sit and have a drink or bite to eat. Rue Perchepinte, the continuation of rue Nazareth, leads to the pretty place Ste-Scarbes, the centre of Toulouse's antique furniture trade.

Further along, towards the place du Salin, was the wealthiest neighbourhood in the city during the age of *pastel*. You'll find a series of grand mansions on the streets near the *place*, notably rue Languedoc and rue Ozenne. One of the best, the compact fifteenth-century **Hôtel du Vieux Raisin** at the junction of rue Ozenne and rue du Languedoc, now houses law offices, but you can still take a peek at the courtyard, which is normally open during the day. On tree-lined rue Ozenne, the old Hôtel Pierre-Bresson houses the **Musée Paul-Dupuy** (Mon–Sat: mid-May to mid-Oct 10am–6pm; rest of year 10am–5pm; €2.20), one of the least inspiring museums in the city. Its holdings represent the collected knick-knacks of Dupuy, which include various medieval artefacts, a transplanted sixteenth-century pharmacy shop and a vast and dull collection of architectural drawings. Try to visit on the first Wednesday of the month at 3pm, if at all, when the ornate nineteenth-century Orientalist-themed automaton, "The Singing Lesson", is put in motion.

The Musée des Augustins

The former home of the city's powerful canons of the Augustinian Order now houses what was, until the opening of Les Abattoirs, Toulouse's largest and most important museum, the **Musée des Augustins** (Mon & Thurs–Sun 10am–6pm, Wed 10am–9pm; ⓦ www.augustins.org; €2.20). The collection is dominated by medieval sculpture, and unless you are an aficionado, you may be surprised by the reputation the museum enjoys. Nevertheless, it deserves a visit – the quality of work here is undeniable and the building itself is well worth a look. An externally featureless fourteenth-century brick precinct, covering an area almost as big as the place du Capitole and dominated by a strikingly huge bell tower, the monastery was founded in 1309 on the authority of Pope Clement V and is a fine example of southern French Gothic style, with an extensive cloister and large chapterhouse surviving from the original construction. Its smaller Neoclassical cloister dates from the seventeenth century, and it also has an apparently medieval refectory, though this is, in fact, one of Viollet-le-Duc's dubious nineteenth-century reconstructions.

The museum's **collection** consists of two disparate sections: superb medieval sculpture and less remarkable eighteenth- and nineteenth-century painting. The former is made up of stone carvings – found in the course of excavations for the museum itself and from the ruins of local churches and cloisters – of exceptional quality, thanks to the wealth of the city's twelfth-century counts. The complex was only restored to its original size in the last thirty years, and in the course of these works, more medieval treasures were discovered and added to the displays. The main floor consists of a series of rooms and chapels opening out onto the cloister; these contain a substantial part of the sculpture collection, with pieces not just from France, but from as far afield as northern England. The star attraction here is the forest of Romanesque **columns** on the bottom floor of the refectory, found just off the cloister on the west side. Rescued from the ruins of the town's various churches, these were crafted by a school of Toulouse sculptors that throve under the patronage of the counts in the first half of the twelfth century, their consummate skill evident in the impressively carved capitals. Moving through the refectory, you can follow the development of the Toulouse school, as the elaborate vegetal forms of the 1120s to 1140s give way to busy narrative scenes in increasingly high relief as the century progresses and draws to a close. The last examples, many taken from the cathedral's destroyed cloister, are the most spectacular – wonderfully carved scenes centred around episodes such as the death of John the Baptist. From the refectory, a monumental staircase leads to the upper floor, which, along with the stifling third storey, contains a collection of largely unimpressive **paintings**, amassed by city councillors of the post-Revolution period. On your way out, back on the ground floor, you'll walk past a series of grounded gargoyles set upright on the floor and apparently yawning, unimpressed by their surroundings.

North of the museum, up rue des Arts is place St-Georges, now packed with restaurants. From here the elegant rue St-Antoine, a narrower version of rue d'Alsace-Lorraine, continues up to place Wilson, and rue de la Pomme heads northwest to arrive at the Capitole.

St-Cyprien and Les Abattoirs

Although the old neighbourhood of **St-Cyprien** was also enclosed within the medieval city's defensive walls, its location on the west bank of the Garonne meant that it became marginalized. Home to tanners and butchers, professionals banned from the main town for sanitary reasons, from the Middle Ages it was also the home of Toulouse's hospitals, where the sick were kept in semi-quarantine. Thus, on this side of the river, you won't find the grand mansions of *capitouls* and merchants, but nondescript streets containing fairly ordinary houses. That said, you should not leave Toulouse without setting foot in St-Cyprien, if only to visit the splendid new modern art gallery, Les Abattoirs, and once you cross over there's a clutch of smaller museums which are also worth a look. Coming from the station or the old town, you can get to St-Cyprien by bus (#1 or #14) and *metro* ("St-Cyprien République" stop), but the best way to get there is to walk, which at the most leisurely pace shouldn't take more than fifteen minutes.

Crossing the Pont Neuf at the western end of rue de Metz brings you over to the broad grassy bank of the Prairies des Filtres. On the left side of the bridge you'll see the **Château d'Eau** (Mon & Wed–Sun 1–7pm; €2.20), a former pumphouse, now a small photographic museum holding good-quality monthly exhibitions. On the north side of the bridge is the old **hospital of St-Jacques**. Modern hospitals grew out of the hospices which cared for pilgrims en route to the Holy Land or Santiago, and which eventually took over the care of sick people in general. Toulouse, being on the pilgrim route and the site of a major university, was a pioneer in medieval medicine. In the plague-ridden centuries preceding the Revolution, the most contagious patients arrived at the hospital directly by boat, so as not to infect the town. Today, these buildings house the administrative offices for Toulouse's centralized medical services, as well as a small **Musée de Médécin** (Mon–Fri 5–7pm, Sat & Sun 1–7pm; free) with collections of surgical instruments and pharmaceutical equipment. Further along the riverbank you'll see the huge dome of the sixteenth-century **hospital of St-Joseph de la Grave**, which is still a working hospital. Hard-core philatelists will want to head over to the Centre Municipal de l'Affiche, a small **stamp museum** and resource centre (Mon–Fri 9am–noon & 2–6pm; free), nearby at 58 allée Charles-de-Fitte.

The main reason for visiting St-Cyprien – indeed a good reason for visiting Toulouse itself – is to see the contemporary art gallery, **Les Abattoirs** (Tues–Sun noon–8pm; €6.10; ⓦ www.lesabattoirs.org) at 76 allées Charles-de-Fitte, the avenue which marks the precinct of the city's former western wall, just behind the great cupola dominating the river's left bank. This splendid venue, opened in 2000, is not only one of France's best contemporary art museums, but also an inspired piece of urban regeneration. The massive brick complex was constructed in 1828, and functioned as an abattoir until 1989, when environmental concerns forced it to close. The space itself is massive, with huge chambers perfectly suited to display even the largest canvases. Comprising over 2000 works by 130 artists, the collection covers everything from painting to multimedia exhibits. Most European and American schools are well represented, with the major post-war French movements, including Support-Surface, Art Brut and Figuration Libre, plus Italian and Spanish works a particular strength. The most striking piece is undoubtedly **Picasso**'s massive 14m-by-20m theatre backdrop, *The Stripping of the Minotaur in the Harlequin Suit*, painted in 1936 for Romain Rolland's *Le 14 Juillet* and towering over the lower gallery. Other avant-garde works which stand out are the untitled canvases of **Tàpies** and **Barceló**, **Bettencourt**'s provocative mosaic *The Conversion of St Paul* and a large collection of **Dubuffet**'s paintings. The collection is so large and varied however – more unusual exhibits include a sculpture made up of transparent pipes into which you drop coins – that whatever your tastes you're unlikely to come away disappointed. The complex also includes libraries and a resource centre, interactive terminals on which you can manipulate digital images and a fantastic children's play area; light meals and refreshments are available in the museum's **café** (Tues–Sun; 11am–9pm). Behind the museum, the grassy Jardin Raymond IV stretches out towards the river, along an impressive section of the city's fourteenth-century **walls**.

South and east of the old town

If you have the time and energy, the areas south and east of the old town are also worth exploring. The southern district is marked off from old Toulouse by the wide Allées Jules-Guesde, the southernmost stretch of the former walls and site of an **antiques market** from Thursday to Sunday. On its northern side is the grassy

Jardin Royal, while at its eastern end, a roundabout encircles the surprisingly tranquil **Grand Rond**, with its pretty flower-rimmed fountain (a favourite for wedding photographs). The town's main park, the formally styled **Jardin des Plantes** (daily 7.45am–dusk), can be entered through a large arch off Jules-Guesde. The park itself is a lively place, complete with kids' rides, ice-cream stands and an ersatz mountain and waterfall. Near the entrance stands the city's natural history museum, optimistically slated for reopening in 2005. At the southern end you'll find the **Monument à la Résistance** (Mon–Fri 10am–noon & 2–5pm; free), where you can enter a solemn stone commemorative chapel.

If this theme interests you, continue down allée des Demoiselles opposite the park; among the fading glory of the Art Deco mansions you'll come across plaques marking the spots where Resistance fighters were shot dead by the Germans in the street-fighting of 1944. Finally, at no. 52, you'll arrive at the **Musée de la Résistance et de la Déportation** (Mon–Fri 9.30am–noon & 2–6pm, Sat 2–5pm; free). Founded to mark the fiftieth anniversary of the liberation of Toulouse on June 19, 1944, this resource centre and museum commemorates through photos, artefacts and dioramas the life of the maquis, the plight of those living under occupation and the crimes of the occupiers, including the massacre of the Forest of Bouconne.

A ten-minute walk up the rue du Japon, just outside the museum's doors, you'll find the tiny mansion belonging to the traveller and collector, Georges Labit. This nineteenth-century pavilion is pure Orientalist fantasy, a Gilbert and Sullivanesque vision of the East, but the **museum** inside (Mon & Wed–Sun: June–Sept 10am–6pm; Oct–May 10am–5pm; €2.20) holds a small but incredibly varied collection of Asiatica, including Chinese artefacts going back to the tenth century, temple carvings from Northern India and two complete samurai suits of armour. Just a stone's throw away, a canalside path leads up to the remains of old Canal du Midi port, **Port St-Saveur**, now being refitted as a modern pleasure port. From here it's a short walk north along boulevard Monplaisir back to the Grand Rond; incidentally, the towpath running parallel forms the first leg of the canalside bike and walking route from Toulouse to the **Seuil de Naurouze** (see box p.113). Heading back north along the west side of the canal, beyond the Halle aux Grains, you'll enter the St-Aubin *quartier* (which extends up to allées Jean-Jaurès). Although it has no sights, this inner-city neighbourhood makes for an interesting evening or afternoon excursion, with its marked North African flavour and increasingly diverse selection of bars, restaurants and nightclubs.

The suburbs

A number of specific sights may tempt you to leave old Toulouse and its immediate environs and head for the suburbs. Most popular among these is the **Cité de l'Espace** (daily: July & Aug 9.30am–7pm; Sept–June 9.30am–6pm; ⓦwww.cite-espace.com; €14, children over 6 €10.50), east of the city centre by exit 17 of the *periphérique est* ring road. This is a massive high-tech science centre, with scores of exhibits on the theme of space and its exploration, including satellite communications, space probes, a real Ariane rocket and, best of all, the opportunity to walk inside a mock-up of the MIR space station – a fascinating, but absolutely chilling and inhuman environment. Many of the exhibits are interactive and, though it's on the pricey side, you could easily spend a half day here, especially if you've got children in tow. Unfortunately, getting here by public transport is a nuisance: the closest bus lines (#16 and #19, from place Esquirol and Gare Matabiau respectively) leave you a good twenty-minute walk north of the park.

Toulouse and the future of air travel

Airbus, which has been giving stiff competition to major American airline manufacturers like Boeing, has upped the ante with its development of a new **super-liner**, the A-380. With a passenger capacity of 656, this two-storey colossus almost doubles the size of Boeing's 747, and promises to usher in a new era of air travel. But the cost of development has not been cheap. The massive components manufactured in Germany, Britain and elsewhere in France can be shipped to Bordeaux, but then must be taken by road to Toulouse. And there's the rub – their size makes transport on existing highways impossible, and thus 250km of highway must be altered or built anew to accommodate trucks bearing loads up to 13m in height and 300m long (travelling at the break-neck speed of 20km/h). Needless to say, there are grave concerns over the environmental impact of such a project, and several *départements*, notably the socialist-run Las Landas, Gers and Lot-et-Garonne, are resisting the development, which promises to radically alter the face of the region. With over 60 A-380s already on order, however, there is little doubt that the project will go through.

Meanwhile, with Toulouse's airport also feeling the pinch, plans are afoot to construct a new larger air hub for southwest France near the city and the authorities are casting around for possible locations. The flat lands of the *pays de Cocagne* on the Tarn's left bank seem to be an ideal site: level, open and with good transport links to the city. This has the villagers of Rabastens and Lisle-sur-Tarn nervous, as they rightly feel that such a monstrosity would spell the end of the bucolic life of their villages, which has continued, unhurried, for almost a thousand years.

Only slightly more down to earth is the tour of **Aérospatiale**'s assembly plant. In 1970 Toulouse became home to the French branch of the European conglomerate Airbus Industries, which manufactures passenger jets. The planes are assembled, painted and tested in a vast hanger, L'Usine Clément Ader, before taking their maiden flights from next-door Blagnac airport. Through "Taxiway", their visitor programme, you can choose between a tour of the assembly bays, where crews of one hundred people churn out five Airbuses per week, assisted by scores of computerized robots (€9), or a visit to the now defunct Concorde (€4.60). The **guided tours** (Mon–Sat) last approximately ninety minutes and must be booked well in advance (July & Aug contact the tourist office, Sept–June ring ☎05.61.18.06.01, ⓦwww.taxiway.fr). The huge factory is in Colomiers, near the airport – the closest bus route is #64 (from *metro* Arènes), and the bus driver will direct you to the site.

In the northern suburbs, you'll find the scant remains of Roman Toulouse's **amphitheatre**, constructed in the first century and used through to the end of the fourth. There are also the vestiges of Roman baths and you can visit a small archeological centre (Sat & Sun: June, Sept & Oct 2–6pm, July & Aug 2–7pm; €2.20). The site is about halfway to the airport, 5km downstream from the centre on the Garonne, on avenue des Arènes-Romaines and can be reached by buses #66 (from *metro* St-Cyprien to "Cautarets") or #70 (from place Jeanne-d'Arc to "Purpan").

Eating and drinking

There's no shortage of good **eating** options in Toulouse, although on Sundays you will find your choice drastically reduced. The city's ethnic mix has engendered a culinary cosmopolitanism, and for French cooking you'll find a multitude of choices in every category of style and price. Toulouse is also a city which loves its **cafés** and **bars** – not surprisingly, given that the population swells by almost a quarter with the annual inundation of university students. The establishments listed below are only a fraction of what's out there – whichever part of town you find yourself in, you're never far from a drink or a meal.

Restaurants

There are several good areas for **restaurants**. Rue de la Colombette in the St-Aubin district, just across boulevard Carnot, has some attractive and fashionable choices. The area surrounding St-Sernin is particularly good: just north, place Arnaud-Bernard and the tiny adjacent place des Tiercerettes have attractive options; between the basilica and place Bernard there's a compact knot of **Arabic** and **Maghrebi** restaurants; and rue du Taur has a number of **Vietnamese** places and sandwich bars. Should you feel stuck for a choice, you can always head south of place Wilson to place St-Georges, where you'll find a gaggle of typical terraced eateries, or to the bottom end of rue des Filatiers where there's a clutster of late-night restaurants and tapas bars. Several of the *bistrots* on place Wilson are distinguished not so much by their fare, but by the fact that you can eat as late as 1am.

If you're on a tight budget you can pick up **picnic** supplies in the Monoprix department store at 39 rue d'Alsace-Lorraine, or head from place du Capitole down rue St-Rome, where there's a string of inexpensive and good kebab and sandwich stands. The best lunch-time bargain is in the covered **market** on place Victor-Hugo (closed Mon), whose upper floor has a group of very cheap food counters. As a last resort, you'll find a late-night grocery store at 67 rue des Pargaminières.

Cheap

Les Abattoirs 97 allée Charles-de-Fitte ☎05.61.42.04.95. A family-run restaurant for two generations, the last of the traditional slaughter-house-side meat emporia, with a reputation for top-of-the-line intestinal delicacies such as calves, brains and pigs' feet. *Menus* from €16. Closed Sun, Mon & Aug.

Asia Fast Food 4 rue Bayard. If you want a quick bite on the way to the station, drop into this cheerful self-service cafeteria at the southern end of rue Bayard. Chinese, Vietnamese and Thai dishes at budget prices. Open daily till midnight.

Benjamin 7 rue des Gestes ☎05.61.22.92.66. A long-standing institution for economical *terroir* food; service is pleasant and service professional, although the atmosphere is somewhat anonymous. A wide selection of duck-based lunch and dinner *menus* €11–19. Open daily.

Le Chateaubriand 42 rue Pargaminières. Named after the politician rather than the steak, this casual little restaurant serves an excellent cassoulet, made with flavourful *haricots Tarbais*, and scrumptious home-made desserts. Lunch *menus* from €11, or €19–29 for dinner. Closed Aug, Sat lunch & Sun.

Chez Atilla In the market at pl Victor-Hugo. The best of the market restaurants, this no-nonsense lunch-time establishment is also one of Toulouse's best options for seafood – their Spanish *zarzuela* stew is a fish-lover's dream. *Menus* from €10. Closed Mon & part Aug.

Chez Fazoul 2 rue Tolosane ☎05.61.53.72.09. Welcoming restaurant serving local dishes in a pleasant, brick-walled dining room. *Menus*, featuring all the usual suspects: steak, cassoulet, *confits* and *cèpes*, for €11.40–27. Closed Sun.

Le Colombier 14 rue Bayard ☎05.61.62.40.05. Cassoulet's the thing in this elegant restaurant, but there are other regional delights, such as *gésiers* ("gizzards") and foie gras, as well as seafood and game. *Menus* from €18. Closed Sat lunch & Sun.

La Embarcadère 11 rue de la Bourse. Good selection of generous-sized salads, dessert crêpes and other light fare for under €8. Closed Mon.

Faim des Haricots 3 rue de Puits Vert ☎05.61.22.49.25. Toulouse's newest vegetarian option, with generous all-you-can-eat salad and dessert buffets (both €8), "bottomless" bowls of soup and a *plat du jour*. Open Mon–Sat lunch & Thurs–Sat dinner; closed first half Aug.

Brasserie de l'Opera 1 pl du Capitole ☎05.61.21.05.56. The *Hotel de l'Opera*'s budget option is a good-quality brasserie featuring a generous lunch-time *formule express* for €14 on weekdays. Open daily lunch and dinner.

Saveurs Bio 22 rue Maurice-Fonvielle
℡05.61.12.15.15. Toulouse's best vegetarian place, offering everything from spinach quiche to alfalfa salads, and with various set meals for under €15 and a *grande assiette* at €8. Closed Sat eve & Sun.
Taverna Casa Manolo 24 rue de 3 Piliers
℡05.61.23.85.06. Lively Spanish taverna hidden away amongst the couscous places north of St-Sernin. Generous tapas from €5 and a massive two-person paella at €28. Open Tues–Sun 7pm to late.
Le Ver Luisant 41 rue de la Colombette
℡05.61.63.06.73. A bar and simple restaurant frequented by the arty set. The good food – mostly regional but with some cosmopolitan touches – is copious and the atmosphere fun. *Plat du jour* €7 at lunch time, or €15–28 for an evening meal. Closed Sat lunch & Sun.

Moderate

La Bascule 14 av Maurice-Hauriou
℡05.61.52.09.51. A Toulouse institution. Its chromy interior is pure Art Deco and the food well preprared and presented. The menu includes regional dishes like cassoulet, *foie de canard* and oysters from the Bay of Arcachon. *Menus* from €19.80. Closed Sun.
Cantine du Curé 2 rue H-de-Grosse. Cosy little *terroir* restaurant, housed in a small but atmospheric old building, complete with wooden beams, by the entrance to the Dalbade church. One of the two tiny dining areas has a fireplace. Evening *menu* from €27. Closed Sun eve & Mon
Au Chat Deng 40 rue Peyrolières. Small, hip bistro with cool blue decor across from the *Petit Voisin* bar. The menu is not overly imaginative, with a solid southern French base and occasional Italian incursions (usually in the form of pasta). *Menus* €18–24, but considerably more à la carte. Closed Sun.
Cosi Fan Tutte 8 rue Mage ℡05.61.53.07.24. Highly-reputed and stylish Italian place with richly garish red decor. Ordering à la carte or dining in the evening is considerably more expensive (€29–58) than the €12 daily specials. Tues–Sat eves only.
La Côte de Boeuf 12 rue des Gestes
℡05.61.21.19.61. This simple and compact street-side restaurant is not the cheapest in the neighbourhood, but the quality of its wood-fire home-cooking (superb duck and foie gras) and the genuine friendliness of the family who run it put it a step above neighbouring *Benjamin*. Extras (such as coffee and liquor) are pricey. Expect to spend €22. Closed Sun.
Kaviar Rouge 21 place Nicholas Bachelier
℡05.61.62.31.19. Toulouse's Russian restaurant

is located in the St-Aubin district. Sample a wide selection of Caucasian delicacies, including caviar (€25–156 per 50g) and the city's best selection of Polish and Russian flavoured vodkas (from €5) in the cosy atmosphere of a *faux* Siberian log cabin. Generous dinner *menu* at €25. Closed Sun.
Au Petit Paradoux 41 rue des Paradoux
℡05.62.26.44.73. Homey and welcoming dining room featuring regional cuisine from the Basque country, Bigorre and Gascony. From €20. Closed Mon.
Semiramis 23 rue des Peyrolières
℡05.6123.66.11. Extremely popular Lebanese and Syrian cuisine, with typical *mezze*, including homemade *kibbeh*, spinach pie and other Middle-Eastern favourites. Dine inside or on the street in the €20 range. Open daily.
Le Sept Place St-Sernin 7 pl St-Sernin
℡05.62.30.05.30. A small house behind the basilica conceals a lively and cheerful restaurant which serves inventive and original cuisine with a constantly changing *carte*, followed by dazzling desserts. *Menus* €23–45. Closed Sat lunch & Sun.
Shun 35 rue Bachelier ℡05.61.99.39.20. Surprisingly well-priced Japanese restaurant at the north end of the St-Aubin district. Basic *menus* at €9–15 but plan on spending more. Closed Mon.

Expensive

Chez Émile 13 pl St-Georges ℡05.61.21.05.56. One of Toulouse's best, and well situated on this busy oblong square. Regional cuisine downstairs and seafood upstairs, at €16–38 on the *menu*. Closed Sun & Mon.
Les Jardins de l'Ópera 1 pl du Capitole
℡05.61.21.05.56. The *Grand Hôtel*'s restaurant is Toulouse's best and most luxurious. If you fancy a splurge this is the place to do it – the food is outstanding – but you will pay for it: a basic *menu* starts at €39.70. Closed Sun & part Aug.
Michel Sarran 21 bd Armand-Duportal
℡05.61.12.32.32. Justifiably renowned *gastronomique* restaurant, a 15min walk from the place du Capitole (follow rue des Lois and rue des Salenques to the end, and turn left). Imaginative dishes with a strong Mediterranean streak are served with style and warmth. *Menus* €40–95. Closed part Aug.
Au Pois Gourmand 3 rue Émile Heybrard ℡05.61 .31.95.95. Great location in a nineteenth-century riverside house with a beautiful patio. The quality French cuisine does not come cheap here (*menus* €22–60), but is of a predictably high standard, and the *carte* presents a pleasant departure from purely regional dishes. Bus #66 or #14 from *metro* St-Cyprien-République. Closed Sat lunch & Sun.

Cafés and bars

Many establishments cater to a mellow coffee and beer clientele during the day and put on the music after 10pm. Regular daytime **café**-lounging can be pursued around the popular student/arty hangout of place Arnaud-Bernard, while place du Capitole is the early evening meeting place. Place St-Georges has been somewhat inundated by restaurant terraces but remains another option, while the more elegant terraces of place Wilson are good if you don't mind the traffic.

Bagdam Café 4 rue de la Croix ☎05.61.99.03.62. Catering for women only, with readings, music and drama as well as coffee, drinks and food. Tues–Sat from 7pm. Closed mid-Aug to mid-Sept.

Bapz 13 rue de la Bourse. English-style bakery and tearoom – definitely not your typical "caff", with good breakfasts and snacks. Smart service (and prices). Closed Sun.

Bar Gambetta 39 rue Gambetta. Quirky place with a long bar and a vaguely 1950s feel, just off the place du Capitole. Closed Sun.

Bar du Matin 16 pl des Carmes. Great old street-corner bar in the finest beer, peanuts and *pastis* tradition. A friendly and deservedly popular place. Closed Sun.

Bibent 5 pl du Capitole. On the south side of the square, this is Toulouse's most distinguished café, with exuberant plasterwork, marble tables and cascading chandeliers. Open daily.

Le Café des Artistes pl de la Daurade. Lively, young café overlooking the Garonne. A perfect spot to watch the sun set on warm summer evenings, as floodlights pick out the brick buildings along the quays. Open daily.

Le Donjon Bar 2 rue du Poids de l'Huile. Tiny bar on the south side of the Capitole building. Impossibly crowded but great fun for watching rugby or having a drink. Open until 2am. Closed Sun.

Dubliners Irish Pub 15 av Crampel. Toulouse's biggest Irish pub. Few surprises. Open until 2am. Closed Sun.

Le Florida 12 pl du Capitole. Relaxed café with a nicely retro air. One of the most pleasant places to hang out on the central square. Open daily.

The Frog and Rosbif 14 rue de l'Industrie. Stop by this friendly British pub, just off bd Lazare-Carnot, for a pint of Darktagnan stout, or one of their other excellent home brews. Quiz nights, foot-ball and fish and chips draw an international crowd. Open until 2am, Sat until 4am. Closed part Aug.

Jour de Fête 43 rue de Taur. Funky tearoom and brasserie with a small street-side patio. Friendly service and a young studenty crowd. Open until 2am Fri & Sat.

Au Père Louis 45 rue des Tourneurs ☎05.61.21.33.45. A lively, old-fashioned bar with *chansons* and music some nights. Open till 10pm. Closed Sun.

St-Philipe 19 rue Arnaud-Bernard. Just off place Bernard to the north of the St-Sernin, on the edge of the Maghrebi neighbourhood, this bar attracts a mixed crowd of locals, students and business people. There's a pool table, *foozball* and video games to keep you busy over your beer. Open daily.

Le Shanti 21 rue Peyrolières. A funky "Indian" tea house featuring a wide range of non-alcoholic refreshments as well as the opportunity to relax with a *narghila* (Arab water-pipe; €6). Open daily 2pm–2am.

Le Sherpa 44 rue de Taur. Another of the city's many tea rooms. Popular with the university crowd and conveniently located by the Cinemathèque. Closed Sun.

Tanygasy 41 rue Paradoux. Bohemian tearoom featuring art exhibits, and occasional "happenings". Tues–Sat noon–8pm & Sun 4–8pm; closed much of July & Aug.

Le Thé l'Ollier 10 pl Saintes-Scarbes. This chilled café makes the perfect break from antique-shopping around the cathedral, or if you just fancy a read to the relaxing sound of the fountain in the *place*. Also does light snacks. Open daily 8am–7pm.

Au Trait d'Union 12 rue des Gestes. Funky tea-house and art gallery down a small street just off pl du Capitole. Closed Sun & Mon.

Nightlife

The annual influx of university students ensures that the city's **nightlife** is active, sustaining a whole range of **music–bars** and **clubs**; if the French are not famous for exuberant partying, Toulouse helps belie the stereotype. Things slow down from July to September, when the academic year breaks, but even in the summer you'll have no trouble drinking and dancing as late as you like. Unfortunately some of the city's best venues lie in the suburbs, which basically condemns you to paying for a taxi. However, as the list below shows, there's no shortage of options closer to the old town. Entrance fees to discos and clubs may be charged depending on the night and event, but generally in these places you're expected to buy a rather expensive drink (€8–10), while at venues which are essentially bars you can enter free of charge.

Music-bars and clubs

L'Ambassade 22 bd de la Gare. Downbeat club where funk and soul rule. Open until 2am, Sat 5am. Closed Sun.

Bar de la Lune 24 rue Palaprat. This evening drinking spot in St-Aubin draws an arty crowd with its occasional exhibitions and concerts. Daily from 7pm.

Bodega-Bodega 1 rue Gabriel-Péri. The old *Telegraph* newspaper building makes a superb venue for this bar-restaurant, with its hugely popular disco after 10pm. Daily until 2am, Sat 4am.

Café Classico 37 rue des Filatiers. Trendy, designer-ish establishment that's a café by day and music-bar by night. House, hip-hop and jungle. Daily until 1am, Sat 4am.

Le Chat d'Oc 7 rue de Metz. Hip bar near the Garonne. Attracts a mixed crowd which gets younger as the night progress. Nightly *animations* include DJs and occasional live acts, with themes from grunge to Goth. Open until 2am, Sat 5am. Closed Sun.

Erich Coffie 9 rue Joseph-Vié. Just west of the river in the *quartier* St-Cyprien, this is one of the city's liveliest and most enjoyable music-bars, with an eclectic music policy. There's food available and live bands most evenings. Open Tues–Sat from 10pm.

Le Griot 3 rue Amélie. Massive super-bar and concert hall, with dance floors, videos, pool room and restaurant. Happy hours 7–8pm & 10–11pm. Daily until 2am.

Hey Joe pl Héraclès. Popular disco with theme nights on Thursdays. Men pay €8, women get in free; happy hour is from midnight to 1am. Daily 11pm–5am.

Le Klub 2bis rue Delpech. Large club with two dance floors and a changing repertoire, including techno, funk, house and rock. Open until 5am, closed Mon. No admission fee.

La Luna Loca 15 rue Pierre Rubens. Cultural centre and club for lesbians. Men admitted on Wed & Fri only. Nightly 8pm–late.

Le Petit Voisin 37 rue Peyrolières. A neighbourhood place, just like the name, "the little neighbour", says. Laid back during the day when workers and businessmen stop for a drink, and livelier at night, when it fills with a student crowd. Open until 2am, Sat 4am. Closed Sun & mid-Aug.

Puerto Habana 12 port St-Etienne. Toulouse's hottest salsa venue, in a superb setting beside the Canal du Midi. Also has an excellent restaurant and a house band Thurs–Sat. Mon–Fri until 2am, Sat till 5am.

Le Rex 15 av Honoré-Serres. Located in an old converted cinema building, just north of the old town, this bar/concert hall usually features ska and punk acts. Opening hours vary so check with the local entertainment magazines for concerts and events.

La Salle des Fêtes de Ramonville 55 chemin des Ētroits, rte de Lacroix-Falgarde. On the city's southern outskirts, this is *the* hangout of Toulouse rockers, and a prime venue for live gigs (formerly known as "le Bikini"). Typical entry charge is €5, including a free drink. Open Thurs–Sun.

Le Shanghai 12 rue de la Pomme. One of the city's most established gay and lesbian clubs, which attracts a mixed crowd including transvestites and transsexuals. Wed–Sun 11pm–late.

L'Ubu 16 rue St-Rome. Long-standing pillar of the city's dance scene, that remains as popular as ever. Mon–Sat 11pm till dawn.

Entertainment and festivals

Drinking and dancing aside, there's plenty to do in Toulouse. Several **cinemas** regularly offer v.o. showings, including ABC, 13 rue St-Bernard (☎05.61.29.81.00), Cinémathèque, 68 rue de Taur (☎05.62.30.30.10, ⓦwww.lacinemathequedetoulouse.com), and Utopia, 24 rue Montardy (☎05.61.23.66.20, ⓦwww.cinemas-utopia.org). The city also has an extremely vibrant **theatre** culture. The official Théâtre de la Cité, 1 rue Pierre-Baudis (☎05.34.45.05.05, ⓦwww.tnt-cite.com) is home to the Théâtre National de

Toulouse Midi-Pyrénées, which has a narrative theatre programme livened up by occasional dance performances, while the workshop Nouveau Théâtre Jules-Julien (6 av des Écoles-Jules-Juliens; ☎05.61.25.79.92) has a reputation for staging provocative drama, with a particular emphasis on Absurdist productions. The large venue Odyssud (4 av du Parc Blagnac; ☎05.61.71.75.15; bus #66) features both theatre and **opera**, but the place to head for the latter, as well as **ballet** and **contemporary dance** performances, is the Théâtre du Capitole, housed in the Capitole building (☎05.61.63.13.13, Ⓦwww.theatre-du-capitole.org), a highly acclaimed venue where you can also hear recitals and chamber music. **Classical music** fans also have the Orchestre National du Capitole, with its base in the Halle aux Grains in place Dupuy (☎05.61.99.78.00, Ⓦwww.onct.mairie-toulouse.fr). The city's biggest **rock music** venue, with nine-thousand seats, is Zénith at 11 avenue Raymond Badiou (☎05.62.74.49.49; *metro* Arènes), which features both French and foreign groups, including visiting jazz and blues performers, while for something a little less energetic, Cave-Poésie (71 rue de Taur; ☎05.61.23.62.00, Ⓦwww.cave-poésie.fr.st) is home to various **literary workshops** and gatherings of a decidedly bohemian spirit.

Toulouse's **festivals** calendar is packed out, with a virtually back-to-back programme of artistic, musical or literary events throughout the year. For a full rundown of these, see the box on pp.76–77. To get the most up-to-date **information** on the latest cultural events check the weekly magazines *Toulouse Hebdo* (€0.90) or *Flash* (€3), which have detailed concert and event listings and are available at news-stands, or Books and Mermaides' monthly *Doings in Toulouse*, an English-language info-mag (free). The monthly *Ramdam* (€2) has listings for the whole region of Midi-Pyrénées, while the *mairie* distributes a free magazine, *Cultures Toulouse*, and has comprehensive event listings at Ⓦwww.mairie-toulouse.fr.

Listings

Airlines Air France ☎08.20.82.08.20, Ⓦwww.air-france.com; American ☎08.10.08.72.08.72, Ⓦwww.aa.com; BMI Baby ☎00.44.87.02.64.22.29, Ⓦwww.bmibaby.com; British European ☎00.44.13.92.26.85.00, Ⓦwww.british-european.com; British Midland ☎05.61.12.62.02, Ⓦwww.flybmi.com; Delta ☎05.62.27.26.05, Ⓦwww.delta.com.

Airport Aéroport Toulouse-Blagnac ☎05.61.42.44.00 & 05.24.61.80.00, Ⓦwww.toulouse.aeroport.fr; for shuttle bus information ☎05.34.60.64.00.

Banks and exchange Most major French banks have offices and ATMs around the place du Capitole. The Banque de France is at 4 rue Deville (Mon–Fri 9am–12.20pm & 1.20–3.30pm). For bureaux de change Banque Populaire Toulouse Pyrénées has an office at the airport (Mon–Fri 8am–7pm, Sat 10am–noon & 1.30–6pm) and C2E Capitole Exchange is in the centre at 30 rue de Taur (July & Aug Mon–Sat 9am–6pm; Sept–June Mon–Sat 9am–12.30pm & 2–6pm).

Bike rental Serious cyclists planning a longer trip may want to contact the Association Vélo, 2 rue de la Daurade, 31000 Toulouse (☎05.61.11.87.09, Ⓦwww.multimania.com/velotlse).

Boat trips Various outfits offer tours on the Garonne and the canals du Midi and de Brienne. Le Capitole has several daily night-time departures for a ninety-minute journey on the Garonne (departs pl de la Daurade; reserve at the tourist office; €5; Ⓦwww.toulouse-croisieres.com). Baladine has a variety of full-day programmes, as well as a 75-minute cruise of historic Toulouse departing from the quai de la Daurade (daily in summer 2.30, 4 & 5.30pm, otherwise Wed, Sat & Sun; €6.10; Ⓔcontact@bateaux-toulousains.com). Alternatively you can rent an electric boat and buzz around yourself: Société AQUALUB has its fleet moored at Port St-Saveur, southeast from the Grand Rond at the end of allée des Soupirs (☎06.86.71.33.46).

Books The best general bookshops are Castéla, on place du Capitole, and FNAC, at 16 allées F-Roosevelt. Toulouse Presse, 60 rue Bayard, stocks a good range of IGN maps and guides while Ombres-Blanches on 50 rue Gambetta is another good choice for travel literature. For English-language books, Books and Mermaides, 3 rue Mirepoix, specializes in second-hand tomes and will exchange, while The Bookshop, 17 rue Lakanal, stocks new titles. There are book markets on Thursday mornings in place Arnaud-Bernard, and all day Saturday in place St-Etienne.

Bus departures *Gare routière* (information booth Mon–Fri 8.30am–4pm; ☎05.61.61.67.67) beside the gare SNCF.

Car rental A2L, 81 bd Déodat-de-Séverac ☎05.61.59.33.99; Avis, gare SNCF ☎05.61.63.71.71; Budget, 49 rue Bayard ☎05.61.63.18.18; Europcar, 15 bd Bonrepos ☎05.61.62.52.89; Hertz, gare SNCF ☎05.61.62.94.12.

Consulates Canada, 10 rue Jules de Resseguier ☎05.61.52.19.06; UK, Immeuble Victoria Center, 20 chemin de Laporte ☎05.61.15.02.02; US, 25 allées Jean-Jaurés ☎05.34.31.36.50.

Gay and lesbian For information contact the gay and lesbian students' group Jules et Julies (Comité des Étudiants, Université du Mirail, 5 Allée Machado, 31058) or Gais et Lesbiennes en Marche (☎06.11.87.38.81, ✉gelem@altern.org).

Hospitals There are two major hospitals, both outside the A61 ring road: CHR Ranguiel, chemin du Vallon (☎05.61.32.25.33) to the south, and CHR Purpan, pl du Dr Baylac (☎05.61.77.22.33) to the west. Emergency ☎15 or 05.61.12.77.77.

Internet access Cyber Media-Net, 19 rue de Lois (Mon–Fri 9am–11.30pm, Sat 10am–midnight), or @fterbug, 12 pl St-Sernin (Mon–Fri noon–2am, Sat noon–5am, Sun 2.30–10.30pm). Aside from these, the CRIJ office at 17 rue de Metz has a free terminal, and you can also get online at the main post office, and at Telecom France kiosks at 11 rue Alsace-Lorraine and 18 place Wilson.

Language courses Alliance Française, 9 pl du Capitole (☎05.34.45.26.10), and Maison de l'Europe, 21 pl St-Sernin (☎05.61.54.11.6930) both run French-language courses.

Laundry Lavomat, 20 rue Arnaud-Bernard (daily 7am–10pm), and Lavaria Auto, 7 rue Mirepoix (daily 7am–9pm).

Markets Antiques in place St-Sernin and allées Jules-Guesde (Thurs–Sun 8am–4pm). Produce and clothes in place du Capitole (Wed & Sun 8am–1pm). There is also a mammoth food and clothing market on Sun and Mon along boulevard Strasbourg. And more produce markets at places des Carmes, St-Cyprien and Victor-Hugo (all Tues–Sun). For a complete rundown of the city's many markets, ask at the tourist office.

Pharmacy There are pharmacies in place du Capitole and dotted throughout the city. The Pharmacie de Nuit, 70–76 allées Jean-Jaurès (entry on rue Arnaud Vidal), is open 8pm.

Police 23 bd de l'Embouchure ☎05.61.12.77.77; emergency ☎17.

Rugby Toulouse is a centre of excellence for French rugby – many players in the national team hail from these parts. You can see their first-rate Stade Toulousain team in action at their stadium at 114 rue de Troenes (☎05.61.57.05.05; bus #16 to "Stade").

Swimming There are several public pools in town. Alfred Nakache is open year-round (allées Paul-Bienes; ☎05.61.22.31.35).

Taxis Allo Association Taxi ☎05.62.16.26.16; Capitole ☎05.34.25.02.50; Taxi Radio Toulousain ☎05.61.42.38.38. For taxis to the airport call ☎05.61.30.02.54.

Train departures Tickets can be bought at the gare SNCF, or at the SEMVAT building, 7 pl Esquirol (Mon–Fri 2–6pm). Information on ☎08.92.35.35.35, ✪www.sncf.fr.

Travel agencies USIT Voyages (✪www.usitconnect.fr) has branches at 16 rue Pierre-Paul Riquet (☎05.61.99.38.47) and 5 rue de Lois (☎05.61.11.52.42); Nouvelles Frontières (✪www.nouvelles-frontieres.fr) is in 2 pl St-Sernin (☎08.03.33.33.33).

Around Toulouse

Predominantly flat, and ribbed by a multitude of small streams, the hinterland fanning out to the north and east of Toulouse has long been the source of the city's wealth. The woad boom of the fifteenth and sixteenth centuries may have powered its prosperous golden age, but the **cereal farming** carried out in this immensely fertile region has been Toulouse's traditional financial mainstay. Field after field of wheat dominates the rolling landscape, cut across by narrow bands of wood, and dotted by the church steeples of modest, introverted hamlets – havens of determined rural existence where elderly farmers speak French

The woad to riches

From the mid-fifteenth to the mid-sixteenth century Toulouse and Albi experienced an unprecedented wave of prosperity, based on the humble **woad** plant (*Isatis tinctoria* or in French, *pastel*). When craftsmen in Albi discovered that the innocuous weed, which was used for medicinal purposes across the Mediterranean, yielded a rich blue dye, they knew they were onto a good thing; blue was one of the colours for clothing most in demand by the growing middle class, and up to that point it could only be produced from rare and expensive raw materials.

With capital from Toulouse, intensive woad cultivation operations were set up across the Lauragais, which had ideal soil and climate conditions for the plant. Once the woad had been harvested, the process of dye production lasted approximately four months, during which time the leaves were picked, crushed and rolled into balls (*coques*) and left to ferment for two weeks, whereafter the sticky dye could be pressed out and rolled into balls (*cocagnes*). Demand from textile manufacturers across Europe brought staggering wealth to the region, which became known in common parlance as the **pays de Cocagne** (a play on words, also meaning "the land of plenty"). Some 30–40,000 tonnes were shipped annually. The woad merchants, many of whom became *capitouls* of Toulouse, erected fine mansions, the *hôtels particuliers*, which even today bear witness to their former wealth. By the late sixteenth century, however, *pastel* began to be superseded by cheaper indigo-based dyes brought over to Europe from the Indies, and production went into decline. The violent upheavals of the Wars of Religion, ravaging fields and interrupting transport, provided the final blow, and the dye, along with the incredible affluence it generated, became a thing of the past. Today, you can purchase traditionally dyed items at La Fleurée de Pastel at 20 rue de la Bourse in Toulouse, near the Hôtel d'Assézat.

with a rounded Occitan accent. The region is hedged to the north by the River Agout and to the west by the rising peaks of the Montagne Noire (see Chapter 3), but is most notable for its southern boundary, the Canal du Midi. With its generally low relief and comparatively little traffic, it makes **cycling** enjoyable and reasonably safe here.

The northern stretch of the region, known as the *pays de Cocagne* (see box above) is dominated by **Lavaur**, once a stalwart Cathar centre, with its beautifully preserved old town. On either side of this, a series of quiet hamlets, **St-Sulpice**, **Giroussens**, **St-Paul** and **Damiette**, line the Agout, crossing it with narrow old trestle bridges. The easternmost town in the area, sitting on the edge of the Parc du Haut Languedoc, is the old *bastide* of **Revel**, with an impressive medieval covered market-place. Just south of here, at **St-Ferreol**, you'll find part of the incredible catchment system of the Canal du Midi, while just to the northeast, **Sorèze** and **Dourgne** embody the past and present of the monastic traditions of the Benedictines and their heirs. The flat Lauragais district stretches southwest of Revel: **St-Félix** is its prettiest town, but **Castelnaudary** – the area's capital – contains a surprising number of monuments and mansions. More significantly, it is also the main town on this stretch of the **Canal du Midi**, the engineering marvel constructed in the seventeenth century to link the Mediterranean and the Atlantic, and now a favourite with boating enthusiasts and cyclists.

Lavaur and around

Thirty-seven kilometres east of Toulouse, **LAVAUR** is the biggest town on the Agout west of Castres, and the traditional capital of the surrounding *pays de*

Cocagne. It's also a key town in the history of Catharism, the twelfth-century heretical movement (see box on p.149). Seat of a Cathar bishop, the "citadel of Satan," as it was known to Catholic forces, was besieged twice by the crusading northern French aristocracy. It resisted in 1181, but when the violent leader of the papal military forces, Simon de Montfort, arrived in March 1211, he meant business. After nearly two months of encirclement the walls were breached, and the town taken – with bloody consequences: Guiraude de Laurac, widow of the town's lord and leader of the defence, was thrown down a well and pelted with stones; her brother, along with nearly a hundred knights, was put to the sword; and some four hundred Cathars were burnt at the stake. Despite such brutality the heresy persisted, prompting the papacy and crown to establish a series of religious foundations here, starting with a Dominican house to run the local Inquisition and finally, in the fourteenth century, a cathedral. In the sixteenth century the town was a Huguenot hotbed, pitting itself once more against the Catholic establishment and the seigniorial powers of the North. Nevertheless it prospered, profiting first from the lucrative woad industry and, later, silk manufacture. Today Lavaur is an attractive if quiet rural centre, surrounded by the wheat fields of the Agout valley.

The town's main landmark, the brick-built former **cathedral** of St-Alain, stands on a wide plaza above the river. The present structure was built in 1254, replacing that destroyed by the Crusaders, and although the interior has been given a hideous nineteenth-century remodelling, the exterior still holds a few surprises. These include a wooden door on the south side, which survives from the original pre-Crusade building, an eleventh-century marble altar, a highly stylized fifteenth-century doorway and an incredible mechanical clock, perched high above the ground in one of its two towers. This *jacquemart* – a clock which strikes using a mechanical figure in the form of a soldier wielding a hammer – dates back to 1523 and still marks every half-hour. Looking across the river from the plaza, you'll be treated to a vista of old mansions set in the fields along its banks, while heading southwest from the cathedral entrance a series of signs leads you on a pleasant stroll past the highlights of the town. Chief among these is the fourteenth-century **church of St-François**, dedicated to St Francis of Assisi, founder of the Franciscans, the first group established to preach against heretics and the Dominicans' great rivals, who also came here to rehabilitate the Cathar population. Set in the town's old main street, the Grande Rue, this church has weathered the centuries, losing its cloister and other appendages to Huguenots and revolutionaries. Nevertheless the graceful simplicity of its single nave and surviving columns make it worth a look. In the adjoining **garden** keep an eye out for the old dovecote, one of the first along the route des Colombiers (see p.104). Nearby, the **church of the Cordeliers**, built in the years immediately following the Crusade, also merits a visit for its elegant Gothic interior. As you walk around the town you'll find that there are quite a number of timber-and-brick houses, many dating from the fourteenth to sixteenth centuries; there may be no major sights in Lavaur, but the narrow old streets make for a pleasantly atmospheric whole. Finishing up, the circuit through the old town leads back towards the cathedral, passing the eighteenth-century Neoclassical *mairie*, which houses the local historical and archeological museum, the Musée du Pays Vaurais, under indefinite renovation at the time of writing.

Practicalities

Trains and buses stop at Lavaur's **gare SNCF**, located northeast of the old quarter on the place de Stalingrad. From here it's a fifteen-minute walk to the **tourist office** (June–Sept Tues–Sat 9.30am–noon & 2.30–6.30pm; Oct–May

The Inquisition

In the thirteenth century the Catholic Church was forced to respond to the threat to its monopoly of religious belief posed by the various heresies, including **Catharism**, which had begun to spring up around Europe. The most dramatic response was the military one, but in the aftermath of the Albigensian Crusade, once Catharism had been destroyed as a political power, the task of converting the "hearts and minds" of the common people still remained. This was taken on by two new religious orders, the Franciscans (1209) and Dominicans (1215), whose members sought, through popular preaching, to reconnect a Church perceived as distant and corrupt to the urban masses. But it was not enough to bring the message of Truth to the people; the danger of heretical Error also need to be stamped out. Thus, the **Inquisition** was instituted in Languedoc. Part secret police, part travelling court, the Inquisition went from town to town investigating local beliefs in order to determine whether they were orthodox or not, and to sniff out secret heretics. Guilt was frequently assumed, and torture not infrequently resorted to – often confession or accusation of others was the only chance, however slim, for the accused to be saved. Once condemned by the Church, whose hands could not be bloodied, the victim was given over to local authorities for execution. The last great inquisition of Cathars was carried out in 1412 against the villagers of Montaillou (see p.145). Not surprisingly, the Inquisition did little to endear the people of Languedoc to the Catholic authorities, and it contributed to the region's residual distrust of "foreign" authority.

9.30am–12.30pm & 4–6pm; ☎05.63.58.02.00, ⓦwww.ville-lavaur.fr), housed in a small turret on the riverside quai Tour de Rondes. Decent **hotels** include the comfortable if unremarkable *Le Terminus* (☎05.63.58.31.14, ⓕ05.63.58.15.11; ❸) by the station, and the basic *Central*, 7 rue d'Alsace-Lorraine (☎05.63.58.04.16; ❷), but the best place to stay is the **chambres d'hôtes** *Taverne de la Dame du Plô*, 5 rue du Père Colin (☎05.63.41.38.77; ❸), an ancient house located just a short walk from the old cathedral with four small but cosy rooms. It also has a great bar, worth a stop whether you're staying there or not. Another option is *En Roque*, 3.5km from town; set in its own grounds, this B&B makes a good base for exploring by car, and can provide babysitting (☎05.63.58.04.58, ⓔenroque@wanadoo.fr; ❹; English spoken).

For eating, the best choice is the **restaurant** *Le Jardin* at 8 allées Ferréol-Mazas (closed Sun & Mon & part Aug) which has hearty *menus* for €18–35 (€13.50 at lunch). A second choice is the dining room *Terminus* (closed Sat), a friendly place serving up inventive *terroir*-based food (around €20). You'll also find a clutch of places in the elongated square stretching up from the tourist office, the most interesting of which is *Bistro Azurro* (closed Sun), a Basque restaurant where you can get a half-chicken lunch with wine for only €9. Lavaur's **country market** is on Saturday morning throughout the old town, and there's a **horse fair** held on the third Saturday of each month near the *gare*.

Giroussens and St-Sulpice

Some fifteen kilometres northwest of Lavaur, the ancient village of **GIROUSSENS** huddles on the slope of a high ridge. For thousands of years and right up to the present day, this town has been a centre of pottery production, as the shops which line the road through town reveal. Pottery fans can also visit the **Maison de la Ceramique**, in place Lucie-Bouniol, a museum/shop featuring local wares (daily 10am–noon & 2–6pm; €2). Aside from this and an attractive thirteenth-century **church**, there's little to draw you here, but if you are walking, cycling or driving by, it makes a good place to spend the night. Just across the river on the south bank of the Agout, you'll find the hamlet of **St-Lieux-lès-Lavaur**, site of a much-touted **steam train** (Easter to mid-July & Sept–Oct Sun & school holidays only same times; mid-July to Aug daily 2.30–6.30pm; subject to cancellation if less than ten tickets sold; €4.70), which runs a one-hour return trip eastwards along the river valley, the highpoint of which is the crossing over a twenty-metre-high viaduct. Beware, however, that the management frequently substitutes a regular diesel model for the trip. Also in St-Lieux is the **Jardin des Martels** (daily: April, Sept & Oct 1–6pm, May–August 10am–7pm; €6), a botanical garden with thousands of varieties of flowers and plants, as well as a petting zoo. The train and garden make a good combination if you are travelling with children. The best place to **stay** or **eat** in Giroussens is *L'Échaguette* (☎05.63.41.63.65, ℻05.63.41.63.13; ❸), in the lower part of the village. This beautiful thirteenth-century building has several well-furnished rooms and a small, intimate dining room, with delicious *terroir*-based *menus* (€21–43 at dinner). Alternatively, you can stay at the Reynauds' B&B, *Le Pepil* (closed late Aug to early Sept; ☎05.63.41.62.84; ❷ English spoken), set in attractive old farm building.

You're only likely to make a stop in tiny **ST-SULPICE**, 8km further west, if changing buses or trains en route to Toulouse or Albi from Lavaur or the Montagne Noire. The village is quite plain, apart from an attractive old suspension **bridge** over the Agout, which flows into the Tarn just west of town. There's also a mildly interesting fourteenth-century **church** just south of the old bridge, whose crenellated facade shows it originally served as part of the town's defences. On one of the doors you can see a depiction of Moses descending from Mount Sinai bearing the Ten Commandments and sprouting ram's horns. The origin of this curious motif, recurrent in Catholic art, is an error on the part of St Jerome, who translated the Bible into its popular Latin version, the Vulgate, in the fourth century. Led astray by the Hebrew text (in which vowels are not written) he confused two adjectives; the original read that Moses returned from his interview with God "radiant", but Jerome read it as "horned". Medieval artists, faithfully following scripture, dutifully depicted the patriarch sprouting horns. Just east of the church, below the ruins of the twelfth-century **château du Castela**, you can visit the castle's underground passages, 142 metres in length, formerly used for storage and defence. Dress warmly for the atmospheric forty-minute tour (on demand; 3–7pm May Sat, Sun & hols, June–Sept Tues–Sun, Oct Sat & Sun 3–5pm; Nov–April on demand via tourist office; €2).

The **tourist office** is at Parc Georges-Spenale (Tues–Sat 3–7pm; ☎05.63.41.89.50). To **stay** the night, you can choose between the *Hôtel Le Relais Fleuri* (☎05.63.41.80.20, ⓦwww.federal-hotel.com; ❷), and several **chambres d'hôtes**, including *Le Cambou* (☎05.63.41.82.66; ❸). There's also a **campsite** in town, *Borio-Blanco* (☎05.63.41.89.55), which is open all year. If you are looking for a **meal**, head out on the RN88 to *L'Auberge de la Pointe* (closed Tues eve, Wed off-season & part Nov; ☎05.63.41.80.14), one of the best *gastronomique* restaurants on this stretch of the Tarn, where you can enjoy subtle and elaborate *menus* overlooking the river for €16–31. If you have transport, the nineteenth-century manor house at St-Lieux has reasonably rooms in impressive surroundings (☎05.63.41.60.87, ⓦwww.gites-tarn.com; ❸; English spoken). Market day is Wednesday (morning only).

The route des Colombiers, St-Paul-Cap-de-Joux and Damiette

If you are cycling or driving from Lavaur, you should take time to explore the **route des Colombiers**, a loose circuit of approximately 20km which you can start on the southern bank of the Agout heading east out of the town. *Colombiers*, elaborate and varied **dovecotes**, have been constructed here among the farm fields since the Middle Ages to house the pigeons which formed a valuable part of the rural economy, providing food and fertilizer. The tourist office in Lavaur has a map with directions to all of the dovecotes (many are private and hardly visible from the road) as well as some explanatory text. If you don't want to do the whole circuit, which leads about 10km east before looping back, you'll pass a good number of dovecotes by taking the small river-side road from Lavaur towards St-Paul (follow signs for "Flamarens"). There are also plenty to see right along the main D112 highway which runs between Lavaur and Castres, in addition to half a dozen in Lavaur itself.

Ten kilometres after the river road and the main road meet you'll come to a bridge over the Agout, abutted on the south side by **ST-PAUL-CAP-DE-JOUX** and on the north by **DAMIETTE**. These two sleepy little towns don't hold any attractions themselves but are the closest places to the castles of Magrin and Roquevidal to the southwest, and make a possible meal stop if you are cutting south by car through the *pays de Cocagne* towards Revel and the Canal du Midi. St-Paul has a small **tourist office** in avenue de Strasbourg (mid-June to mid-Sept Mon–Sat 10am–noon & 2–6pm; mid-Sept to mid-June Tues only 10am–12.30pm & 4.30–6.30pm; ℡05.63.70.52.10), which can give you information for the whole of the valley downstream of Castres. The old *Hotel Central*, on rue Jeanne d'Arc opposite the church, no longer rents rooms, but you can still get a light meal here (*menu* €12), and there is a well-equipped **gîte** (℡05.63.70.66.03, ✉francismalige@wanadoo.fr; ❶) at En Nassalit, 4km from town. Damiette has a **gare SNCF** on the Toulouse–Revel line and a **campsite** (mid-June to mid-Sept; ℡05.63.70.66.07, ✉bernard.belin@wanadoo.fr).

If you have transport, and you would like to visit less frequented sights of the region, ten kilometres down the twisting D40 road from St-Paul you'll come to the **Château-Musée de Magrin** (early July & early Sept daily 10.30am–noon; mid-July to Aug daily 10.30am–noon & 3–6pm; late Sept to June Sun 3–6pm; obligatory guided tour, in French, €6.10). Largely ruined, this castle dates to before the Albigensian Crusade, although most of what survives is from the Renaissance. Included in the visit is a museum of woad, set in the castle's old dye works, featuring displays, reconstructions and models illustrating the techniques of *pastel* manufacture. A few more kilometres along to the west you'll find the **Château de Roquevidal** (Aug Sun 3–7pm; €4), a square thirteenth-century keep remodelled as a manor house in the late fourteenth century. Its collection of antique furniture and knick-knacks, complemented by old typewriters and printing presses, is anything but exceptional, but makes for a pleasant stop if you happen to be driving through.

South from St-Paul towards Revel there isn't much to detain you. The old town of **Puylaurens**, once a centre of local Huguenot learning, is not worth stopping in, despite tourist brochures suggesting otherwise. Midway between Puylaurens and Toulouse, **Loubens-Lauragais** is still dominated by its old seigniorial **castle** (2.30–6.30pm: May, June & Sept to mid-Nov Sun & hols; July first & last Sun, Aug Thurs–Sun; €5); most of its present structure dates from the sixteenth century. The setting is idyllic, with stately white geese lolling in the pond by its gate, while inside you'll find a collection of antique furniture (including some good Aubusson tapestries) amassed by the family that has lived here for 22 generations.

Revel and around

Situated at the westernmost point of the long **Montagne Noire** massif, **REVEL** is a tiny but busy district capital, which serves as a regional bus hub – this is where you catch the bus to Sorèze and Dourgne – and a good base for exploring the surrounding area. It was founded as a *bastide* in 1342 by Philip IV, and the deliberate plan of the town is reflected in its octagonal layout and regular streets; indeed, Revel's original charter prescribed a uniformity which even regulated the size of the houses which could be built. Today, it is still dominated by the immense market which covers the entirety of the town's central square. The market was built soon after the town was founded, its rows of stout pillars supporting a single-gabled roof, converging at a stone-constructed tower. Revel was the principal market town for the farmland of the region before becoming a centre for furniture manufacture in the nineteenth century, taking advantage of the wooded slopes of the Montagne Noire to its east. There's nothing much to see or do here, but if you are changing buses or hiking out of the hills it is a good place to spend a comfortable night and get your laundry done. At any rate, you should take a walk around the compact old town and look at the many medieval houses which remain. Local workshops still turn out exceptionally crafted wooden furniture, and if you are interested in how it used to be done check out the **Conservatoire des Métiers du Bois**, the "Woodworkers' Conservatory", at 13 rue Jean Moulin (Mon–Thurs & Sat 10am–noon & 2–6pm, Sun 2–6pm; €4.60). Here you can see a collection of old tools, watch furniture being made according to traditional techniques and, naturally, make a purchase.

One of the main reasons to pass through Revel is to make your way up to the **Lac de St-Ferreol**, an artificial reservoir created in 1672 with the completion of a massive 780-metre-long dam. This was part of the incredible Canal du Midi project (see p.111), and took some seven-thousand workers five years of hard labour to construct. It was here that run-off from the Montagne Noire was collected to feed the canal, flowing down the Rigole de Canal du Midi to Naurouze, some 25km to the southwest. Nowadays it is a popular weekend spot. The woods make for easy walking, and you can **swim** or **sail** on the lake. A variant of the **hiking** trail GR7 swings by the reservoir, linking up with the G653 west at the Rigole, and passing close to Castelnaudary to the south.

Also worth a stop, particularly if you're travelling between Revel and Toulouse, is the tiny picturesque hill-top hamlet of **St-Félix-Lauragais** – birthplace of the composer Déodat-de-Séverac (1872–1921) – which dominates the flatlands stretching west towards the capital of Midi-Pyrénées. Nothing remains of the time when the town was a meeting place for Cathar clergy, but it does retain a fine wooden **market** with a small stone tower, a curious Gothic-style **church** tucked away amongst the buildings of the main street and a profusion of timber-frame houses.

Practicalities

Buses passing through **Revel** stop on the place de la République, on the main road just north of the town's covered market, where there is a small SNCF bus ticket office (Tues–Fri 9am–noon & 1.30–6.30pm, Sat 9am–noon; ☎05.61.83.53.73). The **tourist office** (July–Sept Mon–Fri 9.30am–7.30pm, Sat 9am–6.30pm, Sun 10am–12.30pm & 3–6pm; Oct–June Mon–Fri 9.30am–12.30pm & 2.30–6.30pm; ☎05.34.66.67.68, ⓦwww.revel-lauragais.com), located in the tower in the market's centre, can give you information about neighbouring towns too (including Sorèze and Dourgne).

The best of the **hotels** here, set in a refined old nineteenth-century mansion, is the *Auberge du Midi* at 34 boulevard Gambetta, just north of the market (closed mid-Nov to early-Dec; ☎05.61.83.50.50, ⓦwww.logis-de-france.com; ❸). Close by, in 7 rue de Taur, you'll find the *Commanderie Hôtel* (☎05.63.46.61.24; closed part Feb, part June, part Sept; ❸), a good second choice, with an old timber-frame facade and a remodelled interior. For **eating**, the *Auberge* also has the town's best restaurant choice (*menus* €29–43; closed Sun eve and Mon lunch) and there are a number of places on the market square to get a drink or a light meal, including *Le Progress*, which has a daily €10.20 *menu*, and the *Café des Arcades*, for sandwiches and drinks. Across the square, the old *Hôtel du Centre* no longer offers accommodation, but still has an atmospheric **bar**. For a chance to see the old covered *halles* in use, try to catch the Saturday morning **market**.

Lac de St-Ferreol has a profusion of **hotels** and **campsites**, most of them clustered along the northwest corner, where the road from Revel meets the lake. Two of the better places to stay are the *Hôtellerie du Lac* (turn right coming from Revel; ☎05.62.18.70.80, Ⓕ05.62.18.71.13; ❸), which also has multiroom suites with kitchenettes, and *La Renaissance* (closed Nov–March; ☎05.61.83.51.50, ⓦwww.logis-de-france.fr; ❷ English spoken), right at the main intersection. The *Hôtellerie* also has a decent **restaurant** (*menus* from €12). The campsites around the lake tend towards the deluxe multifacility type, and the closest to the water is *En Salvan* (☎05.61.83.55.95; April–Oct). You can rent **bikes** and **sailboats** through Le Biouvac (☎05.61.27.53.94), in rue des 4 Vents, behind the *Hôtellerie*.

The excellent **hotel–restaurant** *Auberge du Poids Public* (closed Jan & part Nov; ☎05.62.18.85.00, Ⓕ05.62.18.85.05; ❸ with half-board available) is reason enough to visit and stay in **St-Félix**. Located in a large old house beside the town's public weighbridge, the hotel has been restored and decorated in warm luxury, while the restaurant is widely praised for its regional gastronomic creations – try the rabbit and pigeon dishes (*menus* €24–58) – and served up with fine Gaillac vintages; you'll need to book ahead if you plan to stay or eat.

Sorèze and Dourgne

Taking the D85, the scenic route from Revel to Castres, you'll pass through two small villages, which, with few attractions themselves, are worthy of a visit only if you happen to be driving, walking or biking through, or if you wish to use them as bases for exploring the western reaches of the Montagne Noire. This is cattle-grazing land, an idyllic expanse of rolling green pasture with the wooded ridge of the mountains rising up sharply along the south side of the road. Narrow forest roads (the D45 from Sorèze and the D12 from Dourgne) twist and turn up into the hills, converging in the shadow of Mount Alric (813m) before arriving at Arfons (see p.210).

SORÈZE, just 6km east of Revel, is an ancient town which grew around a monastery founded in 754 by Pepin the Short, forerunner of Charlemagne. The only remaining vestige of the once huge religious complex is the curious octagonal **bell tower**, dating from the fifteenth century and located near to where the mountain road winds out of town. The other sight worth a stop is the old Dominican **convent-school**, which was converted into a military academy in the eighteenth century. The nineteenth-century Latin American hero Simon Bolivar is its most famous *alumnus*. An unremarkable hour-long guided tour takes visitors through the building (July & Aug daily 10.30am, 3pm & 5pm; May–June & Sept–Oct Mon–Fri same times; Nov–April Mon–Fri 10.30am, 2pm & 5pm; €3.10). The convent is also home to a luxurious **hotel-**

restaurant, the *Abbaye-École* (☎05.63.74.44.80, ⓦwww.hotelfp-soreze.com; ❸–❻) which has great old timber-beamed rooms; the restaurant has *menus* from €12. Less luxurious accommodation can be found at the B&B *Le Moulin du Chapître* (☎05.63.74.18.18, ⓔmoulin.chapitre@libertysurf.fr; ❷; English spoken) on the outskirts of town, or at the municipal **campsite**, *Les Vigariès* (July & Aug; ☎05.63.74.18.06). You can also eat or get a drink at the *Pub St-Martin*, in a restored and appropriately rustic stable building in the old town centre (4 rue St-Martin; ☎05.63.74.18.71). The town has a **tourist office** (daily 10am–noon & 2–6pm; ☎05.63.74.16.28, ⓦwww.ville-soreze.com) off the main square, in rue St-Martin, but this will be of less use – in the summer at any rate – than the **Maison du Parc** (July & Aug Wed–Mon 2–6.30pm, rest of year Sat, Sun & hols 2–6pm; ☎05.63.74.11.58), which is on the main road at the west end of town. It is here that you'll find the most up-to-date information on exploring the Parc Naturel de Haut Languedoc, which begins in the hills above the town. There is a lively country market on Friday mornings.

Just a few kilometres beyond Sorèze lies the even smaller village of **DOURGNE**, still marked on the east side by the crumbling walls of an ancient abbey. Today the town's monastic tradition is as alive as ever, revived in the nineteenth century with the founding of two Benedictine communities just up the road at **En Calcat**. The larger of the two is the **Monastère de St-Benoît**, which you can visit to sit in on any of the five daily services and hear a chanted Mass; the smaller convent of **Ste-Scholastique** is the home of nuns who pass the time in devotion and weaving. Although the town is quite pretty, with its old streets and arcaded houses, the only other sight is a rather unexceptional sixteenth-century church. If you are hungry, stop in at the **restaurant** *Hôtellerie de la Montagne Noire*, 15 place des Promenades, which serves up hearty *terroir*-inspired food (*menus* €12.50–31; closed Sun eve & Mon). The *Hôtellerie* also operates as a small **hotel** (closed Feb, late Oct to early Nov; ☎05.63.50.31.12, ⓦwww.logis-de-france.fr; ❷), aside from which there are two **chambres d'hôtes**, run by Rose Pauthe (☎05.63.50.31.30; ❷) and Agnès Kovacs (☎05.63.50.12.97, ⓔlionel.berard@free.fr; ❷) respectively, as well as a tiny one-star municipal **campsite** (☎05.63.50.31.20). The **tourist office** (July & Aug 8.30am–12.30pm & 1.30–6.30pm; ☎05.63.74.27.19, ⓦwww.paysdedourgne-tourisme.com) can be found in the centre of the village, on place Jean-Bugies.

Castelnaudary

The biggest stop on the Canal du Midi between Carcassonne and Toulouse, **CASTELNAUDARY** holds the honour of being the legendary birthplace of that most Occitan of dishes, cassoulet, and is also the capital of the Lauragais region, the flat grain-producing hinterland of Toulouse. With its wide **Grand Bassin**, or reservoir, the town is the major pleasure port on the Canal, and a great place to start a waterborne trip towards the Mediterranean. Like the surrounding region, Castelnaudary's past is intimately linked with Cathar history – the town endured no fewer than three sieges during the Albigensian campaigns, and was also the birthplace of Pierre de Castelnau, the papal legate whose murder prompted Pope Innocent III to proclaim the Crusade. When the Inquisition arrived here in 1235, the grey-robed Dominicans' efforts to root out heretics were thwarted by the solidarity of the townsfolk, who refused to implicate their fellows. It was also just outside the town that the last dream of Languedocian independence died, with the capture in 1632 of the rebellious Henri de Montmorency, who was borne away to Toulouse and executed on orders of Cardinal Richelieu.

Cassoulet

One of the great pillars of Southern French *terroir* ("country" or "local") cuisine is the humble **cassoulet**. A simple but tasty baked dish, made up of white beans and garlic cooked with bits of pork and sausage, cassoulet is a staple you'll find just about everywhere between the peaks of the Pyrenees and the banks of the Rhône. Legend has it that the dish originated in Castelnaudary in the mid-fourteenth century, when the Black Prince Edward besieged the town during the course of the Hundred Years War. The defenders, gathering their last provisions, which amounted to some beans and scraps of meat, not only managed to concoct a culinary triumph under extreme duress but, thus fortified, put the English troops (whose own inferior syrupy brown baked-bean diet could not compete) to flight. Today the "original" recipe is safeguarded by the amusingly solemn Confraternity of the Grand Cassoulet, a collective of local chefs who occasionally dress up in distinctive medieval-style robes for culinary events and fairs. You'll have plenty of chances to eat cassoulet in Languedoc and Roussillon, but be warned, local wisdom (and common sense) says that it is a dish best avoided in the summer.

Arrival, information and accommodation

Trains arrive at Castelnaudary's **gare SNCF** (℡04.68.94.41.55), located on the south side of the Canal du Midi. At the end of the avenue de la Gare, the road running directly from the station, you should turn right onto avenue Arnaut-Vidal, which will lead you over the river and straight to the place de la République, at the centre of town. The **gare routière**, on the other hand, is on the north side of town, on avenue Frédéric-Mistral. Following this street as it veers right (now called rue de 11 Novembre) also takes you to the central *place*, and the town's **tourist office** (mid-July to mid-Sept daily 9am–1pm & 2–7pm; mid-Sept to mid-July Mon–Sat 9.30am–12.30pm & 2–6.30pm; ℡04.68.23.05.73, ✉otsi.castelnaudary@wanadoo.fr). The office can arrange for guided tours (English) of the town and excursions to St-Papoul (€4.50–14). For **Internet** access head to the main **post office**, 18 cours de la République. **Bicycles** can be rented at Trigano Cycles (℡04.68.23.09.77), in St-Martin-Lalande, 4km east on the RN113.

There are several **hotels** to choose from in town, the best of which is the friendly, canalside *Hôtel du Canal* (℡04.68.94.05.05, ⓦwww.hotel ducanal.com; ❸), at 2 avenue Arnaut-Vidal – a comfortable place with all mod cons (including satellite television) and a garage. The second choice is the *Hôtel du Centre et du Lauragais* (closed Jan to mid-Feb; ℡04.68.23.25.95, ℻04.68.94.01.66; ❸), a converted nineteenth-century house, centrally located at 31 cours de la République, close by the post office. Other decent options include the three-star *Hôtel de France et Notre-Dame* (℡04.68.23.10.18, ✉hdf@cassoulet.com; ❷), at 2 avenue Frédéric-Mistral, and the simple but welcoming *Grand Hôtel Fourcade* (closed most Jan; ℡04.68.23.02.08, ✉hotelfourcade@ataraxie.fr; closed Jan; ❶–❸), at 14 rue des Carmes, near the covered market. The municipal **campsite**, *La Giraille* (July to mid-Sept; ℡04.68.23.11.28) can be found west of town, a twenty-minute walk along avenue Georges-Pompidou from the bridge at the foot of cours de la République.

The Town

Although Castelnaudary's main attraction is its canal port (see p.110), there are quite a number of sights worth seeing in the town itself. The first you are likely to encounter is the **halle aux grains**, the former cereal market. It's a handsome building with a plain but dignified arcaded front on the west side of place de la République, and now houses the tourist office, as well as acting as a venue for occasional theatre and dance productions. Heading uphill from the *halles* along allée du Cassieu you can follow the main road west to the thirteenth-century **church of St-François**, inside which you'll find a well-crafted statue of the Virgin and Child, dating from the same period. Another 800m further on (turn up towards the cemetery on the impasse Claude-Chappe), is the curious **Tour Chappe**. This tower (currently being renovated) was once part of the immense semaphore network which covered much of France. Napoleon used the system extensively, and on a clear day messages could be passed from Strasbourg to Paris in just over three hours, using over 180 of these signal stations. The network was a huge success, but the introduction of the electric telegraph in 1859 rendered it immediately obsolete.

Alternatively, you can continue straight uphill from the *halles* to rue de Château; this will take you to the old **Moulin de Cugarel** (July–Aug Mon–Sat 10am–noon & 2–7pm, Sun 2–7pm; €0.75), the last of the town's wind-powered grain mills. With the building of the Canal du Midi, farmers suddenly had access to markets as far afield as Toulouse and the Mediterranean, and so no fewer than 32 mills were built to process the wheat which they brought to be sold. The *moulin* is an attractive stone structure; its superb grinding mechanism was fully restored in 1962. Below the mill the heart of the old town makes a rough trapezoid, marked off by place de Verdun and rue Goufferand on the east and west, and Grande Rue and rue de Dunkerque on the north and south. **Place de Verdun** was the medieval town's main square. Ringed by handsome mansion facades, including that of the Hôtel Dupuy on its north side, the *place* is home to the town's main covered *halles*, as well as the site of the colourful Monday market originally instituted on June 1268 by order of Alphonse de Poitiers, Count of Toulouse, who wanted to spark the town's economy. Following Grande Rue from the market-place will lead you past two more attractive seventeenth-century **mansions**, the Hôtel de Laudun-Courtiade at no. 26, and the Hôtel Latapie, on the corner of rue de la Terrasse. Turning the corner you'll soon reach the southern-Gothic-style collegiate **church of St-Michel**, built in the fourteenth century. Its exterior is notable for its beautiful steeple, towering 55m above the neighbouring place de St-Just, as well as two fine doorways on the north side, but the interior, clinically white, has little to recommend it. Rue du College, which continues from St-Michel, leads on into place Auriol, at the far end of which you'll be able to ascend to the **Présidial**. This sombre stone building was raised on the site of the town's castle in 1585, when Henri III made the town capital of the Lauragais. First serving as a courthouse and later a prison, it now holds a rather dull **museum of pottery** (July & Aug Mon & Sun 2–6.30pm, Tues–Sat 10am–6.30pm; €2.50).

Finally, there are two more points of interest in the old town, both along rue de l'Hôpital, north of place Auriol. The first of these is the chapel of **Notre-Dame-de-Pité**, founded in the eleventh century and a popular stop on the medieval pilgrimage route to Santiago de Compostela. The dazzling interior of the chapel, which was reworked in the sixteenth century (and which you can peek at through the grills), contains a feast of gilt wooden low-relief panels depicting angels and biblical scenes in the most outrageously flamboyant Baroque style. Further along you'll reach the **Apothicairerie** (book first with tourist office; free), a pre-Revolution pharmacy, which has sat on this spot for over two centuries. Nearly two hundred porcelain phials line the shelves, labelled with the kinds of ingredients that make you glad you didn't get sick in the eighteenth century. Castelnaudary's best restaurant, *Le Tirou* (see p.110), is just a short walk beyond.

The Grand Bassin

Castelnaudary's biggest draw is the section of the **Canal du Midi** which runs through the town and is punctuated by the broad **Grand Bassin**. This roughly oblong pool, some seven hectares in area, is the largest reservoir along the length of the navigable canal. Constructed as a port, where barges could turn around, get repaired and load up with the grain harvested in the Lauragais, it now serves as a **pleasure port** and point of embarkation for tours and trips along the inland waterways of the Midi and Languedoc. To the west, the Grand Bassin empties into the Petit Bassin, marked by the two road bridges over the canal, before narrowing to wind its way towards Toulouse. On the east side, a remarkable series of six locks, the **Écluse des St-Roch** lowers barges and boats bound for the Mediterranean. If you want to rent a boat for a few hours or a few weeks, take a tour or simply take in the variety of modern and historical craft which you can find on the canal, this is the place to do it (see Canal du Midi "Practicalities" on p.114).

Eating and drinking

There is no shortage of **restaurants** to choose from for cassoulet and other *terroir* treats. The best, and most expensive, is undoubtedly *Le Tirou* (T04.68.94.15.95; closed Wed, Thus & Sun eve & late Dec to late Jan & part June), at the east end of town at 90 av Monseigneur de Langle. This old stone house has a pleasant garden and an excellent *terroir carte* (€15–40). Of the hotel restaurants, the best is that of the *Centre et Lauragais*, whose traditional Midi dining room is closer to the centre and marginally less expensive than *Le Tirou* (*menus* €13–36), while *La Belle Époque* (closed Tue eve & Wed; T04.68.23.39.72), at 55 rue Général-Dejean, is a great place to taste cassoulet (basic *menu* €15). If you're tired of beans and foie gras, there are several international options in town, including the quality Chinese and Vietnamese cooking of *Le Dragon* at 22 rue Soumet (T04.68.23.33.61), by the market, to the Italian pizza and seafood of *Le Gondolier* at 10 rue Maréchal-Foch (closed Tues, part April & part Aug; *menus* from €12.50), and the local kebab joint, *Agadir*, at 9 Grand Rue.

You can also pick up cassoulet and other regional delicacies "to go" from the town's well-reputed *traiteurs* and *conservateurs*, artisanal butchers and confectioners. There are a number of them in the old town, including Le Regal, at 30 rue Dunkerque, Escudier, at no. 9, and Au Gourmet Chaurien at 38 cours de la République. The local market is held on Mondays.

Around Castelnaudary

If you happen to be in Castelnaudary on April 30 or at Christmas you can get a glimpse of the closed world of France's notorious **Foreign Legion**, whose base, 2km southeast of town on the D33, opens its doors to the public on these two occasions. Another short excursion, 8km east on the D113, is to the **abbey of St-Papoul** (daily: April–June & Sept–Oct 10am–noon & 2–6pm; July & Aug 10am–7pm; Nov–March Sat, Sun & hols 10am–noon & 2–5pm; €3.50, reduction with "Carte Intersite" pass – see box on p.132), set on the edge of the Lauragais plain. Founded in the eighth century by Pepin the Short, it went on to huge success after 1317 when its abbot was elevated to the status of bishop. The church itself is impressive, with some sections dating back to the twelfth century. The most important feature, however, is the **carved capitals** on the upper rim of the exterior of the apse, which can be viewed without entering, and outside opening hours, executed by the "Master of Cabestany" (see box opposite) and depicting Daniel in the lions' den.

The Master of Cabestany

The actual name of the **Master of Cabestany** has long been forgotten, but the work of this genius of masonry comprises one of Languedoc's most important medieval legacies. The twelfth-century itinerant sculptor, whose speciality was human figures in high relief, worked as far afield as Tuscany and Catalonia, but the greatest concentration of his works can be found in a wide band of territory stretching from Castelnaudary to the sea. Doorways, cloisters, tombs and tympanums – over 120 works found so far – all bear the distinctive mark of his vivid style. His large-handed, bulbous-eyed portraits are set apart not so much by their realism, but by the obvious brilliance with which they were executed, which seems to endow the mute stone figures with a life and soul of their own. The most dramatic example of his work can be found at St-Hilaire (see p.133), while others survive at Cabestany (p.354), Lagrasse (see p.317), Rieux-Minervois (see p.320), Passa (p.372) and Le Boulou (see p.372). Several works have been identified just over the border in Catalonia, including at the magnificent monastery of San Pere de Rodes (only 25min by car from Le Boulou) and one piece now resides in the Cloisters collection of the Metropolitan Museum of Art in New York. A museum and resource centre dedicated to this rediscovered master and to the history of Romanesque sculpture is currently under construction in Cabestany, outside Perpignan (see p.354).

Along the Canal du Midi from Toulouse to Carcassonne

The **Canal du Midi** runs a roughly straight path through the wheat–producing lands of the Lauragais, clearing the compact suburbs of Toulouse and steering its tree–lined course east, parallel to the Hers River, towards its highest point, at the Seuil (or "threshold") de Naurouze. From here it descends to the basin at Castelnaudary, as the Montagne Noire, the source of the canal's water, comes into view to the north. From the Grand Bassin, the waterway cuts eastwards across the plain, bridging the 32km to **Carcassonne**, where it begins to adapt to the contours of the Aude valley, and start in earnest its descent towards the sea (see Chapter 6). The towns along the route are not especially notable, but afford you a glimpse of rural France at its most antiquated and peaceful.

The first town of any size which you'll pass is the old *bastide* of **Montgiscard**, some 10km from the port of Toulouse. There's not much to see here, but if you are tempted to stop, take a look at the medieval church, part of which was remodelled by the same architect who designed Toulouse's Hôtel d'Assèzat. Next along you'll come to **Ayguesvives** and **Montesquieu-Lauragais**, both of which have impressive nineteenth–century *châteaux*. Eighteen kilometres out from Toulouse you'll reach the **écluse de Négra**, which is where you leave the canal to reach **Villefranche**, and was once the first post–stop on the way to Agde – several of the old canal–side buildings survive. Just to the east, **Avignonet-Lauragais** was once a wealthy woad town, and is notable for being the place where, in 1242, the Cathars holed up in Montségur launched an attack on and massacred a contingent of the Dominican Inquisition; the resulting counterattack brought about the destruction of Montségur castle and the mass execution of its garrison and population (see p.145). Today the town has a fourteenth–century church with a fine retable dating from 1632. The last stop before you reach Naurouze is the modern **Port-Lauragais**, built specifically for pleasure boating. There's a **restaurant**

The Canal du Midi

The **Canal du Midi** runs for some 240km from the River Garonne at Toulouse, via Castelnaudary, Carcassonne and Béziers, to the Mediterranean at Agde or Sète, and via its subsidiary, the **Canal de la Robine**, to Narbonne, entering the sea at Gruissan. The waterway was the brainchild of Pierre-Paul Riquet, a minor noble and the holder of the lucrative salt-tax concession for Languedoc (the *gabelle* – a tax levied on the sale of salt – was one of the royal treasury's most lucrative sources of income). Riquet succeeded in firing the imagination of Louis XIV (and more importantly, his first minister, Colbert) with the idea of linking the Atlantic and the Mediterranean via the Garonne (in reality the connection wasn't actually to happen until long after the principal stretch had been finished).

The main canal, begun in 1667, took fourteen years to complete using tens of thousands of workers. At the start, an engineering problem automatically presented itself: how to feed the canal with water when the Mediterranean was obviously at sea level, the Garonne at 132m above sea level, and, in the middle, the Col (or Seuil) de Naurouze at 201m. Riquet's solution was to build a system of dams and reservoirs at St-Ferréol, Lampy and on the Alzeau in the Montagne Noire, channelling run-off water from the heights down to Naurouze. He spent the whole of his fortune on the canal (sacrificing even his daughters' dowries) and, sadly, died just six months before its inauguration in 1681. But the waterway, built to accommodate barges of up to 30m in length, was a success and sparked a wave of prosperity along its course, thanks to the access it provided local farmers, manufacturers and raw material industries to foreign markets (via the Mediterranean). Traffic increased steadily until 1856, when it carried 111,000 metric tonnes of material as well as one million passengers, and the official link-up to the Garonne and the Atlantic opened. The next year the Sète–Bordeaux railway came into being and, rail transport being faster and more cost-effective, traffic on the canal dropped to all but nothing almost immediately.

In the last ten years or so, however, the canal has been revived as a course for pleasure craft, and it's not difficult to see why. It remains a marvel of engineering and beauty, incorporating no fewer than 99 locks (*écluses*) and 130 bridges. The various topographical challenges were met with imagination, including the construction of canal **tunnels** and **bridges**, the latter allowing water to cross valleys and gullies, suspended in the air. No less beautiful are the stone foot and road bridges, most of which date back to the first era of construction. The graceful oval **lock-basins**, built in that shape for more strength, are guarded by uniform *maisons d'éclusier*, where the controls of the mechanism are housed; and, as along any major route, inns and restaurants punctuate the canal's course. Even the double file of trees which lines most of the waterway's length, giving it a distinctive "Midi" look, serves a technical as well as an aesthetic purpose: to shade the water and impede its loss through evaporation.

Unsurprisingly, the canal was designated a UNESCO World Heritage Site in 1996, ensuring its conservation. You can follow it by road, and most sections have foot or

here, as well as an **information centre** (daily 10am–6pm; ☎05.61.27.14.63) which houses permanent and temporary exhibitions on the building of the canal. **Naurouze**, the highest point on the canal's path, is where the Rigole, or feeder canal, arrives bearing the water gathered on the slopes of the Montagne Noire; it has long been a point of transit, as the vestiges of Roman road here testify. The area around the canal junction has been set up as a **picnic area** and **park** (unfortunately with no toilets), and nearby you'll find a rather sombre monument to the Canal's founder, Pierre-Paul Riquet. Incidentally, this is also the site where Soult signed his surrender to Wellington in 1814. From bicycle paths, but the best way to travel it (and an ideal way to spend a family or group holiday) is, of course, **by boat**. It's a gentle, restful chug down a tunnel of greenery enhanced in spring by the bloom of yellow iris and wild gladioli, with occasional glimpses of a world beyond: a distant smudge of hills or the pinnacles of Carcassonne. There are outfits in all of the major ports which **rent houseboats and barges** – most of which will also rent **bikes** as an extra, perfect for exploring the sights along the waterway. Or, if you prefer to be driven rather than drive, there are many cruises too. The canal is navigable from March to November, but the high season of July and August is best avoided – boat availability declines, prices rise and the canal gets quite crowded. Finally, if you don't want to commit the time and money to rent a houseboat, most ports also rent smaller **electric boats**, suitable for one to six people by the hour (usually €18–20) or half-day (around €50). Navigation itself is straightforward (quite literally) and an orientation session by the boat rental company is all you need to get you on your way – no licence is required. Generally, **locks** are open daily from 8am to 12.30pm and 1.30pm to 7.30pm, but closed on major holidays. There's no charge for passage, and you can count on about a quarter of an hour for a basin to fill or empty. With a maximum permitted speed of 6km per hour you're not going to break any records, and you should not count on being able to travel more than 250km in a week of cruising. Canal **information** can be found at the port offices of Voies Navigables de France, the government organization in charge of inland waterways – we've given the details of these in the relevant parts of the Guide.

Biking and hiking

The easiest part of the canal's route along which to **bike** or **hike** is the initial – paved – stretch from **Toulouse to the Seuil de Naurouze**, following a path from Port St-Saveur (see p.92). The surrounding farmland, which gradually ascends the further you go, doesn't make for the most spectacular of backdrops, but the canal – its tree-lined placidity interrupted only by the "putt-putt" of passing boats – is beautiful in its own right. The total distance along the paved path is 50km, which can be biked in about five hours and walked in under twenty. If you decide on the latter course of action you need not commit yourself to going the whole way – you can stop at Villefranche-Lauragais at the 30-kilometre-mark to catch a bus back or onwards, or spend the night at *En Jouty* (closed Nov–Feb; ☎05.61.81.57.35; ❷), a **chambres d'hôtes** near the centre of Avignonet. From Port-Lauragais, a further 12km on from Villefranche, you have the option of continuing the rest of the journey to Naurouze on a boat cruise (see "Practicalities" p.114). The paved path ends at Écluse Ocean, shortly after the port, and a gravel towpath (fine for mountain bikes) continues to Carcassonne; should you wish to continue beyond Castelnaudary and on to Bram, you'll find *chambres d'hôtes* at *Domaine de Pigne* (☎04.68.11.40.70, ⊛www.gites-de-france-aude.com; ❷) on the outskirts of the village or the **hotel** *Clos Saint Loup* at 69 av des Razes in town (closed Dec 24–28; ☎04.68.76.11.91, ⊛www.logis-de-france.fr; ❸). There are filling local *menus* in the *Clos*'s dining room, ranging from €11 to €33.

Naurouze it's another 12km to Castelnaudary (see p.107).

The only place of any interest between Castelnaudary and Carcassonne is **BRAM**, an ancient village where the houses are arranged in tight circles around the church; it dates back to the thirteenth century. Bram's villagers resisted the Albigensian Crusaders in 1210, and when the town eventually fell to the Catholic forces, the inhabitants came to a grisly end. Simon de Montfort ordered a hundred prisoners to be blinded and mutilated; the refugees, carrying their amputated body parts, were then sent to the as yet unvanquished fortress of Cabaret, led by the only villager with an eye remaining ungouged.

Practicalities

The head office of Voies Navigables de France is at 2 port St-Étienne in Toulouse (℡05.61.36.24.24, ℻05.61.54.66.50, ⓦwww.vnf.fr); they have English-speaking port offices at Carcassonne (℡06.84.81.96.20), Castelnaudary (℡06.84.81.96.23) and Port St-Saveur (℡06.84.81.96.21). There's also a small **tourist office** at Villefranche, in place Général-de-Gaulle (℡04.61.27.20.94).

If you are interested in **renting a boat** in Toulouse contact Société AQUALUB (℡06.86.71.33.46). In Castelnaudary the biggest boat rental company is Crown Blue Line, Le Grand Bassin, Castelnaudary (℡04.68.94.52.72, ⓦwww.crownblueline.com) – their fleet consists mostly of modern craft, so if you are hoping for a more authentic-looking barge, you may have to shop around and book well ahead. At Carcassonne you can rent from Nautic (℡04.68.71.88.95, ℻04.67.94.05.91), while Locaboat (℡03.86.91.72.72, ⓦwww.locaboat.com) rents out *pénichettes* (traditional canal boats). At any of these firms expect to pay €800–1600 per week, depending on the season, for a three- to five-person boat.

In case you don't feel like navigating yourself, Le St Roch, in Castelnaudary's Grand Bassin (℡04.68.23.49.40), organizes **canal tours** lasting from thirty minutes to two hours (€3.10–8.50 per person), while Croisières Cathy (℡06.09.33.15.96), also in Castelnaudary, has half- and full-day programmes with optional on-board meals. You must book in advance: full-day cruises, which depart at 9am, cost €28–50, depending on whether you have the meal, and half-day tours, leaving at 11.30am, cost €16. Additionally, just west of Naurouze at Port-Laugarais, the *Lucie* runs a thirty-minute circuit to the Seuil and back (daily April–Sept; €4), as well as other longer itineraries whenever ten or more passengers assemble. Small electric boats can also be rented at Castel Nautique in Bram (April–Sept 8am–7.30pm; ℡04.68.76.73.74, ⓦwww.castelnautique.com).

Travel details

Trains

SNCF buses may run in lieu of trains on these lines; services are reduced on Sundays and holidays

Toulouse to: Albi (12 daily; 1hr); Avignonet (4 daily; 42min); Ax-les-Thermes (5 daily; 1hr 55min); Béziers (12 daily; 45min–1hr 30min); Bram (7 daily; 1hr 4min); Carcassonne (15 daily; 45min–1hr); Carmaux (10 daily; 1hr 45min); Castelnaudary (13 daily; 30min–1hr); Castres (11 daily; 1hr 6min); Cordes/Vindrac (6 daily; 50min–1hr 12min); Damiette (2 daily; 50min); Foix (12 daily; 47min to 1hr 12min); Gaillac (18 daily; 48min); L'Hospitalet (4 daily; 2 hr 30min); Latour-de-Carol (5 daily; 2hr 30min); Lavaur (3 daily; 50min); Lisle (12 daily; 38min); Mazamet (10 daily; 1hr 28min–1hr 55min); Montpellier (12 daily; 2hr 15min–2hr 55min); Narbonne (12 daily; 1hr 18min–1hr 50min); Nîmes (20 daily; 2hr

45min–3hr); Pamiers (12 daily; 36min–1hr 10min); Paris (20 daily; 5hr 25min–7hr 10min); Rabastens (12 daily; 29min); St-Gaudens (12 daily; 50min–1hr 15min); St-Sulpice (12 daily; 22min); Tarascon (12 daily; 1hr 20min); and Villefranche (10 daily; 18–33min).

Castelnaudary to: Carcassonne (15 daily; 20–27min); Revel (Mon; 20min); Sorèze (Fri; 54min); Toulouse (13 daily; 30min–1hr).

Damiette/ St-Paul to: Castres (9 daily; 25min).

Lavaur to: Castres (6 daily; 32min); St-Sulpice (8 daily; 12min).

St-Sulpice to: Albi (12 daily; 50min); Castres (11 daily; 45min); Gaillac (12 daily; 12–26min); Lavaur (9 daily; 8min); Toulouse (12 daily; 22min).

Buses

Many lines have no or reduced service on Sundays, holidays and in summer months.

Toulouse to: Albi 6 daily; (1hr 40min); Carcassonne (1 daily; 2hr 20min); Foix (1 daily; 1hr, 45min); Gaillac (4 daily; 1hr 25min); Lavelanet (2–3 daily; 2hr 25min); Mas d'Azil (2 daily; 1hr 50min); Mirepoix (2–3 daily; 2hr); Pamiers (2–3 daily; 1hr 30min); Revel (12 daily; 1hr 10min); St-Félix-de-Lauragais (3 daily; 1hr); St-Girons (3 daily; 2hr 30min); St-Sulpice (6 daily; 30min); Sorèze (3 daily; 1hr 20min); Villefranche (10 daily; 1hr 5min).

Castelnaudary to: Alet-les-Bains (daily; 1 hr 5min); Axat (1 daily; 1hr 50min); Bram (1 or 2 daily; 30min); Carcassonne (5 daily; 45min); Fanjeux (daily; 40min); Limoux (2 daily; 1hr); Quillan (daily; 1hr 30min); Sorèze (Mon; 30min); Villefranche (6 daily; 20min).

Lavaur to: Castres (4–6 daily; 45min–1hr); Gaillac (4 daily; 35min); St-Paul (4 daily; 15min); Toulouse (4 daily; 50min).

Revel to: Castres (4 daily; 1hr); St-Félix (3 daily; 20min); Toulouse (12 daily; 1hr 10min).

St-Sulpice to: Albi (2 daily; 1hr 5min); Gaillac (2 daily; 50min); Toulouse (6 daily; 20min).

2

Carcassonne, Upper Aude and Ariège

CHAPTER 2

Highlights

* **Carcassonne** Southern France's most visited monument, this reconstructed medieval citadel is a must-see. See p.121

* **Rennes-le-Château** A mecca for occultists and conspiracy theorists following the trail of a nineteenth-century priest. See p.136

* **Montségur** The legendary site of the heretic Cathars' last stand. See p.145

* **Mirepoix** The region's best preserved medieval town features a stunningly carved fourteenth-century town hall now converted into a hotel. See p.148

* **Carnaval** Limoux's famous Lenten festival draws crowds from around the Southwest to see its elaborately costumed dancers. See p.132

* **Rafting** The Upper Aude and Ariège provide excellent opportunities for a range of skill levels. See p.138

* **La Grotte de Niaux** Caves painted by our most remote European ancestors. See p.164

▲ Carvings, Carcassonne

Carcassonne, Upper Aude and Ariège

The citadel of **Carcassonne** is quintessential Languedoc: a medieval fortress with the foothills of the Pyrenees rising off to the south, the peaks of the Montagne Noire looming to the north, and the languid waters of the Canal du Midi gliding past towards the Mediterranean. Although it fell to Catholic forces early in the Crusade, Carcassonne was held to be the epicentre of the Cathar heresy in Languedoc: the castles which form a far-flung ring in the Corbières and the Pyrenean slopes to the south were referred to as the heretic capital's "sons". The land fanning southwest of the city rises in a series of ridges and plains, cut through by two rivers. The first, the **Aude**, runs north to Carcassonne, skirting the highlands of the **pays de Sault** on its way down from the mountains; journeying up this valley and into the *pays*, a region littered with narrow gorges and high passes, is like flipping through the pages of Cathar history – from the site of their greatest fortified city to the ruins of their last redoubt, **Montségur**. The second river, flowing down from Andorra to Toulouse, gives its name to the *département* – **Ariège** – constituting the remainder of this chapter. **Foix**, once the thriving capital of a proudly independent county, sits at the centre of the *département*, standing sentinel over the course of the rapid river, after it has twisted through the northern slopes of the Pyrenees past the skiing and hiking country around the spa of **Ax-les-Thermes** and **Tarascon-sur-Ariège**, with its incredible array of **prehistoric caves** – justification alone for a trip to the region. The plain northeast of Foix was the haunt of troubadours and men of religion, be they Cathar *parfaits* (see p.149) or the Inquisitors sent to hunt them. Reduced to a ruin in the Wars of Religion, today its ancient, near-abandoned villages with their arcaded squares and crumbling walls offer the only faded record of the district's rich past. At the southwestern limits of the *département*, the **Couserans**, snowcapped peaks ranged in breathtaking cirques, form a virtually impenetrable barrier to Spain beyond.

Today, the Aude valley – with the exception of ever-popular Carcassonne – and the Ariège *département* are two of the least developed regions in the French Southwest. Isolated by difficult terrain, and afflicted for generations by the emigration of youth to the better prospects of the northern cities, there is little economic base here apart from farming and herding. In recent years, tourism has rescued the area from its relentless decline, and to a certain extent, the construction of **ski resorts**, spas and local museums has served to improve the region's prospects. But these recent initiatives, if they have stimulated the local economy, have not detracted from the essential flavour of the area – a refuge of mountain tradition.

As you'd expect, the region is not the best for **public transport**. There's a good rail service running up the Ariège valley, from Toulouse to beyond the Col de Puylorens (and hooking up with the Tech service of Roussillon), while the other line, from Carcassonne to Quillan, has considerably less service. Bus services, even between larger towns, are infrequent: consult the "Travel Details" on p.168, and obtain current local information before planning a route.

Carcassonne

Your first view of **CARCASSONNE**, its fairy-tale citadel perched high above the grassy verges of the River Aude, is likely to be a memorable one. The famous **cité**, slated as a UNESCO World Heritage site in 1997, enjoys must-see status on any trip through southwest France, and if it has suffered through the ages – beaten, burnt and dismantled – you'd never guess from looking at it. Aside from the walled town, with its castle and basilica, there's the medieval lower town, or **ville basse**, set on the far side of the Aude. Together, the two complement each other: the first is outstandingly beautiful, while the latter is lively, with a sprinkling of good services. Good transportation links by bus, rail, canal and air also make Carcassonne an ideal base for exploring the surrounding areas: the uplands of the Ariège and the Aude covered later in this chapter, and to the north, the ominous Montagne Noire (Chapter 3).

Carcassonne was settled as far back as the sixth century BC, passing through the hands of Romans and Visigoths before its golden age under the great Languedocian family, the **Trencavels**. This family, which had various holdings in Languedoc, became vassals of the counts of Toulouse (the "St-Gilles" family) in 1163, and used Carcassonne as their principal residence, ensuring the town a prosperous economic base. As a consequence of the Crusade against the Cathar heretics, the town was besieged and taken in 1209, eventually passing to the notorious Simon de Montfort, who made it "**capital**" of the extensive territories he was taking over from local nobility. After the feared warrior died outside the walls of Toulouse in 1218, the Trencavel Raymond-Roger VII briefly recovered the town, only to see it pass to royal control in 1229. Some twenty years later, King Louis IX laid out the *ville basse*, a *bastide* which would serve as a regional market and increase the town's wealth, on the far banks of the river. Carcassonne thus prospered until the **Black Prince** invaded during the course of the Hundred Years' War and, frustrated by his inability to seize the strong citadel, burnt the *ville basse* to the ground in 1355. Despite this setback, the town's citizens rallied and rebuilt the lower town, and for the rest of the Middle Ages Carcassonne enjoyed a healthy economy, profiting handsomely from its location – perfect for a market – on the frontier of the old French kingdom. With the annexation of Roussillon in 1659 all of this changed, the border shifted south, and Carcassonne entered a period of stagnation, during which time the citadel was abandoned and eventually quarried for its stones. This is how it remained until it was rediscovered in the nineteenth century by **Viollet-le-Duc**, whose visionary fifty-year restoration project rescued it from obscurity.

Today Carcassonne continues to flourish largely because of that vision, which brings in thousands of visitors every year. Despite the fact that the citadel is the only sight as such, and there is essentially very little to do here, it is nevertheless a great place to spend a relaxing few days. Additionally the *cité* has become something of a symbol of medieval France; its yearly **pageants** and spectacular Bastille Day celebrations (see box on p.122), featuring the second largest fireworks display in France, keep the streets full of both French and foreign tourists.

Arrival and information

Carcassonne's **airport** is just west of town; there's a bank with exchange services, several shops and car rental offices in the arrivals hall. A **navette** service (hourly; 15min; €5) leaves from outside the terminal and stops in town at the

Festivals in Carcassonne and Ariège

July and August are the best months for **festivals** in Ariège. The lively *fêtes locaux* invariably feature live music and dancing, and are a good opportunity to pick up country produce; several have colourful (if not always accurate) medieval re-enactments. The biggest festival is Carcassonne's Bastille Day, but bear in mind that the town packs out for the event, with parked cars lining the route national for several kilometres from the *cité*. Limoux's Carnaval is also a unique event, worth planning for if you're in the area.

Mid-Jan to March Limoux: Carnaval. An extended Lenten celebration featuring vividly costumed dancers in the old town squares. Three sets of performances (11am, 4pm & 10pm) on Saturdays and Sundays.

May–June St-Lizier & the villages of the Couserans: Festival d'Art Sacrée ☏05.61.96.77.77. A two-week celebration of religious artistic expression coinciding with the Ascension, with a heavy emphasis on the medieval. Concerts ranging from Gregorian chant to choral music are performed in the cathedral and in the village parishes, alongside art exhibitions and performances of dramatic works.

19–23 June Saint-Girons: Sent Joan Beth e Gran ☏05.61.04.65.53, ⓦww.ville-st-girons.fr. Celebration of St John's day culminating in the traditional bonfire, celebrated by four days of folk concerts and dances featuring groups of the Couserans and two foreign troupes.

Throughout July Carcassonne: Festival de Carcassonne ☏04.68.25.33.16. Month-long festival of dance, music and theatre with nightly performances in the castle's amphitheatre. The highpoint is the Bastille Day (July 14) celebration, which culminates in a giant fireworks display.

First two weeks July Tarascon: Résistances ⓦwww.capmedia.fr/resistances. Festival of new, cutting-edge film, with a predominantly French programme.

Second week July St-Girons: Festival RITE ☏05.61.96.26.60, ⓦassoc.wanadoo.fr/sigurd/bethmalais. International festival of traditional song and dance, presided over by a group dedicated to preserving the rich culture of the Couserans area, but also featuring music and dance groups from as far afield as South America and Africa.

Second weekend July Seix: Fête de la Transhumance ⓦwww.ville-st-girons.fr. Three-day celebration timed for the traditional passing of the sheep flocks. Market with traditional products and crafts and various events.

Mid-July Pamiers: Fiesta ☏05.61.67.52.52, ⓦpamierstourisme.com/fiesta. Five days of Spanish and Latin American dance and music with a strong accent on flamenco.

Mid-July Foix: Résistances ☏05.61.05.13.30, ⓔrésistences@wanadoo.fr. Annual film festival of national stature. Each year a different theme and over a hundred screenings in ten days.

3rd weekend of July Mirepoix: Les Médiévales de Mirepoix ☏05.61.68.83.76. Medieval horsemanship, pageantry, market and fair in the arcaded squares around the cathedral.

Late July Limoux: Folklore festival. Five-day international festival featuring traditional storytelling, theatre, dance and music.

gare SNCF, place Gambetta and the *cité*; a **taxi** to the centre will cost €8–15. The **gare SNCF** (☏08.36.35.35.35) is on the north side of the *ville basse*, just over the Canal du Midi from boulevard Omer Sarraut. From the station you can catch the *navette* described above, or simply follow the ring road around to place Gambetta and the main **tourist office** at 15 boulevard Camille Pelletan (July & Aug daily 9am–7pm; Sept–June Mon–Sat 9am–6pm; ☏04.68.10.24.30, ⓦwww.carcassonne-tourisme.com); if you don't wish to stop in the lower

Late July Quillan: Festival du Folklore International. Held over six days, this international festival features storytelling and theatre with an impressive repertoire of groups from as far afield as Southeast Asia and South America.

Late July Ax-les-Thermes: Spectacles de Grands Chemins ℡05.61.64.38.00, axanim@wanadoo.fr. A festival of street theatre celebrating local *montagnard* culture, featuring over twenty French companies and held over three days.

Late July Foix: jazz à Foix ℡05.61.01.18.30, ⓦwww.jazzfoix.com. Five nights of jazz, swing and blues featuring a predominantly French and American programme.

Late-July Tarascon: Tarascon-Latino ℡05.34.09.88.87, ⓦwww.tarasconlatino.com. Eight days of music, dance and food from Central and South America.

Late July to mid-Aug St-Girons: Festival de Théatre ℡05.61.96.85.66. French-language theatre festival featuring a programme ranging from the classical (such as Molière) to puppetry.

Late July to mid-Aug St-Lizier: Festival de Saint-Lizier ℡05.61.66.67.89, ⓦaustri-art.chez.tiscali.fr. Long-running three-week music festival with an impressively varied programme, ranging from the Baroque to Prokofiev and Stravinsky.

Late July to late-Aug Foix: Il était un Foix... L'Ariège ⓦwww.foixterredhistoire.fr.fm, ℡05.61.65.03.03. Massive outdoor exhibition glorifying Foix's medieval past, culminating in a fireworks display. Nightly at 10pm, ticket required.

Early Aug Mirepoix: Festival de la Marionette ℡05.61.68.20.72, ⓦfilentrope.free.fr. Three-day festival of puppetry along with a large craft and produce market.

First week Aug St-Girons: Rite ℡06.07.32.77.58, ⓦwww.bethmalais.org. Ten-day festival of traditional culture, including music, song and dance, and featuring over two hundred performers drawn from countries as diverse as Mongolia and Angola.

First two weeks Aug Carcassonne: Spectacle Médiéval ℡04.68.71.35.35, ⓦwww.terredhistoire.com. Medieval costumes and pageantry and a theatrical re-enactment with a different theme each year.

First two weeks Aug St-Lizier: Festival de Musique ℡05.61.96.67.89. Nightly classical concerts, ranging from Mozart to Paganini to classical guitar works, performed in the cathedral by international artists. The *fête locale*, including markets, music and a weekend-long Gallo-Roman festival, is also held at this time.

Last weekend Aug Carcassonne: Fiesta y Toros. A weekend of taurine events including bullfights and *abrivados*, equestrian displays and a Spanish-style street party (bullfights €30; ℡04.68.71.01.00).

First two weeks Sept Foix: Fêtes de Foix. The town's yearly festival, with produce markets, music and a medieval theme, centred on the illustrious figure of Gaston Fébus (see box on p155).

Mid-Sept Mirepoix: Grand Fête de St-Maurice. Held over four days, a lively festival with market and some costumed events.

Sept 21 Vicdessos: St-Matthieu. Transhumant livestock fair, formalized by the Count de Foix in 1313. Nowadays, the tradition continues with a lively market and celebration.

Late Oct/early Nov Lavelanet: Jazz'velanet ℡05.61.01.22.20, ⓦwww.jazz-velanet.com. Eclectic four-day programme of jazz featuring acts from the world over.

Dec 17 Carcassonne: Marche au Gras. Lively Christmas market featuring produce and regional crafts.

town there's a second tourist office (daily 9am–6pm; ℡04.68.10.24.36) in the *cité* itself, just inside the main entrance. At either branch, you can pick up a handy *Rando-Guide* (€1), outlining six walks and hikes in the Carcassonne area. Finally, there's a canal–side information office (daily: April–May 1–6pm; June & Oct 9am–6pm; July–Sept 9am–7pm) at the town's port. The town has no *gare routière* as such; **buses** arrive along the broad boulevard de Varsovie on the west side of the *ville basse*, a ten-minute walk from the tourist office.

The Legend of Dame Carcas

The origin of Carcassonne's strange-sounding name has given rise to a number of interesting stories, the most enduring and popular of which is that of Dame Carcas. This legend asserts that when the town was under Muslim control in the early Middle Ages, the Emperor Charlemagne arrived to lay siege, knowing that if his army attacked for long enough, eventually the town would run short of food. However, just when defeat looked inevitable, Carcas, the Muslim ruler's wife, ordered a pig to be force-fed with the last of the town's precious grain and tossed over the battlements. When the pig hit the ground it immediately split open, and Charlemagne's troops, seeing the contents, despaired, believing that the town must have abundant supplies. They lifted the siege and retreated, and as the town's church bells pealed in celebration, the townsfolk cried "Carcas, sonne!" ("Ring, Carcas!"). It's a great story, but pure fantasy of course. A Muslim ruler, for whom pork would have been considered unclean, would never have kept pigs within the confines of his fortress, and in the early ninth century the locals spoke something more akin to Latin than modern French. Nevertheless it is decidedly more poetic than the truth, which is that the town's name derives from two Occitan roots: carac, for "rock" (after the spur on which it is built), and sonne, for "wood" (for the forests which surrounded it).

If you're arriving **by car**, you can park up by the *cité*, where the mandatory car park charges a €3.50 fee, but there are cheaper options ringing the *ville basse*, as well as free and metered street parking.

Place Gambetta is the **local transport** hub; all city buses and *navettes* (€0.90) leave from here, while a special *navette* to the *cité* (€1) and campsite departs from near the Caisse d'Epargne bank (mid-July to mid-Sept, every 15min: 7am–10.30pm). Local transport information, including maps, can be picked up at the tourist offices, or you can contact Carcassonne's urban transport company (℡04.68.47.82.22). For **bikes** and **motorbikes**, see p.131.

Accommodation

Although your first impulse may be to get a room in the *cité*, beware that if you are hoping to pass the evenings in a medieval idyll you will most likely be disappointed. There is little **accommodation** here and it is expensive; furthermore, the citadel is very busy – verging on lunacy in high season. You may be more satisfied with a room along the slopes down towards the riverbank, or in the *ville basse* (from where you get the view of the *cité*). Be warned, also, that Bastille Day (July 14) is very big here; hotels book up a year in advance and traffic jams clog approaches to the town for kilometres in every direction. From November to March the tourist office operates a "Bon Week-end" programme, which gives you two nights for one at participating hotels.

Hotels

de la Cité Place de l'Église ℡04.68.71.98.71, ⓦ www.hoteldelacite.orient-express.com; see map p.126. If you can afford it, this luxurious hotel with its beautiful enclosed courtyard will separate you from the maddening crowds of the cité. The price matches the opulence. Closed Dec to mid-Jan. ⓽
Le Donjon – les Remparts 2 rue du Comte Roger ℡04.68.11.23.00, ⓦ www.hotel-donjon.fr; see map p.126. The other cité hotel is surprisingly affordable for what you get: a thoroughly renovated hotel with well-equipped rooms. Just a stone's throw from the donjon, with everything you need to stay comfy. ⓺

Éspace Cité 132 rue Trivalle ℡04.68.25.24.24, Ⓔ hotel-espace-cité@wanadoo.fr; see map p.126. What this hotel lacks in charm it tries hard to make up for with amenities such as AC, TV and garage parking. Just downhill from the main gate to the cité; wheelchair accessible. ⓶
Grand Hôtel Terminus 2 av de Maréchal Joffré ℡04.68.25.25.00, Ⓕ 04.68.75.53.09; see map p.129. Fading steam-age luxury in this station-side hotel, which has a splendid fin-de-siècle facade. Also features a good bar and TV in the rooms. Closed Dec–Feb. ⓹

Montmorency 2 rue Camille St-Saëns
☎04.68.11.96.70, ⓦwww.lemontmorency.com;
see map p.126. Like the Éspace, this establishment provides a good range of services and is well
located for those only interested in visiting the
citadel, as it is just one street north of the cité.
Wheelchair access and swimming pool. ❸
Montségur 27 allée d'Iéna ☎04.68.25.31.41,
ⓔinfo@hotelmontsegur.com; see map p.129.
Comfortable rooms in an impressive-looking nineteenth-century townhouse. Located a 15min walk
west of the cathedral, off boulevard Barbès, it is not
the closest hotel to the cité, but it's competitively
priced. Closed late Dec to Jan. English spoken. ❹
du Pont Vieux 32 rue Trivalle ☎04.68.25.24.99,
ⓕ04.68.47.62.71; see map on p.126. Perhaps the
best all-round choice in town, this "olde worlde"
hotel is on a lively, atmospheric little street which
winds up from the medieval bridge towards the
cité. TV and parking; pets are welcome. ❸
de la Poste 21 rue de Verdun ☎04.68.25.12.18,
ⓔhotel.de.la.poste@wanadoo.fr; see map p.129.
A basic no-frills option with a great location on the
main street of the ville basse. The rooms are basic
and the hotel has few amenities or facilities, apart
from a small bar, but if money is tight, this is the
place to stay. ❶
Au Royal 22bd Jean-Jaurès ☎04.68.25.19.12,
ⓔgodartcl@wanadoo.fr; see map p.129. One step
up from the bottom bracket, this hotel has a good
location, and all rooms have TV. Closed late Dec to
late Jan. ❷
St Joseph 81 rue de la Liberté ☎04.68.71.96.89,
ⓕ04.68.71.36.28; see map p.129. Another good
deal in the ville basse, down a quiet side-street not
far from the station. You get TV, a lift and car park
at one-star prices. ❶

Hostels and campsite
Camping de la Cité Rte St-Hilaire
☎04.68.25.11.17, ⓦwww.campeoles.fr.
Exceptional ground with good shady sites, some
bungalows and a shop. Tucked away in parkland
to the south of town, it can be reached by local
bus #8 or by a 20min walk from the cité. If you
point your tent in the right direction you get a view
of the citadel poking up over the trees.
HI hostel Rue Trencavel ☎04.68.25.23.16,
ⓕ04.68.71.14.84, ⓔcarcassonne@fuaj.org; see
map p.126. Excellent, modern hostel in the heart
of the citadel. Its dorms (€12.20) and rooms are
clean and bright and there's a large patio for
respite from the crowds outside, plus a bar.
Membership (available on site) required in summer. Sheet rental €3. Open Feb to mid-Dec.
Notre Dame de l'Abbaye 103 rue Trivalle
☎04.68.25.16.65, ⓕ04.68.72.71.74; see map on
p.126. A second choice for hostel-style accommodation. Great location in a beautiful street, comfortable dorms (€13) and sheet rental available (€3).

The Town

Carcassonne's layout can be a bit confusing initially. The town is divided into
three main parts, the oldest of which is the **cité** – the compact, walled citadel
perched on a hill on the east bank of the Aude. Descending from here you pass
through the medieval suburb of La Barbacane and cross the river to arrive at
the **ville basse**, formally known as La Bastide de St-Louis – a typical grid of
thirteenth-century streets, ringed by a one-way system where there was once
a wall. Splayed out around this is the **new town**, a nondescript series of suburbs which holds nothing of interest for the visitor.

The Cité

From whichever direction you approach, Carcassonne's magnificent citadel, its
stout ramparts and pennant-capped towers piercing the sky, presents one of the
South of France's most striking images – straight out of a medieval fantasy. And
that is mostly what it is – a piece of imaginative reconstruction by the nineteenth-century restorer Viollet-le-Duc, whose enthusiasm for "the medieval"
inspired him to invent inaccurate features like the conical towers and arrow-
slits, which the original medieval fortress lacked. In fact, so much of
Carcassonne is fabrication that it only squeaked by in its application for
UNESCO status.

Nevertheless, as you cross over the moat, passing the wide grassy verges
between the thick double walls, you do feel as though you're entering another world. Although you can enter through the **Porte d'Aude**, on the citadel's

CARCASSONNE: CITÉ

Pont Vieux &
Basse-Ville

ACCOMMODATION

Camping de la Cité	H
de la Cité	G
Le Donjon	F
Éspace Cité	B
HI Hostel	E
Montmorency	D
Notre Dame de l'Abbaye	A
du Pont Vieux	C

RESTAURANTS

Auberge du Dame Carcas	3
Le Barbacane	4
Le Fontaine du Soleil	5
Ponte Vecchio	2
Tête de l'Art	1

PLACE
ST JEAN

Château
Comtal

**Torture
Museum**

Lower Lices

VOIE
MÉDIÉVAL

MONTÉE COMBÉLÉRAN

RUE PORTE D'AUDE

R DU COMTE
ROGER

PLACE
R CROS MAYREVIEILLE
DU CHÂTEAU

**Porte
Narbonnaise**

RUE DU NAZAIRE

RUE SAINT LOUIS

RUE RAYMOND ROGER TRENCAVEL

RU DU PETIT PUITS

PLACE
MARCOU

RUE DU PLÓ

PLACE
AUGUSTE
PIERRE PONT

Basilica

**Musée
de l'École**

PLACE DU
PETIT PUITS

RUE DU PLÓ

Amphitheatre

PLACE
ST NAZAIRE

Upper Lices

CHEMIN DES ANGLAIS

**Musée Mémoires
du Moyen Âge**

CHEMIN DES OURTETS

N

0   100 m

Les Aigles de la Cité

western side (and closer to the *ville basse*), a more visually impressive and evocative option is to head to the main **Port Narbonnaise**, where the local *navettes* and main car park are found – on the far side of the *cité*. From here, following the rue Cros Mayrevieille, with its phalanxes of souvenir shops and ice-cream stands, will lead you to the entrance to the twelfth-century **Château Comtal** (daily: April–Sept 9.30am–6.30pm; Oct–March 9.30am–5pm; 35–40min guided tour only, occasionally in English summer only; €6.10), the castle where Count Raymond-Roger Trencavel made his last stand against the northern knights, and surrendered, in 1209. Although you can wander around the *cité* for free, the ticket office for the Château Comtal is just inside the Porte Narbonnaise, on the left-hand side. The mandatory guided tours of the *château* begin in the main castle courtyard (at the end of the street), from where the guides lead you through the scanty remains of the now open-roofed keep. The tour continues southwards along a section of the citadel's three kilometres of walls and through three of its 31 towers (some of whose Roman foundations can be discerned) before arriving at the modern **amphitheatre**, built on the side of the fortress's former abbey-church and used since 1908 for theatre, dance and musical performances. Take care along the walls, as stairways can be slippery and the inadequate railings are no match for curious children. The ruins themselves are anything but spectacular – Carcassonne is best when looked at from outside – but the views from the walls are good, and the guides' frank account of the history of the town is lively and informative. Appropriately, the castle also hosts an exhibit on the life and work of Viollet-le-Duc (see box on p.128).

The tour ends at place St-Nazaire, behind the **basilica** of the same name (mid-June to mid-Sept Mon–Fri 9–11.45am & 1.45–6pm & Sun 9–10.45am & 2–4.30pm; rest of year closes at 5pm), a late eleventh-century church that was originally Romanesque, but underwent major Gothic and neo-Gothic remodellings, first in the thirteenth century and then again in the nineteenth, by Viollet-le-Duc. As you follow the building round to the entrance in place Pierre Pont look up to see a stunning series of **gargoyles** along the eaves, as well as amusingly carved heads above the door. Inside, the church's plain nave betrays its pre-Gothic origins – the choir and rosette window are thirteenth-century additions – and at the southern end you'll find the tomb where Simon de Montfort lay until his body was transferred to his family's main fief at Montfort l'Amaury near Paris.

There's not a great deal else to see or do in the *cité* apart from wander the narrow, crooked streets, and absorb the convincingly medieval ambience. From behind the basilica, follow the walls east along rue Plô. At no. 3 there's the small **Musée de l'École** (daily July & Aug 10am–7pm, Sept–June 10am–6pm; €3), a reconstruction of a *fin-de-siècle* classroom, and slightly further along you'll pass a little park at place du Petit Puits, with its old well – a good place to pause and soak up the atmosphere – before eventually reaching the restaurant-clogged **place Marcou**. On the nearby place St-Jean, you'll find the small **Musée de la Chivalrie** (Easter–Oct 10am–noon & 3–6pm; €3), further capitalizing on themes medieval, with a collection of arms and armour. The small section of town on the far north of rue Cros Mayrevielle is somewhat less developed and provides a bit of respite from the teeming masses of visitors. Here you can visit a **torture museum** in rue du Grand Puits (daily July & Aug 9.30am–8pm, Sept–June 10am–6.30pm; €6.50), with mock-ups, models and some genuine instruments of pain dating from the Middle Ages to the French Revolution.

Before finishing up your visit of the *cité*, you should also take the time to walk around the grassy **lices**, a narrow space some 1100m in length, created with the building of the second set of walls in 1200s, and divided into two sections. The **lower lices** run from the Porte Narbonnaise to the Porte de l'Aude around the northern perimeter of the citadel; starting out from the former, you'll notice a section of brick-and-stone-constructed wall dating back to the end of the period of Roman occupation. Walking along the slightly longer southern circuit of the **upper lices** gives you good views of the elaborate towers added to the citadel's defences under Philip III in the late thirteenth century. Once a space for medieval archery practice and other military exercises, the *lices* now provide a favourite route for horsedrawn *calèches* and a great place to have a picnic.

Outside the Porte Narbonnaise, on the chemin des Anglaises, you'll find the **Musée Mémoires du Moyen Âge** (Museum of Memories of the Middle Ages; daily 10am–7pm; €4), a collection of dioramas depicting battalions of medieval soldiers hacking and slashing at each other, but all around various parts of Viollet-le-Duc's nineteenth-century version of the *cité* – strictly for kids. Another stop for young travellers is **Im@ginarium**, a glitzy French-

Viollet-le-Duc

It can be something of a disappointment to discover that so many of the buildings of medieval France are in fact, reconstructions, reassembled or repaired in the nineteenth century. Up until then, the Middle Ages was considered to be a period of "Gothic" barbarism best forgotten, but in the early 1800s European intellectuals began to look back at the medieval era as the time when their own nations were born, and all over western Europe projects were undertaken to recover its neglected art and architecture. The major figure in this movement in France was Eugène Emmanuel **Viollet-le-Duc**, the prolific restorer-extraordinaire who left his – sometimes fantastical – mark all over the country, but particularly in Languedoc and Roussillon.

Born in Paris in 1814, Viollet-le-Duc studied art history at the Sorbonne before embarking on an extended tour of France and Italy in his early twenties. On his return to Paris, he assisted in the renovation of the glorious stained glass and stone-carved interior of the **Ste Chapelle**; it was here that he found his calling and made his reputation, and in the years that followed he was inundated with contracts to restore buildings such as Narbonne's Hôtel de Ville (see p.307) and the basilica of St-Nazaire in Carcassonne – accomplished works which served to further his renown. By 1853, when Louis-Napoleon, prince-president of the Second Republic, had given him overall supervision of the restoration of all of France's medieval buildings, Viollet-le-Duc had already begun the massive reconstruction of Carcassonne's walled **cité** – a project which would take fifty years to complete and which he would not live to see finished. After drawing up the restoration plans, he returned to his old university to butt heads with critics and colleagues and dabble as a professor of art history but, finally disillusioned with the criticisms his theories provoked, he left, returning to his work and writing, eventually dying in his adopted home of Switzerland in 1879.

Viollet-le-Duc's idiosyncratic **theory** of restoration dictated that buildings should not necessarily be returned to their exact previous state, but rather modified according to their essential underlying architectural principles (as he saw them, naturally). As a result, the elaborate restorations – in which he sometimes started from nothing more than a pile of stones – are reflections of Viollet-le-Duc's imagination, and bear little or no relation in design or form to their originals. Works such as the Ste Chapelle, which were taken on early in his career and not under his direct supervision, tend to be more faithful, but with later renovations he was more or less given free rein. In Carcassonne's *cité* for example he not only made "improvements", such as adding arrow-slits and crenellation to the walls, but adopted features which are aesthetically pleasing but, quite simply, inaccurate: the pointed roofs on the towers are German-style as opposed to the flat Languedocian version. In this way he created France's medieval heritage almost single-handedly – a heritage which reflects historical reality as much as Sir Walter Scott's *Ivanhoe* or Cecil B. de Mille's movies, but which now forms a focus for French national and Occitan regional identity, as well as the foundation for the booming tourist industry of the twentieth century. Whatever you think about Viollet-le-Duc's easy attitude to verisimilitude, as you travel around Languedoc and Roussillon, bear in mind that – for better or worse – almost all the great medieval monuments here have "benefited" to some degree from his endeavours. There is a permanent exhibit dedicated to the restorationist, including many original sketches and plans, in Carcassonne's castle.

language interactive museum recounting the history of the Cathars in all its drama (Easter-June & Sept–Oct check with tourist office for times; July & Aug daily 10.30am–7pm; €7). A fifteen-minute walk south at Colline de Pech Mary is **Les Oiseaux a la Cité**, which runs exciting 45-minute-long live **falconry** shows (July & Aug daily 2.30–6pm; April–Oct Sun 3pm & 4.30pm; €5).

The Ville Basse

When you leave the *cité*, instead of backtracking through the main gates and past the car park, a better option is to take the gate at the end of rue Notre Dame, off place du Grand Puits, and cut down to rue Trivalle, a world away from the touristy scrum in the fortress above. This leads to the picturesque fourteenth-century **pont vieux**, adorned on its far side by the small and simple Gothic structure of the twelfth-century Notre Dame de la Santé **chapel**. The riverbanks on the *cité* side have been kept free of building and make a nice grassy spot to relax or have a picnic.

Just up from the bridge you reach the southeastern edge of the **ville basse** at place Gambetta, which, despite the traffic, has an airy feel, as well as some attractive nineteenth-century facades. Keep an eye out for the impressive Art Deco facade of the Groupe Scolaire Jean-Jaurès on the northwest corner. Here, by the tourist office, rue Verdun (formerly Grande Rue), will take you straight into the grid of the thirteenth-century *bastide*. Just along there, in an eighteenth-century *hôtel*, you'll find the **Musée des Beaux-Arts** (mid-June to mid-Sept Wed–Sun 10am–6pm; mid-Sept to mid-June Tues–Sat 10am–noon & 2–6pm; free), which, aside from its large but unremarkable collection of eighteenth-century landscapes, sometimes hosts interesting temporary exhibitions. Further along you'll arrive at place Carnot, the heart of the old *ville basse* – a wide square with shops, cafés and bars as well as a good morning **market** (Tues, Thurs & Sat mornings). At the far end of rue Verdun, at no. 53, the **Maison des Mémoires** (Tues–Sat 9am–noon & 2–6pm; free) pays homage to local-born surrealist poet Joë Bousquet (1857–1950). Left paraplegic by battle wounds received at Vailly in 1918, Bousquet lived out the rest of his life bedridden in this house in Carcassonne, comforted by opium and producing dark and mystical poetical reflections which attracted the attention of the interwar intelligentsia. Near the fourteenth-century cathedral of St-Michel you'll find the most substantial remains of the town's once stout defences; the **Porte des Jacobins**, a medieval gate which was widened and remodelled in Neoclassical style in 1778, is in good shape, while beside it lie the remains of the old ramparts. Otherwise, keep an eye out for some of the impressive old private *hôtels* which can be found in the *ville basse*, both along rue Verdun and rue Amié-Ramond, where you'll find the plain, medieval-styled facade of the fourteenth-century Maison du Sénechal, at no. 70, and a more flamboyant Renaissance *hôtel* at no. 50.

If you're heading back to the *cité*, the unpleasant walk along the modern road bridge east of place Gambetta will give you a great view of the citadel and the *pont vieux*. On the other side, cut across to the old bridge and follow rue de la Barbacane up past the church of St-Gimer. From here you can get to the Porte de l'Aude, walking between the double walls to re-enter the *cité*.

Eating, drinking and nightlife

You'll never have a problem getting something **to eat** in Carcassonne, whether in the *cité*, where every other facade seems to belong to a bistro, or in the *ville basse*, which has a good selection of simple and upper-crust establishments. If you don't feel like choosing from the restaurants listed below, head for the mass of indistinguishable patios on place Marcou, all of which have *menus* in the €12 range. For something lighter, rue Cros Mayrevieille at the entrance to the *cité* is crammed with *crêpe* and sandwich stands, while there are traditional café-bars in and around the *bastide*'s place Carnot.

For a small city, Carcassonne does quite well as far as **nightlife** goes, with a good selection of late-night **bars** (normally open until 2am, sometimes 4am or 5am at weekends) in the *ville basse*. Le Café de Nuit, 32 boulevard Omer Sarraut, livens up later with a mixed gay/straight crowd, while nearby, Le Flanaghan, at no. 21, is the town's obligatory Irish-style watering hole. At 49 avenue Henri Goût, La Fiesta Bodega (a rather pricey Spanish-Mexican restaurant by day) stays open late as a lively tapas bar. Tiny rue de l'Aigle d'Or, just off place Carnot, is the centre for local trendies, with bars like Le Conti, at no. 16, which has two dance floors (daily till 5am), or the rockish Le Not, at no. 18 (Tues–Sat till 2am). In the *cité* itself, Bar au Vin, in rue Plô, is the best place for a drink – it's a post-show favourite for visiting actors and musicians. Insular ambience can be found at Pub Sheridan in place Victor-Hugo. For **dancing**, try La Bulle (closed Mon & Tues), just below the *cité* at 115 rue Barbacane, or La Rapière, a house-sound disco popular with under-25s, just outside the main gates.

Restaurants

Auberge du Dame Carcas 3 pl du Château ☎04.68.71.23.23; see map p.126. Large restaurant with several dining rooms, serving up excellent-quality traditional and regional cuisine, including roast meats cooked over an open fire. With menus from €13.50 this is one of the best-value places in town, so call ahead. Closed Sun eve, Mon lunch & Feb.
Le Barbacane Pl de l'Église ☎04.68.71.98.71;

see map p.126. The most elegant (and expensive) of the three restaurants operated by the Hotel de la Cité. Adventurous gastronomique cuisine with four-star service. You'll pay upwards of €60. Open evenings only.
Au Comte Roger 14 rue St-Louis ☎04.68.11.93.41; see map p.126. One of the better choices for terroir in the city. Renowned chef Pierre Mesa imaginatively combines local Lauragais basics with subtle gastronomique touches. Menus

€27–33. Closed Sun & late Jan to late Feb.

La Brochetterie les Saveurs 2 rue Denisse (see map p.129). A friendly restaurant featuring French, Moroccan and Spanish selections just off the place Carnot. Menus start at €12, and you can beat the heat with a pitcher of sangria for €6. Closed Sun & Mon.

La Divine Comédie 29 bd Jean-Jaurès ☏04.68.72.30.36; see map p.129. An Italian restaurant, with decent pasta, as well as local standbys like cassoulet and confit du canard. Menus from €12. Closed Sun & late Dec to early Jan.

L'Écurie 43 bd Barbès ☏04.68.72.04.04; see map p.129. This place, offering elegant dining in a converted eighteenth-century stable, is popular with gays and lesbians. Menus €21–32, offering local cuisine as well as dishes with adventurous touches such as mackerel brochettes in thyme sauce. Closed Sun.

Les Fontaines du Soleil 32 rue de Plô (see map p.126). One of the best deals in the cité: small, friendly and cheap with good local, home-style cookery. You can eat well here for about €13 in a quiet little interior patio. Closed Jan.

Le Jardin de la Tour 11 rue Porte d'Aude ☏04.68.25.71.24; see map p.129. Just outside the citadel's Porte d'Aude, this is a good option for local and Mediterranean cuisine, with a small garden dining area. Menus from €18. Closed Sun eve, Mon & Nov.

Le Petit Couvert 18 rue de l'Aigle d'Or; see map p.129. Snappy and cheerily decorated little restaurant with good cheap menus based around combinations of salads and simple meat dishes (from €10.60) and a small street-side terrace. Also "light" options for vegetarians. Closed Sun, Mon & March.

Ponte Vecchio 22 rue Trivalle see map p.126 ☏04.68.71.33.17. Fine Italian dining and hospitable atmosphere in the shadow of the cité. Menus €14.50–17.50. Closed Mon & mid-Nov to mid-Dec.

Le Quai Bellevue 2 rue des 3 Couronnes ☏04.68.25.05.60; see map p.129. Good regional cuisine served at this riverside patio, which offers excellent views of the medieval bridge and the walls of the cité. Expect to spend about €15. Closed Oct–April.

Tête de l'Art 37bis rue Trivalle ☏04.68.71.23.11; see map p.126. Located on the atmospheric thoroughfare which connects the old bridge and the cité, with an unassuming exterior girded by a tiny sidewalk patio, and an interior festooned with the contemporary painting and sculpture. Excellent terroir fare from €11.50 to €35 with a filling vegetarian option at €13.

Listings

Airlines Ryanair ☏04.68.71.96.65, ⓦwww.ryanair.com.

Airport information ☏04.68.71.96.46 & 04.68.71.96.65, ⓦwwwcarcassonne.cci.fr.

Banks Most major French banks, plus ATMs, are represented. Try, for example, Caisse d'Epargne, 5 bd Camille Pelletan, which also has a 24hr automatic change machine, or Crédit Agricole, 8 pl Carnot; after 5pm use the post office (Mon–Sat till 7pm).

Bicycle rental Evasion 2 Roues, 85 allée d'Iéna ☏04.68.25.28.18; Espace 11/Holiday Bikes, 3 route de Minervoise (☏04.68.25.28.18, ⓔcarcassonne@holiday-bikes.com) also has motorbikes and scooters. Both are closed Sun & Mon.

Boat rental Nautic ☏04.68.71.88.95, ⒻO4.67.94.05.91; Locaboat ☏03.86.91.72.72, ⓦwww.locaboat.com. Voies Navigables de France has an office (☏04.68.71.74.55) at the port.

Bus departures Various bus lines operate from Carcassonne, departing from along bd de Varsovie; tickets and information for destinations within the Aude département (no buses Sun) can be found at the main tourist office. Tickets for long-distance buses and Eurolines can be bought from Verdier Voyages, 1 av Maréchal-Joffre (☏04.68.25.09.06).

Car rental Avis, 52 rue Antoine Marty ☏04.68.25.05.84, ⓦwww.avis.com; Budget, 5 bd Omer Sarraut ☏04.68.72.31.31, ⓦwww.budget.com; Europcar, 7 bd Omer Sarraut ☏04.68.25.05.09, ⓦwww.europcar.com; Garage la Bouriette, 58 bd Denis Papin ☏04.68.47.80.00; Location Occitan de Véhicules, 36 av Franklin Roosevelt ☏04.68.11.74.10. All of these companies, except for Garage la Bouriette, also have offices at the airport.

Hospital Centre Hospitalier Général, rte de St-Hilaire (☏04.68.24.24.24), on the south side of town.

Internet access Alert Rouge, 73 rue de Verdun (Mon–Fri 10am–1am, Sat 2pm–1am).

Laundry 5 sq Gambetta & 31 rue Aimé-Ramond.

Lost property 13 rue Jean Bringer ☏04.68.10.27.00.

Pharmacy There several in rue Verdun: try Pharmacie Serin at no. 56; after 8pm enquire at the police station.

Police 4 bd Barbès ☏04.68.11.26.00.

Swimming pool Grazailles, rue du Moulin de la Seigne (☏04.68.47.81.83) is the one municipal pool open year-round (bus #2 or #3). Locals also head for the Lac de Cavayère, signposted from the Narbonne road, just east of the cité (#7 bus).

Taxi Radio Taxi ☏04.68.71.50.50.

The upper Aude valley

The River Aude, whose course can be followed due south from Carcassonne, is like a highway of Catharism – the majority of the most famous sights and ruins associated with the heretical sect lie along its path as it ascends into the Pyrenees. The river's lower regions hold fewer attractions but are consequently less visited, making quiet towns like **Limoux** and **Alet-les-Bains** good places to get away from the summer crowds, but as the valley winds its way up to the modern service centre of **Quillan** more and more relics of the area's history reveal themselves. On the way you'll pass the mysterious site of **Rennes-le-Château**, a favourite of occultists and treasure-hunters. Just south, the so-called "Cathar castles" (many of which, in reality, postdate the heretics), form a rough chain stretching from Foix in the west, passing Quillan, and on to the Fenouillèdes to the east. South of Quillan, the valley narrows into a series of gorges as you begin the climb into the mountains, eventually reaching the isolated **Donezan** region. This upper portion of the river, skirting the southeastern edge of the highlands of the pays de Sault, has a good network of trails and *gîtes*, stretching out over varied terrain – a great area for **hiking**. From Quillan, you can connect to Foix and access the caves along the River Ariège, while a network of hiking trails leads over the Donezan, southwest towards Tarascon and southeast to the Têt valley of Roussillon.

Limoux and around

Famous for its sparkling white *blanquette* ("little white") wine, first vinted in 1531, **LIMOUX** is the first major town you will arrive at as you follow the course of the Aude upstream from Carcassonne. It is pleasant enough, but there's little to write home about, apart from the Lenten Carnaval **festival**, held from January through to March in the town's main place de la République and featuring displays of masked dancers and live music.

Limoux has dominated this neck of the woods since the Middle Ages and the same **bridge** which spans the Aude today brought prosperity in the form of merchants and traders as far back as the fourteenth century, when the town was rebounding from the repression it suffered as a consequence of its Cathar tendencies. At this time the town, like many of the "new towns" of the era, was governed by a board of consuls rather than by a feudal lord, and was wealthy enough to construct a formidable set of **defensive walls**, part of which can still be seen along the riverside. But these did not prove strong enough to keep out either the Black Death or the Black Prince, and a century and a half later Calvinism arrived, bringing religious strife, quickly followed by a poverty from which it never quite recovered.

The Carte Intersite pass

If you are planning on visiting a few of the Cathar sites in the region, you might consider a "**Carte Intersite**" pass. For €4, this ticket, valid for a year (and available at participating sites and local tourist offices), gives you reductions on the entry price to selected castles and monuments of the Aude *département*, including the castles of Arques, Carcassonne, Caunes-Miknervois, Fontfroide, Lastours, Minerve, Montségur, Peyreperteuse, Puilaurens, Puivert, Quéribus, St-Hilaire, St-Papoul, Saissac, Termes and Villerouge, plus the abbey of Lagrasse. Total savings, if you visit all of these sites, is €13.25.

Today, Limoux is quiet and has something of an air of neglected decay, but at least it provides an opportunity to stretch your legs on the way towards the Pyrenees. The heart of the town is the **place de la République**, a wide square with some fine old stone arcading, a number of timber-frame houses and the requisite café and restaurant patios. Just down rue St-Martin, the town's main **church** has some top-notch stained-glass windows and remarkably restrained sixteenth- and seventeenth-century decor in the side chapels. Behind it the canalized Aude separates the old town from the newer districts. Heading away from the river from place de la République, the quiet streets lead past a hideous nineteenth-century market and on to promenade de Tivoli, the Carcassonne–Quillan highway. Here, you'll find the small **Musée Petiet** (same hours as tourist office; €2.90) in the same building as the tourist office. Its collection of paintings, dominated by local nineteenth-century pointillism and allegory, contains some works of surprising quality. The town's newest attraction is a **piano museum** (July & Aug Wed–Mon 2–6pm; €2), touted as the only one if its kind in France. And, just in case you'd forgotten you were in Cathar country, **Catha-rama** (daily: July & Aug Mon–Fri 10.30am–7pm; €4.50), across the street from the museum, will remind you; it has a cheesy thirty-minute audiovisual show in four languages, emotionally recounting the repression of the religious movement, now a pillar of a manufactured regional identity. Alternatively, if you're more interested in the local *blanquette* (a dry, sparkling white), head to the *domaine* Caves Sieur d'Arques (Mon–Sat 10–11am & 3–5pm; free) on avenue de Mauzac, 1km west on avenue Charles de Gaulle from the main roundabout. Here you can learn about the history of the vintage, as well as sample and buy some to take home.

If you have a car or bike, you may want to follow the winding D104 from Carcassonne to Limoux rather than the main D118, stopping at **ST-HILAIRE**, where you can visit the **abbey-church** (April–June & Sept daily 10am–noon & 2–6pm; July & Aug daily 10am–7pm; Oct Sat, Sun & hols 10am–noon & 2–6pm; Nov–March Sat, Sun & hols 10am–noon & 2–5pm; €3.50) of the same name. This sixth-century foundation, once the choice burial place of the counts of Carcassonne, is best known for a splendid sarcophagus, carved in vivid relief by the Master of Cabestany (see box on p.111), and depicting the martyrdom of Toulouse's first bishop St Sernin. On the right-hand side of the main panel, there is a representation of Toulouse's medieval Capitole building. Aside from the sarcophagus you can visit the compact cloister, and a small wine-cellar. Following the twisting D104 west for the 12km to Limoux will take you past **Notre-Dame de Marceille** (9am–7pm), a Romanesque church with a fine polychrome interior and an eleventh-century Virgin and Child reputed to perform miracles. It is still a place of pilgrimage for local Catholics.

Practicalities

Trains arrive at Limoux's **gare SNCF**, located on the east bank of the river, a good twenty-minute walk from the old town, while **buses** (℡04.68.31.09.64) stop outside the cinema on allées de Marronniers, in the old town. The **tourist office** (July & Aug daily 9–7pm; Sept–June Mon–Fri 9–noon & 2–6pm, Sat & Sun 10am–noon & 2–5pm; ℡04.68.31.11.82, ✉limoux@fnotsi.net) is on promenade de Tivoli, just south of the main roundabout.

There is little reason to spend the night in Limoux, but should you feel obliged, the best two choices are the splendid and stately *Modern & Pigeon* (closed Wed; ℡04.68.31.00.25, ✉hotelmodernepigeon@wanadoo.fr; ❹) in place Général Leclerc, and the humbler *Des Arcades* (closed mid-Dec to mid-

Jan & Wed; ℡04.68.31.02.57, ⓦwww.logis–de–france.fr; ❷), south of the church at 96 rue St-Martin. Both are comfortable and have amenities such as TV and parking. The municipal **campsite** (℡04.68.31.13.63; mid-May to Sept) is on the east bank of the river, south of the old bridge. Limoux's **market** is held on Fridays. If you want to rent a **bike**, contact Cycles Taillefer (℡04.68.31.02.01). At St-Hilaire, the grimey *L'Abbaye* (℡04.68.699.67.23; ❶) offers rooms and generous meals (€15), though with perhaps the slowest service in France. Better accommodation can be found at the **chambres d'hôtes** at 3 avenue de Limoux (℡04.68.11.40.70; ❷).

Restaurants range from the expensive but excellent dining room of the *Modern & Pigeon* (closed Sat lunch & Mon), which has elaborate *menus* starting from €27 to €42, to the *Grand Café* at 25 place de la République, one of several on the square where you can enjoy a *menu* inside or on the sunny terrace for only €9. Otherwise, *Maison de la Blanquette*, at 46bis promenade du Tivoli, is a good place to wash down regional cuisine with the bubbly white (from €14.95), or there's *L'Hibiscus* (€13; closed Mon) Limoux's *gastronomique* restaurant at the edge of town en route to St-Polycarpe.

Alet-les-Bains

Sixteen kilometres further upstream, **ALET-LES-BAINS** is a better place than Limoux to make a stop. This ancient little village still owes its modest prosperity to the **hot springs** which bubble out of the ground on the north side of town, and which were first harnessed for curative purposes by the Romans. From the ninth century the town flourished as the site of a Benedictine abbey, and from the fourteenth as a bishopric, before declining into obscurity with the Wars of Religion. Today it is largely overlooked, a fact which helps to preserve an atmosphere of antiquity in the village, but which is also a shame, given that the quiet streets conceal some surprising relics. A seventeenth-century **bridge** still connects Alet with the Limoux–Quillan highway, and just across it loom the ruins of the **abbey of Notre-Dame** (under renovation and slated for reopening in 2004; daily: July & Aug 9am–7pm; Feb–June & Sept 10am–1pm & 2–6pm; Oct–Jan 9.30am–12.30pm & 1.30–5.30pm; €4), destroyed in 1577 during the Religious Wars and subsequently plundered to strengthen the town's walls. From here, the narrow rue de Séminaire leads back to the town's **square**, boxed in by timbered houses and the stone **Maison de Consuls**, the medieval home of the town council. Following the narrow and evocative rue de la Cadène north from the square will take you through a gate and on to a few **Roman relics**, including a scrap of ancient road. South from the square, sleepy rue de la Rose leads to another gate and a long section of twelfth-century walls. Just inside the gates, to the west, you'll find several tiny **medieval houses**, which, 800 years ago, housed merchants' families.

Practicalities

Buses passing between Limoux and Quillan will drop you on the main road by the old bridge, from where it's a short walk to the town's **tourist office** (daily: July & Aug 9am–7pm; Sept–June 10am–1pm & 2–6pm; ℡04.68.69.93.56, ⓦwww.citaenet.com/Bienvenue1.asp) in rue Nicolas Pavillon, beside the ruined abbey. Staying in Alet-les-Bains is made all the more worthwhile by its excellent **hotel**, the *Hostellerie de l'Évêché* (closed Nov–March; ℡04.68.69.90.25, ⓔclimouzy@aol.com; ❸), in a wooded garden just over the old bridge. If this is full, head for the **chambres d'hôtes** at the friendly, English-run *Maison Val d'Aleth* (℡04.68.69.90.40, ⓔmaison.valdaleth@wanadoo.fr; ●) on the same street. The town's well-equipped **campsite** (☎04.68.69.90.40; book far ahead in summer) is situated on the riverbank, further along rue Nicolas Pavillon. There are two good **restaurants** in town: *L'Évêché*'s dining room (closed Sun; *menus* €22–40), which serves high-quality regional cuisine, and *Auberge de la Main d'Argent* (closed Tues; *menu* from €16), located in a seventeenth-century house in the central place de la République.

Rennes-le-Château and Arques

There is little to detain you along the road from Alet-les-Bains to Quillan, but if you have time, it's worthwhile leaving the course of the Aude at **Couiza** for detours to the ancient abbey-town of Rennes, and the castle at Arques, east of the main highway.

RENNES-LE-CHÂTEAU (not to be confused with the nearby spa town of Rennes-les-Bains) is found at the end of a four-kilometre mountain road winding up from Couiza, with impressive views over the Aude valley. It was here that the enigmatic Bérenguer Saunière, Rennes' parish priest, died in 1917 after having lived in luxury for nearly thirty years, building himself a private villa, conservatory and library, and renovating the church in garish style. Together these sites form the **Espace Bérenguer Saunière** (daily: March–April & mid-Sept to Oct 10am–6pm; May to mid-Sept 10am–7pm, Nov–Feb 10am–5pm; €4), a site cloaked in mystery, and a magnet for treasure-seekers, occultists and crop-circle aficionados (see p.136). Entry to the **church**, a small medieval chapel built on an ancient foundation, is free, as is the pavilion beside it, which served as Saunière's office. Behind this you'll find the cemetery where he lies in eternal rest next to his "housekeeper", Marie Denardaud. The compact church is entered through the side door, above which a Latin inscription welcomes the visitor to this "terrible place" – perhaps a reference to the decor. Inside, you are greeted by a rather sinister wooden carving of a grimacing demon surmounted by four angels. The interior itself is painted in medieval style and filled with a healthy contingent of carved Baroque saints. Although to the uninitiated these may seem to be rather ordinary church furnishings, enthusiasts have uncovered a complex code in their details and arrangement, one which corresponds either to Kabbalistic theory, UFO-influence or the secret "Priory of Zion" society (depending on whom you ask).

Next door to the church is the humble farmhouse in which Saunière lived, now converted into a **museum** and containing important relics, such as the hollow late Visigothic base which once supported the church's altar and which some believe contained ancient parchments which led the priest to a buried treasure. From there you enter Saunière's spacious garden, girded by a fanciful fortified wall capped by two turrets, one of which once served as his library, while adjacent to the farmhouse sits "Béthania", a more luxurious house where he entertained guests and installed his own chapel once he had been banned from conducting the Catholic Mass. The house may seem humble now, but when you reflect on how isolated and poor the hamlet must have been in the late 1800s, it would have seemed like a palace. For more, see the box on p.136.

To reach the **donjon d'Arques** follow the D613 as it winds slowly uphill from Couiza eastwards along the course of the Orbieu. Coming into view 10km later, the perfectly preserved square **keep** (daily: March 11am–5pm; April–May 11am–6pm; June & Sept 10.30am–6.30pm; July & Aug 10am–7.30pm; Oct & Nov 11am–5.30pm; €4) is unmistakable as it rises 25m above the surrounding fields. Both the remains of the walled perimeter and the tower of this so-called Cathar castle date from after the famous Crusade, but it

Bérenguer Saunière arrived to serve as the priest in the tiny and backward hamlet of Rennes in 1885, at 33, a cranky, royalist reactionary whose political views had already earned him the ire of the Church authorities. But his exile was to take an unexpected turn. Within a few years the humble priest was renovating the tiny and ancient **parish church**, decking it with a collection of eccentric fineries bought on order in Paris. By 1891, he began buying up considerable tracts of land, the title to which he put in the name of **Marie Denardaud**. Marie, born in 1868, was the daughter of his first housekeeper in Rennes, and became his lifelong companion. In 1899, Saunière began construction work on the house and gardens of **Béthania**, as he called the smartly appointed villa which he raised next to the church. Luxurious by local standards, it was finished in 1904. Meanwhile, the *abbé* and his consort lorded it over the hamlet, on the one hand dispensing generous donations and throwing magnificent *fêtes*, and on the other maintaining an iron grip on his affairs. Such was the awe Saunière inspired that when villagers begged Marie for access to the priest's cistern to put out a fire, she refused them, rather than rouse him to get his permission.

By 1907 Saunière's activities and outspoken politics had attracted the attention of the Church authorities. He was investigated by the bishop of Carcassonne and deposed on a string of charges, ranging from abuse of power and finances to traffic of Church offices. His initial appeal failed in 1911 and, **defrocked**, he filed a second appeal to the Holy See in Rome. Meanwhile, the construction of the villa continued; banned by canon law from officiating over Mass in the church, he performed the sacraments in the stained-glass annexe built onto Béthania. On January 22, 1917, after giving his last confession, Saunière died of a heart attack and was buried in the cemetery behind the church. Marie Denardaud, much to Saunière's family's disappointment, was his only heir, and she remained faithful to her *"chér disparu"* till her end, refusing to divulge his secrets. Since her death in 1953, they have lain in adjacent graves.

The question, of course, was where Saunière's money came from. It is generally believed he stumbled upon a cache of medieval coins, perhaps after finding ancient parchments either in the hollow stone **Visigothic** altar-support, in a secret compartment in a wooden column or under a carved flagstone which sat before the altar. After his death, Marie made cryptic references to the "gold" over which the "villagers were walking", which would be enough to "support the village for a hundred years". These tales attracted the attention of a steady string of **treasure-hunters** who became so troublesome and disruptive that even today signs forbid any digging in the vicinity of the town.

The story of the treasure and the bizarre symbolism of the church's decor have spawned scores of occult theories over their origin and significance, including possible links to a secret society called the Priory of Zion, the Templars, **Solomon's treasure**, Cathars, the **Holy Grail** and a Christ who escaped crucifixion. In the last decades this has turned into a small industry and there are dozens of books written on the subject. Most are full of the kind of incoherent and self-contradictory pseudo-scientific ramblings which typify this genre. The groundbreaker was Lincoln, Baigent and Leigh's *Holy Blood, Holy Grail*; other titles include Hudson Newman's *Pathways of the Gods* and Gabriel's *The Holy Valley and the Holy Mountain*. Inevitably, this interest in the town has sparked a series of reports of other parapsychological and extra-terrestrial events in the vicinity, including a miraculous image of the Virgin and Child, discernible in a 1967 aerial photograph, UFO visitations and crop circles. With all of this, an open mind and sense of humour makes Rennes-le-Château a unique site in France and, perhaps, Europe.

is without doubt the most beautiful of the region's *château*. The central *donjon*, which dates back to the thirteenth century, is extremely well preserved, with graceful Gothic vaulting sustaining two of its great chambers and a number of ogival (pointed-arch) windows dating from the period of its original construction. The third-floor hall is dominated by an impressively huge fireplace, while the walls, which were constructed in the following century, are breached by a simple gate and buttressed by a square guard tower on the southwest corner. Outside, there's a group of beehives clustered just to the side of the entrance, where you can buy fresh honey.

Arques

The village of **ARQUES** is about 1500m east of the castle – a nondescript little hamlet, which has a fourteenth-century church, some contemporary buildings and a small and dull exhibit on Catharism housed in the **Maison de Déodat Roché** (daily: March 11.30am–5.30pm; April, May & Oct to mid-Nov 11.30am–6pm; June & Sept 11am–6pm; July & Aug 10.30am–8pm; free with castle ticket), the home of the Freemason and pioneering nineteenth-century historian of Catharism. From Arques the road continues (no public transport) through ever more untamed and isolated terrain towards the castles at Termes and Villerouge-Termenès (see p.316), and the abbey-town of Lagrasse (see p.317), a route very much worthwhile exploring either by car or bicycle. Returning to Couiza and following the Aude towards Quillan, you'll run the gauntlet of a series of dubious museums, none of which is particularly worth the effort to see.

Practicalities

If you have no transport, you can reach Rennes and Arques by **taxi** from Couiza (☎04.68.74.25.36), although, if you are up to it, the demanding uphill walk can be enjoyable. Cycling to Arques is another option – Au Fil de l'Aude (☎04.68.74.16.69) in Couiza rents **bikes**. You won't find a **hotel** in Rennes, but you can stay at the **chambres d'hôtes** (☎04.68.74.22.49, ✉ esper-azareservations@hotmail.com; ❹) in the village, or at the luxurious *Château des Ducs* (☎04.68.74.04.20, ⓦwww.chateau-des-ducs.com; ❺) in Couiza. For further information, contact the **tourist office** in Rennes (daily: mid-June to mid-Sept 10am–7pm; mid-Sept to mid-June 10am–5.30pm; ☎04.68.74.72.68, ⓦwww.rennes-le-chateau.org).

In Arques, there's a **B&B** (☎04.68.69.82.74; ❷ English spoken) in the town's old smithy at 19 route des Corbières, and you'll find **campsites** at both Arques (☎04.68.69.88.30, ✉ark19@libertysurf.fr; Feb–Oct) and Rennes (☎04.68.74.09.32; mid-April to Oct). Good *terroir* **restaurants** are scattered throughout the area, the best being the *Château des Ducs de Joyeuse* in Couiza, which sometimes has a dinner-theatre show (closed Sun & Mon eve, & mid-Nov to March; *menu* from €27); *Jardins de l'Abbé* in Rennes with live music on Friday evenings (closed Sun & Mon lunch & Nov–April; ☎04.68.74.31.16; from €19); and *Auberge du Moulin d'Arques* in Arques (closed Sun & Mon, Jan–March; from €15).

Quillan

Clustered on the west bank of the Aude about halfway along its course, **QUILLAN** is a half-heartedly industrialized place with a number of services, its main attraction being its proximity to the pays de Sault (see p.141), plus the river itself, a sturdy torrent running right past the town providing ample canoeing and rafting possibilities (see below). The only monument of interest is the ruined **castle**, on the east bank of the Aude just across the *pont vieux*. Built on the site of a Visigothic fortress, it was burned by the Huguenots in 1575 during the course of the Religious Wars and partly dismantled in the eighteenth century, but the remnants are still worth a scramble.

The **gare SNCF** and **gare routière** are both central, on boulevard Charles-de-Gaulle. The **tourist office** occupies a prominent kiosk beside the train station (summer Mon–Sat 8am–noon & 2–7pm, Sun 9am–noon; ☎04.68.20.07.78, Ⓦwww.ville-quillan.com), and can help with Grotte de l'Aguzou reservations (see below), among other things. Opposite, you'll find the least expensive **hotel** in town, *Le Terminus*, at no. 45 (☎04.68.20.94.67, Ⓕ04.68.20.93.33; ❷) – indeed all accommodation is on this same, noisy street, which doubles as the D117. You won't get much more peace and quiet, but you will get more comfort for scarcely more money at the *Cartier*, at no. 31 (closed mid-Dec to mid-March; ☎04.68.20.05.14, Ⓔhotel.cartier @wanadoo.fr; ❷) or the *Canal* at no. 36 (☎04.68.20.08.62, Ⓦwww.logis-de-france.com; ❷). All have attached **restaurants** (*menus* €11–14), though the *Canal*'s shuts on Sunday evening and Monday. The Centre International de Séjour Sports et Nature, at the southern edge of town en route to Axat, has a **gîte d'étape** (☎04.68.20.33.69; ❶), and organizes **canoeing** and **rafting**, as well as climbing and canyoning trips. *La Sapinette* (☎04.68.20.13.52; March–Oct) at 21 rue René-Delpech, off boulevard Jean Bourrel, is the closer and better equipped of two **campsites**. You can rent **bikes** from Cycles Benassis (☎04.68.20.18.91). The town's produce **market** is held on Wednesdays (8am–4pm).

South from Quillan

The road **south from Quillan** provides a fabulous approach to the eastern peaks of the Pyrenees. Coursing down from the Capcir plateau, the Aude has cut successively through granite, gneiss and schist, and finally soft limestone, carving spectacular **caves** (*grottes*) and ever deeper **gorges** along the way. Public transport here is limited to a summer **bus** service to Quérigut, 44km south of Quillan. There's a map of the region on pp.142–143.

Défilé de Pierre-Lys and Axat

Gorge country begins almost immediately after you leave Quillan heading south, with rock overhangs blasted as necessary to allow passage. The narrowest section is the cliff-lined **Défilé de Pierre-Lys**, 8km to the south, where climbers can usually be seen swinging above the road. Four kilometres beyond the *défilé*, there's a **campsite**, *Le Moulin du Pont d'Aliès* (April–Nov), plus canteen, at the crossroads of the same name, the junction where the D117 highway peels off east towards the Fenouillèdes.

Continuing south 1km beyond the crossroads on the D618 brings you to **AXAT**, where an old bridge, under which rafters often put in, links the through-road district with the east-bank quarter. There's just one **hotel** here, the grubby *Auberge La Petite Ourse* (closed part Sept; ☎04.68.20.59.20; ❹), at 16 route National, the main street.

Grotte de l'Aguzou

A visit to the **Grotte de l'Aguzou**, 15km southwest of Axat towards the upstream end of the Gorges de l'Aude, provides a unique opportunity to get an in-depth and personal look at one of the region's famous caves. The guided tour of this magnificent complex is as close as a non-speleologist can get to

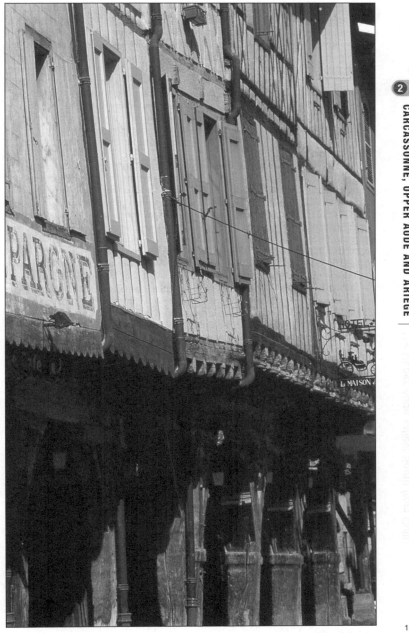

▲ Mirepoix facades

the real thing and is very popular, so book well in advance (contact Philippe Moreno; €50 full day, €30 half-day; ☎04.68.20.45.38, ✉grotte.aguzou @wanadoo.fr). Equipped with overalls, helmet and lamp, groups of four to ten people are taken into the unlit cave system at 9am, to be conducted through the *grandes salles* of stalactites, stalagmites, columns and draperies, some of which are 20m high. Lunch (you bring your own) is taken 600m underground, and then it's on to the so-called "gardens of crystals" – a fantastic array of forms and shapes, some growing from the rock in long, thin needles, or like pine cones dusted by hoar frost, and others clear and convoluted like a Venetian glass-blower's accident. The best place to **stay** for an early start is the designated *camping sauvage* area by the river, 300m from the cave entrance.

The Donezan

In the twelfth century the **Donezan** region, and its then capital Usson – in the southern neck of the Gorges de l'Aude – became a sort of forerunner to Andorra: separated from the rest of Ariège by the **Col de Pailhères** (2001m), it was granted special financial privileges on account of its inaccessibility. Today **USSON**, like the rest of this remote region of seven villages, houses barely enough people to function as a *canton*; the spa of Usson-les-Bains 1km downstream is boarded up and for sale, while the dry-stone walls around the fields are as dilapidated as the **château** (Feb–April & Nov–Dec hols only 2–6pm; May–June Sat, Sun & hols 1–6pm; July & Aug daily 10am–1pm & 3–7pm; most Sept daily 2–6pm; late Sept to mid-Oct Sat & Sun 2–6pm; closed Christmas hols; €4.70), which was the first place of safety for the four Cathars who escaped the massacre at Montségur (see box on p.146). Dating back to at least the eleventh century, the castle, between the thirteenth and sixteenth centuries, marked the eastern boundary of the possessions of the counts of Foix, once champions of the Cathars and resolutely hostile to the French Crown.

Just above Usson, 3km along the D25 to Ax-les-Thermes, **MIJANÈS** is an immensely attractive stone-built village, where you can **stay and eat** year-round at the simple but perfectly adequate *Relais de Pailhères* (☎04.68.20.46.97; ❷), which has well-sized, wooden-floored rooms. This is the only such facility between Quillan and Quérigut, with people coming from some distance away to patronize it, so reservations are advisable at weekends. When there's good snow the nearby **ski station** of Mijanès-Latrabe (☎05.61.20.41.37) opens, but this is not so frequent, given that the lifts only reach an altitude of 2060m. There are also cross-country trails here. For more information on the area, see Ⓦwww.donezan.com.

These days, **QUÉRIGUT**, 7km south of Usson, is the capital of the region. It stands at the head of a slope of neglected terraces, notable only for the stump of the **Château de Donezan**, the last stronghold of the Cathar leadership, who held out here for eleven years after the fall of Montségur. Quérigut makes a good walking base for jaunts southwest through the forest; **accommodation** is either at the ageing *Hôtel le Donezan* (☎04.68.20.42.40, Ⓦwww.hotel-donezan.com; ❷), uphill from the church opposite the fountain (which also has the only **restaurant**), or at the *Auberge du Cabanas* **gîte** (☎04.68.20.47.03; ❶). There is also a **campsite**, *Le Bousquet*, down by the stream below the village. Usson and Quérigut can be reached in about an hour on Monday, Wednesday and Friday afternoons by Petit Charles **bus** from Quillan, making the return trip the same day.

The Pays de Sault

The magnificent **PAYS DE SAULT** – the upland area more or less bounded by the rivers Aude and Ariège and, to the north, the main road from Quillan to Foix – is pure Cathar territory, as evinced by its most famous sight, the cliff-top stronghold of **Montségur**. For visitors it also offers some of Languedoc's most outstanding scenery; the vast highlands are composed primarily of limestone, and thus riddled with caves and ravines like the spectacular **Gorges de la Frau**. Above ground, the region's agricultural methods seem to have changed little since Cathar times – pesticides have yet to infiltrate the region's ecosystem, so the silhouettes of birds of prey can often be seen.

There are various ways to explore the *pays*. The only public transport consists of two regular **bus** services, both of which take you just part of the way to Montségur: the first runs along the region's northern perimeter, linking the train station in Quillan with that in Foix, via **Puivert** and **Lavelanet**; the other runs along the central plateau southwest from Quillan via Belcaire and Camurac to **Comus**, from where you can walk to Montségur via the Gorges de la Frau. Because departures are slightly more frequent from the east, the two routes to the castle described below approach from Quillan.

This is an excellent **hiking** region, which can be crossed in a few days, making occasional use of the sporadic public transport. A network of walking itineraries – the "Tour du Pays de Sault", the "Tour du Massif de Tabe", the "Piémont" and the GR107, plus forestry tracks – provide various routes, but the most popular is the "**Sentier Cathare**". This is best picked up at Foix and arrives at Montségur in two stages via Roquefixade (see p.147), then continues on to the Mediterranean, taking advantage of the descent towards the sea, via Puivert; it's easy walking much of the year (avoid mid-winter and mid-summer), with strategically placed accommodation in *gîtes d'étape*.

Much of the Pays de Sault is a spacious agricultural plateau, but it contains more vertiginous terrain, too. At the southeastern edge, the dramatic D107 road from Axat to Ax-les-Thermes runs through the **Rebenty** and **Joucou** gorges and over the **Col du Pradel** (1673m), a tough but wonderful **cycling** route. Another possible activity in the uplands is **skiing**, although neither of the region's downhill ski stations is worth much effort: the Monts d'Olmes resort, southwest of Montségur, is crowned with a seedy apartment development, while the one at Camurac comprises a "village" of decaying chalets – and both have impossibly low top-lifts of only 1940m. There is, however, good **cross-country skiing** on the plateau, with a small rental and tuition operation at Comus and especially good terrain at the **Col de Marmare**.

Puivert

Although it's just a twenty-minute drive out of Quillan, the countryside around **PUIVERT** feels quite different, a vast upland planted with corn and sunflowers, buzzed by amateur pilots using the small local airport. The village itself offers all amenities, including a **gîte d'étape** just opposite the castle (☎04.68.11.40.70, ℗04.68.11.40.72; ❶, rooms ❸) and the *terroir* **restaurant** *Dame Blanche*. Less than a kilometre south of the village is a small lake – more a large pond really – with a **campsite** (☎04.68.20.00.58; May–Sept) and swimming area (Tues–Sun), a welcome sight whether you've been cycling, driving or hiking.

Puivert's **château** (daily: April–Sept 8am–8pm; Oct–March 10am–5pm; €4), standing alone like a child's cardboard cutout atop a gently rounded hill a

THE DONEZAN, PAYS DE SAULT & UPPER ARIÈGE

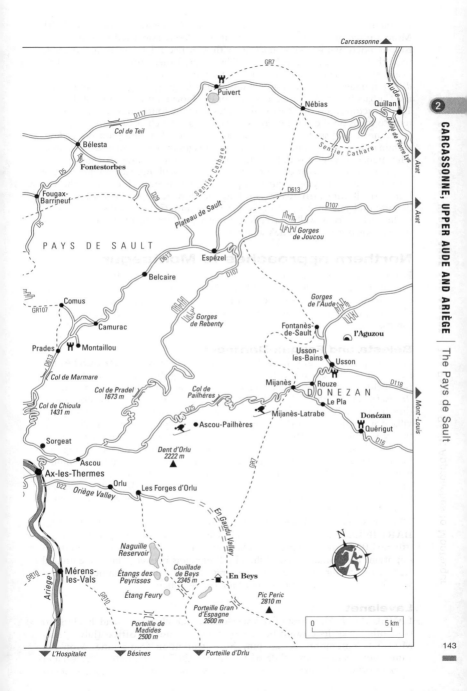

Carcassonne

GR7

Puivert

Nébias

Quillan

D117

Col de Teil

Aude

Défilé de Pierre Lys

Bélesta

Axat

Fontestorbes

Sentier Cathare

Fougax-
Barrineuf

D5

D79

D613

Sentier Cathare

D107

Plateau de Sault

Gorges
de Joucou

PAYS DE SAULT

D613

Espézel

Belcaire

D107

Comus

GR107

Gorges
de Rebenty

Gorges
de l'Aude

Camurac

Fontanès-
de-Sault

l'Aguzou

Prades

Montaillou

D613

Usson-
les-Bains

Usson

Col de Marmare

Col de Pradel
1673 m

Col de
Pailhères

Mijanès

Rouze

D118

DONEZAN

Col de Chioula
1431 m

D25

Mijanès-Latrabe

Le Pla

Mont-Louis

Donézan

Ascou-Pailhères

Quérigut

Sorgeat

D16

Dent d'Orlu
2222 m

GR7

Ascou

Ax-les-Thermes

Orlu

Les Forges d'Orlu

D22

Oriège Valley

En Gaudu Valley

N

Naguille
Reservoir

Mérens-
les-Vals

GR10

Ariège

Étangs des
Peyrisses

Couillade
de Beys
2345 m

En Beys

Pic Peric
2810 m

Étang Feury

GR10

Porteille Gran
d'Espagne
2600 m

Porteille de
Madides
2500 m

0   5 km

L'Hospitalet

Bésines

Porteille d'Orlu

kilometre or so east of the village, fell to the Albigensian Crusade in 1210. More a place of culture than of arms, it was closely associated with the troubadour poets, whose preoccupation with romance might seem incompatible with the asceticism of the Cathars. What united them was the Occitan language, then spoken all across southern France. For the troubadours the *langue d'Oc* ("tongue of Oc") was simply the natural language of poetry and love; for the Cathars it expressed their defiance of the North. Little remains of the pre-1210 structure; most of what's visible dates from the fourteenth century. Visitors tend to focus on the various floors of the *donjon*; the chapel features vigil seats at the north and south windows, a wall font and rib-vaulting on the ceiling, culminating in a keystone embossed with images of the Virgin and St George. The highest chamber is dubbed the "musicians' room" after its eight *culs-de-lamps* or torch sockets at the termini of more rib-vaulting, each sculpted in the form of a figure playing a different period instrument. Back down in the village a small **museum** (daily: April to mid-July & Sept 10am–12.30pm & 2–6pm; mid-July to Aug 10am–7pm; Oct 2–5pm; €4) holds displays of local traditional crafts as well as a collection of reproductions of medieval instruments copied from the castle's sculptures.

Northern approaches to Montségur

From Puivert the road heads west over the Col de Teil, the Pyrenean watershed: east of it, rivers flow to the Mediterranean, while on the west they empty into the Atlantic. You can **walk** from Puivert to Montségur along the "Sentier Cathare", a long but not difficult day of some 25km, mostly through dense fir forests.

Bélesta and Fougax-Barrineuf

A better place to begin the walk, however, is 11km west at **BÉLESTA**, the next stop on the bus route. It's a far more manageable village than Lavelanet (see below), and if you get stranded there's **accommodation** at the *Le Troubador*, on the through road (☎05.61.01.60.57; ❶), which also does meals (lunch from €10.50, dinner from €15), and **camping** on the east side of the village at *Le Val d'Amour* (June–Sept). Attractions begin almost immediately on the way south: some 1500m out of Bélesta, the route to Montségur passes Fontestorbes, an artesian spring (*source intermittente*) under a rock overhang that in summer spurts water for six-minute periods evenly separated by 32-minute pauses (in winter the water flows continuously). From the *source* you can continue directly to Montségur by walking along various marked GRs – roughly a three-hour trip, or taking a longer detour via the Gorges de la Frau, 8km south (see opposite).

The most direct approaches pass through the double village of **FOUGAX-BARRINEUF**, 2km southwest, which offers a fine **restaurant**, *Les Cinq Fours* (☎05.61.01.68.04), occupying an old bone-comb factory (this was formerly an important local industry, established by Protestants between the sixteenth and eighteenth centuries). The portions aren't huge, but they suffice, and the €12.50 *menu* is quite adequate as a four-course lunch.

Lavelanet

LAVELANET, 8km west of Bélesta along the Quillan–Foix road, has little to offer other than its onward bus connections, its **tourist office** (July & Aug Mon–Sat 9am–noon & 2–7pm, Sun 9am–noon; Sept–June Mon–Sat 9am–noon & 2–7pm; ☎05.61.01.22.20, ❶05.61.03.06.69, ✉lavelanet .tourisme@wanadoo.fr) on the central *rond point* and the clean, modern campsite *Camping de Lavelanet* (April–Sept; ☎05.61.01.55.54) southwest of the centre. There's no reason to stay here, but if you do the only **hotels**, the *Parc* (☎05.61.03.04.05, ✉hotel.parc@libertysurf.fr; ❷), on the road out to Bélesta, and the *Espagne*, on the road to Foix (☎05.61.01.00.78; ❷), are adequate. On the other hand, if you have transport and a healthy budget, head 2km south to Villeneuve d'Olmes, where you'll find the luxurious *Le Castrum* (☎05.61.01.35.24, ⓦwww.lecastrum.com; ❻), a small luxury hotel with one of the region's best restaurants (from €35). Lavelanet's **gîte**, *Gréoulou* (☎05.61.01.36.81; ❶), is open year-round. The town's main **market** is held on Friday, but there is also a smaller one on Wednesdays. Further information on this region, including detailed itineraries for numerous walking, cycling and riding trails can be found at ⓦwww.paysdolmes.org; alternatively the tourist office sells a small "rando guide" (€2).

The southern approach to Montségur via Comus

From Monday to Friday there are two late-afternoon buses daily from Quillan to Comus, about 40km southwest. You may, however, want to alight slightly earlier at Camurac, 3km short of Comus, and walk the rest of the way via **MONTAILLOU** village, a detour which takes about two hours. Montaillou subscribed to the Cathar heresy long after the fall of Montségur, until the Inquisition, directed by the bishop of Pamiers, set to work here during the 1320s. The records compiled by the inquisitors were so precise that historian Emmanuel Le Roy Ladurie was able to recreate every aspect of the villagers' lives from them, from the minutiae of domestic economics to the details of their sexual habits, in his book, *Montaillou*. Fewer than twenty people live here permanently now, all of them descendants of the Cathars, as you can see by comparing their surnames with those on the headstones in the ancient graveyard. **CAMURAC** has a **gîte**, *Auberge du Pays de Sault* (☎04.68.20.32.09; ❷), as well as a **campiste**, *les Sapins*.

COMUS isn't a lot bigger than Montaillou, but does have an excellent **gîte d'étape** (☎04.68.20.33.69, ⓦwww.gites-comus-com; ❶) attached to the Centre École Pleine Nature, which specializes in **caving**, the limestone hereabouts being peppered with two hundred known caves. Montségur is 13km away, through the **Gorges de la Frau**. From Comus take the GR107 (formerly the GR7B) which drops down as a mule track between fields to a wide gorge that suddenly becomes a *défilé*, where thousand-metre-high cliffs admit the sun only during the early afternoon. When the gorge widens again, you meet the dead end of the D5 coming south from Bélesta and Fougax-Barrineuf. There are two ways of continuing to Montségur: either along the Sentier Cathare westwards, wrapped in tree shade alongside a stream (turn off at the first farm, 45min along the D5), or via a bridle trail beginning about an hour along the tarmac, offering higher, more open ground. Either way, walking time from Comus is four hours.

Montségur

The ruined castle of **MONTSÉGUR** lives up to the promise of its distant view, its plain stone walls poised emphatically above the straggling, namesake village on a 1207-metre-high *pog* (a local variant on the Occitan *puèg*, or "hill"). The original fortifications were built by Guillaume "Short-Nose", duke of Aquitaine, but between 1204 and 1232 it was reconstructed as a bastion of the Cathars under the direction of Guilhabert de Castres, leader of the sect.

The lost treasure of Montségur

In the 1230s and 1240s, having been subdued by the Albigensian Crusaders, low-land Languedoc was in the grips of the Inquisition, which travelled from town to town, mercilessly rooting out and eliminating any remaining Cathar elements. The remaining heretic forces had gathered at **Montségur**, an isolated redoubt, which up to that point had proved beyond the reach of the French King (later Saint) Louis. In 1242, however, a band of Cathar warriors struck out from the castle and attacked and killed a party of Dominican Inquisitors at **Avignonet-Lauragais** (see p.111), sparking a series of rebellions across the region. The royal response was swift. A massive force was raised for an expedition to impose a **final solution** on the unrepentant heretics, holed up in their "synagogue of Satan".

The **siege** of the castle began in May 1243. Inside, the defenders, 150 knights led by Pierre-Roger of Mirepoix and several hundred Cathars endured eight months of siege and bombardment, before Pierre-Roger negotiated a clemency agreement in exchange for surrender. But the Cathar faithful would not betray their cause and, as a result, when the castle was opened to the French forces, some 225 were led out to a field below the fort and **burnt alive**. A few of the survivors managed to make it to Quéribus (see p.355).

A handful of *perfecti* (see p.149) slipped out of the encirclement during the negotiations and, legend has it, they carried some sort of collection of valuables with them. Within time the story of the **"lost treasure"** of the Cathars grew, and by the time that Berenguer Saunière was living it up in Rennes (see p.136), the legend of Montségur had become tangled up with the usual occultist notions as well as quasi-historical associations with the **Holy Grail** and the **Templars**. In the 1930s, Otto Rahn, a Grail and Cathar enthusiast and quack historian, brought the legend's attention to the Nazi authorities in Germany; for their deluded ideologues the treasure offered a mystical link to the supposedly Aryan Visigoths who overran Rome and Languedoc in the fifth century. **Himmler** took a personal interest in the case and supported the investigations. Like the treasure at Rennes, that of Montségur has encouraged a small army of "experts" to publish a slough of dubious books on the subject which has fuelled the aspirations of treasure-hunters. For a more credible look at the legend, see Markale's *Montségur and the Mystery of the Cathars* (see "Books" in Contexts), which attempts to weigh objectively the evidence for the existence and nature of the Cathar treasure.

Drastically eroded into naked vertical faces and gullies, the *pog* would have been a formidable defence. Only on the western side is it possible to walk up to the summit (about 30min), through what is now called the *prat dels cremats*, where the surviving Cathars were burned to death after the castle fell (a stone memorial pays tribute to them); see the box above.

The beauty of **the site** (daily: Feb 10.30am–4pm; March 10am–5pm; April & Sept–Oct 9.30am–6pm; May–Aug 9am–7.30pm; Nov 10am–5.30pm; Dec 10.30am–4.30pm; €3.50) is what hits you first; the original walls were reduced by half after the siege, and all internal structures are gone except the simple keep, now open to the sky. Then you begin to wonder how that last Cathar community of five hundred people could have held out so long in such a small space. Even given that some lived in now-vanished houses at the foot of the walls on the north and west faces, there was still a sizeable garrison to be accommodated, together with the *faydits* – local aristocrats dispossessed by the crusade against Catharism. What's left of the castle takes no more than a few minutes to explore – rather disappointingly, you're no longer allowed to climb up on the walls, merely to traverse the keep to visit the west *donjon* – but it isn't so much what you see at Montségur that makes the trip unforgettable, as what your imagination can recreate from its remnants.

Down in the village, 1km below, a one-room **archeological museum** (daily: Feb & Nov 2–4.30pm; March & Oct 2–5pm; May 10.30am–12.30pm & 2–7pm; June–Aug 10am–12.30pm & 2–7.30pm; Oct 2–6pm; free) displays artefacts excavated since the 1950s from the original village up beside the walls, from both pre- and post-Cathar periods – mostly food bones, personal effects, tools and surviving fragments of houses.

Practicalities

Despite its small size, tourist numbers at Montségur village have prompted a **tourist office** (July–Sept daily 10am–1pm & 2–6pm; ☎ & ℱ 05.61.03 .03.03, ⓦ www.citaenet.com/montsegur), of most use for information on the precise route of the GR107. If you'd like to stay the night – and the beautiful scenery certainly encourages the notion – there are a couple of **hotels**: the old-fashioned *Couquet* (☎ 05.61.01.10.28; ❶), a rambling country pension of wood-furnished rooms with wash-basins; and the adjacent, en-suite *Costes* (☎ 05.61.01.10.24, ⓦ www.logis-de-france.fr; ❷), just uphill, which also manages the nearby **gîte d'étape** (April to mid-Nov; ☎ 05.61.01.10.24, ⓔ gites-defrance/aude@wanadoo.fr ❶). The closest **campsite** (tents only) is the *Point Acceuil Jeunes* (☎ 05.61.01.10.27), at the lower end of the village on the Bélesta side. The *Costes* has a reasonably priced **restaurant** attached, featuring game and *Ariègeois terroir*, and *L'Occidadelle* specializes in fire-cooked *foie* sausages and local trout (from €15; closed Fri).

Roquefixade

Approximately 8km west of Lavelanet, the village of Nalzen is the best point along the D117 for access to **ROQUEFIXADE**, westernmost of the Cathar castles and last stop on the "Sentier Cathare" before Foix. A two-kilometre side road leads up to the eponymous village, refounded after the Albigensian Crusade as a *bastide*. From the high end of the village it's a twenty-minute climb to the unenclosed castle (free), which takes its name (originally *roca fissada*) from the vast natural fissures augmenting its defences. Perched at the western end of a long ridge, it's bigger than it appears from below but utterly ruined; your main reward is the view over the valley below with its clustered villages, and south – weather permitting – to the high Pyrenean ridge. A **gîte d'étape** (☎ 05.61.03.01.36, ⓔ roquefixade@mail.dotcom.fr; ❶) stands by the base of the path up to the castle, and their outdoor seating is a good place for a drink after the climb; they only have twelve places, so let them know in good time if you wish to stay. Alternative accommodation if they're full is the small inn, *Relais des Pogs* (☎ 05.61.01.14.50, ⓦ perso.wanadoo.fr/gite-relais-des-pogs; ❷ or gîte ❶).

Mirepoix and the lower Ariège valley

The lower part of the Ariège valley winds a leisurely course through a broad, rolling upland, whose rich dairy and wheat farms set it apart from the dry, vine-dominated scrub of most of Languedoc and Roussillon. The plain adjacent to this part of the river, centred on **Mirepoix**, was, like its southern counterpart the pays de Sault, a land of Cathars and castles; today it is home to a series of surprising and unique medieval **monuments**. Along the river proper you'll pass through unprepossessing **Pamiers** to **Foix**. Head of Ariège, France's smallest *département*, Foix was once the capital of a proudly independent principality, whose ambitions of independence were as strong and as fruitless as those of Toulouse county. Today the only testament to this is the town's strikingly positioned castle.

Mirepoix and around

The village of **MIREPOIX**, tucked away amongst the undulating hills of the Hers valley, is one of the region's best-kept secrets. And little wonder, as its only transport connection is made up of four daily buses running each way between Pamiers to the west and Lavelanet to the south. Without a car it would take a day's cycling to cover the 48km from Carcassonne, or a lengthy 30-kilometre trek along the GR7 from Villepinte (near Castelnaudary), via Fanjeux.

Mirepoix was a Cathar stronghold which paid dearly for its heresy, suffering a massacre at the hands of the Catholic Crusaders; but this in fact was only the beginning of its misfortunes, as a generation later it was all but destroyed by a flood. The present town dates back to 1290, when the noble Jean de Lévis laid out a new *bastide* in a safer location. At the centre of the village sits the broad place Général-Leclerc (or place de Couverts), arguably the most beautiful town **square** west of the Rhône. Almost the entire perimeter is rimmed by broad arcades supported by stout old beams, above which rise two storeys of pastel timber-frame houses. Although the *place* as a whole is beautiful, its star attraction is the fourteenth-century **Maison des Consuls** (now a hotel, see p.150) in the centre of the north side, at no. 6. This old council-house, courthouse and prison dates back to the fourteenth century and is decorated by nearly 150 **wooden heads**, carved in high relief at the ends of the beams supporting the second storey. Each carving is individual, the portraits ranging across the gamut of medieval social classes and professions and including exotic and foreign peoples (including some very early portrayals of black Africans), as well as demons, monsters, animals and assorted grotesques. They make a singular masterwork.

By passing through an attractive nineteenth-century wrought-iron **market hall** on the south side of the square, you arrive at another arcaded *place*, Philip de Lévis – not as stunning as its larger counterpart, but also impressive. In the middle stands the fourteenth-century **cathedral of St-Maurice** (Mon–Sat 9am–noon & 2–6pm), whose broad single nave is the widest of any Gothic-style church in France. Local lore attributes the absence of supporting columns to the clergy's desire to monitor parishioners, checking that they were not carrying out forbidden Cathar practices, but this is doubtful given that the cathedral was not consecrated until 1509. The interior itself has suffered a rather excessive Baroque renovation, but the massive pipe organ and large carved gallery are impressive.

Aside from a small thirteenth-century **gate** and a section of the old town wall a few metres west of place Leclerc, all of the town's sights are grouped around the two squares. There is little else to do, but the beauty of the town makes it the perfect spot to relax on a terrace, have a drink and soak up the atmosphere. On Monday mornings both of the *places* fill with the **market** stalls of local farmers – an excellent opportunity to prepare a picnic lunch.

Practicalities

Buses passing through Mirepoix stop within sight of the cathedral, and it's a short walk from there to the **tourist office** (Mon–Sat 9am–noon & 2–6pm; ☏05.61.68.83.76, ⓦwww.ot-mirepoix.fr), located in the only modern building on place Leclerc.

2

Catharism

In the twelfth century the **Catholic Church** in Western Europe was lagging behind the times; geared towards a rural society, it was unequipped to deal with the social and religious problems which the rise of town life posed. This was also the time that the Church began to develop as a wealthy international organization, a fact which encouraged **corruption** among the clergy. Frustrated, the increasingly literate public sought salvation and religious satisfaction in **new beliefs**, qualified by the official Church as heresies.

The most successful of these was **Catharism**. Derived from the Greek *kataros*, or "pure", Cathar beliefs were probably carried to Western Europe by returning **Crusaders**, who had picked them up in the East, where they ultimately derived from Manichean tenets (originally from Persia) and related to the Bogomil Church of the Balkans. Unlike Catholics, Cathars were **Dualists**, for whom good (spirit) and evil (material) were two equal forces locked in a cosmic struggle. There was a strong accent on **asceticism**, of denying the evil of the material world. Thus Cathar believers were presided over by an elite of **perfecti** (or *parfaits*) who led a frugal monk-like existence and eschewed sex and meat (the product of sexual intercourse). When close to death, believers would endeavour to undertake the *consolamentum*, the ceremony which transformed them into *perfecti*, so they could die pure and liberate themselves from the world of matter. Cathars were Christians, but only of a sort – they considered Jesus to have been an angel, and adapted the Bible to suit their own beliefs.

The sect was immensely successful and spread rapidly throughout urbanized northern France and the Low Countries – as early as 1022 thirteen Cathars were burnt in Orleans. Italy, Spain and, of course, Languedoc all become important centres for the religion. By the 1140s, Cathars, some of whom were renegade bishops, had begun to organize a formal Church. In **Languedoc** Catharism was welcomed by a number of different groups, not only the urban tradesmen who favoured it in the north. Here it also appealed to the regional nobility, who resented the papacy's political expansion and feared a Church-backed takeover by the French Crown. Finally, it carried a broad appeal even among peasants because of the charisma of the preaching *perfecti* and the realistic-seeming Cathar cosmology, which seemed to reflect the world they knew. Thus, Cathar beliefs came to be fused with Occitan identity, and although it was not a phenomenon which was unique to southwest France, it came to be associated ever more strongly with Languedoc.

By 1200 the Church could no longer ignore the threat posed by this rival religion. Pope Innocent III (1198–1216) undertook a series of initiatives, including sanctioning the Church's own wandering *perfecti*, the Dominicans and Franciscans, and mounting a concerted military campaign, the **Albigensian Crusade** (see box on p.329), with the aid of the northern French nobility, led by the brutal **Simon de Montfort**. Within half a century Catharism was extinguished as a political force in Languedoc and, with it, the native Occitan nobility. The final military confrontation, at **Montségur** in 1244, ended in a mass execution of several hundred Cathar adherents. Over the following century and a half the **Inquisition** (see box on p.102) struggled to ferret out the remaining heretics. The last **burning** would take place at Pamiers in 1321, and in 1412 an isolated community of Cathars was discovered in the village of Montaillou (see p.145) and prosecuted by an inquisition led by the bishop of Foix. By then Languedoc was French and the Church was secure, but only for the moment – within a little over a century the power of Rome and Paris would be once again challenged by rebels expressing their political discontent through religion, the **Huguenots**. Recently Catharism has enjoyed a revival in the popular imagination as a pole of regional identity for disgruntled Languedocians and a lucrative marketing tactic for modern tourist boards.

CARCASSONNE, UPPER AUDE AND ARIÈGE | Mirepoix and the lower Ariège valley

There are two **hotels** to choose from. Unless you're on a strict budget, try not to pass up a night in the gorgeous *Maison des Consuls* (T05.61.68.81.81, Epyrene@afatvoyages.fr; ❹–❺). The *Commerce*, in cours Docteur Chabaud (closed Jan, part Nov & Sat Sept–June; T05.61.68.10.29, Wwww.logis-de-france.com; ❸), pleasant and well maintained though it is, simply cannot compete. A better option is the **chambres d'hôtes** *Le Patio* (T06.12.21.51.65; ❷) in a fourteenth-century house at 32 place de Couverts. There is also a municipal **campsite** (mid-June to mid-Sept; T05.61.68.84.90).

Mirepoix features a number of **restaurants**, the best of which are the *Porte d'Aval* on cours Maréchal de Mirepoix (closed Mon; T05.61.68.19.19), and *La Flambée* at 27 rue Porte d'Amont (closed Sun eve & Mon; T05.61.68.16.59), both of which are in the €15-and-up range and specialize in cassoulet and dishes based on locally raised beef. Another good choice is *Les Remparts* on 6 cours Louis Pons (T05.61.68.12.15), which has a medieval dining room and features *terroir* specialities from €10.67. On the main square, *Le Cantegril* at no. 25 (closed Wed out of season) has cassoulet and foie gras (from €11), and *Café-Crème* (closed Tues) at no. 32, is the good economy choice (*menus* from €8). Further, at the east end of the same *place*, are two surprisingly hip-looking **cafés**: stylish *Castignolles* and *Atmospher*, which brings in a younger crowd.

Fanjeux

Halfway between Mirepoix and Carcassonne, tiny **FANJEUX** is a town which has fallen from medieval glory into virtual obscurity. Once the capital of Occitan troubadours, it was here that the *jocs florals* ("floral games"), a competition of Occitan poetry and song in which the winners were awarded gilded flowers for their efforts, were first held in 1323 (see p.414). In 1206, St Dominic de Gúzman passed through town and, contemplating the horizon from the town's belvedere, saw a series of miraculous fireballs. Inspired by this divine meteorological phenomenon he founded a convent at nearby Prouille, the precursor of his communities of preaching friars, the **Dominicans**. Nowadays, not even the buses stop in Fanjeux; the streets are quiet, and the various vestiges of its medieval splendour, the old Dominican headquarters and the town's church, moulder away unvisited except by groups of nuns on field trips. The one day it does come to life is August 16, when a medieval-style procession is held. If you are intent on exploring the town, there is an **information office** (Mon–Fri 10.30am–12.30pm & 3–7pm; Efanjeux-brammontreal@fnotsi.net) in the *mairie* which may be able to get you access to the monuments (the tourist office on the main road below the old town remains closed at time of writing). And if you're passing through on the GR7, you might want to stay the night in any of a number of sporadically open **chambres d'hôtes**, including the Dominican convent (T04.68.24.70.16), or grab a meal in the town's **restaurant**, *La Table Cathare* (closed Sun & Mon), on the way out of town on the road to Mirepoix. The local **campsite**, *Les Bruges* (T04.68.24.70.26) is open June to September.

South to Camon

The hamlet of **CAMON**, 13km southeast of Mirepoix along the GR7, makes for a more rewarding stop than Fanjeux, and one which can be visited on a one-day walking trek from Mirepoix. Taking up the trail by the small bridge across the River Hers just east of Mirepoix's main roundabout, you'll walk along the well-marked trail over gentle, hilly farmland for 8km, until you reach **Lagarde**. There is a dramatic-looking ruin here, an ancient **château** (private and closed to visitors) whose empty window-frames set in broken walls romantically frame the blue sky behind. Continuing along for 3km the trail merges into a paved country lane, arriving at Camon shortly thereafter.

This tiny settlement, founded by Charlemagne himself, is still dominated by its **abbey–castle** and surrounded by parts of its two sets of walls (fourteenth- and sixteenth-century). The castle is private and operates as a luxurious bed-and-breakfast, but its richly appointed sixteenth-century interior can also be taken in as part of a guided tour (arranged by the tourist office; €5). The small **tourist office** on Grande Rue (Mon–Fri 9am–noon & 2–5pm; ℡05.61.68.88.26, ℻05.61.68.12.07) can also get you into the town's unexceptional fourteenth-century church. If you want to **stay** the night, *L'Abbaye-Château* (℡ & ℻05.61.68.51.56; ❺) is the obvious choice if you can afford it; if you can't you should at least enjoy a drink in its *salon du thé*, *La Tartine*. The **chambres d'hôtes** *La Besse* (℡05.61.68.13.11; ❶–❹) also operates a **campsite** and has a pool. *La Bergerie*, an old farm 1km west of town towards Mirepoix, has a rustic **restaurant** which serves *terroir* cuisine (closed Wed; *menus* from €12). If you continue south from Camon on the GR7, keep an eye out for the *cabanes*, sturdy little stone shepherds huts, hidden amongst the growth.

Vals

Perhaps the most interesting sight in the vicinity of Mirepoix is the church at **Vals**, 12km west of town on the north bank of the Hers. Vals itself is little more than a cluster of a half-dozen farmhouses – a dusty hamlet, with no services – where you are as likely to encounter a cow as a person walking down the street. About 20m from the main road a small and incredibly ancient **subterranean church** (daily 9am–6pm; free), once a stopping-point on the pilgrims route to Compostela, is built on a rocky spur. Entering through a hobbit-sized doorway you climb a staircase carved in the rock, passing through a pseudo-crypt of pre-Roman origin before reaching the church itself. When you enter, grope for the light switch to the left of the door to illuminate the curious three-chambered vertical structure; in the arches of some of its windows you'll find well-preserved late eleventh and early twelfth-century frescoes of saints and angels, which recall the styles of painted churches of the Pyrenees. Lacking bicycle or car, you can reach Vals by getting off the Pamiers–Mirepoix bus at the turn-off from the D40 (just east of Les Pujols) and walking the remaining 4km.

Pamiers and the Grotte du Mas d'Azil

The town of **PAMIERS** is loaded with history, but suffered so gravely in the Wars of Religion that there is virtually nothing left to see here. Founded by returning Crusaders – who named it after the ancient city of Apamea in Syria, which they had captured – Pamiers later played the role of headquarters for the anti-Cathar Crusaders. In 1321, the Inquisition burned the last Cathar *parfait* Guillaume Bélibaste here. Now, of the town's vanished medieval glory only a scattering of old bell towers survive, poking above the rooftops in the tight knot of streets on the east bank of the Ariège, which make up Pamiers' bland old town. The only reason you might be tempted to stop here is to use the town as a jumping-off point to head east to Mirepoix or west to Mas d'Azil and St-Girons.

Trains and buses stop at Pamiers' **gare SNCF**, just east of the old town, and a short walk from the **tourist office** (July & Aug Mon–Sat 8.30am–noon & 2–6pm; Sept–June Mon–Fri 8.30am–noon & 2–5pm; ℡05.61.67.52.52, ⓦwww.pamierstourisme.com) on boulevard Delcassé, at the southeastern corner of the ring road. If you do want to stay here, head for the *Hôtel de France* on 5 cours du Rambaud (closed late Dec; ☎05.61.60.20.88, ✉df0902@inter-hotel.com; ❸), a welcoming, old-style hotel. The alternatives are *Le Roi Gourmand* (☎05.61.60.12.12, ⦿www.logis-de-france.fr; ❷), an adequate two-star number opposite the train station, and *Hôtel de la Paix*, in place Albert Tournier (☎05.61.67.12.71, ⦿www.logis-de-france.fr; ❷). Each of these hotels has a **restaurant** (the *de France* being the cheapest with a €11.50 *menu*), and there are other places scattered about the town, but nothing outstanding.

Bikes can be rented from Cycles Passion (☎05.61.60.14.05) and Cycle Portet (☎05.61.67.04.12). You will also find a number of **laundries** here, and you can use the terminal in the town's post office to get on the **Internet**.

The cave and village of Mas d'Azil

The swathe of land which sweeps northwest of Pamiers towards the banks of the Garonne and Toulouse holds virtually nothing of interest, its flat landscape peppered by farming hamlets and populated largely by cattle. There is, however, a good route for **biking** (if you're in good shape) or driving (if you're not) across the western spur of the low Plantaurel mountains to the **Grotte du Mas d'Azil**, and on to St-Girons. Pick this up by crossing the Ariège west of Pamiers' old town on the D110 (direction St-Victor); 7km later you'll hook up with the main D119. Thereafter, the road climbs steeply before dipping into the valleys of the Lèze and Arize.

At Sabaret a gruelling series of hairpin curves ascends to the village of **MAS D'AZIL**, whose massive cavern is not only noteworthy for being the most northerly and largest of the great Pyrenean prehistoric *grottes* (see p.163), but also as Europe's only **drive-through cave**. The gaping maw (some 50m in height) opens up just to the south of the town, swallowing the D119 road whole, before disgorging it several hundred metres later. Once a lair of the giant cave-bears which populated the south of France in the days of the great mammals and, roughly 30,000 years ago, a home for our own humble ancestors, historically the cave has provided refuge for a whole series of endangered species, including early Christians, Cathars and Huguenots. Indeed, it was here and in the village that a group of Protestants made a valiant and desperate stand in 1625, fending off a Catholic army which outnumbered them fifteen to one. If you're interested in seeing more than simply what passes by your window, other sections of the cave are **accessible by foot** (March, Oct & Nov Sun 2–6pm; April–May Mon–Fri 2–6pm, Sun 10am–noon & 2–6pm; June & Sept daily 10am–noon & 2–6pm; July & Aug daily 10am–6pm; €6.10, including museum entry), and you can stroll through **galleries** littered and decorated with the vestiges of its former inhabitants.

The village itself, which lost its fortifications to a spiteful Richelieu, has a small **museum** (same hours as the cave) by the church, with prehistoric knick-knacks collected from the cavern and a section on the local glass-making tradition. The same building houses the local **tourist office** (April–Sept daily 10am–1pm & 2–6pm; ☎05.61.69.97.22). The only **hotel** in the hamlet is the family-run *Hôtel Gardelt* (closed mid-Nov to mid-March; ☎05.61.69.90.05, ℗04.61.69.70.27; ❷), and there is a municipal **campsite** (mid-June to mid-Sept) only a twenty-minute walk away. The best place to eat is *Le Jardin de Cadettou* (closed Sat lunch, Sun eve & Mon; ☎05.61.69.95.23), a homely **restaurant** with excellent *menus* of regional cuisine from €20 which also has rooms (❸). A less expensive option is the *Gardel*, whose family-run dining room has *menus* from €12.

Emerging from the cave, the road meanders through attractively forested uplands before meeting the main highway at Lescure, just 8km east of St-Girons (see p.157).

Foix and around

FOIX, 18km upstream from Pamiers, has few specific sights itself but is the most agreeable base in the valley, with connections by train and bus into the mountains. It has a good range of services, and is surprisingly lively for a relatively small town. What's more, people tend to hurry past, so that although Foix is located in the midst of the greatest concentration of prehistoric caves in France, it is never overwhelmed by visitors and retains an appealing intimacy and freshness.

Arrival, information and accommodation

The **gare SNCF** sits on the right bank of the Ariège, a ten-minute walk north of the centre; most **buses** stop on the central cours Gabriel-Fauré, near the Resistance monument, although some will drop you off behind the post office. The **tourist office** at 45 cours Gabriel-Fauré (July & Aug Mon–Sat 9am–7pm, Sun 10am–noon & 2–6pm; Sept–June Mon–Sat 9am–noon & 2–6pm; ☎05.61.65.12.12) can be reached from the train station if you walk south along the east bank of the Ariège and then cross the Pont-Neuf. If you plan on doing any hiking, pick up a free *randonées* booklet here, published by the *département* of Ariège.

Most **accommodation** is found in the old town, on the west bank of the Ariège, though little of it is inspiring. The quietest and most comfortable option is the three-star *Hôtel Lons*, 6 place Duthil, near the *pont vieux* (closed late Dec to early Jan; ☏05.61.65.52.44, ⒺThotel-lons-foix@wanadoo.fr; ❸). *La Barbacane,* 1 avenue de Lerida (☏05.61.65.50.44, ⒻThotel04.61.02.74.33; ❷–❹) seems to be shedding stars every year or so, but is inexpensive, and many rooms have great views. The *Eychenne*, 11 rue Nöel-Peyrevidal (☏05.61.65.00.04, ⒻThotel05.61.65.56.63; ❶), is the only real cheapy, with decent enough rooms but a nocturnally lively bar on the ground floor; across the street at no. 16 is the friendly **youth hostel** *Auberge Léo Lagrange* (☏05.61.65.09.04, ⒺThotelleogagrange-foix@wanadoo.fr; €15), which has one- to four-person rooms. The municipal **campsite**, *Lac de Labarre* (May–Oct; ☏05.61.65.11.58), sits 4km up the N20 towards Toulouse.

The Town

Foix has a well-preserved **old town** of narrow alleys, wedged in the triangle between the Ariège and the Arget rivers. A few of the overhanging houses here date from the fourteenth to sixteenth centuries, and especially attractive are **place Pyrène** and **place St-Vincent** with their fountains, though many junctions in the old quarter sport some sort of water feature. All lanes seem to lead eventually to the conspicuously large **church of St-Volusien** in the east of the old town, originally Romanesque but almost completely reconstructed after being razed during the Wars of Religion. Its eponymous square, along with the Halles des Grains just off cours Gabriel-Fauré, hosts lively Wednesday and Friday **markets** – farm produce and plants at the *place*, and meat, cheese, savouries and pastries at the metal-roofed *halles*, which on other days is a prime drinking venue.

Presiding over the old town is Foix's grey hill-top **castle**, not so much a single fortification as three magnificent, dissimilar towers from different eras: a slender twelfth-century turret, a bulky square fourteenth-century keep and a broad and rounded fifteenth-century tower – dramatic when viewed from any angle. From 1012 the castle on this site was the seat of the counts of Foix, whose association with the Cathar faith led to its being besieged four times by Simon de Montfort, who failed to break the fort's resistance. One of these counts, Roger-Bernard II "Le Grand", was a determined opponent of the Albigensian Crusade, but perhaps made his most lasting contribution to history by marrying Ermensende of Castellbó early in the thirteenth century, thereby linking the fortunes of Foix and Andorra. Although the dynasty ended illustriously with Huguenot king Henri III of Foix-Béarn and Navarre, who annexed what had become a Pyrenean mini-state to the Crown on becoming Henri IV of France in 1589, the biggest name in Foix is that of the fair-haired knight whose features can be seen on postcards all over town – Gaston III, known as Gaston Fébus (see box opposite).

The **castle** (daily: July & Aug 9.30am–6.30pm; May, June & Sept 9.45am–noon & 2–6pm; Oct–April Wed–Sun 10.30am–noon & 2–5.30pm; €4) which looms over the town is reached by ascending a steep flight of stairs. Inside, two of the three towers hold exhibits relating to the history of the building and the County of Foix; others are home to rather uninspiring inter-active displays of local crafts and products. On a clear day the views from the crenellated turrets reward those who puff up the narrow key-stone staircases. On weekend evenings (July & Aug) the castle forms the venue for an elaborate *son et lumière* and theatre performance, "Il était une Foix..." (10pm; €22). If the castle seems rather too cramped to have served as a noble residence, keep

Gaston Fébus

Foix's greatest hero, a towering figure in the history of the central Pyrenees, is **Gaston Fébus** (or Phébus, in French), Count of Foix and Viscount of Béarn (just to the west). Although ultimately frustrated in his plans, Fébus is a local legend, revered as a leader who fought hard for regional independence and whose character epitomizes the ideals of chivalry associated with the Middle Ages. A soldier and poet, Fébus was born in 1331 and died sixty years later, but the details of his life are difficult to disentangle. With his dashing, aristocratic image he naturally became a subject for the songs of troubadours and, a relentless self-promoter, he did everything he could to encourage and embroider tales of his own valour and prowess, even inviting Jean Froissart, the great chronicler of the Hundred Years' War, to write his biography. His surname, Fébus, was his own invention, derived from the Occitan word for sun and celebrating his long, golden hair. What is certain is that he was known as a dauntless soldier, and in battle could be found leading his men with the cry *Fébus avan* ("Fébus forward"). As a ruler he was very much the image of medieval nobility – he had no time for the legislative councils of town dwellers, which he abolished, and set himself up as the highest judicial authority in his realms.

Fébus' great ambition was to create an **autonomous kingdom** in the Pyrenees, adding by conquest the western regions of Bigorre and Soule to the lands of Nébouzan, Béarn and Foix (including all the upper Ariège valley), which he had inherited. This goal was made impossible by the continuing Hundred Years' War, which divided the loyalties of his subjects: in the west lived Gascons who were loyal to the English Crown, and in particular to the Black Prince, who ruled them between 1362 and 1371 – while to the east lay Languedoc, subject to the French king. These divisions exacerbated the feuding of the leading knightly families in his realms, and gave greater purpose to the neighbouring nobles against whom he was pitted. In 1362 Fébus did manage to inflict a crushing defeat on his Gascon arch-enemies, the English-allied Armagnacs, but despite successes such as this, in the end he had to accept the unworkability of his plan. His dreams of **dynastic dominance** were dealt a final, crushing blow in 1380, when he is said to have killed his only son on discovering the latter's role in a conspiracy to assassinate him.

Thereafter, determined that his own dreams fail, those of his enemies would not succeed, Fébus dedicated himself to campaigning for a strong, **united France**, pledging his lands to the Crown by inheritance. But this too was initially thwarted, with the d'Albret family, one of his rivals, gaining the throne of Béarn and keeping it out of French control until 1589. Nevertheless, Gaston Fébus' ideals and endeavours have come to represent all that is romantic about the medieval era, and, in Foix especially, he is celebrated with festivals in July and August and remembered fondly for **l'hypocras**, a spiced wine drink which he invented and which is enjoyed in the region to this day.

in mind that the counts' regular residence was the larger castle of Orthez in Béarn – they just stopped in here on occasion to reassert their power over the town.

Eating, drinking and nightlife

The best area for **eating** is rue Lafaurie, the old blacksmiths' bazaar at the centre of the old town, where the best of several establishments is *Les 4 Saisons* at no. 11 (closed at Sat & Sun in season, plus Sun–Thurs eve off-season), whose gimmick is to bring to your table a hotplate – a *pierrade* – on which you cook fish and meat pieces yourself; they also do a wide range of *crêpes* (you'll spend €13.50–16). *Le Jeu de l'Oie* (closed Sat noon & Sun in winter) nearby at no.

17 is also worth trying for more traditional fare (from €8.60 at lunch; closed Sat lunch & Sun off-season). A pricier, but worthwhile option is *Le Sainte-Marthe* (☎05.61.02.87.87; closed Wed off-season, Tues & part Feb), at 21 rue Peyrevidal, which has a range of specialties (*menus* €33–44) including cassoulet, and a street-side terrace. *L'Atlas* on place Pyrène offers up delicious Moroccan cuisine (€14.50–22; closed Sat lunch & Mon) in the shadow of the town's church.

There is a row of café-restaurants which occasionally double as night-time **music-bars** on the west side of the cours Gabriel-Fauré, on either side of the old market hall. *Café des Rocher*, *Grand Grosse* and *Le Bon Bouffe* all have decent if unspectacular dinner *menus* for €10–15, and stay open for drinking. Later on, you can head to the **disco** *Le Crysco Club* (Wed–Sat 10pm–3am) at 3 cours Irénée Cros, on the far side of the *pont vieux* over the Ariège.

Listings

Car rental ADA, 59 av du Général-Leclerc (☎05.61.68.38.38, ⓦwww.ada.fr), Europcar, Route d'Espagne (☎05.61.02.32.74, ⓦwww.europcar.fr/), and Hertz RN20 Peysales (☎05.61.65.15.99, ⓦww.hertz.fr/), have offices in or near town.

Internet access To get online head to the friendly Bureau de Information Jeunesse (Mon 1–5pm, Tues–Fri 10am–5pm; closed Aug) on rue Roger, off rue de College behind the tourist office, or to the pay-terminal at the post office, also on rue Roger.

Laundry There's a coin-operated launderette (daily 7am–9pm) on place Lazéma.

Swimming pools Indoor and outdoor swimming pools are located at place du Champs du Mars, behind the main post office (€2.30 admission).

Watersports The narrow Lac Labarre reservoir, just north of town, has the usual gamut of water-side facilities; ASPTT (☎05.61.02.62.99) rents kayaks and canoes, and organizes rafting trips.

West of Foix

Heading west from Foix, the main road, the D117, climbs rapidly to the **col de Bouich** (599m) before descending through the Aujole and Baup valleys to arrive at St-Girons and St-Lizier, near the western limit of the *département*. On this particular road, there's little to detain you, although you might stop at **La Bastide de Serou**, just under half way, to have a drink in the square outside its old market building. Just past the village, a treacherous forest road provides cuts up towards Mas d'Azil (see p.152).

If however you take the Vernajoul road from the town centre, which eventually links up with the D117, you'll come to the subterranean **river-cavern of Labouiche** some 3km northwest of Foix (April, May, Oct & Nov Mon–Sat 2–5.15pm, Sun 10–11.45am & 2–5.15pm; June & Sept Mon–Sat 10–11.15am & 12–5.15pm, Sun 10–11.45am & 2–5.15pm; July & Aug Mon–Sat 9.30am–5.30pm, Sun 10–11.45am & 2–5.15pm; €7.50), claimed to be the longest such navigable cave in western Europe, although the water levels in winter are so high as to block access completely. The same amusement-park atmosphere prevails here as at Lombrives (see p.165): twelve-person boatloads travel for 75 minutes in opposite directions along the 1500m of galleries open to the public. Entry is either via the natural entrance, or an artificial one bored at the upstream end, on either side of the ticket office – you're told which to assemble at. Highlights of the cavern are the **waterfall** at the upstream end of the river and a small chamber full of formations below the artificial entry; these and other oddities along the way are described by the guides, who do their best to keep up a witty patter while hauling the crafts via ceiling-mounted cables.

There are also two unusual English-run **chambres d'hôtes** off the road between Foix and St-Girons. At Rimont, 34km from Foix, there is – a rarity in France – excellent and reasonably priced vegan (not even eggs) accommodation, at *Le Guerrat*, Suzanne Morris and Trevor Warman's working organic farm (open mid-May to mid-Oct; ℡05.61.96.37.03, ✉leguerrat@aol.com; ❷), while at Lescure, 4km further on, Nicholas Goldsworthy's *La Baquette* (℡ & ℻05.61.96.37.67; ❷) can arrange guided walks and tours of the local wildlife and flora. Heading south from La Bastide de Serou towards Massat, you'll come upon one of the better hotels in this area, *Auberge les Myrtilles* (℡05.61.65.16.46, ⓦperso.wanadoo.fr/auberge.les.myrtilles; ❸; closed Nov–Feb) in Col des Marrous, a beautiful rustic hotel with amenities such as a covered pool and jacuzzi, as well as a fine *terroir* restaurant (from €15).

The Couserans

Southwest of Foix, the peaks and the northern slopes of the Pyrenees shelter a series of high river valleys known collectively as the **Couserans**. As the Garbet, Salat, Arac and Alet rivers drain off the high glaciers they flow down through a country traditionally as poor and isolated as it is majestically beautiful. Cattle-farming, herding and forest industries were the original means of subsistence for the meagre population of this area, while later, mineral exploitation and spa development brought tenuous fits of humble prosperity and sustain the area today. The two towns which dominate this region, **St-Girons** and **St-Lizier**, are worth a visit if only to appreciate a subtle cultural shift offered by the mid-Pyrenees – the westernmost zone of Occitan influence coloured by contacts with Navarre, the Basque country and the flatlands of Gascony. The most immediate manifestation of the change is the merciful disappearance of cassoulet from *terroir menus*. If you have the time, energy and perseverance, exploring the highlands to the south will lead you through some of the most remote and splendid scenery, and distinctive culture, the Pyrenees have to offer.

Given the area's isolation and poverty, it should come as no surprise that there is little by way of public transport in the region. There are bus links from Toulouse and Foix to St-Girons, and a regular service up into the Couserans, but unless you have a **car**, to do any real exploring you'll have to resort to **hiking** – cycling in these hills is strictly for the dedicated.

St-Girons and St-Lizier

The two complementary towns of St-Girons and St-Lizier, 45km west of Foix along the D117, and separated from each other by only 1500m of riverbank, to all intents and purposes form a single unit. The former is the administrative and commercial centre, which, with good transport links to Toulouse and a range of services, is most useful as a base for exploring the mountains. The latter, which was the capital of the Couserans until the role was ceded to St-Girons, is where you'll find the sights.

Apart from its long association with making cigarette papers, the most striking thing about **ST-GIRONS** is its pavements, made of a local dark-grey marble veined with white, and with finely chiselled gullies to carry away the rainwater. And although there are no other memorable sights, it's a far from unpleasant place, with a couple of decent **festivals**: folklore in mid-July and theatre in early August. The simplest centre for orientation is the **Pont-Vieux**. Straight ahead on the right bank of the River Salat, the bridge points you into the old commercial centre of the town, with some marvellously old-fashioned shops, their fronts and fittings unchanged for generations. To the right is the typically provincial **place des Poilus**, its cachet largely due to the faded elegance of the *Grand Hôtel de France* and the equally old-fashioned *Hôtel de l'Union*, opposite, where you can still stay (see below). The *Grand Café de l'Union* on the square is a splendidly balconied period café that faces the *mairie*. Beside it, along the riverbank, a wide gravelled *allée* of plane trees, the **Champ de Mars**, provides the site for a big general market on the second and fourth Mondays of every month, and for a regular produce market every Saturday morning.

St-Girons' older and prettier sibling, **ST-LIZIER**, occupies a little hillock, still partially enclosed by walls and towers built under the Romans in the third and fourth centuries. Strolling along its narrow streets, keep an eye out for the carved facades of its numerous fifteenth-century palaces, particularly around the places de l'Église and des Entends, and on the rues des Nobles and d'Horloge. Of special note is the late seventeenth-century **bishop's palace**, from the terrace of which you get a great view over the Couserans rising to the south, with the snowcapped peaks of the Pyrenees as a backdrop. Inside, the **museum** (April–May & Oct Tues–Fri & Sun 2–6pm; June daily 10am–noon & 2–6pm; July & Aug daily 10am–7pm; €4) contains an uninspiring collection of local handicrafts, bric-a-brac and household items.

The main attraction here is the **cathedral of St-Lizier** (daily 10am–3pm; free) an eleventh-century structure built on Roman foundations, with a magnificent array of Romanesque frescoes on the walls and ceiling of its twelfth-century apse; the figure of Christ, as *Pantocrator* ("Lord of all") presides over angels, apostles and various other figures who descend in hierarchy towards the floor. The adjacent **cloister** (daily 9am–noon & 2–7pm) is particularly noteworthy for the carvings of its capitals – in addition to the usual floral motifs and monsters are extraordinary narrative scenes illustrating the highlights of the Old and New Testament. Over the five centuries after its founding the church was completed piecemeal, with sections added on in a strange higgledy-piggledy manner, and though there hardly seems to be a right angle in the floor plan, somehow it all holds together. Apart from the building itself, the church's **treasury** (May–Sept Mon–Sat 10am–12.30pm & 2–7pm & Sun 2–7pm; Oct–April Mon–Sat 10am–noon & 2–6pm; free) is host to a stunning sixteenth-century reliquary bust of St Lizier, as well as other pieces dating back to the eleventh century. The town's other cathedral, Notre-Dame-de-Sède, has long been closed for renovations.

Practicalities

Buses from Toulouse and the Couserans arrive in St-Girons on the left bank of the river at place des Capots. There's a **tourist office** here, in the central place Alphonse-Seintein (July & Aug Mon–Sat 9am–7pm, Sun 10am–1pm; Sept–June Mon–Sat 9am–noon & 2–6pm; ☎05.61.96.26.60, ⓦwww.ville-st-girons.fr), and another one up in St-Lizier (same hours as St-Girons; ☎05.61.96.77.77, Ⓔsaintlizier@wanadoo.fr). The best **accommodation** in the area for both atmosphere and comfort is St-Lizier's *Hôtel de la Tour* (☎05.61.66.38.02, ⒺHoteldelaTour@Hotel-Restaurant.net; ❷) in a remodelled old building down by the riverbank. Otherwise *La Clarière* (☎05.61.66.66.66, Ⓕ05.34.14.30.30; ❷–❺), on the south side of St-Girons, comes a close second (very close, if you factor in the pool), and the *Hôtel de Union* (☎05.61.66.09.12, Ⓕ05.61.04.81.73; ❶–❸), on allée Champs de Mars, has some cheaper rooms. If you look like a hiker, the St-Lizier tourist office will arrange a berth in the hamlet's pilgrim **hostel** for a single night (€12), and the nearby **campsite** *Parc des Palettes* (☎05.61.66.06.79), is open from March to September and rents out bungalows. The departmental website,

@www.ariege.com, has comprehensive listings of *gîtes*, B&Bs and hotels in the isolated hinterlands.

The *de la Tour* and *La Clarière* both have **restaurants** (*menus* from €14; both closed Sun eve), the first with a strong *terroir* streak, and the second somewhat more adventurous. For lighter fare, head to *Chez Alain et Dominique* at 8 place Jean-Jaurès (closed Sun); expect to spend €14 and up. Vegetarians will be grateful for *La Végé'table* at 13 rue Joseph Pujol (*menus* from €8; closed Sun & Mon out of season). Look for the local *croustade aux cèpes* – mushroom pie.

Bikes can be rented at Horizon Vertical (☎05.61.96.08.22; they also do caving trips) in St-Girons and at Cycles Carbonne (☎05.34.13.31.31) in St-Lizier. You can check your email at the **Internet** terminal in the St-Girons post office.

Over the Couserans to Tarascon

Looping back from St-Girons to Tarascon (see p.161) in the Ariège valley provides an opportunity to take in the stunning terrain of the **COUSERANS**, which buttress some of the highest peaks in the Pyrenees and, culturally, remains a unique and independent zone, quite different from Languedocian Foix. Gascon is still spoken here, and if you have the good fortune to visit during local festivities, you'll be treated to the area's singular costume and music: men wearing white embroidered jackets (reminiscent of traditional Greek styles) and red *baretos* (hats) sport curious wooden shoes with high (up to 30cm) pointed toes, while women wear long dresses draped with colourful scarves; the clarinet-like *hautbois*, accompanied by drums, supplies the sounds for traditional dances. The villages in the region are likewise distinctive, built low in stone and timber to resist the high mountain clime. The Couserans has traditionally been a difficult area to access and even more so to govern, the proud mountain people resentful of any infringement of their liberties or threat to their way of life. As late as the nineteenth century, the villagers waged a guerrilla war against the French government – the so-called Guerre des Demoiselles ("war of the girls"), when they dressed up as women in a surprise attack on local property owners, government foresters and police.

The magnificent landscape is accessible by road and trail, with a number of rewarding circuits. Most of the villages of the Couserans have tourist offices, but hours can be irregular and confirmation is best made at the office in St-Girons, which has information and **walking** itineraries for the whole region. You may also want to contact the Ariège tourist board for **information** (CDT Ariége Pyrénées, 31bis avenue du Général-de-Gaulle, BP 143, 09004 Foix; ☎05.61.02.30.70, ☏05.61.65.17.34, @www.ariegepyrenees.com). There are two main **routes** which traverse the Couserans from west to east, only one of which is partially accessible by public transport from St-Girons (a single bus route climbing from St-Girons to Aulus-les-Bains), and both of which are fairly demanding drives.

Via Massat

Striking out from the Salat, south of St-Girons, through the dramatic **Gorges de Riabouto** will bring you to the confluence of the Arac and Riabouto. Here, you can take the more direct of the two routes to Tarascon by heading due east to the village of **MASSAT**. As you approach, the fifteenth-century bell tower of its church rises 60m above the village in a marvellous Pyrenean tableau. There is a **tourist office** here (☎05.61.96.92.76, @massatourisme @libertysurf.fr) and good shops and services, and the *Hotel Le Globe* (☎05.61.96.96.96, ☏05.61.04.91.63; ❶), and the *Hostellerie des Trois Seigneurs* (closed Nov–Easter; ☎05.61.04.90.52, @www.logis-de-france.com; ❷) provide food as well as lodging. A **market** is held on the second and fourth Thursday of every month, and Sundays in summer. Continuing east, the road climbs in a seemingly endless succession of hair-raising bends until you reach the 1250m-high Col de Port. On the left rise the wooded slopes of the **Montagnes de l'Arize**, while on your right the barren **Pic de Trois Seigneurs** (2199m) scratches the clouds. A steep eighteen-kilometre descent then brings you to Tarascon, passing the Parc de la Préhistoire (see p.162) at the entrance to the town.

Via Seix and Aulus-les-Bains

From the mouth of the Riabouto gorge, the bus will take you further up the Salat to **SEIX**, where the peaks of the **cirque** at the valley's head come into view. This market town, still lorded over by a fifteenth-century castle and with a distinctive church tower, provides another opportunity to stock up on supplies, and is a good base if you plan to do some hiking in the region; you can get up-to-date information at the village **tourist office** (☎05.61.96.52.90, ⓦwww.haut-couserans.com) in the town centre – if **mountain biking** is your thing, enquire about the circuit just south of town. There are two **hotels** in town, the *Auberge des Deux Rivières* (☎ & ⓕ05.61.66.83.57, ⓕ05.61 .04.42.63; ❷) and the *Auberge du Haut Salat* (☎05.61.66.88.03; ❶), both with restaurants. There is also a **gîte**, *Pyrénées Anes* (☎05.61.66.82.15, ⓔpyrenees.anes@free.fr; ❶). La Marmotte (☎05.61.66.91.60) rents **bikes**, and the local Crédit Agricole bank handles currency **exchange**. In summer a **market** is held on the second and fourth Wednesday of the month, and local products are also sold at the annual **horse fair** on October 18.

From Seix, the bus line continues up the Alet river to its terminus **AULUS-LES-BAINS**, a spa village and adjunct to the mediocre ski station of **Guzet-Neige** (☎05.61.96.00.11), separated from Spain's Vall de Cardós by a ten-kilometre-wide mountain wall, and lying among lush and fragrant meadows ringed by dramatic peaks. The most remote point of the traditionally poor Couserans, Aulus was once famous for its bear trainers, who toured the wealthier lowlands. The classic walk here involves heading south along the GR10 to the **Cascade d'Ars** waterfall, a round trip of about five hours. Aulus' **tourist office** on allée des Thermes (☎05.61.96.01.79, ⓔtourisme@haut-couserans.com) can provide detailed information regarding hikes, as well as accommodation options. Thanks to the spa industry which keeps the town busy from May to November, and the skiing which brings people in winter there are a number of places to eat and stay. In Aulus, the best deal for **accommodation** is the *Hôtel de France* (closed Nov; ☎05.61.96.00.90, ⓕ05.61.96.03.29; ❶), which has comfortable rooms and an excellent and affordable **restaurant** (from €10.67). A more expensive and attractive choice is the *Hôtel les Ousaillès* (☎05.61.96.03.68, ⓔjcharrue@free.fr; ❷), while the cheapest digs are at the **gîte**, *Présbytère* (☎05.61.96.02.21,ⓔhel-aulus@hotmail.com; ❶). For light meals, the tearoom and bar *Les Fontanalia* (weekends only in winter) can fix you up with snacks from about €5. The nearest **campsite** to Aulus is *Le Couledous* (☎05.61.96.02.26; year round) in a holiday complex neighbouring the town. Sunday is **market**-day (morning).

From Aulus, a narrow mountain road and the GR10 wind separate paths along the northern fringe of the **Pic Rouge de Bassiès** (2676m), weaving in and out of the tree line. Looking back, you'll see the high-walled crenellated cirque formed by the peak and its nearest neighbour, the Pic des Trois Comtes; the drama of the cirque's heights is underscored by wedges of snow lying beneath the sheerest faces, while below, the steep slopes are luxuriant with

❷

beech. The road rises to the east, then the north, skirting the small Étang de Lers and passing herds of grey cows grazing the alpine meadow, to arrive at the pass, the **Port de Lers** (1517m). Eventually passing the waterfall, the **cascade d'Arbu**, some 3km beyond, you begin a sharp descent towards Vicdessos. The GR10, on the other hand, continues due east to the Port de Saleix (1794m) where it meets two other paths. The main trail takes a right, arriving 2km later at the CIMES **refuge**, *de Bassies* (☎05.61.64.89.98; meals available June–Oct; open weekends only May & Sept–Oct; ❶), and then, passing a series of reservoirs, it branches east, crossing the **Pic du Far** and descending to Auzat and Vicdessos – in total some 16km of often demanding trail. On the final leg of the hike, keep an eye out for the squat stone shepherds' shelters, or *orris*, hidden among the underbrush – some are as much as 700 years old.

There is little to detain you in **VICDESSOS**, the capital of a remote and poor *canton*, and nearby **AUZAT** is remarkable chiefly for the large and ugly aluminium factory which dominates it. It is however at these villages that the footpath and road route converge again, and where the main road descends the river valley, passing the Grotte de Niaux (see p.164), shortly before entering **Tarascon**. You may want to take a **room** or **meal** at the homely *Hôtel Henri Hivert* (☎05.61.65.88.17; ❶) in Vicdessos. Alternatively the farmhouse, *Les Marmousets* (☎05.61.86.00.82; ❷), between Auzat and Vicdessos, has two *chambres d'hôtes*, and the local **campsite** (☎05.61.64.82.22) also rents bungalows off-season. For those on a budget, *La Bonne Auberge* (☎ & ℱ05.61.03.80.99; ❶) in Auzat has cheap rooms and well-priced *menus* (from €10.37). The town is also the headquarters of the departmental association of *accompagnateurs* (1 rte de la Prade ☎05.61.64.83.96), which can set you up with a reliable **guide** for hikes up into the Couserans. Vicdessos' **market** is held on Thursdays, and there is an annual fair on 21 September.

The upper Ariège valley

South of Foix, the **upper Ariège** narrows rapidly, and forest slopes rise sharply on either side as the riverbed twists and cuts down through gneiss and schist of the Pyrenean foothills towards **Tarascon**. It is along this part of the river that you'll find in thick concentration many of France's best and most famous prehistorically inhabited **caves**, decorated by hand-prints, etchings and animal figures left by our ancestors up to a quarter of a million years ago. This, along with the beauty of the countryside, has made the upper Ariège an extremely popular destination, especially for French tourists. High season, particularly August, is mayhem, and if you're hoping to see the renowned cave art you should plan (and reserve) as far ahead as possible. Further up in the hills towards the Spanish and Andorran frontiers, the high peaks of the Pyrenees loom ever closer. Here, around **Ax-les-Thermes**, there is breathtaking mountain scenery and great possibilities for **walking**. There's a map of the region on pp.142–143.

Tarascon-sur-Ariège and the caves

A small, utilitarian mining and metallurgy centre with traffic roaring past on the bypass highway, **TARASCON-SUR-ARIÈGE** has nothing about it to suggest that this is the heart of one of the most fascinating areas in Europe. Yet any account of the emergence of the human species must include the **caves** around the town, which taken as a group constitute an unequalled display of prehistoric painting and artefacts. The *grottes* served as shelters – and, arguably, as places of worship – for early humans, later coming in handy as hideouts for religious dissidents during the Christian era. Their high concentration in the Ariège is due to the limestone which constitutes the hillsides here – permeable rock ideally suited to the millennial work of cavern-creation. There are four main sites, all accessible in a single day if you have your own transport.

Tarascon itself is rather dull and hardly worth a stop, although riverside cafés provide pleasant vantage points over the Ariège, past which you can follow a narrow pedestrian lane past a string of craft shops into the old quarter. Here the church of St-Michel presides over a partly arcaded square, and various surviving bits of the medieval walls, razed in 1632, crop up here and there: the **Tour St-Michel**, and the **Porte d'Espagne** with a fountain inside. From the gate, the short hike past walled orchards up to the **Tour du Castella**, now a clock tower, is worthwhile for the views over the five valleys which converge here. Tarascon is the sight of two lively livestock **fairs**, on May 8 and September 30, timed for the passing of the transhumant herds. A regular **market** is held on Wednesday morning in the place de l'Horte, and Saturday morning in the place de l'Ayroule as well as during the annual fairs on May 8 and September 30.

If you haven't managed to make reservations at the caverns, you can still experience the Neolithic era, albeit vicariously, at the **Parc de la Préhistoire** (April–May & Sept–Oct Tues–Fri 10am–6pm, Sat & Sun 10am–7pm; June–Aug Mon–Fri 10am–6pm, Sat & Sun 10am–7pm; €9), just 5km outside Tarascon (take the N20 north towards Toulouse, you'll see it signposted at the junction for St-Girons). This rambling park contains nature trails, and prehistory-related exhibits including replica bison and reproductions of some of the more important and inaccessible cave art – a good alternative to the real thing if you have children along.

Practicalities

Buses and trains call frequently from nearby Ax-les-Thermes and Foix, on the line from Toulouse to Latour-de-Carol; the **gare SNCF**, which also serves as the bus stop, is on the left bank of the Ariège, in the northern half of town. The **tourist office** (July & Aug daily 9am–7pm; Sept–June Mon–Sat 9am–6pm; ☎05.61.05.94.94, ✉pays.de.tarascon@wanadoo.fr) is inside the multipurpose hall known as the Espace François Mitterand, on avenue des Pyrénées in the centre.

Quietest and most attractive of the **hotels** is the *Confort* on the riverside quai Armand-Sylvestre (☎ & ℱ05.61.05.61.90; ❸), with some rooms facing a courtyard. For more comfort, with the quieter rooms facing the river, try the *Hostellerie de la Poste*, 200m north on the main through road (☎05.61.05.60.41, ✉hostellerieposte@aol.com; ❷), which has a cosy fireside lounge. The best option, however, is the eighteenth-century manor house, *Domaine Fournie* (☎05.61.05.54.52, ✉Contact@domaine-fournie.com; ❸), 1km from the town centre on rte Saurat, and set within impressive grounds. There are two **campsites**: *La Bernière*, near the junction of the road to Bédeilhac, and the municipal *Pré Lombard*, upstream from town on the right bank.

All of the hotels have attached **restaurants**, with the best food and service at *Hostellerie de la Poste*, which offers a reasonably priced Gascon *menu* featuring *auzinat*, a rich hotpot of cabbage, potato, sausage, game and other goodies; while the *Domaine Fournie*, offers a €15 *table*.

Pyrenean cave art

The **painted caves** of the Pyrenees are known to have been created by nomadic and semi-nomadic communities of Cro-Magnon *Homo sapiens* during the Late Paleolithic period, between 10,000 and 35,000 years ago. Almost everything else about them is conjecture.

According to the pioneering French paleo-anthropologist **Father Breuil** (1877–1961), known as the "Pope of Prehistory", cave art served a **magical function**, to ensure "that the game should be plentiful, that it should increase and that sufficient should be killed." The frequency with which ibex, wild boar, reindeer and bison appear on the walls makes this notion attractive, but there are objections to it, the most obvious being that the animal remains found in the caves show that the species depicted were not the main food supply. Moreover, although some of the animals are marked by symbols that might be arrows, over ninety percent of them are not. His disciple **André Leroi-Gourhan** (1911–86) and his colleague **Annette Laming-Emperaire** focused on the **layout** of cave designs. As a result of extensive surveys, they observed, for example, that hands were depicted only at the entrance to caves or in the centre, and that mammoths and bison were confined to the centre. They suggested that the arrangement reflected a sexual polarity, with bison symbolizing the female element, and horses the male. Some people have raised the objection that the weak illumination available to the cave-dwellers – since they had only grease and a wick perhaps, or wooden torches – would not have allowed them to see the cave decorations as a unity. A problem is also posed by the way successive outlines were superimposed to the extent that they became indecipherable, even though suitable areas of blank rock were available to either side. Nevertheless, most experts agree that there is some sort of pattern: bison and horses, for example, are thirty times more likely to occur in the central area than are deer, a statistic impossible to dismiss as coincidence.

The most cogent refutation of the above theories was published in 1996 by Jean Clottes, a French prehistorian and cave-art expert, and David Lewis-Williams, a South African archeologist specializing in the art and beliefs of the Kalahari Bushmen, one of the last surviving hunter-gatherer societies with strong parallels to European Paleolithic culture. Their *Les Chamanes de la Préhistoire* (Editions Seuil) proposes that many of the images may have been executed by **shamans** in a trance or other altered state, and that "the paintings and engravings do not represent real animals that are hunted for food in an actual landscape; rather they are visions drawn from the subterranean world of spirits because of their supernatural powers and ability to help the shamans."

Undoubtedly the caves will continue to stimulate speculation. The apparent stylistic development of the paintings, for example, along with similarities between decorative work in caves hundreds of kilometres apart suggests that there was some sort of coherent "school" of artistic development, as well as communication between widely dispersed groups. A great many decorated caves of the Pyrenees are closed to the general public, an essential precaution if they are to be preserved; application through a caving organization might gain access to some of these. The most spectacular examples, though, are open to all. After the Tarascon group, the major Pyrenean cave is **Gargas**, with its vast array of hand-prints in red and black, many with apparently mutilated fingers. Whatever the uncertainties about its significance and the ways in which it was made, Pyrenean cave art offers an extraordinary aesthetic experience, marvellously conjuring shape and movement from the most basic natural materials, and even, in places, exploiting the very contours of the rock. Niaux itself contains an excellent example of such artistic opportunism: one of the bison carved on the clay floor is formed around holes caused by dripping water, which function as an eye and wound marks.

Grotte de Niaux

Unquestionably the finest of the Pyrenean caves is the **Grotte de Niaux**, 2km southwest of Tarascon. Rivals like Lascaux in the Dordogne and Altamira in Spain are now closed or very nearly so, but the only restriction on access to Niaux is the mandatory **reservation** for places on the twenty-person 45-minute **guided tour** (daily: July & Aug 9.15am–5.30pm, English tours at 9.30am & 1pm; Sept 10am–5.30pm, English at 1pm; Oct–June Tues–Sun tours at 11am, 2.30pm & 4pm; ☎05.61.05.88.37, ⓦwww.sesta.org; €9).

The contemporary entrance to Niaux is a tunnel created in 1968 near the low and narrow natural opening under an enormous rock overhang. Using torches for illumination, you penetrate 900m (from a total 4km of galleries) to see just some of the famous black outlines of **horse** and **bison**, minimally shaded yet capturing every nuance. Analysis has established that these drawings, and those of the ibex and stag in the recess further back, were produced around 10,800 BC with a "crayon" made of bison fat and manganese oxide. A line of **footprints** left by the artists can be seen in a part of the cave that was opened up in 1970, while their primitive form of **writing** is represented by the dots and bunches of lines on the wall of the main cavity.

NIAUX village itself, between the cave and Tarascon, has a small, private **Musée Pyrénéen** (daily: July & Aug 9am–8pm; Sept–June 10am–noon & 2–6pm; €6) which displays a splendid collection of tools, furnishings and archival photos illustrating the vanished traditions of the Ariège. Exhibits also explain local Pyrenean architecture, with its use of *lauzes* (stone slabs), *ardoise* (slate) and occasionally *chaume* (thatch) for roofing. About halfway between Niaux and Tarascon, keep your eye peeled also for the picturesque remains of a medieval smelting works by the riverside.

Grotte de la Vache

The **Grotte de la Vache** (Easter–June & Sept Mon & Wed–Sun 2.30–4.15pm; July & Aug daily 10am–6pm other times by arrangement – ring ☎05.61.05.95.06; €7) at Alliat is well worth the couple of kilometres' journey across the valley from Niaux, south on the road to Vicdessos; a path, beginning some 150m before the Niaux museum, slightly shortcuts the road. Excavations here over two decades sifted through the detritus of ten thousand years of habitation, beginning between 15,000 and 12,500 BC and ending in the Bronze Age. Around 30,000 fragments of flint tools were unearthed and over 6000 complete tools, mainly for engraving in rock; some pieces are displayed in the cave.

Grotte de Bédeilhac

To reach the **Grotte de Bédeilhac** (Easter–June & Sept to mid-Dec Mon–Sat 2.20–4.15pm; July & Aug daily 10am–6pm; mid-Dec to Easter Mon–Sat 2.30–4.15pm & Sun 3pm; ☎05.61.05.95.06, €8) above the eponymous village, you have to return to Tarascon and cover 5km along the D618 towards Saurat. This cave, a hollow in the ridge of Soudour, contains examples of every known technique of Paleolithic art, including polychrome painting (now faded to monochrome). The imposing entrance yawns 35m wide by 20m high, making it easy to understand how the Germans managed to adapt the cavern as an aircraft hangar during World War II. Although the art within is not as immediately powerful as that at Niaux, diversity compensates: low reliefs in mud, paintings of bison, deer and ibex, and stalagmites used to model figures.

In the village below, **beds** are provided by the *Relais d'Étape* (☎05.61.05.15.56; ❷) and **meals** by the adjacent *Auberge de la Grotte*, on the through road next to the *mairie* and the post office.

Grottes de Lombrives

The **Grotte de Lombrives** (Easter–May & Oct to early Nov Sat & Sun tours at 10am, 10.45am & 2.30pm, plus May Mon–Fri 2–5.30pm; June & Sept daily tours at 10am, 10.45am & 2–5.30pm; July & Aug daily 10am–7pm; or by appointment, ℡05.61.05.98.40; €6.60), 3km south of Tarascon along the N20, near Ussat-les-Bains, could only disappoint if you've already seen Niaux, Vache and Bédeilhac. The access by underground train gives it something of an amusement-park feel – as do the nocturnal *spéctacles* regularly staged here in July and August – but the stalagmite formations are superb, and the sheer size of the complex is impressive. It is, in fact, the largest cavern in the EU open to tourists, and would take five days' walking to see it in its entirety. For groups of eight or more, you can arrange for three- or five-hour walk-throughs by ringing the number above. Lombrives was inhabited around 4000 BC, but all the material found here now rests in museums such as that at Foix. Its later history is embellished by legends of the last Cathars walled up inside in 1328, and of 250 soldiers subsequently disappearing without trace, the victims of cave-dwelling bandits. For a more serious visit, you can book on one of the "Visites longue durées caractère spéléologique", which are run from June to September.

Ax-les-Thermes and around

AX-LES-THERMES, 26km southeast of Tarascon on the main N20 road, is an unobjectionable spa resort with little specifically to see – owing to numerous disastrous fires in centuries past – other than a lively Monday market along the river promenade, but it makes the most convenient centre for skiing or walking in the Ariège region. **Hikes** can be routed in circuits, permitting use of the town as a base, and several **ski resorts**, both downhill and Nordic, are scattered in all directions within a convenient distance.

Ax dates back to at least Roman times, while the commercial exploitation of its hot springs goes back to the thirteenth century; the smell of sulphur that early twentieth-century travellers commented on can still be whiffed from the spring water coursing through the gutters, and the ambience of a spa remains. Four *thermes* still exist, all of them part of the central *Hôtel Royal Thermal*, and

---

Skiing around Ax-les-Thermes

The nearest **ski station** to Ax is **Ax-Bonascre** (t05.61.64.20.64), 8km south up the D820. In winter there are ski-bus services from the town centre. Bonascre itself is a hideous knot of high-rises, but once you get into the télécabine (to Bonascre €6, to Saquet €9) and up to the **Plateau du Saquet**, with the beautiful Andorran frontier peaks as a backdrop, it's a different matter. The snow record here is good, there are 75km of pistes (some over 3km long), and the top lift is at 2305m. An alternative station is to be found 13km east of Ax at **Ascou-Pailhères** (℡05.61.64.28.86), which has 15 downhill runs and a top station of 2020m. It's a pretty drive up to the station, and though it only has one black piste, it's quite a challenging one.

Three valleys west of Bonascre, the **Plateau de Beille** is a likely area for **cross-country skiing**. The 55km of pistes range in length from one to twenty kilometres, at an altitude of just under 2000m – which should ensure adequate snow. For the Beille resort, see ⓦwww.lespyrenees.com. You reach the plateau by taking the "route Forestière" (an unpaved "forest road") from the village of Les Cabannes, 15km north of Ax along the main N20 road. You can also get good cross-country skiing to the north of Ax around the **Col de Chioula** (1431m).

in total there are more than forty *sources*, producing a volume of water in excess of 600,000 litres per day, at temperatures hotter than 70°C in a few cases. The town itself is small and pleasant enough, but there's little to see once you've wandered a couple of streets in the quarter to the right of the N20, which forms the main street. Rue de l'École and rue de la Boucarie retain a few medieval buildings, and above place du Breilh, the **church of St-Vincent** is of architectural interest for its Romanesque tower. Just across the road you can join the locals and dangle your feet for free in the **Bassin des Ladres**, a pool of hot sulphurous water (77°C) dating to 1250, which was once incorporated into the now-vanished hospital founded in 1260 by St Louis for leprous soldiers returning from the Crusades.

Practicalities

The **gare SNCF** is on the northwest side of town, just off the main avenue Delcassé; **buses** stop in the town centre. The helpful **tourist office** (July & Aug daily 9am–1pm & 2–7pm; Sept–June 9am–noon & 2–6pm; ℡05.61.64.60.60, ⓦwww.vallees-ax.com) is on the north side of the main road, halfway through town. Here you can find information on hiking, contact guides, and purchase a range of *Topoguides* and maps. Thanks to the baths and the local skiing there is a wide selection of hotels in and around town. *Le Bellevue* (℡05.61.64.20.78, ℻05.61.64.65.44; ❶) is the cheapest option, but *Le Roy René* (℡05.61.64.22.28, ✉denoizeroger@wanadoo.fr; ❷) at 11 avenue du Dr F. Gomma and *L'Auzeraie* (℡05.61.64.20.70, ✉auzeriae@free.fr; ❷) give much better value for money. Both have restaurants (from €13). The municipal **campsite**, *Malazéou* (℡05.61.64.22.21; open year-round), is beside the Ariège, 500m from the train station. Ax Sports, near *La Paix*, will replace any lost or worn-out mountaineering and ski gear.

Other than the hotel dining rooms and restaurants, **eating** prospects aren't brilliant in Ax, but the hip new *La Petit Fringale* on rue Piétonne is worth a stop for its "montagnard" cuisine and its shady terrace (menus from €15). Otherwise the *Terminus Bar* near the station and *Grand Café*, beside *Les Pyrénées*, serve passable light fare. For **snacks** on the hoof, there are numerous cheap *boulangeries* and over-the-counter pizza places in rue de l'Horloge, leading off the place du Marché. More atmospheric venues for a **drink** are the *Grand Café* and *Brasserie Le Club* on place Roussel. The **market** is held Tuesday and Sunday mornings (also Thurs in summer). **Bikes** can be rented in nearby Saivgnac at L'Eskimo Sport (℡05.61.64.02.85).

The Oriège valley

Extending east from Ax, the damp, leafy **Oriège valley** allows access to both the Carlit peaks for hikers (see opposite) and the **Réserve Nationale d'Orlu**, created south of the road in 1975 to benefit a growing herd of isards (Pyrenean chamois, a goat-like animal) as well as roe deer, golden eagles and lammergeiers (Europe's biggest birds of prey). Under the shadow of the distinctive Dent d'Orlu, beloved of technical climbers, the D22 road heads up the valley to **ORLU**, where there's camping at the *Municipal* (℡05.61.64.30.09) and a popular *gîte d'étape* aimed at walkers, the *Relais Montagnard* (℡05.61.64.61.88; ❹). A path from **Les Forges d'Orlu** further up the valley permits a link-up with the "Tour des Montagnes d'Ax" (see below), via a climb from near the power station to the dam at Naguille.

At a popular picnic area some 8km beyond Orlu, the asphalt ends and a jeep track, from which all private cars are banned, climbs south into the *réserve* through the En Gaudu valley, before meeting the GR7 below the Étang d'en

Beys, with its refuge. If you're approaching the Carlit via the Oriège, it's well worth splashing out for a taxi to the picnic grounds: the walk in is tedious and steep, with little chance of a lift in either direction.

Walks near Ax-les-Thermes

With an office next door to the tourist office in Ax, the Bureau des Guides et Accompagnateurs Montagne des Vallées d'Ax (℡05.61.64.31.51) maintains a list of seventeen brief **walks** around the town, ranging in length from twenty minutes to seven hours, though most of these prove rather short and over-generously timed; it also keeps information on all the mountain huts and refuges, climbing courses and weather forecasts. To fill a day properly, take the suggested itinerary to the attractive village of **SORGEAT** and link this hike with other sections.

Among the long-distance hikes in the area, the five-day, four-night **Tour des Montagnes d'Ax** is most recommended, since it covers a variety of terrain, including parts of the Carlit. You can begin at **Le Castelet**, on the main road 5km northwest of Ax, climbing south for a day to hook up with the GR10 at the **Col de Beil** (2247m); the closest crude shelter is at **Prat Redon**. The route then heads eastwards to cross the Ariège valley at Mérens-les-Vals, your second overnight stop, from where you stick with the GR10, and later the GR7, all the way to the *Refuge d'en Beys* (℡05.61.64.24.24; late May to Sept & weekends in May & Oct by arrangement; ❶) – the refuge will be your third night out, after a very long day unless you spend the night at the refuge *Les Bésines* (℡05.61.05.22.44; meals available June–Sept, otherwise open weekends only by reservation; ❶) at the junction of the two trails. From the refuge, you've a shorter day up to the gentle **Couillade de Beys** (2345m), then past the easterly Étang des Peyrisses and the Naguille dam before the descent to the floor of the Oriège valley.

Mérens and L'Hospitalet

The reputation of **MÉRENS-LES-VALS**, 8km south of Ax along the N20, rests on the stocky frame of the **Mérenguais horse**, a breed which – partly on the strength of the Niaux cave paintings (see p.164) – is considered the closest thing in western Europe to the wild horse of prehistory. Nowadays there are more specimens outside the mountains of Mérens than in them, but the village remains a place of pilgrimage for horse lovers. Mérens itself, though, is unexceptional, one part clustered on the main road, the other spread out on the slopes to the east around a Romanesque church. The village straddles the GR10, which accounts for the attractively restored **gîte d'étape** in the upper village (℡05.61.64.32.50, ℻05.61.64.02.75; ❶), a congenial place to base yourself for a few days' walking, serving excellent food – luckily enough, since there are no other hotels or restaurants open in the town at present, though there is a **campsite** just off the main road, near the river.

Mérens makes a good base for **walks**, short or long. A popular one-day circuit involves following the GR10, and then a local path, southwest up the Mourgouillou valley, where Mérenguais horses still graze, to the **Étang de Couart**, and then dropping back down to the train station at L'Hospitalet by using the **HRP** (the Haute Route des Pyrénées, a trail which traverses the whole range). Alternatively, heading southeast, the GR10 offers a more appealing, if more strenuous introduction to the **Carlit range** than the HRP from L'Hospitalet (see below), but be warned that both French and translated *Topoguides* sketch the route on the wrong bank of the River Nabre.

L'Hospitalet

Ten kilometres further south from Mérens is **L'HOSPITALET-PRÈS-L'ANDORRE**, whose sole interest – in the absence of any monumental or natural attraction – is as a route convergence: the HRP goes through here, as do buses to and from adjacent Andorra, and trains south into the Cerdagne and north to Toulouse. There is a basic and unremarkable one-star **hotel**, the *Puymorens* (⚎05.61.64.23.03; ❶), plus a **gîte** (⚎ & ⊜05.61.05.23.14, ✉gitedetape.lhospitalet@libertysurf.fr; closed Nov; ❶), and a **campsite**. Heading into the Carlit massif, the **HRP** gets you quickly to grips with the mountains, offering the shortest approach from the west as it climbs unusually gently to the dam and pair of refuges at Bésines, where you link up with the GR10. Heading south of L'Hospitalet, a 7km-long road tunnel pierces the Col de Puymorens (1915m), reducing the road distance to Latour-de-Carol to only 20km.

Travel details

Trains

SNCF buses may run in lieu of trains on these lines; services are reduced on Sundays and holidays.

Carcassonne to: Alet-les-Bains (3 daily; 35min); Castelnaudary (22 daily; 20–30min); Limoux (16 daily; 25min); Montpellier (18 daily; 1hr 30min–4hr); Narbonne (22 daily; 35min); Nîmes (26 daily; 2hr 5min–3hr 10min); Perpignan (24 daily; 1hr 15min–2hr); Quillan (6 daily; 1hr 15min); Toulouse (22 daily; 45min–1hr).

Foix to: Ax-les-Thermes (6 daily; 50min); L'Hospitalet (7 daily; 1hr 10min–1hr 30min); Latour-de-Carol (6 daily; 2hr); Pamiers (13 daily; 15–25min); Tarascon-sur-Ariège (13 daily; 15–25min); Toulouse (13 daily; 45min–1hr 15min).

Latour-de-Carol to: Ax-les-Thermes (6 daily; 55min); Bourg-Madame (5 daily; 15min); Foix (6 daily; 2hr); L'Hospitalet (10 daily; 25min); Mont-Louis (4 daily; 1hr 20min); Tarascon-sur-Ariège (11 daily; 1hr 25min–1hr 45min); Toulouse (6 daily; 2hr 30min); Villefranche-de-Conflent (4 daily; 2hr 25min–2hr 45min).

Limoux to: Carcassonne (16 daily; 25min); Quillan (10 daily; 30–45min).

Pamiers to: Foix (13 daily; 15–25min); Latour-de-Carol (6 daily; 1hr 55min–2hr 10min); Toulouse (13 daily; 50min–1hr 10min).

St-Girons/St-Lizier to: Toulouse via Boussens (8 daily; 1hr 45min–2hr).

Buses

NOTE: In the Aude département no buses run on Sundays; many lines are reduced on Saturdays, holidays and school vacation periods.

Axat to: Castelnaudary (1 daily; 1hr 50min); Limoux (1 daily; 50min).

Caracassonne to: Albi (1 daily; 2hr); Axat (1 daily; 1hr 45min); Castelnaudary (5 daily; 45min); Castres (8 daily; 1hr 50min); Homps (2 daily; 55min); Lézignan (6 daily; 45min); Marseillette (2 daily; 22min); Narbonne (2 daily; 1hr 25min); Quillan (2 daily; 1hr 20min); St-Hilaire (2 daily; 45 minutes); Toulouse (1 daily; 2hr 20min); Trèbes (8 daily; 15min).

Comus to: Quillan (2 daily Mon–Fri; 1hr 5min).

Foix to: Auzat (2 Fri; 1hr); Ax-les-Thermes (2 daily; 1hr); Lavelanet (3–4 daily; 30min); Mirepoix (2–3 daily; 1hr 30min); Niaux (2 Fri; 35min); Pamiers (8 daily; 30min); St-Girons (3–4 daily; 45min); Quillan (1 daily; 2hr).

Latour-de-Carol to: Font-Romeu (4 daily; 50min); Perpignan (4 daily; 3hr 5min).

Lavelanet to: Foix (3–4 daily; 30min); Mirepoix (2–3 daily; 40min); Quillan (2 daily; 1hr); Toulouse (2–3 daily; 2hr 25min).

Limoux to: Castelnaudary (3 daily; 35min).

Mas d'Azil to: Toulouse (2 daily; 1hr 55min).

Mirepoix to: Lavelanet (2–3 daily; 40min); Pamiers (2–3 daily; 30min); Toulouse (2–3 daily; 2hr).

Pamiers to: Ax (4 daily; 1hr 40min); Foix (8 daily; 30min); Tarascon (6 daily; 45min).

Quillan to: Axat (2 daily; 20min); Carcassonne (2 daily; 1hr 20min); Comus (1–2 daily; 1hr 5min); Perpignan (2 daily; 1hr 30min); Quérigut (3 weekly in summer; 1hr 45min).

St-Girons to Aulus-les-Bains (1–2 daily; 1hr 15min); Foix (3–4 daily; 45min); Massat (1–2 daily; 45min); Toulouse (3 daily; 2hr 30min).

Tarascon-sur-Ariège to: Vicdessos/Auzat (2 daily; 30min).

Albi and Haut Languedoc

CHAPTER 3 Highlights

* **Albi Cathedral**
  Distinctive brickwork
  construction gives this
  medieval cathedral a
  surreal look. **See p.178**

* **Toulouse-Lautrec** See
  the largest collection of
  the diminutive
  Impressionist's distinctive work. **See p.178**

* **Cordes-sur-Ciel** Once a
  refuge for heretics, now
  a town of artisans,
  perched "on the sky"
  west of Albi. **See p.186**

* **Gaillac wines** Sample
  one of the country's oldest and most venerable
  AOCs. **See p.188**

* **Rabastens** A brilliantly
  restored painted church
  set by the tranquil banks
  of the Tarn.
  See p.190

* **Parc du Haut
  Languedoc** A wild and
  under-populated area,
  perfect for hiking and
  cycling. **See p.198**

▲ Cordes-sur-Ciel

Albi and Haut Languedoc

Tarn, the *département* to the east of Toulouse, consists of two contrasting zones. The northwest is wine country: the rolling landscape on the banks of the river after which the administrative area is named is punctuated by towns which grew up on the modest prosperity of the grape and other products of the soil, including garlic and woad. The southeast, on the other hand, is a rugged upland where herding and wool have sustained a precarious living for the villagers of the high valleys as far back as can be recalled. Today Tarn is not the most of dynamic of regions – it has fallen victim to the rural depopulation which typifies much of southern France, with the result that there is almost no industry. Nevertheless, there's much to see here and though, like Toulouse, it falls outside the modern administrative *région* of Languedoc-Roussillon, it is culturally and historically inseparable from the Occitan coastal lands.

In the northwest, **Albi**, Tarn's principal town, was ruled for centuries by the counts of Toulouse, and its name is synonymous with the Cathar sect with which modern *languedociens* still proudly identify. The undulating lowlands which surround the town are defined by the flow of the Tarn: to the east, descending from the Grandes Causses, it follows a rapid, rocky course, cutting down through forested hills and meandering dramatically around **Ambialet**; north of the capital, gritty **Carmaux** sits atop a coal-rich landscape, the Ségala, scarred by the centuries-long search for the black stuff; to the west, the stunningly preserved medieval citadel of **Cordes** marks the transition to the Aveyron valley; and finally, passing Albi, the Tarn flows west toward **Gaillac** and one of the most praised wine regions of the South of France, veering south, past the ancient *bastides* of **Lisle** and **Rabastens**, before being met by the tributary Agout. The region's interior, south of Albi, has a scattering of sleepy old towns set amidst fields of corn and wheat, slumbering since the leather industry which sustained them in the Middle Ages declined. Moving away from the river past Graulhet and Réalmont, the land becomes more hilly, and here you'll find **Lautrec**, the most beautiful town of the Albigeois.

To the southeast, **Haut Languedoc** ("Upper Languedoc"), a wild hinterland of rocky hills that provides an unexpected contrast with the bustle of the nearby coast, has a history of religious and political nonconformity – it was once a remote hotbed of Protestant Huguenots. At its base lies **Castres**, Albi's poorer cousin, a lively little provincial town, birthplace of the socialist hero Jean Jaurès and home to an important collection of Spanish art. In the uplands, most of which have been incorporated into the **Parc Naturel Régional de Haut Languedoc**, dark woods and high pasture are interspersed with a series of largely forgotten villages, including Lacaune, La Salvetat and St-Pons. This is easy walking terrain, crisscrossed by *grand randonnées* and local trails like the Gijou Valley Railway Path. Further south the **Montagne Noire**, rising south of **Mazamet**, presents an even more isolated and untamed landscape, guarded

Millau

St-Affrique

Tarn

Ambialet

GR36

D999

GR71

Gijou

Lacaune-
les-Bains

MONTS DE LACAUNE

Vèbre

Murat-
sur-Vébre

D922

Sommet de
l'Espinouse
(1124 m)

Brassac

Lac de la
Ravière

Lac Laouzas

La Salvetat

Agout

Agout

GR7

Angles

GR71

PARC NATUREL RÉGIONAL DE
HAUT LANGUEDOC

MONTS DE L'ESPINOUSE

D908

Lac de Stes-Payres

GR7

Olargues

Mazamet

La Devèze

St Pons

Orb

Pic de Noire
(1153 m)

St Chinian

N O I R E

N112

GR36

Clamoux

GR111

Limousis

Clermont/l'Hérault

Béziers

See Haut Languedoc & Montaigne Noire

on its southern side the ruined fortress of **Saissac** and the Cathar castles of **Lastours**. Chilling out in Castres is a good option, especially given its museums and amenities, while the rest of the region features rugged countryside, ideal for rambling or back-road motoring and cycling.

Despite its general isolation, the area of Albi and Haut Languedoc is well served by public transport. The main Toulouse–Rodez rail line follows the course of the Tarn up to Albi and Carmaux, with branch-offs to Cordes and companies. Cordes acts as a bus hub for the western part of the Parc Naturel

Festivals in Albi and Haut Languedoc

As elsewhere in Languedoc and Roussillon, most towns have their local **fêtes** between June and August, here featuring dances, fireworks and *pétanque* competitions. Some of the more exceptional ones are listed below; where we haven't given a number for information, contact the town's tourist office.

Feb–March Albi: Carnaval. Held from the last Sunday in February to the first Sun in March, Albi's traditional French Lenten festival coincides with "reBonds", a festival of sculpture, modern dance and contemporary music.

Late Feb to early March Albi, Castres & Mazamet: reBonds ☎05.63.38.55.56, Ⓦwww.athanor.asso.fr. Since 1989 this festival has brought together a wide range of French choreographers and musicians, in conjunction with sculpture and art exhibitions.

1st weekend April Albi: Un Week-end avec Elles ☎05.63.60.55.90, arpegesettremolos.com. Female vocals and music, featuring *chanson française* (Jane Birkin headlined in 2003) as well as European and North African acts.

Mid-May Gaillac: Wine contest. Held over four days, this competition is one of the two most important dates on the Gaillac calendar, when the new year's vintages are debuted and judged.

June–July Albi: Open-air theatre festival. Nightly performances of mostly French works, covering everything from the classics of Molière to the avant-garde, at the Palace de la Berbie (9.45pm), running from the last week of June through to mid-July.

June–August Blayes-les-Mines: Open-air concerts Ⓦwww.capdecouverte.com. Daily performances (4pm–midnight) of comedy drama and music, including, rock, soul, reggae, jazz, and *chanson*. The 2003 series featured Alpha Blondy, Marcus Miller and Mateo Parker.

1st weekend July Monastiès: Pause Guitare ☎05.63.60.55.90, arpegesettremolos.com. Free concerts dominated by *chanson française*, but also featuring solid world-music acts (Johnny Clegg in 2003).

Early July Albi: Jazz festival. Held over one week this festival draws French and international musicians alike, playing in a range of venues, both indoor and outdoor.

Mid-July Cordes: Fêtes du Grand Fauconnier. This four-day medieval festival converts the town into a costumed extravaganza, complete with concerts, exhibitions on medieval crafts and falconry. Daily admission to the old town is €7 (Ⓦwww.cordes-sur-ciel.org).

Mazamet, while other routes are now served by regular SNCF buses or local de Haut Languedoc, but getting to smaller villages is more difficult; penetrating the heart of the park is best done from St-Pons.

Albi and around

A provincial town with a population of 65,000, **ALBI** has a sleepy atmosphere which belies its role as *préfecture* of Tarn. Despite its visitors, in the evening its streets are deserted, even in summer. By ten o'clock the restaurants shut down, and it lapses into a village-like slumber. The highlights are the hulking brick-built **cathedral** and the **Toulouse-Lautrec museum**, which houses the world's largest collection of paintings by the native artist. In addition, the town offers a well-conserved **medieval quarter** of winding cobblestone alleys and centuries-old mansions. Set picturesquely on a high bank of the Tarn, it makes a comfortable base for exploring the nearby sights: the medieval vestiges of **Lescure** and **Castelnau**, and the coal country to the north. Albi is easily

Mid-July Castres: Les Extravadanses ☎05.63.71.56.58, ⓦwww.ville-castres.fr. A ten-day festival featuring music, dance and cinema in free open-air venues and at the town's theatre. An eclectic programme with a strong Caribbean flavour.

Mid-July Mazamet: Fanfares sans Frontières ☎05.63.61.27.07, ⓦwww.fanfares-sans-frontieres.org. Massive three-day gathering of dancers and musicians from around Europe, performing in free outdoor venues.

Mid-July Cordes: Musique sur Ciel ☎05.63.56.00.75, acadoc.festival@libertysurf.fr. Each year this ten-day festival focuses on the work of a different contemporary composer, and features the most promising of young French soloists playing programmes of classical music.

Last two weeks of July Castres: Goya festival. Nightly performances of classical music, theatre and opera, all performed on an outdoor stage in the place 1er du Mai. Brings in symphonies and companies from around France and western Europe.

Late July Blayes-les-Mines (Cagnac): Summer festival ☎05.63.38.55.57, info@rock-time.org. Long-running outdoor summer rock festival (camping available) held over a weekend, featuring international acts as well as notable local acts, such as Zebda.

Late July Réalmont: Ré'alcroche ☎05.63.55.52.89, ⓔreal.croche@wanadoo.fr. Massive outdoor weekend festival of bluegrass, rock, blues, Celtic and Cajun music, bringing in world-class acts and attracting over 30,000 spectators.

1st three weeks Aug Castres: Couleurs du Monde ☎05.63.71.59.84. Free world-music performances held nightly in the place 1er du Mai, and featuring performers from Africa, the Caribbean, Latin America and across Europe.

1st weekend Aug Gaillac: Fête du vin. Gaillac's second wine festival is timed to coincide with the beginning of the grape-harvest season, with wine contests and tastings, as well as concerts and cultural events.

Mid-Aug Rabastens: Grande Cavalcade. Typical village *fête* held for two days and featuring dancing, fireworks, and a parade through the town centre.

Mid-Nov Albi: Les Œillades. A one-week festival of new French feature films (with some entries from Belgium and Québec) with an emphasis on young film-makers. Plenty of seminars, and prizes are awarded for the films, actors and directors. Held at Ciné-forum, 104 av Colonel-Teyssier ☎05.63.38.25.17, ⓦwww.oeillades.free.fr.

Nov 23 Albi: Ste Cécile Day. Feast of the patron saint of the cathedral, with a special Mass held, and a market in the adjacent square.

explored on foot, and you can take in the main sights in a single day.

After the decline of Roman power, the former Celtic settlement here passed through the Visigothic and Frankish hands before coming under the power of the counts of Toulouse in the eleventh century. It was under them that the *pont vieux* was built over the Tarn, stimulating the town's growth as a centre for trade and attracting immigrants from as far away as the Rhine. The anti-Cathar Crusade let the town's burghers and bishops play the counts and kings against each other, increasing their own autonomy, and under the rule of the bishops from the 1300s onwards, Albi rode a wave of prosperity, based on the same woad trade that powered Toulouse (see box on p.100). But when demand for the dye declined, the town dropped out of history, and by the 1700s the adventurous were turning to the sea, some becoming renowned navigators. Industrialization came with the development of coalfields to the north; glass-working and textiles becoming the mainstay. These industries persist in Albi on a modest scale, and today the town is something of a backwater, living on under the shadows of its cathedral and the legacy of its most famous son, the artist Henri-Toulouse Lautrec (see box on p.179).

ALBI

▲ **1** _Castelnau & Lescure_

◀ **2** (1 km)

Musée
Lapéyrouse

Old Mills **A**

LA MADELEINE

RUE STE MARIE
RUE DE LA MADELEINE
RUE RINALDI
RUE PERROTY
RUE POR'A
RUE DU PORT
RUE RINALDI
RUE DU TENDAT

3

Tarn River

PONT DU 22 AOÛT 1944

PONT VIEUX

R. BASSE DES MOULINS
RUE DE LA RIVIÈRE

Gabares
Pier

SENTIER DES BERGES DU TARN

ACCOMMODATION

Camping de Caussels	B
Georges V	H
Hostellerie de Vigan	E
Hostellerie St-Antoine	F
Mercure les Bastides	A
Régence	G
St-Clair	C
Le Vieil-Alby	D

4
QUAI CHOISEUL

RUE DE LA GRD CÔTE
RUE DE LA VIGAN
RUE ÉMILE GRAND
R ST APRIC

LICES GEORGES POMPIDOU

RUE DE LA RÉPUBLIQUE

▶ **8** & Ambialet

Palace
de la Berbie

RUE DE LA SOUQUE
R ST ÉTIENNE

Covered
Market

R D FOUSSANTS
RUE STE CLAIRE

RUE DE
PL STE RHONEL
CLAIRE

BONNE-CAMBO D'ELBÈNE

Musée de
Toulouse-
Lautrec

_i_
RUE DE LA TEMPORALITÉ

B.D FARGUES
PLACE DU
MARCHÉ
RUE SAINT JULIEN

RUE CANDEIL

PLACE DE LA TREBAILLE

RUE DE LA MAITRISE

PLACE
SAINTE
CÉCILE

RUE AUGUSTIN MALROUX

Hôtel de
Reynès

Cathédrale Ste-Cécile

RUE MARIES

Church of
St-Salvy

PLACE DU
CLOÎTRE

Pharmacie des
Pénitents

RUE TIMBAL

IMP TIMBAL

R CAMINADE
RUE DE LA PIALE

5 **6**

RUE STE CÉCILE

IMP STE MARIE
RUE PEYTOUL
RUE DES PÉNITENTS
IMP DU PUITS DE LA GRÂCE

RUE DE LA CROIX VERTE

P

R DE LA CROIX BLANCHE

RUE DE L'OULMET

IMP PEYROLIÈRE
RUE D'EMPEYRALOTS

PLACE
DU
VIGAN

R SÈRE DE RIVIÈRE

BD GÉNÉRAL SIBILLE

Maison de
Vieil-Albi

C

R DU BIROT
R P BÉRENGUIER

R ST SÉCALIN
R DE L'HÔTEL DE VILLE

R DE L'HÔTEL DE VILLE

Hôtel
du Ville

RUE DE L'HÔTEL DE VILLE

LICES JEAN MOULIN

R ST ANTOINE

7

Wax Museum

8

D

BD LAUTREC

BD RANCAT

R DE VERDUSSE
R DES NOBLES

RUE DE L'HÔTEL EN SALVY

9

R DU BOURGUET

E

F

Hôtel du Bosc

BD GÉNÉRAL SIBILLE

BD GÉNÉRAL SIBILLE

RUE DU SEL

PLACE DU
PALAIS

RUE DE LA PORTE NEUVE

RUE DE LA VIOLETTE
RUE DU MAIN

RUE MATHE

CAMBOULIVES

▶ _Rue Balzac & Place de Fernand Pelloutier_

0 — — **200 m**

RESTAURANTS

Auberge du Pont Vieux	3
Auberge la Viguiere d'Alby	8
La Calèche	5
La Casa Loca	7
L'Esprit du Vin	4
Le Jardin de Quatre Saisons	1
Moulin de Mothe	2
La Tête de l'Art	6
Tournesol	9

PLACE
LAPEROUSE

R DOCTEUR TEIXISON

RUE DU DOCTEUR

Jardin National

RUE HIPPOLYTE SAVARY

AV CHARLES DE GAULLE

R DU CORBIERS

AV DE GENÈVE

Gare
Routière

AV GAMBETTA

BD ÉDOUARD ANDRIEU

▼ **G** , **H** & _Gare SNCF (250 m)_   _Castres & Toulouse_ ▼

Arrival, information and accommodation

Albi's **gare SNCF**, midway along the Toulouse–Rodez line, is southwest of the old town on place de Stalingrad, which can be reached in fifteen minutes by foot, or by local bus (#1; every 30min; €0.80) to place du Vigan, on the eastern side of the old town. There's not much to the *gare* itself: a ticket office, car rental office and small café; there's no left-luggage service. The **gare routière** is on place Jean-Jaurès, southeast of the old town, a little over ten minutes by foot from the cathedral, while you'll find the **tourist office** (July & Aug Mon–Sat 9am–7pm, Sun 10am–12.30pm & 2.30–5pm; Sept–June Mon–Sat 9am–12.30pm & 2–6pm, Sun 10am–12.30pm & 2.30–5pm; ☏05.63.49.48.80, 🌐www.tourisme.fr/albi) housed in the Palace de la Berbie, beside the cathedral; it will change money when banks are closed. The tourist office also offers a *Carte Avantage* (€5) which gives slight discounts on museums and activities.

Given its size, Albi offers a surprisingly wide selection of **hotels**, and even those located near the train station are only a short walk from the historical centre; rock-bottom budget places though are scarce. The FJT youth hostel has now closed but the local diocese operates a **hostel**, the *Centre Saint-Armand* (☏05.63.48.18.29, 📠05.63.48.18.21), at 16 rue de la République, which offers dorm accommodation (€16). The two-star **campsite**, *Camping de Caussels*, is a thirty-minute walk east of the centre in Parc de Caussels (Easter–Oct; ☏05.63.60.37.06; Albibus #5 to "Camping" from place Jean-Jaurès). Ask at the tourist office for the "Bon Séjour à Albi", a set-price hotel package (from €21–85 per person) which includes a *Carte Avantage*.

Georges V 29 av Maréchal-Joffre ☏05.63.54.24.16, 📧hotel.georgev@ilink.fr. Located by the train station, a small 80-year-old hotel in a converted house. Each room is individually decorated in modern pastel tones, and there's a garden to breakfast in. You'll need to book ahead. ❷

Hostellerie St-Antoine 17 rue St-Antoine ☏05.63.54.04.04, 📧stantoine@ilink.fr. Classy establishment founded in 1734 and run by the same family for five generations. The sumptuous rooms are appointed with antique furnishings, but the hotel also has modern facilities such as parking and AC. ❺

Hostellerie de Vigan 16 pl du Vigan ☏05.63.54.01.23, 🌐www.logis-de-france.com. Near the *gare routière*, this modern building is more functional than charming, with big but bland rooms. Comfortable, clean and quiet, it has all the amenities. ❹

Mercure les Bastides 41 rue Porta ☏05.63.47.66.66, 📧mercure.albi@wanadoo.fr. A luxury establishment in a restored eighteenth-century mill building, with modern facilities and decor, and a highly rated and well-priced restaurant. Try for one of the riverside rooms, which have spectacular views over the river to the cathedral. ❺

Régence 27 av Maréchal-Joffre ☏05.63.54.01.42, 🌐www.hotellaregence.com. Next door to, and a virtual replica of the *George V*, and a fine second choice when that hotel is full. ❶

St-Clair 8 rue St-Claire ☏05.63.54.25.66, 📧michelandrieu@hotmail.com. In a converted old brick-and-timber house in the heart of the old town only 50m from the cathedral, this friendly establishment is clean and well maintained. Also has parking. Closed part Jan. ❷

Le Vieil-Alby 25 rue Toulouse-Lautrec ☏05.63.54.15.69, 📠05.63.54.96.75. Comfortable and quiet, this hotel, set in a renovated medieval house in the centre, is possibly the best deal in town. It also has a great restaurant (closed Sun eve & Mon) with *menus* at €12–35 and very friendly management. Closed part Jan & early July ❸

The Town

All of Albi's sights are within or adjacent to the compact limits of the once-walled **old town**, whose northern boundary is formed by the steep banks of the Tarn, and which is now completely surrounded by the sprawl of the new town. Across the river, the eighteenth-century suburb of **La Madeleine** is also worth a look, primarily for the spectacular views of the Tarn which it affords, with medieval Albi perched above.

The Cathédrale Ste-Cécile

The rounded arches and towers and red-brick construction of the **Cathédrale Ste-Cécile** (June–Sept daily 8.30am–7pm; Oct–May Mon–Sat 9am–noon & 2.30–6.30pm, Sun 8.30am–7pm; free) dominate Albi, evoking a mix of the Middle Ages and Art Deco that makes it without doubt the most curious medieval cathedral you are likely to see. Financed by the proceeds of the Inquisition, the first bricks were laid in 1282, some fifty years after the Cathar defeat, but the 30-metre-wide nave and 78-metre-tall tower were not complet-ed for more than a century after. The cathedral's clean lines, narrow windows and hulking mass reflect its role as a bastion of militant Catholicism in a region plagued by heresy, but two alterations spoil its unity: a gaudy and incongruous sixteenth-century stone porch, and a Baroque frenzy of *trompe-l'oeil* festooned about the interior. In better harmony with the structure are the fifteenth-cen-tury **statues** of saints and biblical figures which decorate the rood screen to the right of the entrance, while the west wall is dominated by a giant contempo-rary **mural** of the Last Judgement – sadly marred by the later construction of a chapel – replete with nasty devils carrying off teeth-gnashing souls to the infer-no. To the immediate right of the entrance, a doorway leads to the **choir** (€1), consisting of wooden stalls backed by elaborately carved stonework and more statuary, similar to that of the nave. The **treasury** (€3), reached by a spiral stair-case on the north wall, is disappointingly small. If you can, catch the **organ recitals** held in the cathedral in July and August (Wed 5pm & Sun 4pm; free), or the tourist office's night-time **tours** (June–Sept daily 9.30pm; French only; €5). Weekend nights in summer (10.15pm), the cathedral is the venue for an elaborate French-language *son et lumière*, "La Légende du Gaucelm" (€9).

The Palace de la Berbie and the Musée de Toulouse-Lautrec

Next to the cathedral, the matching brick-built **Palace de la Berbie** ("bish-op", in local parlance), the fortified redoubt of Albi's lord-bishops, squats over the slow-passing Tarn. This complex began as a simple keep in the thirteenth century, but was elaborated in succeeding centuries by its wealthy owners, who strengthened its fortifications, linked it to the cathedral and laid out a classical garden. Today the palace houses the **Musée de Toulouse-Lautrec** (March & Oct Wed–Mon 10am–noon & 2–5.30pm; April–June & most Sept daily 10am–noon & 2–6pm; July to early Sept daily 9am–6pm; Nov–Feb Wed–Mon 10am–noon & 2–5pm; €4.50), the most important public collection of the painter's work, and the only part of the palace interior which is open to the public. Conceived and endowed by the artist's mother and opened in 1922, it is comprehensive (boasting both his first and last works) – a must for any fan of the diminutive Albigeois. His famous depictions of the entertainers and prostitutes of *fin-de-siècle* Paris, such as the provocatively matter-of-fact *In the Salon in Moulin Street*, or the erotic *Woman Disrobing*, are complemented by many **posters** and lesser-known works inspired by his family life in the local countryside. Off in a corner up a spiral stairway, you'll find a sumptuous thir-teenth-century **chapel**, with a beautiful ceiling of gold-painted stars on a blue background – once the audience chamber of the bishops. The topmost of the museum's three storeys houses works by other modern French artists, includ-ing Brayer, Gauguin and Matisse.

Henri de Toulouse-Lautrec

Perhaps the most famous of Languedoc's artists is the painter and illustrator **Henri de Toulouse-Lautrec**. Born into the venerable family of the viscounts of Toulouse-Lautrec in 1864, Henri was deprived of a traditional aristocratic upbringing due to a congenital bone condition; his frailty kept him out of school, and after two falls at his home in Albi resulted in broken legs, any hope of pursuing a "normal" life ended. He thus turned to painting, and his earliest works, scenes from his family's milieu such as *Artilleryman Saddling a Horse*, and portraits – particularly of his mother – showed great promise. With the support of his family and the encouragement of their friend, the painter René Princeteau, Henri moved to Paris to study under Bonnat and Cormon, two successful conservative artists. Settled in bohemian Montmartre and accompanied by his friend and fellow student **Vincent Van Gogh**, he came under the spell both of the Impressionists and of the seedy underside of the city, and it was here that his own vivid style began to flourish. Seduced by the subversive Parisian **nightclubs**, he began to convey their dynamism in charcoal sketches like *Gin-Cocktail* and *Chocolate Dancing*, which were published in popular newspapers and magazines. By the early 1890s he was renowned as an illustrator, doing colourful line-drawn adverts, posters for the famous **Moulin Rouge** cabaret and covers for magazines like *La Revue Blanch*. By 1894, when he began his series of sketches and paintings of Paris **brothels**, including *In the Sitting Room at Moulins Street* and *The Two Girlfriends*, he was already successful.

Henri's disabilities did not prevent him from living life to the full: he travelled widely, drank copiously and, of course, patronized with gusto the brothels he depicted (he was known to Parisian prostitutes as the "teapot", owing to his short rotund figure and excessive endowment). In the end his vices aggravated his already fragile state, and by 1899 he was seeking treatment for **alcoholism**. In September 1901, at the age of 37, he died in a family castle near Bordeaux. What compelled Lautrec's dissolute lifestyle is uncertain (it wasn't his family relations, as he remained close to his parents throughout his life) but his contribution to the artistic world is unquestionable; with a unique illustrative style – a peculiar outgrowth of Impressionism – he not only influenced successive movements such as the Fauvists, but set the precedent for innovative poster design; to this day his Moulin Rouge adverts remain some of the most reproduced pictures in the world. His other great legacy is the **chocolate mousse**, a dessert invented by the painter, for whom culinary experimentation was also a passion.

The palace also has a partly covered gallery (free) with a shady outdoor **café** providing views of the old bridge and the far riverbank, as well as access to the **garden** (July & Aug 9am–6pm; Sept–May 8am–noon & 2–6pm); you enter it from the place de l'Archevêché, on the east side of the complex.

The old town and La Madeleine

Albi's **old town** is a chaotic jumble of narrow streets spreading east and south of the cathedral–palace complex. From the square by the tourist office, you'll see the red-brick spire of the much mistreated **church of St-Salvy**, which marks the old town's centre. While the interior of the building is nothing special, its simple Romanesque **cloister** can be entered from the streets to either side (daily: 7am–8pm; free) – a great place to read or just take a break. Just east, in rue Timbal, sits the sixteenth-century brick-and-timber "**Pharmacie des Pénitents**", once a wealthy merchant's mansion and now a pharmacy, with playfully carved faces on its wooden beams, while across the street lies the rather more austere Renaissance and Gothic **Hôtel de Reynès** (courtyard open Mon–Fri 8am–noon & 1.30–5.30pm; free). To the south a hulking Renaissance mansion, now housing the **Hôtel du Ville**, holds a huge, timbered council chamber within its regal interior (Mon–Fri 8am–noon & 1.30–5.30pm; free). West from the town hall, the narrow cobbled streets overhung with balconies of medieval houses evoke the age when the bishops and woad merchants held sway. Here you'll find the medieval **Maison de Vieil Albi** (Mon–Sat 10.30am–12.30pm & 3–7pm; €1), a museum displaying items of local interest, including memorabilia of the young Toulouse-Lautrec, but – more interestingly – a period town-house interior. Close by are the artist's childhood home, the **Hôtel du Bosc** (no entry), and a laughably shabby **wax museum** (March–May & Oct–Dec Tues–Sat 2.30–5pm; June–Sept Tues–Sat 10am–noon & 2.30–6pm; €3.20).

Across the river from the main body of the old town lies the eighteenth-century suburb of **La Madeleine**, best reached by the oft-repaired eleventh-century *pont vieux* to the east of the bishop's palace. Before you cross over, however, you might want to explore the banks of the Tarn, where under the shadow of the palace walls, *gabares* (traditional river boats) depart downriver for half-hour **excursions** around town (30min; May–Sept 10.45am–6.30pm; €5) or to Aiguelèze (2hr; July & Aug Mon & Wed 5.45pm & Sun 9am; €15) about halfway to Gaillac. La Madeleine itself is a compact knot of residential houses, with a number of disused eighteenth-century mill buildings clustered along the riverbank on its eastern side. Part of the mill complex, back from the river, holds the **Musée Lapéyrouse** (April–Sept Mon–Fri 9am–noon & 2–6pm, Sat & Sun 10am–noon & 2–7pm; Oct–March Mon–Fri 10am–noon & 2–5pm, Sat & Sun 2–6pm; €2.50), named in honour of the adventurous navigator (1741–88) who fought the British in New France before embarking on a scientific voyage to South America, Japan, Siberia and the East Indies, where he perished in a shipwreck. The museum reviews the admiral's career in a lively display of personal and period artefacts, maps and dioramas.

Eating, drinking and nightlife

Culinary variety is not a high priority in Albi and most of the **restaurants** specialize in local *terroir* ("country cooking"), with the usual dishes – cassoulet, foie gras and duck, accompanied by fine Gaillac wine. You can also get *lou tastou*, tapas-sized portions which permit you to sample a variety of dishes without breaking the bank. Pizzas and *briques*, quick and cheap, can be found on the place du Vigan. Numerous **cafés** and **bars** lining place de l'Archevêché and place du Vigan have terraces for a daytime drink, including *Café de la Poste* on the north side of the latter, which has a good selection of Belgian beers, while others offer night-time **music** (predominantly Latin), including *Ó Caliente* (nightly till 2am) opposite the Palace de la Berbie and *Les Gargouilles* (weekends till 2am) in the place de l'Archevêché. *Le Shamrock*, 57 avenue Charles de Gaulle, and *Le Connemara*, 6 rue Honoré-de-Balzac, are Irish-style options.

Restaurants

Auberge du Pont Vieux 98 rue Porta ☏05.63.77.61.73. On the north bank of the Tarn, this popular establishment serves traditional Albigeois cuisine and offers both a vaulted dining room and a riverside terrace. *Terroir menus* go from €10. Closed Wed lunch & Tues off-season.
Auberge la Viguière d'Alby 7 rue Toulouse-Lautrec ☏05.63.54.76.44. Now under new ownership, the cuisine here, best enjoyed on the shady little patio, has taken a *gastronomique* twist. *Menus* from €11.50 at lunch to €53 in the evening. Closed Jan, part June & July, Sun eve & Mon.
La Calèche 8 rue de la Piale ☏05.63.54.15.52. Comfy dining room built under the supporting vaults of the cathedral, and a wide range of lunch and dinner *menus*, including cassoulets, *escargots*, excellent salads and Moroccan dishes (starting from €9.15). The service is fast and professional, yet friendly. Wheelchair accessible.

La Casa Loca rue Puech Bérenguier ☎ 05.63.47.26.00. A cosy and informal little place, featuring genuine Spanish food, with tapas (from €3 each) and, of course, paella (from €9), all made by ex-pat Spaniards. Closed Sat lunch & Sun.

L'Esprit du Vin 11 quai Choiseul ☎ 05.63.54.60.44. Under the shadow of la Berbie, this place scores on both decor and quality with imaginative *gastronomique* cuisine, balancing sweet and savoury with duck, lamb and fish dishes as well as excellent home-made desserts. Dinner *menus* €42–60. Closed mid-Feb to May.

Le Jardin de Quatre Saisons 19 bd Strasbourg ☎ 05.63.60.77.76. Hearty *terroir* fare prepared with market-fresh ingredients. Dine in AC comfort inside, or on a shaded terrace. *Menus* from €17. Closed Sun eve & Mon.

Mercure les Bastides 41 rue Porta ☎ 05.63.47.66.66. A luxurious, but nevertheless affordable restaurant in the hotel of the same, with fine views of the old town across the river. Match this with quality food and good service and you

have a winner. Lunch *menus* from €18. Closed Sat & Sun lunch & late Dec.

Moulin de Mothe Rue de Lamothe ☎ 05.63.60.38.15. Albi's well-established home of excellent Tarnais fare, located on the Madeleine side, a pleasant 1km stroll west from the *pont vieux*. Dishes include heartwarming *pot au feu* stews, first-rate foie gras and roast pigeon in a delicate fruit and nut sauce, with *menus* at €25–28. Wheelchair accessible. Closed Sun lunch.

La Tête de l'Art 7 rue de la Piale ☎ 05.63.38.44.75. Decidedly unrestrained atmosphere and wacky decor makes a pleasant change from its more formal rivals. *Menus* consisting of plentiful portions start at €13.50. Closed Tues & Wed off-season & Aug.

Tournesol Rue de l'Ort-en-Salvy, off pl du Vigan ☎ 05.63.38.44.60. Albi's herbivorous option; expect to pay €12 for a variety of salads, quiches and other organic options. Open lunch only, Tues–Sat.

Listings

Banks Most of the major French banks have branches in the old town offering currency exchange and ATMs. After bank hours, change money at the tourist office.

Bike rental Rey Sport, 39 rue Soult ☎ 05.63.47.24.22.

Bus information ☎ 05.63.53.31.28.

Car rental ADA, 173 av François-Verdier ☎ 05.63.38.96.48; Europcar, 24 av François-Verdier ☎ 05.63.48.88.33; and Hertz, 15 rue Jacques-Monod ☎ 05.63.60.89.89.

Hospital Centre Hospitalier, bd Général Sibille (☎ 05.63.47.47.47), southwest of the old town.

Internet access Les Royaumes Virtuels, 44 rue Croix Verte (daily 2pm–midnight); Ludi.com, 62 rue Séré de Rivère (daily 11am–midnight).

Laundry 10 rue Emile Grand (daily 8.30am–8pm).

Police Police Municipal, Hôtel du Police, 11 licés Georges-Pompidou.

Shopping and markets Flea market in the Halle de Castelviel (Sat 8am–noon), just west of the cathedral, and produce markets in pl Ste-Cécile and pl du Marché (Tues–Sun 8am–noon). Organic foods are sold in pl F-Pelloutier (Tues 5–7pm) and at Aliments Naturels, 1 rue Puech Bérenguier (☎ 05.63.54.44.86).

Swimming Espace Caussels is a waterpark just north of town on the Cordes road with an Olympic-sized pool and activities for children. Daily June–Aug 10am–8pm, €3.30 (€2.20 children).

Taxi Albi Taxi ☎ 05.63.54.20.69.

Train information ☎ 08.92.35.35.35, ⓦ www.sncf.fr.

Around Albi

Albi makes a good base for a number of easy excursions, most of which are well served by public transport (either Tarnbus or private firms). On the north bank of the Tarn, 6km west of Albi, tiny **Castelnau-de-Lévis** boasts the ruins of a hill-top **castle** (free entry) founded after the Albigensian Crusade by a rehabilitated Raymond VII of Toulouse. Little remains apart from a single slender tower, but climbing its 198 steps provides breathtaking views of Albi and the plains of the *pays de Cocagne*. La Taverne (☎ 05.63.60.60.16; closed Mon & Tues) in rue Aubijoux in the hamlet of Castelnau makes a very worthy lunch or dinner stop (*menus* €22–44).

Another vantage point from which to take in the panorama of Albi is the

The Albi–Castres rail line trail

The most pleasant, if not the fastest way to get from Albi to Castres is to follow the former rail line, now converted into a **hiking**, **cycling** and **riding** trail, which connects Albi and Castres. There are no major sites on the way, but this is an excellent way to enjoy a typical slice of Midi landscape – gently rolling hills with alternating pastures, wheat fields and sunflowers. The walk is suitable for all ages and fitness levels. The total distance is 45km, which can be walked in approximately sixteen hours, making an overnight stop at Lautrec (see p.192), 26km along. The trail can be picked up 1km south of the Albi ring road, on rue Bourgelat, near the old cemetery, just off the southbound N112. After 800m you'll meet the D71, which should be followed south for 900m to regain the trail. A further 7km will lead you past the ruined church of Monstalvy and along the N112 until you reach a parking lot. Following the yellow trail markings you'll take a small lane on your right, and continue straight, over the quiet N120, as the trail once again becomes dirt. After 400m, branch off to the right (southeast) to regain the rail line. Turning right it continues for 3.5km, passing below the hamlet of Lombers, and continuing 12km to Lautrec, the turn-off for which is marked by a disused crossing-house. Leaving Lautrec the trail can be regained at the same point, or by taking the D83 (direction Castres) south for 1.5km, where you'll pass a grain silo on the left. From here the trail continues the remaining 16km to Castres, emerging near the town's *gare*.

nineteenth-century octagonal sanctuary of **Notre-Dame-de-la-Drèche**, set on a rise 6km north of town. Founded by returning missionaries, the working church has a small **museum** (Mon–Sat 9.30–12.15pm & 4–6pm; free) recalling their efforts overseas; the grassy grounds outside the church are a popular picnic spot, and make an ideal rest stop for those returning by foot or bike from Cagnac (see p.184). A visit to the sanctuary can also be combined with a trip to **Lescure**, on the northeast edge of Albi, whose draw is the must-see eleventh-century **chapel** of St-Michel (hours vary). Founded by the monks from Gaillac and presently used for photography and art exhibitions, the ancient church boasts a striking twelfth-century Romanesque doorway and is festooned inside and out with carvings of gargoyles, animals and biblical scenes. Die-hard Toulouse-Lautrec fans will want to trek 45km north to **Château du Bosc** (daily: 9am–7pm; 45-min guided tour in French; €5), the family's principal estate, easily accessible from Albi by car or train to Naucelle-Gare, and then 3km southeast (follow signs for "Bosc"). The rambling estate is presided over by a magnificently appointed manor house still owned by the painter's family. In addition to family furnishings and *objets*, there are galleries featuring temporary exhibitions.

Ambialet

Following the twisting and rocky bed of the Tarn 21km east from Albi you reach **AMBIALET** (on the GR36), a mandatory stop on the way to Millau and not unworthy of exploration in its own right. Here the river doubles back in a dramatic oxbow, leaving a spit of land only 25m across at its narrowest point – a truly striking location. First mentioned in 924 AD, Ambialet belonged to Toulouse until it was seized by Simon de Montfort during the Albigensian Crusade. Over the following centuries it suffered in the Hundred Years' War and Wars of Religion; by the nineteenth it lay abandoned and even today it exudes a certain sleepy desolation. The main sight here is the austere Romanesque **church** (daily 7.15am–10pm; free), still used by the resident monks whose chanted masses are open to the public. Perched on the top of the hill it provides an impressive panorama of the town below. You reach the church by climbing up a path from the "old town", which sits at the narrowest part of the river's meander (the "new town" is above the road tunnel), and return either the same way, or by following the road behind the monastery for 2km. The countryside south of Ambialet is agricultural land – high plains deeply etched by winding rivers. Apart from pleasant scenery, there is little of interest until you reach the Monts de Lacaune of the Parc du Haut Languedoc (see p.199), some 35km south.

Buses stop in the car park on the south bank, near which you'll find Ambialet's summer **tourist office** (July & Aug 10am–noon & 2–6pm). On the north bank, the village's only **hotel**, the well-appointed *Du Pont* (closed Jan–Feb; ☎05.63.55.32.07, ⓦwww.hotel-du-pont.com; ❸), has been run by the same family for almost two centuries. Its **restaurant** (open daily) offers *menus* in the range €18–48. Ambialet also has three **campsites** (May to mid-Sept), all clustered along the riverbank near the bridge: the municipal site (☎05.63.55.32.93), the *Pont de Couris* (☎05.63.55.32.25) and the *La Moulinquié* (☎05.63.56.43.53), which also has two *gîtes*. **Bikes** can be rented at the hotel, while **kayaks** and **canoes** can be rented near the bridge on the same side of the river, and at other locales along the length of the river on the way to Albi. Wednesday's "country" **market** is strictly a tourist affair.

Carmaux and around

Lying 16km north of Albi, down-to-earth **CARMAUX** owes its minor wealth to the thirty-square-kilometre coalfield over which it sits, and its few visitors are drawn by the relics of the defunct mining industry around the town: the open pit of **Ste-Marie** and the museum of **Cagnac**. These sights can be taken in by car, bicycle or even by foot, and, combined with a visit to the church of Notre-Dame-de-la-Drèche, make a good day's outing from Albi. The countryside hereabouts is flat, scarred by excavation, and not particularly welcoming, but it improves as you head west towards Cordes, passing through **Monestiés**, home to a well-preserved ensemble of late medieval statues. If you're reliant on public transport, you'll have to catch one of the frequent buses which follow the old highway to see the mining sites, but there's no public transport link between Carmaux and Monestiés.

Carmaux's **coal** vein has been used since the twelfth century, but mining on a grand scale didn't begin until the 1700s, when the local squire, Georges Solages, received a royal licence to exploit the deposit. Late in the nineteenth century, the massive coalface at nearby Cagnac was discovered and became the focus of a boom. By the end of that century though, brutal conditions prompted miners, supported by Jean Jaurès, to unionize; in the half-century that followed the mines enjoyed their greatest period of production. In the 1970s things began to wind down, and the last mine, the great open pit, closed in 1997.

Carmaux itself offers little to visitors aside from a refreshing roughness – a relief after the pretensions of one too many polished-up *bastide*. In fact, the only "attraction" is the deceptively named **Musée de Château**, the former Solages estate 1km west of the centre, now housing a **museum** of mining and glass-working (June–Sept Mon–Sat 9am–noon & 2–6pm, Sun 3–6pm; Oct–May Mon–Fri 9.am–noon & 2–6pm, Sat & Sun 3–6pm; French-only 1hr guided visits; €4). With its unremarkable and run-down appearance, the mansion is an eyesore, and is unfortunately not redeemed by the subterranean exhibition, which, dominated by examples of local glass products and over-technical displays on coal mining, is insubstantial and dull.

Practicalities

Carmaux's **gare SNCF**, on the Albi–Rodez line, sits on the west side of the town centre. Turning left out of the station, boulevard Malroux leads north 100m to avenue Jean-Jaurès, the main street; at the junction turn right and you'll arrive three minutes later at the *place* of the same name, the town's centre. Two streets beyond lies place Gambetta, where the same kiosk serves as **gare routière** and **tourist office** (Mon–Sat 10am–noon & 2–6pm; ☎05.63.76.76.67, ✉otsi.carmaux@wanadoo.fr). Of the town's **hotels**, the non-descript *Terminus* (closed Sat, mid-Aug & late Dec; ☎ & ℻05.63.76 .50.28, ⓌÐwww.logis-de-france.fr; ❶), across from the train station on avenue Jean-Jaurès, is the best option, while the more basic *Gambetta* (☎05.63.76.51.21; ❶), on the *place* of the same name, is cheaper. The **campsite** (May–Oct) is beside the museum. *La Mouette* (closed Sun & Mon eves & mid-Feb; ☎05.63.36.79.90), the town's best **restaurant**, is on place Jean-Jaurès, and offers original and varied *menus* featuring grilled meats and *confits* starting at €10.50 for lunch, up to the deluxe dinner-time "*menu* surprise" at €43. **Bikes** can be rented from Patrick Gelac (☎05.63.56.05.64) on boulevard Augustin-Malroux, near the station.

Blayes, Cagnac and the Cap Découverte

With the land sloping down towards Albi, it makes the most sense to start a trip through the once coal-filled landscape to **Cagnac** from Carmaux. Just 2km south of town, the mining hamlet of **Blayes-les-Mines** has now become a centre for industrial-history tourism, and makes an interesting stop, particularly if you are travelling with children. The first thing you'll come upon is the abandoned *découverte*, or **open pit**, of Ste-Marie, where the silent hulks of rusting machinery parked along its rim have been revived as the **Parc de Titans** (June–Sept daily 10am–7pm; Oct–May Mon–Fri 10am–noon & 2–5pm, Sat & Sun 10am–noon & 2–6pm; €4). The adjacent **Jardins du Carbonifère** (same hours and ticket) feature nature trails among local fauna. Further along the D90 you'll pass the **Cité du Homps**, a little industrial suburb of single-storey wooden huts, built for the Polish miners who immigrated in the Fifties, until you reach the **Musée Mine de Cagnac** (same hours; €7, or €8.80 with Parc and Jardins), a vivid recreation of the world of the coal mine, and undoubtedly the region's most original museum. It consists of a stimulating, if claustrophobic, ninety-minute guided tour through 350m of galleries, excavated by out-of-work miners, and over a century of mining history, as you're shown different types of tunnels and machinery, a broad coal face and the miners' day quarters.

In Blayes there's a **tourist office** (hours irregular; ☎05.63.80.15.10, Ⓦwww.capdecouverte.com). You can stay at the newly opened *L'Auberge* (☎05.63.80.21.35, ℻05.63.80.21.36; ❷) near the Cap and *La Grand Couverte* serves up traditional fare (from about €12). There's a **picnic** area with a pond beside the museum, and in Cagnac village, a kilometre further along, you'll find a couple of simple **café-bars**. From the village, the D90 begins a rapid descent, reaching Notre-Dame-de-la-Drèche (see p.182) after 3km, before continuing to Albi. You may, however, be tempted to stay the night or enjoy a meal at

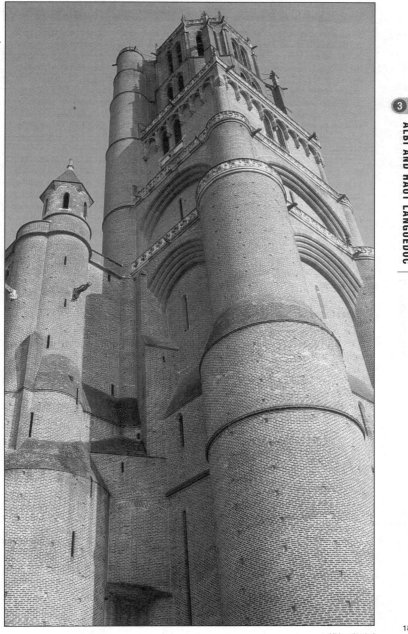

▲ Albi cathedral

The Cérou Valley

From Monestiès to Cordes-sur-Ciel the **Cérou** river meanders down from the scrub-by highlands of the Ségala towards the rocky hills of the Tarnais *causses*, before emptying into the Lot. The pleasant and unchallenging sixteen-kilometre trip along the wooded riverbank can be made by car or bicycle, but can also be **hiked**, following a gentle path, in four to five hours. Leaving from the sports ground on the north side of Monestiès, follow the disused rail-bed which runs parallel to the D91 highway for 6km to the hamlet of Salles. Crossing the river, follow the directions though town for Virac, but turn right when you come to Salles' medieval church. At the end of that street follow the sealed road which ascends towards the Vignasse farm. After 200m or so, take the first trail branching off to the right. After 800m or so, following the yellow trail markings, you should reach the top of a T-junction. Cross this and proceed 30m, before the trail turns off left through the trees. Regaining a country lane 60m later, turn right, passing a bridge on your right, and a turn on your left, before coming to a T-junction. Here, take the left branch, which descends, becoming a dirt trail for 250m before reaching the D7 road. Cordes should now be in view. Descending along the D7 for just over 1km you'll pass a sign saying *"virages sur 2000m"*; here you can pick up the trail which leads to the town itself (1km further).

the welcoming B&B *Les Campagnes* (☎05.63.53.92.97, Ⓦwww.gites-du-tarn.com; ❸ English spoken); which features organic cuisine (Thurs & Fri only) for €16.

Monestiés

Some 8km west of Carmaux is the rather run-of-the-mill village of **MONESTIÉS**, remarkable only for a much-touted set of fifteenth-century religious **statues** housed its **Chapelle St-Jacques** (daily: mid-March to June & Sept–Oct 10am–noon & 2–6pm; July & Aug 10am–noon & 2–7pm; Nov to mid-March 2–5pm; €3.50). The stone carvings on display are a set of four works representing together a group of figures in Christ's tomb, the Crucifixion and a *pietà*; they are well executed and preserved, but most likely only fans of late medieval art will feel that the admission price is justified. The town is also home to the small **Bajén-Vega Museum** (daily 10am–noon & 2.30–6.30pm; €3 or €5 with chapel), with works by the two unexceptional local twentieth-century artists after whom it is named. It is housed in the same building as the **tourist office** (same hours; ☎05.63.76.19.17, Ⓦwww.monesties.com). The only **hotel** is the intermittently open *L'Orée des Bois* (☎05.63.76.11.72, Ⓦwww.logis-de-france.fr; ❷), opposite the *chapelle*, but you can also stay at the B&B *La Bouysse* (☎05.63.76.48.78, Ⓦwww.lesvoisins.nl; ❷ English spoken) There is a basic riverside municipal **campsite** off the road to Cordes. *Auberge Occitane* (closed late Aug to Sept & Wed), on the main street, is friendly and serves two-course **meals** from €8; the grocery store rents **bikes** (☎05.63.76.11.51).

Cordes-sur-Ciel

CORDES-SUR-CIEL, 27km northwest of Albi and just west of Monestiés, is the most spectacularly preserved of the Albigeois fortified planned towns, or *bastides*. Dramatically situated on a steep hill, the origin of the town's surname *sur-ciel* ("in the sky") can be appreciated on mornings when fog cloaks the foot of the hill and the medieval *cité* pokes through, apparently suspended in the clouds. No single sight brings people to Cordes; rather, the town as a whole, girded by several concentric medieval walls and endowed with a score of old houses, is something of an open-air museum and artisanal centre. It can be seen in an afternoon, but if you can afford the relatively expensive hotels, it makes for an atmospheric place to spend a night or two.

Founded in 1222 by Count Raymond VII of Toulouse at the height of the war against his Cathar subjects, Cordes provided a durable and defiant strong-hold against Simon de Montfort's attacks. Its forename comes from the **leatherworking** industry (a craft associated with Córdoba, in Spain) which supported and enriched the town, bringing rapid growth; in the 1200s alone the walls had to be enlarged no less than seven times. Things took a downturn, however, with the arrival of the plague in the 1400s. Although Cordes later recovered, and had a notable lace industry in the nineteenth century, its real renaissance didn't come until the 1970s, when hippies, including the **crafts-men** and **artisans** whose wood, metalwork and other studios now cram the upper town, arrived to put Cordes back on the map, attracted by the place's beauty and air of antiquity.

The Town

The traveller, who from the terrace of Cordes regards the summer's night, knows that he has no need to go further, and that if he allows it, day after day, the beauty here will raise him out of any solitude.

Albert Camus

Camus' words give some idea of the town's allure, and hard though it may be to achieve such a placid state when the streets are packed during summer days, in the evening or out of season the romance of Cordes returns. To watch the sun rise from the ramparts is worth getting up for, and with every other build-ing a medieval mansion, walking the town before the crowds arrive is a delight. Its layout is simple: the old citadel – the "**upper town**" – runs along and down the sides of the long and narrow ridge which juts up from the plain, while the modern "**lower town**" consists of a clump of streets at the foot of the old town's eastern tip. The best route to the upper town is the knee-cracking Grande Rue Basse ascending from the lower tourist office (see below), although at busy times, it is more pleasant to take one of the picturesque but less crowded side-streets. Alternatively, a *navette* ("minibus"; July & Aug; €2) makes frequent trips from outside the tourist office. Along the way a series of medieval **gates** leads to the compact upper town.

Entering the last of the fortified entrances, you'll reach the **Musée Charles-Portal** (April & May Sun 3–6pm; June & Sept Sat & Sun same times; July & Aug daily 11am–12.30pm & 3.30–6.30pm; €3), housing a display on the medieval wells which riddle the town, and which were used in time of siege for water supply or to store grain. Further along on Grande Rue, the elegant and symmetrical arcaded face of the fourteenth-century **Maison du Grand Fauconnier** conceals the **Musée Yves-Brayer** (daily 10.30am–12.30pm & 2–6pm; closed Jan; €4), which features works by the local figurative painter, a French-only audio presentation explaining the town's lace-making tradition and a motley collection of modern art, including minor pieces by Picasso, Miró and Klee – hardly worth the stop. Across the street squats the ancient covered market, where you can peer down one of the town's famously deep wells. Continuing along Grande Rue, you'll see the **Maison de Grand Veneur**

("House of the Great Hunter") – whose otherwise plain stone facade is festooned with amusingly sculpted and extremely well-preserved medieval caricatures of beasts and hunters. A few doors down is the similarly impressively carved frontage of Raymond of Toulouse's old palace, now home to the hotel *Grand Ecuyer* (named after the finely sculpted horse figure) while, just beyond, the contemporary **Porte des Ormeaux** ("Gate of the Birds") takes you out of the old town.

There are more than forty **boutiques** in Cordes, including some which are thinly disguised as "museums". If you would like to shop for leatherwork, metal and handicraft items and price is not an issue, you could easily spend an afternoon or two (and a considerable sum) here. Many of the stores double as workshops, so even window-shopping is quite interesting. One of the better deals is *Le Petit Bois*, in the place de l'Église, which has ingenious toys and gifts.

Practicalities

Trains stop 5km to the west of Cordes at **Vindrac** (☎05.63.56.05.64), from where it's a pleasant hour-long walk. Alternatively, a **taxi** (☎05.63.56.14.80) will cost around €3.80. **Buses** arrive near the lower-town summer-only **tourist office** (May to mid-June & 1–15 Sept Sat 2–6pm, Sun 10.30am–12.30pm & 2–6pm; mid-June to Aug Mon 2–6pm, Tues–Sun 10.30am–12.30pm & 2–6pm), while the main tourist office (July & Aug daily 10am–1pm & 2–7pm; Sept–June Mon 2.30–6pm, Tues–Fri 10.30am–12.30pm & 2.30–6pm, Sat & Sun 2–6pm; ☎05.63.56.00.52, ⓦwww.cordes-sur-ciel.org) is in the heart of the *cité*. If you're driving, **parking** can be a challenge – in the summer months the area a few metres east of the lower tourist office soon fills up and cars line the roads leading into town. Don't be tempted to drive into the old town.

The best **hotel** in town is the magnificently atmospheric *Grand Ecuyer* (☎05.63.53.79.50, ⓔgrand.ecuyer@thuries.fr; closed mid-Oct to Easter; ❺), housed in Raymond's former palace. Across from the Charles-Porte museum, *Hôtel de la Cité* is a lower-priced alternative offering the same medieval trappings (closed Nov–April; ☎05.63.56.03.53, ⓔcite@thuries.fr; ❹), or there's an upmarket **chambres d'hôte**, *La Chevance*, just inside Porte des Ormeaux (closed Oct–April; ☎05.63.56.14.65, ⓕ05.63.56.28.72; ❺), with a good restaurant (*menus* €19–37). There's also a decent **campsite**, *Le Moulin de Julien* (open May–Sept; ☎ & ⓕ05.63.56.11.10), 1km southeast on the Gaillac road. The best **restaurants** are in the town's hotels, including that in the *Grand Ecuyer*, a one-star Michelin restaurant known for its foie gras and other regional dishes (*menus* €38–72). Aside from these, there's plenty of choice around the central place de la Halle and adjacent place de la Bride, while *Le Grand Veneur*, at 53 Grande Rue (closed Mon; main dishes €6–9), serves decent salads, pizzas and *crêpes* among incongruous nautical bric-a-brac.

Gaillac and around

Twenty-three kilometres west of Albi along the Tarn, **GAILLAC**, located at the heart of the wine region bearing its name, is a town built on the grape. It has a climate ideal for viticulture, and its inhabitants started putting corks in bottles more than 2500 years ago. But the industry really took off in the eighth century with the founding of the Benedictine abbey of St Michel – as part of their rule, monks are given a healthy daily ration of wine which, along with that needed for Holy Communion, ensured a high demand for the local product. In the tenth century the entrepreneurial Order decided to guarantee the quality of their vintage by laying down the rules as to which wines could quality as Gaillacoises – and thus one of France's most famous AOCs was born. Today, Gaillac continues to live off the deserved reputation of its wine, but the commercial success of such a class-conscious product has led the simple town to adopt certain pretensions unmerited by its provincial reality. The chief reason for staying here longer than a few hours is to use it as a base for exploring the old *bastide*-villages of **Lisle** and **Rabastens**, further downstream.

The Town

Gaillac, with its compact medieval core, sits on the north side of the river. The focal point of the old town, though not its geographic centre – set as it is by the old bridge over the Tarn – is the ponderous **abbey-church of St-Michel**, constructed in the eleventh century, and impressively large for its era. The interior is unadorned, apart from a fourteenth-century painted Virgin and Child in the left-hand side of the nave. The uninspiring **Musée de l'Abbaye de la Vigne et du Vin** (July & Aug daily 10am–1pm & 2–6.30pm; Sept–June 10am–noon & 2–6pm; €2.30), adjacent to the church, is dedicated to winemaking, with a twenty-minute French-only audiovisual show and displays of old grape presses, barrels, tools and bottles, but its chief attraction is its location in the old monastery cellars. The real business in Gaillac goes on down in the **Maison de Vins de Gaillac** (daily 10am–noon & 2–7pm; free) in the same complex, where you can sample, and are encouraged to buy, local vintages.

The old town spreading out to the north and east of the abbey-church retains a number of brick-and-timber houses worth seeking out, while a few minutes' walk northwest from place Lapérouse across the old Pont Château-de-Homps sits the **natural history museum**, the Musée Philadelphe Thomas (May–Oct Fri–Sun 10am–noon & 2–6pm; €2.30), with a collection of specimen cases stacked with the usual stuffed birds, dead bugs and sea creatures. Behind the monastery, off place Eugénie de Guérin, lies the medieval *faubourg*, whose twisting lanes lack grand monuments but are loaded with atmosphere. On its eastern side, shady **Parc Foucaud** surrounds the surprisingly good **Musée des Beaux-Arts** (June–Sept Wed–Sun 10am–noon & 2–6pm, Oct–May Fri–Sun 10am–noon & 2–6pm; €2.30). The nineteenth- and twentieth-century Impressionist works of local artists Raymond Tournon and Henri Loubat deserve a look, and some of the contemporary art rises well above the quality of a country museum.

Practicalities

Gaillac's **gare SNCF** (℡05.63.57.00.23), which is also where **buses** stop, is off to the north of the old town, a good twenty-minute walk from the wine centre and the **tourist office** (July & Aug daily 10am–1pm & 2–6.30pm, Sept–June 10am–noon & 2–6pm; ℡05.63.57.14.65, ⓦwww.ville-gaillac.fr) at the heart of things. **Accommodation** is plentiful and relatively cheap, with the best digs at *La Verrerie* (closed mid-Oct to mid-April; ℡05.63.57.32.77, ⓦwww.la-verrerie.com; ❸; English spoken), a converted glass factory set in its own grounds in rue de l'Egalité. A good budget choice is the cosy *Hôtel du Parc* (℡05.63.57.02.07; ❶; *menu* from €12), and Lucile Pinon has **chambres d'hôtes** (8 place St-Michel; ℡05.63.57.61.48, ⓕ05.63.41.06.56; ❸) in her comfortable seventeenth-century *faubourg* house. Heading south out of town on the route de Lisle, you'll find the adequate new **gîte** *Bel Aspect*

(☎05.63.81.21.50, ✉mfrbelaspect.81.gaillac@wanadoo.fr; ❶), which also provides affordable meals (€10). The municipal **campsite** (June to mid-Sept;
☎05.63.57.18.30) is nicely situated along the river, under the shadow of the
abbey. The best **restaurant** in town is *Les Sarments* at 27 rue Cabrol (closed
Sun eve & Mon; ☎05.63.57.62.61; *menus* from €22), a *gastronomique* place
tucked away in a medieval cellar in the *faubourg*. But the much cheaper *Aux
Charmes Gaillacois*, on rue Denfert-Rochereau near the train station, offers
inexpensive and abundant four-course *menus* which include wine and home-
made desserts (from €9.80). The local market is held Tuesday, Friday and
Sunday mornings.

Lisle-sur-Tarn and Rabastens

Only a ten-minute ride (7km) south on one of the frequent buses or trains
from Gaillac, **LISLE-SUR-TARN** is a tranquil twelfth-century *bastide* known
for its *pountets*, the overhead covered passages which connect many of its brick-
built medieval houses. There is little to detain you here apart from a stroll
through the town and a relaxed drink in arcaded place Saissac, at its centre. The
small local **museum** (same hours as tourist office; €2) is tucked away to the
southeast of the square and contains works by the native designer Raymond
Lafage (who studied under Michelangelo). To the east, a street descends to the
riverside and a point which long ago was the town's pier – an evocative spot.
By the modern bridge just downstream sits the town's strikingly bold fourteenth-century brick **church**.

Lisle's **tourist office** (April to mid-Oct Wed–Mon 10am–noon & 2–6pm;
mid-Oct to March Thurs & Fri 2–6pm; ☎05.63.40.31.85, ⊛www.ville-lisle-
sur-tarn.fr) is on the east side of place Saissac. *Le Princinor* (☎05.63.33.35.44,
🄵05.63.33.89.84; ❷), on the road to Rabastens, is the town's only **hotel**; don't
be fooled by its box-like exterior – the rooms are comfortable and the *menu*
(from €10 at lunch and €15 at dinner) has a distinctly northern French flavour.
The tiny one-star **campsite** (July–Sept; ☎05.63.33.35.18) near the *Princinor* is
another option. Méridiac on avenue d'Albi (☎05.63.33.38.96) rents **bikes**.

RABASTENS, the next village downriver on the Tarn, can be reached easily by bicycle or foot and is a better choice than Lisle for an overnight stop. On
weekend evenings the streets fill with young people, giving it a vivacity surprising for its size and making it a welcome contrast to the sleepier villages of
the Albigeois. Still guarded by vestiges of its brick ramparts, Rabastens was born
in the time of the fifth-century barbarian invasions, when it served as a refuge
for the inhabitants of a huge Gallo-roman villa. In the Middle Ages, the tanning
industry brought it considerable prosperity, reflected in its surprisingly rich
architecture. The sight which makes Rabastens an obligatory stop is the twelfth-
century **Notre-Dame du Bourg**. In the 1860s its incredible painted interior
was rediscovered and restored. The magnificent, vibrant **frescoes** cover virtually every surface, and provide a rare chance to see what medieval churches really looked like, before the "puritans" of the Catholic Reformation scrubbed
them clean. Also of note is a chapel dedicated to St James, donated by the archbishop of Santiago, grateful for the wealth which the pilgrimage route was
bringing his diocese. The **Musée du Rabastinois** (May–Oct Tues–Sat
10–noon & 2–6pm, Sun 3–6pm; Oct–April Tues–Sun 2–6pm; €2) is just down
the street and contains pieces from the Gallo-Roman and medieval periods.

Buses from Lisle pass through the centre of Rabastens, but the **gare SNCF**
is located just across the river in Couferoul – about a ten-minute walk from
the centre. The **tourist office** (mid-Feb to Nov Tues–Sat 10am–noon &

2–6pm, Sun 2–6pm; ☎05.63.40.65.65, ✉ot-rabastens@wanadoo.fr), at 2 rue Amadée-Clausade, is by the old bridge and the church. The best **hotel** in Rabastens is the *Hostellerie du Pré-Vert* (closed Sun, Mon & Jan; ☎05.63.33.70.51, ✉info@leprevert.com; ❸), an eighteenth-century mansion on the promenade des Licés. The one-star **campsite**, *Les Auzerals* (May–Aug; ☎05.63.33.70.36), is situated 3km northwest of town, on a small lake. As far as food and drink goes, any of the bistros and **restaurants** on the main promenade will provide solid Tarnaise sustenance, but for something different head to the *Hotel de la Poste* on place St-Michel (just off the main road), which has authentic Andalucian ambience and *menus* from €12, including wine.

Graulhet, Réalmont and Lautrec

The undulating wheat lands stretching southeast from Gaillac towards Castres are dominated by three small *bastides*. Of these, **Graulhet** and **Réalmont** are better served by transport (both falling on the Albi–Toulouse line) but are less interesting; unless you have a car, they do not merit inclusion in your itinerary. **Lautrec**, on the other hand, picturesquely set on a windmill-capped spur, is a nice place to spend an afternoon or evening, but can only be accessed from Albi either via Graulhet or Castres.

Graulhet

One of the possible bus routes from Albi to Lautrec involves a change in **GRAULHET**, located 16km southeast of Gaillac and 30km northwest of Castres, on the Dadou river, and the transfer is about the only reason you would want to stop here – it is a grim, unsmiling town, whose unremarkable old quarter has been allowed to decay into a shambles. The town's name is derived from *groule*, the Occitan word for leather, which has been the source of the town's meagre prosperity since the Middle Ages – as early as the twelfth century raw hides from the pasture lands of the Montagne Noire were brought here to be tanned and finished. **Buses** stop in place du Jourdain, across the river from the main road, below the old quarter capping the low rise on the north side of the square. The **tourist office** (Mon–Sat 9am–noon & 2–6pm; ☎ & ☎05.63.34.75.09, ✉graulhet.ot@wanadoo.fr) on place Foch has maps of the town's paltry highlights. If you do need to **stay** here, *Le Grandgousier* (☎05.63.34.50.32, ✉paul.fernandez@wanadoo.fr; ❷), also in place du Jourdain, has reasonable rooms and a **restaurant** (€8.50–30). Finer dining can be found at *La Rigaudié* (closed Mon & Sat & Sun eves, Aug & late Dec; ☎05.63.34.50.07), 2km east of town out on the St-Julien-du-Puy road, and with an excellent fish *menu* (€19–37). The town is at its best on Tuesday, Thursday and Sunday when the local market is held.

Réalmont

Seventeen kilometres east of Graulhet, **RÉALMONT** is one of the "royal *bastides*" founded by the twelfth-century Capetian kings to weaken the power of the local nobility. Today, only a few vestiges of its medieval past – the arcades of the main square and the grid of streets typical of medieval "new towns" – survive. The town's **church**, dating from the sixteenth century, is unremarkable. Wednesday morning is the best time to stop in here; the country **market** has local produce at excellent prices, making it a great opportunity to stock up for a picnic. The **tourist office** (June–Sept Mon 2–6pm, Tues–Sat 10am–noon & 2–6pm, Sun 3–6.30pm; Oct–May Tues–Fri 2–6pm, Wed & Sun 10am–noon; ☎05.63.45.52.05) is in rue Cabroult, behind the charming but slightly decayed *Hôtel Noël*. This, the town's only **hotel** (closed Sun eve, Mon & Feb; ☎05.63.55.52.80, ⓦwww.logis-de-france.fr; ❷), has been run by the Granier family for six generations and provides excellent meals (from €15; closed Sun eve & Mon). There is also a basic **campsite** 2km away on the Graulhet road (May–Sept; ☎05.63.55.50.41). The best **restaurant** deal is *Les Routiers* (closed Sun & part Aug; ☎05.63.55.65.44) on boulevard Armengaud, which serves up massive *menus* (from €10.50), including dessert and wine. A country market is held on Wednesday morning (July & Aug).

Lautrec

The most picturesque of the towns between Albi and Castres, **LAUTREC** is located on a minor road 15km southeast of Graulhet. The vanes of the windmill still churn on top of the hill where the castle once stood, and the hamlet gathered around it is a warren of steep, twisting streets, interspersed by little arcaded squares. It was here that a marriage alliance of 1196 established the family of the counts of Toulouse-Lautrec (the artist Henri's forebears). Nowadays the town prides itself on its pungent pink **garlic**, first brought by Spanish merchants in the eighteenth century. Celebrated with a festival (Aug 6), four thousand tonnes of the stuff are harvested here every year, but smaller quantities can be purchased at the town's Friday **market**.

Entering the old town through rue Mercadiel, where the main road passes on the north side, the *mairie* is just on the left, in a building which also houses the tourist office and the two-room **archeological museum** (open sporadically; €1.50). The latter is a fairly humble affair, with a display on local medieval burial customs and information on the scores of wells which perforate the old town and, as at Cordes, served primarily for grain storage. Continuing from the museum to the first crossroads, you can either descend on the left towards Lautrec's remaining twelfth-century **gate** or continue to the fourteenth-century collegial **church**, now a Baroque monstrosity inside. To get to the functioning seventeenth-century **windmill** perched above the town (July & Aug daily 2–7pm; Sept–June Sun 2–5pm; €2), climb the street to the right immediately before the church. As you enter the mill on a windy day, the sight and sound of the large, rapidly spinning wooden mechanisms are exhilarating. The hill top also offers a superb panoramic **view** towards the south.

There is no **hotel** here, but a number of **chambres d'hôtes** in or near the town can put you up. The **tourist office** (July & Aug Mon–Sat 10am–12.30pm & 2.30–6.30pm, Sun 2.30–6.30pm; Sept–June Sun & Mon 2–5pm, Tues–Sat 10am–noon & 2–5pm; ☎05.63.75.31.40, ⓦperso.wanadoo .fr/crea-fm) in rue de Marcadiel has a complete list, but the most homely of the lot is Alain Routier's house in place du Monument (☎05.63.75.98.77; ❸). Those on a strict budget should head to the **gîte** 4km from town at Bramtourte (☎ & ⒻF05.63.42.05.04; ❶). The two best **restaurants** are *Le Trois Gargouilles*, 5 rue St-Esprit, below the windmill (June–Sept daily for lunch & Thurs–Sat dinner; from €15), which serves home-made food made with garden-grown ingredients, and the superior *Le Garde Pile* (☎05.63.75.34.58; Fri lunch to Sun lunch only), located in a converted grainery, just outside of town on the Castres road, which features a selection of varied dishes, strong on the local pink garlic (*menus* €14.50–27.50). Friday is **market** day (morning).

Castres and around

Southeast of Lautrec, the rolling agricultural landscape comes to an abrupt end as the land begins to rise and you approach Haut Languedoc, a highland ridged by peaks rising up to 1100m. **CASTRES**, on the western edge of the uplands, 42km south of Albi, began some two thousand years ago as a Roman military base (as its name, from the word for "camp" or "fort" recalls). An important Benedictine monastery was built here in the seventh century but, like the Roman town, its traces have all but vanished. In the twelfth century Castres was swept up in the Cathar movement, and it was here that the first Albigensian **martyrs** were burned at the stake in 1209. The ever-rebellious population took up the Protestant banner four centuries later, and the town became an important centre of **Huguenot** administration. Today, still supported by the textile industry which boomed in the eighteenth century, Castres is a town with energy – worth visiting in its own right and an ideal point of access to the northern and western parts of the Parc Naturel Régional du Haut Languedoc (see p.198). Boasting a colourful medieval core and a pleasantly diverse populace, it is also enlivened by two summer **music festivals**. In

▲ Albi ▲ **Ⓐ**, Parc Gourjade & Campsite

Covered Market
PLACE DE L'ALBINIQUE

CASTRES

ACCOMMODATION
Domaine de Gourjade	A
L'Europe	D
Le Périgord	C
Renaissance	E B
Rivière	B

RESTAURANTS
La Mandragore	4
Le Belee	2
Le Médiéval	5
Yankee Grill	1
Bar 3 Rois	3
La Mouclade	6

Musée Jean-Jaurès

Hôtel Nayrac

Riverboat Pier

Centre for Contemporary Art

Cathédrale St-Benoît

Hôtel Jean-Leroy   Hôtel de Poncet

Hôtel de Ville & Musée Goya

▶ Brassac & the Sidorbe
▶ Gare Routière, Mazamet & St Pons

◀ Gare SNCF
◀ Lavaur

0   100 m

▼ Revel & Toulouse   ▼ Post Office (30m)   Sorèze & Labrugière ▼

addition, it has a couple of good museums: one dedicated to Castres' native son, the nineteenth-century socialist Jean Jaurès, and the other to Spanish art. The Sidorbe, a granite massif to the east famed for its peculiar rock formations, makes an easy excursion. Castres is also the end-point of the Gijou Valley Trail, a hiking, riding and mountain-bike route, leading up into the isolated heights of Haut Languedoc (see p.201).

Arrival, information and accommodation

Castres' **gare SNCF** is at avenue Albert 1er, west of the old town, which can be reached by bus #7 ("Arcades" stop; €0.90) or a 25-minute walk. The **gare routière** on place Soult is on the far eastern edge of the centre – a short walk west from the river. For those driving, **parking** on the street in old Castres is possible, but check the signs carefully: between the market days and street-cleaning schedule, you could easily get your car towed. The **tourist office**, at 3 rue Milhau-Ducommun (April–Oct Mon–Sat 8.30am–7pm, Sun 10am–noon & 2–6pm; Nov–March Mon–Sat 8.30am–12.30pm & 1.30–6.30pm, Sun 2–6pm; ℡05.63.62.63.62, ⊛www.ville-castres.fr), sits along the riverbank in the old town, by the *pont vieux*; in summer it offers a "**Passe culturel de l'été**" (€3.81 summer only), which includes admission to the town's three museums and is valid for one month.

Castres has two marvellous seventeenth-century mansions converted into luxurious but affordable **hotels**; the more deluxe is the *Renaissance* at 17 rue Victor Hugo (℡05.63.59.30.42, ℻05.63.72.11.57; ❹), while close behind is the *L'Europe*, just up the same street at no. 5 (℡05.63.59.00.33, ℻05.63.59.21.38; ❹). Otherwise, the *Rivière*, 10 quai Tourcaudière (℡05.63.59.04.53, ℻05.63.59.61.97; ❷), has pleasant views over the Agout and helpful staff, and the very friendly and clean *Le Périgord*, 22 rue Zola (℡05.63.59.04.74; ❶), is a bargain, with a *bain complet* in every room and great half- and full-pension plans. The best bargain however is the magnificent *Domaine du Gourjade* (℡05.63.62.41.72, ✉gourjade@ville-castres.fr; ❶), set in a rambling seventeenth-century manor house in Parc Gourjade. The three-star **campsite** (April–Sept; ℡05.63.59.72.30) nearby also has bungalows – you can reach the site and the Parc, which has walking trails and watersports facilities, by buses #3, #6 or #7 (direction Borde-Basse) or by the *Miredames* river-boat (see "Listings" p.197).

The Town

Don't let yourself be fooled by the drab suburbs which surround it; Castres' **old town**, spilling just over the River Agout to the east, its rough square outline reflecting the Roman layout, is a delight. The brightly painted riverside **dyers' houses** are the town's hallmark, while the impressive sixteenth-century mansions hidden among its narrow streets make the medieval quarter a pleasure to stroll through. At its centre, café-girded **place Jean-Jaurès** is home to a bustling produce market four days a week, while just south of the square, the unprepossessing **Cathédrale St-Benoît**, constructed in 1677, stands on the site of the old monastery church. It's a squat and not especially noteworthy Baroque building, although the marble statues of saints around the choir are worth a look.

Across the street, the **Hôtel de Ville** reposes within the former bishop's palace, a dour, hulking square edifice, whose grey sobriety contrasts with the bright formal gardens, the **Jardins de l'Évêché**, which stretch out on its southern side. The town hall shares the building with Castres' foremost

Jean Jaurès, the nineteenth-century labour activist, politician and martyr, is a figure whose presence travellers can scarcely escape in Languedoc and Roussillon. Nearly every town has at least one street or square – usually a main one – and a building or two named after this **socialist hero**, whose tireless struggle for workers' rights and international peace eventually cost him his life.

Born in Castres in 1859, Jean Jaurès showed exceptional promise as a student and was sent by scholarship to complete his studies in Paris. When these were finished, rather than stay in the capital he returned to his home *département* of Tarn and took a post teaching philosophy in **Albi**'s *lycée* (high school), and giving lectures at the University of Toulouse. But the miserable conditions under which his **working-class** neighbours toiled drew him out of the academy; their dangerous working environment, underpayment and near-total lack of rights and representation could have been lifted straight from the pages of **Emile Zola**'s contemporary *Germinal*. Jaurès ran for political office and at the young age of 26 was elected a deputy (or legislative representative) of Tarn. One of his first projects was to help the glass-workers at Albi found the collectively run V.O.A. bottle factory, which still operates today. Continuing in politics and the cause of social justice, in 1893, as socialist deputy for **Carmaux**, he supported the miners' struggle for better working conditions (see p.183), and his renown as a social reformer began to spread.

However, Jaurès' desire for reform went beyond simply improving the lives of those around him. Five years later he joined other liberals, including Zola, in defence of the Jewish army captain, **Alfred Dreyfus**, convicted on unfounded charges of espionage. National feelings of resentment against Dreyfus were running high, but despite this Jaurès persisted in his defence of the underdog, and – eventually – got him pardoned. The patriotically charged issue temporarily cost Jaurès his popularity, but he was soon back on the stage, founding the Communist daily *L'Humanité* in 1904 (still one of France's major newspapers; ⓦ www.humanite.fr) and the following year helping found the socialist SFIO party. With the dawn of World War I, however, Jaurès' internationalist brand of socialism revealed itself again in an outspoken and unpopular **pacifist** stand – and led to his **assassination** in Paris by a nationalist extremist in July 1914. On his death he was hailed as a martyr, the perfect hero for the Tarn – a local politician who improved the quality of life in this underdeveloped and marginalized region, and who wasn't afraid to take on the political establishment of Paris in order to defend a higher justice.

museum, the **Musée Goya** (Aug daily 9am–noon & 2–6pm; Sept–June Tues–Sun same times; July–Aug €3, otherwise €2.30), which was established a century ago by private donation, and now holds the biggest collection of Spanish paintings in France apart from the Louvre. Dominating its largest salon, the core of the exhibition is, as you'd expect, taken up by the artist after whom it is named, but the paintings here are not the dark, sinister visions for which **Francisco Goya** is most famous, but rather his portraiture, including his *Self-portrait with Glasses*, and politically inspired works like *The Junta of the Philippines Presided over by Ferdinand VII*. A separate room features several series of his satirical pen-and-ink cartoons, depicting vices and virtues and popular adages, as well as series on bullfighting and war. Other rooms contain numerous pieces by other seventeenth-century Iberian masters – including **Velázquez**'s *Portrait of Philip IV*, **Murillo**'s *Virgin with Rosary* and **Zurburán**'s *Carthusian Martyr*. Flemish-influenced medieval paintings by fifteenth-century Catalan and Spanish artists round out the collection. There are also displays of old coins, royal seals and assorted archeological knick-knacks, as well as a room dedicated to the local war-time Resistance. An adjacent gallery (separate admission) houses temporary exhibits of impressive quality.

West of the Goya Museum along rue Chambre de l'Edit are three palatial residences dating from the sixteenth and seventeenth centuries. On rue Guy, the first street on the right, the seventeenth-century **Hôtel de Poncet** stands out, with its classically inspired Renaissance facade and caryatid columns supporting an elegant Ionic-columned loggia. Further along rue Chambre de l'Edit you'll find the earlier **Hôtel Jean-Leroy**, notable for its stately carved casement windows and topped by a defensive tower. Next door to that, **Hôtel de Viviès**, built along the now-vanished city walls, was once the seat of the town's Huguenot judicial court and now houses the small **Centre for Contemporary Art** (July & Aug daily 10am–6pm; Sept–June Wed–Fri 10am–12.15pm & 1.15–5.30pm, Tues 10am–12.15pm & 1.15–7pm, Sat, Sun & Mon 3–6pm; €1), home to temporary exhibitions of local and international modern works. Castres' shopping district stretches north from here, on the far side of which, in rue Thomas, you'll find Castres' grandest *hôtel particulier*, the **Hôtel de Nayrac**, built in the brick-and-stone style of the Toulouse mansions, with three sober facades boxing in a broad symmetrical courtyard. Just beyond is the **Musée Jean-Jaurès** (July & Aug daily 9am–noon & 2–6pm; Sept–June Tues–Sun 9am–noon & 2–5/6pm; €1.50), which pays homage to the life of Castres' favourite son (see box on p.195), recounting the martyred activist's career with newspaper reports, memorabilia and contemporary artefacts.

Over on the far side of the river, the scruffier east bank of the Agout is home to a number of interesting little restaurants and cafés, and although it lacks historical buildings the neighbourhood's proletarian feel is refreshing. The sparsely adorned medieval **fountain** in place Fagerie, just north of the Pont Neuf, is also worth seeking out, if only for the "undiscovered" atmosphere of the square in which it sits.

Eating, drinking and nightlife

For its size, Castres has an impressive range of **restaurants**. Of the hotel options, the best is *L'Europe*, which has an excellent all-you-can-eat buffet (€10) both at lunch and dinner-time (daily noon–2pm & 8.30–10.30pm), featuring a range of *terroir* fare and an impressive selection of desserts. *La Mandragore*, 1 rue Malpas (closed Sun & Mon lunch; ☎05.63.59.51.27) is praised both for its *gastronomique* cuisine (*menus* €15–30) and selection of wines, while for a no-nonsense quality **brasserie**, try *Le Belge* beside the *Rivière* (meals from €15) or *Le Médiéval* (closed Sun & Mon; ☎05.63.51.13.78) at 44 rue Milhau-Ducommun, whose eleventh-century dining room sits above the Agout, and has a funky pseudo-medieval decor (*menus* from €18). Along rue Fuzies, which runs east from the bridge by the tourist office, you'll find a number of cheaper but no less interesting options: in addition to a selection of kebab stands and Chinese places, the *Yankee Grill* (closed Sun noon) offers Tex-Mex à la carte from €12. The jazzy *Bar 3 Rois*, in the street of the same name, also has a small upstairs dining room. For lighter food fare, *La Mouclade*, at 6 rue d'Empare, is a small mussels bar whose owners do up the delicious bivalves fifteen different ways, and afterwards you can get a pint at the very un-Irish *Moran's Pub* a few doors down at no. 18.

A good café is *Saveurs du Temps*, 4 rue Fuziers and, aside from this, any of the **bars** around place Jean-Jaurès will do for a coffee or drink, and *Glacier* (on the south side) sometimes has live music and his popular with locals for its gigantic ice-cream sundaes (€6). Late-night diversion is provided by the rock **club**

One-Two-Two (after 11pm), through the graffitied door (no sign) in passage Henri IV, and the cool cocktail and tapas bar *Cuba Cafe* at 8 rue d'Empare (Wed–Sun 6pm–2am).

Listings

Banks There are several banks with ATMs in the old town, including Crédit Agricole in pl Jean-Jaurès.

Bike rental You can rent bikes from Cycles 3000, 21 de Melou ☎05.63.50.14.14, and the *gare* SNCF. Alternatively the tourist office lends bicycles for two-hour periods.

Boat trips The Miredames river-boat does a 45min round trip down the Agout (June–Aug noon, 2.20pm, 3.40pm & 5.10pm; Sept noon & 2.20pm; €4), leaving from the pier outside the tourist office.

Bus information ☎05.63.35.37.31.

Car rental Ada, 32 av Charles de Gaulle ☎05.63.51.10.26; Avis, rte de Toulouse ☎05.63.72.82.21; Budget, rue Albert 1er

☎05.63.71.31.28; Europcar, 67 rue Maillot ☎05.63.72.24.69; Hertz, av François Mitterand ☎05.63.59.01.14; and Lavail, rte d'Albi ☎05.63.71.93.34.

Hospital Centre Hospitalier, pl Alsace-Lorraine, just south of the Hôtel de Ville (☎05.63.71.15.15).

Internet access Cyberspace, 31 rue Fuziers (Mon–Sat 2–9pm; ☎05.63.62.00.80).

Laundry Lavanderie Express, 8–9 rue Fuziers (daily till 9pm).

Market Tue, Thurs, Fri & Sat in pl Jean-Jaurès and pl l'Albinique.

Police 2 av Charles de Gaulle (☎17 or ☎05.63.35.40.10).

Taxis ☎05.63.71.55.55.

Train information ☎05.63.59.37.03.

Around Castres

Castres is not only a comfortable place to rest for a day or two, but an ideal base for exploring a number of day-trip destinations in the vicinity. Just to the east lies the hundred-square-kilometre granite plateau known as the **Sidorbe**. This heavily promoted area is known for the boulders which litter it, either eroded into evocative shapes or balancing precariously. Many are found within a three-kilometre radius of Lacrouzette, including the rock-strewn waterfall, **Saut de la Truite**, and while some of the formations are truly remarkable, others are really rather lame – the **Trois Fromages** ("Three Cheeses"), for example, merely comprises a group of three roundish boulders set on top of each other. South of these groups lies the **Peyro Clabado**, an 800-tonne boulder perched on a smaller stone, and the **Rochers de Sept-Faux**, two giant stones balanced in such a way that upper one, 900 tonnes in mass, can be rocked simply by pushing on it. The wooded paths which lead to the sites are well maintained and make for pleasant walking, although on weekends they're crowded with families and pensioners. Bring sufficient water or be prepared to pay over the odds at the cafés and drinks stands near the trails. To explore the region by foot or bicycle, pick up the free "Les Circuits du Tarn" brochure in Castres, which provides detailed descriptions of routes. Otherwise, all the sights of the region are easily accessed by **bus** from Castres, and **accommodation** can be found in nondescript Lacrouzette, at *L'Auberge du Crémaussel* (open Easter–Nov; ☎05.63.50.61.33; ❷), which also has a restaurant (*menus* from €15, including wine; closed Sun eve, Wed all year, Jan & winter weekends) or the less expensive *Au Relais du Sidorbe* (☎05.63.50.60.06, ⓦwww.logis-de-france.com; ❷). For something more unique, head for the *chambres d'hôtes* of the luxurious fourteenth- to sixteenth-century castle in **Burlats** (☎05.63.35.29.20, ⓔle.castel.de-burlats@wanadoo.fr; ❹). Nearby **St-Salvy** also has a great lunch or dinner stop: *Le Clos du Roc* (closed Wed eve, Sun eve & part Feb; ☎05.63.50.57.23; *menus* €10–25; call ahead), located in a converted barn, has excellent cuisine at economical prices.

③

> ## Circulades
>
> A curious feature of southern Languedoc are **circulades**, or circular villages, concentric rings of streets at the centre of which is, or was once found, a castle or fortified church. The origin of these hamlets, thought to go back as early as the ninth century, is uncertain, but it seems likely that their peculiar design was the result of the military uncertainties of the era and the challenges posed by defence in flat countryside. A circular town, the entrances of which can be barricaded, is more easily defensible than a dispersed settlement. Few of these towns contain much of interest to today's traveller, but it is worth stopping in one or two if only to take in the unmistakable medieval character of their streets. Circulades mentioned in this guide include Bram (p.113), Frontignan (p.242), Gruissan (p.313) and Labrugière (below); for more, see ⓦwww.circulades.com.

South of Castres on the way to Mazamet, you may pass through **LABRU-GIÈRE**, a quaint *circulade*, or "round village" (see box above), laid out in concentric circles around the village church. Dating back to 985 AD, the town owes its notoriety to the 1484 **witch trial** of Péronne Bachère. Accused of making a pact with the Devil, casting spells and killing a neighbour with magic powder, she confessed all when interrogated and was burnt at a nearby crossroads. The parchment which recorded her trial can be seen today in a display at the *mairie* on the town's main square.

The Parc du Haut Languedoc

The southeastern half of the *département* of Tarn is dominated by the mountain -ridged highlands of Upper Languedoc. In this region of isolated hamlets the scant population has traditionally subsisted on herding and agriculture, supplemented nowadays by a growing outdoor recreation industry. Long a backwood of proudly self-sufficient Calvinist Huguenots, these hills later proved a fertile recruiting ground for anti-German resistance after the occupation of Vichy France. The zone is dominated by the sprawling **PARC NATUREL RÉGIONAL DU HAUT LANGUEDOC**, an imprecisely bounded region which, in the thirty years or so since its establishment, has grown to encompass additional territory almost yearly. Its designation as a park is primarily administrative, which can lead to confusion – the boundaries aren't well marked, and there's no change in the landscape or villages which distinguishes the park from the surrounding area. That said, a good approximation is to define the park more or less by the mountains which cross it: the **Monts de Lacaune** in the north, the **Monts de l'Espinouse** to the east, and the north face of the Montagne Noire range (see p.207), tacked onto the park's southwest. The man-made **lakes** which punctuate the highland near **La Salvetat**, **Fraïsse** and **Anglès** are the focus of a thriving tourist industry: each is ringed by campsites and boat-rental outfits which do a brisk trade in the summer months. Although public transport across the park is poor, it serves **hikers** well, crisscrossed by a network of footpaths: *grand* and *petit randonnées*, and local routes, such as the **Gijou Valley Railway Trail** linking **Lacaune-les-Bains**, **Vabre** and **Brassac**. Native wildlife, which still includes some wild boar and deer, is less frequently encountered as the park becomes more popular – although you might see the ancient breed of mouflon sheep if you cross the

Monts de l'Espinouse – and despite straddling the border of the Atlantic and Mediterranean climatic zones, the bulk of the park lies in the cooler, humid northern zone, where the flora is dominated by forests of sturdy oak and chestnut. Detailed park **information** can be obtained at the **Maison du Parc** offices in **St–Pons**, the "capital" of the park, and **Murat**; local tourist offices sell a guide to fifteen **bicycle** itineraries in the area.

Lacaune-les-Bains and around

Poised on the northern edge of the park, slate-roofed **LACAUNE-LES-BAINS** lies east from Castres, at a distance of either 67km along the tortuous Agout and Gijou valley road, or 46km along the mountainous route which passes through Brassac. At 885m, it sits just below the source of the Gijou river in the **Monts de Lacaune**, whose sheep are the exclusive source of milk for the famous blue cheese of Roquefort. The town was a curative spa (specializing in urinary tract ailments) in the Middle Ages, a role commemorated by a fourteenth-century iron **fountain** in the town centre known as "Les Pisseurs", featuring four tiny but impressively endowed male figures peeing into a pool below. Beside the fountain, in place du Friggoul, is the hokey **Musée de Vieux Lacaune** (April–June & Sept–Nov Tues–Sun 2.30–6pm; July & Aug daily 10am–noon & 2–6pm; free), which offers an unexceptional look at local nineteenth-century rural life. In similar vein, you can also visit the **Filature Ramond**, a wool workshop from the same era, where you can see the various tools and machines used (Mon, Wed & Fri 11am, 2 & 3pm; €2). Aside from taking in the surroundings there is little to do in Lacaune, apart from enjoying the Sunday-morning local **market** and a larger regional **fair** on the 21st of each month. The town has good bus connections, but the best way to leave is along the old Gijou Valley Trail, a disused narrow-gauge railway line heading west towards Castres, which has been converted to a foot and bike path (see p.201).

Buses trundle through Lavaur stopping at place de la République, on the far side of which is a small **tourist office** (mid-June to mid-Sept Mon–Fri 9am–noon & 2–6.30pm, Sat & Sun 10am–noon & 2–6.30pm; mid-Sept to mid-June Mon 2–5pm, Tues–Fri 9am–noon & 2–5pm, Sat 10am–noon; & 2–5pm; ☏05.63.37.04.98, ⓦwww.lacaune.com), which has detailed information on walks in the area, and also provides **bikes**. If you want to **stay** the night, the *Central Hôtel Fusies* (closed most Jan; ☏05.63.37.02.03, ⓔespoutis@infonie.fr; ❸) on rue de la République offers all the three-star amenities. More attractive and cheaper is the *Calas* (closed mid-Dec to mid-Jan; ☏05.63.37.03.28, ⓔhotelcalas@wanadoo.fr; ❷), tucked away in the place de la Vierge. Claude Calas, the owner of this small family hotel and a fourth-generation chef, also runs a highly praised **bistro** (closed Fri–Sat eves & Oct–Easter; *menus* €14–29). Even if you're not on a budget you might consider the local **gîte** (☏05.63.37.04.98, ⓔoffice-tourisme@lacaune.com; ❶), set in the town's château. The local municipal **campsite** is on the Murat road (☏05.63.37.03.59).

Murat-sur-Vèbre

Twenty-six kilometres east of Lacaune lies **MURAT-SUR-VÈBRE**, an ancient but otherwise unremarkable hamlet bisected by a tributary of the Vèbre, which undoubtedly saw its heaviest traffic passing through when it was a way-stop on the pilgrim route to Santiago. Hikers who want to relive a bit of the Middle Ages can follow the "chemin de St-Jacques" (now the GR653) east to Castres. If you stop here it will most likely be to pick up information

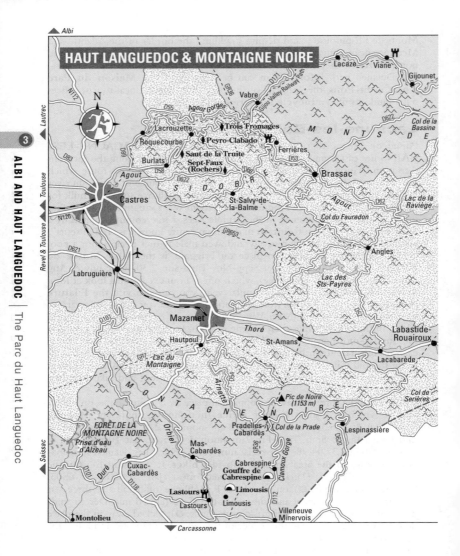

from the **Maison du Parc** (July & Aug Mon–Sat 10am–noon & 2–6pm; Sept–June 10am–noon & 2–5pm; ☎05.63.37.45.76), an annexe to the local **tourist office** (same hours; ☎05.63.37.47.47). Should you decide to stay, the only **hotel**, the rather basic *Durand* (☎05.63.37.41.91, ⊛www.federal-hotel.com; ❷) has a reasonable but unexceptional **restaurant** (closed Fri eve & Sat out of season), and there's also a **campsite**, *Les Adrets* (☎05.63.37.41.16; June–Sept). Alternatively, Cristiane Roque's farm, *Félines* (☎05.63.37.43.17, ℻05.63.37.19.85; ❷), just outside town, has rooms and can provide meals. Those who want to make Murat a temporary base can rent **bikes** from the tourist office.

The Gijou Valley Railway Trail

Half a century ago locomotives still threaded the tortuously meandering Agout and Gijou valleys, steaming up the cliff-hanging **narrow-gauge railway** connecting Castres with Vabre and Lacaune to the east, and branching off to Brassac to the south, 16km up the Agout valley. The trains have long disappeared, but the rail-bed has been brought back to life as a well-set-out **hiking-** and **mountain-biking** trail – a route best travelled from Lacaune westwards for the simple reason that it descends in that direction. This defunct railway winds along steep and forested banks, dramatically crossing the riverbed on ancient trestle bridges and only rarely passing tiny hamlets of slate-shingled houses and solitary farmsteads.

The Huguenots of Haut Languedoc

The rugged and isolated hills of Haut Languedoc remain a bastion of France's once much-mistreated but stubborn Protestant community, or **Huguenots**. During the sixteenth century, Protestantism, like Catharism before it, exercised a strong attraction on the inhabitants of Languedoc. In an age when political and religious obedience were perceived as parallel, the people of the south felt exploited, on the one hand by an absolutist monarchy in Paris and on the other by a Church which manifested itself most visibly as a tax-collector.

The new faith arrived in the Haut Languedoc close on the heels of Martin Luther's defiance of Church authority in 1519; the first Protestant was burned in Toulouse only eight years later. The Huguenot movement – named after an obscure Swiss political event – however, tended to follow the Frenchman **John Calvin**'s teachings, which had a more politically revolutionary message: his principle of "Inferior Magistrates" dictated that people were morally justified in disobeying and deposing an unfit ruler. The established order was clearly under threat from the dangerous new religion, and when the Crown and Church attempted to eradicate it, arresting reforming theologians and preachers and impounding French-language versions of the Bible, the people of the south, backed by the equally dissatisfied local nobility, retaliated, and the long and bloody **Wars of Religion** ensued. In a dynamic reminiscent of the Cathar era, the nobility, already divided into factions, used the theological conflict as justification for open warfare: the princely house of Guise and their allies championed Catholicism, while the rival Bourbons took up the Protestant flag. After a prolonged series of military campaigns and massacres the wars ended, or rather paused for while, with a compromise when the formerly Protestant Henry IV passed the **Edict of Nantes** in 1598, recognizing limited Huguenot rights. Castres became a "protected zone" for Protestants, and eventually home to one of the four courts of the land empowered to mediate legal disputes between Catholics and Huguenots. Almost a century later however, this uneasy accommodation ended when the supreme autocrat Louis XIV outlawed Calvinism again in 1685, and set in motion a harsh period of **repression** in Haut Languedoc. Soldiers were billeted in suspected Protestant homes, and possession of the Bible in French (instead of the official Latin) became a criminal offence. Huguenots reacted by escaping into exile or going underground, like the community in Ferrières, which hid Bibles in secret wall-compartments or women's bonnets, and held clandestine services in the forest. Eventually many villages fled en masse to the even more isolated Cévennes to the east, out of reach of royal officials and the army. Many returned only in 1787, when the **Edict of Toleration** finally established Protestant liberties; with the foundation of the secular revolutionary government two years later, Catholicism ceased to be an official measure of "Frenchness". Although Protestantism declined as a result of centuries of persecution, today nearly every hamlet in the highlands and every sizeable town in Languedoc has a Huguenot church (or *temple*), and country folk of Haut Languedoc still recall the stalwart nonconformity of their ancestors with pride.

Leaving from Lacaune, the trail arrives at **Gijounet** after a couple of hours, just after a small waterfall. Continuing along for 5km, it skirts the slightly larger **Viane**, with a ruined *château* perched above, and then at **Lacaze**, several hours further, a medieval bridge spans the river, beside a once-stately fifteenth-century **mansion**. From this point the river gains force and begins to wind erratically through the cliffs girding it; fifteen kilometres now remain to **Vabre**, a larger town, which conserves a twelfth-century bridge. The distance from Lacaune to Vabre is 40km, which will take around eleven hours on foot. A few kilometres after Vabre, the Gijou empties into the Agout, and it is here that the railway branches off southwards and uphill towards **Brassac** 16km away (see below), passing the still fiercely Huguenot village of **Ferrières**, which has a much advertised but private **castle** (closed), and a paltry **Musée du Protestantisme** (April–June & Sept–Oct Sun & hols 2–6pm; July & Aug Mon & Wed–Sun 10am–noon & 3–7pm; €3) at the halfway mark. From the Vabre junction, the mainline trail continues to Roquecourbe, threading the gorges which mark the northern limit of the Sidorbe; from here the D89 can be followed 8km to Castres. Alternately, 3km out of Roquecourbe, take the tarmac road towards the Le Carla generating station to regain the river and follow it to Castres via Burlats (adding 12km to the route). The trail is also manageable if you start from Castres (as detailed in the Topoguide *Le Tarn ...à pied*), but heading upriver entails travelling uphill along the route.

There are few opportunities to pick up supplies en route – Lacaze, with a **store** and **café**, is the first good spot to refuel – but for those who plan on making the journey over a night or two, each of the villages along the line has a very basic and free **campsite**. Vabre has a number of services, including a **tourist office** in the *mairie* (Mon–Fri 10am–noon & 2–5pm; ☎05.63.37.27.18), and a Thursday-morning **market**. A short walk 2km east of town on the Berlou river, the Clarensons' comfortable **farm/gîte**, *Le Mouline* (☎05.63.50.41.91, ⓦwww.lamouline.free.fr; English spoken) has several cabins for four to eight people, with a four-person cabin from €185 per week (€95 per weekend). In Ferrières, Davina Doughan's B&B *La Ramade* (☎ & ⒻF05.63.73.47.08, ⒺEddoughan@aol.com; ❸; English spoken) also provides meals (€15). The best deal, however, is the municipal **gîte** (❶), which can be booked through the *mairie* (☎05.63.74.40.60, ⒻF05.63.74.40.64).

Brassac

BRASSAC, lying some 20km southwest of Lacaune, is undoubtedly the most attractive town on the west side of the park. Here the Agout, girded by nineteenth-century textile plants and the towers of a small medieval **castle**, is crossed by a picture-postcard twelfth-century **bridge**. Something of a focal point for the even smaller hamlets of the countryside, Brassac has some decent amenities: its **stores** and **ATMs** recommend it as a possible base for exploring the western sector of the park. The former stage-post, the *Café de Paris* (closed Sun & Mon out of season; ☎05.63.74.00.31, ⓦwww.tables-aubergemidipyrenees.com; ❶) offers **accommodation**, and has a **restaurant** (closed Sun Sept–June) which serves *menus* from €11. Across the street, the *Centre* (☎05.63.74.00.14; ❷), with a little **bar**, also offers rooms and meals. You'll find the basic municipal **campsite** (☎05.63.74.09.11) just to the north of the village.

The Plateau des Lacs

Sandwiched between the mountains of Lacaune and l'Espinouse, and stretching from Murat in the northeast almost as far as Mazamet to the southwest, the rambling upland of the park, the **Plateau des Lacs**, is punctuated by three large, artificial lakes along the Vèbre and Agout rivers, which converge here. **LA SALVETAT-SUR-AGOUT**, smack in the middle of the uplands, is the hub of the plateau, and the terminus of the Béziers–St-Pons bus line. The attractive little town has not been spoiled by the souvenir shops which dot its centre, and when the daily hubbub subsides, the tangled knot of streets which makes up the old town evokes the eleventh century, when La Salvetat was founded. There is nothing in particular to look at in the village, but two historical relics lie just outside of town: the twelfth-century Romanesque **chapel** (July & Aug daily 3–7pm), which contains a "black Virgin"– a Romanesque statue discoloured by time – and the stone bridge next to it, used by medieval pilgrims on the way to Santiago. The town is a short walk from the ten-kilometre-long **Lac de la Ravième**, which has been extensively developed as a holiday spot – here you'll find **beaches**, and plenty of **canoe**, **sail** and **motorboat** rental outlets. Those wishing to explore the surrounding area on foot can purchase a booklet with twelve well-laid-out *petits randonnées* for €1 at the tourist office.

La Salvetat's **tourist office** (Mon–Fri 9am–noon & 2–6pm, Sat & Sun 10am–noon & 2–5pm, Sept–June closed Sun; ℡ & ℻04.67.97.64.44, ⓦwww.lasalvetatot.com) can help find furnished flats and cottages, but otherwise the English-owned *La Pergola* (℡04.67.97.55.48, ℻04.67.97.56.76; ❶), just off the main road by the *place* where the **buses** from St-Pons stop, has inexpensive **rooms** and serves generous portions of home-cooking (for guests only) in its restaurant. There's also a cosy **B&B** in the centre, on rue de Poterie (May–Oct; ℡04.67.97.65.13, ℻04.67.97.50.97; ❷) as well as the *chambres d'hôtes*, *La Moutousse* (closed Nov–Easter; ℡04.67.97.61.63; ❷), in an old farm 4km out of town on the GR653, and *Hameau de Meges* (℡04.67.97.56.65, Ⓔpommier.pierre@wanadoo.fr; ❷; English spoken). **Bikes** can be rented at the shop on place de Compostela. There are no fewer than four **campsites** within walking distance; the nearest is *La Blaquière* (April–Aug; ℡04.67.97.61.29) on allée St-Étienne de Cavall just north of the centre, while down by the lake you'll find the small *Calcia* (℡04.67.97.63.45). Of the several **restaurants** in town, none merits special mention, apart from *La Ficelle* (℡04.67.97.56.01), on the route de Lacaune, which is open all year.

Fraïsse-sur-Agout and Lac de Lauzas

Although **FRAÏSSE-SUR-AGOUT**, 10km east of La Salvetat by road (D14) or trail (GR71), is only 2km south of **Lac de Lauzas** as the crow flies, the winding of the road which crosses the intervening hills clocks in at nearly 10km. This hamlet, set at a hilly crossroads, has become rather touristy in summer, but still retains its bucolic air thanks to its diminutive size and the isolated beauty of its surroundings. From the ancient bridge over the Agout, a short trail leads southwards uphill for 2km to the **Prat d'Alaric** and a traditional working **farm museum** (Thurs 10am–noon; free). Lac de Lauzas to the north is purely of interest to those who are looking for developed waterside **camping**, with the gamut of activities which this implies. Fraïsse has a **tourist office** (May, June & Sept Sat & Sun 10am–12.30pm & 2–5pm; July & Aug daily 10am–12.30pm & 2–5pm; ℡04.67.97.53.81), and you can **stay** at the municipal **gîte** (℡04.67.97.61.14, ⓦwww.gites-de-france-herault.asso.fr; ❶). Lac de Lauzas' main **campsite** is *Rieu Montagné* (mid-June to mid-Sept; ℡05.63.37.15.42) on the north side of the lake, and *Le Pioch* (℡04.67.97.61.72; May–Sept) is in Fraïsse.

Anglès

Some 16km south from Brassac on the St-Pons road, **ANGLÈS**, a collection of houses which is home to no more than a handful of families, is only likely to be of interest to hikers following the GR71 west from La Salvetat or the GR653 east from the Sidorbe, but the hamlet can also be reached by regular buses from Mazamet. Although in Julius Caesar's time it served as a border post guarding the frontier against the Gallic barbarians, its oldest presently surviving monument is a small twelfth-century **gate**. The village is about 5km from **Lac des Sts-Peyres**, on the westernmost edge of the plateau, which remains undeveloped for tourism and is a good spot for a bit of peace and quiet. Anglès'

seasonal **tourist office** (Easter–Aug 10.30am–12.30pm & 2–7pm; ℡05.63.74.59.13, Ⓔotespinouse@wandoo.fr) is adjoined by two **hotels**, of which *Auberge de la Souque* (March–Nov; ☎05.63.70.98.53, ⓦwww.federal-hotel.com; ❶) is the most economical. The other, *Le Manoir de Boutaric* (☎ & Ⓕ05.63.70.96.06, Ⓕ05.63.7096.05; ❷), just south of town, is a two-star rural affair with a **campsite** (April–Oct). The *Manoir's* **restaurant** is open in July and August only; the rest of the year you can eat at *Aux Épis*, in Anglès itself, where you can get a hearty meal for about €15.

St-Pons-de-Thomières and around

Deep in the folds of the Jaur valley, 52km from Castres and 35km due east on the N112 from Mazamet, sits **ST-PONS-DE-THOMIÈRES**, the park's principal information centre, separated from the Plateau des Lacs to the north by a high ridge, the western spur of the Monts de l'Espinouse (see p.206). It is also a transport hub for the park, with two main **bus** lines, the Béziers–La Salvetat and Castres–Montpellier, intersecting here. This ancient town's curious compound name originates with local count Raymond Pons, who founded a monastery (hence, the "St" part of the name) across the river, north of the hamlet of Thomières in 936.

St-Pons' old quarter is worth a walk around – on the edge of it, on the north side of the modern road, is poised the twelfth-century **cathedral** (€3), with its incongruous, slapped-on seventeenth-century facade, around the back of which you can still see the statues on the medieval tympana, faces chipped off by iconoclastic Huguenots in the sixteenth century. The bulk of the old town, however, lies south of the main road on both sides of the Jaur, which is crossed by a medieval **bridge**. Amidst the ancient alleys the square fourteenth-century defensive tower, the **Tour de la Évêché**, pokes above the rooftops. To the west of the old town, the **Musée de la Préhistoire** (mid-June to Oct daily 10am–noon & 2.30–6pm; Nov to mid-June Wed, Sat & Sun 10am–noon & 2–5pm; €3.50) has information on the area's menhirs as well as an exhibition of local Flintstonian relics, and also arranges speleological **safaris** in the neighbouring Ponderatz cave complex (☎05.67.97.22.61; check for availability of English-speaking guides). Cave fans will also want to check out the **Grotte de Devèze**, 5km west of St-Pons on the N112, and its **Musée Français de la Spéléologie** (July & Aug daily 10am–6pm; April–June & Sept daily 2–5pm; otherwise call to book; ☎04.67.97.03.24, ⓔcourniou.les.grottes@wanadoo.fr; €6). Opened in 1932, the cave contains a variety of rock forms, including an impressive stone cascade and several calcite "draperies".

Buses pull up near the main crossroads of St-Pons, on the south side of which is the town's **tourist office** (July & Aug daily 9am–7.30pm; Sept–June Mon–Fri 10am–noon & 2.30–6pm, Sat 10am–noon; ☎04.67.97.06.65, ⓦwww.saint-pons-tourisme.com); the central information office for the park, the **Maison du Parc**, is also located nearby – beside the cathedral, at 13 rue du Cloître (Mon–Fri 8am–noon & 1.30–6pm; ☎04.67.97.38.22, ⓦwww.parc-haut-languedoc.fr). The best **hotel** is *Le Somail* (☎04.67.97.00.12, Ⓕ04.67.97.05.84; ❶), near the tourist office, which also has a reasonably priced dining room (May–Aug daily; Sept–April Sat & Sun only; *menu* from €13.50), but the best place to eat in these parts is undoubtedly *La Route du Sel* (closed Wed; ☎04.67.97.05.14) at 15 Grande Rue, which combines friendly service with an excellent-value *carte* (*menu* from €16). The municipal **campsite** (reserve through the tourist office) is open in summer only, while the all-year *Cerisiers du Jaur* (☎04.67.97.06.65) is just out of town on the road to Bédarieux.

Olargues and around

From St-Pons, the Jaur river snakes northeast, skirting the **Monts de l'Espinouse** that loom over the north bank, to arrive at **OLARGUES**. Approached from the west, this hamlet presents an impressive vista: a high and gracefully arched medieval **bridge** backed by the steep hill where its castle once stood. From a covered staircase just west of the parking area along the main street, a ten-minute climb through the steep medieval alleys leads up to the lonely **clock tower**, the only remaining vestige of the eleventh-century fortress. Nearby, the Romanesque **priory** of St-Julien makes a good hike or a short drive, its shady wooded surroundings providing a great picnic spot and wonderful **views** of the Jaur Valley; take the Bédarieux road east for 2.5km and climb steeply on the left up the narrow signposted road a further 1500m.

The Monts de l'Espinouse

Olargues is a natural place to begin a circuit of the **Monts de l'Espinouse**, an area whose isolated beauty is preserved in part by its inaccessibility; there's no public transport here. From the village the D14 switchbacks steeply up past slate-covered hamlets clinging to near-perpendicular slopes until you reach the central pass of the **Col de Fontfroide** (971m). Here, **trails** (including the main GR7-71) crisscross the barren hillsides, and a sombre **monument** commemorates the German occupation. To the east on the lonely D53 the forest gets thicker (a picnic paradise) as you approach the 1124m **summit** (sommet de l'Espinouse). A few kilometres later, rounding the Col de l'Ourtigas, the country opens up dramatically into a series of broad gorges, the vibrant green landscape contrasted with dull grey rock. Continuing for 4km, you come to the turn-off for **Douch**, after which the road descends to **Lamalous-les-Bains**. Douch is a good place to pick up the GR7 trail to reach either **Mont Caroux** (1091m; 2hr round trip) or the **Gorges d'Héric**, which you access via the tiny stone hamlet of Héric, 2km west of Douch. The deep and narrow gully of sparkling red granite shaded by thickly covering oak descends rapidly to the River Orb, 6km below, and the beauty of the gorge accounts for its popularity with day-trippers. Easier access to the trails of the gorge is found in **Mons la Trivalle**, just off the main St-Pons–Bédarieux highway.

Practicalities

Olargues' summer-only **tourist office** (July & Aug daily 10.30am–12.30pm & 4.30–8pm; ☎04.67.97.71.26, ✉mairie.olargues@libertysurf.fr) is on the main road. There is a deluxe country **hotel**, the *Domaine de Rieumégé* (☎04.67.97.73.99. ⓦwww.tbsfrance/com/rieumege; ❺) just outside town on the St-Pons road, but a better deal is Pauline Giles' homely *Les Quatr' Farceurs* in rue de la Comporte (☎ & Ⓕ04.67.97.81.33, ⓦwww.olargues .co.uk; ❸), which also serves huge meals with free-flowing wine for €18. A further option is *La Mazate* (☎ 04.67.97.33.80, ✉la-mazette@wanadoo.fr; ❷), a B&B set in an old *relais* on rue du Tour des Ponts.

There is a municipal **campsite** (mid-April to mid-Sept; ☎04.67.97.71.50) and **bikes** can be rented from Oxygène (☎04.67.97.87.00). Walking the Gorges d'Héric or westwards through the mountains you'll find a **gîte** in Héric (☎04.67.97.80.43; ❶). There's also a comfortable new B&B, *Manoir la Trivalle* (☎04.67.97.85.56, ⓦwww.monslatrivalle.com; ❺), at Mons.

Mazamet and the Montagne Noire

The highlands of Haut Languedoc are bounded on their southwest side by the deep valley of the River Thoré, which empties into the Agout just west of Castres. A separate massif, the **MONTAGNE NOIRE**, stretches in a narrow 50km band along the south side of the river course and westwards to Revel (see p.105), its highest peak, the **Pic de Noire** (1153m), located more or less at the centre of the range.

The two sides of the Montagne Noire present a stark contrast: the north face, which has been incorporated into the Parc du Haut Languedoc, is thickly covered in a mixed forest of oak, beech and spruce, while the south presents a scrubby Mediterranean landscape of brush and vine. This whole district has traditionally been even poorer and more isolated than Haut Languedoc proper: near-subsistence farming and herding continue to be the only activities through most of the zone now that the mining of Salsigne and cloth industry of **Mazamet**, which boomed in the nineteenth century, have been reduced to shadows of their former selves. The Montagne Noire's chief attraction is its isolated wilderness, even more extreme than that to the north; you'll find that the outdoor facilities which have sprung up in the main body of the park are lacking here. South of Mazamet, which is the closest service town to the range, the ruin of medieval **Hautpoul** is a popular stop.

There are two direct **routes** over the mountains: the first starts at Hautpoul before continuing to the Pic de Noire and Carcassonne via the **Clamoux Gorges**; the second, ten kilometres west and roughly parallel to this route, follows the dark and evocatively lush Orbiel valley down to the Cathar castles of **Lastours**. Further west still, on the far side of the main Mazamet–Carcassonne road, you can skirt the massif to medieval **Saissac**, a good base from which either to ascend to the forests around Arfons, or descend via **Montolieu** – known for its bookshops – past the ruined abbey at **Villelongue** and on into the open country around Carcassonne. Public transport in this neck of the woods is more or less non-existent, the only regular service being the Mazamet–Carcassonne bus.

Mazamet and around

Lying 17km southeast of Castres, **MAZAMET** is a pale imitation of that town, owing its meagre prosperity to the cloth industry. Its only allure is as a place to recharge your batteries – and even in this case Castres is a better choice. The town's single sight is the **Musée Mémoire de la Terre** (July & Aug 9am–noon & 2–6pm; free) in the old Fuzier-family mansion – an unimpressive exhibition consisting mainly of a fifteen-minute French-language slide show lamenting the fate of the Cathars. More interesting is a short trip to **Hautpoul** – the precursor of Mazamet – a Cathar redoubt perched on a hillside above, which was all but levelled by the unstoppable de Montfort in 1212. The trip up to the village follows the serpentine **Route des Usines**, climbing the bed of the Arnette, where windowless relics of hulking nineteenth-century factories lurk at every hairpin. Now consisting of nothing more than one winding street and the sparse vestiges of the **castle**, Hautpoul is lorded over by the **Maison du Bois** (April, May & Oct–Dec Sat & Sun 2–6pm; June & Sept daily 2–6pm; July & Aug daily 10am–noon & 2–6pm; €4), an artisanal operation churning out wooden toys which really doesn't merit the entry charge. Despite having relatively little to offer, Hautpoul is a popular spot for excursions, in part because of the strong Cathar connection. But even if you aren't a Cathar fan, you'll still enjoy the hamlet's breathtaking setting, with views over the seemingly endless forested hills. If you have neither a car nor the desire to walk up to the hamlet, take one of the tourist office's **organized trips** (regular departures March–Oct; €5).

Practicalities

Mazamet's **gare SNCF** (☎05.63.61.19.00) is located just off the Castres road, a fifteen-minute walk from the town centre; **buses** stop here or 300m further south on avenue Rouvière, by the post office. The **tourist office** (Mon–Sat 9am–noon & 2–6.30pm; July & Aug also Sun 10.30am–12.30pm; ☎05.63.61.27.07, ✉officedetoursime.mazamet@wanadoo.fr) is further south on the cours René Reille, where you can park. Inexpensive **hotels** are plentiful in Mazamet; the cheapest is the basic and ageing *Le Nord* at 4 place Olombel (closed part June & Sun; ☎05.63.61.00.53, ℉05.63.61.57.74; ❷), while the other two options – *Le Boulevard*, 24 boulevard Soult (closed late Dec; ☎05.63.61.16.08, ✉degruel@aol.com; ❷), and *Le Jourdon* at 7 avenue Albert Rouvière (closed Sun eve; ☎05.63.61.56.93, ℉05.63.61.83.38; ❸) – offer a higher comfort level. The three-star **campsite** *La Lauze* (☎05.63.61.24.69; May–Sept) lies some 5km east of town. Once again, the hotel **restaurants** are the best bet for food here – *Le Boulevard* has a good-value *menu* with wine included (€11–23), but *Le Jourdon* beats it on quality at a comparable price.

St-Amans-Soult and the Thoré valley

Climbing east from Mazamet, the **Thoré valley** still maintains its long-established role as a transport link between Castres and the Mediterranean coastlands, now the N112. Not far east of Mazamet you reach **ST-AMANS-SOULT**, a nondescript town which changed its name in honour of its native son, Field Marshal **Nicolas Soult** (1769–1851), Wellington's would-be nemesis of the Peninsular War. The warrior's sombre and monolithic tomb is hardly worth stopping to see, but not so his palatial estate, **Château de Soult-Berg** (June–Sept Wed & Sun guided tours at 3 & 4pm; €5), set amidst a wooded park. The richly furnished rooms here are immaculately preserved, and the mansion's rich library reflects the eighteenth-century ideal of the Renaissance man: aristocratic, learned and soldierly. From here the highway continues, passing through tiny **Labastides** and eventually reaching St-Pons.

St-Amans and Labastides will be of interest to hikers in need of supplies or yearning for a hotel. The former is crossed by the **GR36** on its way to the Pic de Noire, and the latter by the **GR7**, descending from the Monts de l'Espinouse. In St-Amans the only **hotel** is the *Hostellerie des Cèdres* (☎05.63.98.36.72, ⓦwww.logis-de-france.fr; ❷), while 1.5km north of Labastides, *La Bouriotte* offers comfortable **farm accommodation** and plentiful home-cooked food (☎05.63.98.07.64; ❸). Both St-Amans (☎05.63.98.87.31) and Labastides (☎05.63.98.49.74) have **campsites**.

South via the Pic de Noire

If you are heading towards Carcassonne from Mazamet, and you have your own transport, there are a couple of interesting routes which you can take across the Montagne Noire. To cross via the **Pic de Noire**, continue up the Arnette, past the turn-off to Hautpoul, for 3km, until you reach a junction from which the massive transmission tower crowning the summit should be in easy view. An arm-wrenching series of switchbacks then takes you to the flat and barren mountain-top around the antenna's base, and a breathtaking combination of cool, thin air and sweeping panorama. From the peak, the tortuous road descends several kilometres to the hamlet of **Pradelles-Cabardés**, with its medieval **church**, before threading through the steep and forested cliffs of the **Clamoux gorges**, where, after 12km, you'll pass the turn-off for the **Gouffre de Cabrespine** (daily: March–Nov 10am–noon & 2–6pm; €7), a huge vertical subterranean cavern with a main chamber 250m in height ("higher than the Eiffel Tower!"). The route continues to **Villeneuve-Minervois**, a quiet little town with some traces of medieval buildings, including the remains of its **castle**. Services along this route are minimal and you should plan to complete it before nightfall. In Pradelles there is a basic **campsite** on a nearby reservoir, and a **café** which also serves simple meals, while in Villeneuve the **restaurant** *Au Chanoine Gourmand* (*menu* from €13) also has **rooms** (T04.68.26.15.69; ❷).

South via the Orbiel valley

An alternative route across the Montagne Noire, which you pick up by turning east off the D118 just after Lac du Montagne, is via the **Orbiel valley**, and south to the castles at **Lastours**. As you descend the valley, the blanket of iridescent green forest threatens to swallow the steep and narrow stone-buttressed road, and the continuous series of hairpin curves makes the 11km to Mas-Cabardés seem at least twice as long as it should. Driving here is an effort, however, which the scenery makes worthwhile.

After the long descent you'll pass the romantically ruined church of St-Pierre-de-Vals, just outside **Mas-Cabardés**, a village which makes a good spot to stretch your legs before the tortuous second leg of the trip. While here check to see if the medieval **church**, crowned by a fifteenth-century bell tower, is open; if it is, step inside to see the fourteenth-century statuary within. Onwards from Mas-Cabardés, the road bends sharply as you approach Lastours, where the old textile mill which serves as the entrance to the grounds of the **Châteaux de Lastours** (Feb–March & Nov–Dec Sat, Sun & hols 10am–5pm; April–June & Sept daily 10am–6pm; July & Aug daily 9am–8pm; Oct daily 10am–5pm; €4) looms on the right. A cluster of four separate forts, perched dramatically on the points of the rocky hill dominating the river-bend, these are the northernmost of the Cathar castles, although in fact, only two of them, eleventh-century Cabaret and twelfth-century Surdespines, date from the era of the Crusade. When Simon de Montfort had conquered Minerve to the east and Termes to the south, the survivors took refuge in these forts, which were the redoubt of the Cathar-protecting lord, Pierre-Roger Cabaret. Efforts to besiege them proved vain and de Montfort only took the castles in 1211, when Pierre-Roger surrendered in exchange for pardon. Two more castles were built in the fourteenth century. A path climbs the steep and scrubby hill, and leads from one small castle to the next – an exhilarating walk which takes about two hours. The *châteaux* are quite ruined, and really their location is more evocative than their remains, so if you don't want to climb, you can drive to the look-out point (same ticket), set on a ridge to the west, which affords the best perspectives.

Before continuing south, cut over 5km on the D111 to **Limousis**, whose **cave complex** (daily: March & Oct 2–5pm; April–June 10am–noon & 2–6pm, July & Aug 10am–6pm, Sept 10am–noon & 2pm–5.30pm; €6.20) boasts impressive calcite formations, including the largest known cluster of the crystalline mineral, aragonite. The lively English-speaking guides also make the visit enjoyable. Although there are simple **restaurants** in Mas-Cabardés and Lastours, you'll enjoy the trip more by packing a picnic lunch before departing and finishing up in Carcassonne or another substantial town. This said, the basic **campsite** (T04.68.77.56.01; June–Sept) beside the belvedere at Lastours is recommendable for its location overlooking the castles.

Saissac and around

By traversing the Montagne Noire and heading west along its lower slopes you'll arrive at **SAISSAC**, an ancient hamlet whose steeply sloping lanes lead downhill from the main road to a large ruined fortress looking out towards Carcassonne – the medieval walls and towers can be clearly made out in the distance. Although little remains of the fifteenth-century **castle** (Feb–March & Nov–Dec Sat, Sun & hols 10am–5pm; April–June & Sept daily 10am–6pm; July & Aug daily 9am–8pm; Oct daily 10am–5pm; €3.50), which can be reached from the road in about ten minutes, the hollow ruin is evocative – and a great place for viewing sunsets, but hardly worth the price of admission. Up on the road itself, a solitary tower surviving from the town's now-vanished walls holds a dull **museum** (April–June & Sept daily 10am–1pm & 2–6pm; July & August daily 9am–1pm & 2–6pm; Oct–March Mon–Fri 10am–1pm & 2–5pm, Sat & Sun during school hols; €2.50) containing an exhibition of tools used in local crafts and agriculture.

If you are leaving Saissac by car, you can easily reach the **Bassin du Lampy**, the smallest of the Park du Haut Languedoc's reservoirs, and a quiet place to have a swim, 5km up the D4 (picked up just west of Saissac). From the reservoir, the road continues north, through ever-thickening forest, to **Arfons**. Set among a series of grassy clearings, this little hamlet has an enchantingly forgotten air and is a great place to buy freshly picked mountain produce, including splendid wild mushrooms in late summer. The forest road continues north, eventually forking off to Dourgne and Sorèze. South of Arfons a turn-off to the east leads towards Lacombe, following a narrow path through the **Forêt de la Montagne Noire**, lush, dark and green woods which make for another prime picnicking zone. In the heart of the *forêt*, at the hamlet of La Galaube, a path leads south for twenty minutes to the **Prise d'eau d'Alzeau**, the uppermost reservoir of the Canal du Midi's catchment system. The easy-to-follow trail to the site, where a statue to the visionary engineer stands, is a good way to get a feel for the forest of this region.

Saissac's **tourist office** is in the same tower as the museum (July & Aug daily 10am–12.30pm & 2–6.30pm, ☎04.68.24.47.80, ⓔsaissac@fnotsi.net). Its only **hotel**, *Montagne Noire* (☎04.68.24.46.36, ⒻFAX04.68.24.46.20; ②), is nothing special, and it's certainly better to eat in the town below at *Au Beau Site* (closed Sat & Sun Sept–June; ☎04.68.24.40.37), which also has good views and *menus* from €20. The L'Ambinets run a comfy two-room **gîte**, *La Salamandre*, to the east at **St-Denis** (☎04.68.26.42.13; ②), and they also rent **bikes**. At the Bassin du Lampy, the *Domaine du Lampy-Neuf* (☎04.68.24.46.07, ⒻFAX04.68.24.44.81; ②) offers deluxe **chambres d'hôtes** and *gîte* dorms (①), while *La Galaube* (closed mid-Sept to mid-Jan; ☎04.68.26.51.23, ⓦwww.federal-hotel.com; ②) by the *prise* has simpler rooms and an inexpensive year-round restaurant. You'll find basic **campsites** at the reservoir and at Arfons (ask at the bakery). The *bassin* also has a snack-bar, while Arfons has a bar and **restaurant**.

Montolieu and Villelongue

A short drive south of Saissac, **MONTOLIEU** has striven to make a mark since 1990 as a "town of books", a contrived (and pale) imitation of England's famous Hay-on-Wye. One shop, the aptly titled English Bookshop in rue de la Mairie, specializes in English-language titles, while several of the rest concentrate on New Age and occult books. You can also visit the **Conservatoire des Arts et Métiers du Livre** (daily 10am–noon & 2–6pm; free) at the north end of the village, with a collection of old presses and book-binding tools. West of Montolieu, tucked away in a wooded vale down a seemingly endless country lane, lie the ruins of the twelfth-century Cistercian **Abbey of Villelongue** (May–Oct daily 10am–noon & 2–6.30pm; €4) – worth driving to if only for the picturesque location on the banks of the Vernassonne. The remains of the abbey include the thirteenth-century vaulted cellar, a fourteenth-century Gothic cloister and the ruins of the abbey-church, now surrounded by a garden. In Montolieu you can **stay** at the very funky *Café du Livres*, two streets south of the town's church (T04.68.24.81.17; call ahead; ❷), but greater luxury can be enjoyed at the *Château de Villeneuve* (T04.68.24.84.08, Ela-calle@wanadoo.fr; ❸), a wine *domaine* just north of town. At Villelongue, the former monastery also offers **rooms** (❹), but these are rather spartan and monkish given the price. For more information contact the **tourist office** in the *mairie* at Montolieu (Mon–Fri 10am–noon & 2–6pm; T04.68.24.80.80, Wwww.montolieu.net).

Travel details

Trains

SNCF buses may run in lieu of trains on these lines; service is reduced on Sundays & holidays.
Albi to: Carmaux (20 daily; 30min); Gaillac (17 daily; 20–40min); Naucelle (10 daily; 1hr); St-Sulpice (10 daily; 22min); Toulouse (17 daily; 1hr).
Castres to: Damiette (8 daily 20min); Labrugière (11 daily; 8min); Lavaur (8 daily; 40min); Mazamet (11 daily; 20min); St-Sulpice (8 daily; 1hr 5min); Toulouse (11 daily; 1hr 5min).
Gaillac to: Lisle-sur-Tarn (17 daily; 8min); Rabastens (17 daily; 15min); St-Sulpice (17 daily; 22min); Toulouse (17 daily; 50min); Vindrac (for Cordes; 5 daily; 20min).
Mazamet to: Castres (11 daily; 20min); Labrugière (11 daily; 10min); St-Amans (2 daily 15min); St-Pons (2 daily; 40min); Toulouse (11 daily; 1hr 28min–1hr 55min).

Buses

Many lines have no or reduced service on Saturdays, Sundays and holidays, and in the summer months.
Albi to: Ambialet (3 daily; 1hr 15min); Blayes (daily; 30min); Carcassonne (1 daily; 2hr); Carmaux (6 daily; 30min); Castres (6–8 daily; 1hr 15min); Cordes (2 daily; 35min); Gaillac (6 daily; 45min); Graulhet (2 daily; 40min); Lacaune (1 daily; 1hr 30min); Lisle (6 daily; 40min); Rabastens (2 daily; 50min); Réalmont (6–8 daily; 20min); St-Sulpice (2 daily; 1hr 5min); Toulouse (6 daily; 1hr 40min).
Carmaux to: Albi (6 daily; 30min); Blayes (2 daily; 10min); Cagnac (2 daily; 20min).

Castres to: Albi (6–8 daily; 1hr 15min); Béziers (2 daily; 2hr 50min); Brassac (3–6 daily; 50min); Carcassonne (8 daily; 1hr 50min); Dourgne (6 daily; 40min); Gijounet (4 daily; 1hr 15min); Labrugière (2 daily; 15min); Lacaune (daily; 1hr 15min); Lautrec (2 daily; 30min); Lavaur (4–6 daily; 45min–1hr); Mazamet (2 daily; 30min); Murat (daily; 2hr); Réalmont (2–4 daily; 25min); Revel (3 daily; 40min); St-Pons (2–4 daily; 1hr 15min); the Sidorbe (frequent; 20min); Sorèze (3 daily; 45min); Toulouse (2–4 daily; 1hr 40min–2hr); Vabre (4 daily; 45min).
Gaillac to: Albi (4 daily; 45min); Graulhet (4 daily; 30min); Lavaur (4 daily; 35min); Lisle (4–8 daily; 10min); Rabastens (4–8 daily; 20min); Toulouse (4 daily; 1hr 25min).
Graulhet to: Albi (2 daily; 40min); Gaillac (4 daily; 30min); Lautrec (4 daily; 30min).
Mazamet to: Anglès (2 daily; 20min); Labastide (2 daily; 35min); Labrugière (2 daily; 10min); Lacabarède (2 daily; 30min); La Salvetat (2 daily; 45min); Lavaur (2 daily; 1hr 10min); Réalmont (2–4 daily; 55min); St-Amans (2 daily; 20min); St-Paul (2 daily; 55min); St-Pons (4 daily; 45min); St-Sulpice (2 daily; 1hr 30min); Toulouse (2 daily; 2hr).
Réalmont to: Graulhet (daily; 20min).
Revel to: Dourgne (daily; 5min); Sorèze (daily; 10min).
St-Pons to: Bédarieux (6 daily; 1hr 20min); Béziers (4 daily; 1hr 20min); Lamalou-les-Bains (6 daily; 55min); La Salvetat (2 daily; 45min); Montpellier (2 daily; 2hr 20min).
Sorèze to: Castres (3 daily; 45min); Castlenaudary (Mon; 30min); Saint-Félix (3 daily; 20min); Toulouse (3 daily; 1hr 20min).

4

Nîmes and around

N

4

Nîmes and around

N

CHAPTER 4

Highlights

✳ **Tauromachie** The "art of the bull" is practised in the Gard with a passion and intensity unparallelled north of the Pyrenees. See p.226

✳ **Nîmes Amphitheatre** Once the scene of gladiatorial combats, this 20,000-seat stadium still functions after 2000 years. See p.226

✳ **Pont du Gard** France's most famous Roman monument, a testament both to brilliant engineering and slave labour. See p.237

✳ **The Monastery of St-Roman** An underground monastery cut from the living rock, tucked away in the hills above the Rhône. See p.243

✳ **Aigues-Mortes** A picture-perfect medieval walled town, set among the swamps and dunes of the Mediterranean coast. See p.249

✳ **La Petite Camargue** Durrell's "Little Argentina", an open expanse of salt-pans and meadows, populated by horses, bulls and wide array of birdlife. See p.253

▲ Flamingos, the Camargue

4

Nîmes and around

îmes is Languedoc's most revitalized city, on the way up after an eighteen-hundred-year slump following its decline as an imperial settlement. Chock-full of the region's most impressive Roman monuments, and a showcase for its most exciting new architecture, it's a busy little place, embodying an intriguing combination of ancient glory and modern style. The lands around the city comprise the southern half of **Gard**, the easternmost *département* of Languedoc-Roussillon – hemmed in on the east by the mighty Rhône river and on the west by the humble River Vidourle. On the Mediterranean coast, the **Petite Camargue**, the western section of the Rhône delta, rises tentatively out of the sea. This is desolate and windswept country, dominated by bull and horse farms near the seaside, and vineyards closer inland. As you move away from the sea, the sand dunes gradually give way to the brushy hills known as the **garrigues**, around Nîmes itself and to the north. These in turn are cut through by the deep gorge of the Gardon river, on the far bank of which runs the band of flatland once dominated by the ducal castle of **Uzès**. Vineyards cover the river valley, but in the scrub-covered hills stunted holm oaks compete with hardy thistles, lavender and thyme.

Although the numerous and majestic **Roman ruins** of southern Gard, including Nîmes' **Les Arènes** and the magnificent **Pont du Gard**, attest to the area's prosperity in Roman times, this corner of the south has for centuries been something of a poorer cousin of neighbouring Provence, relegated to secondary status as the House of Toulouse collapsed in the wake of the Albigensian Crusade. This traditional economic marginalization is reflected in the faded glory of the former medieval port towns of **Beaucaire** and **St-Gilles**, although further south, recent revival has drawn developers to the **beaches** and **pleasure ports** of the Camarguaise coast. To the west, the gentle Vidourle is still spanned by **Roman bridges** and dotted by all but forgotten hamlets.

The weather in Gard tends to extremes: hot summers and mild winters, punctuated by violent rainstorms in autumn and the merciless buffeting of the cold mistral wind in spring. The best season to visit is undoubtedly summer, but if you want to see Nîmes and Gard at their most traditional, try to visit during the local **festivals**, which invariably entail *tauromachie* – bullfighting and horsemanship, both Camarguaise and Spanish-style.

Getting around in southern Gard presents some difficulties if you're reliant on **public transport**, and want to get off the main routes. Nîmes is the hub, with good train and bus services to most of the region's towns, services to the coast becoming more frequent in summer. Crossing between the various

Festivals in and around Nîmes

Festivals in the *département* of Gard have a decidedly bullish flavour to them. In the bigger places – Nîmes, Beaucaire and St-Gilles – full-blown Spanish-style *corridas* are held for the most important occasions, but otherwise, nearly every small town will somehow involve **bulls** in their celebrations. Aside from these there are a number of fairs and events which commemorate the area's medieval past or its regional products. Where no specific information number is given, contact the relevant tourist office for details.

Fourth week before Easter Nîmes: Feria de Primavera. The local celebration for pre-Lenten Carnaval, and the first of Nîmes' famed *ferias*, a street festival including music and *tauromachie*.

Late March St-Gilles: Carnaval. Held for one week and similar to the Nîmes event, but on a much smaller scale and with emphasis on the traditions of the Camarguaise cowboy culture: horsemanship, *courses camarguaises* and *corridas*.

Late March to Sept Le Grau/Port Camargue: *Courses camarguaises* are held every weekend in order to decide the year's winners of the Trophée de As and the Trophée de l'Avenir.

April Sommières: Medieval festival. On the first weekend in April, a street festival with costumed merchants and performers, markets, music and cookery.

May Nîmes: Feria de Pentecôte. The city's most important festival and a frenzied rite of spring, held on the fifth weekend after Easter. The festival has a heavy emphasis on bullfighting, along with music, dancing and a large street market in the old town.

Early June Beaucaire: Fête du Drac. A three-day medieval festival, held in conjunction with neighbouring Tarascon, and celebrating the legend of the river beast, La Tarasque, a child-eating amphibious monster of local medieval folklore. Admission charge of €9 per day.

Mid-June Le Grau-du-Roi: Fisherman's festival. Along with the traditional *courses camarguaises*, water-jousting competitions are held in the harbour and canals in this four-day celebration of Le Grau's traditional industry.

Throughout July Nîmes: Les Jeudis. Thursday nights. Street market with live music running the gamut of styles and nationalities in nearly every square (and many restaurants).

Mid-July Nîmes: Mosaïques Gitanes. A four-day festival of Romany ("Gypsy") culture including music, dancing and an outdoor market.

Mid-July Sauve: African festival ☎04.66.77.59.96, ⊛www.enfance-action.org. Yearly three-day festival which brings in performers of traditional and modern music from across Africa. Concerts held in the town's Théâtre de Verdure. Admission €20.

routes from Nîmes, or accessing out-of-the-way areas like the Petite Camargue or the *garrigues*, however, is more inconvenient. That said, the flattish terrain makes for relatively easy walking and, as elsewhere in the south, local drivers are generally helpful when it comes to hitching. Unfortunately for **cyclists**, heavy traffic makes the country roads of the coastal plain unpleasant and dangerous, but amongst the *garrigues* and along the Vidourle there are some excellent and not overly challenging routes.

Mid-July to mid-Aug Uzès: Autres Rivages. A World-Music festival featuring primarily African groups. Performances are held in sites of architectural and archeological interest in the countryside around town.

Fourth week July Beaucaire: Estivals. A ten-day-long summer festival with a medieval emphasis, including market, parades, fireworks and bullfights. The grand finale, on the last Friday of the month, is marked by a 100-bull *abrivado*.

Throughout July & Aug Beaucaire: Les Beaux Quais du Vendredi. Friday-night open-air concerts, featuring live acts ranging from blues to World Music, plus a lively canalside street market.

Throughout Aug Aigues-Mortes: Les Nuits d'Encens ☎04.66.73.91.23. The town's "Nights of Incense" offer an eclectic musical programme, with styles from around the world and across the ages – from European chamber music to medieval Hispano-Arabic sounds. Nightly performances at 10pm in the courtyard of the Logis du Gouverneur.

Early Aug Quissac: Les Vidourlades ☎04.66.77.15.13, ⓦwww.vidourlades. com. A three-day World-Music festival with a Spanish and North African bent. Nightly performances are held in the medieval ruins atop the town's hill.

Mid-Aug St-Gilles: Feria de la pêche et de l'abricot. A one-week harvest festival, celebrating two of the area's major agricultural products, peaches and apricots, with emphasis also on ranch culture and *tauromachie*.

Late Aug Aigues-Mortes: Fête de St-Louis. Held on the closest weekend to August 25, a medieval pageant and reconstruction of St Louis' departure for the Crusades, celebrating the day when the saint-king set out to fight the Muslims.

First week Sept Fourques (near Beaucaire): Foires aux Chevaux. A traditional two-day horse-market, which brings together *manade*-owners and *gardians* from across the Camargue, in addition to some 10,000 spectators, for a boisterous carnival.

Second week Sept Le Grau/Port-Camargue: Fête locale. A major event on the taurine calendar, the twin towns' festivities include bull-running, *courses camarguaises*, water-jousting and the usual markets, street parties and general exuberance.

Third week Sept Nîmes: Feria des Vendanges. The third great *feria* in Nîmes, celebrating the wine harvest. Another *tauromachie* extravaganza, with live open-air concerts, parades and a market.

Mid-Oct Aigues-Mortes: Fête local. A three-day annual party featuring Gardois *tauromachie* performed alongside the medieval walls of the old town.

Nîmes

NÎMES is a city inextricably linked to its Roman past. Its location on the Via Domitia – the main chariot route from Spain to Rome – helped make it a favourite with a series of emperors of the first and second centuries AD, who endowed it with the outstanding collection of monuments which dominate the place today; the **Maison Carrée**, the **amphitheatre** (or "Arènes") and the **Temple of Diana** are all testament to the city's bright, if short-lived, splendour. Since then, over the last eighteen hundred years, Nîmes has had something of a tough time of it, having to vie with neighbouring rivals Arles, Avignon and Montpellier (see p.262), which each in their time stole the city's limelight. Through the Eighties and Nineties, however, a succession of two

Tour Magne

Temple of Diana

Jardin de la Fontaine

2 & Uzès

Uzès & Beaucaire

Motorway, Airport, Beaucaire, & Pont du Gard

Castellum Divisorum

Fortress/ University

Les Halles

Carrée d'Art

Maison Carrée

Cathedral

Porte d'August

Musée de Vieux Nîmes

Meynier de Salinelles

Hôtel Bernis

Archeological/ Natural History Museum

Hôtel Régis

Hôtel de Ville

Galerie des Arènes

Les Arènes

Roman Gate

Musée de Cultures Taurines

Musée des Beaux-Arts

Gare SNCF

Gare Routière

Nemausus Development

Stade, Roundpoint & Motorway

ACCOMMODATION

Alcanthe du Temple	D
Atria	K
Audrans Terminus	L
La Baume	C
Central	F
Imperator Concorde	A
Kyriad	G
Lisita	I
de la Maison Carrée	E
Nouvel	J
de Provence	H
Royal	B

RESTAURANTS

L'Ancien Théâtre	8
Aux Plaisirs des Halles	4
La Bodeguita	3
Le Bouchon et l'Assiette	2
El Rinconcito	10
Le Jardin d'Hadrien	1
Le Magister	6
Ophélie	11
Le Paradis du Couvent	5
Le P'tit Bec	13
Simple Simon	7
Le Tango	12
La Truye qui Filhe	9

N

0   200 m

flamboyant mayors have promoted the city within and without, engaging in a
series of audacious building projects (including a retractable cover for the
Roman amphitheatre), sponsoring concerts and festivals and drawing in artists
and musicians. Their efforts have succeeded, kindling a spark that not even the
massive mudslide of 1988, which covered the city in two and a half metres of
muck and claimed the lives of seven people, could extinguish. Nowadays,
crowds come not only to see the shrines of the Caesars and the dusted-off
mansions of the cloth-making bourgeoisie, but a collection of provocative
contemporary urban architecture in a city which is redefining itself. Nîmes also
has two surprisingly good **art galleries**, and hosts some of the South of
France's most colourful **festivals** – February's Carnaval, and the *ferias* of

Pentecost and September, when the arena fills with **bullfighting** aficionados and the bars and restaurants are packed late into the night with noisy revellers.

Some history

Nemausus had been a Roman colony since 40 BC, but didn't really take off until Augustus Caesar (then, Octavian, and not yet emperor) defeated Mark Antony and Cleopatra at Actium in 31 BC, bringing Egypt under his power. As a reward, he settled his veterans here, laying out a Roman grid-plan city and endowing it with powerful fortifications. In honour of their victory in Egypt, his soldiers adopted the ensign of a crocodile (the Nile) chained to a palm tree, which subsequently became the city's **symbol**. As the town grew, water-demand outstripped the resources of its sacred spring and, under Claudius, a 50km-long canal, of which the Pont du Gard (see p.237) is part, was constructed to supply water. A century later, the city was at its zenith, enjoying the special patronage of the emperor Antoninus Pius, whose mother's family hailed from these parts. It was a sprawling city enclosed by some 7km of thick walls (which survived as late as 1786), reinforced by thirty stout towers and pierced by seven monumental gates. From that glorious era, however, things went rapidly downhill. Within a decade of Antoninus' death, the Roman Empire spun into a temporary political crisis, and by the time the situation had restabilized, Christianity had replaced paganism in the empire, and Christian Arles had supplanted polytheistic Nîmes as the local capital.

With the Roman decline, Nîmes was to suffer conquest by Germanic "barbarians". For 250 years the town was held by the Visigoths, in turn displaced by Muslims who came up from Spain in about 724. Only seven years later the Muslims were forced out, and for the next four hundred years the town was incorporated into a series of rapidly dissolving principalities including West Francia, Aquitaine and Septimania. In 1185 it came under the control of the **counts of Toulouse**, under whom the town briefly flirted with Catharism; the mere sight of de Montfort's powerful army, however, was enough to make it "repent" and return to the Catholic fold. Nîmes was absorbed by the French Crown in 1226, but by this time little was left of the glorious Roman city – only two clusters of houses huddled around the cathedral and amphitheatre.

After three sleepy centuries as a poor market town, Nîmes began to discover a new vocation as a textile centre – until the **Wars of Religion** wracked the region. Calvinist preachers found eager ears in Nîmes' new prosperous class of cloth-makers, to the extent that local Huguenots destroyed the eleventh-century cathedral and, on St Michael's Day of 1567, massacred some two hundred clergy. Following their repression in the wake of the Wars, Protestants from Nîmes as well as exiles from Haut Languedoc rose up together in the Camisard rebellion, brutally suppressed by royal forces in 1704, following its leader's defection to the Catholic forces at Nîmes. Many Protestants fled, while others persevered, having to disguise their faith. After the Revolution, religious issues were laid aside, and Nîmes, still predominantly Protestant, got back down to making money, which it did by spinning silk and cotton. The town's product became so successful that the cotton cloth "de Nîmes" (thus "denim") went west, where in 1848 an American, Levi Strauss, hit upon the idea of attaching small red labels to pants made out of the material. Recent city history is dominated by mayors Jean Bousquet and Alain Clary, who embarked on a daring policy of reconstruction, including drawing leading avant-garde architects to the city, and opening its first university. The 2001 elections, which marked a swing to the right across France, swept Jean-Paul Fournier into the mairie; whether Nîmes' recent élan continues or not remains to be seen.

Arrival and information

Garons **airport**, which also serves Arles, has few facilities, basically limited to an ATM and car rental desks. Located 10km south of Nîmes along the D42, just outside St-Gilles, from here the trip to the city can be made by *navette* (2–4 daily; ☎04.66.29.27.29; "Gambetta" or "Imperator" stop; €5). By taxi, the trip will cost at least €23 (€30 at night). Nîmes' **gare SNCF** and **gare routière** are both located at the end of avenue Feuchères, about a ten-minute walk south of the old town – the gare SNCF has **left luggage** lockers, and a **tourist office**, currently closed for renovations but slated to reopen soon. Arriving **by car** on the A9, take either exit and follow signs for the centre (north of the *autoroute*); there are underground parking spaces on the ring road, and street parking is also legal, if often difficult. The **main tourist office** (Easter–June & Sept Mon–Fri 8am–7pm, Sat 9am–7pm, Sun 10am–6pm; July & Aug Mon–Fri 8am–8pm, Sat 9am–7pm, Sun 10am–6pm; Oct–Easter Mon–Fri 8.30am–7pm, Sat 9am–7pm, Sun 10am–5pm; ☎04.66.58.38.00, ⊛www.ot-nimes.fr) is about a twenty-minute walk from the *gares* at 6 rue Auguste, and can also be reached by bus #8 ("Antonin"). Up-to-date information on Nîmes and other places covered in this chapter can be found at ⊛www.tourismegard.com.

Unless you're staying at the campsite, hostel or one of the far-flung motels, you'll most likely have no use for Nîmes' city transport system. The **bus** network's hub is avenue Feuchères, through which all the main lines pass, the most useful of which, line #8, circles the city centre. Transport **maps** are available from tourist offices, and single **tickets** (€1) can be bought from the drivers. If you want to cycle around Nîmes, the youth hostel (see below), gare SNCF and campsite **rent bikes** to guests, and there's also Cycles Rebour, at 38 rue Hôtel Dieu (☎04.66.76.24.32). Alternatively, TRAN **taxis** (see "Listings", p.232) charge €24 for a fifty-minute tour of Nîmes for a maximum of six people (€6 extra for hotel pick-up and drop-off).

Accommodation

Accommodation options in Nîmes are plentiful, although rock-bottom budget places aren't so easy to come by. You can reserve many hotels in the city through a **central reservation** office (☎04.66.36.96.30, ☎04.66.67.65.25), and should book ahead as far as possible for visits during any of the city's celebrations. If you are here for a weekend, you may want to check the tourist office's **hotel package**, the "Pass Romain", which includes admission to the city's museums, the Pont du Gard, a "Roman" meal and one night's accommodation (from €70 per person, depending on hotel rating). Nîmes' comfortable **FUAJ/HI hostel** (☎04.66.23.25.04, ⊛www.fuaj.org/aj/nimes; July & Aug membership required; Sept–June no curfew; €9), which also has camping facilities, is on Chemin de la Cigale, 2km northwest of the centre (take bus #2 dir: Ales or Villverte to "Stade"). In addition, there are several private hostels (*résidences*), some for under-25s, others with self-catering suites (contact the tourist office for details). The municipal **campsite** (☎04.66.38.09.21; open year-round) is further out, on the route de Générac, 5km south of the centre, beyond the A9 *autoroute* (bus #D: "La Bastide" stop).

Hotels

With the exception of the *Imperator*, none of the city's hotels offer anything unique, but all of the establishments listed below are solid possibilities. Most of the cheaper **hotels** are located between the Arènes and the train station. At *feria* times, you may have to resort to the cluster of motels around the Nîmes-Ouest exit of the A9, which includes the *Holiday Inn* (T04.66.29.86.87, Econtact@holidayinn–nimes.com; ⑥), *Mercure* (T04.66.70.48.00, Wwww.mercure.com; ⑤), *Mas de Galoffre* (T04.66.38.15.36, Wwww.gallofre.com; ②) and *Formule 1* (T04.66.38.14.05, F04.66.29.77.85; ①).

Alcanthe du Temple 1 rue Charles Babout T04.66.67.54.61, Wwww.hotel-du-temple.com. This is one of the old town's best bargains. Friendly, well-kept and quiet, set in an eighteenth-century house. Rooms have fans, TV and en-suite showers. Closed Jan. ③

Atria 5 bld de Prague T04.66.76.56.56, Wwww.novotel.com. Just south of the old town, this modern building is something of a monstrosity compared with Nîmes' other hotels, but it has all the mod cons – at a price. ⑥

Audras Terminus 23 av Feuchères T04.66.67.66.20, Wwww.hotel-terminus-nimes.com. Right by the train station, this is a well-decorated and lively hotel, with attentive staff. Amenities include cable TV. ②

La Baume 21 rue Nationale T04.66.76.28.42, Wwww.new-hotel.com. Located in a former mansion, tastefully decorated, with friendly and professional service, this hotel is at the high end of this bracket, but worth it. ⑥

Central 2 pl du Château T04.66.67.27.75, F04.66.21.77.79. Just behind the temple and the Porte d'Auguste, with English-speaking management, this is a small but cosy hotel which also has secure parking. ③

Imperator Concorde Quai de la Fontaine T04.66.21.90.30, Ehotel.imperator concorde@wanadoo.fr. Nîmes' best and most prestigious hotel, with top service and amenities in an atmosphere-loaded *fin-de-siècle* mansion with a stately garden. Prices quadruple during *ferias*. ⑥

Kyriad 10 rue Rossy T04.66.76.16.20, Wwww.kyriad.nimescentre.wanadoo.fr. One of

Nîmes' newer hotels, the *Kyriad* is a solid two-star option with an impressive range of amenities. Its location just outside the old town makes street parking a convenient possibility. ③

Lisita 2bis bd des Arènes T04.66.67.66.20, F04.66.76.22.30. Long-established place, and one of the funkier digs in town; the Spanish flavour is popular not only with travellers but with visiting bullfighters. Rooms have AC and TV. Also a highly recommended restaurant specializing in – what else? – beef (expect to spend €35; closed Sun & Mon). ②

De la Maison Carrée 14 rue de la Maison Carrée T04.66.67.32.89, Eaaaaa@abtel.fr. Right by the famous temple, this small hotel has cheery decor and a great rooftop breakfast terrace. Extras include AC and TV. Reception closes at 11pm, and the check-out is a rather early 10am. ③

Nouvel 6 bd Amiral Courbet T04.66.67.62.48. Surprisingly good amenities for the rock-bottom price, including TV in every room. ①

De Provence 5/7 square de la Couronne T04.66.76.04.92, Wwww.hoteldeprovence.com. Well located near the train and bus stations and the amphitheatre. Rooms have cable TV; parking is extra. ②

Royal 3 bd Alphonse-Daudet T04.66.58.28.27, F04.66.58.28.28. Near the *Imperator*, the *Royal* has a cool Spanish-style decor which also draws in passing *toreros*. The rooms are individually decorated with a distinctly Iberian flavour, and the place exudes a certain cool chic. This is also home to the *Bodeguita* tapas bar. ③

The City

The heart of Nîmes can be found in the place de la Masion Carrée, where an august two-thousand-year-old temple, the **Maison Carrée**, faces off against its gleaming twentieth-century doppelganger, the **Carré d'Art**. Fanning off from here to the east, a compact warren of pedestrian streets makes up the city's **old town**, a triangle hemmed in by the boulevards Gambetta on the north, Amiral-Courbet on the southeast, and Victor-Hugo on the southwest, and home to the city's medieval and early modern sights. Nîmes' oldest remains – its **Roman**

monuments – lie for the most part on the edge of the old town, like the famous **Arènes** coliseum, and off to the north and east, clustered around the blunt Mont Cavalier. There are several worthwhile museums here, all to be found in the city centre, whereas Nîmes, famous modern architecture, is concentrated in the far south, in the newer suburbs.

The Maison Carrée and Carré d'Art

The **Maison Carrée** ("square house"), a tiny but perfectly proportioned temple, once the centrepiece of the city's forum, was founded in 4 or 5 AD and dedicated to Augustus' adopted grandson. Size, of course, is not everything, and as Henry James remarked, it is precisely because of its compactness that "it does not overwhelm you, you can conceive it." This is perhaps the world's best preserved Roman temple (rivalled only by Lebanon's stupendous Temple of Apollo at Baalbek), and can still boast all of its columns, an intact roof and *cella* (inner sanctum). If over the ages its functions – including use as a stable – haven't always done it justice, its aesthetic perfection has long drawn notable admirers: Colbert, Louis XIV's prime minister, wanted to carry it off lock and stock to Versailles; Thomas Jefferson modelled the Virginia Capital building on it; and Napoleon took it as inspiration for the Magdalene church in Paris. Today it houses a **museum** (Tues–Sun 9am–7pm; free), which contains a small but somewhat overly detailed exhibition on the building itself, and odds and ends of recovered Roman masonry.

The Carré d'Art

On the far side of boulevard Victor-Hugo sits Norman Foster's 1993 **Carré d'Art** (July & Aug 10am–5pm, Sept–June 9am–7pm; free), a twentieth-century descendant of the Roman temple. Four fine columns support the high portico with seeming effortlessness, paying homage to the chunkier Ionic columns of the smaller Maison Carrée, reflected in the inscrutable glass face of Foster's building. The building is home to a library and resource centre, and the top two floors house the city's **Musée d'Art Contemporain** (Tues–Sun 10am–6pm; €4.55), which contains an impressive survey of French and Western European art of the last four decades. Emphasis is on Gallic movements such as Nouveau Réalisme and Support-surfaces, but Mediterranean and northern European art is also strongly represented.

The Cathedral and around

With the core of the Roman city long buried and built over, and most of the medieval buildings destroyed in the course of the Wars of Religion, Nîmes' **old town** is for the most part a testament to the success of the local cloth-merchants of the seventeenth to nineteenth centuries – the builders of the grandiose *hôtels* which pepper the streets emanating south and west from the **Cathédrale de Notre-Dame et St-Castors**, a five-minute stroll east of the

Maison Carrée. This church serves as a fitting transition point from Roman to early-modern Nîmes, set as it is on the foundations of the former temple of Apollo. Of the original cathedral, founded in 1069, only the bell tower and the badly chipped friezes of the facade survived the Huguenots' wrath – the rest was rebuilt in the 1700s. The new building is rather nondescript and the drably remodelled interior is hardly worth a visit. On the south side of the square sits the seventeenth-century **bishop's palace**, now home to the **Musée de Vieux Nîmes** (Tues–Sun 10am–6pm; €4.55), whose lively collection focuses on the city's artisanal and industrial past, including, of course, the manufacture of denim, and will appeal to both adults and children. It is a well-organized exhibition, rounded out by a noteworthy furniture collection, which includes a nineteenth-century billiard table and sedan chairs.

Northeast of the cathedral, following the narrow lane which runs along its north wall, you'll eventually come upon the excavated **Porte d'Auguste**. This surprisingly well-preserved triumphal entryway into the city, sunk by the rising ground level, was only discovered in the eighteenth century with the destruction of the medieval palace which had been built around it. It is through this gate that the **Via Domitia** entered Nîmes from the east: the larger central passages were for chariots and the smaller side entrances for pedestrians. Just beyond, in place des Carmes, the Protestant Grand Temple and the Catholic church of St-Baudille contemplate each other uneasily,

The Hôtels of the denim lords

Heading south from the cathedral on rue des Marchands, you'll pass the plain facade of a medieval shop at no. 15 – a rare "commercial" survivor of the Middle Ages – before passing **Hôtel Régis**, a former merchants' house with a stately sixteenth-century courtyard in rue de Chapitre. The street ends at Grande Rue, where you'll be confronted by the clean Neoclassical lines of the former **Jesuits' Chapel** (Tues–Sun 10am–6pm; same ticket as the archeological museum; see below). Inside, there's a spacious and luxuriously appointed Baroque interior, now used for exhibitions and concerts. In rue des Greffes, to the south, sits the late Renaissance **Hôtel de Ville**, built in 1700 – look for the stuffed crocodiles suspended above the staircase inside the entry hall, gifts to the city from contented (and rich) eighteenth-century burghers.

West from here, the saurian theme continues in place de la Marché, where a twentieth-century homage to the city's emblem has been paid in a **fountain** designed by Martiel Raysse and Silvio and Vito Tongiani. Just to the northwest, innocuous among the colourful boutiques and restaurants, sits the **Hôtel Bernis**, one of the town's earliest surviving mansions, its fifteenth-century facade studded by casement windows and concealing an atmospheric old courtyard with a well in the centre. Nearby, at 8 rue l'Aspic, you can see three early Christian sarcophagi incorporated into the walls of the **Meynier de Salinelles** mansion, as well as a splendid staircase leading up from its courtyard. Further along rue l'Aspic is the place de l'Horloge, whose solitary eighteenth-century **clock tower** is now crowded by the tables of café terraces; place aux Herbes is just to the east.

The Museum of Archeology and Natural History

Butting up against the back of the Jesuits' Chapel, is the **Museum of Archeology and Natural History** (Tues–Sun 10am–6pm; €4.55) – two collections whose only thing in common is the roof which they share. The archeological section is disappointingly poor in Roman artefacts considering the city's ancient Latin glory; items are limited to a sizeable but visually monotonous collection of Latin epigraphy and an assortment of household goods, though it does have some fine Greek lacquerware and pre-Roman Etruscan.

The quirky natural history exhibition comprises a jumbled collection of Polynesian masks and spears, and a hotchpotch of stuffed animals, including a Royal Bengal Tiger. In fact, the museum rather resembles a large curio cabinet – a journey into the nineteenth-century European mind, which saw the world beyond its borders as a hunting ground for collectables.

Les Arènes and around

The city's other famous Roman monument squats at the south end of boulevard Victor-Hugo, and although not the largest surviving Roman amphitheatre, **Les Arènes** (daily: July & Aug 9am–7pm; Sept–June 10am–5pm; closed during special events; €4.55) may well be the best preserved. Dating back to the first century, the 133-metre-long and 101-metre-wide oval surges 21 metres above the street, thanks to its uniquely intact upper galleries, and still holds the crowds of 20,000 spectators for which it was designed. An ingenious access system allows the public to enter and exit through the *vomitoria* – the great arched entryways which ring the building – quickly and with minimal jostling. Back before the stick-in-the-mud Christians banned gladiatorial matches in the fourth century, these entertainments, along with spectacles involving killing exotic animals, were the big draw. In the intervening centuries

Bullfighting and tauromachie

Bulls have been raised in the Petite Camargue and the plains to its north for centuries, and for the people of the ranchlands around St-Gilles, **tauromachie** or *la bouvine* – the art of bull-handling – has come to represent a measure of virility, testament to their proud rural roots. Its significance however, is also region-wide: in addition to the exciting action and dangerous elements of bull-handling – which naturally began to attract audiences – the growing cultural awareness of the mid-nineteenth century prompted intellectual Occitan patriots to find in it a further mark of the uniqueness of their local culture, thus sealing *tauromachie*'s transformation into a popular spectacle throughout Languedoc and Roussillon.

The traditions of the **bullfight**, which seem now to be so essential to the spirit of Gard, are in fact almost exclusively recent innovations. A *jeu taurin*, wherein ranch hands and sometimes other animals were pitted against bulls as entertainment, had developed by the Middle Ages, but it wasn't until the Iberian customs arrived, thanks to a visiting Spanish nobleman, that French *tauromachie* came into its own. The first real **corrida** (Spanish bullfight) in France was held in 1853 at Bayonne. It was a great success and soon spread throughout the Midi and into Provence. At Nîmes' Les Arènes the first official *corrida* was held in 1865, and by 1880 the spectacle could be seen across the south. Meanwhile, the local tradition, the **course** – in which men on foot would try to pull ornaments off the foreheads of charging bulls – had also been formalized, and achieved such popularity that when the government tried to ban it because of high fatalities, the population defiantly opposed the plan.

The standard Spanish-style *corrida* which can be seen at the *ferias* of Nîmes, Beaucaire, St-Gilles and Sommières is a highly ritualized **ceremony** – a fatal dance in which the bull is an unwitting but respected partner. In a typical afternoon, three matadors will dispose of six bulls, each of which will face a series of torments: first, after a few initial passes with the large cape (*capote*), the bull is subjected to the long, barbed spear of the mounted *picadores*; next, the graceful *banderilleros* run at the bull and plant their colourful barbs in its shoulder; and finally, the matador executes a series of choreographed passes with his small red *mula* until, to the minor strains of a *paso* since the decline of these games the building has only managed to escape destruction thanks to its more or less continued use. With its occupation by the Visigoths it was used as a fortress, a role in which it remained through the twelfth century (in the east section, two contemporary windows remain). Thereafter it quickly filled up with houses, shops and churches, coming to constitute a veritable slum, which was only cleared out when restoration work began in 1809.

Since the nineteenth century the amphitheatre has been used again for public spectacles, including bullfights. Once you have appreciated the grandness of its structure, however, the inside of the arena holds little interest; the long series of impressively vast but near-identical passages, stairways and bench-rows is a tribute to Roman engineering, but hides few surprises. Unfortunately, the concerts and events held here often obscure the building with scaffolding and stage-works, and although the retractable cover which was added in the late 1980s makes winter-time shows possible, it frustrates efforts to imagine the building's ancient ambience. The best way to visit Les Arènes is to come for a **bullfight** (see box below) during one of Nîmes' *ferias*. Outside the main entrance of the arena you'll see a sombre reminder of the seriousness of the *corrida*, the statue of Christian Moncouquiol, a promising young *torero* who performed under the name of "el Nimeño II," who was gored to death in 1991.

doble, the president of the *corrida* gives the order for the bullfighter to finish off his partner. Crowds at the event are extremely vocal and demonstrative: a poor matador and bull will be pelted with seat cushions, while a very successful matador will be greeted with cheers, showered with roses, rewarded with a gift of the bull's ears and tail and borne out of the ring on the shoulders of the crowd. The happiest ending, however, is the rare *indulto*, when the bull is also rewarded for his performance, and retired, to be used for breeding and allowed to die of contented old age.

The French *course* is quite distinct, although it has been permeated by an undeniable Spanish flavour. Less expensive and elaborate, it is more common in village *fêtes*, such as at **Uzès** or **Aigues-Mortes**. The bulls (or cows) are first led to the ring in an *abrivado*, herded by a tumult of mounted *gardians* – if this takes place within a confined area, it is called an *encierro* (a "running" of the bulls). Once in the ring the animals are outfitted with a rosette and tassels suspended between their horns, and for fifteen minutes *raseteurs* (named after the hooked handgear they wear) provoke the animal into charging, and attempt to snatch the rosette or tassels without getting trampled or gored. When all is complete, the bulls are herded out with great fanfare and frenzy (the *bandido*) and back to the pen.

Aside from these entertainments, a rather more workaday manifestation of *la bouvine* has also become a staple of local spring-time festivals. This is the *ferrado*, in which year-old bulls are driven from their pens by mounted *gardians*, wrestled to the ground by their colleagues on foot and then branded with a hot iron, marking them with the arms or initials of the *manade* to which they belong.

La fé di bioù ("love of the bull") has proved contagious, and today *tauromachie* is more popular than ever. The *ferias* of Nîmes draw thousands of enthusiasts from all over France and the rest of Europe and are universally acknowledged as southern France's liveliest and most colourful festivities. And the practice has taken firm root even in the smallest of villages far from the *manades* of the plains; even if they can afford no more than an *encierro*, villagers pool their money in order to pay for some sort of taurine display, without which no *fête* would be seen as complete.

Whether or not you manage to see a matador in action, be sure to check out the two taurine museums near the Arénes, the small **Galerie des Arénes** (Tues–Sun 11am–6pm; free) on the north side of the boulevard des Arénes and the new **Musée des Cultures Taurines** (Tues–Sun 10am–6pm; €4.55). The former is a gallery featuring local painters, while the latter is a museum dedicated to *tauromachie*, with a permanent collection of posters and relics, and engagingly themed annual exhibits (2003 was on "Women and Bulls").

From the temple, it's a fifteen-minute jaunt southwest to rue Cité Foulc and the **Musée des Beaux-Arts** (Tues–Sun 10am–6pm; €4.55). This is worth a visit if only for its huge Roman mosaic, depicting the mythical "marriage of Admetus", which is its centrepiece, but the collection – mostly Flemish, Italian and French paintings of the sixteenth to eighteenth centuries – is endowed with works of surprising quality, including Rubens' uncharacteristically static *Portrait of a Monk*, and a fine example of the transition from medieval to humanist style in Giambono's *Mystical Marriage of St Catherine*.

Along the way, in rue Porte de France, you'll pass through the **Roman gate** of the same name. It's worth pausing here to consider the immense size of the Roman city – the whole area between here and the Tour Magne was contained by its walls.

The Castellum Divisorum, La Tour Magne and Temple of Diana

Tucked away north of boulevard Gambetta, beside the cold and sinister facade of the town's eighteenth-century **fortress** (now the Centre Universitaire du Vauban; Oct–June; free) sits one of Nîmes' most important but least known Roman artefacts – the **Castellum Divisorum** (daily: mid-March to mid-Oct 7.30am–10pm, mid-Oct to mid-March 7.30am–6.30pm; free), the rare remains of a first-century waterworks (the only similar ones are at Pompeii in Italy and Tiermes in Spain), which mark the start of the Roman circuit. It was from this innocuous-looking open basin that the water carried to the town via the Pont du Gard was distributed to the various parts of the Roman city by lead pipes, which are still partly visible – at the Pont du Gard museum (see p.238) multimedia installations show how the complex worked. Following the quiet residential streets west from here takes you to the **Jardin de la Fontaine**, a formal eighteenth-century garden with a complex series of fountains and pools, at the foot of the forested **Mont Cavalier**.

La Tour Magne and Temple of Diana

From the *place* at the foot of the Mont, follow the signs up the serpentine path which takes you to the ruins of the **Tour Magne**. This **watchtower** (Tues–Sun: July & Aug 9am–7pm; Sept–June 10am–5pm; €2.45), based on an earlier Celtic structure, dates from about 15 BC, and as the Roman settlement grew, was eventually incorporated into the city walls. The tower has suffered its share of indignities, including the loss of the top fifteen of its original 45-metre height and the frantic diggings around the foundations by a treasure-hunting seventeenth-century gardener deluded by a prediction of Nostradamus, but it is impressive even in its ruined state. Broken off and eroded, the tower evokes the romantic etchings of the nineteenth-century travellers who marvelled at it, and it is still the best place from which to survey Nîmes and its surroundings. As you return to the foot of the hill, to the right of the Jardin sit the shambolic ruins of the "**Temple of Diana**" (daily: mid-March to mid-Oct 7.30am–10pm; mid-Oct to mid-March 7.30am–6.30pm; free). Originating

Nîmes' avant-garde architecture

Through the mid-Eighties and Nineties Nîmes embarked on an audacious project of **urban renewal**, contracting high-flying architects from around the world to construct public housing developments, sport centres and civic spaces. These new buildings – Nîmes' modern pride – vary in originality and effect; you may judge them to be either wonders or monstrosities. Some of them you'll pass as you make the rounds in the centre, while the rest (which will really only be of interest to hard-core modern architecture fans) are scattered around the southern edge of the city and are best visited either by bike or taxi.

The best work by far is Norman Foster's great **Carré d'Art** (1993; see p.224). Also in the old town are two remodelled urban *places*: Martiel Raysse's **la place d'Assas** (1989) and Philippe Starck's **Arbibus** (1987), both offering simple landscape architecture and decidedly underwhelming modern sculpture. The peripheral sites include the whale-like and rapidly ageing social housing development **Nemausus 1** (Jean Nouvel, 1987), its monstrous rejoinder, **Nemausus 2** (Alain Amedeo and Jacek Padlewski, 1989), and three sports complexes – **Stade des Costières** (Vittorio Gregotti and Marc Chausse, 1989), **Salle Omnisports** (Gregotti, 1993) and already-dated **Le Colisée** (Kisho Kurokawa, 1991) – which, with their lunging surfaces of concrete and glass, complete the discordant collection.

as a *nymphaeum*, a sacred fountain dedicated to Nemausus (the god of the spring), the structure was taken over by Benedictine monks in the Middle Ages, in whose care it remained until destroyed by Huguenot mobs. Today the hulking half arches and ruined walls are the only remnants of the temple, but are enough to give you an impression of the scale of the building in Roman times.

Eating, drinking and entertainment

On the culinary front, Nîmes is a city of plenty, where three culinary traditions – Spanish, *gastronomique* and, of course, Gardois *terroir* dominate the local **restaurant** *cartes*, with Indian and North African establishments adding a cosmopolitan flavour. The cuisine of Gard has a distinctly Mediterranean taste, with a strong current of olive and garlic, plus rosemary, basil, bay and mint, all of which sprout up in the *garrigues*. Look out for *boeuf à la Gardianne* (slow-cooked marinated beef), *soupe au pistou* (vegetable soup with pesto), and *brandade de morue* (cod and olive-oil purée); wash these down with the wines of the Costières, or with the famous Côtes-du-Rhône vintages.

Bars in Nîmes are smoking – literally. Over the course of an evening many establishments fill with the thick blue haze of Galloises and Gitanes; appropriately enough, given that the person who introduced the evil weed to France in the sixteenth century was the city native Jean Nicot (also the drug's namesake). But despite the newly opened university, Nîmes' bar scene is still quite sedate – nothing to compare with nearby Montpellier, and the **clubs**, as is frequently the case, are located in far-flung suburbs or out of town altogether, making them all but impossible to get to without a car. Nîmes has a **cinema**, Sémaphore, 25 rue Porte de France (☎04.66.67.83.11), showing films in v.o. Generally, the city's high-brow cultural programme is pretty disappointing, possibly because of its proximity to more prestigious centres like Avignon and Montpellier. That said, there's a steady stream of theatre groups and musicians,

The ferias

The most important dates on the Nîmes calendar are those of the **ferias**, lively street festivals featuring parties, music and *tauromachie*. The city is the French capital of the *corrida*, the Spanish tradition of bullfighting which the Occitans have striven to make their own, and during the three great annual *ferias* – **Primavera** (February), **Pentecôte** (seven weeks after Easter) and **des Vendanges** (mid-September), the best local and Spanish *toreros* come to Les Arènes to practise the brutal pageantry of their art. During the *ferias*, particularly Pentecost, the centre of Nîmes becomes a massive round-the-clock party; the bars fill with boisterous revellers and the best hotels have already been booked a year in advance. If you plan to visit the city during one of the festivals, it is essential to make reservations for accommodation; for tickets to **bullfights** throughout the year, contact the Bureau de location des Arènes, at 1 rue Alexandre-Ducros (☎04.66.67.28.02).

ranging from symphonies to rock and blues acts, coming to town – drawn primarily by the presence of an excellent venue in the Roman amphitheatre; groups who can't fill Les Arènes play on various smaller stages scattered about the town. For information and reservations for concerts and plays, contact the main tourist office and also check the annual *Guide Culturel* booklet for major shows. Of course, if Nîmes' nightlife is somewhat lacking in vibrancy, its famous **festivals**, the *ferias* (see box above), more than make up for it.

Restaurants

Many of the cheapest **restaurants**, including self-service cafés and cheap sandwich stands, can be found along the boulevard Amiral-Courbet, and the whole of the old town is thick with small restaurants and brasseries. As an alternative to the establishments listed below you can find a veritable colony of street-side bistros in the narrow alleys around place du Marché (many in the €12–18 range). When weather permits, you'll be threading through the tables which spread into the streets and squares.

L'Ancien Théâtre 4 rue Racine ☎04.66.21.30.75. Just a 5min stroll west from the Maison Carrée, with zippy Mediterranean cuisine. *Menus* from €13. Closed Sat noon, Sun, Mon & early July.

La Bodeguita Pl d'Assas ☎04.66.58.28.27. A solid choice for Spanish food and tapas, with a good view of the Maison Carrée. A meal costs about €25.

Le Bouchon et l'Assiette 5bis rue de Sauve ☎04.66.62.02.93. Worth the walk out past the Temple of Diana – come here for elaborate *gastronomique* variations on traditional *tarnaise* themes. Very reasonably priced, with *menus* from €15 to €39. Closed Tues & Wed, part Jan & most of Aug.

El Rinconcito 7 rue des Marchands ☎04.66.76.17.30. Nîmes' Chilean restaurant offers a range of South American favourites, including *ceviche*, *empanadas* and fish pie. Wash it down with Chilean vintages or *pisco*, inside or on the indoor patio. But get there early, the last dinner

order is taken at 9.30pm. From €17 to €88. Closed Sun & Mon.

Le Jardin d'Hadrien 111 rue Enclos-Rey ☎04.66.21.86.65. Inventive cuisine based on local southeastern Gard tradition. Reasonable prices, too, with *menus* €17–26. Closed Mon & Wed lunch & Sun (July & Aug), Wed, Tues & Sun dinner (Sept–June) & late Aug to early Sept.

Le Magister 5 rue Nationale ☎04.66.76.11.00. Daring experimentation is the order of the day at this good *gastronomique* restaurant. Cod and salmon act as a springboard for the most adventurous combinations, which blend tangy herbs with the sweetness of fruit, while the lamb cutlets are also of exceptional tenderness. The €30 *menu* is a solid option, and includes wine; otherwise *à la carte* is pricey. Closed Sat lunch & Sun, part of Feb, July & Aug.

Ophélie 35 rue Fresque ☎04.61.21.00.19. An excellent choice, with good-value, quality food served in a seventeenth-century setting with roman-

tic atmosphere. Open later than most. *Menu* €22.
Dinner only, closed Sun & Mon, part Feb & Aug.

Le Paradis du Couvent 21 rue du Grand Couvent
℡04.66.76.26.30. Housed in a former convent, a
large restaurant dishing out typical Provençal and
Nîmoise cuisine. Open till midnight and you can
eat from €14.30, so good value. Closed Mon out
of season.

Le P'tit Bec 87bis rue de la République
℡04.66.38.05.83. The best mid-range place for
typical Gardoise cuisine, including the ever-present
bouef à la gardienne and *brandade de morue*.
Good *menu* options from €16, plus children's
menus. Closed Sun eve & Mon.

Aux Plaisirs des Halles 4 rue Littré
℡04.66.36.01.02. Located between the tourist
office and the new *halles*, serving up market-fresh
food combining a traditional olive oil base with the
enticing flavours of the herbs of the *garrigues*.

Menus €16–22. Closed Sun & Mon.

Simple Simon 11 rue Xavier Sigalon
℡04.66.76.01.21. Any restaurant in France daring
to advertise English cuisine deserves credit. If
you're tired of duck and "under-cooked" meat with
too much sauce, you can savour the culinary glory
of Britain, including fish'n'chips and pasties, for
€8–15. Closed Sun & Mon.

Le Tango 6 rue Thoumayne ℡04.66.67.40.77.
Street-side bistro specializing in the cuisine of
Collioure. Franco-Catalan dishes, strong on
seafood, are prepared *à la plancha*, with *menus*
costing €14–25. Closed Sun & Mon.

La Truye qui Filhe 9 rue Fresque. Basic self-
service place, incongruously tucked away in a
fourteenth-century building. Fill up with *croque-
monsieurs*, salads and the like from €8.40. Lunch
only, closed Sun & Aug.

Bars and cafés

Nîmes' two dominant types of drinking establishments are sedate neighbourhood **café–bars**, and louder and larger **music–bars**, which usually feature a DJ
(or more rarely, unexceptional live music) on weekend nights. Smaller bars can
be found scattered among the narrow streets of the town core, while the large,
traditional–style café–bars are found on the wider streets such as boulevards
Amiral–Courbet or Victor–Hugo, on either side of the old town.

Café des Beaux-Arts Pl aux Herbes. A cheerful
and airy place with a good patio that's well located
for people-watching, or simply for soaking up the
ambience of the old medieval heart of Nîmes.
Closed Sun.

Café Carré d'Art Bd Daudet. Great views of the
city from inside the glassed-in interior or outside
on the patio atop the museum of the same name.
Open the same hours as the museum.

Café Napoléon Top end of bd Victor Hugo.
Famous old neighbourhood café – complete with
faded wood decor, cigar-chomping old men in
cardigans and unbeatable Gallic ambience. Great
place for a refreshing mid-afternoon *pastis* break
and right on the edge of the old town. Closed Sun.

Le Diagonal 41bis rue Émile-Jamais. Lively tapas
bar which keeps hopping until 2am during
Tues–Thurs & Sun, 3am Fri & Sat. Closed part Aug.

Le Grand Bourse 2 bd des Arènes. Solid, late-
night bar and eatery. *Menus* from €15. Open daily
till midnight.

La Casa Don Miguel 18 rue de l'Horloge. This popular and late-opening Spanish-style *bodega* is known
for its cocktails and large variety of tapas. Occasional

flamenco, salsa and jazz shows. Closed Sun.

La Movida 2 la Placette. A Spanish bar with decent
tapas and a Romany/flamenco atmosphere that
explodes during the *ferias*. Closed Sun & most of Aug.

O'Flaherty's 26 bd Amiral-Courbet. British beer –
seven kinds on tap – plus food and regular
Thursday concerts of Irish, country and bluegrass
(except July & Aug). Open till 2–3am daily.

Pub "Au Bureau" 24 bd Amiral Courbet. Massive
bar and pool hall which also features live music on
most weekends from Oct to May. Open late.

Le Shaker 1 square de la Bouquerie. Traditional
piano bar, featuring live *chanson française* and
good cocktails. Mon–Sat evenings.

Les Trois Maures 10 bd des Arènes. Fantastic old
high-ceilinged bar beside the Arènes, festooned
with bullfighting and rugby memorabilia and
exceptionally busy during *ferias*. Open late. Closed
Sun in July & Aug.

Wine Bar Chez Michel 11 square de la Couronne.
This is *the* place to begin your acquaintance with
the wines of Languedoc (at €17–185 per bottle).
All served up with traditional Gard cuisine. Closed
Sun & Mon lunch.

Listings

Airlines Air France ☎08.02.80.28.02 ⓦwww.air-france.com; Air Littoral ☎08.25.83.48.34, ⓦwww.airlittoral.fr; Ryan Air ☎08.92.55.56.66, ⓦwww.ryanair.com.

Airport The Aéroport International Garons ☎04.66.70.49.49.

Banks and exchange A number of banks have branches in the old town which offer currency exchange and ATMs.

Books Secondhand English books can be bought and sold at Bouqinerie, 21 av Amiral-Courbet (beside *O'Flaherty's* pub).

Bus departures Intercity service leaves from the *gare routière* on bd Natoire (☎04.66.29.52.00; ⓦwww.stdgard.com), connected by a footbridge to the gare SNCF. The main carriers are the SNCF and Cévennes Cars (☎04.66.29.27.29), although Sommières is served by Cariane Cars (☎04.66.38.13.98).

Car rental ADA, 2614 rte de Montpellier ☎04.66.04.79.99; Apex 2, 72 rue de la République ☎04.66.38.09.66; Avis, 1800 av du Maréchal Juin ☎04.66.29.05.33; Budget, 1800 av du Maréchal Juin ☎04.66.38.01.69; Europcar, 1bis rue de la République ☎04.66.21.31.35; National, 14 av Carnot ☎04.66.21.03.62; Hertz, 5 bd de Prague ☎04.66.76.25.91. All except Apex have airport offices as well and Avis has an office at the *gare*.

Children's activities A good place to take the kids is Parc Aquatropic (☎04.66.38.31.00), a waterslide theme park near the Nîmes-Ouest *autoroute* exit, accessible by bus #D from outside the Halles shopping centre on bd Gambetta. Adults pay €4.27, kids €0.91. Open summer only 9am–10pm.

Hospital Hôpital Gaston Doumerge, rue de la Biche (☎04.66.68.68.68) is slated to close in 2004, to be replaced by Carremeau Hospital at Nîmes University (☎04.66.68.68.68). Emergency (☎15).

Internet access Cyber Café Vauban, 34 rue Clérisseau (daily 10am–11pm).

Laundry There's a launderette on rue de Grand Couvent, at the corner of rue de Agau (daily 7am–9pm).

Market Farmers' market (Fri) and flea market (Mon morn) on bld Jean-Jaurès; also general open-air crafts market throughout the old town in July & Aug (Thurs 6–10pm).

Police *Mairie*, rue Hôtel de Ville (☎04.66.76.70.54); emergency (☎17).

Taxi TRAN ☎04.66.29.40.11. Their excursion to the Pont du Gard with a thirty-minute wait costs €39.

Train information ☎08.92.35.35.35, ⓦwww.sncf.fr.

Around Nîmes

For such a small area, the southern portion of Gard contains a surprising number of draws for visitors. Just across the river Gardon to the north of Nîmes lies **Uzés**, the "First Duchy" of France, its castle still in the hands of a family which traces its roots back to Charlemagne. A few kilometres east of the city lies the **Pont du Gard**, perhaps the most famous of all Roman aqueducts, now developed into a major attraction, while along the Rhône, medieval **Beaucaire**'s castle and the uniquely sculpted facade of the church of **St-Gilles** deserve a visit. The southern edge of the *département*, sweeping west of here, is dominated by the westernmost branch of the swampy Rhône delta, the **Petite Camargue** – an important way-station for migratory birds. On the west, the medieval walls of **Aigues-Mortes** are now besieged only by invading sun-seekers who crowd the beaches south of the town, around **Le Grau-du-Roi** and **Port-Camargue**. Upstream from Le Grau, on the River Vidourle, **Sommières** and **Sauve** lie quietly languishing in forgotten obscurity, far from the bustle of the coast. Roman ruins pepper the entire area, including aqueducts, arches and stretches of road still marked by milestones, and towns throughout the region share Nîmes' enthusiasm for the *corrida*; if possible trips should be planned to coincide with village *ferias*. The best time to visit the southern Gard is during the summer, when pleasure ports and beaches are busy, although inland towns follow a rhythm not so dependent on the sun.

Public transport in the region is fairly good and, with the unfortunate exception of Uzès, the main towns are served by frequent bus and train routes. Distances, however, are not great, and the generally even landscape makes **hiking** a good option. Unfortunately, south of the *garrigues*, **cycling** is made hazardous by the intense and rapid traffic on the area's narrow highways.

Uzès

Long disdained by the French literati as the proverbial "middle of nowhere", **UZÈS**, nestled among the rocky *garrigues* twenty kilometres north of Nîmes, has now been discovered. Like so many towns of the Gard, Uzès traces its history back to the time of the toga, when it served as an agricultural and local market centre, and it became the seat of a bishop as early as the fifth century. Changing hands many times over the following centuries, it eventually came under the control of the counts of Toulouse. When they lost the town to the French Crown in 1229, their former underlings, lords of Uzès, battled it out with the bishops for local control. These barons served the French kings well and were rewarded when the town was given the rank of the "First Duchy of France" in 1632. The title had belonged to the dukes of Montmorency until then, but they lost it as a consequence of Henri de Montmorency's failed revolt (see p.398). Like Nîmes, Uzès violently embraced Calvinism – becoming the fifth most important Huguenot centre in France – but once the movement was suppressed and the majority of Protestants fled, those "Catholics" that remained turned it into a wealthy silk town, which it remained for the next three hundred years. The early twentieth century brought depression, and when the railway bypassed the town, the writing of Uzès' decline was on the wall. The history of the town's celebrities is also one of near misses: Guillaume de Grimoard, later to become Pope Urban V, was not from Uzès, but did live here for a while; the great seventeenth-century poet Jean Racine had an uncle from the town, and spent a year and a half here; and Charles Gide, father of Nobel-laureate author André, was a native – the junior Gide passed his childhood summers here.

But Uzès, historical marginalization belies its beauty. As André Gide remarked, "O little town of Uzès! Were you in Umbria, the tourists of Paris would rush to see you!" In fact, today the town fairly packs out with tourists in summer months; each medieval stone arcade now conceals a bistro, and when the weather is good the restaurant patios which dominate the squares are frequented by buskers of surprising quality. Saturday's traditional **market** is particularly lively, while gourmands will want to sample the **truffles** for which the town is renowned. If you're reliant on public transport and short on time the town is best visited on a day-trip that also takes in the **Pont du Gard**, 20km southwest; with only one bus daily to and from Uzès to Nîmes, and services to Remoulins (see p.237) far more frequent, heading for the aqueduct first gives you the most time in each spot.

Arrival, information and accommodation

Uzès' **gare routière** (℡04.66.22.00.58) is located just west of the old town on Esplanade Maréchal de Lattre de Tassigny; from here it's a five-minute walk north along boulevard Gambetta to the **tourist office** (July & Aug Mon–Fri 9am–6pm, Sat 10am–noon & 2–5pm, Sun 10am–5pm; Sept–June Mon–Fri 9am–noon & 1.30–6pm, Sat 10am–1pm; ℡04.66.22.68.88, ⓦwww .ville-uzes.fr) in place Albert 1er, just north of the Duché. To check your email, head for the *Cyberland* **Internet** café on place Austerlitz (daily noon–2am); **bikes** can be rented at Et Paysan on avenue General Vincent, one block west of the tourist office, which has a free brochure of bike routes, including one to the Pont du Gard.

Most of the town's **hotels** reflect its noble past – which is to say, luxurious but pricey. The cheapest beds are found at the friendly *Hostellerie Provençal* (℡04.66.22.11.06; closed Sun & Mon eve Sept–June & Feb; ❷) at 1 rue Grand Bourgade, near the church of St-Etienne. Next up is the attractively renovated *La Taverne* (℡04.66.22.13.10, ⓔlataverne.uzes@wanadoo.fr; ❹), behind the tourist office at 4 rue Xavier Sigalon. The only other option in town is the deluxe *General d'Entraigues*, 8 rue de la Calade (℡04.66.22.32.68, ⓦwww.lcm.fr/savry; ❹–❾), in a converted fifteenth-century mansion opposite the cathedral. And if you really want to treat yourself, the same owners also have rooms at the *Château d'Arpaillargues* (March–Oct; ℡04.66.22.14.48, Ⓕ04.66.22.56.10; ❼), a rural mansion converted into a hotel, located 4km northwest of town. Two **campsites** accommodate tenters in the warmer months: the municipal site (mid-June to mid-Sept; ℡04.66.22.11.79), set on the riverside 500m northeast of town on avenue Pascal, and *La Paillote* (mid-

March to mid-Oct; ☎04.66.22.38.55), 500m along rue Xavier Sigalon. The local **gîte d'étape**, *L'Oregon* (☎04.66.22.16.25; April–Oct), is 1.5km north of Uzès, following avenue Pascal. It has one private room (❷), in addition to its dorm (❶) and guests have use of a kitchen.

The Town

Uzès, the core of which can be walked in about an hour, is extremely easy to find your way around; the compact **old town** – shaped roughly like a kidney bean – is ringed by a broad one-way system. Within this perimeter the town is still dominated by the twelfth-century castle, **the Duché**, just south of the tourist office, while its other focal point, the place aux Herbes, lies a bit further southwest of the fortress. The **cathedral** sits overlooking the Alzon river on the eastern edge of the old town, as if pushed aside by the power of the town's dukes.

The Duché

The old ducal castle of the de Cressol family, the **Duché** (daily: mid-June to mid-Sept 10am–6.30pm; mid-Sept to mid-June 10am–noon & 2–6pm; ☎04.66.22.18.96), is the centrepiece of Uzès, and the sight of its towering *donjon* topped by the family's red and yellow-banded pennant makes a Hollywoodesque but authentic medieval tableau. The compact walled *enceinte* rises dramatically from amidst the old town's buildings, concealing a courtyard presided over by a majestically columned Renaissance facade, and a small garden, as well as the bulky and crude keep. Claiming roots which go back to Charlemagne and St Louis, the de Cressols are proud of their long lineage, and their motto *ferro non auro* – "by iron [i.e. the sword], not gold" – sets them apart from the later families who bought rather than fought their way into the aristocracy. Their stay in Uzès has not been continuous, however, as the Revolution precipitated a hiatus which lasted until 1954. Among the most colourful of its members was the Duchess Anne, grandmother of the present Duke; monarchist, suffragette and enthusiastic hunter (she killed over 2000 animals), this energetic woman rode until the age of 87, and was France's first female driver –and the first to receive a speeding ticket. Despite the fact that it is still a part-time residence for the dukes, the castle can be visited on a lively hour-long **guided tour** (€11; an English-language handout is provided), although given its price the budget-conscious may opt only to climb the tenth-century **Tour Bermonde** (€6), from the top of which you can peek out between the battlements and admire fine views. The main tour through the family's apartments is entertaining and offers an intimate look at a disappearing aristocratic world, with personal effects set amongst the rare furnishings and ancient books. The visit wraps up in the castle's ancient cellars, where guests are invited to taste the Duke's own vintage (also on sale, of course) and buy grossly over-priced Provençal statuettes.

The rest of the old town

The castle is far from Uzès' only attraction, and a wander through the dense and evocative alleys of the old town is a true pleasure. Leaving the Duché and following it around to the left, rue Dampmartin leads towards the arcaded **place aux Herbes**, the route punctuated by the carved stone doorframes and casement windows of several elegant sixteenth- to eighteenth-century mansions. Crossing the *place* towards the eighteenth-century St-Étienne **church**, with its thirteenth-century belfry, brings you past the old Gide house, and the streets behind the church are pleasantly quiet, unlike the café- and boutique-

André Gide

André Gide was born in Paris in 1869, the son of a wealthy Huguenot family from Uzès. A sensitive, nervous soul, the young Gide's introspection and uncertainty was no doubt nourished by the tensions he felt regarding his sexual identity. His disquietudes came to be expressed through literature, and his exceptional promise was reflected in the fact that he published his first work at the age of 20. Five years later he married his cousin and childhood sweetheart, Madelaine. Their marriage was never consummated, although in 1923, he had a daughter by another woman. His *Si le grain ne meurt* ("If It Die"; 1924–26), recalls in part the summers of his youth, spent in Uzès. Like so many nonconformist contemporaries he was drawn to exotic and liberating French North Africa, where he confronted and eventually came to celebrate his bisexuality, as in the landmark "The Fruits of All Earth" (1897) – a work which decisively influenced young up-and-comers Albert Camus and Jean-Paul Sartre. He became a close friend of Oscar Wilde, whom he met in Algiers. In the English-speaking world his best-known novels are "The Immoralist" (1902) and "The Counterfeiters" (1926). He died in 1951, recognized as a seminal moral and social iconoclast of the modern age, four years after having received the Nobel Prize for Literature. In 1952 his books were placed on the Catholic Church's Index of forbidden reading.

crammed area around the *place* to the west. Rue Foussat leads back up into the heart of the old town; on rue Port Royal, off to the left, look out for the entrance to the recreated **medieval garden** (daily: April–June & Oct–Nov 2–5pm; June & Sept 2–6pm; July & Aug 3–7pm; €2) – set in the courtyard of the former bishop's palace, it contains the herbs and plants which were collected or cultivated in the area during the Middle Ages and makes a great stop for children. Further up, at the dour entrance to the plain **Hôtel des Monnaies** (the former bishop's mint), you can either loop back to the Duché, or turn right to pass the sumptuous Hôtel du Baron de Castille to arrive at the cathedral.

Following the fate of other churches of the region, the medieval **cathedral** of Uzès fell victim to the violence of the Wars of Religion but, thankfully, the twelfth-century bell tower, the **Tour Fenestrelle** (daily 10am–noon & 2–6pm; €2.50) survived. Rising 42m above the plaza on which it sits, the six levels of arched windows on this round structure – unique in France – recall strongly the Leaning Tower of Pisa. The new cathedral, on the other hand, dates from the seventeenth to nineteenth centuries and is hardly of interest, apart from its flamboyantly styled seventeenth-century organ. The broad verge to the south of the cathedral, the **promenade de Racine**, provides pleasant views of the countryside and river, and sports a curious eighteenth-century **pavilion** resembling a Victorian bandstand, built on one of the town wall's old towers. On the north side of the cathedral the sombre and hulking episcopal palace is now home to the **municipal museum** (Tues–Sun: July & Aug 10am–noon & 3–6pm; March–June, Sept & Oct 3–6pm; Nov, Dec & Feb 2–5pm; free), which holds Polynesian relics carried home by local missionaries, some decent eighteenth-century portraiture and a room dedicated to the Gide family, consisting of manuscripts, photographs, furniture and personal effects.

Eating and drinking

Uzès' recent tourist boom has been good news for diners, as the town has a surplus of **eating** establishments – stiff competition meaning good prices.

Among the terraces which clutter the old town and line the ring road, a number of establishments stand out. The finest (and most expensive) dining is found at the restaurant of the *General d'Entraigues*, where *menus* are €22–49, and can be enjoyed on the panoramic terrace. For cheaper *terroir* cuisine, try *L'Abbaye*, 24 boulevard Charles-Gide (closed winter; ☏04.66.22.91.21) – a traditional family-run bistro with *menus* from €12. *San Diego* (closed Mon & Feb; ☏04.66.22.20.78) a few doors away at no. 16 is a better option both for its refreshing decor and generous servings; the plentiful *menus* here can be enjoyed from €12. The *Provençale*, on rue Grande Bourgade (☏04.66.22.11.06) has lunch *menus* featuring savoury dishes from neighbouring Provence from as low as €7.95, while vegetarians should head for *Zaïka* (☏04.66.03.27.37), an Indian restaurant on passage du Marchands. Couscous is the speciality at *Le Passage*, 37 boulevard Gambetta (from €10.95), but also check out the four-course French *menus* from €14.95.

For a **drink**, try *Au Suisse d'Alger* on rue République, near place aux Herbes; it has a lively terrace and wine by the glass is very reasonably priced. Later in the evening *Bar l'Encas*, at the corner of Gambetta and République, is the place to head for – in addition to its pool table and good selection of beers, it has a terrace where off-duty buskers often sit down for an impromptu jam.

The Pont du Gard and around

No one with even a passing interest in history or architecture should go through the Gard without seeing what is arguably the world's most famous Roman aqueduct, the **PONT DU GARD**, 20km to the northeast of Nîmes. The area around the Pont was devastated by serious flooding in 2000, but since then the site has been developed as a major tourist attraction, with an activities centre which, together with the pleasant but stony river-beach and excellent **picnic** and **hiking** possibilities, makes it easy to spend more than a full day here, particularly if you are travelling with children. The wide range of accommodation and activities makes this a good area for a base. In fact, the new **museum** is one of the most modern and impressive in the South of France. Several of the hamlets nearby are worth checking out too, as is the **medieval bridge** of St-Nicholas, further up the Gardon river. The aqueduct can be visited as a day-trip from Nîmes and combined with a visit to Uzès but if you're planning an overnight sojourn, you can stay by the Pont itself, in the service town of **Remoulins**, 2km away or, particularly if you have some transport, in one of the hamlets which cluster between Uzès and Remoulins.

The Pont du Gard

When the Romans needed to supply growing Nîmes with water, they found that the nearest suitable source was some 50km away on the Eure river, near Uzès. Despite the deep Gardon gorge which cut through the route, with Roman single-mindedness (and slave labour), they set about to construct a waterway. This remains nothing short of a technical marvel, descending only 17m in altitude along its course and bridging the Gardon with a monumental aqueduct, the **Pont du Gard** (free access). Most likely constructed in the mid-first century, the Pont's three tiers of arches span an incredible 275m in length, carrying water 49m above the riverbed below. Pillaged for stone through the ages, and first used as a bridge in 1295, the aqueduct has suffered various misfortunes, including an earthquake of 1448, but there was enough of the structure remaining to begin a comprehensive restoration in the eighteenth century. Such was its impact that when Rousseau passed by shortly after this work had been undertaken, the sight of the monument was enough to make him say he wished he'd been born a Roman. A visit here used to be a must for French journeyman masons on their traditional tour of the country, and many of them have left their names and home towns carved on the stonework. Among these, the markings made by the original builders to facilitate construction can also still be found. For the moment, the top tier is under renovation (reopening has been continually postponed), and you can only cross the broad lower level. The best way to enjoy this ancient engineering wonder, however, is to take it in from different perspectives, climbing up to the lookout areas at the top of either end, or viewing it upriver from the bed of the Gardon. Seen from here on a sunny day, the utilitarian but gracefully symmetrical beauty of the aqueduct's yellow-stone structure presents a striking contrast to the blue sky.

The new **Site de Pont du Gard** visitors' complex offers a whole range of activities and attractions. The **museum** (daily May–Sept 9.30am–7pm, Oct–April 9.30am–5pm; €6) is an incredible multimedia installation, fully multilingual and incorporating archeological finds, working models, film, sound effects and interactive terminals. Themes include the role of water in Roman society and culture, the building of the aqueduct and its later decay and rediscovery. This is a must-see, not only for technology and engineering buffs and children, but for anyone remotely interested in the past. In the same building you'll find the **Ludo**, an interactive activity centre for **children** (closed Mon morn; €4.50), a resource centre and a cinema. Out back, the **Mémoires de Garrigue** is a 37-acre garden with **nature trails** highlighting the local fauna (April to mid-Oct daily 9.30am–6pm; €4). A **combined ticket** for all of these attractions costs €10 (or €20 per family). Finally there are a number of activities and displays particularly suited to children, including **workshops** for making Roman-style crafts and weapons (daily 10am–6pm), and **gladiator** demonstrations (daily noon & 5.30pm). The whole site is designed to accommodate with visitors with disabilities.

Around the Pont du Gard

The Pont du Gard is a great place to cool down on a hot day (although the river slows to a trickle in August), and this part of the Eure is an easy stretch for **canoeing** and **kayaking** (see opposite). Two kilometres south of the aqueduct lies the **château de St-Privat**, the site where Richelieu signed the Peace of Alés with the Huguenots in 1629 (the lords of the castle, the Faret family, were Protestants) and famous for its elaborate formal garden, which dates back to 1644. One of the garden's three sections, the "Avant-park", is home to the War Sacrifice Chapel, commissioned after World War I by then-owner Jacques Rouché; its walls are decorated with painted works of metaphysical allegory, mixing biblical figures with depictions of *poilus* (French common soldiers). Unfortunately the property can only be visited on a ninety-minute **guided tour** (May to mid-Nov Sat & Sun 3pm; July & Aug daily 3pm; €5) leaving from the Pont's tourist office (see opposite).

Moving on from the aqueduct, the best way to leave is to hike along the Gardon gorge to the Pont St-Nicholas. The GR6 on the north bank and the AR6 on the south (passing St-Privat) lead to **Collias** 4km away, formerly a hippie Mecca, from where the GR6 can be followed upriver. Aside from the rugged beauty of the riverbed's red cliffs, look out for the **Grotte de la Baume**, on the north bank after Collias, a cave with a medieval chapel set amongst what were once the rocky abodes of hermits. Finally, some 10km after Collias, you reach the ponderous and chunky thirteenth-century **Pont St-Nicholas**, now incorporated into the main Uzès–Nîmes highway. There are also some interesting hamlets along the Uzès–Remoulins road, the most intriguing of which (and also the one where the most buses stop) is **Vers**, 4km north of the Pont, where you'll find bits of ruined arches and chunks of Roman road lying around town, and an eleventh-century church. Other nearby villages include **St-Hilaire** and **Castillon-du-Gard**, ancient and picturesque farming settlements which don't have any particular sights, but are worth wandering around.

Practicalities

The Pont itself can be reached by **bus** direct from Nîmes (there is a stop on the south riverbank), or via **Remoulins** (a thirty-minute walk away), which is served by buses from Uzès and Nîmes. Those arriving by **car** can park in official spaces (€5 per day, or €8 for an annual pass) on either bank of the river, or for free in Remoulins, 3km from the site. **Tourist information** is provided at the ticket counter of the activity centre on the north bank (la rive gauche), where you'll find the closest parking. This centre also has a couple of fast-food outlets, while on the far bank, the pleasant **restaurant** *Les Terraces* makes for better dining (*menu* from €14). For **canoe rental**, head to Kayak Vert (☎04.66.22.80.76, ⓦwww.canoe-france.com) on the south shore. They arrange for trips (including pick-up or drop-off) in either direction, the best being the downstream paddle from the Pont St-Nicholas. They also rent mountain **bikes**. If you're just going to splash around, keep your sandals on or buy some cheap plastic shoes to survive the pebbly bed of the Gardon; on the upriver side of the aqueduct there are places deep enough to dive in, but the river level varies considerably, so check carefully before taking the plunge. Conveniences such as **banks** and **supermarkets** can be found at Remoulins.

Accommodation

In addition to the hotels listed below, the Turions also have several well-appointed rooms at their farm in Vers (Easter–Oct; ☎04.66.37.16.25; ❷), as well as providing the cheapest option in the region around the Pont with their three-room **gîte d'étape** located near the farm (open May–Sept; ☎06.86.90.44.84; ❶).

There are four **campsites** in the area, all with cabins or trailers for rent. *La Sousta* (March–Nov; ☎04.66.37.12.80, ⓔlasousta@aol.com) has the widest range of facilities and lies on the south bank of the Gardon, right by the Pont. *La Soubeyranne* (April to mid-Sept; ☎04.66.37.03.21, ⓔsoubeyranne @wanadoo.fr), on the other side of Remoulins, is more expensive but you may have little choice as campsites here often book up in high season. The *Gorges du Gardon* (mid-March to Sept; ☎04.66.22.81.81, ⓕ04.66.22.90.12) in Vers is the cheapest around, while *Le Barralet* (open April–Sept; ☎04.66.22.84.52, ⓕ04.66.22.89.17) in Collias wins out on both location and value – located on the riverside, it is cheap and far from the maddening crowds.

L'Arceau 1, rue de l'Arceau, St-Hilaire ☎04.66.37.34.45, ⓔarceau@avignon-et-provence.com. One of the best value-for-money options, an eighteenth-century home set in a picturesque hamlet 3km from the aqueduct. Closed late Nov to mid-Feb. ❸
Auberge le Gardon Collias ☎04.66.22.80.54,

ⓦwww.logis-de-france.com. Another excellent mid-range choice. An old farmhouse in a village just up-river from Remoulins. Closed mid-Oct to mid-March. ❸
Bégude St-Pierre CD 981, Vers ☎04.66.63.63.63, ⓕ04.66.22.73.73. Excellent value, good location and a swimming pool make

this seventeenth-century former post-house on the edge of Vers village a first-rate option. ❹

Le Colombier Rive Droite, Pont du Gard ☎04.66.37.05.28, ⓦwww.logis-de-france.fr. This cosy hotel on the right bank close by the aqueduct offers facilities including parking, TV and a restaurant. ❸

Hostellerie Le Castillas Grand' Rue, Collias ☎04.66.22.88.88, ⓦwww.lecastellas.com. Three luxuriously if idiosyncratically restored seventeenth-century houses are home to this small and welcoming hotel. Closed Jan & Feb. ❻

Mas de Raffin, Chemin Mas de Raffin, Castillon ☎04.66.37.45.79, ⓕ04.66.27.14.78. A good mid-range option, this small but stately restored five-room mansion sits on the outskirts of the village and also boasts a swimming pool and has English-speaking staff. ❹

Le Moderne 8 av Perret-Geoffroy, Remoulins ☎04.66.37.20.13, ⓔhotelmoderne@wanadoo.fr. The best of Remoulins' hotels: a mid-sized establishment with good amenities and helpful staff. Closed during early Nov. ❸

Tuilleries RN 86 Castillon ☎04.66.37.08.47, ⓕ04.66.37.02.43. One of the cheaper options in this neck of the woods, with basic amenities. ❷

Vieux Castillon Rue Turion Sabatier, Castillon ☎04.66.37.61.61, ⓦwww.relaischateux.com. This gloriously restored rambling country estate provides top-end accommodation. Amenities include a swimming pool. Closed Jan & Feb. ❾

Le Vieux Moulin Rive Gauche, Vers ☎04.66.37.14.35, ⓕ04.66.37.26.48. Just 200m from the aqueduct on the left bank, this three-star hotel has excellent views and good amenities. Closed mid-Nov to mid-March. ❺

Eating

The most pleasant option for **eating** is to have a **picnic** on the banks of the river. Each of the hotels listed above has a restaurant, most with *terroir menus* in the €15–26 price range: the most sophisticated are those of *Le Vieux Castillon*, which features an eclectic *carte* (and *menus* from €45), and *La Bégude St-Pierre* in Vers (*menus* from €28), which features variations on local *terroir* themes (notable in the predominance of beef) as well as the surrounding country's best selection of wines. There's also *Le Clos de Vignes* (closed Mon & Tues lunch & mid-Jan to mid-Feb; ☎04.66.37.02.26) in Castillon, which serves up good, inexpensive local food on two pleasantly situated terraces (€16–25).

Beaucaire and around

BEAUCAIRE doesn't necessarily merit making a special effort to visit, but can be a rewarding stop for those passing through. This is particularly worth considering if you have your own transport, as the interesting **Roman** and **medieval** vestiges around the town are better reached by car, although **hiking** and **biking** are possible as well. The best time to visit Beaucaire is during June's Fête du Drac, a traditional festival in honour of the town's dragon mascot, marking the arrival of summer and featuring parades and *tauromachie*, or July's Estivales, a medieval pageant celebrating the town's once-famous fair. Located on the banks of the Rhône and crossed by the Roman Via Domitia, Beaucaire is a town whose success was grounded in its position as a crossroads, and as one of the region's main gateways – Provençal Tarascon lies just across the river.

From the second century BC Beaucaire was a Roman wine entrepôt known as Ugernum, but this disappeared along with the empire. Centuries later, the town was throve under the patronage of the counts of Toulouse. During the Albigensian Crusade, de Montfort's forces seized the castle, and when Raymond VII of Toulouse re-took the walled town in 1216, Simon's men would not let him into the castle. So, aided by the townsfolk, Raymond laid siege to the castle from within the town, while Simon, who had arrived in the meantime, encircled the town from without. Raymond prevailed in this strange double siege – a rare defeat for the fierce de Montfort – and the jubilant count granted the town the right to hold a yearly **trade fair** as a reward. Bringing merchants from all over Europe, the Middle East and North Africa, the market survived the town's transition to the French Crown in 1229 and continued to be held through the nineteenth century. Trade routes shifted, however, and by the time Richelieu ordered the castle torn down in 1632, Beaucaire was already a backwater.

Nowadays, the town presents a strange dichotomy. Although in summer, the tree-lined canal is alive with waterfront restaurants and the busy leisure of the boaters who ply the canals to Sète and Montpellier, the old town is a singularly decrepit area – a marginalized industrial neighbourhood which shows the stresses of high unemployment and unintegrated immigration. At night it takes on a fairly unpleasant aspect: dark and narrow streets and small deserted squares where care should be taken when walking; you should also avoid parking here.

The Town

The limits of Beaucaire are roughly defined by the Sète canal on the south, the Rhône river on the east, and the castle-topped hill which rises sharply on the north side. Walking from the canal, there are only one or two sights as you make your way across the old town towards the castle. Just north of the tourist office sits the town's most noteworthy building, the Neoclassical **Hôtel de Ville**. This fine seventeenth-century edifice has a colonnaded facade and window casements lavishly carved in floral motifs; inside, the courtyard (Mon–Fri 10am–noon & 2–5pm) is girded by slender columns and dominated by a monumental staircase. Unfortunately the *hôtel*'s beauty is diminished by its surroundings; the scruffy and inhospitable place Georges-Clémenceau. On the south side squats the small nineteenth-century metal-and-glass **market**, whose picturesque quality is offset by the decaying shop fronts and miserable-looking bars neighbouring it. Beaucaire's main **church**, Notre-Dame de Pommiers, lying two streets beyond, has a plain facade which hides a gaudy and unexceptional late Baroque marble interior. The church's real treasure is found on the building's exterior, which you will pass if you follow rue Charlier towards the castle – here, high up on the east wall, is the only remaining part of the original Romanesque structure: a remarkable low-relief frieze recounting scenes from the eve of the Crucifixion. Aside from these specific sights, you should also keep an eye out in Beaucaire for the seventeenth-century merchant's **mansions** which pop up en route to the castle, notably along rue de la République at the foot of the hill. The palace at no. 23, for example, has a strikingly elaborate facade, including caryatid columns on either side of the entrance. From the west end of rue de la République a stiff climb leads up the rise, dramatically crowned by the remains of the former keep.

Poised on a rocky promontory rising 35m above the Rhône, Beaucaire's **castle** provides dramatic views of the surrounding countryside, including one down over Tarascon's own castle. Fortunately, Richelieu did not manage to destroy the fortress completely. The fourteenth-century **curtain wall** survives, as do several towers, including the striking **Tour Polygonale**, shooting dramatically skyward out of the living rock of the hill. The castle now hosts an entertaining medieval **falconry** display, "Les Aigles", with hourly live demonstrations (daily except Wed off-season: March & Sept–Nov 2.30–4.30pm, April–June 2 pm, 3 pm, & 4.30pm, July & Aug 10am–noon & 2–7pm; €7.50) – the only way of visiting the castle ruins. On the other hand, the eighteenth-century listed **gardens** which fill the outer courtyard can be visited free of charge (daily except Wed off-season: April–Oct 10am–noon & 2.15–6.45pm;

The Rhône–Sète canal

Although not as famous as its sister to the west, the **Rhône–Sète canal** is an inland waterway which also offers great sightseeing and leisure possibilities, either on its own or combined with a trip along the Canal du Midi. Not only is the Rhône–Sète waterway less crowded than its more popular counterpart, the general evenness of the landscape means that there are no locks (on the main line) and fewer queues to contend with, even in high season. The various **subsidiary canals** also offer the opportunity to explore the backwaters of the Camargue in relative isolation.

The canal begins from the River Rhône at **Beaucaire**, heading southwest 11km through the flat Camarguaise wine-country past Bellegard. From here, a further 11km brings it to **St-Gilles**. Here you can turn off on a secondary canal to **Vauvert**. This town has no boat rental and no sights to speak of, but makes a handy stop for supplies, particularly when its market is in swing, on Wednesday and Friday mornings. Otherwise, if you keep on the main canal, after 30km of salty marshland, rich in birdlife, this will lead you past the medieval **Tour Carbonnière**, which marks your arrival at **Aigues-Mortes**. From that town, St Louis' thirteenth-century canal can be followed to **Le-Grau-du-Roi** and **Port-Camargue**.

Alternatively, from Aigues-Mortes follow the main canal west as it weaves its way past the Étang de Maugaio, before arriving at Carnon and **Palavas-les-Flots**, the latter of which provides a handy base for exploring **Montpellier**, and whose branch-canals lead inland to **Villeneuve-lès-Maguelone** and Lattes. Heading west, the canal threads a series of *étangs*, gliding past the ancient **cathedral** of Maguelone, before the Montaigne de la Guardiole rises to the north, and **Frontignan**, an ancient *circulade* with a **medieval church**, is reached. Finally the canal arrives at its terminus, Sète; from here you can continue into the broad expanse of the Bassin de Thau, skirting the mussel-beds, to visit its colourful fishing towns: Balaruc, **Mèze** and Marseillan. At the far end of this salt-water lagoon, an access canal leads 5km to **Agde**, from where the **Canal du Midi** can be accessed.

Boats can be rented at most of the ports of call along the canal (see the entry for each town in this guide), which also have sanitary facilities and fresh-water supplies. The local Capitainneries can also direct you to the nearest **bicycle** rental, handy for exploring the canalside towns.

Nov–March 10.15am–noon & 2–5.15pm), and within these sits the municipal **Musée Auguste-Jacquet** (same hours; €2.20) – a conglomeration of small collections of medieval bits and bobs, local rocks and paraphernalia relating to Beaucaire's annual fair. The town's other museum, **Le Monde de Daudet** (daily: July–Aug 10am–7pm; Sept–June 2–6pm; €5.50) uses models to recreate the nineteenth-century world of the local poet and author, but holds little appeal for most non-French visitors. On Friday nights during the summer the castle is the backdrop for the *son et lumière* "Raymond VII and the Siege of Beaucaire" (July & Aug daily 10pm), which floods the castle buildings in garish colour while recounting the town's moment of medieval glory.

Practicalities

To get to Beaucaire by **train** you will arrive at Tarascon's **gare SNCF** (℡08.36.35.35.35) on boulevard Gustave-Desplaces, just across the Rhône. From here, you cross over the bridge, a ten-minute walk which brings you to the Rhône–Sète canal, or take a Nîmes-bound bus from the "Café de Fleurs" stop across from the station. Arriving by **bus** (information on ℡04.66.29.27.29), make sure to get off at "Passarelle" (the footbridge), which is the third stop coming from Nîmes, and the first from Tarascon. Those who come by **car** should be wary of the more isolated public parking spaces; it's safest to park outside the tourist office or on the far side of the canal. Beaucaire's friendly **tourist office**, 24 cours de Gambetta (Jan–June & Sept–Dec Mon–Fri 9am–12.30pm & 2–6.30pm, Sat 9am–12.30pm & 3–6pm; July & Aug Mon–Fri 9am–12.30pm & 2–6.30pm, Sat 9am–12.30pm & 3–6pm, Sun 9am–noon; ☏04.66.59.26.57, ⓦwww.ot-beaucaire.fr) is on the north side of the canal, opposite the footbridge. The staff can give you information on a number of package excursions to the Camargue. Beaucaire's **pleasure port** offers everything from pedal-boats to yachts for rent, as well as cruises and custom trips down the Rhône into the bird-rich delta of the Camargue. One of the best itineraries is to the bird sanctuary at Pont de Gau, off the Petit Rhône. To **rent a boat** in Beaucaire, try Arolles Marine (☏04.66.01.75.15) or Connoisseurs Cruisers (☏04.66.59.46.08). There are two **car rental** outfits: Avis, in the Total petrol station at 6 rue Général-de-Gaulle (☏04.66.59.29.89), and ADA, in the Le Mistral petrol station on route de Nîmes (☏04.66.59.37.77).

Accommodation

Beaucaire does not have the widest selection of **hotels**, but at least there is some range of price. At the lower end of the scale, the tiny and basic *Napoleon* at 4 place Frédéric Mistral (☏04.66.59.05.17; ❷) reposes in the shadow of the *digue*, the massive flood dyke which protects the town from the Rhône. *Le Jardin d'Isis* (☏04.66.59.30.74; ❸), no. 3 on the tree-lined boulevard Maréchal Foch, is more pleasant and only slightly more costly. Finally, for those willing to splash out, the three-star *Doctrinaires* (closed mid-Dec to mid-Jan; ☏04.66.59.23.70, ⓦwww.logis-de-france.fr; ❸–❹) on Quai Général de Gaulle wins for comfort, atmosphere and location, set as it is in a seventeenth-century building overlooking the port. The 65-bed **HI hostel** is over in Tarascon at 39 boulevard Gambetta (closed mid-Nov to Feb; ☏04.90.91.04.08, ⓦwww.fuaj.org/aj/tarascon/; €8.40), a ten-minute walk north of the Tarascon train station; it has dining facilities and a washing machine, but also a distressingly early 11pm curfew. For those with transport, rooms are available at the *Domaine des Clos* (☏04.66.01.14.61, ⓦwww.domaine-des-clos.com; ❸; English spoken), an eighteenth-century Provençal farm located 6km south of Beaucaire on the route de Bellegard.

Eating

For **restaurants** the best deals are the *Brasserie du Midi* along the canal at 29 quai de Gaulle (open daily; *menus* for €8–12) and, next door, *Le Soleil* (lunches from €9), both of which have traditional regional-based *cartes*. More interesting are the Portuguese *Churrasqueira*, no. 5 on quai de Gaulle (closed Sun; lunch only, but dinners on Fri July & Aug; *menus* from €12), and *Ugernum Taverne* on place de la République (closed Sun), which has an eclectic *menu* (various options from €9.80). For those looking for something more formal, the restaurant of the *Jardin d'Isis* (open until midnight) features Provençal fare for €18 and up, while the *Doctrinaires* (closed Sat lunch) is as fancy as it gets here; service and atmosphere are good and there is a solid range of meat and fish options for up to €40.

Around Beaucaire

Four kilometres northwest of Beaucaire, off the Remoulins road just before the dam on the Rhône, lies the turn-off for the **underground monastery of St-Roman** (April–June & Sept daily 10am–6pm; July & Aug daily 10am–6.30pm;

Nov–March Sat & Sun 2–5pm; €5 including €2 parking charge); to get there, follow the narrow road (no RVs) 3km to the monastery car park, then walk 500m to the site itself. This incredible complex, founded in the fifth century, is one of the oldest monasteries in France. Later covered over by a castle which was subsequently destroyed, the huge abbey was not rediscovered until 1966. The subterranean main chapel – built to house the sacred remains of St Roman – still contains the impressive carved seat from which the abbots presided over their community until the sixteenth century. Inside you'll also find small tombs carved in the floor, and set with recesses in which oil-lamps were placed in honour of the dead. This church, the monks' cells and other chambers were cut into the living rock of the hill in what must have been gruelling labour. The terrace of the monastery offers a sweeping panorama of the Rhône, with the hills of Provence easily visible in the distance.

Also worth a trip is a well-preserved eight-kilometre stretch of the **Via Domitia** leading west from Beaucaire, which still boasts three Roman **milestones**. One of the better ways to visit the site is to combine it with a visit to the recreated Roman winery of **Le Mas de Tourelles** (April–June & Sept daily 2–6pm; July & Aug daily 10am–noon & 2–7pm; Nov–Easter Sat 2–6pm; €4.60), 8km west of town on the D38 (no public transport). This is an entertaining stop, where you can see toga-clad types making wine using first-century AD technology; you can taste the final result before drawing your own conclusions as to its "Roman" accuracy. From the vineyard it's a thirty-minute signposted walk north to the Roman road; when you reach it, turn right and you will arrive shortly at the milestones.

Finally, while visiting Beaucaire it would be a shame not to walk or drive across the bridge which spans the Rhône to visit the **castle** at **Tarascon** (July & Aug daily 9am–7pm; Sept–June Tues–Sun 10.30am–5pm; €6.10). This immaculately preserved fortress, rising majestically from the banks of the Rhône, provides a stunning contrast to the ruins of Beaucaire's fortress. The rectangular *enceinte* was constructed in the 1200s by the count of Provence to guard his western border; the present towers were raised in the following two centuries. It was here that the anonymous medieval poem (possibly a musical play), *Nicolette and Aucassin*, was written, recounting the tale of the star-crossed love affair between Aucassin, a fictional heir of Beaucaire, and Nicolette, a beautiful Saracen slave girl who had been bought by the viscount of Tarascon and raised as a Christian. Close by, the **church** of St Martha features a masterful Romanesque portal on the south side, and in the crypt you'll find a carved third- to fourth-century sarcophagus.

St-Gilles and around

Twenty-six kilometres southwest of Beaucaire and 20km south of Nîmes lies the former pilgrims' stop of **St-Gilles**, another town whose candle blew out in the late Middle Ages, and whose only present attraction is the magnificent and fortunately preserved facade of its former **abbey-church** (a UNESCO World Heritage monument). St-Gilles is also one of the gateways to the vast and swampy Petite Camargue (see p.253) which surrounds it on the eastern and southern sides; moving away from town, the stony ground becomes increasingly sandy and marshy, and vineyards give way to flower farms, rice paddies and bull and horse **ranches** (*manades*), as the Rhône spills out to sea. The band of flat grape-growing land which stretches west from the town to the River Vidourle is punctuated by nondescript hamlets; it is here, near the town of **Vauvert**, that the famous **Perrier spring** and bottling plant sits – a site of modern Gallic pilgrimage.

St-Gilles

Perched on the edge of the Camargue, quiet **ST-GILLES** – with its tiny, entirely residential old centre – is, like Beaucaire, a town rescued from complete oblivion only by its medieval monuments and the Rhône–Sète canal, each of which ensures a steady stream of passers-by in summer months.

The town takes its name from a legendary sixth-century hermit who converted the Visigothic king Wamba to Christianity. The ever-astute Cluniac monks promoted the cult of the saint in order to make the town (already on the Arles route to Santiago de Compostela) a lucrative stopping point early in the twelfth century. By this time it was already a favourite of the counts of Toulouse, and the Crusader Raymond IV even preferred to be called "de St-Gilles". A good port and liberal market privileges further boosted prosperity and drew traders from around the Mediterranean, but within a few hundred years the unstoppable silt of the Rhône and the tide of the Reformation conspired to kill both the port and the pilgrim route. The **Wars of Religion** were especially bitter in St-Gilles – at one point a Protestant mob is said to have thrown the church's choristers down a well – and by the time the great abbey-church was virtually destroyed by Huguenot mobs in 1622, the town had already passed into history. Today the town's two principal roles have been revived: it has both a busy canalside **pleasure port** and the pilgrim route to Compostela, which lives on as the GR653, coming into town from Arles and heading on west through the flat vineyards to Vauvert (see below) and on to Montpellier. The biggest festivities of St-Gilles take place in mid-August, with the Feria de la Pêche et de l'Abricot ("The Peach and Apricot Festival") featuring *abrivados*, *encierros* and full-blown *corridas*.

The Town

The only part of St-Gilles which is likely to interest you is the **old town**, which lies on the eastern side of rue Gambetta, the main Arles–Montpellier road. Rue Gambetta ends at the tourist office, opposite which an arched passageway leads into the rue Porte des Marchaux, which takes you into the old centre and up to the **abbey-church**; as you round the last bend in the street and enter the compact place de la République, you'll be greeted by the stunning sight of its broad facade.

Although the Religious Wars destroyed almost all of the church, fate spared the most interesting work of medieval art of the region: the great twelfth-century Romanesque **frieze** of the church's west entrance. Spreading between and over the three great doorways (reminiscent of a Roman triumphal arch), a series of bas-reliefs convey the story of Jesus' return to Jerusalem and subsequent Crucifixion, representations of the Apostles, the three Marys and St Paul, and scenes based on the Old Testament and medieval iconography. These carvings are of superlative workmanship, a unique blend of Byzantine, Classical and medieval stylings setting them apart from the mass of contemporary work; they're best viewed (and photographed) in the afternoon, when the sunlight plays across the carvings. Aside from this entrance, two other interesting remains of the medieval church can be seen: the **choir** and the **crypt** (Mon–Sat: June & Sept 9am–noon & 2–6pm; July & Aug 9am–noon & 3–7pm; Oct–May 9am–noon & 2–5pm; €3.50 guided visit). Located

The pilgrimage route to Santiago de Compostela (known in Spain as the "Camino de Santiago") was Languedoc's and Europe's first grand tourism venture (and inspired the first European guidebooks). It all started in the ninth century when a priest at Iria Flavia in northwestern Spain miraculously discovered the burial site of **St James the Greater**, the Apostle, in a local cemetery. The remains were shifted to a nearby hamlet, which was subsequently renamed as **Santiago** (St James) de Compostela (traditionally attributed to the "field of stars" which signalled the saint's resting place, but actually derived from the Latin for "little burial ground"). The tomb became a rallying point for the Christians of northern Spain, who lived under the shadow of the Muslim Caliphate of Cordoba. But it was in the late eleventh century that things really got going. By this time, the Catholic Church had introduced pilgrimage as a way of doing penance for sins, and although Rome, the home of the papacy, was the most prestigious site, it was soon exceeded in popularity by Santiago. Pilgrimage became popular with common folk and nobles alike, who saw it as a way to travel, see the world and escape the mundanities of daily existence, as well as a way to score points for salvation of the soul. The volume of travellers brought wealth and prosperity not only to Santiago, but to the churches and monasteries along the route which, like **St-Sernin** in Toulouse (p.83), **St-Guilhem** in Hérault (p.296) and **St-Gilles** in Gard, made showcases of their own relics to attract the faithful on the way. Today hikers, whether out of faith or for fun, continue to follow the pilgrimage route, a fascinating window into a world long past.

behind the modern building, the ruins of the former choir hint at the grandeur of the medieval church. On the north side lies the *vis* ("screw"), a twelfth-century stone **spiral staircase** which once climbed to the church's upper gallery: an architectural marvel – a massive self-supporting key-stone stairway – it was another mandatory stop on the traditional masons' tour of the country. From a gate on the south side of the church entrance, you can enter the massive vaulted eleventh-century crypt, which contains the **tombs** of St-Gilles and Pierre de Castelnau, and which is where services for the crowds of passing pilgrims were also held.

Opposite the church sits the **Maison Romane**, a restored medieval house in which it is claimed Gui Folques, who became Pope Clement IV in 1265, was born; it now houses a municipal **museum** of slight interest (Mon–Sat: June & Sept 9am–noon & 2–6pm; July & Aug 9am–noon & 3–7pm; Oct–Dec & Feb–May 9am–noon & 2–5pm, closed Jan; free), mostly full of chunks of carved stone salvaged from the wrecked abbey-church as well as a dusty exhibition of stuffed birds. Before leaving St-Gilles, it is well worth taking a few minutes to wander around the narrow lanes and arch-covered streets of the old town – many of the tiny houses here retain their medieval details and it won't take long for you to discover small doors set in slowly sagging walls, and half-open windows revealing pastel-toned plaster walls and ceiling beams within.

Practicalities

St-Gilles' **gare routière** (☎04.66.87.31.32), 100m south of the tourist office and just north of the canal, is a fifteen-minute walk from the centre, to the northeast. Arriving by **car**, stop in the free municipal car park on the west side of the old town – just off rue Gambetta. You'll find the **tourist office** at place Frédéric Mistral (July & Aug Mon–Sat 9am–noon & 3–7pm, Sun 10am–noon; Sept–June Mon–Sat 9am–noon & 2–5pm; ☎04.66.87.33.75 ⓦwww.ot.saint-gilles.fr), at the northern end of rue Gambetta. The town's **hotels** all lie within a few minutes' walk of the *gare routière* and the canal. *Le Provence*, 7 rue Gambetta (℡04.66.87.31.38; ❷) is the best budget option – a tiny hotel in a converted house, with simple but clean rooms. Only slightly more upmarket, the *Ste-Gillois* (℡04.66.87.33.69, ℻04.66.28.99.57; ❷) at 1 rue Nueve also does good-value half-pensions. For better amenities, head for *Le Cours*, 10 allée Griffeuille (closed late Dec to late Feb; ℡04.66.87.31.93, ⓦwww.hotel-le-cour.fr; closed mid-Dec to Feb; ❸), or the three-star *Heraclée*, 30 quai du Canal (℡04.66.87.44.10, ⓦwww.hotel-heraclee.com; ❸). The **campsite**, *Chicanettes* (closed Nov–April; ℡04.66.87.28.32), is in town, just behind the public car park. For eating, St-Gilles offers a number of unremarkable but adequate *terroir* **restaurants** and pizzerias around the canal port, while those intent on dining well should head to the restaurant of *Le Cours*, where, for €11–27, you can enjoy well-executed and imaginative cuisine in the recently renovated dining room – the local speciality is *taureau* (beef) *à la gardianne*. The local **market** is held on Thursday and Sunday mornings in avenue Emil-Cazelles.

Around St-Gilles

Although Aigues-Mortes is better situated for exploring the **Petite Camargue**, St-Gilles can also serve as a jumping-off point to the region by either boat or on horseback. The portion of the delta near St-Gilles is far from the coast, and comparatively dry and uniform: an expanse of salt marshes, with a bull or horse farm set wherever the land rises far enough above the water table. Several of the horse farms near St-Gilles offer half- and full-day **horseback** and **carriage tours** around their land, the cheapest of which is Manade Lebret (℡04.66.87.22.04), some 10km from St-Gilles (east on the N572 to the D37, and then south). Whether you approve of the *corrida* or not, a visit to a bull farm (or *manade*) is an interesting experience – a chance to see the traditional lifestyle of the ranches of the delta, and witness the impressive equestrian skills of the *gardians* ("cowboys") who manage the herds. The tourist office in St-Gilles has a list of the twenty or so ranches in the area and can indicate which have English-speaking guides and which charge admission to visitors. Crown Blue Line (℡04.66.87.22.66) in St-Gilles operates a **boat** rental service, and L'Isle de Stel (℡06.80.83.82.01) has a combination cruiseboat-bar which runs various itineraries along the network of canals and the Petit Rhône.

The flat band of plain between St-Gilles and the Vidourle river 20km to the west comprises a sort of transition zone between the salty swamps to the south and the rocky hills around Nîmes. A shadeless countryside of vineyards and indistinguishable hamlets, it is, however, home to one of France's proudest commercial institutions, the **Perrier spring and bottling plant**, located a few minutes' drive north of **Vauvert**, just before you reach the village of Vergèze. The source of France's second most famous bubbly stuff, the much-advertised **spring** (Feb–June & Sept–Dec Mon–Fri 9.30–10.30am & 1–4pm, Sat & Sun 1.30–5pm; July & Aug Mon–Fri 9.30–10.30am & 1–6pm, Sat & Sun 10–10.30am & 1–6.30pm; €6) is a site venerated by the Gallic hordes who arrive daily, blissfully shelling out for the two-hour **tour**, sharing vicariously in the glory of the water which has come to signify France abroad. The spring was known in Roman times, but subsequently languished in obscurity until 1894, when a certain Dr Perrier of Nîmes bought the property and set up the Perrier Spring Company in partnership with a young, disabled English aristocrat, who came up with the distinctive shape for the bottle inspired by the

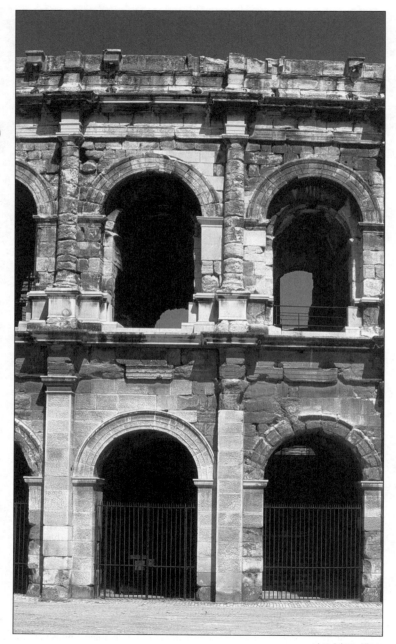

▲ Les Arènes, Nîmes

dumbbells he used for his physiotherapy. The **guided tour** includes a walk through the vast and modern bottling complex, a visit to the spring itself and ends at the former owner's mansion, this last now the Perrier "museum" – a thinly disguised shop where you can pay ridiculously high prices for various bits of merchandising. Judging by the guest-book, the tour is a big domestic hit, but non-French – unless they are avid spring-water enthusiasts – are likely to regard the experience as time and money misspent.

If you head to the Perrier plant from Vauvert keep an eye out for the turrets of **Château du Candiac,** more or less at the halfway point, on the riverbank off the right-hand side of the D56. This is the birthplace of the Marquis of Montcalm (1712–59), who unsuccessfully defended Québec against the English general James Wolfe. Montcalm could not save the French colony from the invaders, and both he and his adversary died in the battle fought on the Plains of Abraham outside the city.

The Camarguaise coast

Lying 35km south of Nîmes, set amidst the flat swampy land of the western-most reaches of the Rhône delta, sits **Aigues-Mortes**, its perfectly intact rectangular walls rising out of the plain like a storybook image of a medieval town. An ancient canal leads southwest to **Le Grau-du-Roi**, once a humble fishing town, now a teeming **summer resort**, exploiting the great unbroken band of dunes which stretches along the coast from the town's eastern limits all the way to the mouth of the Petit Rhône. **Port-Camargue**, a modern adjunct to Le Grau, is a purpose-built yachting complex – the biggest pleasure port on the whole of the Mediterranean. Heading east from Aigues-Mortes, you penetrate the heart of the **Petite Camargue**, the western portion of the Rhône delta, a ten-thousand hectare band of inhospitable terrain which forms a temporary home to a wide variety of migrating birds and, along the coast, crowds of summer-time sunbathers. Driving, cycling or horse-riding is the best way to explore the hinterland of the Carmargue.

Aigues-Mortes

Originally intended to be France's principal Mediterranean port, **AIGUES-MORTES** was swallowed up in short order by the silt of the Rhône, which pushed the sea south and consigned the town to stagnation among the "dead waters" surrounding it. Founded by Louis IX in 1246, it was from here that the saint-king embarked on two of his expeditions: to Cyprus on the Seventh Crusade of 1248, and to Tunis in 1270, where he met his death. His son, Philip, gave the medieval town its present form – commissioning Genoan engineers to build walls in emulation of those of Damietta in Egypt, the site of Louis' early triumph. Local salt beds and trade privileges brought initial success, but by the end of the fourteenth century it had become a backwater, stranded by the waves of silt brought downriver by the Rhône. Aigues-Mortes' misfortune, however, has preserved the town's striking profile, which may have otherwise been built over and around. Today it is a mandatory photo-stop, and a tour of the **fortifications** and the grid of thirteenth-century streets is a pleasant way to pass an hour or so, combining well with a trip to the **beaches** to the south. If you have the fortune to visit during a festival, try to catch a bit of the *course Camarguaise*; watching the crowds and the bulls beneath the medieval ramparts is a truly evocative sight.

Arrival and accommodation

The **gare SNCF** (℡04.66.53.74.74), on the spur line which runs down from Nîmes to Le Grau-du-Roi, is on the route de Nîmes, about 100m north of the old town, while **buses** stop on avenue de la Liberté, across the canal from the *gare*. From either of these head south towards the massive Tour de Constance (see below) on the northwest corner of the old town. Drivers are directed by a signal system to free spaces in the **car park** along the east wall of the town. The **tourist office** (late June & early Sept Mon–Fri 9am–7pm, Sat & Sun 10am–7pm; July & Aug Mon–Fri 9am–8pm, Sat & Sun 10am–8pm; mid-Sept to mid-June Mon–Fri 9am–noon & 1–6pm, Sat & Sun 10am–noon & 2–6pm; ℡ & ℻04.66.53.73.00, ⓦwww.ot.aiguesmortes.fr) is found just inside the Porte de la Gardette, one of the old town's five monumental gates, just east of the Tour de Constance on the north wall. **Bikes** can be picked up at Les Enganettes, 12 rue de Marceau (℡04.66.52.69.11), and Rive de France (℡04.66.53.82.21) hires out canal **boats**.

If you are planning on staying in this area, you may want to choose between Aigues-Mortes and Le Grau (see opposite), which are only 8km apart. There are a number of **hotels** in and around Aigues-Mortes, but even so it is wise to book ahead in high season. Unfortunately those who do opt to stay here have to pay for the privilege – room prices are relatively high and do not offer great value for money. *L'Escale* (℡04.66.53.71.14, ℻04.66.53.76.74; ❶), right by the Tour de Constance, is the best deal, with a traditional homely atmosphere as well as a good restaurant. More expensive but with more amenities (TV and AC), *Le Victoria* (℡04.66.51.14.20, Ⓔlevictoria@wanadoo.fr; ❸) is on the same square as the tourist office. Moving upscale, *Les Arcades*, 23 boulevard Gambetta (℡04.66.53.81.13, ⓦwww.lesarcades.fr; ❺), is a small, tastefully appointed hotel located in a beautiful old building; the rooms are not huge, but the service is attentive. Just outside the old-town walls, the *Tour de Constance* at 1 boulevard Diderot (closed Nov–March; ℡04.66.53.83.50; ❷) lacks the ambience, but is economical and has larger rooms for families and groups. The **campsite**, *Le Petite Camargue* (late April to late Sept; ℡04.66.53.98.98) is a four-star super-site, a massive complex with a café-bar, laundry facilities and a gamut of other services, located 3km west of town.

The Town

Aigues-Mortes' **old town**, where the sights, hotels and restaurants are concentrated, is laid out on a rectangular grid, girded by stout walls. It is well maintained, but its success as a day-trip and weekend destination has cluttered the streets with photo-developing shops and souvenir boutiques, the regular street pattern adding to an air of artificiality and tweeness. Henry James's observation of a hundred years ago is equally valid today: Aigues-Mortes, he wrote, "can hardly be said to be alive; but it has been very neatly embalmed."

On the far side of the open *place* where the tourist office sits, looms the massive **Tour de Constance** (daily: May–Aug 10am–6pm; Sept–April 10am–1pm & 2–4.30pm; €6), the main fortress of the town – once a lighthouse and for many years a prison for uncooperative nobles and stalwart Huguenots. Protestant women were confined in the cells on the top floor, including the stoic Marie Durand, who spent almost forty years here in the eighteenth century, and whose graffiti remain etched in the stone to this day. It is also through the tower that you access the walk along the **town walls**, which provides sweeping views over the flat terrain of the delta and allows a close-up look at the city's defences: arrow-slitted battlements, and stone ducts for pouring boiling oil on would-be attackers. Those on a budget, however, should almost certainly skip this steeply priced visit; a pleasant (and free) option is to walk across town from the Porte de la Gardette and take in the walls from the fields to the south. Looking back at the town from here, the tower which you see on the far left is "**the tower of the salted Bourguignons**", the curious nickname dating back to a grisly episode of the Hundred Years' War. When the town was seized in a raid by English-allied Burgundian forces in 1418, royalist Armagnacs came to try to retake the town. They were foiled by the strong fortifications, but one night a local citizen opened one of the smaller gates to let their forces in. Sneaking up on the sleeping Burgundian garrison, the Armagnacs slaughtered them before they knew what was happening, but rather than bury the bodies (no easy task in the fetid marshes surrounding the town), the victorious forces stuffed them into this tower, and layering them with salt so they would not putrefy – leaving them, literally, in a pickle. There's little more to see in Aigues-Mortes, but the country **market**, held on Wednesday and Sunday mornings on the broad esplanade of avenue Frédéric-Mistral (75m north of the town walls), has excellent produce and prepared dishes, and you could do much worse than buy a **picnic** and enjoy it with a bottle of the local *vin du sable*, "sand wine", on the grassy verge by the ramparts.

Eating and drinking

On the **restaurant** front the old town fares quite respectably. Without a doubt, however, the culinary champion of Aigues-Mortes is the highly praised *Café de Bouzigues* at 7 rue Pasteur (☎04.66.53.93.95) – here (for about €10 at lunch) you can enjoy plentiful, elaborate *menus* on the cosy interior patio or in the comfortable dining room. Many establishments specialize in seafood, most in the €11–22 range. Other than these places and the hotel restaurants, *La Citadelle*, 10 place St-Louis (☎04.66.53.86.68), for seafood, and *La Goulue*, 2 rue Denfert-Rochereau (☎04.66.53.69.45; April–Sept), for *terroir*, are solid, inexpensive options. *Casa de Tora Luna*, 16 place St-Louis (☎04.66.53.68.75) is the local Spanish joint, with the requisite tapas and paella (*menus* from €10.90).

Le Grau-du-Roi and Port Camargue

LE GRAU-DU-ROI and its sister PORT CAMARGUE comprise, between them, a bustling contrast to Aigues-Mortes. Like its fortress neighbour, Port Camargue is also a purpose-built port complex, but one dedicated to pacific hedonism rather than violent idealism. Le Grau (Occitan for "sand bar") has been a fishing village since the time of Henry IV in the sixteenth century, but it was only with the building of Port Camargue in 1969 that prosperity finally arrived. Now summer months fill the town with boaters from around the world, and sun-worshippers from France and abroad who seek out the duned expanses stretching off towards the mouth of the Rhône in the east. If on one hand the town resembles a package-tour nightmare, on the other, there's no shortage of bars, cheap food and beachside fun. Off season, of course, it's another story entirely; things wind down quickly and, as happens in so many seaside towns, a certain air of cold desolation sets in.

Basically, the only reason to stay in Le Grau or Port Camargue is the beach. West of the mouth of the canal which passes through Le Grau's centre, a narrow band of sand, hemmed in closely by road, leads 5km west to La Grande-Motte (see p.277), whose curious triangle-shaped buildings can easily be made out on a clear day. This is the most accessible swimming area, but the best **beaches** are east of town, once you pass the busy little bay between Le Grau and Port Camargue. Just beyond Pointe de l'Espiguette, the spur of land jutting westwards on the south edge of Port Camargue, is where the real beach starts – an uninterrupted swathe of dunes stretching 5km east to the lighthouse and from there towards the horizon. Naturally the busiest area is around the **lighthouse** itself, which can be accessed by road from Le Grau, and where you will be charged a hefty €4.50 fee to park. The further east you go, the more the crowds thin out, and the more laid-back beach etiquette becomes. **Nudists** have staked their claim on one stretch of beach to the east of the lighthouse, and if you are prepared to go far enough away you can find seclusion even at the busiest time of year. The main attraction here aside from the seaside is the **Seaquarium** (daily: 10am–6pm; €8.60), one of the biggest indoor aquariums in Europe, located between the two towns in the Palais de Mer. The fairly steep admission price also gives access to the **Musée de Mer** ("The Sea Museum") in the same building, which features exhibits on local marine life and nautical history. Le Grau/Port Camargue is a big centre for **bull**-related activities, including a series of *courses* (held every weekend late March to Sept), the climax of which is the Trophée de As competition in mid-August, and *corridas* (held throughout July & Aug).

Apart from swimming there are facilities for a wide range of other water-related **activities** in Le Grau and Port Camargue, including outfits which rent sail-boards, sailboats, kayaks and jet-skis, many offering instruction (see below). For children, no fewer than three **water parks** have been set up around the towns. Summer months also provide an opportunity to enjoy regional diversions including *courses* and waterborne jousting competitions during the *fêtes* of mid-June and September.

Practicalities

Both **buses** and **trains** approach the town along the narrow sandy spit leading from Aigues-Mortes and deposit passengers more or less smack in the middle of Le Grau, at the small **gare SNCF** (☎04.66.51.40.93) just off the canal on the east side. The large and efficient **tourist office**, 30 rue Rédarès (daily: June & Sept 9am–8pm; July & Aug 9am–11.30pm; Oct–May 9am–noon & 2–6pm; ☎04.66.51.67.79, ⓦwww.ville-legrauduroi.fr), is on the east side of Le Grau, five streets south from the train station. To rent **bicycles**, try Vélo Evasion, 1291 rue de Camargue (☎04.66.51.48.65), or Loca Loisirs, avenue Jean Lasserre (☎04.66.53.45.12), while for **watersports** try Surf Loisirs on boulevard Front de Mer (☎04.66.52.40.01) or Société Nautique on quai d'Escale (☎04.66.53.29.47); Espace Mer (☎04.66.51.75.25) in the Nouveau Port de pêche will handle your **diving** needs. For canal **boats** try A2M (☎04.66.51.42.54, ⓔa2mglad@wanadoo.fr) or contact the tourist office for a full list of establishments.

Accommodation

The dozen or so **hotels** which serve Le Grau and Port Camargue range from smaller and more attractive establishments in the old town to typical beachside monsters. Surprisingly, prices tend to be fairly reasonable. In the **old town**, the least expensive choices are the small *Le Provençal*, 45 rue des Combattents (☎04.66.51.41.68, ⓕ04.66.51.40.46; ❷), and the basic *Quai d'Azur*, rue du Vidourle (March to mid-Nov; ☎04.66.51.41.94, ⓕ04.66.53.41.94; ❷). The best of the smaller, old town hotels is the *Bellevue et d'Angleterre*, quai Colbert (closed Jan; ☎04.66.51.40.75, ⓦwww.bellevued'angleterre.com; ❹) which is a pleasant, airy and clean establishment with good views. In **Port Camargue** things tend to be more expensive, but have a greater number of facilities. *Le Spinaker*, pointe de la Presqu'île (March–Oct; ☎04.66.53.24.91,

Ⓦwww.spinaker.fr; ❼), is cosy and discreetly set in a green patch in the midst of the port, while *Oustau Camarguen*, 3 route des Marines (March–Nov; ☎04.66.51.51.65, Ⓔoustaucamarguen@wanadoo.fr; ❺), is larger but has a more authentically maritime feel. **Campsites** abound, but three are set conveniently between Le Grau and Port Camargue, and all have excellent facilities: *Les Mouettes*, avenue Jean Jaurès (March–Sept; ☎ & Ⓕ04.66.51.44.00), and *A.C.C.C.F*, route de l'Espiguette (March–Oct; ☎04. 66.51.46.21) are both two-star rated, while *L'Eden*, on the same road (March–Oct; ☎04.66.51.49.81, Ⓕ04.66.53.13.20) is a four-star, four-hundred-pitch monster-site, which also rents chalets.

Eating

Eating in Le Grau and Port Camargue means **seafood**, and it seems that on every corner there is a restaurant serving up the same bouillabaisse, *moules frites*, *coquiallages* and fish. Competition means prices are good, even if the product is often indistinguishable – most establishments have *menus* in the €12–24 range. The bargain places are *La Pichouline* on place de la Libération and *Le Provençal*, 45 rue des Combattents, which serve up lunch from €10. At the other end of the scale, *Le Spinaker*'s restaurant is recognized as the best eatery in the area, and *menus* are priced accordingly (€26–77). Of the towns' many **bars**, the only one which stands out from the crowd is *Leon* at 2 avenue de la Gare, the home turf of the local bullfighting aficionados association. **Markets** are held every morning (except Sunday) either at place de la République or Boucanet on the far bank of the *grau*.

The Petite Camargue

The **PETITE CAMARGUE**, which Lawrence Durrell called "Little Argentina", stretches east from Le Grau and Aigues-Mortes, an inhospitable expanse of marshes, crisscrossed by canals, and dominated by great saltwater *étangs* ("lagoons"). This is a lightly populated and unwelcoming area, with no villages to speak of, only isolated ranches, rice farms and salt works. It is temporary home, however, to an incredible variety of **waterfowl** – some four-hundred different species – including a steady stream of migrating birds crossing the Mediterranean between Europe and Africa; look out especially for pink flamingos, herons, grand cormorants and egrets. The delta is also where Gard's strong traditions of horsemanship and *tauromachie* originate, on the great ranches where wild bulls are left to graze the salty scrub freely. The *gardians*, whose simple huts dot the plain, have been the proud masters of the delta since at least 1512, when they established a formal confratierny. Riding their distinctively small "Camargue" ponies they pursue and corral the black bulls, rounding them up for branding in the springtime *ferrade*. The Camargue proper, which lies in Provence, has been incorporated since 1970 into a national park, but there is no visible characteristic which distinguishes the official parkland from the section of the delta near Aigues-Mortes and Le Grau.

Heading east from Aigues-Mortes into the Petite Camargue you pass the curious **Tour Carbonnière** on the left. Once the guard-post on the only land access to the medieval port-town, this twenty-metre-high tower, perched on a rare mound of *terra firma* and pierced by a gate through which the road once led, is now a popular place for a picnic. Penetrating the heart of the area, the road rolls by a flat, unchanging landscape until you reach the bridge over the Petit Rhône. Heading in the other direction from Aigues-Mortes down to Le Grau you'll see the **saltpans** of the Salins du Midi to the south – if you're interested in visiting these, a *petit train* (March–Oct daily 10am–5.45pm) does circuits of the area (1hr 15min; €6.80) and bus (2hr 15min; €9), with a guide explaining their history and the techniques of salt harvesting. Book the train at the tourist office in Aigues-Mortes (see p.250), but if you need an English-speaking guide check ahead of time that one is available. Just past these salt works are the **Caves de Listel**, a wine *domaine* where locally produced "sand wine" can by sampled and purchased. On the far side of Le Grau, on the way to the lighthouse, you'll pass the **bird observatory**, a discreet cabin overlooking one of the shallow, salty *étangs*; early morning and evening in summer are the best times to look.

If you are exploring the Petite Camargue with your own vehicle, don't be tempted onto the unpaved roads and lanes leading out through the fields; quite often they are deceptively soft and you may find yourself walking back to civilization. The best ways to visit the more remote areas are either to sign up for one of the one-day "**safaris**" offered by travel agencies, or join a boat tour. Among outfits that can arrange organized visits are Cabane de Boucanet of Port Camargue (☎04.66.53.25.64), which sets up **horseback** rides, and Le Gitan in Le Grau (☎04.66.70.09.65, ⓦwww.francemarket.com/gitan), which deals with **four-wheel drive** expeditions; Isle de Stel in Aigues-Mortes (April–Oct; ☎04.66.53.60.70) offers a half-day **boat** tour of the nearby *étangs* and canals.

The Vidourle valley

West of Nîmes, the border of Gard is marked by the **Vidourle valley**, which begins as a trickle on the southern edge of the Cévennes mountains at the northwest of the *département*. This is a quiet corner of Gard, relatively unexplored, and on the whole the villages here, some of which are impressively ancient, lack both the sights and amenities to draw travellers. Notable exceptions though are **Sommières**, where the breadth of the river is still spanned by a Roman bridge and watched over by the richly preserved castle of Villevieille; **Sauve**, an ancient hamlet which makes a convenient stopping-point en route from Nîmes to Ganges; and, further on, at the edge of the *département*, just 15km from Ganges to the west, **St-Hippolyte-du-Fort**.

Sommières

SOMMIÈRES, the largest town along the Vidourle, lying halfway between Nîmes and Montpellier, is one point on the way west from Nîmes which definitely merits a stop. Its easy, unspoilt charm seduced the English author Laurence Durrell into spending the last 33 years of his life here, and prompted him to remark, in the *Spirit of Places*, that he had seen "nothing prettier". Walking through the old town or along the riverbank it's hard not to sympathize with Durrell's judgement – Sommières remains a peaceful, idyllic village. Strongly Protestant, it was all but destroyed during the Wars of Religion as it repeatedly changed hands before being conquered personally by Louis XIII in 1622. Today Sommières makes a pleasant stop for a bite to eat and a wander around, and those looking for a few days of quiet relaxation could fare a lot worse than to spend some time here, away from the crowded beaches of Le Grau and the busy streets of Nîmes. April through to September is the season for *courses Camarguaises*, held on Sunday afternoons.

The **Roman bridge** which spans the river remains an integral feature of Sommières, uniting the newer town on the west bank with the old town on

the east. Something of a curiosity, it was built in the first century and originally consisted of seventeen arches, but half a dozen have been gradually covered
over by the encroaching town. A testament to Roman engineering, it continued to carry all of the car and truck traffic passing through the town up until
the recent opening of a new bypass. At the bridge's western end the walled old
town is entered by passing through the **tour de l'horloge**, home to a ponderous seventeenth-century clock. From here you can descend to the left to
the **bas marché** (low market), now the place des Docteurs M. et G. Dax, or
proceed along the course of the old Roman road to the **haut marché** (high
market), the place Jean-Jaurès – both arcaded squares still serve as market places
for local farmers. From the upper market, an alley leads to the steep stairs at the
foot of the town's **castle**. Not much remains of this fortress, built in the tenth
century and all but destroyed by Catholic forces in 1573, but you can climb to
the top of the square **tower** (July & Aug daily 4–7pm; €2) for a dramatic
panorama of the Vidourle plain. Aside from the confines of the old *enceinte*, the
quai Griolet, between the town walls and the riverbank, makes for a particularly evocative stroll downriver, with the geese which mill about the small dam
honking emphatically at each other and passers-by.

Practicalities

Buses arriving in Sommières currently drop passengers off at the place de la
République, along the northern wall of the old town. The **tourist office** (July
& Aug daily 9am–12.30pm & 3–7pm; Sept–June Tues–Sun 9am–12.30 &
2–6pm; ☎46.68.80.99.30, ⓦwww.ot-sommières@wanadoo.fr), on rue du
Général-Bruyère, just west of the Place de la République, distributes a pamphlet detailing local walking routes. The best **hotel** in Sommières is the *Relais
de L'Estelou* (☎04.66.77.71.08, ⓦwww.relaisdelestelou.com; ❹), an arty hotel
set in the town's old *gare*. Amenities include a swimming pool, and the service
is genuinely personable. Other choices are the **chambres d'hôtes** *L'Orangerie*
(☎04.66.77.79.94; ❻), a seventeenth-century mansion tucked away in rue de
Baumes in the shadow of the castle, Colette Labbe's home in 8 avenue Emile
Jamais (☎ & Ⓕ04.66.77.78.69; English ❸), which has a pool set in a verdant
garden (meals from €9), and Billy Gérard's cosy **gîte** at 8 rue Docteur
Chrestien (☎04.66.80.35.66; ❷). The **campsite** (☎04.66.80.33.49;
Easter–Sept) is on rue Eugène Rouché, on the west bank of the Vidourle,
heading north out of town.

For **eating**, *L'Olivette*, 11 rue Abbé Fabre (closed Tues; ☎04.66.80.97.71), is
indisputably the best place in the area for exciting regional cuisine, with *menus*
from €24, and you'll also find good *terroir* fare at *L'Estocade* on the same street
(closed Mon–Fri eve Sept–June; ☎04.66.77.77.01; *menus* from €10). The
restaurant of the *Commerce* (Mon–Fri lunch only, Sat & Sun lunch and dinner)
has *menus* from as little as €12. On Saturday morning a **market** is held in place
de Marché.

Near Sommières: the Château
de Villevieille and around

If you are passing Sommières you shouldn't miss the opportunity to visit the
Château de Villevieille, perched on the rise which dominates the old town.
Villevieille itself is a beautiful little hamlet of stone-built houses, but the **castle** (May & June daily 2–7pm; July–Sept daily 2–8pm; Oct–April school hols
only 2–7pm; €6) is a must-see. Owned by the same family for some 750 years,
it is one of the few noble castles to escape appropriation or destruction during
the Revolution (due to the lord's friendship with Voltaire and Condorcet, who

interceded on his behalf). Today it boasts a sumptuous interior; the furnishings, including sixteenth-century Flemish leather "wallpaper" and the first mirror in France are classed as national monuments, plus the beds in which three kings of France and Cardinal Richelieu slept are still in their respective rooms. One of the best things about the visit is that you're shown around by members of the family – an unassuming, friendly bunch who are disarmingly frank, and genuinely welcoming. Next door, the restaurant *Les 4 Vents* (T04.66.77.79.66) has home-cooked *menus* (€16–22) and **chambres d'hôte** (❷), handy also if rooms in Sommières are booked up.

If you feel like staying a few days in Sommières, have a look at the tourist office brochure which details local walks. The best of these is the excursion to the twelfth-century **church of St-Julien**, 5km north of town along the right bank of the Vidourle (the turn-off is marked on the left after 3km). The church is usually closed, so if you want to visit the inside, check first at Sommières. Otherwise, it makes a good stop for a picnic. The villages of the *garrigues* stretching north from town do not contain any sights of particular interest, but the relative tranquillity of the highways makes for very pleasant **cycling**.

Sauve

The first town of any interest on the road from Nîmes to Ganges is **SAUVE**, 40km to the west of the capital of Gard and 20km upriver from Sommières. It's a quiet little town, once fortified and still presided over by the castle which was centuries ago the summer retreat of the bishops of Maguelone, and although there are no monuments here, it is a particularly good example of a typical medieval-era town of northern Gard. The **old town** is a maze of twisting alleys, some of which are covered, and the **view** from the other side of the bridge over the Vidourle is inspiring. In recent years it has been revived due to an influx of cosmopolitan urban refugees who have opened up interesting, ethnically flavoured eating establishments and now organize an annual African music festival in mid-July.

Sauve's only **bus** link is with Nîmes and Ganges: the stop is just off the main road, at the edge of the village. The small **tourist office** in place René Isouard (July & Aug Mon–Sat 10am–noon & 2–6pm, Sun 10am–noon; Sept–June Mon–Sat 10am–noon & 2–5pm; T04.66.77.57.51, Wwww.office-tourisme-sauve.com) has information on local excursions. As for accommodation, there is the very comfortable **hotel** *La Magnanerie* (T04.66.77.57.44, Wwww.lam-agnanerie.fr; ❸) and an agreeable *gîte*, *La Pausamanque* (T04.66.77.51.97; English spoken; ❷), 2km east on the Nîmes road. There are two good **restaurants** in town: *Le Micocoulier* (Easter to Oct Mon & Thurs–Sun dinner only; July & Aug daily; T04.66.77.57.61; *menu* €15), at 3 place Jean-Astruc, is a cosy little *auberge* serving up intriguing un-French food and lavish desserts; while *L'Auberge au Volet Verts*, 6 place Pascual-Vallongue (closed Tues & Oct; T04.66.77.53.28) is also open for lunch – a bargain at €9.15. Alternatively, Anne Tourneux's *Villa Eugénie* on route de Villesèque (closed Dec–March; T04.66.77.05.22) provides excellent dinners and lunches (€15–25) in a garden setting. Finally, you can stock up on your own supplies at Sauve's country **market**, held on Thursdays and Saturdays in the town centre.

St-Hippolyte-du-Fort

ST-HIPPOLYTE-DU-FORT, eight kilometres west of Sauve, across undulating farmland, is the highest town on the Vidourle's course. Beyond lies Ganges, where the road dips into the Hérault valley, having crossed over into the *département* of the same name. St-Hippolyte, like so many old cloth towns of the Cévennes, switched over to silk production in the period before the Revolution, and prospered until a nineteenth-century epidemic wiped out the mulberry plants on which the silkworms depended. Today the town is trying to generate interest as a tourist stop, encouraging its inhabitants to attach **sundials** to the fronts of their houses in order to develop a rather contrived identity. Some of the solar clocks are quite attractive, but most are unremarkable; the tourist office distributes a route map which takes you past all of them. Rather more interesting is the **silk museum** (daily: April–Nov 10am–12.30pm & 2–6.30pm; €4.20) behind the old military school, a five-minute walk west of the main square, place de la Canourgue. In addition to reconstructed silk-weaving machinery, it houses an exhibition of live silk worms doing their stuff; the museum makes for a good stop for both adults and children.

Kids big and small may also want to stop at the nearby **Musée du Sapeur Pompier** (June to mid-Sept daily except Tues 10am–noon & 12.30–6.30pm; mid-Sept to May Sat & Sun 10am–noon & 12.30–6.30pm; €2.30), a new museum featuring a collection of historical fire trucks and fire-fighting equipment.

Buses roll through the town centre, stopping just before place de la Canourgue. The town's **tourist office** (Tues 9am–noon & 3–6pm, Wed 3–6pm, Thurs 9am–noon, Fri 9am–noon & 3–5.30pm; ☎04.66.77.91.65, ⓦwww.multimania.com/sainthippolyte) is located within the courtyard of the same building as the silk museum. For **accommodation** you can choose between the hotel *Auberge Cigalois* (☎04.66.77.64.59, ⓔauberge cigaloise@aol.com; closed Dec–Feb; ❷), off the D999 a kilometre or so east of town, or at Arlette Naintre-Collin's B&B (closed Nov–March; ☎ & ⓕ04.66.77.94.10, ⓔNaintre-Collin@libertysurf.fr; ❸; English spoken) at 14 rue Blanquierie. There are several functional if unexceptional **restaurants** and **cafés** clustered around place de la Canourgue. The town has two **campsites**: *Figaret* (☎04.66.77.26.34) and *de Graniers* (☎04.66.85.21.44).

Travel details

Trains

SNCF buses may run in lieu of trains on these lines; services are reduced on Sundays and holidays.

Aigues-Mortes to: Le Grau-du-Roi (5 daily; 5min); Nîmes (3 daily; 50min).

Nîmes to: Agde (18 daily; 1hr 10min); Aigues-Mortes (3 daily; 50min); Beaucaire (2 daily; 24min); Béziers (36 daily; 1hr 15min); Carcassonne (26 daily; 2hr 5min–3hr 10min); Le Grau-du-Roi (3 daily; 55min); Lunel (26 daily; 15–25min); Montpellier (26 daily; 30min); Narbonne (20 daily; 1hr 45min); Paris (23 daily; 3hr–9hr 30min); Perpignan (12 daily; 2hr 45min); Sète (22 daily; 48min); Toulouse (26 daily; 2hr 45min to 3hr); Vauvert (5 daily; 20–45min).

Tarascon/Beaucaire to: Montpellier (2 daily; 1hr 5min); Nîmes (2 daily; 25min).

Buses

Many lines have no or reduced service on Saturdays, Sundays, holidays and in summer months. In summer extra services run from Nîmes to Aigues-Mortes, Grau and La Grand-Motte.

Aigues-Mortes to: Le Grau-du-Roi (17 daily; 10min); Montpellier (5 daily; 1hr 20min; increased service in summer); Stes-Maries-de-la-Mer (summer 1 daily; 30min).

Beaucaire to: Remoulins (2 daily; 45min); St-Gilles (2 daily; 30min).

Nîmes to: Aigues-Mortes (17 daily; 55min); Avignon (4 daily; 1hr 30min); Beaucaire (7 daily; 45min); Collias (3 daily; 1hr 5min); Ganges (2–3 daily; 1hr 30min); La Grand Motte (9 daily; 1hr 30min); Le Grau-du-Roi (17 daily; 1hr 15min); Montpellier (2 daily; 50min); Pont du Gard (8 daily; 45min); St-Gilles (10 daily; 50min); Sauve (4–6 daily; 50min); Sommières (8 daily; 45min); Uzès

(12–13 daily; 30min–1hr); Vauvert (4 daily; 35min); Villevieille (8 daily; 40min).
St-Hippolyte to: Ganges (3 daily; 15min); Montpellier (2 daily; 1hr 45min); Nîmes (3 daily; 1hr 20min); Quissac (3 daily; 35min); Sauve (3 daily; 30min).

Sommières to: Montpellier (4 daily; 1hr 10min); Nîmes (8 daily; 40min); Villevieille (8 daily; 5min).
Uzès to: Nîmes (12–13 daily; 30min–1hr); Pont du Gard (8–9 daily; 25min); St-Hippolyte (2 daily; 25min).

Montpellier and
around

CHAPTER 5

Highlights

* **Beaches** A long swathe of sand girds the Mediterranean coast: you can find both solitude and crowds here. See p.261

* **Cafés-litteraires** Take in Montpellier's lively student culture and these provocative salons. See p.274

* **Water-jousting** This curious Sètoise sport has grown in the last centuries into a regional tradition. See p.282

* **Seafood** Whether cultivated in the Bassin de Thau or fished from the sea, the coastal cuisine of this area is a gourmet's delight. See p.285

* **Pézenas** Walk the streets of Languedoc's old capital for a taste of life in the age of Molière. See p.285

* **Cirque de Navacelles** A spectacular ox-bow canyon, etched deep into the *causse* of upper Hérault. See p.293

▲ Montpellier

Montpellier and around

ogether **Montpellier** and the surrounding country comprise the most varied and exciting region in Languedoc. The city is a capital in every sense of the word – a zesty centre of government, education, culture and economy for the whole of Languedoc-Roussillon *région* and, best of all, it is minutes from the beach. While Languedoc's **coast** may not be able to hold a candle to the likes of Provence's Côte d'Azur, if you can put up with the often-strong wind, its some forty kilometres of nearly uninterrupted sand bar – as well as providing ample opportunities for sun-soaking and watersports – means you can escape the crowds if you wish. Moreover, the seaside towns, although unavoidably busy in high season, have not sunk into the irretrievable triteness of their Provençal counterparts; the continuing role of **Palavas**, **Mèze** and **Sète** as fishing ports balances their beach-town roles, endowing them with life and energy throughout the year. Just inland, **Pézenas** was the capital of Languedoc in the glory days of French Absolutism, and the many palaces which cram its old town preserve it as one of the most beautiful in the Southwest. The River Hérault gives its name to the *département* of which Montpellier is the administrative centre, and dominates its **interior**. Less travelled than the coast, its beautiful highlands are home to a wealth of natural wonders and historic sites. Dusty and provincial **Clermont-l'Hérault** acts as a gateway to the dramatically varied landscape at nearby **Lac du Salagou**, while **Lodève** – still lorded over by its hulking medieval cathedral, is the best place to set off for the breathtaking **Cirque de Navacelles**. East of the cirque, Ganges sits on the banks of the Hérault at the point where the river completes its descent from the high Cévennes mountains to the north; just downstream you can visit one of France's most celebrated caverns, the **Grotte des Demoiselles**, before following dramatic gorges southwest past the ancient monastic centre of **St-Guilhem-de-Désert**, or bearing due south towards the towering **Pic-St-Loup**.

Getting around by **public transport** in the region around Montpellier is easy. The city sits on the main coastal rail artery, uniting it with Sète to the west and Nîmes to the east, while the area of greater Montpellier, the *agglomération*, is served by the city's transport network (TAM), whose far-ranging buses reach Palavas and Maguelone on the coast. Inland, the lack of train lines is compensated by regular bus services connecting the bigger towns. Only the smaller villages, such as the hamlets around Lac du Salagou and Navacelles, do not have useful bus services; to explore these you'll need a car or bike, or be prepared to hitch-hike.

Montpellier

MONTPELLIER is a great place. Home to a youthful and dynamic university culture and a host of artistic festivals and events, and a beautiful architectural fusion of the classical and the avant-garde, it is the most exciting city in Languedoc proper – it's even close enough to the Mediterranean to have the beach within reach of public transport. Since his first election in 1983, Mayor Georges Frêche has continued the successful policies of his socialist predecessors, pouring money into the city's infrastructure and arts and drawing in investment – the effects of which are immediately obvious to the visitor. With fine museums, a charming old centre and a bouncy rhythm of life, you'll find that Montpellier offers an ideal place for either a longer, relaxing stay, or a whirlwind two-day tour of its highpoints, notably the many Renaissance **mansions** of the old town and, when it reopens in 2006, the **Musée Fabré**.

Montpellier is a medieval city, and can't claim the same venerable Roman past of rival Nîmes. Starting off as a market town for nearby **Maguelone** in the tenth century, in 1204 it was acquired by marriage by the count-kings of Barcelona, who favoured it as a residence – both Jaume I "the Conqueror" and his son Jaume II of Mallorca were born here. By the late thirteenth century it had become second only to Paris in size, thanks partly to its famous **university**, and a major centre for medicine, law and the arts. With Jaume I's posthumous divison of his realms, the city was incorporated into the Kingdom of Mallorca until 1349, when Jaume II sold it – afflicted with plague, banditry and famine – to the French Crown. In the era that followed the city was sustained by its university, through whose doors passed the pioneering Renaissance poet Petrarch and, later, the satirist Rabelais, who received his doctorate here in 1537. Despite the transfer of the bishopric of Maguelone here in 1537, Montpellier became strongly **Protestant** in the sixteenth and seventeenth centuries, losing many of its old church buildings in factionalist struggles, and was only saved from destruction at the hands of Louis XIII, who had personally waged war on the Huguenot stronghold in 1622, by an eleventh-hour truce. In a good position for trade and with a varied economic base, Montpellier managed to escape the post-Religious Wars depression which afflicted most of Languedoc, and the wealthy burghers vied with each other to build decadently outfitted **manors** in the surrounding vineyards. The city's leftist tradition began with a bang in 1789, and the revolutionary anthem known as "Le Marseillaise" was in fact first sung by a local medical student. Another wave of serious unrest came during the wine crisis of 1907, during which it was the strongest centre of popular agitation in reaction to plummeting grape prices (see p.402). The last shake-up was in 1962; with the dismantling of the Algerian colony, 13,000 French (*pieds-noirs*) and Maghrebi (*harki*) refugees arrived in the city, two groups whose integration into Montpellier society generated considerable friction, but whose presence brought a revitalizing dynamism to the city. Not long after this, Montpellier became the official capital of the administrative *région* of Languedoc-Roussillon.

Arrival, information and city transport

The city's **airport**, which has various **car rental** outlets, is 8km to the southeast of the centre, beside the Étang de Mauguio; from here buses run to the *gare routière* (hourly; 15min; €4.60), or it will cost you €18–25 by **taxi**. The **gare SNCF** and **gare routière** are next to each other at the southern end of rue Maguelone – it's a five-minute walk along this street to the central place de la Comédie. The gare SNCF has no **left luggage** facilites. If you're driving, the simplest option for **parking** is to head for the "Comédie" car park, under the famous *place* – if however you want to avoid paying, you will be banished to the metered zones on the periphery of the old town. Alternatively, the outlying public parking places offer a €3 special which includes parking and a return tram fare for each passenger.

The main **tourist office**, (July & Aug Mon–Fri 9am–7.30pm, Sat 10am–6pm, Sun 10am–1pm & 2–5pm; Sept–June Mon–Fri 9am–6.30pm, Sat 10am–6pm, Sun 10am–1pm & 2–5pm; ☎04.67.60.60.60, ⓦwww.ot-montpellier.fr), which has **exchange** facilities (Mon–Fri 9am–6.30pm; July & Aug also Sat 9am–6pm) is on the northern edge of place de la Comédie while there are seasonal annexes at the gare SNCF (July & Aug Mon–Fri 9am–1pm & 3–7pm) and in the Antigone, at 78 av de Pirée (April–Oct Mon–Fri 9am–1pm

Festivals in and around Montpellier

Most of the action in Hérault *département* is centred on Montpellier, which is renowned for its cultural vitality, hosting a range of annual **festivals**. Also worth looking out for are the *fêtes* on the coast, which invariably feature the local tradition of water-jousting – throughout July and August in Palavas and Sète (see box on p.282) – as well as *tauromachie* (both Spanish and Camargue styles). The uplands of the Hérault valley also have a few small local festivals which you may have the good fortune to happen upon. Where no specific information number is given, contact the relevant tourist office for details.

1st or 2nd weekend Feb Montpellier: Swing Danse Festival ⓦ www.montpellier-swing.com. One of France's biggest swing festivals, featuring lindy-hoppers, boogie-woogiers and swingers from around the country.

Feb or March Pézenas: Carnaval. Lent kicks off with a three-day Mardi Gras (Shrove Tuesday) festival here, featuring folkloric displays and a parade led by the local totem-animal, *Le Poulain*.

Pentecost (5 weeks after Easter) Lunel: Estivales. Early summer celebration featuring three days of *courses camarguaises*, a massive street market and livestock fair.

Weekend in May Pézenas: Cavalcade. A popular festival with a bustling handicrafts market, culminating in a medieval period-costume parade led by *Le Poulain*.

Throughout June Palavas: Maguelone music festival ☎04.67.60. 90.92. Medieval and Baroque music concerts held several nights a week in the cathedral.

Weekend in June Pézenas: "Pézenas sous regard de Molière". A historical reconstruction of Pézenas in its greatest period of glory. Lots of costumed townsfolk, activities and a market.

Mid-June to mid-July Montpellier: Le Printemps des Comédiens ☎04.67.01.04.04, ⓦ www.printempsdescomediens.com. Theatre, dance and music festival held in the grounds of Château d'Ô, a mansion northwest of Montpellier (tram #1 to "Chateau d'Ô").

Mid-June to mid-Aug St-Guilhem: Musique Sacrée ☎04.67.63.14.99. Religious and Baroque music series, performed in the former abbey-church.

Late June to mid-July Montpellier: Montpellier Danse ☎04.67.60.83.60, ⓔ info@montpellierdanse.com. A three-week festival of traditional music and dance from around the world, held in the old Ursuline convent, the Comédie, Le Corum and

& 2–6pm). All of these offices manage reservations for the official **guided tours** (Wed & Sat 3pm, prior reservation obligatory ☎04.67.60.19.19, ⓔ guides@montpellier.fr; €6.50–8), the advantage of which is that they allow you to visit certain normally off-limits sights, like the medieval *mikvé* (Jewish ritual bath) or the interior of the Arc de Triomf. For information on all sorts of practicalities and events, pick up the student guide *L'Indic*, the fortnightly *Sortir*, which has entertainment listings, or *Montpellier Côte Coeur*, which also lists shops – all are available free at the tourist offices.

The star of the city's transport system (TAM; 27 rue Maguelone; ☎04.67.22.87.87, ⓦ www.montpellier-agglo.com/tam) is its new fleet of **trams**, which has its hub at place de la Comédie. At present, one line is in service, which runs a twisting course northwest to southeast across town. Coupled with **buses**, it makes an incredibly comprehensive network, the real advantage of the buses for visitors being that they run out to Palavas on the coast. Both buses and trams operate from 5am to 1am, and **maps** and **passes** (one-day pass €3.20, weekly pass €11.10) are available at the TAM office (see above), although you can also buy tickets (valid for both; single €1.10 valid for one hour including transfers, ten-trip ticket €9.50) from drivers, at tobacconists or other venues around town.

First weekend July Sète: Fête de la St-Pierre. Traditional fishermen's festival with a religious procession, street party and jousting.

Second Sunday July Palavas: Fête de la Mer ☎04.67.07.73.34, ⓦwww.palavasles-flots.com. Religious procession and blessing of fishing boats, followed by jousting, fireworks and *tauromachie*. Also night-time *joutes* on July 14.

Mid-July Mèze: Festival du Thau ☎04.67.18.92.80, ⓦwww.festivaldethau.com. A week-long "alternative", ska and World-Music festival on the banks of the Bassin du Thau, with three concerts per evening – all on the same ticket.

Mid- to end July Montpellier: Le Festival de Radio-France et de Montpellier ☎04.67.02. 02.01, ⓦwww.festivalradiofrancemontpellier.com. Musical festival representing styles from classical to jazz, held at Le Corum and other venues. Half of the concerts are free.

Mid- to end July Sète: Festival de Sète. Mediterranean-music festival featuring folk and pop music from African and European shores.

July 21–23 St-Guilhem: Fête. Local *fête* of the town, featuring costumes, music and traditional market.

Late July to early Aug Sète: Fiest'a Sète ☎06.67.74.48.44, ⓦwww.fiestasete.com. Two-week celebration. Nightly performances of music and dance at the Théâtre de la Mer (from €26), as well as street theatre and plenty of parties.

Throughout July & Aug Pézenas: Mirondela des Arts ☎04.67.98.36.40. International theatre festival with excellent quality performances held at the town's Théâtre de Verdure, in the old town's squares and other venues.

End Aug Sète: Fête de St-Louis. One-day extravaganza of fireworks, street parties, jousting and medieval pageantry.

Sept 29 to Oct 1 Palavas: Feria d'Automne ☎06.61.46.68.85. Local Camarguaise-style festival, with horsemanship and *tauromachie*.

Mid- to end Oct Montpellier: Festival du Cinéma Méditerranéen ☎04.99.13. 73.73. Festival of feature-length films and shorts, with symposiums and awards.

Third week Dec Pézenas: Occitan Christmas. Christmas festivities featuring the folk traditions and customs of the Languedocian plains.

at the vending kiosks at major stops (credit cards accepted). Other green transport initiatives include the city's comprehensive **bike** path network, which has now topped 120km in length; bikes can be rented at Vill'a Vélo at the *gare routière* (☎04.67.92.92.67) or direct from TAM (€6 per day). Finally, if you have come on your own bike and want to store it safely, TAM also provides this service for only €1 per day.

Accommodation

With its roles as a student and administrative centre, Montpellier has abundant **hotel** facilities in all price ranges. Most accommodation is concentrated in the compact grid of streets between the *gares* and the place de la Comédie. You may be tempted to stick to this area for convenience, but there are options in the old town which are worth searching out, particularly in the area west of the central place des Martyrs-de-la-République. The city's tourist office runs a "Bonne Weekend" programme which gives you a free second night at selected hotels (Nov–March).

Montpellier's **HI hostel** (closed mid-Dec to mid-Jan; ☎04.67.60.32.22, ⒺMontpellier@fuaj.org; bus #6 "Ursulines"), fifteen minutes' walk from place

Comédie, is in a renovated old building on impasse Petite Corraterie, off rue des Écoles Laïques at the northern boundary of the old town; the curfew is at 2am and it has amenities such as a bar and billiards room and a luggage check. Another option for low-budget accommodation is to contact L'Association des Residences Internationales (Mon–Fri 8am–noon & 1.30–5pm; ☎04.67.60.36.00, ℱ04.67.60.36.58) at 2 rue Germain (just north of the Marché aux Fleurs), which administers a network of over six hundred rooms and apartments in the greater Montpellier area – a good option for medium to long stays and popular with students. The closest **campsite** to Montpellier is *L'Oasis Palavasienne* (☎04.67.15.11.61; April to mid–Oct), just south of town on the D21 (to Palavas; bus #28). There are also plenty in Palavas itself (see p.280).

Les Alizés 14 rue Jules-Ferry ☎04.67.12.85.35, ℱ04.67.12.85.20. Perhaps over-priced, but with a convenient station-side location. Amenities include en-suite bath, satellite TV in every room and a restaurant serving from 5am–1am. ❹

du Commerce 13 rue Maguelone ☎04.67.58.36.80, ℱ04.67.58.10.64. Centrally located and well-kept, despite the ageing and increasingly seedy-looking reception area. Good-sized rooms, some en suite with TV. ❷

Edouard VII 10 rue Aristide-Ollivier ☎04.67.58.42.13, ℱ04.67.58.93.66. Friendly place in a great nineteenth-century building with a striking facade and spacious interior. Every room has en-suite shower, toilet and TV. ❷

des Étuves 24 rue des Étuves ☎04.67.60.78.19, ⓦwww.hoteldesetuves.fr. Simple, spotless rooms in the south of the old city, all with en-suite bathrooms and TV. ❷

Floride 1 rue François-Perier ☎04.67.65.73.30, ℱ04.67.22.10.83. Friendly and clean, a young travellers' favourite in a pleasant neighbourhood, even if the rooms are a bit small. Some rooms with private bath, all with TV. ❷

Le Guilhem 18 rue J-J-Rousseau ☎04.67.52.90.90, ⓔhotel-le-guilhem@mnet.fr. Beautifully restored sixteenth-century town house whose cheerful rooms mostly overlook quiet gardens, and with a sunny breakfast terrace. ❺

L'Hôtel 6 rue Jules-Ferry ☎04.99.13.33.44, ⓔlhotel@wanadoo.fr. Newest and best of the station-side hotels – modern, clean and soundproof, with good amenities. Some rooms with bath. ❸

Majestic 4 rue de Cheval-Blanc ☎04.67.66.26.85, ℱ04.67.66.11.42. Very basic but clean, quiet and central, with rooms with en-suite showers. ❶

Le Mistral 25 rue Boussairolles ☎04.67.58.45.25, ℱ04.67.58.23.95. Comfortable and clean, a good option in the middle price range, offering satellite TV and garage parking (€5 extra). ❷

New Hôtel du Midi 22 bd Victor-Hugo ☎04.67.92.69.61, ⓦwww.new-hotel.com. A luxury option, but good value considering the level of service and the beauty of the building, right on the Comédie, in the old "Grand Hôtel du Midi" building. ❻

du Palais 3 rue du Palais ☎04.67.60.47.38, ℱ04.67.60.40.23. Tastefully renovated eighteenth-century mansion on the west side of the old town, blending modern and antique touches. Cosy rooms, most with en-suite facilities. ❹

Royal Hôtel 8 rue Maguelone ☎04.67.92.13.336, ⓦwww.hotel.royal-34.com. An ageing but well-maintained three-star hotel between the Comédie and the *gare*, with old-world service and comfortable if not overly large rooms. ❸

Sofitel Antigone 1 rue des Pertuisanes ☎04.67.99.72.72, ⓦwww.sofitel-montpellier.com. Suitably futuristic design, with a somewhat cold predominance of concrete over glass set in the city's flagship Antigone development. Four-star service and amenities including a pool. ❾

des Touristes 10 rue Baudin ☎04.67.58.42.37, ℱ04.67.92.61.37. Friendly, inexpensive hotel with well-maintained if somewhat spartan rooms. ❶

The Town

More or less everything you will want to see in Montpellier can be found in or on the edge of its compact and largely pedestrian **old town**, which spreads out north and west from the **place de la Comédie**, at the heart of the city. Bounded on the north by the boulevards Pasteur and Louis Blanc, on the east by the **Champ de Mars** park and on the west by the **Jardin des Plantes** and **place du Peyrou**, the terminus of the town's old aqueduct, the old centre is marked off into two unequal halves by the avenue made up of rues de la Loge and Foch.

▲ Water-jousting, Sète

The north side was the most prosperous part, as the **mansions** which pepper it testify, and is also home to the city's old university buildings and **cathedral**. The crowded lanes of the south side were inhabited by the city's workers and artisans; its buildings are correspondingly less showy. East of the place de la Comédie you'll find the sprawling **Antigone** development, Montpellier's boldly designed but sterile modern quarter. Beyond the old town are mixed commercial and residential quarters, which provide interesting backdrops to stroll past, if lacking in significant sights, while further out still, various **châteaux** ring the town.

ACCOMMODATION		RESTAURANTS	
Les Alizés	O	A. Cerdan	11
du Commerce	L	Abarcante	13
Edouard VII	I	Le Bistrot St-Côme	17
des Étuves	G	Chez Marceau	3
Floride	N	La Churrascaria	15
Le Guilhem	B	La Diligence	7
HI Hostel	A	Eden	14
L'Hôtel	M	Le Jardin des Sens	2
Majestic	H	L'Olivier	18
Le Mistral	J	Le Pastis	9
New Hôtel du Midi	F	La Pomme d'Or	6
du Palais	C	Le Prévert	10
Royal Hôtel	K	Le Prince de Menorque	16
Sofitel Antigone	E	Le Saleya	5
des Touristes	D	Salmon Shop	8
		Tripti Kulai	12
		Le Tropezienne	1
		Le Vieux Four	4

The place de la Comédie and the Champs de Mars park

The **place de la Comédie** is a broad plaza which was opened up in the mid-nineteenth century with the inauguration of the then new **opera hall** at its southern end. Although superseded by the new Corum hall, the gaily domed building still hosts music and theatre performances. Today the *place* to its north-east is a busy crossroads for both pedestrians and trams, and is lined on each side by a series of old cafés and fast-food joints, although it retains its traditional role as morning market-place (Mon–Sat 7.30am–1pm). At the northern end, the tourist office's pavilion marks the beginning of the **Champs de Mars**, a park with both a formal promenade and a network of paths and ponds which attract sunbathers and strollers in good weather.

The main attraction in the vicinity of the park is the huge **Musée Fabré** situated halfway up its west side, and containing an immense collection of paintings – overwhelmingly French and post-eighteenth century in content and bridging a range of styles including the local "luminophile" movement of the early nineteenth century. Works by better-known names include David's *Portrait of the Doctor, Alphonse Leroy* and Delacroix's *Fantasia*, as well as pieces by Dufy, Maillol and the local Frédéric Bazille. In addition to these, there are works by well-known foreign artists such as Reynolds, Zurbarán and Rubens. Unfortunately, the museum is undergoing an extensive renovation and is **closed** until 2006. In the meanwhile you can visit the museum's **pavilion** in the park opposite (Tues–Sun 1–7pm; €3), which houses rotating exhibitions featuring a selection of the main collection. To the south of this you'll find the small **Galerie Photo** (Tues–Sat 1–7pm; free) which hosts temporary exhibitions of contemporary photographers from around Europe. Across a small bridge by the pavilion you'll see the city's massive star-shaped seventeenth-century **citadel**, built in 1622 to guard the suspiciously Protestant-leaning town and now converted into a school. Finally, at the northern end of the park looms the concrete and pink granite **Le Corum** (July & Aug Sat & Sun 2–7pm; Sept–June Sat 2–7pm), designed by Claude Vasconi to house the city's new 2000-seat opera hall – the Opéra Berlioz – plus a convention centre and exhibition hall. During opening hours you can poke around the building and take in the sweeping **views** of the old city from its terrace.

Back at the place de la Comédie heading east brings you to the Triangle shopping centre, which marks the beginning of the Antigone development (see p.272); south down to the *gares* you'll find a bustling neighbourhood of shops and restaurants; while northwest from here is the core of the old town.

From place de la Comédie to place de la Canourgue

After the Musée Fabré, Montpellier's greatest attraction is its old town, richly adorned by elaborate mansion facades and home to a series of small museums. Rue de la Loge, the city's main shopping street, leads northwest into the old centre from in front of the former opera. Just off this at 7 rue Jacques-Coeur is the impressive fifteenth-century facade of the Hôtel de Trésoriers de France, now home to the **Musée Languedocien** (Mon–Sat 2–5pm; €5). This museum is worthy of a visit not only for its collection of medieval artefacts, which include thirteenth-century ceramics and a curious lead baptismal font, but for the impressively vaulted Gothic interior of the main exhibition room. You'll also find luxurious Flemish tapestries, pre-Revolution furniture – including a seventeenth-century Italian celestial globe – and a collection of *faïence*, whose manufacture was an important industry here throughout the 1700s. Just northwest of here, the compact, triangular place de Pétrarque is closed in by a clutch of palaces, the largest of which is the **Hôtel de Varennes**, at no. 2, whose ground floor is almost entirely Gothic in style, and includes the beautiful fourteenth-century **salle de Petrarch**, a long hall vaulted with delicate stone ribs. On the first floor is the **Musée de l'Histoire de Montpellier** (Tues–Sat 9.30am–noon & 1.30–5pm; €1.50), whose dull collection is dominated by portraits of city luminaries and assorted regalia of the town's public offices. On the next floor up, the **Musée Fougau** (Wed & Thurs 3–6pm; free) houses a similarly unexciting exhibition on traditional rural life, including nineteenth-century costumes, tools and household implements.

From place Petrarch you can head back down to the main street via the live-ly café-lined place Jean–Jaurès, or follow rue Foch west into the wide *place* dominated by the city's *préfecture*, adjacent to which is a colourful market square, the place du Marché-aux-Fleurs. Around here you'll find a concentra-tion of mansions, particularly on **rue du Cannau**, whose string of facades, decked out with ornately carved doorways and casement windows, attest to the wealth of this street – a prestigious neighbourhood three centuries ago. If you continue north along Cannau you'll eventually reach the hulking stone mass of the former **Ursuline convent**, built in the seventeenth century and later converted into a prison; today it is a centre for dance performance. Heading west from Marché aux Fleurs, will take you past the **Hôtel de la Vieille Intendance**, the former governor's mansion at no. 9 on the street of the same name, a stately palace which was later home of the philosopher Auguste Comte and writer Paul Valéry. South of here, quiet place du Chabanneau, whose mod-est old houses box in a gurgling eighteenth-century **fountain**, makes a good place to pause and enjoy a terrace-side drink before you continue to **place de la Canourgue**. This larger plaza served as the eighteenth-century adminstra-tive hub of the city. Its eastern side is dominated by the huge **Hôtel de Richer**, the former town hall, whose broad square courtyard is decorated in the finest Neoclassical pomp of the late 1700s. The square is ringed by further magnificent frontages; including the stone-carved faces which cap each win-dow of the Hôtel de Cambacères across the square at no. 3.

The cathedral and around

From here it's just a short descent north to Montpellier's **cathedral** (Mon–Sat 9.30–noon & 2.30–7pm, Sun 9am–1pm), with its strikingly bizarre entrance, a porch flanked by two straight towers capped with high conical roofs. The effect, which resembles two old-fashioned rockets, smacks of a Viollet-le-Duc initia-tive but is, in fact, original – dating back to the church's fourteenth-century foundation. It is also the most interesting feature of the cathedral, whose dark and bare interior is hardly worth poking your head inside. The cathedral has a covered cloister, which you can't enter, but can view from the back porch of the **Faculty of Médecin**, next door in rue de l'École du Médecin. The stately Neoclassical faculty building occupies the grounds of the now-vanished Benedictine monastery which the cathedral once served as chapel. Passing through the main doors, flanked by bronzes of local medical giants Barthez and Lapeyronie, you'll find the interior is decorated with marble columns and rich low-relief detailing around the windows and ceilings. The back porch is oppo-site the entrance, while up on the first floor, you'll find two noteworthy muse-ums. The larger of these is the **Musée Atger** (Mon, Wed & Thurs 1.30–5.45pm; free), an art museum named after the local artist Xavier Atger, whose sketches make up the core of the collection, although you'll also discover contemporary southern French art, as well as paintings by noteworthy Flemish artists such as Rubens and Van Dyck. While on the first floor, the strong of stomach can also visit the **anatomy museum** (daily 2.30–5pm; free) a library of specimens, models and manuscripts relating to vivisection.

At the end of rue de l'École de Médecine, which is lined with nineteenth-century university buildings, the **Jardin des Plantes** (July & Aug daily noon–8pm; Sept–June 2–5pm; free) marks the transition to the new town. Managed by the university's botany department, its well-maintained paths lead among an impressive variety of plant specimens, from tropical to temperate. The garden dates back to 1593, when it was founded by order of the former Huguenot king, Henry IV, in order to cultivate and study herbal remedies.

Place du Peyrou and south of rue Foch

Rising above the Jardin on the edge of the old *enceinte*, the flat paved expanse of the **place du Peyrou** stretches west, flanked on either side by wide beds of colourful flowers. The plaza itself is dominated by a Roman-style equestrian statue of the "Emperor" Louis XIV – an 1838 replacement of the original statue of 1692, which was destroyed during the Revolution. The great bronze king is frozen in motionless stride towards the **Arc de Triomf**, opposite the eastern end of the park, at the head of rue Foch. The arch, designed on the ancient Roman model, consists of a single, free-standing entryway, whose sides are covered with low-relief sculptures celebrating the military victories of the "Sun King" over the Dutch and the Huguenots, the revocation of the Edict of Nantes and the construction of the Canal du Midi. Behind Louis' statue, at the western end of the place du Peyrou, an octagonal, colonnaded pavilion marks the terminus of the 880metre-long aqueduct of St-Clément, built in the late eighteenth century to carry water to the city from a nearby spring. The Neoclassical pavilion was the work of Jean Giral, the same architect who designed the Faculty of Medicine. From the two levels of terraces over which the pavilion stands, you can enjoy views over the city and a hazy panorama of the flat Languedocian littoral fading off towards the distant Mont St-Loup.

From Peyrou, passing through the triumphal arch you'll come face to face with the striking Neoclassical **Palais de Justice**, which features a Doric-columned facade capped by an impressive tympanum in relief. From here, rue Foch sets out eastwards towards the *préfecture*, but before you reach it take a right into rue Petit Scel; here, at no. 4, sits the former palace of Francese de Cazelli, a noblewoman named as governor of the coastal town of Leucate by the king in 1590 after she commanded its defence, refusing to surrender even in exchange for the life of her captured husband. The nearby plain stone nineteenth-century **church of St-Anne** is only really of interest for the occasional art exhibitions it houses; it's also the epicentre of the "L'Isle aux Createurs", a collective of a dozen or so designers of decorative goods who have set up workshop-boutiques throughout the zone. South of the church on rue de l'Huile, you'll enter the city's old **artisanal quarter**, containing houses that survive from as early as the thirteenth century.

This neighbourhood is bounded on the east by rue St-Guilhem, a street of functional, quotidian shops, beyond which you'll find a succession of squares – good territory for restaurant-hunting. At the northernmost of these, place St-Ravy, are the scant remains of the **palace** of the kings of Mallorca and, crossing the colourful rue de l'Ancien Courrier, you'll pass the ruined church of St-Roch to arrive at a busy little bar-lined plaza at the end of rue Plan d'Agde. Just to the east, on the far side of the terrace-choked place St-Côme, squats the marvellous **hôtel** of the same name, girded by a double row of columns and capped by a low cupola. This edifice, built by Giral in the eighteenth century as an anatomical theatre, was donated to the city at the bequest of the Royal Surgeon François Gigot. Just to the south of it you'll come upon a final small *place*, set in the shadow of the **Tour de la Babote**, the only surviving portion of the town's twelfth-century defences. Crowned by an observatory in the 1700s it was also incorporated into the same semaphore system used at the Tour Chappe in Castelnaudary (see p.109).

The Antigone

Cut off from the main part of the old city by the hideous sprawl of the Le Polygone shopping complex and defended on the north and south by a whizzing expressway, the **Antigone**, twenty-first-century Montpellier, is a world apart from that of the eighteenth. Laid out on an esplanade stretching east from the city for almost 2km, this self-contained and car-free development of residences, shops, services and restaurants is endowed with an uncompromising unity of form and design. The Catalan architect Ricard Bofill has created a massive low-rise building complex, drawing largely on Classical motifs, including smooth columns, triangular window lintels and roof cornices reminiscent of ancient temples, but with a net effect that looks somehow futuristic–Georgian. The first section, the westernmost part of the complex, was inaugurated in 1984, and the latest, a library designed by Paris-born architect Paul Chemetov, opened in late 2000. The whole thing, a striking if not entirely convincing Utopian landscape of broad cypress-lined courtyards, culminates in the monumental Esplanade de l'Europe on the bank of the River Lez, across which it gazes at the recently inaugurated Hôtel de Région, the governmental seat of Languedoc-Roussillon. It's an ambitious project, and you cannot deny it a certain graceful beauty, but it is somehow disappointing – perhaps it just needs some weathering to shake off the air of contrived novelty. For the time being, the grandeur of the buildings and the breadth of its plazas only serves to reinforce a feeling of emptiness. As a visitor to Montpellier, it would be a mistake not to see Antigone for yourself, but in the end it is nothing more than an elaborate suburb, and a quick walk through will likely exhaust your interest.

Beyond the old town

Aside from those in old Montpellier and the Antigone, there are number of sights scattered around the city. Just to the southwest of the old town in the local military academy on avenue Lepic, you can visit an **infantry museum** (Mon & Wed–Sat 2–5.30pm; bus #7 from the *gare*; €3), which holds a collection of uniforms and memorabilia from over the last five centuries. To the north, you'll find the city's eighty-hectare **Parc Zoologique de Lunaret** (July & Aug 8am–7pm; Sept–June 8am–6pm; bus #9 to "René Bouginol"; free), a sprawling park with nearly 10km of paths leading through to spacious animal enclosures. Also, in the north end of town, you'll find Montpellier's newest attraction, **Agropolis** (Wed–Mon 2–6pm; €5), located at 951 av d'Agropolis (shuttle bus from tram stop "St-Eloi"). This original multimedia museum explores the history of agriculture and food, with a particular emphasis on Languedoc; its interactive displays make it an entertaining stop for children.

The main attraction of Montpellier's hinterland, however, is the series of **follies** raised by the town's wealthiest citizens as summerhouses in the 1700s. In a game of social one-upmanship, merchants and aristocrats vied to construct ever more luxurious estates, a few of which have been opened to the public, and are accessible by city transport. To the east of the centre at 2235 route de Vaugières (tram #1 "Odysseum"), the eighteenth-century **Château de la Mogère** (June–Oct daily 2.30–6pm; Nov–May Sat & Sun 2.30–6pm or by appointment ✆04.67.5672.01; €5) is one of the most sumptuous of the mansions, and contains a considerable collection of period furniture and artwork, but perhaps the oldest and most elegant is the **Château de Flaugergues** (visits by appointment only; ✆04.67.56.66.37, ✉colbert@flaugergues.com; €6.50), just to the north of la Mogère at 1744 avenue Albert Einstein (bus #12 "Louis Lépine"). Still lorded over by the original family which built the palace in 1696, the luxurious apartments, decked out with contemporary tapestries and *objets d'art*, and accompanying formal French gardens, sit amidst the vineyards of its *domaine* (Mon–Sat 9am–12.30pm & 2.30–7pm, also Sun 2.30–7pm in July & Aug). The furthest out is former bishop's palace, the **Château de**

Lavérune, which involves a considerable walk from the bus stop ("Les Bouisses", lines #4, #7 & La Ronde); it's worth it, however, to visit the **Hofer-Bufy museum** (Sat & Sun 3–7pm; €2), host to temporary painting exhibitions (check with the tourist office for the current programme).

Eating, drinking and nightlife

No other city in Languedoc and Roussillon, with the possible exception of much larger Toulouse, can compete with Montpellier in terms of either dining possibilities or cultural life. Cuisine in Montpellier is a combination of the bounty of the sea, the rich garden produce of the plain and the meats of the hills. Fish lovers should look out for the savoury, tomato-based seafood stew known as *tielle*, or crab-stuffed squid tails (*enornets farcis*) while *gâteau d'áubergine* (aubergine cake) makes a delicious meat-free option. Far from the *manades* of Gard, pork makes a triumphant reappearance here as sausage, cured ham and paté, with duck and goose in strong supporting roles. In addition to its *terroir* options, the city has a wide range of ethnic **restaurants**, rich *gastronomique* pickings and a lively **café** culture sustained by the university community.

The **nightlife** in Montpellier is also excellent, with an incredible number of **bars**, **clubs** and **live music** options. You'll be able to find everything you need in the old town and its environs, but die-hard clubbers will want to head for the string of nightclubs (*boîtes de nuit*) on the route de Palavas in Lattes. Fortunately, many of these are served by l'Amigo, TAM's night service (till 5am), so you may not have to take a taxi home (TAM can provide a list of nightclubs served by the route). These clubs are supplemented by a profusion of **café-littéraires** on a variety of themes (some permanent, some occasional); the restaurant *Le César*, 17 pl du Nombre d'Or (☎04.67.20.27.02) holds two regular *café-littéraires* (both 6.30–8.30pm) – a general colloquium on the third Monday of each month, and a feminist one on the first Monday. **Concerts**, ranging from chamber music to classical as well as opera, are held at l'Opéra de la Comédie (☎04.67.60.19.99), the L'Opéra Berlioz in Le Corum (☎04.67.61.66.16), which also serves as a major venue for pop music, and at other venues – the tourist office has a complete list. The **theatre** scene thrives here too, with nearly a dozen regular stages scattered throughout town. Major performances are held at the Opéra, while you'll also find informal *café-théâtres*, like Le Cicrane on 9 rue St-Ursule (☎04.67.60.74.11). If you fancy the **cinema**, the Diagonal complex at place Pierre-Enaidel (☎04.67.58.44.74) is the place to head for.

Naturally, things tend to be quieter out of academic season, but there is still plenty to do, and the beaches and bars of Palavas are only a bus ride away.

Restaurants

Practically every one of the squares of Montpellier's old town has a **restaurant** or two, so if you don't feel like searching out something special, you need do no more than wander around and pick from among the many terraces.

A. Cerdan 8 rue Collot ☎04.67.60.86.96. High-quality cuisine combining Norman and Algerian specialities, just off the *Comédie*. Lunch from €8 and dinners €12.60–32.50. Closed Sun.
Abarcante 18 rue de St-Sépulchre ☎04.67.60.20.91. Funky little one-man show run by Arnaud, who cooks market-fresh food here

daily. *Plat du jour* at €7 and *menu* for €9.80. It's also an antique shop. Closed Sun.
Le Bistrot St-Côme 2 pl St-Côme. The best of a phalanx of open-air eateries dominating the south side of pl St-Côme. Service from noon till 11.30pm, and a range of *menus* and standard but dependable French fare (€12–21.50).

Chez Marceau 7 pl de la Chapelle Neuve ☎04.67.66.08.09. Excellent-value Languedocian cuisine (both inland and coastal varieties) with a wonderful shaded terrace. The *pâtés de canard* are particularly notable. *Menus* €10–20. Closed Sun lunch in summer, otherwise Sun & Wed.

La Churrascaria 17 pl du Nombre d'Or ☎04.67.22.10.75. Brazilian restaurant in the west of the Antigone, with a large terrace and small but cheerful dining room. Roast meat is the speciality, from €16. Closed Sun & Aug.

La Diligence 2 pl Pétrarque ☎04.67.66.12.21. Atmospheric vaulted medieval setting for innovative French dishes. *Menus* are €18–58, and offer a good-value dip into the finest French cuisine. Closed Sat lunch, Sun & Mon lunch.

Eden 12 bd Sarrail ☎04.67.66.18.04. An airy bistro, featuring Lyonnaise cuisine as well as the usual Gallic stand-bys. Expect to spend €12 and up. Also has a parkside patio. Open daily 8am–midnight.

Le Jardin des Sens 11 av St-Lazaire ☎04.67.79.63.38. One of the highest-rated restaurants in Languedoc and universally acclaimed as Montpellier's best, just north of Le Corum. Excellent *terroir*-based creations in elegant surroundings. *Menus* €46–130. Closed Sun, Mon & Wed lunch.

L'Olivier 12 rue Aristide-Olivier ☎04.67.92.86.28. Pretty little restaurant north of the station offering excellent-value traditional French cuisine. *Menus* €26–43. Closed Sun, Mon and Aug.

Le Pastis 3 rue Terral ☎04.67.02.78.59. Great southern French cooking in a fine old mansion. Lunch *menu* at €14, dinner from €23. Closed lunch Mon & Sat, all day Sun.

La Pomme d'Or 23 rue du Palais des Guilhem ☎04.67.52.82.62. Arty restaurant-bar with a predominantly gay clientele. A very wide selection of inventive *menus* at €15.

Le Prévert 8 rue Ste-Anne. A funky little place in the shadow of the Church of St-Anne. The tiny dining room with its clutch of tables is supplemented by a terrace which spills out into the adjacent square. Imaginative combinations in the €9.50 *formule*. Open for lunch Tues–Fri.

Le Prince de Menorque 1 rue des Tessiers ☎04.67.66.05.77. Great-value Mediterranean food, in a cheerful setting with a streetside patio. Solid *plats du jour* at only €8.50, *menus* from €16. Open for lunch Tues–Sat, dinner Thurs–Sun.

Le Saleya Pl du Marché aux Fleurs ☎04.67.60.53.92. In fine weather, join the locals at the outdoor tables to feast on a daily selection of market-fresh fish and regional fare for €12. Open for lunch mid-March to Oct, and also evenings June–Sept, depending on the weather.

Salmon Shop 5 rue de la Petite-Loge. Novel "mountain cabin" interior offering oak-smoked salmon main courses in half-a-dozen guises from €11 to €28 (including wine). Just off place Jean-Jaurès. Closed Sun lunch.

Tripti Kulai 20 rue Jacques-Coeur. Quirky, friendly women-run vegetarian restaurant. Dishes with oriental-influenced flair, including a good choice of salads, from €7. Closed Sun.

Le Tropezienne 55bis rue de la Cavalerie ☎04.99.58.18.91. Elegant but modern restaurant featuring a range of dishes, from fresh shellfish to specialities of Aveyron. Open for dinner till 11.30pm with *menus* from €15 to €25.50 and a lunch special for €10. Closed Sat & Sun lunch, all day Mon.

Le Vieux Four 59 rue de l'Aiguillerie ☎04.67.60.55.95. Meat-eaters should head for this cosy, candlelit place specializing in *grillades au feu de bois* – meats roasted on an open spit. *Menus* €19.50–25. Eves only; closed Sun in summer.

Cafés, bars and clubs

Antidote Pl de la Canourgue. Snappy bar which attracts the arty set. Techno-music dominates, and there are occasional art exhibitions. Mon–Thurs till 1am, Fri & Sat 2am.

Arts et Buffet Pl St-Roch. Tucked behind the St-Roch church, this delightful *salon du thé* is great for breakfast, a tea break or light meals of salads, home-made pies and cakes. Magazines and books available, some in English. Closed Mon & Tues.

Café de la Mer 5 pl de Marché-aux-Fleurs. Popular gay-friendly establishment with a busy terrace. Mon–Sat 8am–1am, Sun 3pm–1am, open till 2am in July & Aug.

Cargo Pl Ste-Denis ☎04.67.92.56.05. Montpellier's best nightclub and live venue for blues, funk and soul. A ten-minute walk south of the old town. Tues–Sat 7pm–1am. Entry free or up to €4.50 on weekends, or for concerts or special events.

Charlier Bière 22 rue A. Olliver. Grungy beer bar for the under-25 crowd. The slogan "Helping ugly people have sex since 1862," says it all.

JAM (Jazz Action Montpellier) 100 rue Ferdinan-Lesspes ☎04.67.58.30.30. Jazz bar, concert venue and home of the regular *café-littéraire* "Ethnologue" on the first Wed of month (8pm–midnight).

Aux Mille et une Feuilles d'Or 20 pl du Nombre
d'Or. Funky little tearoom/bookshop in the
Antigone. Relax over a pot of any one of a range of
herbal or regular teas. Open Mon–Sat 11am–7pm;
also serves lunch.

Rockstore, 20 rue Verdun. Legendary Montpellier
club and concert venue. You can't miss the half-
Cadillac protruding from the front of this former

Calvinist temple. Free except for concerts.
Mon–Sat 6pm–4am.

Ysis 1384 av de la Mer ☎04.67.20.25.40,
ⓦwww.ysis.fr. Flash new nightclub, open nightly
from midnight till 6am, with an in-house restaurant,
Club 379 (8.30pm–4am). Features the "price shaker" drinks system whereby, like the stock market,
booze prices rise and fall according to demand.

Listings

Airlines Air France ☎04.67.22.65.05, ⓦwww.air-
france.com; Air Liberté ☎08.03.80.58.05; Air
Littoral ☎08.03.83.48.34, ⓦwww.air-littoral.fr;
British Airways ☎08.02.80.29.02,
ⓦwww.britishairways.com; Ryanair
☎04.68.71.96.65, ⓦwww.ryanair.com.

Airport Aéroport de Montpellier Méditerranée
☎04.67.20.85.00, ⓦwww.montpellier.aeroport.fr.

Banks All major French banks are represented,
most with branches in rue de la Loge, place de la
Comédie or rue de Maguelone.

Books English books at: As You Like It, 8 rue du
Bras de Fer; Book Shop, 4 rue de l'Université.
Travel books at Les Cinq Continents, 20 rue
Jacques-Coeur.

Bus information ☎04.67.92.01.43.

Car rental ADA, 58bis bd Clémenceau
☎04.67.58.34.35; Avis, 900 av Prés d'Arènes
☎04.67.92.51.92, ⓦwww.avis.com; Europcar, 6
rue Jules-Ferry ☎04.67.06.89.00, ⓦwww.europ-
car.com; Hertz, 18 rue J-Ferry ☎04.67.58.65.18,
ⓦwww.hertz.com; Rent-a-Car, 111 av de Palavas
☎04.67.22.42.52.

Consulates Britain, 64 rue Alcyone (by appointment only, ☎04.67.15.34.04).

Cultural associations Centre Culturel Juif, 5000
bd Antigone ☎04.67.15.08.76; Institut Franco-
American, 55 rue du Mistral ☎04.67.20.05.09;
Maison de Cambridge, 1 rue du Général-Riu
☎04.67.64.07.86.

Internet access There are lots of cybercafés
around town; try Cybersurf, 22 pl du Millénaire in
Antigone (Mon–Fri 8am–9pm, Sat & Sun
10am–6pm).

Language courses French courses are offered by
several academies including: AICF, 3 rue
Boussairolloes ☎04.67.34.07.79,
ⓔas.inter@wanadoo.fr; École Méditerranée de
Langue Française, 32 rue de l'Argenterie

☎04.67.66.14.51, ⓦwww.ecolemed.com;
Langues Sans Frontières (☎04.67.91.31.60,
ⓦwww.lsf.fr); and various others (consult tourist
office)

Laundry 11 rue Serane (daily 7.30am–10pm).

Markets There are two main covered markets:
Castellane, rue de la Loge; and Laissac, pl A.-
Laissac (both Mon–Sat 7.30am–1pm). There are
also outdoor markets (Mon–Sat 7.30am–1pm) in
Antigone (Wed & Sun only), bd des Arceaux (organ-
ic food), av de Heidelberg (flea market, also Sun),
cours Gambetta (food and clothes) and pl de la
Comédie (food and clothes).

Medical emergencies ☎04.67.22.81.67 or ☎15;
Centre Hospitalier de Montpellier, 555 rte de
Ganges (☎04.67.33.93.02) – take bus #16 from
the *gare* to "Route de Ganges" or the tram to
"Hôpital Lapeyronie" and walk.

Police Hôtel de Ville ☎04.67.34.71.00.

Regional Products Maison Régionale des Vins et
des Produits du Terroir, 34 rue St-Guilhem
(Mon–Sat 9am–8pm).

Swimming Piscine Olympique d'Antigone, av
Jacques-Quartier (☎04.67.15.63.00; tram to
"Léon Blum").

Taxis Allo Taxi d'Oc ☎04.67.47.26.80; Taxi 2000
☎04.67.03.45.45; Taxi à Montpellier
☎04.67.20.35.20; Taxi Bleu or 5 ACTM
☎04.67.0.20.00.

Train information ☎04.99.74.15.10.

Travel agencies USIT Connect, 1 rue de
l'Université ☎08.25.08.25.25, ⓦwww.usitcon-
nect.fr; Nouvelles Frontières, 4 rue Jeanne d'Arc
☎04.67.64.64.15.

Youth information CRIJ, 3 av Charles-Flahault
☎04.67.04.36.66. Youth information and a ride-
sharing service, Allostop ☎04.67.04.28.28. Also
Espace Montpellier Jeunesse, 6 rue Maguelone
(Mon–Fri noon–6pm; ☎04.67.92.30.50).

The coast: La Grande-Motte to Pézenas

From its narrowing point at Le Grau-du-Roi, south of Nîmes, the Petite Camargue trails off westwards in fits and starts – a string of salty *étangs* and scrubby flats populated by birds and bulls respectively, passing close by Montpellier and continuing as far as Agde (see p.330). The easternmost town along this stretch is **La Grande-Motte**, a bizarre 1960s planned resort handy for getting to the ruins of **Ambrussum** a few kilometres inland, where the great Via Domitia once carried goods from Cadiz, past Gibraltar, all the way to Rome. The other towns along this coast – **Palavas**, **Sète** and **Mèze** – have been fishing centres for generations, and their maritime heritage lives on in popular local traditions, such as the water-joust. Only **Maguelone**, once a bustling port, was unable to stand the test of the ages, and has been reduced to an ancient and romantically sited **cathedral**. Extremely popular and flooded with people in the summer months, all of these towns offer the makings of a good beach holiday, but they are far from being merely soulless seaside resorts. Finally, Languedoc's first modern capital, **Pézenas**, sits a few kilometres inland, now a town of beautifully preserved pre-Revolution palaces.

La Grande-Motte and around

Separated by only a few kilometres of sandy beach from Le Grau-du-Roi to the east and less than 20km southeast of Montpellier's centre, **LA GRANDE-MOTTE** is undoubtedly the oddest resort town on the French Mediterranean. A Sixties-era beachside version of Montpellier's Antigone development, this "futuristic" planned community, executed by Jean Balladur has aged about as gracefully as the beanbag chair and eight-track tape. Begun in 1967, the town consists of an immense array of weirdly shaped sand-coloured condos and apartment complexes with evocative names like "Le Calypso" and "Temple du Soleil", set on a long boardwalk. Traffic is banished to the background; you park (if you can find space) in the back streets, and reach the beach on foot. The strange aspect of the seafront is compounded by the absence of trees – nothing breaks up the pale beige landscape sandwiched between sea and sky – and, to cap it off, the proliferation of restaurants and shops on the promenade makes the whole place feel like an enormous shopping mall that just happens to have a beach. Aside from its peculiar looks though, the town is a run-of-the-mill family-holiday seaside resort, where apartments and hotels usually book for two- to four-week blocks. It's as good a place as any to stop for a swim, and if you want to spend a couple of days on the beach, you'll find all of the facilities and services you would expect.

Practicalities

La Grande-Motte's **tourist office** (July & Aug 9am–9pm; Sept–June 9am–12.30pm & 2–6pm; ☎04.67.56.42.00, ⓦwww.ot-lagrandemotte.fr) is on allée des Parcs, at the entrance to the town. **Buses** come in at the *gare routière*, located just to the east of the tourist office on avenue de Megueil. The most appealing among the town's dozen or so near-identical **hotels** is the *Azur Bord du Mer* (☎04.67.56.56.00, ⓦwww.hotelazur.net; ❷–❺); set out dramatically on the extremity of the town's quay, it is no more expensive than the larger, uglier places stuck in the town itself. A cluster of seven **campsites** sits just west of the tourist office, among them *Louis Pibols* (☎04.67.56.50.08; April–Oct) and *Le Garden* (☎04.67.56.50.09; March–Oct) – both close to the beaches and with good facilities. The only **restaurant** which stands out above the uniform beachside fare is *Alexandre* (☎04.67.56.63.63; closed Sun eve & Mon) on esplanade de la Capitainerie, with good views of the port (menus from €25; closed Sun lunch & Mon). **Bikes** and scooters can be rented at Bumpcycles at 172 rue des Artisans in the *Zone Industrielle* (☎04.67.29.87.73, Ⓦwww.rosalies.fr), and Holiday Bikes at 476 avenue de Melgueil (☎04.67.24.19.30, Ⓔgrand-motte@holiday-biks.com), as well as at numerous other beachside outfits.

Lunel and Ambrussum

Marking the northwestern extent of the Petit Camargue, **LUNEL** is just 14km north of La Grande-Motte, on the western side of the Vidourle river. Aside from a few medieval buildings scattered about the decaying old town, the place is unforgivingly nondescript, and the only reason you should contemplate stopping here is to visit the nearby but scant ruins of Roman Ambrussum, or to partake in the town's lively tradition of *tauromachie* – bullfights are held occasionally from the spring to mid-autumn.

If you're interest lies with the former, you'll most likely want to catch the first bus to Villetelle, which can drop you within a few kilometres (just before the A9 motorway; follow the signposted gravel road) of the Roman remains of **Ambrussum**. This settlement (guided tours June–Aug Wed 3pm & Sat 10am; free entry) once commanded the bridge which carried the Via Domitia over the Vidourle, and which is now reduced to a couple of massive supports rising romantically out of the river. To get to the ruins, climb the stairs on the hillside, to the old Roman **road**. Where this forks, taking the left will lead you past a series of indecipherable foundations and on to the remnants of the town's once formidable five-metre-thick walls. There are good **views** from up top, but the ruins themselves are disappointingly insubstantial. The visit is further frustrated by a total lack of informative plaques, but despite these shortcomings, the ruins are a popular spot for locals – the riverside is quite beautiful, its trail makes for a pleasant walk and the area is prime for picnicking.

A stop on the Montpellier–Nîmes line, Lunel's **gare SNCF** is on rue Verdun; from here it's a fifteen-minute walk south to the **tourist office** (July & Aug Mon–Sat 9am–7pm, Sun 9.30am–12.30pm; Sept–June Mon–Sat 9am–noon & 2–6pm, Sun 9.30am–12.30pm; ☎04.67.71.01.37, Ⓦwww.ot-paysdelunel.fr) on cours Georges-Péri, beside the church in the old town. The summer-only (mid-June to mid-Sept) "Comet" **bus** service from La Grande-Motte stops at the main roundabout by the rue République, which is also where you get the bus towards Ambrussum. If you get stuck here for the night, *Las Mimosas*, on avenue de Vidourle (☎04.67.71.25.40; ❷), makes for cheap and adequate digs, and you can get a decent meal at *L'Auberge des Halles* (closed Sun eve, Mon & Feb; *menus* from €15) beside the tourist office. There are several **campsites** in the neighbourhood, including *Bon Port* on route de Camargue, just south of town (☎04.67.71.15.65; April–Sept).

Palavas and Maguelone

PALAVAS-LES-FLOTS is Montpellier's own beach town, now absorbed into the metropolitan *agglomération* and even served by regular city buses. The town has been a popular seaside destination for almost a century, a fact attested to by the satirical caricatures of its inhabitants and visitors drawn by Montpellier artist Albert Dubout (1905–76). It's not as dismal as it seems, either, for once you penetrate the surrounding developments you'll find that the oldest part, where the banks of the canalized River Lez reach the sea, still retains the air of a pretty old fishing town. That said, Palavas is a busy, modern resort complete with all that that implies: restaurants of dubious quality, stores selling colourful junk and crowds of people enjoying themselves swimming, sunbathing, sailing and cycling. Like so much of the coast, the town is built on a sand bar which encloses a series of *étangs*, the smallest of which, the Lac du Levant, on the north side of the old quarter, has a small eighteenth-century fort, La Redoubte, in the middle. Reached by a long causeway, the fort now houses the **Musée Albert Dubout** (Jan & Dec Sat & Sun 2–6pm; Feb, March, Oct & Nov Wed–Sun 2–6pm; April–June & Sept Wed–Sun 2–7pm; July & Aug daily 4pm–midnight; €3.10 including the Musée du Train), which holds works of the artist. Back on the mainland, a **Musée du Train** (same hours and ticket as Musée Dubout) houses the steam locomotive which used to run between here and Montpellier and was a favourite subject of Dubout (you'll see it in several of the works on display in the museum). The *étangs* themselves are replete with birdlife, and are one of the few places on the French coast where you will see flamingos in their habitat; the tourist office can arrange **bird-watching** trips (Mon–Fri 9am–noon; €5).

The most interesting section of **beach** and the best for swimming and sunbathing lies west of the main town, past the campsite. You can get there by TAM bus or, if you drive, you will be obliged (mid-June to mid-Sept) to use the free car park. From the parking area, a narrow sand spit stretches west, separated from the *étang* behind by a shrubby embankment; the beach here is a popular gay spot and given over generally to nude (rather than topless) bathing. A road runs along the inland side of the embankment on which a free *petit train* runs every twenty minutes, ferrying people from their cars to the beach and on to the isthmus of **MAGUELONE** (TAM buses do the route out of season).

You wouldn't guess it, but the Romanesque **cathedral**, built in the 1100s and dominating the green promontory today, was for centuries one of the most important churches in the medieval South of France. Before accumulating silt linked it to the mainland, Maguelone was an island, most likely first settled by the Phoenicians. In the early eighth century, the town here was taken by Muslim forces, but Charles Martel, court chamberlain and de facto ruler of France, pushed back the Muslim advance and destroyed the settlement in 737 to prevent its recapture and use as a forward base for further attacks. Refounded in 1030, the strongly fortified church became an important religious centre and a place of refuge for bishops and popes in their quarrels with the nobility and kings of Europe. In 1096, Urban II proclaimed Maguelone as the second church after Rome – an indulgence which guaranteed the complete forgiveness of sins of whoever was buried there. Shortly thereafter, the church was rebuilt in its present form. With the papal blessing and in its recovered role as port, the town throve from the Middle Ages until the Wars of Religion, when Louis XIII destroyed it for its unrepentant Protestantism. Nowadays, all that remains is the ancient church. The building is still a place of worship, so you won't be able to enter it in beachwear, although you'll be able to see its marble **portal**, with excellent mid-twelfth-century low-relief carvings of apostles Peter and Paul. The **interior** (daily 10am–6.30pm; free), which has suffered total looting through the ages, is dominated by a huge overhanging gallery. You'll find some ancient tombstones down by the altar, and from the gallery you can look down through the sluices over the entrance, which were intended to pour hot oil on the heads of attackers. The rest of the island is a verdant idyll, and on the north shore, some restored fishermen's huts evoke the Maguelone of the early twentieth century, when the once glorious town had revived as poor fishing hamlet.

Practicalities

TAM **buses** (line #17; pick it up from tram stop "Port Marrianne") from Montpellier circulate throughout the town. Palavas' **tourist office** (April, May & Sept daily 9am–noon & 2–6pm; July & Aug daily 10am–8pm; Oct–March Mon–Sat 9am–noon & 2–6pm; T04.67.07.73.34, Wwww.palavaslesflots.com) is in the unmistakable lighthouse building which towers above the port. For **accommodation**, try the comfortable beachside *Le Golfe* (T04.67.68.01.87, F04.67.68.30.88; April–Sept; ❹), just under 1km east of the tourist office, or the central *Le France*, at 9 quai Clémenceau (T & F04.67.74.00.35; ❷), both of which are good value, with excellent locations. There are several **campsites** around town, most along avenue St-Maurice, but the best-situated is the beachside *Palavas Camping* (T04.67.68.01.28; mid-May to mid-Sept) at the westernmost part of town. You'll have no problem finding a **restaurant** here; the ones that stand out from the bunch include the riverside *La Marine* (T04.67.68.00.05; €28 and upwards), for its original seafood creations, *Les Flots Bleus* (T04.67.68.01.73; *menu* from €17; closed part Jan) at 21 quai Georges-Clémenceau, for its grilled monkfish, and the elegant *Les Embruns* (T04.67.68.16.95; menu €19–42) at 3 av Général-de-Gaulle, which specializes in lobster and turbot and has fine views over the canal.

Sète

Some 38km west along the marshy coast from Maguelone, and a twenty-minute ride by train or car from Montpellier, the cranes and winches of **SÈTE**'s busy port rise above the expanse of *étangs*. Entering town from this direction you find yourself surrounded by grey warehouses, fenced-in storage yards and stacks of freight containers. This initial vision is somewhat disconcerting, but if you fight the impulse to turn back, you'll cross the wide Canal Maritime and arrive at the colourful old quarter, which straddles the westernmost of the two north–south canals, the Canal Royal. On the west bank of the canal, the land rises dramatically, hedging in the historical centre. This slope is the eastern side of the 175m-high rocky promontory, **Mont St-Clair**, whose presence has determined the growth of the town. As it expanded early in the last century, Sète grew as a long corniche completely circling the *mont*, but recently suburbs have begun to climb its steep slopes. The attractive town has a couple of small museums and a park, but primarily makes a good base for enjoying the twenty-kilometre long unbroken stretch of beach west towards Agde – it also has accommodation, excellent pleasure-port facilities and lively nightlife in summer. The best beach reachable by public transport (buses #6, 7 & 9) – and with showers and other amenities – is the plage de la Corniche, where you'll also find restaurants and accommodation (see below). It's also worth trying to time your visit to coincide with one of the many **water-jousting** tournaments (see box on p.282) which are held on the town's canals; the quaysides jam with people watching the boat-borne combatants, and afterwards the bars fill with boisterous revelry.

You're likely to spend most of your time in Sète along the Canal Royal, which is lined on the west side by restaurants and bars, or in the tight scrum of streets between the water and the hill. On the water, you'll find the quirky new **Musée International des Arts Modestes** (daily except Tues 10am–noon & 2–6pm; €5) at 23 quai Maréchal-Lattre, which features a collection of art made from cast-off goods, and explores popular culture themes. Apart from this, the closest attraction to the old quarter is the **Musée Paul Valéry** (Wed–Sun 10am–noon & 2–6pm; €3.05), southwest of the canal on rue François-Desnoyer, about a ten-minute walk west of the old port. This

SÈTE

QUAI DE LATTRE DE TASSIGN ●A

RUE HONORÉ EUZET

AV MAX DORMOY

R GEN DE GAULE

Gare Routière

Ferry Terminal

Montpellier

R ALSACE LORRAINE

R DÉPUTÉ SALIS ●B

R COL FABIEN

RUE JEAN JAURÈS

QUAI LÉOPOLD SUQUET

RUE MAURICE CLAVEL

R DE LAPEYRADE

R P SEMARD

QUAI DE LA REPUBLIQUE

QUAI DE LA RESISTANCE

RUE GAMBETTA

RUE LEFÈBVRE

RUE DOUMET

R F MISTRAL ●C

Market

QUAI CH LEMARESQUIER

RUE LAZARE CARNOT ●2

R DE METZ

RUE P VALERY

PL L-BLUM ▣P

GRAND RUE

RUE SAVONNERIE

QUAI D'ALGER

Nouveau Bassin

R VILLEFRANCHE CH DU MAS ROUSSON

RUE LOUIS BLANC

RUE PASCAL

RUE DU PALAIS

R RIBOT

QUAI GENERAL DURAND

RUE R ROLLAND

RUE GARENNE

GRANDE RUE

R RAPIDE

ⓘ

Canal Royal

RUE J-F BAZILLE

Pierres Blanches Park ◀

RUE DU PARC

R E BONNET

RUE HAUTE

RUE 3 JOURNÉES

GRAND RUE

RUE M LICCIARDI

QUAI ASPIRANT HERBER

RUE MARTIN

RUE FRANKLIN

RUE VILLARET JOYEUSE

RUE LACAN

R DES MARINS

QUAI M LICCIARDI

RUE RICHELIEU ●D

RUE ELIE D'ELIAS

R DES PÊCHEURS

●3
●4 ●5

QUAI DE LA MARINE

QUAI RICHELIEU

Vieux Port

N

RUE TRAVERSIÈRE

Citadel

RUE J B MARTY

PROM DE J B MARTY

Musée Paul Valéry

GRANDE RUE HAUTE

RUE J R PINET

Sailors' Cemetery

ACCOMMODATION
Le Castellas Campsite	E
Le Grand Hôtel	A
Grand Hôtel de Paris	C
L'Orque Bleu	D
Le Venice	F
Villa Salis Hostel	B

RESTAURANTS
Le Bistro-Quais	4
La Galinette	1
Marcel	2
La Palangrotte	5
Table St-Jean	6
Toit de Calou	3

0 ————— 250 m

▼ ● , ● , ● , *Plage de la Corniche, Espace Bressens & Agde*

doubles as a municipal historical museum, whose collection focuses on the
nautical traditions of the town and includes documents, models and paintings
relating to the sport of water jousting. Valéry's (see box on p.284) remains lie
in the **sailors' cemetery** across the street from the museum, along with many
Sètois fishermen who have lost their lives at sea. From this museum, or from
the canal front, you can take a long ride on bus #3 to the northwest side of
Mont St-Clair. Here you'll find the **Espace Georges-Bressens** (Tues–Sun:
June & Sept 10am–noon & 2–6pm; July & Aug 10am–noon & 2–7pm; €5;

Water-jousting

The origins of the curious Sètois sport of **water-jousting** are lost, but the practice seems to have originated in the late seventeenth century, when Sète throve as a port thanks to its link to the Canal du Midi and the Canal à Rhône. The sport consists of two sleek boats, each manned by eight oarsmen, charging at each other on a near head-on course. At the stern of each boat, a long, raised tail supports the platform on which a jouster stands, dressed in white. Six other jousters provide a counterweight to the platform, while the rest of the crew, a coxswain and two musicians, keep the boat on course and in time. As the boats approach each other, the jousters steady their small shields, aim their long lances and attempt to strike their adversary from his mount. The spectacle is repeated seven times in each tournament, or *joute*, and the winning team is the one that unseats its opponents the most times. There are about a dozen *sociétés des joutes* in Sète (other Languedocian ports also have their own teams). The season runs from late spring through early autumn, with more frequent tournaments taking place in the summer. The most important championships are held here on August 25, the *fête de St-Louis*.

French-only voice-recorded commentary), another local shrine. Bressens (1921–81) was perhaps France's most popular folk singer of the postwar era, a sort of Gallic Bob Dylan, whose simple guitar melodies served as platforms for irony-edged sentimental lyrics. Looking over the Valéry museum, on a broad plateau on the west of Mont St-Clair, you'll see the park of **Pierres Blanches** (bus #5 from the Hôtel de Ville or the museum), a scrubby habitat for lavender, thyme and rosemary, which provides impressive views over the shellfish beds of the Bassin de Thau to the north, particularly towards sunset. This is also a great spot for a picnic, but if you come without supplies, you can get a snack at the small on-site café. Further east, at the summit of the *mont*, you'll find the nineteenth-century church of **Notre-Dame-de-la-Salette** (bus #5), built on the remains of a medieval fort; the church is nothing special but the **views** from here over the ports, old and new, are spectacular.

Practicalities

Sète's **gare SNCF** (℡04.67.46.51.00) is on quai Maréchal-Joffre, on the north bank of the Canal Latéral; from here it's a forty-minute walk into town so your best bet is to take bus #3 to the "Les Pénitents" stop, near the tourist office. The **gare routière** is a little bit closer in, on quai de la République; from here it's a ten-minute walk west along rue Honoré Euze to the Canal Royal, and then another fifteen minutes south to the tourist office, or you can take bus #4 to the Hôtel de Ville, at the northern end of the old town. Across the Canal Maritime, to the east of the *gare routière*, you'll find the **ferry terminal**, Gare Maritime Orsetti (℡04.67.46.68.00; bus #4), which has regular departures for Mallorca and Morocco. The **tourist office** (July & Aug Mon–Sat 10am–1pm & 3–8pm, Sun 10am–1pm; Sept Mon–Fri 9.30am–noon & 2.30–6pm, Sat 9.30am–noon; Oct–June Mon, Wed & Fri 9.30am–noon & 2.30–6pm, Sat 9.30am–noon; ℡04.67.74.71.71, ✆www.ville-sete.fr) is at 60 Grand'rue Mario Roustan. It has exchange facilities, and can also provide local bus tickets (€1 for a one-way fare). Buses #6, 7 or 9 will take you to the plage de la Corniche, the town's best beach. You can get on the **Internet** at Le Cyber Snack, 10 av Victor-Hugo (Mon–Fri 9am–noon & 2–6pm) and rent **bikes** at Déferlantes, 6 quai Commandant Semary (℡04.67.74.82.30) or **scooters** at Cabello, 9 quai Vauban (℡04.67.74.50.29). **Car rental** is available from inter-

national companies, including ADA (☎04.67.74.24.26), Budget
(☎04.67.74.37.78), Europcar (☎04.67.74.51.69.90) and Hertz
(☎04.67.74.51.68). For **boat** rides, see Sète Croisières on quai Général-
Durand; they run regular trips in the summer (€10–29). **Markets** are held
every morning except Tuesday; check with the tourist office for locations.

Accommodation

There's no shortage of **hotels** in town, starting with the decaying but funky
Grand Hôtel de Paris (☎04.67.74.98.10; May–Sept; ❸) at 2 rue Frédéric-
Mistral. *Le Grand Hôtel* (☎04.67.74.71.77, ⓦwww.sete-hotel.com; ❺), 17 quai
de Lattre de Tassigny, alongside the northern part of the Canal Royal, is more
elegant, but the best deal is *L'Orque Bleu* (☎04.67.74.72.13, ⓔlorque-
bleu@wanadoo.fr; ❸), 10 quai Aspirant-Herber, at the same canal's southern
end – try to get a quayside room in this converted nineteenth-century mansion, as the views over the canal to the old town are great. The unhospitably
basic **youth hostel**, *Villa Salis*, is on rue du Général-Revest (☎04.67.53.46.68,
ⓕ04.67.51.34.01; March–Nov; ❶), a stiff half-hour walk west of the *gare
routière* on the eastern slopes of the *mont*. The biggest and best **campsite**
around is the mammoth *Le Castellas* complex (☎04.67.51.63.00, ⓔcamping-
lecastellas@wanadoo.fr; mid-May to mid-Sept), 10km west on the RN112,
although many people camp for free in the car parks along the road. A good
alternative to staying in the centre is to head out to the beach, where *Hôtel le
Venise* (☎04.67.53.02.86; ❷; closed Dec & Jan) on plage de la Corniche is a
stone's throw from the sand.

Eating and drinking

There's a barrage of **restaurants** along quai Général-Durand, from the pont
de la Savonnerie right down to the pleasure port, all offering seafood in the
€12–28 bracket. *Le Toit de Calou*, just south of the tourist office at 82 Grand'rue
(☎04.67.74.04.24; closed Sun), offers some respite from the culinary monochrome – a dark and cosy place with *à la carte* selections from €15 and a good
cellar of regional wine – as does the tranquil *Le Bistro-Quais* (☎04.99.04.99.90;
closed Sun eve), at no. 90 Grand'rue (*menus* €9.50–19.50). *The Marcel*
(☎04.67.74.20.89) on rue Lazare-Carnot is a great deal, with a meal of grilled
fish and local wine from €13. A local favourite is *La Palangrotte*
(☎04.67.74.20.89; closed Sun noon & Mon) at 1 quai de la Marine, famous
for its mussels, *bouillabaise* (€20–30) and solid wine list. For a more upscale
seafood meal, you might head to *La Galinette*, 26 pl des Mouettes
(☎04.67.51.16.77; closed Sun eve, Fri lunch & Sat lunch out of season), on the
north side of town (*menus* from €35). Another good bet is the *Table de St-Jean*
(☎04.67.53.02.57; closed Mon), next door to the *Le Venise*. Local specialities
to look out for include "La Tielle", a spicy octopus pie, and biscuits, including
the sweet "Zézette", best washed down with muscat or champagne.

For **nightlife**, the bar *Grand de la Marine* at 90 quai Durand is a good place
to start, while *La Bodega*, on 21 quai Noel-Guignon, is a cocktail bar with jazz,
Latin and rock music (nightly 10pm–4am).

The Bassin de Thau and Mèze

North and west of Sète sits the shallow expanse of the **Bassin de Thau**,
which, at 18km long and some 5km wide, is one of the biggest salt lakes in
Languedoc. From its northeastern end above Sète, it accompanies the town's
fourteen-kilometre stretch of beach southwest to Agde. Although there are no

Paul Valéry

Though of Corsican and Italian parentage, **Paul Valéry** was born in Sète in 1871, and spent his childhood and adolescence in the town. An introspective youth, he whiled away his hours contemplating the sea. On reaching adulthood, he moved to Paris, where he took up work as a legal clerk; by this time he had already begun writing **Symbolist poetry** influenced by Poe and Mallarmé. His great and largely unrequited love, however, was for science, and despite his literary successes, he turned towards more pragmatic intellectual pursuits in the sciences. He was a great admirer of da Vinci, in whom he saw the "universal man" – a cerebral Renaissance figure whom he brought to life in his stylized novel *Monsieur Teste* (1895). Valéry did his best to live up to the da Vincian ideal which he professed. In his forties, at the urging of André Gide, he returned to poetry, while his scientific pursuits brought him into personal contact with contemporaries such as Albert Einstein. His acute observational powers and political insights made him a popular *salon* guest in inter-war Paris, and official accolades followed with his election in 1925 to the Académie Française and his appointment to the Collège de France as the first Professor of Poetry. Valéry remained in Paris through the Nazi occupation and, having lived to see the Liberation, died the following year and was buried as a national hero.

major sights on the length of road that runs from Sète around the eastern section of the *étang*, there are a number of interesting little villages along the way. On the eastern bank of the Bassin, **Balaruc-le-Vieux**, an ancient fishing village, still retains its medieval walls and eleventh-century church, and the remains of a third-century paleo-Christian basilica (free) in the village centre. Close by on the north shore, the old town of **Bouzigues** looks out onto the oyster and mussel beds which crowd the lagoon – here you can visit the **Musée de l'Étang de Thau** (daily: Jan, Feb, Nov & Dec 10am–noon & 2–5pm; March–May, June & Aug 10am–noon & 2–7pm; Sept & Oct 10am–noon & 2–6pm; €4), whose array of imaginative multimedia displays explains the art of shellfish-raising (including tanks with live specimens), as well as traditional fishing techniques. Non-French speakers will want to skip the video presentation, but the museum is worth a look if you are passing by.

MÈZE, a few kilometres to the west, is an ancient fishing hamlet whose old town is a dense maze of narrow streets flanked by low houses – the largest village on the Bassin de Thau's northern shore. As it isn't situated directly on the sea, it gets relatively few visitors, so provides some respite from the crowds of the coastal towns. It also has a surprising number of points of interest in and about town. A compact **Écosite** (July & Aug daily 10am–7pm; €4.60), located along the shore, 3km southwest of town, was set up to preserve the habitat of the salt lagoon, and features exhibitions on the flora and fauna of the *étang*, and on techniques of aquaculture (lagoon exploitation). Also near Mèze, 5km north, and just off the main RN 113 road towards Pézenas, is the **Musée-Parc La Plaine des Dinosaures** (daily: April–June, Sept & Oct 2–6pm; July & Aug 10am–7pm; Nov–March 2–5pm; €6) a museum and excavation area established on the site of a major paleological find, including one of the biggest caches of dinosaur eggs yet discovered. Just to the east of town, on the road to Loupian, you can visit a recently excavated **Gallo-Roman villa** (daily: mid-June to mid-Sept 10.30am–6.30pm; €4.60). Dating from the very tail end of the Roman period, it contains some impressive figurative and geometric mosaics. Finally, 12km north of Mèze along the D161 and a good detour on the way to Pézenas, the ruined twelfth-century Cistercian **abbey of**

Valmagne (daily: mid-June to mid-Sept 10am–noon & 2.30–6.30pm; mid-Sept to mid-June 2–6pm; guided tours in English available; €6; Ⓦwww.val-magne.com), once one of the richest in the south of France, sits in a romantic wooded park, and is now used to host temporary art exhibitions and occasional concerts.

Mèze is the main service town for the Bassin de Thau; its **tourist office** (July & Aug Mon–Fri 9am–12.30pm & 2–8pm, Sat 9am–12.30pm & 2–7pm, Sun 9am–12.30pm; Sept–June Mon–Fri 9am–12.15pm & 1.30–8pm, Sat 9am–12.30pm; Ⓣ04.67.43.93.08, Ⓦwww.ville-meze.fr) is near the village centre on rue Massaloup. If you are looking to stay, the town also has a good **hotel**, the economical *de Thau*, on rue de la Parée (Ⓣ04.67.43.83.83, Ⓕ04.67.43.69.45; ❷). You'll find a string of **restaurants** along the waterfront quai Descournut, all serving up shellfish fresh from the *bassin*: *Le Chabichou* or *Le Coquillou* are well regarded by locals, but any of them will do (*menus* from €15). The sprawling **campsite** *Beau Rivage* (Ⓣ04.67.43.81.48; April–Sept) is located off the highway RN-113. Sailboats, ideal for exploring the broad and calm *bassin*, can be rented at Le Taurus (Ⓣ04.67.43.59.51).

Pézenas and around

PÉZENAS, 54km southwest of Montpellier along the N113, and more or less halfway between Mèze and Béziers (see p.325), is the last large inland settlement on the Hérault river, as it meanders south to Agde through the vineyards of the Languedoc plain. One of the most singularly beautiful towns in the French Southwest, endowed with an almost overwhelming concentration of grand architecture, it is also a centre for **arts and crafts**, and thus very popular – packing out with tourists in July and August.

Although it had been an important market centre for centuries, Pézenas catapulted to glory when it became the seat of the Languedoc parliament and the residence of its governors in 1456, and reached its zenith in the late seventeenth century, when the Armand de Bourbon, prince of Conti and governor of Languedoc, made it a "second Versailles", drawing artists and writers of the stature of Molière to his court with his wealthy patronage. On and off, the playwright spent a good four years here performing for the prince and garnering inspiration for the plays which would later make him famous. But with the prince's death in 1666, stagnation soon set in, and Pézenas reverted to the sleepy provincial town which – outside high season – it remains today.

The Town

Pézenas' compact **old town** is set on the west bank of the Peyne river, occupying the area between the hill on which the town's castle once stood, and the village church. It is best accessed from the broad café-lined place du 14 du Juillet, a lively square which now hosts the town's market and is set on the riverside just to the west of the *gare*. Entering from here, the first of the fine *hôtels* which you'll encounter is the **Hôtel Lacoste** (daily 10am–noon & 3–7pm; free) at 8 rue Oustrin, a fifteenth-century palace with a beautiful but compact vaulted courtyard framed by a monumental staircase; the mansion now houses temporary painting exhibitions. As you continue west, place de Gambetta is home to the tourist office (see p.287), once the shop where Molière idled away his afternoons. Across the narrow, cobblestoned *place* stands the handsome sixteenth-century council house, whose broad and square vaulted interior once held sessions of the Estates of Languedoc, but now houses the **Maison de Métiers des Arts** (daily 10am–noon & 3–7pm; July & Aug also

PÉZENAS

Castle

Clermont l'Hérault ▲

PLACE DES ÉTATS
DU LANGUEDOC

Peyne River

N

Musée
de la Porte

RUE MONTMORENCY

RUE LITANIES

RUE DU CHATEAU

JEWISH
QUARTER

RUE JUIVERIE

PLACE
LEDRU
ROLLIN

RUE MALVIC

RUE MARCEAU

RUE BARÈME

RUE VENEL

RUE EMILE ZOLA

RUE FOUR VILLE

RUE CANABASSERIE

Maison
de Métiers
des Arts

RUE A SABATIER

RUE DE LA FOIRE

RUE MARÉCHAL DE PLANTAVIN

R BÉRANGER

RUE A ALLIÉS

Musée
Vulliod-
St-German

PLACE
GAMBETTA ℹ

RUE FRANÇOIS OUSTRIN

Hôtel
Lacoste

AVENUE FRANÇOIS HUE

P

PLACE DU
14 JUILLET

✉

RUE A ROUZIÈRE

Ⓐ

Gare
Routière

Béziers & Montpellier

COURS JEAN-JAURÈS

RUE TRIPERIE VIELLE

RUE MERCIÈRE

❷

RUE CHEVALIERS SAINT-JEAN

RUE COMMANDEURS

RUE ORFÈVRES

PLACE DU MARCHÉ
DES TROIS SIX

R TAUCHE

St-Jean ✝

RUE KLÉBER

RUE CONDORCET

PLACE DE LA
RÉPUBLIQUE

RUE DOCTEUR MARTIN

RUE JOSEPH CAMBON

RUE ANATOLE FRANCE

RUE RASPAIL

R C CASSAN

RUE BARBATERIE

RUE RABELAIS

RUE DE JUVENEL

RUE BARRES

RUE CONTI

R DU VIEUX SAINT

R MICHELET

RUE DES FABRES

RUE J MOUSSEAU

R DU CAPT DAVID

R FRANKLIN

ACCOMMODATION
Genieys   B
Molière   A

RESTAURANTS
Le Pomme d'Amour   1
Les Palmiers   2
Le Conti   4
Le Vietnam   3
La Tasca   5

0   200 m

❸ ▼ Hôtel d'Alfonce, ❹ ❺ ▼ Ⓑ

Wed & Fri 8.30–11pm; free), a showcase for local crafts, including painting, decorative sculpture, stained-glass items and the like.

From here, wandering off in any direction will lead you to the carved stone facades of the wealthy merchants and nobles of Renaissance Pézenas; a glance up as you stroll around will almost certainly reveal a playful human face, a stately lion or regal sun carved out of a window casement or doorframe. North of the square, down rue Alliés, is the mansion housing the **Musée Vulliod–St-German** (Mon–Sat 10am–noon & 2–5pm, Sun 2–5pm; €2) – purportedly dedicated to the life and times of Molière, but in fact containing all manner of sixteenth- and seventeenth-century artefacts, from classically themed Aubusson tapestries to displays dwelling on the daily life of the humbler classes. The famous playwright is recalled in a room containing some of his papers and personal effects. Beyond this museum, you'll see the watchtower that forms the sole remnant of the medieval fortifications, while on the hill at the end of rue Béranger lie the ruins of the **castle** (closed) destroyed by Richelieu and dating back to as early as 1500 BC. At the foot of the castle's rise, sits the small and rather dull **Musée de la Porte** (July & Aug Mon–Fri 10am–12.30pm & 3.30–7pm, Sat & Sun 3.30–7pm; Sept–June Sun 2–6pm; free), celebrating Pézenas' tradition of ironwork, most evident in the elaborate balustrades which can be seen around town.

On the far side of the castle's base through rue Litanies, is the town's old

Jewish quarter, marked off by gates, as was the custom during the Middle Ages – there's not much of interest here but snaking east, between the gate of rue Juiverie and place Gambetta, are a warren of narrow streets jammed with magnificent *hôtels*; make sure you check out the doorway of the **Hôtel Grave** on rue de Château, the fifteenth-century **Hôtel de Jacques Coeur** at 7 rue Émile-Zola and the impressive ironwork railing in the courtyard at 12 rue Sabatier. From the old Jewish quarter, rue de la Foire eventually leads to the incongruously plain **church**, the Collegiate of St-Jean; south of this, at no. 32 rue Conti, the **Hôtel d'Alfonce** (June–Sept Mon–Sat 10am–noon & 3–7pm; €2) features a spacious courtyard girded by an ornately balustraded stone balcony; it was here that Molière's players put on performances during the winter of 1655–56.

If you like to **shop** while travelling, Pézenas will not disappoint, as two out of every three frontages seem to conceal a store or workshop. Quality varies incredibly, and if you persevere, you may turn up some interesting and original *objets* amongst the tack. Cheaper and considerably less durable souvenirs can be bought in the form of "petits pâtés", bite-sized mince-tarts based on the recipe of an Indian cook in Lord Clive's household – the British Governor of India holidayed here in 1768 and the recipe stuck. The best place to pick these up, piping hot, is at Maison Aleary, 9 rue de Chevaliers de St-Jean. Another town speciality, the "Berlingot," is a hard candy which comes in a variety of flavours and continues to be made in the town. If you happen to be around for one of the local festivals (see box on p.264), keep an eye out for **"Le Poulain"** – the town's traditional totemic animal. A mock horse, constructed of a cloth-draped wooden frame and borne through the streets by a bunch of burly men, Le Poulain was adopted in honour of a foal which King Louis VIII's favourite mare gave birth to here in 1226.

Around Pézenas
The immediate surroundings of Pézenas offer good possibilities for walking, cycling or exploring by car. **Montagnac** lies halfway between Pézenas and the abbey of Valmagne to the east and has an attractive old town with a well-preserved fourteenth-century church. To the south, **Castelnau-de-Guers** was once a way-station on the Roman Via Domitia. Most worthy of visit, however, is the priory, **Château de Cassan** (Easter–Sept daily 3–7pm; €7), 10km west of town, just after Roujan. Founded originally by Charlemagne, it enjoyed great prosperity under the Trencavels, who added a Romanesque church that still survives, and in the 1700s it was rebuilt as a huge Neoclassical palace. Aside from the church, and the remains of a medieval hospital, the main attraction today is its immense cloister, which contains a fine iron-forged staircase. Also in the grounds is an elaborate oriental garden, founded by Armand de Bourbon.

Practicalities
Buses stop in Pézenas at the open-air *gare routière* on place Molière, five minutes' east of place Gambetta on foot, which is where you'll find the main **tourist office** (July & Aug Mon–Tues, Thurs & Sat 9am–7pm, Wed, Fri 9am–10pm, Sun 10am–7pm; Sept–June Mon–Sat 9am–noon & 2–6pm, Sun 10am–noon & 2–5pm; ☎04.67.98.36.40, ⊛www.paysdepezenas.net). For **Internet**, head to Le Web Conti (daily 9am–midnight), at 30 rue Conti, while **bikes** can be rented at Cycles Garin (☎04.67.98.34.04). The town centre becomes a busy **market** on Sundays from 10am to 6pm. You can **rent cars** at *Citer* on rte de Béziers (☎04.67.98.82.08).

There are two **hotels** in Pézenas, both of which have good amenities: *Genieys* (☎04.67.98.13.99, ⓦwww.logis–de–france.fr; ❷) at 9 rue Aristide-Briand, near the end of rue Conti, and the splendid old *Molière* (☎04.67.98.14.00, ⓕ04.67.98.98.28; ❸) on place du 14 Juillet. If these are full, you can try *Les Rocailles* (☎04.67.24.00.27, ⓕ04.67.24.06.70; ❸) on the N113 in Montagnac, and if you make the trip out to Cassan you can stay 'at the luxurious **gîte** *Domaine l'Eskillou* (☎ & ⓕ04.67.24.60.50, ⓦperso.wanadoo.fr/domaine-eskillou; April–Sept; ❸), whose price includes breakfast, in nearby Pouzelles. **Campsites** in the area include the municipal site *Castelsec* (☎04.67.98.04.02; April to mid-Oct) and *St-Christol* (☎04.67.98.09.00; mid-April to mid-Sept), and there is a quiet, rural municipal **gîte** (☎04.67.98.05.80, ⓔcommunaut-edecommunes@paysdepezenas.net; ❷) at Castelsec, 1km west from town.

Restaurants in Pézenas tend, somewhat surprisingly, to be unremarkable, falling into either the *terroir* or pizzeria bracket with *menus* for under €15; *Le Pomme d'Amour* (March–Dec; closed Mon eve & Tues in winter) on rue Albert-Paul-Alliés and *Brasserie Molière* (on the same *place* as the hotel of that name, and notable for a good whiskey selection) fall into the first category, while *Le Conti*, 27 rue Conti (closed Mon in winter & Sun) belongs to the second. The exception to the rule is *Les Palmiers* in 50 rue de Mercière (☎04.67.09.42.56; June–Sept only), a beautiful and welcoming establishment featuring inventive Mediterranean-style cuisine from about €25. International alternatives are *Le Vietnam* (closed Sun noon) at 11 rue Barbès, and the tapas bar *La Tasca* (closed Sun & Mon off-season), at 15 rue Anatole-France (both from €8).

Inland from Montpellier

The area **inland from Montpellier** is dominated by two rivers: the mighty Hérault, which cuts down southwest from the Cévennes mountains through the plains above the city, and the Vis, which runs along the northern rim of the *département* and into the Hérault at Ganges. Between them, their underpopu-lated and lesser-travelled valleys – a world apart from the fishing towns and beaches of the coast – offer some remarkable scenery and attractions, and, taken in conjunction with a couple of absorbing towns, also form a naturally cir-cuitous tour of the region by car, with plenty of hiking opportunities along the way.

The circuit starts with quiet **Clermont-l'Hérault**, poised on the eastern edge of the Haut Languedoc uplands 40km west of Montpellier, which pro-vides access to the nearby reservoir **Lac du Salagou** and an array of interest-ing sites: **Villeneuvette**, an old industrial centre; **Cabrières'** prehistoric cop-per mines; and the eerie landscape of **Cirque de Mourèze**. North of here is **Lodève**, an eminently explorable town which boxes in the Orb valley to the west and provides a good base for local excursions, as well as for the route east-wards across the high plateau des Garrigues to the beautiful **Cirque de Navacelles** in the Vis valley. From here, you pass down through the Vis gorge to link up eventually with the Hérault just north of **Ganges**. The area on the southern border of the Cévennes – with its gnarled olive trees and sturdy oaks – is a far cry from the Mediterranean scrub of the plains further south, a zone whose cloth industry was supported by the flocks of sheep which still roam its long valleys. Ganges provides easy access to the cavernous chambers of the **Grotte des Demoiselles**, which open up under the calcite plateau – you'll pass the *grotte* on either of two routes south to Montpellier. The first follows the **Hérault valley** itself, veering southwest to the deep Hérault gorge and the ancient hamlet and UNESCO World Heritage site of **St-Guilhem-le-Désert**, while the second, more direct route heads straight south via the **Pic-St-Loup**, standing sentinel above the coastal plain, and the old town of **St-Martin-de-Londres**.

Clermont-l'Hérault, Lac du Salagou and around

Some 40km west of Montpellier, a short distance from the banks of the River Hérault, lies quiet **CLERMONT-L'HÉRAULT**, a dull little cantonal capital whose only recommendation is as a jumping-off point for visiting the area around **Lac du Salagou**. A brief walk around the town, with a stop to look at its thirteenth-century **church**, fortified in the fourteenth century to defend it against the English, more or less exhausts all the possibilities. Otherwise, at 8 rue Louis Blanc, you'll find the small Gothic chapel of **Notre-Dame-du-Peyrou**, once a way-station on the Chémin St-Jacques. Instead of sticking around, head west by car, foot or bike, towards **Villeneuvette**, 4km away. A model factory town founded by Colbert in the seventeenth century to produce high-quality wool for sale in the Mediterranean, Villeneuvette stayed in business until 1954 and still has 85 inhabitants. The walled-in compound is entered through a monumental gate bearing the legend *Honneur au Travail* ("honour to work"), and inside, a square, flanked by the church and *mairie*, opens onto neat rows of low, flower-bedecked workers' houses and the decaying factory. In its wooded surroundings, the little settlement presents a curious but enchanting idyll. A detour 5km south from Villeneuvette will take you to **Cabrières**, where you can visit the site of the **copper mines** of Pioch Farrus (April–Nov daily 10am–7pm; €7), which were exploited by the region's Neolithic inhabitants over 5000 years ago – the engaging hour-long tour takes you through 200m of galleries. Wrap up warm; the temperature in the mine is 15°C.

Alternatively, heading northwest from Villeneuvette leads to the village of Mourèze, located in the midst of an eerie zone of eroded dolomite known as the **Cirque de Mourèze**, featuring a landscape of ancient seabed eroded by rainfall into a forest of rocky pinnacles. You can stroll though the myriad of paths which crisscross the area, or enjoy an impressive panoramic view from the **Courtinales** (daily 10am–7pm; €5), a private park whose footpaths lead through a garden of local fauna and reconstructions of the prehistoric dwellings of the region – good fun for adults and children. Mourèze was also the first town which the Resistance group, the Maquis Bir Hakeim, liberated from the Germans – a monument to 140 of their dead (including one English officer) sits a kilometre or two south of the entrance to town.

Continuing towards **Salasc**, a tiny crossroads hamlet 4km further west, the landscape becomes almost Martian, as the ground gives way to red iron-rich dunes. From Salasc, the road marked for Laiusson leads to the south shore of **LAC DU SALAGOU**, a reservoir whose shallow waters teem with birdlife, as well as fish and tiny crabs. The north shore, east of the larger village of **Octon**, is more developed and the landscape less striking. As the road follows the cliffs above the shore, it passes the ghost town of **Celles**, which was expropriated in the 1970s when the reservoir was built. The waters, however, never reached the hamlet, which now sits abandoned. Today, it is the scene of a lively mix of families on outings and nude bathers. After another eight kilometres of winding road, you'll join up with the busy *route national* just north of Clermont.

In 1942, with the dissolution of the puppet **Vichy regime**, the formal **German occupation** of Languedoc began, and once again the natives of the region found themselves fighting an outside power against enormous odds. Although research has dispelled the romantic vision that every Frenchman was pro-Resistance (in fact, it seems, just as many were against it), in Languedoc the movement was particularly strong and determined. This was due to a number of factors, not the least of which was a sense of regional identity. The highlands of Languedoc were traditionally a home to nonconformists, originally Cathars and Huguenots, but in the 1940s to "white" royalists, "red" communists, supplemented by refugee leftists from Franco's fascist Spain (some of whom were wanted by the Gestapo), Wehrmacht deserters and Jews escaping from occupied northern France. Local people were additionally embittered by the fact that citizens had suffered involuntary transportation to Germany to substitute factory workers gone to the front, and others, who had volunteered, seeing this as the only escape from a devastated rural economy, had found themselves in concentration camps. Given these conditions, men and women of the highlands of Languedoc took up arms with determination. Soon they became known as "maquisards" or **"maquis"**, a term which refers to the scrubby Mediterranean landscape – the isolated and difficult terrain which was their home and their refuge.

In the first two years of German occupation, the maquis groups were comprised of mere handfuls of individuals, who tended to be those who were ideologically committed enough to die for the anti-Nazi cause, mostly **Communists**. The main resistance group, which operated primarily in the Cévennes and eastern Haut Languedoc, was known as the Maquis "Bir Hakeim", named after the heroic defence of Bir Hakeim in Libya by Free French Forces in June 1942. They were extremely active in the region until surprised by German forces in the hills near La Parade in May 1944 and wiped out. In the Sidorbe of western Haut Languedoc and Tarn, the **Resistance** was more durable, and the feared Maquis de Vabre carried out a campaign of raiding and sabotage despite the brutal retaliations which such acts provoked. In 1944, with the invasion of Normandy, Allied successes in Italy and Russian advances in the East, the writing was clearly on the wall for the Germans, and more and more French began to join the Resistance. Meanwhile, the Allies began to provide support for the Resistance, supplying them with air cover and sending in agents. In August of that year, fifteen commandos of the OSS (the fore-runner of the CIA) were parachuted into Vabre, one day before a British agent, Major Davies, arrived. Davies' notebook, which he called a report on "the war in Languedoc Rouge", recalls the fighters as "mainly youths who were not very experienced, but they made a profound impression on me. They were fine upstanding fellows with fresh keen faces, from all social classes. In England, of course, they would (still) have been at school." Davies was also impressed by the participation of people from all walks of life. "This was the sort of war that Mr. Smith, Jones and Robinson of France were engaged in, nothing very tremendous perhaps but brave work nonetheless..." Despite their lack of arms and equipment, in August 1944, maquis action turned the German withdrawal from Albi into a military debacle – many vehicles were lost and the 4500-strong garrison of Castres surrendered. In the wake of this retreat, the Resistance squads were organized into the Forces Françaises de l'Interieur and sent to Lyon to bolster the Allied presence.

Practicalities

Trains and **buses** arrive in Clermont-l'Hérault at the **gare SNCF** on place Frédéric-Mistral, five minutes' walk south of the town centre. The **tourist office** (Mon–Sat 9am–noon & 2–6pm, Sun 10am–noon; ℡04.67.96.23.86,

@www.clermont-herault.fr) for the town and surrounding area is at 9 rue Gosse, between the station and the church. **Bikes** are available at Ozone (T04.67.96.03.99), and other facilities in town include banks and laundry services.

If you have to stay overnight in Clermont itself, the best bet is the basic but cheap **hotel** *Le Terminus* (T04.67.88.45.00, @leterminus@wanadoo.fr; ❷), 11 allées Salegro, by the station, but the Lac du Salagou area offers better possibilities. Chief among these is Villeneuvette's *La Source* (T04.67.96.05.07, @www.hotellasource.com; closed Jan to mid-Feb & late Nov; ❸; English spoken), a friendly place with great amenities and a good restaurant (*menu* €17–28), while in Mourèze, *Les Hauts de Mourèze* (T04.67.94.04.84, F04.67.96.25.85; closed Nov–March; ❹) is a comfortable inn with a rustic setting. Salasc has a **gîte**, the *Auberge Campagnard* (T & F04.67.96.15.62; ❸ with breakfast), and at Octon you can stay or eat at the comfortable old *La Calade* (T & F04.67.96.19.21; March to mid-Dec; ❸) in the village centre (*menu* €15; closed Tues & Wed out of season). There's a **campsite**, *Les Rivières* (T04.67.96.75.53; June to mid-Sept) just west of Clermont, and two on the lake: *Le Salagou* (T04.67.96.06.18) at the eastern end, and the nudist *Village du Bosc* (T04.67.96.07.37, @www.villagedubosc.fr.st; April to mid-Sept) near Octon.

The **restaurant** situation in Clermont is rather bleak, and the choice, by default only, is *L'Arlequin* in place St-Paul, by the church (*menus* from €14; closed Sun & Mon). In Mourèze, you'll find a couple of pizzerias by the entrance to Les Courtinales.

Lodève and around

Located on the eastern spur of the massif that forms the bulk of the Parc de Haut Languedoc, and just 10km north of Lac du Salagou, **LODÈVE** is everything which Clermont-l'Hérault is not – a pleasantly situated and friendly little town with a couple of surprisingly good sights. Heading southwest from the *gare routière*, you'll arrive in a few minutes at the greatest of these, the **Cathédrale St-Fulcran** (€2.50), built in the town's second great period of prosperity in the twelfth and thirteenth centuries (the first was under Nero in the first century BC, when it had been important enough to have an imperial Roman mint). The current cathedral was raised on the riches of the woollen cloth industry, which dominated this area in the Middle Ages, and named in honour of a local tenth-century bishop. Although it's mostly late medieval, traces of an earlier cathedral's sixth-century foundations can be seen, while the **cloisters** preserve part of the cathedral building raised by the saint himself in the tenth century. The nave's dimensions are impressive – 58m in length and 25m high – and its biggest bell weighs in at 2000 kilograms; in a small interior chapel opposite the door, you'll find where the remains of the town's 84 bishops lie interred. Next door to the church, the later **bishop's palace** has been converted into the *mairie*, and during business hours you can peek in at the Italianate salons and staircases.

From the cathedral, the old town spreads out east, bounded on three sides by a dramatic bend in the Lergue river. Just southeast of the church, you'll find the beautiful medieval bridge, the **Pont de Montifort**, while in the centre of town, up nearby rue de la République, is the surprisingly decent **Musée Fleury** (Tues–Sun 9.30am–12.30pm & 2–6pm; €6), a gallery which draws the best fine-arts exhibitions between Castres and Montpellier, as well as a good selection of archeological finds and historical items dating from the prehistoric

LODÈVE

ACCOMMODATION
du Nord — B
de la Paix — C
Les Vals Campsite — A

RESTAURANTS
Le Petit Sommellier — 1
Café de la Bourse — 2

Atelier National de Tissage de Tapis & Clermont

& Priory of St-Michel-de-Grandmont

to the post-Revolutionary. Just east of this museum, in the place du Marché, the nineteenth-century *halle* has been converted into the **Hôtel Dardé** (daily 9am–7pm; free), a showcase for local sculptor Paul Dardé (1888–1963). Unfortunately, little survives of medieval Lodève, as the town was nearly razed in retribution for its support of Montmorency's revolt. You can, however, get a glimpse of the cloth-making industry (which only ceased in 1960) by visiting the **Atelier National de Tissage de Tapis** (Tues–Thurs 2–6pm; €3.20; call ahead to book ☎04.67.96.40.40) south of the old town, across the river – an exhibition of looms and other machinery where you can see textiles being woven according to traditional methods.

Lodève makes a pleasant base for exploring the surrounding area, including the upper Orb valley to the west and Lac du Salagou to the south, but the nearest attraction is the **priory of St-Michel-de-Grandmont**, just 8km away, on a wooded rise to the east of town. The old monastery and its grounds can be visited as part of a **guided tour** (Feb–May 3pm; June, Sept & Oct 10.30am, 3.15pm & 4pm; July & Aug 10.30am, 3.15pm, 4pm & 5pm; Nov to mid-Dec Sat & Sun 3.15 & 4pm; €5.40), but you can also poke around the buildings on your own (June–Oct 1–2.45pm; €3.85). Built in 1128, this was one of the first convents of the extremely strict Grandmontine Order of hermits, whose alarming popularity with the faithful prompted the power-jealous John XXII to clamp down on them in 1317. The buildings which remain today comprise one of their best-preserved houses, including a cloister, reception hall and an austere late thirteenth-century church. The spacious **grounds** are well worth a visit; their shaded woods are stocked with deer and other wildlife and punctuated by prehistoric dolmens and menhirs (going back some 4000 years) as well as Visigothic sarcophagi.

Practicalities

Lodève's **gare routière** (℡04.67.88.86.44) is on place de la République, right beside the town's **tourist office** (Mon–Fri 9am–noon & 2–6pm, Sat 9am–5pm & July & Aug only also Sun 9.30am–1.30pm; ℡04.67.88.86.44, ⓦwww.lodeve.com). You can rent bikes at Club House (℡04.67.96.46.48). The best place to stay is the well-renovated *Hôtel du Nord* (℡ & Ⓕ04.67.44.10.08, ⓦwww.hotellodeve.com; ❷) at 18 bd de la Liberté, just down from the post office. The young couple that run it are very welcoming, and rooms range in size from singles to family-sized suites with kitchen. Another good choice is *De la Paix* (℡04.67.44.07.46, Ⓔhotel-de-la-paix@wanadoo.fr; closed Feb to mid-March; ❸) on 11 bd Montalangue, run by the same family for over a century. The nearest **campsite** is *Les Vals* (℡04.67.44.36.57: closed Feb), just south of town. The *De la Paix* has one of the better **restaurants** (*menus* €18–25; closed Sun eve & Mon Oct–April), with solid, home-cooked regional dishes, and *Le Petit Sommelier* (*menus* from €12; closed Mon), at 3 pl de la République, is another good option. You can also pick up light meals at the *Café de la Bourse*, 1 av Fumel and *Le Grand Café du Nord*, in the hotel of the same name, and there's a **snack bar** out at St-Michel. On Saturdays, a large **market** is held throughout the centre of Lodève, while in the summer months (mid-June to mid-Sept), a *terroir*-produce market convenes on Tuesday, Wednesday and Thursday afternoons in the place de la République.

North to Ganges via the Cirque de Navacelles

Taking the D25 eastwards from just north of Lodève, you'll climb 15km up the wooded Brèze valley before reaching an open plain stretching a similar distance to the hamlet of St-Maurice-Navacelles. Here the road drops into the Vis valley, descending with it all the way to Ganges (see p.294). If you turn off to the north at St-Maurice, you'll come to the **CIRQUE DE NAVACELLES**, a breathtaking section of the valley where the river, carving down sharply through the surrounding plain, has doubled back on itself, leaving a small hillock stranded in the middle of the cirque; at its base huddles the ancient hamlet of **Navacelles**. The cirque can also be reached in a day's **hiking**; the GR653 east from Lodève links up with the GR7, which winds its way north, entering the Vis valley near St-Maurice before heading on into the Cévennes. Arriving by car, you'll first reach the belvedere on the south side of the cirque, from which you can contemplate the incredible sweep of the gorge and look down on the village 600m below. From the lookout point, the road follows a dramatic series of switchbacks descending to Navacelles itself – a tiny stone hamlet with a medieval bridge – before climbing to another lookout point on the north side. The **information centre** (daily 10am–noon & 2–6pm) for the cirque is located at the southern belvedere; it has a small exhibition explaining the formation of the curious canyon and conducts two- and three-hour walking tours (€5; frequently in English). A good alternative walk which you can easily manage without assistance is the spectacular six-kilometre hike to the underground *source de la four*, along a trail leading west along the canyon floor from Navacelles itself.

East of St-Maurice, the road snakes down into the Vis gorges for the remaining 26km to Ganges. Contrasting with the open scrub around Navacelles, this section of the valley is a steep and lush canyon, whose tree-clad banks at times close off the sky above with thick boughs. As you continue, it gradually widens, passing occasional signs of life – riverside *relaises*, ancient bridges and abandoned factories – before opening up abruptly when it reaches the Hérault at Ganges.

As you'd expect, services are rather minimal in this neck of the woods. Navacelles has only one **hotel**, *Auberge de la Cascade* (℡04.67.81.50.95, Ⓕ04.67.81.53.45; ❷), as well as the **gîtes** *Le Mas de Guilhou* (℡04.67.81.50.69; ❶) and *Casa Lou Haîdouc* (℡04.67.81.51.54; ❶). A CAP *gîte* at La Vacquerie, halfway between Lodève and St-Maurice (℡04.67.44.56.05; ❶), provides shelter if you're hiking along the GR7. You can also stay at *Les Tilleuls* (℡04.67.44.61.60; March–Nov; ❷) in St-Maurice itself, and there are other possibilities along the Vis gorge, the most luxurious of which is the *Château de Madières* (℡04.67.73.84.03, Ⓔmadieres@chateaux-country.com; closed Nov–March; ❾), a renovated fourteenth-century castle. All of these establishments serve **meals**, as does the café *Baume Auriol* at the southern belvedere (*plat du jour* €9).

Ganges and around

GANGES, the largest town in the upper Hérault valley, is primarily of interest as a transport hub and service centre for the more interesting places just to the south (which you can also access travelling along either of the two routes down to Montpellier – see p.288), and for the busy recreation industry which has grown up on the banks of the river. The town, like many villages of the Cévennes region to the north, enjoyed prosperity first as a hub for the wool trade then subsequently as a silk centre, until the advent of synthetic fabrics and ravages of phylloxera disease in the late 1800s drove the industry under. It was also here, in August 1944, that the local maquis managed to repulse a column of three thousand German troops after a fierce ten-hour battle. Nowadays, there's little to see or do, although a walk through the old quarter will take you past a few remaining medieval houses, a pretty eighteenth-century market square and an imposingly dour Huguenot temple. All in all, though, these do not suffice to dispel a certain lingering air of stagnation.

The **gare routière** is on rue Jules-Ferry, just west of the central plan l'Ormeau, which is where you'll find the **tourist office** (Mon–Fri 10am–noon & 2–6pm, Sat 10am–noon; ℡04.67.73.00.56, Ⓦwww.otcevennesmediterranee.com). There are various banks with exchange services (look along rue Frédéric-Mistral), and you can connect to the **Internet** at Médi@gora, beside the *gare routière*. L'Atelier (℡04.67.73.69.20), by the tourist office, rents **bikes**. Also on plan l'Ormeau you'll find a **hotel**, the basic *De la Poste* (℡04.67.73.85.88, ✉hotel.dela.poste@wanadoo.fr; closed Jan; ❷). The *Domaine de Blancardy* (℡04.67.73.94.94, ⊛www.blancardy.com; ❶), 7km out of town in the direction of Nîmes, also operates a comfortable and well-equipped **gîte** with some private rooms (❷). The municipal **campsite** (℡04.67.57.92.97), along the river at the southern end of town, has the only laundry. Of the local **restaurants**, the best is *Le Josyln' Melodie* (℡04.67.73.66.02; closed Wed), a homely little Lyonnais place on 4 pl Fabre d'Olivet (*menus* €7.35 at lunch, €12.50 at dinner), although *La Rose de Saigon* at 12 pl des Halles (closed Tues) serves good Vietnamese cuisine (from €7.50 at lunch, €11 at dinner). For something lighter, try the crêperie *La Luciole* next door at no. 11.

Laroque, the Grotte des Demoiselles and St-Bauzille

A couple of kilometres south from Ganges, the first place you come to is the hamlet of **LAROQUE**, attractively situated on a hillside along the Hérault river. It has a cheerful bank-side promenade, with narrow medieval streets zigzaging up to the remains of its castle. At the entrance to the town, there is a small twelfth-century church, while on the south side lie the ruins of a huge nineteenth-century textile plant. A few kilometres further south, you'll come upon the area's biggest draw, the **Grotte des Demoiselles** (daily: April–June & Sept 9am–noon & 2–6pm; July & Aug 9am–7pm; Oct–March 9.30am–noon & 2–5pm; ⊛www.demoiselles.com; €7.50), a little more than 2km east off the road. This incredibly vast cavern, discovered in 1770, stretches out below the plateau de Thaurac, the highland southeast of Ganges, and is famous for its huge stalactite and stalagmite formations. The obligatory one-hour **guided tour** (expect a long wait in high season; last departure 1hr before closing) is made aboard an underground funicular (hourly; last departure 45min before closing), which lends the whole thing an amusement-park air, and though the cave is spectacular, it can be a bit of a let-down after all the crowds and fuss. Just south of the grotto, **ST-BAUZILLE** is of note only as a stopping point in the vicinity of the cave and as a centre for river-oriented sports; it's a good place to shop for a canoe trip south down the Hérault.

Without doubt, the nicest place to **stay** in this area is Laroque, where you can get a room or a meal (from €12) at the comfortable *Aux Trois Arches* (℡04.67.73.86.80; April–Oct; ❸) on the main promenade. In a park on the northern edge of town, *Le Parc aux Cedres*, 120 av de l'Europe (℡04.67.73.82.63, ✆04.67.73.69.85, ❹), also has a restaurant, while *Bar de Ramparts*, near the *Trois Arches*, has decent Belgian beers and home-made desserts. There is also a **campsite**, the two-star *Le Tivoli* (℡04.67.73.97.28; June–Aug), near the *Cédres*.

South to Montpellier

Heading south from Ganges to Montpellier, you can choose between two routes, whose paths diverge at **St–Bauzille** (see above). The longer, more spectacular of the two leads down the Hérault gorge to the medieval abbey-town of St-Guilhem-le-Désert, emerging from the canyon shortly before Gignac, from where you can either head 30km east to Montpellier or continue to Clermont-l'Hérault. Unfortunately, only the St-Guilhem–Gignac leg of this route is served by buses, and then only in summer, so if you don't have your own transport, doing the whole thing will involve some walking or hitching. The other option is to head due south, a forty-kilometre route which takes you to St-Martin-de-Londres, from where you can hike to the Pic-St-Loup and surrounding sights. St-Martin is, in fact, only 6km from the banks of the Hérault, but is separated from the river by a series of low peaks; if you have a car or are willing to hitchhike or walk, you could link up the two routes by heading first to St-Martin and then doubling back on the treacherously winding D122 to the village of **Causse-de-la-Selle**, north of St-Guilhem on the valley route (a distance of 14km). Stopping at Causse also gives you the opportunity of making the trip to St-Guilhem by river raft (see opposite) – the most thrilling way to take in the gorges.

Via St-Guilhem-le-Désert

The route from Ganges to St-Guilhem follows the course of the Hérault via the D4 on the river's right bank, which you access by crossing the bridge at St-Bauzille. After 15km, the road cuts southwest across a plateau, passing the hamlet of Causse-de-la-Selle – the turn-off for St-Martin-de-Londres (see above) – before rejoining the river midway through the dramatic **Gorges de l'Hérault**. Hugging the western bank, the road follows the tortuous canyon to reach the stunningly situated hamlet of **ST-GUILHEM-LE-DÉSERT**. There is no mistaking the great antiquity of this village; nestled in a steep and wooded ravine rising from the gorge, the reddish roofs of its medieval houses contrast with the electric green of the surrounding trees. The town grew up around the abbey founded by Charlemagne's counsellor Guilhem, who returned from Rome in 800 with three pieces of wood said to be remnants of the Cross. Thanks to these relics, the monastery and the village around it throve through the centuries that followed, both as a pilgrimage destination in its own right, as well as a stopping point on the way to Santiago de Compostela. Today, the immaculately preserved town, designated a UNESCO World Heritage site, is still presided over by the eleventh-century **abbey-church of Gellone** (daily 8am–12.10pm & 2.30–6.20pm; free), at the upper end of the village, by the obligatory car park (€5; the lower car park is €3). Crowned by a chunky, fifteenth-century bell tower, the church is the only surviving part of the once powerful monastic house. Its magnificent entryway, flanked by columns pillaged from Roman ruins, passes through a small vaulted narthex and opens into the cavernous but plain nave, ending in a curiously oversized transept and apse. Inside the church is the casket holding the remains of Guilhem (who was canonized after his death) and a reliquary holding one of the famous bits of wood. From the church you can climb down to the **crypt**, which dates back to the eighth century, as well as the ruined **cloister**, whose north and west galleries are still in place. There is also a small **museum** here (July & Aug Mon–Thurs & Sat 11am–noon & 2–5pm, Sun 2–5pm; Sept–June Mon & Wed–Sat 2–5pm, Sun 2.30–5pm; €1.50) containing religious sculptures recovered from the destroyed abbey. The rest of the village consists of low, ancient houses which follow the narrow lanes leading down the ravine, interrupted by medieval pilgrims' fountains marked with the scallop-shell symbol of St James. Looking back as you descend past the church, you'll be treated to views of its impressive apsidal chapels.

Alternatively, a one-hour **hike** leads up from the car park to the ruins of a castle, from where you get the best **views** of the town. Just after this, the GR trail splits, with the GR74 climbing through a canyon towards Mont St-Baudille, and the GR653 looping south before merging again with the GR74 to proceed west to Lodève. The tourist office (see opposite) can give you information on the several AR trails which run through the hills hereabouts.

Leaving St-Guilhem by road, the D4 continues 4km further along the dramatic canyon, passing the mouth of the **Grotte de Clamouse** (daily: Feb–May & Oct 10am–5pm; June & Sept 10am–6pm; July & Aug 10am–7pm; Nov–Jan noon–5pm; €6.80), famous for its immense and delicate crystalline formations. Only 500m later, the gorge abruptly opens up at the beginning of the low Languedocian coastal plain; the transition is marked by a great medieval *pont du diable*, which crosses the river above a gravelly bank now serving as a popular river-beach. Shortly beyond, you pass the uninteresting hamlets of Aniane and Gignac, the latter of which serves as a bus interchange.

St-Guilhem's **tourist office** (July & Aug 9am–7pm; Sept–June 10.30am–12.30pm & 2–7pm; ℡04.67.57.44.32, Ⓦwww.saint-guilhem-le-desert.com) is at the foot of the village, just above the main road; the office has an ATM, and they can give you a coupon offering you €2 off entry to the Grotte de Clamouse. The best of the town's two hotels is *La Taverne de l'Escuelle* (℡04.67.57.72.05; ❸) in 11 chemin Val Gellone. A number of **gîtes** in and around St-Guilhem can put you up for the night, including the English-speaking *Gîte de la Tour* (℡ & ℻04.67.57.34.00; ❶), located in a medieval tower in the village, and the CAF *gîte* (℡04.67.52.72.11; ❶), also in town. A dramatic approach to the town can be made from the riverbank 3km east of Causse on the D122, from where Canoë La Vallée de Moulins (℡04.67.73.12.45) runs **canoeing** excursions downriver to St-Guilhem. St-Guilhem's **rafting centre** is at the bottom of the hill, across the road (℡04.67.55.75.75).

Via the Pic-St-Loup and St-Martin-de-Londres

Some 20km due south of St-Bauzille looms the great **Pic–St–Loup** (658m), which, dominating the plain of Hérault, can be seen from Béziers almost to Nîmes. **ST-MARTIN-DE-LONDRES**, 13km south from Ganges by road or hiking trail (the GR60, leaving St-Bauzille), makes the best base for hiking the remaining 10km to the *pic*'s wooded summit – a site from which you can enjoy impressive panoramas, but which cannot be reached except by foot (car drivers can get as close as 4km away by taking the D113 to the hamlet of Cazevielle). St-Martin is another town of great antiquity and, contrary to appearances, its name has nothing to do with England's capital, London ("Londres" in French); it is named after the Plaine du Londres (from the Celtic word for "swamp") in which the town is located. Testament to the town's history is the beautiful knot of buildings focused around the eleventh-century Romanesque **church**, founded by monks from nearby St-Guilhem. Its interior is plain, but is more than made up for by the three-lobed Byzantine-style exterior, which blends in harmoniously with the surrounding buildings. Elsewhere in the town, you can see how the two concentric sets of walls and towers were swallowed up by houses over the centuries.

If you're **hiking** into town, or if you're not up to tackling the *pic*, about 2km north of St-Martin a leg of the GR60 leads off eastwards into the Ravin des Arcs, a high but narrow canyon which makes an excellent two-hour walking circuit; be sure to bring water along, as there is no potable source on the way – you can fill up at the public fountain in front of the tourist office (see p.298). Another option is the ninety-minute walk south of St-Martin (but also on the Montpellier bus route) to Viols-en-Laval, where you'll find the excavated **pre-historic village** of **Cambous** (April–June & Sept Sat & Sun 2–6pm: Easter hols daily 2–7pm: July & Aug Tues, Wed & Fri–Sun 2–7pm; Oct–March Sun 2–6pm; €2.50), once home to the "Fontbouisse" culture, which practised copper-smelting and ceramic production as well as agriculture and herding some 5000 years ago.

St-Martin's **tourist office** (May to early July & late Aug to mid–Sept Mon & Tues 9.30am–12.30pm; July & Aug daily 9am–1pm; ☎04.67.55.09.59, ⓦwww.tourismed.com) is on the main road in the centre of town. For accommodation, there is the **gîte**, *La Bergerie du Bayle* (☎ & ⓕ04.67.55.72.16, ❶), which also does very affordable half-pension. The **campsite**, *Pic de Loup* (☎04.67.55.00.53, ⓔcamping-pic@tourisme.com; April–Sept), is just east on the main road. A recommendable **restaurant** in St-Martin is *Les Muscardins* (☎04.67.55.75.90; closed Feb & Mon & Tues), which has superb Cevennoise *menus* from €25 (weekdays) and €45 (weekends), while a more economical yet very worthwhile option is *La Pastourelle* (call ahead, ☎04.67.55.72.78), for excellent *terroir menus* (from €18).

Travel details

Trains

SNCF buses may run in lieu of trains on these lines; services are reduced on Sundays and holidays.

Montpellier to: Agde (18 daily; 35min); Beaucaire (2 daily; 1hr 5min); Béziers (18 daily; 40min); Carcassonne (18 daily; 1hr 30min–4hr); Lunel (26 daily; 15min); Narbonne (26 daily; 45min–1hr 15min); Nîmes (26 daily; 30min); Paris (16 daily; 3hr 15min–6hr); Perpignan (12 daily; 2hr 15min); Sète (22 daily; 15–20min); Toulouse (18 daily; 2hr 15min–2hr 55min).

Buses

Many lines in Hérault have no Sunday service; service on Saturdays and holidays may be reduced. Summer lines, *lignes estivales*, serve St-Guilhem and other tourist sites.

Clermont-l'Hérault to: Lodève (3–4 daily; 35min); Pézenas (6 daily; 35min)

Ganges to: Montpellier (6–7 daily; 1hr 10min); Nîmes (3 daily; 1hr 15min); Quissac (3 daily; 45min); St-Hippolyte (3 daily; 15min); St-Martin-de-Londres (6–7 daily; 25min); Sauve (3 daily; 25min).

Gignac (summer only) to: Pont du Diable (1–5 daily; 20min); St-Guilhem (1–5 daily; 35min).

La Grande-Motte to: Le Grau-du-Roi (9 daily; 10min); Lunel (2 daily; 35min); Nîmes (9 daily; 40min).

Lodève to: Béziers (5 daily; 1hr 50min); Clermont-l'Hérault (5 daily; 45min); Pézenas (5 daily; 1 hr 20min).

Lunel to: Villetelle (for Ambrussum; 4 daily; 20min).

Montpellier to: Béziers (11daily; 1hr 30min); Clermont-l'Hérault (6–12 daily; 40min); Ganges (4–5 daily; 1hr 15min); Gignac (for St-Guilhem; 6–8 daily; 40min); La Grande-Motte (8–12 daily; 1hr 5min; in summer hourly); Le Grau-du-Roi (8–12 daily; 1hr 10min); Lodève (4 daily; 1hr 15min); Lunel (8 daily; 35min); Nîmes (2 daily; 50min); Palavas (local service); Pézenas (10 daily; 1hr); St-Hippolyte (2 daily; 1 hr 45min); St-Martin-de-Londres (6 daily; 50min); St-Pons (2 daily; 2hr 20min); Sète (10 daily; 1hr 10min); Sommières (4 daily; 1hr 10min).

Pézenas to: Béziers (10 daily; 32min); Clermont-l'Hérault (6 daily; 35min); Lodève (4 daily; 1hr 20min); Montpellier (10 daily; 1hr).

Narbonne, Béziers and around

N

Highlights

* **Lagrasse** A sleepy little village which grew up around a once-powerful monastery. See p.317

* **Canal du Midi** France's seventeenth-century engineering wonder is now a sublimely beautiful thoroughfare for cyclists, walkers and boaters. See p.318

* **Oppidum Enseurune** A pre-Roman settlement, perched on a ridge above the vineyards of Béziers. See p.324

* **Old Béziers** Atmospheric streets and a splendid cathedral which provides views as far west as the Canigou. See p.327

* **The Orb valley** Rarely visited, this river course boasts unique micro-climate zones and near-forgotten hamlets. See p.333

▲ Béziers

6

Narbonne, Béziers and around

T he provincial towns of **Narbonne** and **Béziers** dominate the flat expanse of marshy alluvial plain formed by the outpourings of the Hérault, Orb and Aude rivers, whose mouths all reach the Mediterranean within a 15km strip. The former town is the smaller, but generally livelier centre, with a compact medieval core and vibrant nightlife, while the latter is a historically proud and defiant place which, though some- what more sedate these days, springs to life in the summer with its renowned *feria*. Poised just north of the Étang de Bages' long expanse, Narbonne is best situated for excursions into the **Corbières**, an isolated range of hills stretch- ing south to Roussillon; once forming the Cathar heartland, they harbour the idyllic village of **Termes**, with its *château*, and the strikingly beautiful hamlet of **Lagrasse**. Swinging sharp east at Carcassonne, the River Aude makes its way along the northern edge of the Corbières, shadowed by the **Canal du Midi**, the incredible waterway which has dominated the whole of this area since the seventeenth century, and which links both Narbonne and Béziers. The canal route takes you past the various monuments of the **Minervois** – the region squeezed in between the Corbières and Haut Languedoc – and attractive Languedocian scenery before it splits, with the Canal de la Robine heading south towards Narbonne and the main waterway meandering on, via Béziers, to the Bassin de Thau. Skirting Béziers, the route up the **Orb valley** threads north along the border of the Parc Naturel de Haut Languedoc, pass- ing a succession of villages which have survived the centuries thanks to the river's fertile banks. The coastal stretch curving between the two towns is, for the most part, an area of uninviting marsh, but at either end two chunks of terra firma, the Montagne St-Loup and de la Clape, provide anchors for a couple of old ports, **Agde** and **Gruissan**, each of which have modern beach- resort alter egos. Although those interested in sun and swimming will find prettier surroundings in the Côte Vermeille to the south, both of these old set- tlements are worth a visit for their gentle ambience – Agde from Béziers and Gruissan from Narbonne.

  Public transport facilities in this region vary considerably. At Narbonne, the busy coastal rail line to Perpignan branches off from the main Toulouse–Marseille route, on which Béziers can be found. In the hinterland, you'll have to depend on bus services, which are fairly good for the major

6

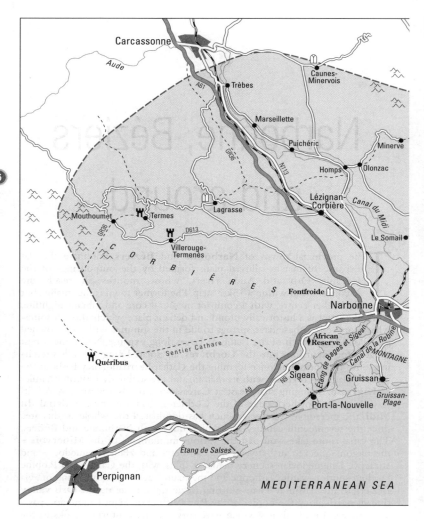

towns along the coast and the Orb valley. Out-of-the-way sites are more difficult: Minerve, for example, isn't served at all by public transport (although the
narrow-gauge ATM train does approach it). But in any case – if you have time
– the best way to travel through the region is by canal, either by piloting a
houseboat, or biking or hiking along the towpath.

Narbonne and around

There's no mistaking **NARBONNE** as you approach it, its towering cathedral rising up over the rooftops and dominating the coastal plain for miles around. Once the capital of the Roman province of Gallia Narbonensis, it flourished as a port and communications centre from ancient times into the Middle Ages, and was home to an important Jewish university in the twelfth and thirteenth centuries. But in the mid-1300s things suddenly went awry: the Jews were expelled, the plague struck, the Black Prince burnt down the town, the dykes

A, B, C, I, Gare SNCF, Béziers & Montpellier

ACCOMMODATION

Alsace	A
Camping Club Les Mimosas	C
La Dorade	G
Les Floralys	L
de France	K
de la Gare	B
Grand Hôtel du Languedoc	I
du Midi	H
MJC	E
Le Regent	J
La Résidence	F
Will's	D

RESTAURANTS

L'Agora	4
L'Alsace	1
Aux Trois Caves	5
CO	9
L'Estagnol	7
Palais du Vin	3
La Petite Cour	6
Royal Kebab	8
La Table St-Crescent	2

NARBONNE

L & Gruissan

of the Aude burst and the port silted up, a series of disasters which brought ruin to Narbonne's economy. A tentative prosperity returned only in the late 1800s with the birth of the modern wine industry, which continues to support the town. Today, it's a pleasant provincial town with a small but well-preserved old core, centred on the great truncated choir of the **cathedral** and bisected by the **Canal de la Robine** (see p.322), whose banks provide a grassy esplanade in the heart of things. Narbonne also makes a handy base for exploring surrounding attractions, including the old port of **Gruissan**, Sigean's **nature reserve** and the abbey of **Fontfroide**, which you can also visit en route to the Corbières hills (see p.315).

In the summer of 1991 Narbonne acquired notoriety as a flashpoint in France's continuing problems with its ethnic minorities, this time a long-suffering and disregarded minority desperately forcing itself on public attention. Among its mixed population of relative newcomers, Narbonne has for thirty-

In this little corner of Languedoc, Béziers is the hot spot for popular festivals, with its five-day *feria* the prime attraction. Narbonne, for its part, is big on theatre and also has a good Carnaval. There are summer music cycles and parties throughout the area and, as can be expected from a wine region, local festivals timed with the grape harvest. Where no specific information number is given, contact the relevant tourist office for details.

Late Jan to early March Narbonne: Carnaval. A series of parades, dances and street entertainment held on the weekends leading up to Lent.

Late April Béziers: Fête de la Ste-Aphrodise. The feast day of the town's patron saint, usually held on the third Sunday, and featuring a curious procession with a camel float.

Late June to early July Narbonne: Festival National de Théâtre Amateur. Free nightly theatrical performances (9.15pm) on the cours de la Madeleine and at the Archbishop's Palace. ℡04.66.32.40.50.

Throughout July Narbonne: Orgues d'Été. Evening organ recitals every Sunday in the cathedral.

First two weeks of July Béziers: Festival de Musique de Béziers. Classical choral performances of international quality held in various venues.

July 12–15 Narbonne: Bastille Day. Huge four-day outdoor party in cours Mirabeau.

Late July Cap d'Agde: Fête de la Mer. After an open-air Mass for victims of the sea, the boats are blessed, and there's water-jousting and general celebration.

Late July Gruissan: Fête des Pêcheurs. Sea-faring rituals, including boat blessings and a procession with the statue of St Peter.

Throughout July & Aug Bédarieux: Soirées Musicals. Evening performances of comedy and music (from medieval to jazz to reggae), which are usually free, in the place Nouvel.

Throughout July & Aug Lamalou-les-Bains: Festival National d'Operettes. Operetta troupes from around France perform in Lamalou's casino. ℡04.67.95.70.91, Ⓦwww.lamalou.free.fr

Throughout July & Aug Villerouge-Termènes: Fête Médiéval. Medieval market, fair and events held in even-numbered years. ℡04.68.70.06.24

Mid-July to mid-Aug Orb valley: Festival de la Vallée de l'Orb. Choral music and folk activities related to wine, held in town squares and churches throughout the region. ℡04.67.89.65.32

Late July to early Aug Sigean: Musical. Street festival featuring music, theatre and children's activities. ℡04.68.40.40.95

Aug 5 & 6 Narbonne: Fête du Commerce et du Vin. Wine festival.

Aug 10 & 11 Narbonne: La Via Mercadaria. Medieval street market and fair.

Mid-Aug Béziers: La Feria. Four-day festival with street entertainment, fireworks, music and a daily Spanish-style *corrida* (tickets €24–83).

Aug 25–28 Narbonne: Semaine Bavaroise. Narbonne's summer version of the Munich Oktoberfest, with plenty of lager and lederhosen.

Throughout Sept Narbonne: Orgues d'Été. September's version of the July series of recitals.

Late Oct Béziers: Les Primeurs d'Oc. The best of the local wine festivals, with wine contests, music and traditional activities.

odd years been home to a group of *harkis*, Algerians who had enlisted in the French forces and fought with them against their own people in the Algerian war of independence in the late 1950s. After the war they were settled in France for their own protection, and since then have received little or no help. Eventually the *harkis'* children, now French citizens, broke out in open protest, angry at finding themselves still last in the pecking order in spite of their parents' sacrifice. In the intervening years little has been resolved, and occasional sit-ins and protests continue, with *harki* claims supported by the French Socialist Party but still not leading to any comprehensive settlement.

Arrival and information

Narbonne's **gare SNCF** is situated at the eastern end of the railyard that runs along the northern edge of the city centre, at the head of the RN9 as it leaves town. It has **left luggage** facilities; enquire at the information desk. From here it's about a fifteen-minute walk to the place de l'Hôtel de Ville in the centre, or a short hop on buses #1, #2 or the Petit Bus. Just to the southwest, on the far side of the freight terminal, you'll find the **gare routière**. If you're **driving** into town, you can park just about anywhere you find a spot – most plazas and streets have meter-parking. The town's main **tourist office** (April–Sept daily 9.30am–12.15pm & 2–6pm; Oct–March Tues–Sun 10am–noon & 2–5pm; ☎04.68.65.15.60, ⓦwww.mairie-narbonne.fr) is on tiny place Roger-Salengro, just to the north of the cathedral, but there is also canalside **information kiosk** at the southern end of the centre on quai Victor-Hugo (June–Sept Mon–Sat 10am–7pm; Nov–May 8am–noon & 2–6pm). Information on festivals and events can be picked up in the free fortnightly events magazine, *Olé!*, which also covers the surrounding area; available at the tourist office and news-stands.

Narbonne has an efficient municipal **bus** system. You can buy single tickets (€1) from drivers and ten-trip TICTEN passes at tobacconists. If you want to rent a **bike**, try Cycles Cancel, 50 boulevard Frédéric-Mistral (☎04.68.65.12.26).

Accommodation

It's easy to find reasonable **accommodation** in Narbonne. In addition to a fair number of hotels, whose prices are relatively good compared with many other cities in the South of France, there's a hostel and a couple of decent campsites. The two main concentrations of accommodation are in the immediate vicinity of the gare SNCF and along the Canal du Robine, which flows through the centre.

Hotels

Alsace 2 av Carnot ☎04.68.32.01.86, ⓔhotel-lal-sace@wanadoo.fr. Just across from the station, this small, old-fashioned two-star is clean, but the rooms are on the small side. ❷

La Dorade 44 rue Jean-Jaurès ☎04.68.32.65.95, ⓕ04.68.65.81.62. Founded as a hotel in 1648 and a traditional favourite of visiting nobility, this beautiful building is in good repair despite its age, having been fully renovated in the early 1990s. Great location facing out onto the canal, and excellent service; amenities include TV and garage. ❸

De France 6 rue Rossini ☎04.68.32.09.75, ⓦwww.hotelnarbonne.com. Just south of the old town, and steps from the covered market and the canal, this quiet nineteenth-century establishment has TVs in the rooms and parking facilities, and is wheelchair accessible. ❷

De la Gare 7 av Pierre-Sémard ☎04.68.32.10.54. This stationside hotel is a bit run-down, but does the trick if you're looking for cheap, basic accommodation. ❶

Grand Hôtel du Languedoc 22 bd Gambetta ☎04.68.65.14.74, ⓕ04.68.65.81.48. One of the better deals in town, this is another attractive old building – a nineteenth-century house – which has been converted into a well-appointed and comfortable hotel. Located on the ring road, a five-minute walk south of the cathedral. ❷

Hotel du Midi 4 av de Toulouse ☎04.68.41.04.62, ⓦwww.le-midi-narbonne.com. A comfortable but affordable all-mod-cons option, with a parking garage and wheelchair access. ❸

Le Regent 5 rue Mosaïque/13 rue Suffren ☎04.68.32.02.41, ⓦwww.leregentnarbonne.com. Reasonable accommodation in the quieter and newer part of the city centre, two minutes' south of boulevard Gambetta. Rooms have TV. **❸**

La Résidence 6 rue 1er du Mai ☎04.68.32.19.41, ℱ04.68.65.18.48. Another early nineteenth-century converted house, with a great location on a quiet street near the pont Voltaire. Comfortable rooms, and comes with AC, a garage and lift, but you pay for the privileges. **❻**

Will's 23 av Pierre-Sémard ☎04.68.90.44.50, ℱ04.68.32.26.28. Friendly place and a travellers' standby, which accepts pets and has amenities like TV and cable, but fills up quickly. Right by the train station. **❷**

Hostel and campsites

Camping Club Les Mimosa's Chausée de Mandirac ☎04.68.49.03.72, ⓦwww.lesmimosas.com. Big 3-star site with all mod-cons, located 6km south of town on the Étang de Bages (no public transport). Open late March to Oct.

Les Floralys rte de Gruissan ☎ & ℱ04.68.32.65.65. The closest campsite to town, located 3km from the centre on the road heading south towards the coast, this is a small, thirty-pitch site with good services (including laundry and restaurant). Open all year round.

MJC Centre International de Séjour pl Roger-Salengro ☎04.68.32.01.00, ℱ04.68.65.80.20. Modern hostel right by the tourist office, with dorm (€12) and – limited – private room (**❶**) accommodation. Nice lounge with TV and a simple restaurant.

The Town

If Narbonne's name lends itself to a certain sense of grandeur, you'll be shocked by its diminutive size. The whole of the **old town** – which is where all the sights are – fits snugly into a 1km-by-750m rectangle, bisected north–south by the **Canal de la Robine**. Of the two halves it is the eastern that holds the main draws, with the **archbishop's palace**, its **museums** and the **cathedral** dominating affairs, plus a number of medieval attractions on their periphery. The western side of the canal, though less salubrious than its eastern counterpart, also harbours a couple of interesting sights.

A single ticket costing €5 and valid for three days gives you entry to all of Narbonne's museums (unless otherwise noted).

The Archbishop's Palace

The broad square of the place de l'Hôtel de Ville, in whose centre you'll find a recently uncovered section of the Roman Via Domitia, is marked on its southern side by the grand old Aux Dames de France department store, while the entire north side is taken up by the great facade of the **Archbishop's Palace**, peppered by pointed ogival windows and decorated with Gothic-looking vegetal flourishes. But while you marvel at its medieval beauty, it is worth bearing in mind that what you are looking at is in fact one of Viollet-le-Duc's imaginative repair jobs (see box on p.128), an ersatz bit of medievalia. Now the town hall, the palace's rambling complex also incorporates the city's two major museums, plus the entrance to the cathedral (see below). Passing through the main doors of the palace, which are directly on the square, on the left you'll find the entrance to the towering **donjon** (Mon–Fri 9am–noon & 2–6pm) commissioned in the late thirteenth century by the town's lord and archbishop, Gilles Aycelin. This ponderous 42m defensive tower is a fine example of late thirteenth-century military architecture – its splayed-out base, which was constructed over the remains of the previous Roman wall, was designed to prevent battering and better withstand attempts to undermine the keep. There's not much to see inside, but from the top (after managing a 162-step key-stone staircase) you can enjoy excellent **views** of the cathedral and the surrounding countryside. Back at the main entrance, heading straight ahead leads you out into a broad courtyard, occasionally the scene for concerts and exhibitions, and from here you can access the two museums: the **art and history museum** and **archeological museum**.

The art and history museum

On the left you'll see the entrance to the **art and history museum** (May–Sept daily 9.30am–12.15pm & 2–6pm; Oct–May Tues–Sun 10am–noon & 2–5pm), which is located on the upper floors of the palace. The collection, featuring scores of canvases of mediocre seventeenth-century portraiture and landscape, plus some early modern pottery and *faïence*, is on the whole less than stunning, and at times you'll find it more rewarding to take in the luxurious interior of the palace itself, with its *artesonado* ceilings and other details; rooms to look out for in particular are the audience hall, the king's chamber – with seventeenth-century painted walls – and the grand salon. That said, a smattering of medieval pieces certainly warrant attention, and the museum's highlight, the **Orientalist collection** in the salle Hippolyte Lazerges, alone almost justifies the admission price. Here some thirty-odd works, dating from the seventeenth to twentieth centuries, reflect the European fascination with the world of the desert: paintings depicting sultry Berber girls staring enigmatically at the viewer, or eyes flashing from under turbans, as bearded men pose with cruel-looking swords on horse- or camel-back. On your way out, poke your head in the **Hall of the Synods**, accessed from the same grand staircase as the museum. Built by one of the archbishops in 1628, it was used for clerical meetings and sittings of the *parlement* of Languedoc and is decorated with impressive Aubusson tapestries.

The archeological museum

A much better collection can be found just across the courtyard at the **archeological museum** (same hours as the art and history museum), which strikes a good balance between the artefact and explanation. It begins with the Neolithic period, represented by various skull parts and a series of footprints preserved in solidified muck, and follows with Bronze Age finds (the usual brooches and weapons) from the *oppida* of the region. The mainstay of the exhibition, however, is its **Roman collection**, whose strong maritime streak reflects the role which Narbonne played as a major port of Roman Gaul. Various stone carvings illustrate ships of the period, and there's a towering 3.5-metre wood-and-lead ship's **anchor** on display. Combined with the seafaring items is a collection of first-century BC **Roman paintings** – the best of its kind in France. Most of the pieces came from a villa in the northern part of the Roman town, and include elaborate borders, depictions of country scenes and "portraits" of gods. The collection winds up with an impressively large mosaic from the same period as the paintings, and a number of paleo-Christian sarcophagi.

The Cathédral de St-Just et St-Pasteur

From the archeological museum a narrow alley, the passage de l'Ancre, leads further into the complex, towards the entrance to the **Cathédral de St-Just et St-Pasteur** (April–Sept 9.30am–12.15pm & 2–6pm; Oct–March 10am–noon & 2–5pm; free). Christianity in the city dates back at least to the time when Constantine the Great proclaimed it the empire's official religion in 328 AD; as a provincial capital Narbonne became seat of an archbishop, and a cathedral was raised. Its exterior is pure Gothic – the tall and narrow core of the building, dominated by expanses of stained-glass window, is braced by sturdy buttresses, from which delicate-looking flying buttresses launch up to support the highest points on the walls. The building which you see today is the fourth to sit on this site, and was begun in 1272. With the completion of the hulking 49-metre choir some fifty years later, construction of the nave, which

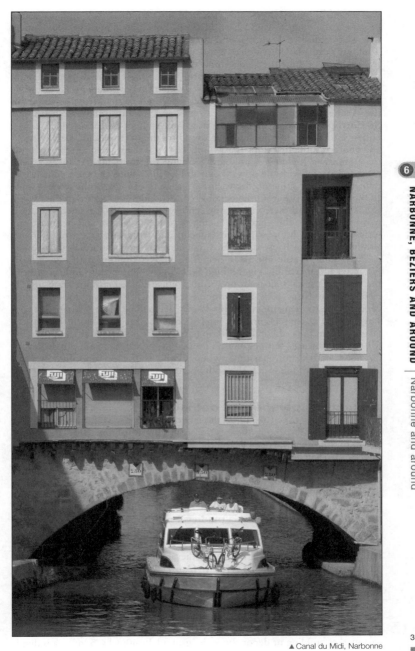

▲ Canal du Midi, Narbonne

was meant to extend westwards, was held up after the first couple of stages, because extending it would have involved knocking down the old Roman defensive wall – still very useful in those uncertain times. Thus, as with Toulouse's cathedral, the project was never completed, leaving the church with its strikingly odd form. As you climb the short flight of stairs from the street you'll arrive first at the compact **cloister**, from where there's a good view of the seemingly delicate array of buttresses which support the light Gothic-style walls. A door on the west side of the cloister leads to the formal-style **Jardin des Archevêques**, with even better views, and around to the so-called **Cour St-Eutrope**, which is in fact the sealed-off stub of the aborted nave. The entrance to the church itself can be found on the north side of the cloister.

On entering, the first thing that will strike you is the tremendous space inside the unfinished building – its soaring ceiling the third highest for a French cathedral. Along with the upward dynamic of the design, the predominance of stained glass over stone on the walls is a hallmark of high Gothic style – some of the windows date from the original construction. The centre of the church is taken up by elaborate eighteenth-century **choir stalls**, presided over by a massive **organ** of the same era. Facing it is the high altar, and behind this a series of chapels hung with fine Gobelin and Aubusson tapestries. Directly behind the altar, a badly damaged – but nevertheless beautiful – fourteenth-century stone **retable** illustrates themes of the Redemption with exceptionally carved and incredibly kinetic high-relief figures. From the southernmost of the chapels, a spiral stair leads up to the beehive-shaped chamber housing the cathedral's **treasury** (€3), the centrepiece of which is a sumptuous fifteenth-century tapestry depicting the Holy Trinity, personified as three kings. On your way out of the church complex, after descending the stairs from the cloister, take a peek in the cathedral's gift shop (same hours as the church), not so much for the stuff on sale, but because it's housed in the elegant **Salle au Pilier**, an airy fourteenth-century chamber whose Gothic vaulting is supported by a single delicate pillar, and in which you'll find carvings dating back to the Visigoths of the sixth century.

Around the palace and cathedral

It's worth taking time to explore the lesser sights in the vicinity of the palace and cathedral. First among these is the small **chapel of the Blue Penitents**, just steps from the tourist office on the west side of place Salengro, in the heart of the "quartier de Europe", as this part of the old town is called. Originally founded in 1149 for the Hospitaller Knights, the chapel has suffered a bout of Baroque, and its interior (hours vary) is a bland white with pale blue detailing, but you can still recognize the fine Romanesque features of its doorway. South of the square two small streets lead directly away from the massive east wall of the cathedral and into a compact **medieval neighbourhood**, which was once the *quartier* of the choristers and other functionaries of the great church: rue de Lieutenant-Colonel-Deymes and the next street along, rue Rouget de l'Isle, both contain houses with distinctly medieval windows and doors. On the latter street, at no. 7, is the **Horreum** (April–Sept daily 9.30am–12.15pm & 2–6pm; Oct–March Tues–Sun 10am–noon & 2–5pm). Despite Narbonne's importance in Roman times, this is the only structure in the city which has survived from that era – in fact it disappeared until 1838, when the building covering it was demolished. It's name means "granary" in Latin, and that's precisely what it was: an underground grain store which was most likely attached to a market building or depot above the ground. Its 40m-by-50m area is divided into a series of small storage chambers leading off a rectangular passage.

There's not much to see inside, apart from some ancient graffiti, but it does make for an atmospheric visit.

From the Horreum, head east to the bend in rue Maréchal, where an ancient Roman **stela** sits in the courtyard of the grandiose Hôtel de Poulhariez **building** (now apartments). Following this street further will take you to place Bistan, where you'll see the meagre remains of the Roman forum and capitol, while the once graceful yet flamboyant Gothic **church of St-Sébastian** rises up in rue Michelet, just to the south of the square. From the *place*, atmospheric rue Droite traces the route of both the Roman and medieval main street west back to the place de l'Hotel de Ville.

West of the Canal de la Robine

Narbonne's old town extends over the Canal de la Robine to the west, but in the Middle Ages, as today, this neighbourhood on the far side is a humbler section of town. The narrow lanes and crooked streets are home to the city's marginalized North African community, and the plethora of police who comb it are testament to the social problems which grip the area. Even so, it is eminently explorable; there are fewer shops and restaurants here, and the tiny windows of the ageing buildings hang with laundry but the main reason for visiting is to see the two parish churches which share this side of the river. The first is the **Basilique de St-Paul** on rue Dupleix, which you can reach by crossing the canal at pont Voltaire and proceeding south. It's a tall thirteenth-century construction, chipped and battered on the outside over the years, but inside possessing a pleasant mixture of Romanesque and Gothic. The main attraction is the **crypt** (Mon–Sat 9am–noon & 2–6pm; free); built over a paleo-Christian necropolis and dating back to the fourth century, it is where the town's first bishop was buried. Scattered about the low-ceilinged room are various amphora, sarcophagi and a small mosaic.

Leaving the crypt, around the far side of the church, pick up rue de l'Hôtel Dieu, at the corner of which, with rue Quinet, you'll find the magnificent sixteenth-century facade of the **Maison de Trois Nourrices**. Taking the next left will lead you to place and rue Belfort, and another crop of medieval dwellings, while at the end of the street, a car-filled *place* opens up in front of the former abbey-church of Notre-Dame-de-la-Mourguié. This is now home to the town's **lapidary museum** (July–Sept daily 9.30am–noon & 2–6pm; rest of the year by request at the tourist office), with a large – but monotonous – collection of over a thousand statues, inscriptions, tombstones and sarcophagi, most dating back to the days of Roman glory. The town's beautifully restored nineteenth-century **covered market** (daily 7am–1pm) is right beside the church on the banks of the canal, while along its south side runs the boulevard de Dr-Ferroul, whose stately facades braced by elaborate wrought-iron balustrades testify to the wealth which the wine industry brought in the late 1800s. Finally, the town has a quirky new attraction in the home of native **Charles Trénet** (April–Sept 10am–noon & 2–6pm, Oct–March 2–6pm; €5), at 13 avenue Charles Trénet. A local legend (1913–2001) known as the "singing fool," he was half of the popular 1930s act "Charles and Johnny", and in post-war France became an international cabaret star. Jammed with personal effects, his house recalls in a campy spirit the nostalgic simplicity of still-colonial 1930s and 1950s France.

Eating, drinking and nightlife

Narbonne is definitely not the culinary capital of the Southwest, but you won't starve. There are a couple of **restaurants** which stand out, as well as an array of unexceptional brasseries and bistros where you can eat for under €18. The best place to browse is along the cours de la République on the southern portion of the canal, where you'll also find lots of informal snack places, and the boulevard Gambetta which runs off it to the east.

The **nightlife** situation is quite the opposite, with a profusion of energetic bars and clubs – curious in a town so quiet and lacking a university. A good place for an early evening **drink** is *Café le Soleil Noir* in place de l'Hôtel de la Ville (open till 2am in July & Aug, otherwise till 9pm), a small corner café with sleek decor, a mixed crowd and good sandwiches. Livelier late-night venues include *Le Cyrano*, 26 boulevard Gambetta, a bar with pool table, or *Le Galion* on avenue Anatole France (nightly 9pm–2am), which has different nightly themes and dancing. The coolest places are the cocktail bars *Why Not Café* and *Le Bal Masqué*, at no. 4 and no. 6 rue Marcelin-Coural, respectively. The former (Mon–Sat until 2am) has live music and DJs with a predominantly Sixties playlist, while the latter (daily till 2am) has better musical variety (including salsa on Fridays), with live bands occasionally playing on Thursday nights. Another **club** option is *Le Talgo*, at 8 avenue des Pyrénées (Tues–Sun 6pm–2am) with an eclectic programme of DJs. If you're in the mood for a quieter drink, head to the pub *Chez Fred* (June–Sept 5pm–1am), in the beautiful old *Hôtel Dorade*.

Narbonne does have a reasonable **theatre**, le Théâtre-scène Nationale de Narbonne, 2 avenue Domitius (Mon–Fri 12.30–6.30pm, Sat 3–6pm; ☎04.68.90.90.20, ⓦwww.letheatre-narbonne.com; bus #2 to "MI Juin"), but otherwise the city's cultural programme is nothing to write home about.

Restaurants

L'Agora 9 pl de l'Hôtel de la Ville ☎04.68.90.10.70. Despite the Roman name, this is a *terroir* which specializes in foie gras and *magret en confit*, as well as doing a fine line in tapas. *Menus* €12.

L'Alsace 2 av Pierre-Sémard ☎04.68.65.10.24. Just opposite the train station, this is Narbonne's best restaurant, hands down, featuring *terroir* and northeastern French dishes. Great decor, mammoth servings and *menus* from €16. Closed Tues.

CO 1 rue Rossini ☎08.20.39.12.91. Narbonne's newest eating establishment is surprisingly sophisticated, with arty decor, modern furniture and subtle lighting. The *gastronomique carte* is a welcome relief after one too many *steak frites*. *Menus* are an inexpensive €9 for lunch, or €12 and up at dinner.

L'Estagnol cours Mirabeau ☎04.68.65.09.27. On the market side of the canal, this good no-frills *terroir* restaurant also has a good fish selection. Solid *menus* in the €16–20 range; less at lunch time. Closed Sun.

Palais du Vin Domaine de St-Crescent le Viel rte de Perpignan ☎04.68.41.47.20. A *terroir* restaurant, with *menus* starting around €17, that's part of the local vintners' complex – a showroom for over 2500 regional wine growers. *La Table St-Crescent*, below, is part of the same complex; to get there, walk 30min west of the town centre or take bus #3 to "St-Crescent".

La Petite Cour 22 bd Gambetta ☎04.68.90.48.03. Fish and seafood are the order of the day in this high-ceilinged room decked with seascape murals. There's a good choice of *menus* from €14 at noon, or up to €45 in the evening.

Royal Kebab 14 bd Docteur-Lacroix. The town's Turkish *table*, with all the usual suspects: shish and doner kebabs, salads and sweets.

La Table St-Crescent Domaine St-Crescent-le-Vieil ☎04.68.41.37.37. It's worth the effort of getting to this excellent *gastronomique* located in an ancient eighth-century oratory, amongst vineyards and olive groves on the same *domaine* as the *Palais du Vin*. Expect to spend about €40 per person. Closed Sun eve & Mon.

Aux Trois Caves 4 rue Benjamin-Crémieux ☎04.68.65.28.60. Quirky place whose modern decorative touches clash incongruously with their surroundings. Inventive dishes based on local standbys are served in an excavated Roman cellar. Expect to spend €16–28.

Listings

Banks and exchange Narbonne has branches of several major French banks; all have ATMs and most will change money during normal banking hours. Try the Caisse d'Epargne in bd Docteur-Ferroul, beside the indoor market, or the Crédit Lyonnaise opposite the *passarelle* in cours de la République.

Boat rental For canal trips, Berges de la Robine, cours de la République (☎06.11.75.36.98) rents electric boats by the hour (from €19), while Connoisseurs Cruisers, promenade des Barques (☎04.68.65.14.55), is the best place for house-boats.

Car rental ADA, 12 av des Pyrénées ☎04.68.42.44.81; Avis, 21 bd Marcel-Sembat ☎04.68.32.43.36; Europcar, 52 bd Frédéric-Mistral ☎04.68.32.34.54; Locabest, 2 rue Romain ☎04.68.65.35.50.

Hospital Centre Hospitalier de Narbonne, bd Docteur-Lacroix (☎04.68.41.00.00; bus #1, #2 or #3 to "Hôpital").

Internet access Versus, nos. 73 & 82 rue Droite (Mon–Thurs 10am–8pm, Fri 10am–midnight, Sat 2pm–midnight, Sun 2–8pm).

Launderettes 24 av des Pyrénées; 25 bd Docteur-Ferroul; 3 av Karl-Marx.

Pharmacies Pharmacie de l'Hôtel de la Ville, pl de l'Hôtel de la Ville. For night-time and weekend, check the notice on the door.

Police Gendarmerie, rue Anatole-France ☎04.68.90.38.50.

Rugby Local team RCNM play at the Parc des Sports et de l'Amitié, southeast of the old town (bus #3 to "Parc des Sports"; ☎04.68.41.76.93).

Swimming Éspace Liberté, rte de Perpignan ☎04.68.42.17.89; bus #3 to "Roches Grises" or "Hautes de Narbonne".

Taxi ☎04.68.32.03.00.

Train departures All trains leave from the main gare SNCF (☎04.68.80.77.74), except the ATM (Autorail Touristique Minervois) service to Sallèles and Bize (see p.323), which leaves from a separate station on place de la Constituante, just off place des Pyrénées; the fare from Narbonne to Bize is €9.50 return.

Gruissan and Gruissan-Plage

Some 20km southeast of Narbonne, the quiet fishing town of **GRUISSAN** cuts a striking figure from the distance, with its circular streets huddled around an ancient tower, and filling a dramatic-looking promontory in the inland *étang* which bears its name. Arriving, you may be surprised to find little sign of life among the fading colours of Gruissan's houses, or even around the ruins of the **watchtower** (no set hours; free entry) – development has turned its back on the town, which basically consists of an array of low-roofed houses. The "action" is to be found on the long shore, partly in a smattering of bars and restaurants, but mainly in the daily business of the fishermen, tending to their boats or bringing in the catch. The salty Étang du Grazier separates Gruissan from the narrow spit of sand marking the Mediterranean's shore. Here, a concrete expanse of low-rise hotels has choked the banks of the inlet, and spreads north to the equally vacuous development of **GRUISSAN-PLAGE**. Apart from the traditional array of beachside activities and sights for which the towns are admirably equipped, there is virtually nothing to see or do on this stretch of the coast. When you tire of wandering Gruissan's near-deserted streets, you can head to the tourist office, which distributes a series of **biking** and **walking** itineraries in the low but rugged mountain of La Clape, separating Narbonne from the coast. The most popular is the one- to three-hour (depending on whether you start from town, or a car park up the hill) excursion to the local sailors' graveyard and hill-top chapel of Notre-Dame-des-Auzils. The landscape along the way is archetypically Mediterranean, with scrubby pines and slender cypress sprouting up between the red stones; from the top of the hill, there's a dramatically sweeping panoramic view: the slender band of yellow sand set against the turquoise sea to the east, and the vineyards and *châteaux* of the La Clape *appellation* to the west.

Arriving by **bus** in Gruissan, you'll be left by the new **tourist office** (July & Aug daily 9am–1pm & 3–7pm; Sept–June Mon–Sat 9.30am–noon & 2–6pm; ☎04.68.49.09.00, ⓦwww.ville-gruissan.fr), on boulevard Pech-Maynaud between the old and new towns. Given the town's proximity to Narbonne, there's really no reason to spend the night here, but if you are intent on a bout of beach-side hedonism, you'll find a selection of modern, near-identical two- and three-star **hotels** ready to serve you. Right on the beach-front, *Le Floride* (☎04.68.49.04.06, ⓦwww.hotellefloride.com; ❸) is a reasonable choice with good amenities, while closer to the old town, the *Port* (☎04.68.49.07.33, ⓦwww.gruissan-hotel-du-port.com; ❹) is a good, if slightly expensive, option. Among the several **campsites** in the area, the best deal is the municipal site (☎04.68.49.07.22, ⓔcamping@ville-gruissan.fr; June–Sept), on route des Salins. If you're looking for a **meal**, well-priced seafood and fish can be enjoyed at *L'Estangol*, on avenue de Narbonne (☎04.68.49.01.27; April–Sept; *menus* from €21), whose patio dining area has good views, and *Le Phoebus* (☎04.68.49.03.05; *menus* €18–38) in old Gruissan, at 4 rue Amiral-Courbet.

South to Sigean

Heading south from Narbonne, the road hugs the base of the rising hills, separated from the sea by a wide buffer – a series of salty *étangs* – and accompanied by a landscape characterized by scrubby trees, red soil, and an impossibly blue sky in summer. Travelling by rail south from Narbonne provides a different perspective, as the line threads the marshy spits connecting the saltpans and lagoons; on board you'll feel no hint of the steady and unforgiving wind which lashes in from the east. There's little along the coast to detain you until you arrive at **SIGEAN**, just north of which is a large **African nature reserve** (daily: mid-April to early Sept 9am–6.30pm; rest of the year 9am–4pm; €9). This immense drive-through park (no motorcycles) recreates several equatorial habitats, including brushland, savannah and plain, and lazing around you'll see lions, giraffes, rhinos and hippos, as well as graceful oryx and springboks. There's also a bear area and a bird reserve, while chimpanzees are exiled to their own island at the southern end of the park. For those without cars, a series of footpaths have been laid out among the habitats in a limited area. Sigean itself is nothing special, although it does have a small **archeological museum** by the tourist office (June–Sept daily 10am–noon & 2–5pm, Oct–May Mon, Wed, Thurs & Sat–Sun 9.30am–5.30pm, Fri 9.30am–12.30pm; €4.60), holding artefacts recovered from the nearby *oppidum*; the remains of this hill-top settlement, just outside of town and dating back to the sixth century BC, can also be visited (no public transport; same ticket). There's little to see there, but if you are intent on going, check with the tourist office for directions and to verify that the site is open.

Buses from Narbonne, Perpignan and Port-la-Nouvelle stop right in Sigean's centre, near the **tourist office** (July & Aug Mon–Sat 9.45–11.45am & 4–7pm; Sept–June Tues & Wed 10am–noon; ☎04.68.48.14.81, ⓦwww.sigean.org) on place de la Libération. Accommodation hereabouts is limited to two **campsites**: the municipal site, a few minutes' walk from the town centre at the Étang Boyé (☎04.68.48.43.68; July & Aug), and *La Grange Neuve* (☎04.68.48.58.70), near the reserve. To eat, head to the **restaurant** *Le Ste-Anne* on 3 avenue Michel-de-l'Hôpital (closed Mon; *menu* €14). If you're just passing through, you might pause for a drink in the wonderful old glassed-in *Café La Rotunda*, in the centre of town on the main street.

The Corbières

To journey into the heart of the hilly **Corbières** region, which fans out south-west of Narbonne, bordered to the west by the upper Aude valley and to south by the Fenouillèdes hills of northern Roussillon, is to enter a world very distinct from the coastal plain. As the land rises, the roads narrow, twisting and writhing up into the forests of the low mountains, tenaciously following the streambeds which cut into the slopes. Once the heart of Cathar territory, this district has suffered centuries of abandonment and neglect, and many hamlets lack even a café or a proper payphone, let alone a restaurant or hotel. For all of this, it is a splendid place to drive through, offering the ancient monasteries of **Fontfroide** and **Lagrasse**, and the Cathar sites of **Villerouge–Termenès** and **Termes**. Without your own transport, however, the Corbières is difficult to access, the only bus route following the D613 from Narbonne.

Fontfroide

Passing through the rocky *garrigues* west of Narbonne, the D613 leads you past the narrow turn-off to the **Monastery of Fontfroide**, 22km out of town. Following this road south for four kilometres, you'll come across the stout walls of the ancient Cistercian foundation, tucked inside a shallow valley hidden amongst cypress groves. Founded in the late eleventh century by a count of Narbonne, it saw its greatest prosperity in the two subsequent centuries, after which, like so many monastic centres, it began to decline. The monastery's best-known abbot was Jacques Fournier, who as Bishop of Foix commanded the Inquisition which investigated the Cathars of Montaillou (see p.145), and went on in 1337 to be elected pope as Benedict XII. In private hands for the last hundred years or so, the abbey can only be visited as part of a one-hour **guided tour** (daily: early Jan by appointment only; Feb–March & Nov to early Jan 10am–noon & 2–4pm; April to early July & Sept–Oct 10am–12.15pm & 1.45–5.30pm; early July–Aug 9.30am–6pm; €6.25). It's best to come early in the morning or late in the day in order to avoid crowds; but be warned, this is a popular stop on bus tours, and in high season is frequently too busy to be enjoyable.

The visit starts in the open courtyard, the *cour d'honneur*, built by the sixteenth-century abbots. From here, you're led to the refined beauty of the **cloister** – originally built in the 1200s, but added to as late as the seventeenth century. From the east side you enter the marvellously vaulted **chapterhouse**, and then the **church**, a simple twelfth-century Romanesque basilica, on the south side of which is an interesting ossuary, the salle des Morts, which contains a fifteenth-century Crucifixion scene. After a visit to the storage **cellars** which, going back a thousand years, are the oldest surviving part of the monastery, the tour concludes with the monks' living quarters above. Afterwards, you can wander freely along the paths which lead through the surrounding groves and gardens.

There's no accommodation at Fontfroide, so if you're travelling by **bus** you'll want to make sure you are back at the main road in order to catch the last one back to Narbonne or further on up into the hills. There is, however, an excellent **restaurant** at the monastery, *La Bergerie* (closed Dec–Feb). The establishment is divided into two parts: the less expensive lunch-time dining room, which serves traditional but well-executed dishes (*menus* from €13), and the evening-only *gastronomique*, where you should be prepared to spend at least €30 (closed Mon).

Villerouge-Termenès and Termes

If you continue west from Fontfroide along the D613, you'll arrive at St-Laurent-de-la-Cabrerisse, where the road forks right for Lagrasse (see opposite), and left towards the hills. Following this second route will lead you into some of the wildest back-country of the region, where forested uplands are capped by the tumbled remains of nameless castles. The road first climbs to the 404-metre-high Col de Villerouge, and as you round the top, you'll get a startling view of the castle and **VILLEROUGE-TERMENÈS** below. The village is dominated by the tall keep of its impressively restored **castle** (Feb–March & late Oct–Dec Sat, Sun & hols 10am–5pm; April–June & Sept to mid-Oct daily 10am–6pm; July & Aug daily 9.30am–7.30pm; €4). The earlier Cathar fort here was destroyed in the wake of its conquest by Crusaders in 1210, and the present structure, dating from the 1300s, was designed not to protect but to dominate the inhabitants of the surrounding hills. A visit involves an engaging audiovisual show which recaps the history of the area and recounts the tale of Guilhem Bélibaste, the Cathar *parfait* who was burned at the stake here in 1321. Afterwards it's worth taking a walk through the village huddled around the castle; the town was almost certainly fortified in the twelfth century, but the walls which are visible today were built to fend off the English and their allies during the Hundred Years' War. South of the *enceinte* you'll find the **church** of St-Étienne, which houses an immense sixteenth-century retable.

Leaving Villerouge, another steep ascent takes you to the **Col de Bedos** (485m), where a narrow paved road veers off to the right. Carefully following this relentless succession of hairpin curves will take you over hill and into valley until you make a sharp descent to **TERMES**. Little more than a cluster of ancient houses set on cramped but orderly streets, this extraordinarily beautiful hamlet would be worth a visit even if it weren't for its famous castle. Trees crowd over the narrow stream, bridged by a centuries-old stone bridge, and the sharply rising slopes above are covered by a blanket of beech, ash and stunted oak. The only thing which ruins the effect is the modern reception centre across the river, which is the point at which you begin the arduous ascent to the ruins of the **castle** (March, mid-Oct–Dec & school holidays Sat & Sun 10am–5pm; April–June & Sept to mid-Oct daily 10am–6pm; July & Aug daily 10am–8pm; €3.50). You wouldn't know it from either the ruins or the village, but this castle was dominated by one of the greatest feudal domains of Languedoc. Ruled by an unrepentant heretic lord, Raymond, it was a prime target for de Montfort, who besieged it for four months, until the disease-ravaged garrison could resist no more. After it was taken the castle continued to be used, and it was not destroyed until the seventeenth century, when Richelieu systematically cleared the land of possible points of resistance to central rule. Clambering among the remains of the two concentric sets of walls, you'll find the chapel and take in breathtaking **views** over the hills around. From Termes, you have two options: continue on for another twenty hair-raising kilometres to reach the main road heading north to Lagrasse, or double back the way you came, and descend the Col de Bedos to **MOUTHOUMET**. This sleepy village serves as the end for the bus line which runs up from Narbonne and, if nothing else, makes a welcome rest stop on the GR36 as it winds its way south from Termes to Peyrepertuse, or on the west towards Arques and Rennes-le-Château.

Practicalities

Services are extremely thin on the ground in this neck of the woods. **Accommodation** is especially rare; aside from Madame Lefranc's chambres d'hôtes (℡04.68.70.00.42 or 04.68.48.85.95, ℻04.68.48.46.20; ❷; English spoken) in Villerouge, all you'll find is an unofficial campsite on the riverside outside Termes, just before you enter town. **Eating** is a little better: in Villerouge you can enjoy a lively meal in the castle's *Rôtisserie Medieval* (℡04.68.70.06.06; closed Sun eve & Mon except hols & closed all Jan) for about €29, while in Mouthoumet, on what passes for a main square, you'll find the *Auberge du Terroir* (lunch only; closed Sat Oct–May), a homely little place which has excellent salads, and *menus* from €10.52 (wine included).

Lagrasse

Just over halfway from Narbonne to Carcassonne and separated from the Aude valley by the low ridge of the Montagne d'Alaric, **LAGRASSE** is the largest and most beautiful village of the Corbières highlands. A compact walled hamlet set idyllically where the Orbieu opens up in a broad hollow, it hugs the right bank of the shallow river, while the magnificent abbey squats on the far side. Delightfully, but surprisingly, Lagrasse does not seem to have been discovered yet by the tourist industry; the grid of streets in the old town is almost strictly residential, and you'll hardly see a postcard stand or gift shop. It's a real pleasure to wander the cobbled lanes down to the arcaded *place* and its ancient **covered market**, with flowers cascading from the windows of the houses which hem the streets and crowd around the fort-like **church**. Much of the old *enceinte* is intact, and as you cross the eleventh-century bridge, try to crane over its protective walls to look at the town's riverside fortifications, now pierced by the scores of windows of the houses built against them – an especially evocative sight at dusk. It's only about a five-minute walk from the far side of the river to the **abbey of Ste-Marie d'Orbieu** (mid-Jan to mid-Feb Sat & Sun 2–5pm; mid-Feb–April daily 2–5.15pm; May–June & Sept–Oct daily 10.30am–noon & 2–6pm; July & Aug daily 10.30am–6.15pm; Nov to mid-Dec daily 2–5pm; €4.50). This is one of the region's oldest monastic houses, founded in an era when it was a dangerous, underpopulated frontier of the eighth-century Carolingian empire. Cultivating the extensive lands with which they had been endowed, the monks slowly increased the monastery's wealth until its golden age in the fourteenth century, which saw the building of the town's walls and market. The complex is now a pastiche of styles, with components dating from the tenth to eighteenth centuries. The abbot's Renaissance **palace** and cloister were built during the monastery's second great period of revival – just before the storm of Revolution swept it away – whereas the bulk of the **abbey-church** and the old Romanesque-style **cloister** date from the thirteenth century, although both have suffered substantial remodellings. Look for the distinctive mark of the "Master of Cabestany" (see box on p.111) in the cloister and on one of the abbey's entrances. You'll also get a look at the monks' cavernous **dormitory**, and have the chance to climb the Gothic-tinged fifteenth-century **clock tower**, whose heights afford impressive vistas of the town and valley. Leaving the abbey, continue along the riverside to a low dam bridging the river – you can walk across here and re-enter the town.

Heading on from Lagrasse towards Carcassonne, the most scenic route takes you west through the Gorges d'Alsou.

Lagrasse's services and shops are mostly strung along the tree-lined boulevard de la Promenade; the **tourist office** (July & Aug daily 10am–12.30pm & 2–6pm; ☎04.68.43.11.56, ⓦwww.lagrasse.com) is at no. 6. Further along at no. 9, you'll find the friendly *Auberge St Hubert* **hotel** (closed part Feb, & Sun & Mon Sept–Easter; ☎04.68.43.15.22, ⓔdupont.ghislain@wanadoo.fr; ❷), which also has a pleasant restaurant (*menu* from €16). Otherwise, there are **chambres d'hôtes** in the old town at *Les Trois Grâces*, 5 rue de Quai (☎ & ⒻO4.68.43.18.17; closed Wed & Thurs, and all Jan & Feb; ❷), which also serves meals; and with the English-speaking Hughes family (☎04.68.43.14.54, ⓦwww.gites-de-france-aude.com; ❸), who can also provide bicycles. There's also the option of the basic municipal **campsite** (March–Oct; no phone) on the western edge of town. The most interesting **restaurant** here is *Les Temps de Courges* (☎04.68.43.10.18; closed Wed & Thurs lunch), at 3 rue des Mazels, where you can order vegetarian or meat dishes and dine on a cosy little ter-race (*menus* €16–24). Otherwise there are a string of family-run establishments on the boulevard de la Promenade, including *Le Petit Saint* and *L'Affenage*, both of which have basic *terroir menus* for under €20, and offer the possibility of eat-ing on street-side terraces.

Along the Canal du Midi east from Carcassonne

Heading east from Carcassonne, the **Canal du Midi** (see p.112) follows the course of the lower Aude valley, past the shady port at **Trèbes**, and on into the wine country of the **Minervois**, bounded by Haut Languedoc to the north and the hills of the Corbières to the south. Here the small port of **Homps** pro-vides a jumping-off point for the old Cathar stronghold of **Minerve** and the monastery at **Caunes**, while bustling **Lézignan** is a hub for non-fluvial trans-port. Just after the old way-station of Le Somail the canal splits; the offshoot **Canal de la Robine** glides past the ancient wine centre of **Sallèles**, and on through Narbonne to reach the sea near Gruissan, while the main channel edges on to pass the magnificent **Oppidum d'Ensérune**, before reaching Béziers and, eventually, Agde (see p.330). As with the western leg of the canal system, you needn't commit yourself to boating to enjoy this archetypal south-ern French landscape, since the two towpaths which run along the canal's length make for excellent **biking** and **walking**.

Trèbes and Puichéric

The first and prettiest port of call along the eastern stretch of the Canal du Midi is **TRÈBES**, just a few kilometres east of Carcassonne. The canal makes a broad curve here, following the wide meander of the Aude; arriving at Trèbes, two canal bridges, the second designed by the military architect Vauban in 1686, carry the watercourse over the Frequel and Orbiel rivers. Aside from being an attractive place with a canal port overlooked by the town walls at its western end, Trèbes is home to the remarkable **church of St-Étienne** (July & Aug Mon–Fri 10am–noon & 3–7pm; free), the wooden-beamed ceiling of which, dating back to the early fourteenth century, has over 350 individual faces painted on the ends of its roof supports, including caricatures of various professions and social classes, exotic foreigners and grotesques. For boaters the

The Black Prince: Languedoc's first English tourist

The end of the Cathar Wars ushered in an era of peace and prosperity for Languedoc, but it wasn't fated to last, as events far off at the courts of Westminster and Paris brought warfare once again to the already severely devastated region. This time the occasion was the **Hundred Years' War**, which flared up in 1330 when Edward III of England, who already controlled a significant part of north and western France, claimed that he, rather than Philip VI, was the rightful king. At that time, Edward III's eldest son and heir, also named Edward, was only two years of age, but by the time he was 16, he was experienced enough in war to be given partial command at the Battle of Crécy in 1346, which saw a resounding victory over the forces of the French king.

Young Edward, who was the first heir to the throne to carry the title "Prince of Wales", was also duke of Aquitaine, and once he had proven his mettle, he was sent off to Bordeaux to take command of the province. Here the local Gascons were only too happy to join the English in looting and pillaging their neighbours; contemporary chronicler Jean de Froissart commented that the Gascons "love the English in preference to the French, for the war against France is the most profitable; and this is the cause of their preference." Edward, by then known as the **Black Prince** after the colour of his armour, would give them every opportunity.

Although most of the war was being fought in northern France, Edward mounted a massive *chevauchée* – a scorched-earth campaign designed to terrorize civilians and destroy infrastructure – into Languedoc in 1355. Striking out towards Toulouse, he and his men covered nearly 675 miles in 68 days of raiding. Castelnaudary, as well as the *bastide* of Carcassonne, Trèbes, Limoux and Narbonne, were just a few of the towns he and his troops sacked and put to the torch; in all his troop of five thousand men laid waste to nearly 18,000 square miles of territory. The following year Edward went on to further glory by capturing the French king, John II, in battle at Poitiers. It would be many years before the horror of the raid would be forgotten. For his part, Froissart ventured a rather restrained assessment of the foreign forces, saying that he had "witnessed the great haughtiness of the English, who are affable to no other nation than their own."

town is a well-equipped stage-post, just as it was in the seventeenth century, with mooring facilities and a range of services.

From Trèbes, the canal meanders east to **PUICHÉRIC**. This Cathar town survived the Crusade, but was put to the torch by the Black Prince a century later. There's not much to see, as its medieval castle is now private, but it makes a good accommodation stop for cyclists and walkers.

Trèbes' **tourist office** is by the former canal *auberge*, on rue Pierre-Loti (July & Aug daily 10am–12.30pm & 2–8pm; June & Sept Mon–Sat 10am–12.30pm & 2–7.30pm, Sun 10am–12.30pm; May Mon–Sat 10am–noon & 2–7pm; April & Oct Mon–Sat 3–7pm; ☎04.68.78.89.50, ⓦwww.ot-trebes.fr.st). The nearby Sautès Le Bas commercial zone holds two decent **hotels**, *La Gentilhommière* (☎04.68.78.74.74, ⓦwww.lagentilhom.com; ❸) and the *Andalousie* (☎04.68.78.88.48, ⓕ04.68.78.63.48; ❶). The town's **campsite** is on chemin de la Lande, on the west side of Trèbes (☎04.68.78.61.75; April–Sept). There are a number of inexpensive **restaurants**, including *Les 3 B*, on avenue Pasteur, and *Le Relais de Capuchins*, at 34 rte de Narbonne – either of which can set you up with a €9 midday *menu*. For **boat rental** see the port office (☎04.68.78.83.08); Connoisseur Cruisers (☎04.68.78.73.75) have houseboats, and La Forcola (☎04.68.78.89.92) electric boats (half-day €50).

The Minervois

As the canal arcs northward it passes **HOMPS**, a town which suffered destruction in the Crusade and the Wars of Religion, but revived with the construction of the waterway. It's the main port of the **Minervois** region, a sun-bleached wine-producing territory stretching from the north bank of the Aude up to the hills of Haut Languedoc. The principal town of the Minervois, **OLONZAC**, lies just 2km north of the canal, linked to Homps by the D910. There are no sights here but it makes a convenient stop on the road to the former Cathar stronghold of **MINERVE**, a further 15km north. A tiny medieval hamlet, located at the cirque where the deep gorge of the River Cesse doubles back on itself, Minerve's main attraction is its stunningly dramatic location – only a single pile of stones remains of its **fortress**, which resisted Simon de Montfort for five months in 1210. When it was taken, 140 Cathars who refused to recant their beliefs voluntarily jumped into the fire which the Crusaders had prepared for them. Neither of the town's museums merit much attention: the **archeological museum** (daily 10am–6.30pm; €2), with its shambolic collection set in dusty fly-specked display cases, is quite a specimen itself, while the **Musée Hurepel** (April–Sept daily 11am–12.30pm & 2–6pm; €2) is nothing more than a thinly disguised shop, where you can pay to see a series of cheesy miniature dioramas recounting the Cathar saga. A visit to the town is best spent hiking the path through the **canyon** which surrounds it, and where you can walk in natural tunnels bored through the cliffs. The trail can be picked up just over the bridge which enters town. It's best to avoid Minerve in high season and at weekends, when the volume of visitors threatens to obliterate its charms.

If you have a car, you might want to drive 20km west of Olonzac (or alternatively a short drive from Carcassonne) to the far western edge of the Minervois, where you'll find the town of **CAUNES-MINERVOIS**, the centre of which is dominated by its hulking **abbey** (daily: April–June & Sept–Oct 10am–noon & 2–5pm; July & Aug 10am–7pm; Nov–March 10am–noon & 2–5pm; €3.50). There's not much to see here, although the crypt holds the foundation of the original fourth-century church, and some eleventh-century pavement has been uncovered in the cloister. Otherwise, the town is fairly unremarkable, although a wander through its streets discloses a peppering of the abbots' luxurious mansions, which were constructed in the Middle Ages and through to the sixteenth century. Caunes is most famous for its marble quarries, which supplied stone for many of the churches throughout the region. Along the way you may want to stop in **Rieux-Minervois**, where the town's **Église de Notre Dame** contains a fine example of the handiwork of the "Master of Cabestany" (see box on p.111) in its chapel of the Assumption, as well as a fine fifteenth-century tomb.

Practicalities

There are **tourist offices** in the centre of Olonzac, at 3 place de la Mairie (July & Aug daily 9am–noon & 2–6pm; ☎04.68.91.34.95, ℻04.68.91.21.08), and behind the church in Minerve, at 2 rue des Martyrs (July & Aug daily 10am–noon & 2–6pm; ☎04.68.91.81.43). Comfortable **hotels** in the region include the *Hôtel du Parc* on avenue de Homps in Olonzac (☎04.68.91.14.55; ❷) and *D'Alibert* in the place de la Mairie at Caunes (☎04.68.78.00.54, ℮frederic.dalibert@wanadoo.fr; ; closed Sun & Mon in low season, and late Dec–Feb; ❷), which also has a good restaurant. In Minerve you can choose between the overpriced **chambres d'hôtes** *Ulysse Martin*, at 23 Grand Rue

(℡04.68.91.22.97; ❺), or the better *Relais Chantovent* (closed mid-Dec to mid-March; ℡04.68.91.14.18, ℻04.68.91.81.99; ❸), which is also a decent spot for a locally-flavoured meal (*menus* from €14.95). Caunes also has a municipal **campsite** (June–Aug; no phone). For those following the canal route, there are additional accommodation opportunities en route, including *Hôtel la Muscadelle* (℡04.68.79.20.90, ✉la-muscadelle@atarizie.fr; ❶), on the route de Languedoc in Marseillette; *Auberge de l'Arbousier* (℡04.68.91.11.24, ⓦwww.logis-de-france.fr; closed mid-March to mid-April; ❷–❹) in Homps; and the *Logis de Merinville* (℡04.68.78.12.49, ✉cathy.morin@wanadoo.fr; ❸) on avenue Général-Clemenceau in Rieux.

You can **eat** in Olonzac at the simple *Du Minervois "Bel"*, 2 rue des Écoles (℡04.68.91.20.73; *menus* from €18.30; closed Sun & Mon), but a better option is to head for the *Auberge de l'Arbousier* in Homps (℡04.68.91.11.24; closed Wed & Sun eve & Mon only in summer), which has *terroir menus* from €13.

Justfun (℡04.68.91.56.22) in Olonzac rents **bikes**, while for boats and cruises, contact Camargue Plaisance (℡04.68.91.25.99), Luc Lines (℡04.68.91.24.00) or Les Croisières du Midi (℡04.68.91.24.00, ⓦwww.croisieres-du-midi.com) in Homps' port.

Lézignan-Corbières and Le Somail

Veering south and east after Homps, the Canal du Midi enters a particularly beautiful stretch, passing a series of castles as the landscape settles into vine-covered plain. Some 5km south of the canal sits **LÉZIGNAN-CORBIÈRES**, the capital of the rugged region rising gradually to the south. Lézignan has been in the business of wine production since the time of the Romans and today remains a small but bustling centre of the viticulture industry. There's no overwhelming reason to visit, although if you're dependent on public transport you may find yourself here to change buses or board a train. While in town, you can stop in at the **Musée de la Vigne et du Vin** (daily 9am–noon & 2–7pm; €4), right by the gare SNCF (see below), whose interesting exhibition focuses directly on the wine business that has brought prosperity to the countryside here since the nineteenth century.

This leg of the canal continues, over the canal bridge of Répudre – France's first, and an invention of Riquet himself – and on to **LE SOMAIL**, the last port before the Canal de la Robine splits off to head south towards Narbonne. As a whole, the town, mired among modern housing developments on a broad expanse of flat land, looks unpromising as you approach, but the area along the canal, which formed the seventeenth-century port, is a world apart. Here a single-arched stone **bridge** dating from the eighteenth century spans the canal, still attached to the old post-house *auberge* on the east bank and a small **chapel** on the west. There's little to do here aside from enjoy a drink or meal and soak up the canalside ambience before moving on, although if you're not in a hurry you might take a look at the private **hat museum** (June–Sept daily 9am–noon & 2–7pm; Oct–May Mon–Sat 2–6pm, Sun 2.30–8pm; €4), located at the south end of town, which displays more than six thousand hats from around the world.

Practicalities

In Lézignan-Corbières, **buses** will let you off as they pass through the town's centre, while **trains** stop at the **gare SNCF**, 3 rue Turgot. There's also a **tourist office** (July & Aug Mon–Sat 9am–9pm, Sun 10am–noon; Sept–June

Mon–Fri 10am–noon & 3–6pm; ℡04.68.27.05.42, ℮tourisme-lezignan@wanadoo.fr) at 9 cours de la République, on the southern side of the ring road which skirts its old town. You'll find a good selection of shops and services in Lézignan, plus a number of **hotels**, the best of which is the *Tassigny*, on rond-point de Lattre-de-Tassigny (℡04.68.27.11.51, ⓦwww.logis-de-france.fr; ❸), which has clean rooms and good amenities. You can also get a bed at the local MJC **hostel**, 25 rue Marat (℡04.68.27.03.34, ℮MJC.lezignan-corbieres@wanadoo.fr; €12), while Lézignan's **campsite**, *La Pinède* (℡04.68.27.05.08; March–Oct) is on the main road on the eastern edge of town. On Wednesday morning the local market convenes.

In Le Somail, there is a small canal **information office** (℡06.84.81.96.20; irregular hours) by the old bridge, around which you'll find **accommodation** options. The old canal *auberge* on the east side of the bridge offers chambres d'hôtes (℡04.68.46.16.02; ❸), while satisfying meals can be enjoyed at the neighbouring *Auberge Lou Somaillou* (℡04.68.46.19.41; March–Nov), which has a comfortable dining room and a canalside terrace (*menus* €16–36). If you're tempted to continue from Le Somail by **boat**, Minervois Cruisers (℡04.68.46.28.52) can help you out, or you can putter by the hour on an electric boat from Comptoir Nature at 1 chemin de Halage. Landlubbers can rent **bikes** from Plancade (℡04.68.27.29.13), at 33 avenue Président-Wilson in Lézignan.

Routes from Le Somail

From Le Somail you have a choice of two routes: the first follows the subsidiary Canal de la Robine on a course through the southern portion of the alluvial plain, passing the old wine town of **Sallèles**, while the second stays with the main Canal du Midi heading east to Agde and the northern section of the plain, via the ancient **Oppidum d'Ensérune**.

Along the Canal de la Robine

The **CANAL DE LA ROBINE**'s short trajectory carries it almost directly south, crossing the course of the wide and, here, tame Aude, and continuing through Narbonne before penetrating the marshy extent of the Étang de Bages et de Sigean. After Narbonne there are two legs; the longer tracks the same spit of land as the railway, skirting the bird-lovers' paradise of Île de Ste-Lucie, before arriving at Port-la-Nouvelle and the sea, while the shorter cuts east past the vineyards of La Clape, passing Gruissan (see p.313) and the saltpans of St-Martin before reaching the Mediterranean.

The only major port of call on the Canal de la Robine, a few kilometres before it merges with the Aude, is **SALLÈLES**. Like Lézignan, Sallèles is a wine town of great antiquity, whose vintages graced the tables of Rome more than two thousand years ago. Bearing testimony to this are the town's Roman pottery works, now incorporated into the **Amphoralis** museum on Sallèles' northern edge (July–Sept Tues–Sun 10am–noon & 3–7pm; Oct–June Tues–Fri 2–6pm, Sat & Sun 10am–noon & 2–6pm; €4). Named after the distinctively tapered vessels (*amphorae*) once made here, it's a well-laid-out and entertaining museum, which includes the excavation site of the pottery itself. The walk out to the museum from the tourist office is interesting too, thanks to the six sets of **locks** which grace that part of the canal. While you're in town, you might also head to the rather less imaginative **Musée de Vieux Sallèles** (May–Sept Sat & Sun 2.30–6.30pm; €3) in the centre, a rather traditional small-town French museum with extensive but familiar collections of tools relating to traditional crafts, viticulture and nineteenth-century life. The old town itself, a tight knot of narrow lanes, is also as good a place as any to stretch your legs. Finally, at Sallèles' canalside station, you can hop on board the narrow-gauge **Autorail Touristique Minervois** (℡04.68.27.05.94, Ⓦwww.perso.wanadoo .fr/autorail.touristique.minervois), a 1950s-era tourist train which uses the old line connecting Narbonne in the east with Bize-Minervois to the west. The ATM runs on Saturdays (July & Aug; 2 daily), Sundays (July–Sept; 2 daily) and occasional weekdays. The fare for the half-trip leg from Sallèles to Bize is €5.50; Narbonne to Bize is €9.50.

Sallèle's canalside **tourist office** (Mon–Fri 10.30am–12.30pm & 4–6.30pm; ℡04.68.46.81.46, Ⓦwww.salleles-daude.com) is just southeast of the centre at 2 quai de Lorraine. The only place to stay in the village is the municipal **camp-site**, *Les Sablous* (℡04.68.33.61.30; mid-June to mid-Sept), a ten-minute walk from the centre on the east side of the canal, or at Ms Evan's canalside **B&B** (℡04.68.46.83.03, Ⓦwww.gites-de-france-aude.com; closed Dec to mid-March; ❸; English spoken), which has comfortable rooms and can provide meals (€18). Otherwise, you'll find a couple of **cafés** along the main road where you can also get something to eat., **Bikes** can be rented from VTT Sallelois, 13 rue Victor Hugo (€13 per day, left baggage €1), and electric boats are available at Comptoir Nature Somail (℡04.68.46.01.61).

Capestang and Bize-Minervois

East of Le Somail the Canal du Midi enters its most picturesque stretch, snaking through a rugged landscape of low and rocky vine-clad hills whose only reminder of civilization is an occasional bell tower. Sixteen kilometres after the Robine it passes under the old hill-top town of **CAPESTANG**, whose small castle is capped by a distinctive tower. With a tree-lined square snuggled up against its medieval church, Capestang is an exceedingly pleasant little town, where you can climb the church's **bell tower** to enjoy sweeping views over the Aude valley, or simply enjoy a snack or drink and observe the unhurried life of the *place*. The nondescript-looking **castle** is currently private property, but there are plans to open it in the next few years, at which time its 161 fourteenth-century **ceiling paintings** will become a must-see for those following the canal route. These vivid caricatures depict monsters, musicians, court ladies and even a mischievous jester pulling a rather exaggerated "moon" at the viewer (enquire at the tourist office).

The final stop on the Narbonne–Sallèles rail line, **BIZE-MINERVOIS**, lies 20km west of Capestang and is not situated on the waterway itself. Nevertheless, this quiet, walled hamlet makes a pleasant detour. In summer months the canalized Besse river here is a favourite local bathing spot, and though there are no obvious sights, the town provides a break from some of the more touristed and less appealing towns of the region.

Practicalities

In Capestang, the **tourist office** (Mon–Fri 10am–noon & 3–6pm, Sat 10am–noon; ℡04.67.93.34.23, Ⓔot-capestang@wanadoo.fr) is located on main street, adjacent to the castle. The *mairie* runs a **gîte**, *Lo Castel* (℡ & Ⓕ04.67.93.40.90, Ⓔfr.capestang@wanadoo.fr; ❶) at 5 boulevard Pasteur, as well as a **campsite** (℡04.67.49.85.95; July & Aug), or you can stay at the two-star *Franche Comté* **hotel**, 39 cours Belfort (℡04.67.93.31.21; ❷). In terms of **restaurants**, there are several popular ones across on the main square, as well as the slightly fancier *Le Provence* (℡04.67.93.36.54) on the west side of the square, with *menus* at €16–25. For delicious *grillades* (€10–16) and wonderful atmosphere, head to the nearby *domaine* Cros-Reboul's *La Table du Vigneron* (℡04.67.93.48.90; open May–Sept Tues–Sun).

If you arrive at Bize-Minervois by train, it's a twenty-minute walk north to the bridge to the old town. Here you'll find the rustic but well-appointed **chambres d'hôtes** *Du Menhir* (℡04.68.46.16.90, Ⓦwww.force10.net/menhir; June–Sept; ❹) at 3 chemin de la Touleyre, which has a pool. Some 3km south of Bize on the main road (a twenty-minute walk from the station), there's also *La Bastide Cabezac* (℡04.68.46.23.05, Ⓦwww.labastidecabezac.com; ❺), a *domaine* in Hameau de Cabezac, whose restaurant *L'Olivier* (closed Mon & Tues & Sun off-season) has menus from €20. The best place to **eat** in Bize is *La Toye*, a funky art-gallery/restaurant which specializes in *tartouille* and has abundant *menus* (lunch €10, dinner €12–22; closed Wed lunch).

Colombiers to Villeneuve-lès-Béziers

After cutting through the ancient hamlet of Poilhes, some 5km beyond Capestang, the Canal de la Robine passes through a long tunnel, eventually arriving at **COLOMBIERS**, a tiny village which merits a stop if only because it's the closest town to the exceptional excavations of the Oppidum d'Ensérune, which lies just 2km to the west. While here, however, you might stop to check out the **Cave des Ducs de Castries** (daily 10am–12.30pm & 4–8pm; €2) in place du Millénaire, a sumptuous nineteenth-century *bodega* designed by wood carvers who studied under Eiffel, which hosts art and archeological exhibitions.

Set on a long ridge towering over the surrounding plains, the site of the **OPPIDUM D'ENSÉRUNE** (*oppidum* being Latin for "town", referring generally to pre-Roman hill-top settlements) has attracted settlers for over 2500 years. Even before Hannibal and the Romans took it over in turn, it was an important centre for trade, maintaining commercial ties with Greece, while under the Romans it served as one of the postal way-stations on the busy Via Domitia. The site itself, a rocky spur crowned with cypress and brambles, is characteristically Mediterranean, and climbing to the top, looking north, you'll get a view of a strange array of fields resembling a spoked wheel. This was once the *étang* of Montady, one of the many salt lagoons of the lowlands here that were drained and cultivated in the thirteenth century. The **excavations** (April & Sept Tues–Sun 10am–12.30pm & 2–6pm; May–Aug daily 10am–7pm; Oct–March Mon & Wed–Sun 9.30am–5pm; €4.60) of the ancient ruins, covering most of the hill-top, are impressive, with remains of defensive walls, villas and a large array of cisterns and sunken grain stores. The small **site museum** inside the grounds holds a collection of statuary found here, including small devotional pieces and larger civic portraits.

If you have the time, **NISSAN-LEZ-ENSÉRUNE**, the largest town near the ancient settlement – just 4km to the south on the main road – is also worth a look. The thirteenth-century Gothic **church** contains inscriptions in Occitan and some fine medieval statuary, and it also has a small **museum** (open by prior arrangement through the Nissan tourist office; free), housing Roman finds from the surrounding area. At the roadside leaving Nissan, there's an extremely ornate country cemetery, with several impressive mausoleums.

As it arrives at the foot of Béziers' ridge, the canal descends another set of multiple locks, the **neuf écluses**. Billed as a tourist attraction, and endowed with footpaths and snack bars, the lock complex draws families and tour groups who dutifully stand around watching the boats make their slow descent – altogether about as exciting as watching someone take the lift. Only 5km later, tiny **VILLENEUVE-LÈS-BÉZIERS** is the last mooring point on the Canal du

Midi before it follows a flat and featureless course to Agde (see p.330) and empties into the Bassin de Thau. From this lagoon you can reach the sea or connect with the other great inland waterway of Languedoc, the Rhône–Sète Canal (see box on p.242), which carries on past the Petite Camargue into Provence.

Practicalities

At the time of writing, the only **tourist office** in the vicinity of the *oppidum* is at Nissan, in place Rene-Dez (Mon–Sat 9am–noon & 2–5.30pm; ☎ & ℱ04.67.37.14.12), although a new office at Colombiers (ⓌWwww.colombiers.com) should open soon. Villeneuve also has a tourist office, on rue de la Fontaine (July & Aug daily 9am–7pm; Sept–June Mon–Fri 9am–noon & 2–6pm; ☎ & ℱ04.67.39.48.83).

Nissan also has the best **hotel** hereabouts, the *Résidence* (☎04.67.35.00.63, Ⓦwww.hotel-residence.com; closed late Dec to early Jan; ❹), set in an old mansion at 35 avenue de la Cave; just outside Nissan, there's also a pretty and well-equipped **chambres d'hôtes**, *Domaine Salabert* (☎04.67.37.19.43; ❸). Other local options include the well-sited *Via Domitia* (☎04.67.35.62.63, ℱ04.67.35.62.00; ❷) in Colombiers and, in Villeneuve, *Las Cigalas* (☎04.67.39.45.28, Ⓦwww.las-cigalas.com; ❶), at 28 boulevard Gambetta, as well as a municipal **campsite** (☎04.67.39.36.09; mid-April to mid-Sept).

The only **restaurant** which stands out is *La Tour Sarrazine* (☎04.67.93.41.31; *menus* from €25; closed Sun eve & Mon), which serves imaginative *terroir*-based cuisine in a cosy old house, 5km west of Nissan, at 27 boulevard du Canal in Poilhes. Villeneuve's country market is held on Tuesdays and Sundays, and you can rent **boats** from Rive de France (☎04.67.37.14.23) at Colombiers.

Béziers and around

Just inland from the mouth of the Orb river and dominating the strip of plain between the coast and Haut Languedoc, **BÉZIERS** could be held up as a metaphor for Languedoc – it's a town with a long and proud past, and a history of independent spirit, which it has more than once paid for in blood. Like neighbouring Narbonne, Béziers was already a sizeable settlement when the Romans took it over in the second century BC; it thrived under *pax romana*, and was the seat of a bishop and a prosperous market town through the Middle Ages. The last great event here was the attack it suffered in the Albigensian Crusade, and since then it has been something of a sleepy bywater – Paul Riquet, the genius behind the Canal du Midi, is the town's biggest claim to fame. Still, its former grandeur is evident from afar; as you approach, its great **cathedral** towers over the Orb river, high up on a dramatic ridge. Until only recently the city had fallen into decay, its dusty streets and deteriorating shopfronts betraying the slump into which the town has settled in the last century or so. Determined civicism has turned the situation around, however, and Béziers has become a delight, its atmospheric **old quarter** now bustling with busy shops. Modern Béziers is the home to two great Languedocian adopted traditions: English **rugby**, and the Spanish **corrida**, both of which it follows with a passion. The best time to visit is during the mid-August **feria**, a raucous four-day party which you will enjoy even if you don't find bullfighting to your taste. Béziers is also a useful staging point for excursions up the **Orb valley** (see p.333) towards Haut Languedoc, or down to **Agde** and the coast.

BÉZIERS

Cimitière Vieux ▲▲ Cimitière Vieux ▲▲ ▲ St-Aphrodise Church

La Madeleine

Gare Routière

PLACE DE LA VICTOIRE

R G MANDEL

AV DU 22 AOÛT 1944

Théâtre Municipal

RUE PORTE OLIVIER

R C LABUR

R C FERET

R TRENCAVEL

RUE ST VINCENT

PL DE LA MADELAINE

RUE PAUL RIQUET

RUE DE LA RÉPUBLIQUE

RUE DE LA TOUR

RUE ÉTIENNE FORCADEL

RUE FRANÇAISE

R OH GIBAL

RUE MAIRAN

A

B

C

Market

PLACE PIERRE SÉMARD

R OEN VEREL

R CARLES

RUE DU 4 SEPTEMBRE

ALLÉES PAUL-RIQUET

COLLÈGE

RUE

Musée Fayet

RUE DU GAL CROUZAT

R FLOURENS

PLACE GABRIEL PÉRI

ⓘ

R H MONTMORENCY

RUE PAUL PEISSON

RUE DES BALANCES

Place G. de Gaulle ▲

Montpellier ▲

RAMPE DES MOULINS

BOULEVARD D'ANGLETERRE

RUE BOUDARD

R CAPUS

RUE VIENNET

②

③

AVENUE ALPHONSE MAS

R DE LA CITADELLE

AVENUE VALENTIN DUC

R DE LA JUVERIE

④

Musée des Beaux Arts

R DU BT TRGEN VERT

R ESTÈVE

PLACE JEAN-JAURÈS

ⓘ ⓔ Camping Clariac, Gare SNCF & Plateau des Poètes

PLACE DE LA RÉVOLUTION

RUE DE BONSI

RUE DE MASSOL

R A FABREGAT

T DU DE BOURGUET

RUE JEAN JAURÈS

D

St-Nazaire Cathedral

Jardin de L'Évêché

BD TOURVENTOUSE

PLACE CANTERELLETTES

R DE LA CONCORDE

AV DU M JOFFRE

RUE DU COQ

PLACE GARIBALDI

RUE GAVEAU

AVENUE GAMBETTA

Orb River

PONT VIEUX

RUE DES SAINTS SIMONIENS

RUE CANTERELLES

R DES PUITS DES ARÈNES

BD DE LA MALPAS

RUE SAINT JACQUES

RUE DU MIDI

PONT NEUF

R DE L'ABREUVOIR

BD JEAN MACE

Roman Amphitheatre

AVENUE DES CASEMES

RUE SAINT JACQUES

RUE DE L'HORTEL

RUE DE CHÈVRELETTE

AVENUE COLONEL D'ORNANO

R DES LONGUES ANNES

RUE DAME DU PLO

PLACE DES CASEMES

RAMPE DU SOLEIL

Musée du Bitterois

RUE DE LA MARNE

R GÉNÉRAL CHANZY

R B S MARGUERITTE

PLACE SAINT JACQUES

RUE FR RASPAIL

QUAI DE L'ORB

N

BOULEVARD DE VERDUN

Gare SNCF

⑤

Narbonne ▼

ACCOMMODATION
Angleterre	D
France	B
Imperator	C
des Poètes	E
du Théâtre	A

RESTAURANTS
L'Ambassade	5
Le Bistrot des Halles	1
Le Cep d'Or	3
Le Petit Table	2
La Table Bretonne	4

0   200 m

Arrival and information

If you arrive at the **gare SNCF** on boulevard de Verdun, about fifteen minutes' walk southeast of the old town, the best way into the centre is through
the landscaped gardens of the Plateau des Poètes, opposite the *gare* entrance,
and up allées Paul-Riquet to place de la Victoire. The **gare routière** is on place
Général de Gaulle, just to the east of Victoire, while the **tourist office** is in
the new Palais des Congrès at 29 avenue Saint-Saëns (July & Aug Mon–Sat
9am–7pm, Sun 9.30am–12.30pm; Sept–June Mon–Sat 9am–noon & 2–6pm;
☎04.67.76.47.00, ⓦwww.ville-beziers.fr). There's also a small summer-only
office (Mon–Fri: May–June 10am–noon & 2–6pm; July & Aug 10am–1pm &
2–7pm) in place Lavabre in the old town. If you're **driving**, there is no need
to park in the underground garage at place Garibaldi – there's plenty of

metered street parking in and around the town centre. You can rent **bikes** at La Maison du Canal (T04.67.62.18.18) beside the Port Neuf, south of the gare SNCF. For entertainment **listings** and activities, consult the monthly *Paus'cafe* magazine (free) available at news-stands and businesses.

Accommodation

For a central place to **stay**, try *Hôtel des Poètes*, 80 allées Paul-Riquet (T04.67.76.38.66, F04.67.76.25.88; ❷), at the southern end overlooking the gardens, the smarter *Hôtel du Théâtre*, 13 rue Coquille (T04.67.49.13.43, F04.67.49.31.58; ❷), right beside the municipal theatre, or the new *France* (T04.67.28.44.72, Wwww.hotel2france.com; ❷) at 36 rue Boiëdieu. The town's deluxe option, *Hôtel Imperator* (T04.67.49.02.25, Wwww.hotel-imperator.fr; ❸), at 28 allées Paul-Riquet, is a notch above the rest but won't break the bank. There's no **campsite** in Béziers, but you can head to nearby Villeneuve-lès-Béziers (see p.325) or 6km east to Clariac (T04.67.76.78.97; April–Sept).

The Town

Béziers' vaguely semicircular **old town** snuggles into a gentle meander of the Orb, which, along with the canal – the Ruisseau de Bagnols – bounds it on three sides. The eastern limit is marked by allées Paul-Riquet, which has a broad pedestrian concourse running down its centre. From place Jean-Jaurès, which opens up off allées Paul-Riquet, you can descend rue due la Citadelle to place Gabriel Péri, the old town's centre.

The Cathédrale St-Nazaire

Béziers' main attraction is undoubtedly the majestic Romanesque **Cathédrale St-Nazaire** (free entry), about five minutes' walk west from place Péri on the western rim, just off place de la Révolution. Constructed in the thirteenth century, the cathedral's marriage of style and function is immediately apparent in its west face, which has a great rosette window flanked by two fortified towers. From the entrance here, the first part of the cathedral you enter is the cloister. Within its low and austere gallery, there's a collection of old funerary stones, including one with Hebrew characters, while on its east side a stairway descends into the airy gardens, the **Jardin de l'Évêché**, built off the south side of the great church. The cathedral's voluminous, predominantly unadorned **interior** is dominated by an outrageous Baroque retable – a gaudy starburst of saints and cherubs which clashes with the sobriety of the building. The high point of the visit is the dizzying climb to the **upper galleries** (free) – a rare opportunity to get a pigeon's eye view of a cathedral's interior. Climbing the well-worn, narrow keystone staircase, you traverse a small landing before continuing up to the top – the balconies which circle the pinnacles afford spectacular **views**. Almost directly below the cliffs on which the cathedral stands, you'll see the evocative twelfth-century *pont vieux* as it crosses the Orb below and, beyond to the west, the whole of the Bitterois plain stretching off into a haze – on a clear day you might make out the form of Le Canigou on the horizon. Take care when climbing the stairs and circulating up top, particularly if you're travelling with children – the only protective fencing here is the old stone balustrade.

The rest of the old town

North of the cathedral, at the far end of the pleasant place de la Révolution – where republican protesters were fired upon in 1851 – is the Hôtel Fabrégat, a mansion which houses the **Musée des Beaux Arts** (Tues–Fri 9am–noon & 2–6pm; €2.35), a collection of works by local painters as well as better-known artists such as Delacroix and Dufy. The museum's sculpture annexe is lodged in another aristocratic residence, the nearby **Musée Fayet**, whose collection is dominated by nineteenth-century works, notably by local sculptor Injalbert (same hours and ticket). Continuing north from here, you'll pass the beautiful wrought-iron covered **market** (Tues–Sun 7.30am–12.30pm), set in the attractive place Pierre-Sémard and, further on up rue Paul-Riquet, the **church of La Madeleine** (Mon 3–6pm, Tues–Sun 10am–1pm & 3–6pm; €2.50), scene of the murder of the Trencavel viscount in 1167 and the **massacre** of seven thousand Catholics by the Crusaders in 1209 (see box opposite). Continuing north from La Madeleine, for some 250m, up to place St-Aphrodise – follow the pedestrian signs – you'll come across **St-Aphrodise church** (briefly open some days at 5.30pm), an incredibly old structure with a tenth-century nave and Gallo-Roman crypt. A further five minutes' walk north along rue de la Faïence you come to the *cimitière vieux* (daily 8am–noon & 2–6pm; free); founded in 1838, it contains a series of impressive mausoleums and monuments raised by the town's prospering bourgeoisie, featuring sculptures by Jean-Antoine Injalbert (a town native) and other noteworthy artists.

Heading east from La Madeleine, rue Trencavel takes you towards the pretty Art Nouveau-style **Théâtre Municipal Molière** at the top end of allées Paul-Riquet, a broad, leafy esplanade lined with cafés, *crêpes* stalls and restaurants; on Friday mornings, the weekly flower market is held here. The boulevard ends at the gorgeous little park of the **Plateau des Poètes**, whose ponds, palms and lime trees were laid out in the so-called English manner by the same team, the brothers Denis et Eugène Bülher, who created the Bois de Boulogne in Paris. Finally, to the west of the park on rampe du 96ème, you'll find the impressive **Musée du Biterrois** (Tues–Sun: July & Aug 9am–7pm; Sept–June 9am–noon & 2–6pm; €3.10), housed in an old barracks and containing three sections: natural history, ethnography and archeology. The first two, respectively illustrating the biological diversity of the marshy coast and the rural and craft traditions of the region, are passable, but it's the last section, most of which is given over to the Gallo-Roman period, which makes the museum well worth a stop. This important collection ranges from locally produced pottery and ceramics, to funerary monuments and milestones, and there are also various artefacts dredged from ancient shipwrecks off the coast, but the highlight is the "treasure of Béziers" – a rich cache of silver platters found in a nearby field. The medieval period is represented by locally sculpted medieval capitals and bas-reliefs.

You can finish off your visit to Béziers by taking a look at the remains of a modest Roman **amphitheatre** two streets to the north of the museum. This is being developed as an open-air museum at the time of writing, and should be ready by 2005.

Eating and drinking

There's a whole string of economical **restaurants** (with patios) along the west side of allées Paul-Riquet, serving the usual *steak-frites* type menus for about €12. Better fare can be found in the old quarter, where rue Viennet has a good choice of places. The best value for money is found at *Le Petit Table* at no. 12, where you can enjoy an excellent home-cooked meal for €11, including wine. Otherwise, the elegant *Le Cep d'Or*, at no. 7, serving mostly seafood (*menus* €15–20; closed Sun eve & Mon) is a bit pricier, while lighter fare can be found at *La Table Bretonne*, at no. 21 (closed Mon), an airy crêperie with a large street-side patio where savoury or sweet pancakes start at €8.80. *L'Ambassade* (closed

Simon de Montfort and the Albigensian Crusade

On July 22, 1209, a massive host of armed knights surrounded **Béziers** under the leadership of Arnaud-Amaury, Abbot of Cîteaux, the most powerful monastery in northern France, who had been charged by Pope **Innocent III** with leading the Crusade against the **Cathar heretics**. Raymond-Roger, the viscount of the city, had already left, and with him the town's Jewish community. But the majority of the townsmen, Cathar and Catholic, were not prepared to surrender their homes and property. The assault came swiftly and, unable to resist, the surviving townsfolk took **refuge** in the Church of the Madeleine, within which according to Catholic law, no blood was to be shed. The abbot and his knights, however, were merciless. Arnaud-Amaury gave the order to set **fire** to the church. When a subordinate protested that innocent Catholics would die, he is said to have exclaimed, "Burn them all, God will know his own!"

This was the opening scene for the Albigensian Crusade (see p.392), the ferocious military campaign waged against the counts of Toulouse and their subjects by a vengeful papacy and a ravenous **northern French nobility**. One of these soldiers of fortune was **Simon de Montfort**, a veteran knight and a northern French magnate. His plan was to take over Raymond VI's lands for himself. After the siege of Béziers he was appointed military commander of the Crusade and embarked on a **brutal campaign of terror** and conquest, which saw town after town, from Carcassonne up to the walls of Toulouse, fall or burn before him. His treatment of the native populace was pitiless – massacres and mutilation were the order of the day. Nor did he respect **chivalric values** – when Raymond's liege-lord King Peter "the Catholic" of Aragon was drawn into the fray, Simon had him singled out and killed on the field of battle at Muret in 1213. De Montfort's career came to an appropriate end in June 1218 at the siege of Toulouse, when a missile from a catapult fired by a squad of women and children bashed his brains out. Simon de Montfort may have failed in his ambition to rule the lands of the counts of Toulouse, but his relentless attacks had left them unable to withstand the pressure of the French Crown; after **Raymond VII** reorganized the Cathar communities in the 1220s, French royal forces responded with a second scorched-earth campaign, which ultimately brought about the extinction of Raymond's line and the fall of independent Languedoc.

Sun & Mon; ☎04.67.76.06.24), at 22 boulevard de Verdun, is one of the town's fancier places (*menus* from €25), while *Le Bistrot des Halles*, further north behind the market square on place de la Madeleine, is popular for its varied, well-priced *menus* (from €15; closed Sun & Mon). A good **café** is *La Bourse* at the corner of place Jean-Jaurès and allées Riquet, while a livelier time can be enjoyed at two tapas bars, *Charlie & Carlos* and *Le Mondial*, which square off at the corner of rues Boieldieu and Solferino.

In addition to the town's covered **market** (Mon–Sat mornings), a regional produce market is held Fridays in place 14-Juillet.

Listings

Banks All major French banks are represented here, and most have offices in allées Paul-Riquet or place Jean-Jaurès. On the former you'll find BNP at no. 34, Banque Populaire du Midi at no. 39 and Crédit Lyonnais at no. 16.

Boat rental At Béziers' port, try Ad'navis-Amica Tours (☎04.67.62.18.18) or Béziers Croisières

(☎04.67.49.08.23); the latter also runs canal trips.

Bus information ☎04.67.28.23.85.

Car rental ADA, 23 bd Verdun ☎04.67.62.65.39; Avis, 18 bd Verdun ☎04.67.28.65.44; Europcar, 70 allées Paul-Riquet ☎04.67.62.09.89; Hertz, 83 av Pt-Wilson ☎04.67.62.82.00.

Internet access Cyberia, 7 rue St-Ferignon

☎04.67.72.99.91 (Mon–Fri 10am–12am, Sat
1pm–2am, Sun 2am–12am).
Police Pl Général-de-Gaulle.
Rugby Béziers has one of the star rugby clubs in
France, A.S.B.H., based at the Stade de la

Méditerranée in the eastern suburbs
(☎04.67.11.03.76, @www.asbh.net).
Taxis ☎04.67.35.00.85
Train information ☎08.36.35.35.35

Agde and the coast

Thanks to the few kilometres which separate it from the sea, **AGDE**, just 12km
east of Béziers, is one of the most unspoilt towns on the Languedocian coast.
It boomed as port 2500 years ago under the Phoenicians and on through the
Middle Ages, until competition from neighbouring towns and the silting up of
the Hérault pushed the seashore from its walls. Today, its compact old town has
resisted intensive development and remains a quiet respite from the crowds –
the best time to arrive is on one of Agde's market days: Thursday for produce
and Wednesday and Saturday for the flea market. Set along the now canalized
river, the town is dominated by a twelfth-century fortified **cathedral**, St-
Étienne, on its south bank, whose appearance is more castle than church, its
three-metre-thick walls and hot-oil sluices having formed the strongpoint of
the town's defences. A series of *places* follows the riverside from east to west:
the lively Jean-Jaurès, with its sidewalk cafés; Picheire, where you'll find the
small porticoed medieval **market**; and de la Marine, a grittily authentic fishermen's quarter. Heading south from place de la Marine, the residential rue
Poissonerie is a step back in time – a neighbourhood of fishermen's families
living in modest and ancient houses. Following rue Poissonerie to the end,
you'll arrive at the old convent housing the **Musée Agathois** (July & Aug
daily 10am–noon & 2–6pm; Sept–June Mon & Wed–Sun same times; €3.80).
It's one of the better of the region's "local" museums, with exhibitions on life
in the area from the prehistoric era to the present day; relics of the town's sea-
faring past range from ancient Greek *amphorae* to nineteenth-century naviga-
tional instruments. Continuing, you'll pass the new market building and the
church of St-André, occupying a site on which there's been a church since
as far back as 506 AD, when an episcopal council was held here. Just south is
the wide tree-lined La Promenade, with its multitude of terraced bars, while
close by, rue de l'Amour and rue Jean-Roger are lined with tacky souvenir
shops.

Cap d'Agde and Grau d'Agde

Agde's evil twin, **CAP D'AGDE** lies to the south of Mont St-Loup on the
seashore, some 7km south. A sprawling and characterless modern resort, its only
redemption is the abundance of colourful plants and flowers which line its
broad streets, only partially concealing a uniform sea of cream-coloured holiday villas behind. But, the Cap has everything you would want for a mindless,
cultureless beach holiday – nightclubs, watersports and restaurants, although
here you will pay dearly for them. If you're just passing through though, a
worthwhile stop is the **Musée de l'Éphèbe** (July & Aug daily 9am–12.30pm
& 2.30–6.30pm; Sept–June Wed–Sat 9am–noon & 2–6pm, Sun 2–6pm;
€3.80), in the central Parc de la Clape, which holds a collection of Greek and
Roman relics retrieved from the sea bed, including the beautiful little
Hellenistic bronze statuette known as the Éphèbe d'Agde, until recently one
of the treasures of the Louvre. There is also an **aquarium**, at 11 rue des Deux-
Frères (daily: June & Sept 10am–7pm; July & Aug 10am–11pm; Oct–May
2–6pm; €6), though it's not as good as that at Le Grau-du-Roi (see p.252), and

There are two very distinct sides to Cap d'Agde. On the one hand there is the conventional and somewhat tacky tourist resort – the largest in France – with its over-priced restaurants, busy beaches and homogenous personality. Meanwhile, on the western edge of the town lies the largest and most legendary nudist resort in the world.

Cap d'Agde's **quartier naturiste**, which in the height of summer attracts as many as 60,000 visitors, owes its existence to a small group of lost German tourists and two enterprising winegrowers. Looking for a secluded spot away from prying eyes, a caravan-load of German naturists arrived more or less by accident at the modest beachside vineyard owned by René and Paul Oltra in 1958. Next year they returned, now in a small convoy of caravans, and the rest is history. The Oltra brothers were granted permission by the local council to establish a naturist campsite on their land, and by the early 1960s a small office had been set up at the entrance, while the campsite itself was full of bungalows, tents and caravans. The first brick construction went up in 1971 next to **Port Ambonne**, to be followed soon after by other apartment complexes and commercial centres such as **Héliopolis** and **Port Nature**. Nowadays, the *quartier naturiste* is really a small town in its own right. There are supermarkets, restaurants, cafés, bars, discos, thousands of holiday apartments for rent, a hotel and a campsite with more than 2500 places, all catering to a naturist clientele. Nudity is permitted – although not absolutely required – at all times anywhere within the confines of the resort, and while not everyone chooses to do their shopping or go to the bank in the nude, the two-kilometre stretch of sandy beach around which the resort has developed remains almost entirely "textile free".

Just as the landscape of the *quartier naturiste* has changed dramatically over the years, so has the type of people who visit the resort. Until about the early 1990s, most of the people who came to Cap d'Agde did so simply because they enjoyed spending their time naked, with no other connotations attached. Gradually, however, another type of naturist, described by French commentators as "*à poilistes*", began to arrive. For these people nudity and sex were inextricably linked, and soon the beach became unofficially segregated into various sections: for families, for sexually liberated heterosexuals and for gays. The resort's infrastructure also evolved to cater to this new breed of visitor. For example, there are more boutiques selling X-rated clothing in the *quartier naturiste* than in most large cities, and some of the raunchiest and most famous **swingers clubs** in Europe are located here. Cap d'Agde is now perhaps the world's ultimate "sea, sex and sun" destination.

The nudist **season** in Cap d'Agde runs from mid-March to mid-October, although most of the shops, restaurants and bars are open from around mid-May to mid-September. One-day access is €9 per car or €2.80 for pedestrians and cyclists. No tickets are sold after 8pm. For more information, contact the Bureau d'acceuil (☎04.67.26.00.26, ⊛www.agdenaturisme.com), or read Ross Velton's *The Naked Truth About Cap d'Agde* (⊛www.wordcrafting.com).

a huge Aqualand **amusement park** (mid-June to mid-Sept daily 10am–7pm; €15.50–18.50), on the west end of town. The former prison of **Fort de Brescou**, built in 1680, lies just offshore and can be reached by ferries departing from the ports at either Cap d'Agde or Grau d'Agde (Mon, Tues & Thurs–Sun 10.30am, 2.30pm & 6.30pm; €7). Evoking Marseille's famous Château d'Îf – of *Man in the Iron Mask* fame – this rather grim fortress can be visited on a **guided tour** (mid-June to Aug, timed with boat arrivals; €2.50), or you can simply scamper about the rocky seagull-infested island for free.

If you fancy a dip, the best **beaches** are on the west side of the cape stretching over towards La Guirandette; there's also a huge, self-contained **nudist** colony here on the east side (see box on p.331). Nearby **GRAU d'AGDE** is the beach-town antithesis of the Cap: a dispersed settlement of weathered houses and ageing bungalows, this dissipating suburb distils into an old fishing town as you reach the lighthouse-capped wavebreak.

Practicalities

Trains and **buses** arrive in Agde just across the river from the old town. To continue south to the Cap you can take a municipal bus (€0.60) from the *gare*, or use the superb network of cycle paths – once there you'll realize it's no place to walk, and end up using one of the two *petits trains* which circulate around the town (€2), or the various **water taxis**. Agde's **tourist office** (July & Aug daily 9am–7pm; Sept–June Mon–Sat 9am–noon & 2–6pm; ☎04.67.94.29.68, €ot-agde@wanadoo.fr) is on place Molière, near the main roundabout; two-hour English-language **guided tours** of the town (Tues & Thurs 10am; €5) leave from outside. Cap d'Agde's **tourist office** (daily: July & Aug 8.30am–8pm; May, June & Sept 9am–7pm; Oct–April 9am–noon & 2–7pm; ☎04.67.01.04.04, ⓦwww.capdagde.com) is on the huge roundabout which marks the centre of the settlement.

You can get **Internet** connection in Agde at Globe Trotter, 4 place de la Marine, and **bike rental** at La Cadotière, 1 place Jean-Jaurès (☎04.76.94.26.20), while **river trips** are available from Les Bateaux du Soleil (☎04.67.94.08.79) at the port. Nautic (☎04.67.94.78.93) and Locarama (☎04.67.26.26.45) rent **boats**.

Accommodation

The best hotel in **Agde** is the Dutch-run *La Galiote* (☎04.67.94.45.58, ⓦwww.lagaliote.fr; ❷), located in the old bishops' palace on place Jean-Jaurès, while a close second is *Le Donjon* (☎04.67.94.12.32, ⓦwww.hotel ledonjon.com; ❸) on the same square. Some of the cheapest – but still decent – digs can be had at the *Hôtel des Arcades* (☎04.67.94.21.64; ❷) in an old convent at 16 rue Louis-Bages. In **Cap d'Agde**, a good option is *La Voile d'Or* on place de Globe (☎04.67.01.04.11, ⓦlavoiledor.com; ❺), while **Grau d'Agde** has the seaside *El Rancho* (☎04.67.94.24.35, ⓦwww.logis-de-france.fr; closed Feb–Nov; ❸). If you plan on staying in the **nudist colony**, try the *Eve* (☎04.67.26.71.70, ⓦwww.hoteleve.com; April–Oct closed Nov–March; ❼) in impasse Siassan, or its campsite (☎04.67.01.06.36).

There are no fewer than 24 basically indistinguishable **campsites** in the area – you might start with *Sud Loisirs* (☎04.67.21.09.10) near Agde, or *La Clape* (☎04.67.26.41.32, €clape@capdagde.com; March–Oct) at the Cap.

Eating

The area's best **restaurant** is at *La Tramissière* (☎04.67.94.20.87; closed Nov–March & frequently on Sun & Mon; *menus* from €27.50), a *gastronomique* halfway between Agde and Grau on the far bank of the Hérault, which also has some rooms (❹–❾); take bus #275 from the main road through Agde. Good choices at the Cap are the seafood specialist *Le Brasero*, at Port Richelieu II (☎04.67.26.24.75; *menus* from €16), or the *gastronomique*, *Le Caladoc* (☎04.67.26.87.18; *menu* €20) in the Ile des Loisirs. In Agde itself, you could do worse than *La Fine Fourchetté* (☎04.67.94.49.56), at 2 rue du Mont-Saint-Loup, featuring a delightfully intriguing *carte* (*menus* from €10); there are also a number of places right on the quayside or on rue Chassefière, which runs along it.

The Orb valley

The **River Orb** winds a twisting path down from its source in the hills of Haut Languedoc north of Béziers, descending some 120km through the highlands and across the broad coastal plain to skirt the city before emptying into the Golfe du Lion. Heading up its valley from Béziers provides rapid access from the coast to the lesser-travelled uplands of Haut Languedoc. Just after **Roquebrun**, a centre both for viticulture and rafting, the valley delves into the rugged uplands, wheeling off to the east to pass **Hérépian** and the old spa town of **Lamalou-les-Bains** – both good bases for walks into the Parc Naturel de Haut Languedoc – and following the park's edge round until the land opens up into a compact but fertile plane around **Bédarieux** – another possible departure point for exploring the highlands. Heading further north into the **upper valley** you eventually reach a series of tiny hamlets high up at the river's origins.

Roquebrun and around

Journeying 21km upriver from Béziers, the D14 joins the course of the Orb at Cessenon, just before it ascends into the rugged uplands. The border of the Parc du Haut Languedoc (see p.198) has recently been pushed south to incorporate the area around **ROQUEBRUN**, less than 10km further along. This old town, clumped on a hillside beneath the ruins of its medieval tower, is located in an exceptionally mild microclimate, making the valley floor, which is still wide here, an idea place for vine cultivation – indeed the town has produced several award-winning vintages (AOC Saint-Chinian), which you can sample and buy at the various *domaines* scattered around the valley. The good weather also provides a suitable climate for the town's **Jardin Méditerranéen** (daily: mid-Feb to June & Sept to mid-Nov 9am–noon & 1.30–5.30pm; July & Aug 9am–7pm; €4), a collection of exotic, primarily arid-climate plants from around the world, while in winter the valley around the town bursts into colour with the blooming of mimosas. After Roquebrun the valley begins to meander drunkenly, reeling between the ever-higher peaks which gird it until, at last, you reach the mill at **Terassac** 14km on, where the Jaur and the Héric join the Orb; here the river course takes an abrupt swing to the east on towards Lamalou. The mill is also the place to rent **canoes** (℡04.67.97.74.64) for the exciting rafting journey downstream to Roquebrun, the terminus for this and trips from higher up in the hills.

There is a small **tourist office** (July & Aug Mon–Sat 10am–1pm & 3–7pm; Sept–June Mon–Fri 9am–noon & 2–6pm; ℡ & ℻04.67.89.79.97, ✉otroquebrun@bechemail.com) in Roquebrun, while for **accommodation**, you can choose between the *Campotel* **campsite** (℡04.67.89.61.99, ℻04.67.89.78.15; mid-March to mid-Nov; ➋) or the Anglo-run **chambres d'hôtes** *Les Mimosas* (℡04.67.89.61.36, ℻04.67.89.61.36; ➍), set in a nineteenth-century house in avenue Orangers, which also does meals (€25).

Lamalou-les-Bains and Hérépian

Built on the hot springs which have brought it prosperity for the last thousand years, **LAMALOU-LES-BAINS** lies just a kilometre north of the river course. In the late nineteenth and early twentieth century it came into fashion, and notables such as the writers Alphonse Daudet and André Gide came to enjoy its curative waters. It's still a popular therapeutic spot today, and the more or less constant parade of ailing people moving among its faded *fin-de-siècle* mansions gives it the strange air of a large outdoor hospital. The town is most useful as a stopover for hikers making their way through the hills, but there is also a beautiful old parish church here, **St–Pierre–de–Rhèdes**, which dates back to the spa's earliest beginnings. The church's pastiche of stylistic touches, overlaying its basic Romanesque form, results from immigrants to the region, including Mozarabs from Spain, who left Christian inscriptions written in Arabic.

A pleasant workaday town with only the most basic of services, **HÉRÉPIAN**, a few kilometres upstream, has a much more salubrious air. While here you can visit the Bruneau-Garnier **bell foundry** (daily: April–June & Sept 10.30am–noon & 2–6pm; July & Aug 10am–noon & 2–7pm; Oct–March 10am–noon & 2–7pm; €5) – one of the last in France still functioning – or you might hike up to the ruins of the **Castle of St-Michel**, 300m above the riverbed on the slopes of the **Pic de la Coquillade**. The trail head begins on the Orb's south bank, just west of the hamlet of Les Aires, and the gruelling 6km will take you first to the extensive ruins of the castle, which was founded in 990, and on to the summit, where you'll find a small chapel.

Lamalou's **tourist office**, on avenue Dr-Ménard (June–Sept Mon–Fri 9am–noon & 2.30–6.30pm, Sat 9am–noon & 2–5pm, Sun 10am–noon; Oct–May Mon–Fri 9.30am–noon & 2.30–6pm, Sat 9am–noon; ☎04.67.95.64.17, ⓦwww.ot-lamaloulesbains.fr), has information on nearby towns and also sells SNCF bus tickets, and you'll also find several banks, a laundry and even a car rental office in town. There's no shortage of accommodation either: the **hotels** *De la Paix l'Arbousier*, 18 rue A-Daudet (☎04.67.95.63.11, ⓔarbousier.hotel@wanadoo.fr; ❸), and *Galimar*, 17 boulevard St-Michel (☎04.67.95.22.99, ⓔhotelgalimar@wanadoo.fr; ❷), are both good deals. Both are adequate, and there are many others to choose from around town. There are **campsites** at both towns: *Le Riviéral* (☎04.67.95.19.25) at Hérépian, and *Le Verdale* (☎04.67.95.86.89; May–Sept) at Lamalou.

Bédarieux

Continuing from Hérépian, the valley broadens suddenly, forming a wide pocket of flat land dominated by **BÉDARIEUX**, the biggest place north of Béziers on the course of the Orb. The town is something of a transport hub and, as an administrative centre, it's also busy, but you're not likely to want to stay too long. Bédarieux's one tourist attraction is the predictably mediocre **Maison des Arts** (Wed–Fri 3–6pm; €3), on avenue Abbé Taroux, whose collection is dominated by local painter Pierre-Auguste Cot. Otherwise, the tourist office can set you up with detailed information on **walks** in the local countryside (€1 for their booklet). One of the better short ones is the trail, through vines and bulrushes, to the twelfth-century pre-Romanesque **chapel** of St-Raphaël, on the far bank of the river, while a more challenging option is the ascent of the Pic de Tanajo (518m) to the southwest.

Bédarieux's **gare SNCF** (☎04.67.95.02.92), which is also where **buses** call in, is a good twenty-minute hike north of the old centre, where you'll find the regional **tourist office** (Mon, Tues, Thurs & Fri 9am–12.30pm & 2–7.30pm, Sat 9am–12.30pm; ☎04.67.95.08.79, ⓦwww.bedarieux.fr), on place aux Herbes. The town's only **hotel**, *Le Delta* (☎04.67.23.21.19; ❷) is on rue de Clairac, while the **campsite**, *Trois Vallées* (☎04.67.23.30.19), is on the south bank of the Orb, just west of town. The municipality also operates a **gîte** (☎04.67.23.30.05, ⓔgites.bedariuex@wanadoo.fr; ❶) on boulevard Jean Moulin. The best **restaurant** deal is *Le Rapier*, by the Hôtel de Ville on rue de la République, where you can get a four-course meal including dessert, coffee and wine for around €14. If you want to **rent a car** and explore the uplands of the Orb and the Parc Naturel, try Wallgren, 4 rue de la République (℡04.67.23.18.23), while Passion Sauvage (℡04.67.23.69.33) will rent **bikes**. There are markets in the town's *places* on Monday and Saturday mornings.

The upper Orb valley

Moving north, the valley continues to rise, with the river petering out to little more than a brook near its sources in the Monts d'Orb. Proceeding from Bédarieux, you should take the turn-off 6km north of town and ascend to the tiny medieval hamlet of **BOUSSAGUES**, an extremely well-preserved walled town, replete with church, fountain and *donjon*, which is surprisingly unvisited; the only service you'll find here is a (frequently closed) café. The ruins of its castles, on the hill above, are little more than foundations overgrown by vine and bramble, but the views they provide are great. **Hikers** on the GR7 will pass by Boussagues as they make their way between Lamalou and Lodève. **LE-BOUSQUET**, 10km further up the valley, has a strange air, as if everyone is waiting for something to happen – nothing ever does, however, and aside from taking a fleeting look at the old quarter gathered in a mound on the right bank, there is no reason to stay. **LUNAS**, just a few kilometres further (and on the GR653) makes a much more pleasant option. Here the river glides past the walls of a pitched-roof *château*; you'll find an old bridge and a church which, it is claimed, dates back to the fifth century – nothing particularly stunning, but, with the low, forest-clad hills rising on either side of the river valley, an attractive and peaceful scene, and a good stop before braving the spectacular mountain road which leads east along the steep ridge to Lodève (see p.291).

You can **stay** in Le-Bousquet at the small and homely *Hôtel Berthomieu* (℡04.67.23.80.45; closed Jan & weekends in winter; ❶), whose restaurant has basic home-cooked meals from €10. At Lunas, there's a **hotel**, *Auberge Gourmand* (℡04.67.23.81.41, ℻04.67.23.79.57; ❷), whose restaurant (closed Fri–Sun in winter) has menus at €12–40, wine included. A more unique choice and a great bargain, however, is to take one of the simple rooms in the castle, *Le Château* (℡04.67.23.87.99; ❶) which also has a **bar** (till 1am) and an excellent restaurant (*menus* from €18). Finally a more bucolic option, in the hamlet of Laval du Nize, 3.5km from Le-Bousquet, is the *Domaine du Laval la Nize* (℡04.67.23.43.23, ⓦwww.gites-de-france-herault.asso.fr; ❸; English spoken), a **chambres d'hôtes** with comfortable rooms and good amenities including a pool. There are also seasonal (mid-June to Aug) **campsites** Laval du Nize (℡04.67.23.77.62), and Le-Bousquet (℡04.67.23.80.89).

Travel details

Trains

SNCF buses may run in lieu of trains on these lines; services are reduced on Sundays and holidays.
Note that the Autorail Touristique Minervois (see p.323) also connects Narbonne to Sallèles and Bize.
Béziers to: Paris (30 daily; 4hr 30min–12hr);
Toulouse (14 daily; 1hr 35min).
Narbonne to: Agde (18 daily; 28min–1hr); Béziers (18 daily; 14min); Carcassonne (22 daily; 35min); Lézignan (16 daily; 14min); Montpellier (26 daily; 45min–1hr 15min); Nîmes (20 daily; 1hr 45min); Paris (30 daily; 5–11hr); Perpignan (24 daily; 36–45min); Salses (9 daily; 30min); Sète (23 daily; 45min); Toulouse (18 daily; 1hr 30min).

Buses

Note that in Aude *département*, no buses run on Sundays, and that in Hérault many lines have no Sunday service. Services may also be reduced on Saturdays, holidays and school vacation periods.

Agde to: Cap d'Agde (6 daily & half-hourly in summer; 15min).

Bédarieux to: Béziers (6 daily; 1hr–1hr 20min); Le Bousquet (2 daily; 15min); Lamalou-les-Bains (3 daily; 20min); Lunas (2 daily; 15min); St-Pons (3 daily; 1hr 20min).

Béziers to: Agde (2 daily & 5 in summer; 25min); Bédarieux (6 daily; 1hr–1hr 20min); Capestang (8 daily; 30min); Castres (2 daily; 2hr 50min); Colombiers (6 daily; 23min); Montpellier (11 daily; 1hr 30min); Nissan-les-Ensérune (6 daily; 35min); Pézenas (10 daily; 32min); Roquebrun (4 daily; 50min); St-Pons (4 daily; 1hr 20min).

Carcassonne to: Caunes-Minervois (1–4 daily; 30min), Lagrasse (1–2 daily; 1hr 40min).

Narbonne to: Bize (1–2 daily; 40min); Carcassonne (2 daily; 1hr 25min); Gruissan (3–5 daily; 30min); Lézignan (6 daily; 35min); Mouthoumet (1–2 daily; 2hr 5min); Perpignan (1 daily; 2hr 30min); Sallèles (1–3 daily; 30min); Salses (1 daily; 1hr 55min); Sigean (1 daily; 35min); Sigean Reserve (4 daily; 30min); St-Julien/Fontfroice (2–5 daily; 40min); Villerouge-Termenès (1–3 daily; 1hr 40min).

7

Roussillon

CHAPTER 7

Highlights

* **Christmas festivals**
Roussillon celebrates
Christmas in distinctive
Catalan style featuring
traditional folk art:
pessebres, *caganers* and
cagatiós. See p.349

* **Le Canigou** The
Catalans' sacred moun-
tain; join the mid-sum-
mer firelight pilgrimage.
See p.362

* **Train Jaune** A revived
narrow-gauge line takes
you up through a string
of villages that make

perfect hiking bases.
See p.364

* **Romanesque churches**
A series of rural church-
es painted and sculpted
by local masters one
thousand years ago.
See p.378

* **Collioure** The region's
most beautiful
beach-town; swim in the
shadow of the royal
castle and soak up the
atmosphere that inspired
the town's Fauvist
artists See p.380

▲ Quéribus

7

Roussillon

R oussillon, bordered by the Mediterranean to the east, the hills of the Corbières along the north, and the upper Aude and Ariège valleys to the west, is France's southernmost region, sometimes known as French Catalonia; the peaks of the eastern section of the Pyrenees, which it shares with Spain, mark its southern limit. Although absorbed by France some three and a half centuries ago, and now known officially as the *département* of Pyrénées-Orientales, it hasn't entirely lost its Catalan flavour: in the mountains there are many people whose language of choice is Catalan, and even in the larger towns you'll find the survival of customs such as the *sardana* dance or Paschal rituals. You'll also notice the influence of traditional Catalan ingredients and recipes in the region's *terroir* cuisine. But despite these particularities, and recent efforts by Catalan speakers to broaden the currency of the language, Roussillon is fundamentally French in cultural orientation, and unlike other French regions, such as Corsica, it has no significant separatist movement or regionalist political party – most likely, your only encounter with the language will be overhearing the conversations of the many visitors to the region from Catalonia proper. Traditionally a poor and neglected area, Roussillon's people have historically lived off fishing on the coast; agriculture, herding and lumber in the hills; and, until recently, smuggling, which, with the region's frontier position and the inhospitality of its landscape, provided a meagre source of income. In the last decade or so though, Roussillon's mild climate has provoked its resurgence as a retirement spot for northern French, viewed by some of the local inhabitants with a jaundiced eye as "foreign" encroachers.

Roussillon is a beautiful region, marked by the variety and contrasts of its landscape. North of the cosmopolitan main city, **Perpignan**, a marshy coastline hems in the **Fenouillèdes** hills stretching up to the northeast corner of the *département* – home to the easternmost Cathar castles and a number of prehistoric caves. Southwest from the capital you can follow the course of Roussillon's jugular, the River **Têt**, up the valley to **Canigou**, the peak which still symbolizes all of Catalonia, and the scene of a patriotic torchlight procession on midsummer's eve. Roussillon's mountains begin with the Canigou massif and include the zones of the **upper Têt** – shadowed by the spectacular route of the *Train Jaune* – the **Capcir** plateau, stretching up to the Aude, the **Cerdagne**, tucked away in the far southwest corner of the *département* and, north of that, the forbidding **Carlit massif**; all of these regions offer excellent **hiking** and **skiing** amidst superb scenery. There are also many architectural treasures worth seeking out here, in particular the sturdy Romanesque **monasteries** which cropped up along this length of the Pyrenees in the eleventh and twelfth centuries. The **Tech valley** runs a vaguely parallel course to the Têt, leading up from the plains south of Perpignan and along the Spanish border; a favourite zone with refugees from Franco's repression, its villages are some of the most traditionally Catalan in the whole region. Finally, the rugged **Côte Vermeille**, the seashore to the north of the frontier, is ideal for swimming and relaxing, its rocky harbours, cut out of wind-blown precipitous hills, forming a mirror image of Catalan Empurdà on the far side of the Pyrenees.

Despite its relative lack of development, Roussillon is fairly easy to get around, as long you stick to the main **transport** routes, which run along the coast, and up the major valleys – the Têt, Tech and rivers of the Fenouillet. Travelling between the valleys is more problematic, and unless you have your own transport you'll have to resort to hiking or hitching. The main road and rail links to Spain head south from Perpignan, the latter passing through the towns of the Côte Vermeille.

Perpignan and around

PERPIGNAN (or Perpinyà, in Catalan), the capital of Roussillon, is the most multinational city in the Southwest. A substantial part of its population is descended from Spanish Catalans who poured across the border in the final days of the Spanish Civil War, desperate to avoid reprisals at the hands of Franco's Castilian and Moroccan troops. There's also a sizeable Romany contingent, while some of the suburbs were settled by French colonists who fled the upheavals associated with the Maghrebi independence movements of the 1950s and 1960s. Finally, a run-down zone in the centre has become the quarter for recent arrivals from Morocco and Algeria, who moved here fleeing unstable and repressive political regimes or simply in search of a brighter economic future. The melting-pot atmosphere of the city makes it difficult for a distinctly Catalan ambience to coalesce, but the people are nonetheless happy

The Roussillonaise seem to have inherited a penchant for **festivals** from their Spanish cousins south of the Pyrenees, as just about every village has at least one cheerfully energetic celebration – usually the local saint's day, or *festa major* (*fête majeur*, in French). It is in these that the region's Catalan and Spanish character come to the fore, with *sardanas*, *corridas de toros* and Holy Week processions. The last of these, a solemn barefoot march by taper-carrying and hooded penitents, is best seen in places like Collioure, Arles-sur-Tech and Céret. Lest you forget that you are in France, there are also mid-October grape-harvest festivals in the wine-producing regions, two of the best of which are at Banyuls and Elne. Where no specific information number is given, contact the relevant tourist office for details.

First weekend Feb Arles-sur-Tech: Fête de l'Ours. This ancient festival, rooted in prehistoric shamanistic ceremonies and hunting traditions, marks the time when bears come out of hibernation.

End Feb Prats-de-Molló: Fête de l'Ours. Similar festival to Arles' festival above.

April Perpignan: Confrontation. Retrospective film festival with a different theme each year. Held in the Palais du Congrès.

April 23 Perpignan: San Jordi. Festival of Catalonia's patron saint, St George. Also the birthday of Cervantes and Shakespeare, now declared International Day of the Book; the – slightly sexist – custom on this day is for the men to present their sweethearts with a red rose, and the women to reciprocate by giving their loved ones a book.

Late May Perpignan: Medieval Market. The old town centre is transformed into a medieval open-air market replete with costumed food-and-craft vendors, jugglers and street entertainers.

Early June Céret: Grand Fête de la Cerise. "Festival of the Cherry", held over several days; Céret is the cherry capital of the Pyrenees, and it celebrates the traditional source of its prosperity with music, dancing and bullfights.

June 23 Têt valley: Nit de Sant-Jaume. On the eve of St John's Day people come from all over Catalonia for the torchlight pilgrimage from the Castillet in Perpignan to the peak of El Canigó – one of the symbols of the Catalan nation. Banyuls: St John's eve is celebrated here with the traditional Catalan bonfire: leap over it for good luck in the coming year.

End June Arles-sur-Tech: Fete de St-Éloi. This three-day festival culminates in the Sunday morning blessing of the mules – traditionally indispensable here, as the only transport over the surrounding mountains.

Second weekend in July Céret: Feria de Céret ☏04.68 87.47.47. A month-long festival featuring regular bullfights, as well as bull-runnings. Also a Flamenco programme around the middle of the month.

July 14–21 Perpignan: Día de Sant-Jaume. The second biggest Catalan holiday kicks off a week of medieval pageantry in Perpignan, with a medieval-style market held in the place de la Loge and around the cathedral on July 14 itself.

Mid-July Céret: Céret de Toros. A three-day celebration featuring bullfights and bull runnings.

Mid-July Prades: Ciné-Recontres ☏04.68.05.20.47. A week-long film festival with an international but essentially retrospective programme.

July 28–30 Arles-sur-Tech: Festa Major. Typically boisterous Catalan festival, featuring processions and loaded with medieval traditions.

to set themselves apart from the rest of their countrymen by promoting this identity – even if their own spoken Catalan is frequently nonexistent or limited to a few phrases pronounced with a distinctly Gallic accent. Unfortunately,

Late July Thuir: Tuïr la Catlana. Festival celebrating Catalan culture and cuisine of Roussillon and La Cerdagne.

Late July Saint-Génies-des-Fontaines: Festival Lyrique. Celebration of Catalan song and verse.

Late July Céret: International *Sardana* Festival ☎04.68.87.46.49. Three days of traditional dance renditions and contests, held in the town's streets, as well as a market, and evening concerts and dancing.

Throughout July Perpignan: Estivales ☎04.68.35.01.77, Ⓦwww.estivales.com. Music and dance festival featuring international acts; the varied programme tends to have a heavy Spanish influence.

July & August Villelongue-des-Monts: Festival Lyrique ☎04.68.89.68.35, Ⓦmairie.wanadoo.fr/..mairie.villelonguedelsmonts/Associations/santamaria.htm#lyrique. On Saturday evenings at 9pm, the Romanesque chapel of Santa Maria Vilar hosts top-notch medieval music ranging from Gregorian chant to troubadour recitations.

Mid-July to late Aug Perpignan: Les Jeudis de Perpignan. Thursday evening festival, featuring street performers and live music in many bars and squares.

End July to mid-Aug Prades: Festival Pablo Casals ☎04.68.96.33.07 Ⓦpro.wanadoo .fr/festival.casals. A world-famous classical music festival. Over 25 concerts with soloists and groups from around the world, and a programme which ranges from Bach to Ravel. The venues include the monastery at Cuxàc and other regional churches.

Aug 16 Collioure: Festa Major. The town's saint, Vincent, is feted in the finest Catalan and Spanish styles, with merrymaking, fireworks, dancing and a *corrida*. It's a very popular event, and you must book ahead with the town's tourist office if you want to see the *corrida*.

Mid-Aug Argelès-sur-Mer: Festival Lyrique. Celebration of Catalan song and verse.

First week Sept Elne: Festival de Musique en Catalogne Romane. A classical music festival featuring mostly French artists, held in the medieval cathedral.

First weekend Sept Arles-sur-Tech: Fête Médiéval. A rollicking medieval festival, complete with dancing bears and fire-eaters.

First two weeks Sept Perpignan: Visa pour l'Image Ⓦwww.visapourlimage.com. International festival of photojournalism held at the Palais de Congrès, with seminars, exhibitions and screenings of journalistic photos by leading photographers and rising stars.

Late Sept Céret: Méditerranéennes de Céret ☎01.44.79.00.36, Ⓔazimuthprod @wanadoo.fr. Huge three-day Latin and Mediterranean music festival, which draws crowds in excess of 12,000. Book ahead.

Last two weekends Oct Perpignan: Jazzebre ☎04.68.51.13.14. Eclectic programme ranging from mainstream jazz to klezmer, performed by musicians and groups from around the world.

Penultimate weekend in Oct Banyuls-sur-Mer: Vendîme. Grape harvest and wine festival.

November Perpignan: Foire de la Saint-Martin. Perpignan's month-long autumn fair, complete with midway, games and the usual, corny fare. Held at the Palais des Expositions, across the river from the Palais du Congrés (free *navette* service).

Last two weeks Dec Perpignan: Christmas activities that include a market, *pessebres* (Nativity scenes), a public *cagatió* and concerts.

though, Perpignan is far from a model of tolerance – Le Pen's Front National party and its derivatives have done well here at the polls, peddling a racist vision of white French nationals "swamped" by outsiders.

Airport 5 km ▲ Camping la Garrigole, Centre du Parc Ducup & Roussillon Camping Catalan ▲

PERPIGNAN

River Têt
PONT JOFFRE
AVENUE LOUIS TORCATIS
COURS PALMAROLE
i Promenade des Platanes
COURS LASSUS
BOULEVARD WILSON
SQUARE BIR HAKEIM
Gare Routière
AVENUE DU GENERAL LECLERC
PL. DE LA RESISTANCE
Cinema Castillet
BOULEVARD JEAN BOURRAT
Jardin d'Enfants
BOULEVARD CLEMENCEAU
le Castillet
PL. DE VERDUN
Cathédrale St-Jean
RUE F. RABELAIS
RUE DU CASTILLET
Campo Santo
PL. GAMBETTA
RUE F. RABELAIS
RUE REMPART VILLENEUVE
QUAI VAUBAN
RUE SAD CARNOT
Loge de Mer
PL. DE LA LOGE
PL. JEAN JAURES
PL. DE LA REV FRANÇAISE
RUE DE L'ARGENTERIE
Palais de la Députation
R. ALSACE LORRAINE
RUE DE L'ANGUILLE
PL. DU PUIG
Jardin de la Miranda
St-Jacques
PL. PERI
PL. ARAGO
RUE DE L'UNIVERSITE
RUE LLUCIA
PLACE CATALOGNE
RUE ANGE
PL. DE LA REPUBLIQUE
PL. RIGAUD
RUE ZOLA
PL. CASSANYES
Musée Rigaud
RUE DE LA LOGE DE OR
R DES AUGUSTIN
R DE LA FUSTERIE
Natural History Museum
QUAI DE L'DE TASSIGNY
i PL. DU PONT D'EN VESTIT
RUE GRANDE
PETITE LA REAL
RUE GRANDE LA REAL
Ste-Marie-la-Réal
PL. DES ESPLANADES
Musée d'Algerie Française
RUE MARECHAL FOCH
LA MINRALE
LA MONNAIE
RUE DES ROIS DE MARJORQUE
N
AVENUE DES BALEARES
Palais des Rois de Majorque
0   200 m
BD. FELIX MERCADER
BOULEVARD HENRI POINCARE

▼ Céret & Spain

Gare SNCF Musée Numismatique HI Hostel Mediterranean & B & G

7 ROUSSILLON | Perpignan and around

RESTAURANTS

Au Père Pernot	8
Casa Sansa	3
Le Divil	2
des Expéditeurs	B
La Fontaine	7
Le Perroquet	9
Le Poissonerie	5
Le Route de Tanger	11
Le Sud	4
Tarteline	12
Le Tire Bouchon	10
El Triquet	6
Les Trois Soeurs	1

ACCOMMODATION

Avenir	M
La Cigale	E
Domaine de Mas Boloix	F
des Expéditeurs	B
L'Express	L
de France	C
Le Helder	I
Le Maillol	H
Le Mediterranée	K
Mercure	A
Le Metropole	G
Poste et Perdrix	D
Terminus	J

Perpignan has had a quiet history. Too far from the sea to serve as a port itself, it was a sizeable if unremarkable town until the thirteenth century, when it began to boom as a cloth-making centre. Jaume II of Mallorca and Roussillon enhanced this prosperity in 1276, when he made the town his alternative mainland capital (Montpellier being the other, and Palma de Mallorca the king's principal residence). When that kingdom evaporated in 1349, however, the city was absorbed by the Catalan-Aragonese Crown, whose own main capital, nearby Barcelona, brought an end to Perpignan's elevated status. In the centuries that followed it was the object of repeated campaigns of conquest by France, finally becoming French territory in 1659 with the Treaty of the Pyrenees.

Aside from taking in the pleasant Mediterranean ambience of the place, there are a number of interesting monuments and museums worth seeking out here, and the one sight that shouldn't be missed is the **Palais des Rois**, in the south of the old town. In addition, Perpignan is the principal transport hub of the region and serves as a handy base for exploring nearby **Salses**, as well as **Tautavel** on the way into the Fenouillèdes (see p.354), plus the beaches of the Côte Vermeille.

Arrival, information and city transport

Perpignan's small **airport**, Perpignan-Rivesaltes, 5km north of town, handles daily flights to and from Paris, Montpellier, Lyon and Strasbourg, as well as services from London in summer; its meagre facilities include shops, a bar and restaurant, and car rental offices (see pp.351-2). An airport **navette** (shuttle service) (€4.50) makes the twenty-minute trip into the centre up to six times daily (and is rather tightly timed to meet the flights), stopping at the gare SNCF, place de Catalogne and the *gare routière*; a **taxi** into the centre will cost around three times the bus fare.

Perpignan's **gare SNCF**, at the west end of avenue Général-de-Gaulle, was once dubbed "the centre of the world" by Salvador Dalí; the milestone which once announced "Centre du Monde: 0.0km" has been removed, but the station is now topped by a large statue of the artist, falling over backwards or reaching out to embrace the heavens (your interpretation depending on what you think of his *oeuvre*). To get into the heart of the city from here, walk along the avenue, over place de Catalogne and cross the River Basse at **place Arago**, close by the *quartier de piétonnes* (pedestrian zone) – a twenty-minute walk – or take one of the frequent #2 buses (€1.05 one-way) to "Castillet". If you arrive by local or long-distance bus or airport *navette*, you'll be dropped at the **gare routière** just off avenue Général-Leclerc near Pont Arago, a short distance northwest of place de la Résistance. From the station you can grab the free *navette,* which does a circuit of the old town (does not run during lunch hour). If you're arriving by **car**, follow signs for the "Centre" to get to the old town. There are car parks –the Palais des Rois' is a good option – as well as free and metered street parking on most roads outside the pedestrian area; avoid leaving your car in the seedier areas of the old town.

The **municipal tourist office** (mid-June to mid-Sept Mon–Sat 9am–7pm, Sun 10am–4pm; mid-Sept to mid-June Mon–Sat 9am–6pm, Sun 9am–noon; ☎04.68.66.30.30, ℻04.68.66.30.26, ⓦwww.perpignantourisme.com) is in the Palais des Congrès, the white building at the eastern end of the leafy promenade des Platanes which runs parallel to boulevard Wilson – they can supply you with the free *Perpignan Mag* (monthly in summer, otherwise quarterly), which will keep you abreast of cultural events in the city. There's also a less useful **departmental tourist office** (Mon–Fri 9am–12.30pm & 1.30–6pm;

T04.68.51.52.53, @www.cg66.fr) at 1 avenue des Palmiers, just off boulevard Georges-Clemenceau.

As far as city transport goes, your feet are the best bet, as the compact old town can be crossed in twenty minutes. Alternatively, you can rent **bikes** at Véloland, 95 avenue Mal Juín (T04.68.08.19.99). Finally, there are plenty of **city buses** – the CTP kiosk in place Peri, near the *Palmarium* café, supplies information and tickets (€1.05 one-way, also available from drivers) – as well as a free *navette* which circulates through the old town.

Accommodation

Accommodation is plentiful in Perpignan, with a selection of establishments in all price and luxury ranges, although the most common are small and service-able, few-frills hotels. For a start, there's a range of reasonable **hotels** strung along the lively avenue Général-de-Gaulle, beginning just as you leave the train station. This is a fair distance from the old town though, so if you prefer to be more central there are some good options here, particularly around the place de la Loge or along the promenade des Platanes. Perpignan also caters well for the budget-conscious traveller, with a number of **hostels** and **campsites**.

Avenir 11 rue de l'Avenir T04.68.34.20.30, @www.avenir.com. Unprepossessing, simple comfort near the train station, with a wide range of rooms from singles to a family room; also has secure parking. ❸

La Cigale 78 bd Jean-Bourrat T04.68.50.20.14, @hotelcigaleperpignan@wanadoo.fr. Renovated and comfortable hotel at the far end of the promenade des Platanes, near the church of St-Jacques. Good facilities and service. ❸

Domaine de Mas Boloix Chemin du Pou de les Colobres T04.68.08.17.70, F04.68.08.17.71. Well-appointed B&B with five rooms, sitting room and garden. ❹

des Expéditeurs 19 av Général-Leclerc T04.68.35.15.80. On a rather desolate stretch near the *gare routière*, this small place is by far the cheapest in town. Also has a good restaurant (see p.351). ❶

L'Express 3 av Général-de-Gaulle T04.68.34.89.96. One of the small, old hotels near the station. The rooms don't rise much above functional but they do all have TV. ❷

de France 16 quai Sadi Carnot T04.68.34.92.81, @francehotel@wanadoo.fr. Beautifully appointed nineteenth-century hotel perfectly located on the edge of the old town, overlooking the canalized Basse river. ❹

Le Helder 4 av Général-de-Gaulle T04.68.34.38.05, F04.68.34.31.09. A few steps down from the *Terminus* and a few steps up in quality. Another clean but run-down budget hotel, but with larger rooms for groups or families. ❷

Le Maillol 14 impasse des Cardeurs T04.68.51.10.20, @hotellemaillol@worldonline.fr. Funky decor and friendly service in this clean and

well-kept hotel. Located in a cul-de-sac in the heart of the old town, this is the most convenient accommodation for enjoying the town at night, and one of the best deals going. ❸

Le Mediterranée 62bis av Général-de-Gaulle T04.68.34.87.48, @www.hotelmediterranee.com. Hip new hotel near the station which is very popular with the backpacking crowd. The building isn't the most modern or in the best repair, and the service is relaxed to say the least, but its bar, cybercafé and laid-back atmosphere more than compensate. ❷

Mercure 5bis cours Palmarole T04.68.35.67.66, F04.68.35.58.13. Ideal for families, this distinctive-looking hotel has five suites in addition to its well-outfitted rooms. Just within the confines of the old town, north of the tourist office. ❺

Le Metropole 3 rue des Cardeurs T04.68.34.43.34, @www.hotelmet.com. Basic and very cheap, this is another backpacker haunt in a narrow, bistro-lined street just to the east of the Loge. ❶

Poste et Perdrix 6 rue Fabriques-Nabot T04.68.34.42.53, F04.68.34.58.20. Central, beautiful old nineteenth-century hotel with period details. One of the better deals around. Closed Jan–March. ❷

Terminus 2 av Général-de-Gaulle T04.68.34.32.54, F04.68.35.48.16. Clean but getting tattier with each passing year, this is station-side accommodation with few frills; rooms are available with and without private baths and TV. ❷

La Villa Duflot Rondpoint Albert Donnezan (Serrat d'en Vaquer) T04.68.56.67.67, @www.villa-duflot.com. Halfway between the city centre and the airport, Perpignan's most luxurious hotel is set among a sixteen-acre spread of ancient olive gardens and has an excellent in-house *gastronomique* (*menu* from €30.50). **❼**

Youth hostels and campsites

Camping la Garrigole 2 rue Maurice Lévy ☎04.68.54.66.10. Small and basic but shady campsite 5km to the northwest of the city. Bus #19 will drop you off nearby. Open all year.

Centre du Parc Ducup Rte de Prades ☎04.68.68.32.40. Large park-side hostel run by the local Catholic diocese, some 5km north of the city centre. Singles from €26 up to a family-sized room, with full pensions available. No membership necessary, but no cheaper than a hotel. On the bus

#19 route.

HI Hostel Av de la Grand-Bretagne ☎04.68.34.63.32, ©04.68.51.16.02. Modern, well-run hostel beside a park, fifteen minutes' walk from the centre, between the *gare routière* and the gare SNCF, but with a noisy road running behind it. Curfews 11am–4pm & 11pm. Closed mid-Dec to mid-Jan. Dorm beds €11.50. Camping is permitted.

Roussillon Camping Catalan Rte de Bompas ☎04.68.62.16.92. Large two-star site, 8km northeast of the city, with shop, swimming pool and laundry service. Also rents caravans and is wheelchair accessible. No service by municipal bus. March–Oct.

The City

Perpignan's medieval walls, though spared by Richelieu, were demolished early last century to allow for expansion, and replaced by wide boulevards. This, in fact, maintained the separation of the city's older districts from the new, and it's still easy and enjoyable to get around the compact **old town** on foot. The overriding impression is favourable: the Mediterranean is visible to the east, the River Têt skirts the town to the north, while the narrow River Basse threads through the centre, dispensing welcome greenery along its banks. Most of the city's sights are concentrated in the dense clutch of pedestrian streets northeast of riverside **place Arago**, and stretching towards the geographical centre of the old town, while between **place de la Loge** and place Rigaud just to the southeast, you could be on the Left Bank in Paris, the old streets now a maze of chic boutiques. On the north side of the pedestrian area you'll find the **cathedral**, from where you can follow the course of the old walls, through the Romany and **Maghrebi quarter** to the church of St-Jacques, marking the eastern limit of old Perpignan. To the south of this the land rises towards the massive **Palais des Rois de Majorque**, crowning the hill which dominated the southern quarter of the medieval town. In the **new town**, to the west of the River La Basse, you won't find many sights, but the avenues leading west towards the train station make for excellent hotel- and restaurant-hunting.

Place Arago to Le Castillet

The heart of the city is café-lined **place Arago**, on the flower-decked bank of the canalized La Basse river. From here you can head south along rues Proted'Assaut and Maréchal Foch to bring you to a tiny old thirteenth-century *faubourg*, whose quiet grid of streets contains well-restored houses and the odd café; Maréchal Foch itself contains a small **Musée d'Algérie Française** (Wed 3–6pm; free), at 52 rue Maréchal Foch, commemorating France's domination of North Africa with bitter nostalgia. But you'll most likely prefer to dive directly east into Perpignan's historical centre. Heading from the *place* along rue Ange, you'll find the **Musée Rigaud** (Wed–Mon: May–Sept noon–7pm, Oct–April 11am–5.30pm; €4) on the right at no. 16. This museum is housed in a seventeenth-century palace, originally the workshop of local artist Hyacinthe Rigaud, a favourite of Louis XIV, and it later served as studio and living space for Picasso, Dufy and Cocteau. Today it holds a good collection of modern art, including works by Maillol, Alechinsky and the aforementioned artists. Just beyond the museum, rue Ange crosses the evocatively named rue Cloche d'Or ("street of the Golden Bell"); turning right on this street will lead you uphill towards the hulking Palais des Rois (see p.350), while turning left you delve further into the medieval quarter.

At the northern end of Cloche d'Or, is place Jean-Jaurès; this is the centre of the pedestrian zone, now serving as the city's shopping district – bustling with life during the day, and all but deserted at night. Next along is **place de la Loge**, the centre of activity in fourteenth-century Perpignan: here you'll find three of the city's most important administrative buildings, lumped together on its eastern side. The first of these is the fifteenth-century Gothic-style **Palais de la Députation**, where the Catalan count-kings once convened the Roussillon parliament, while next door, the sixteenth-century **Hôtel de Ville** is worth a peek for the Aristide Maillol bronze, *La Méditerranée*, which sits in the courtyard. The last of the three great buildings is Roussillon's famous **Loge de Mer**; built in 1397, it served as the region's stock exchange – the meeting place and court for its merchants. High on the south wall is a blazon bearing three arms, which stand for the three classes of city folk who ran the town council: merchants and drapers, doctors and notaries, and artisans and gardeners. The building remains a marvel, with a gracefully vaulted interior and gargoyles adorning the upper parts of its facade – a fine and rare example of Gothic civic architecture – that is now home to a tastefully arty café-restaurant. Until recently, it suffered the ignominy of housing a fast-food restaurant until public outcry demanded change. The square, which spreads around the Loge, long served as the scene of grisly executions, notably of the rebels housed in Le Castillet (see below), while during World War II, the *place*'s busy pavement cafés were the place to find *passeurs*, the men and women who guided refugees across the Pyrenees into Spain.

If you feel like exploring around place de la Loge, take a wander through the series of ancient lanes which run off towards the river, including tiny rue Fabriques d'En Nabot, where you'll come across a number of notable thirteenth- and fourteenth-century houses, with magnificent doorways and ogival windows. Following any of these streets, or taking wider rue Louis-Blanc at the north end of place de la Loge, will lead you to Perpignan's distinctive red-brick **Le Castillet**, the lone surviving tower of the old town walls. Also known as the Casa Païral ("House of the Ancestors"), it now houses a **museum** celebrating Roussillonaise rural culture (Wed–Mon: May–Sept 10am–7pm; Oct–April 11am–5.30pm; €4) and in particular commemorating the anti-French rebellions of 1661–74, when the tower held captured Catalan insurgents. The place de Verdun, on the south side of Le Castillet, is the setting for summer evening performances of the *sardana*, the perplexingly insipid Catalan folk dance. Nearby, at 1 boulevard Wilson, is the battered but splendidly ornate **Cinema Castillet**, the oldest cinema in France, now converted into an eight-screen complex.

The cathedral and east

Two hundred metres east of Le Castillet, but most easily accessed from the north end of place de la Loge, is another ancient square, place Gambetta, scene of the town's open-air market since the Middle Ages. On its eastern end towers the **Cathédrale St-Jean** (Mon & Wed–Sat 10am–noon & 2–5pm, Tues & Sun 2–5pm; free), commissioned in 1324 and elevated to cathedral status in 1602 when the diocese of Elne was transferred to Perpignan. Next door, its predecessor, the impressive Romanesque St-Jean le Vieux (currently closed for renovations), is linked to the cathedral by mammoth buttresses. The cathedral's striking exterior sports bands of rounded river stones sandwiched by brick, while inside there's a majestically columned nave, whose side chapels, though badly damaged, retain some elaborate sixteenth- and seventeenth-century retables. Leaving through the south transept, poke your head in the **chapel** on the left, which is presided over by an excellent fourteenth-century polychrome Crucifixion, known as the *Dévot Christ*, and most likely the work of a Rhineland sculptor. Past the chapel, on the left, is the entrance to the **Campo Santo**, one of France's oldest cemeteries, going back some 600 years (April, May & Sept Tues–Sun noon–7pm; Oct–March Tues–Sun 11am–5pm; closed July & Aug) – it is now used for concerts in summer.

On the far side of Campo Santo, the lively rue de la Revolution Française, populated by arty cafés and hip bars, runs east to the *place* of the same name. From here you can turn right to ascend into the slums of old Perpignan, which spread south from here almost as far as the great palace, and east to place Cassanyes, at the former limits of the city walls. Inhabited almost exclusively by recent arrivals from North Africa, with a Romany enclave centred on **place du Puig** (pronounced "pooch"), this can seem an intimidating district, although it has improved in recent years; the cramped quarters are littered with refuse and hung with washing, a stereotype of immigrant poverty. But it's

The caganer and cagatió

Among the many Catalan folkloric customs which have survived centuries of French domination are two rather strange practices associated with **Christmas**. Like the Provençals, the Roussillonaise are known for their elaborate Nativity scenes (*pessebres*), populated by hordes of figurines. However, if you look carefully at the Catalan version, among the various shepherds, angel choirs and wise men you'll note a small figure, usually dressed in peasant garb and sporting a traditional Catalan red cap. This is the **caganer**, a crouching man, poised with pants around his ankles, in some stage of the act of defecation. Similarly, although Catalan children customarily receive presents on the Epiphany (Jan 6), the **cagatió** (literally, the "shitting log") ensures that they don't go completely empty-handed at Christmas. It consists of a log with a painted-on face, draped with a red cloth at its posterior end. As children gather round the *cagatió*, beating it with sticks and singing a song invoking bowel movement, the blanket is withdrawn to the delight of all, revealing the sweets which it has apparently "excreted". You can purchase your own *caganers* (which now come in various forms, including policemen, referees and political figures) and *cagatiós* at Perpignan's Christmas market, held in front of the cathedral during the four weeks of Advent.

worth persevering – the various squares dotted around are rich with history, such as the innocuously named place Fontaine-Neuve, which dates back some 700 years, to the time when the "new well" after which it is named was dug here. If its interminable renovations have finally been concluded, you might also stop at Perpignan's **natural history museum**, at 12 Fontaine Neuve (Wed–Mon: May–Sept noon–7pm; Oct–April 11am–5.30pm; €4), which holds the usual stuffed specimens of local fauna, as well as a prized Egyptian mummy.

Northeast of place Fontaine-Neuve and just east of place du Puig is the fourteenth-century **church of St-Jacques** (daily: July & Aug 3–7pm; Sept–June 2.30–5.30pm), the nucleus of Perpignan's oldest parish, originally founded by Jaume I in honour of his patron saint (Jacques being French for Jaume) a hundred years earlier. The king was also a donor to the confraternity of Sanch – a parish-based social organization typical of the Middle Ages, dedicated to the Holy Blood of Christ ("sanch" means "blood" in old Catalan). On the Maundy Thursday of each year, they hold a Spanish-style procession of penitents, who walk from the church through the town hooded (so as not to take pride in their piety) and barefooted, carrying heavy candles or crosses. Behind the church, the **Jardin de la Miranda** (daily: July & Aug 3–7pm; Sept–June 2.30–5.30pm), built on a section of the city's old fortifications, provides an airy respite for the inhabitants of this quarter. If you want to avoid the seedy part of the old town, the church and garden can also be reached from place de la Révolution Française, by heading north and following rue Pierre Ronsard, in the shadow of the city's remaining **walls**, or, further north still, alongside the square Bir Hakeim, and the adjacent Jardin d'Enfants, a grassy, tree-lined park crisscrossed by paths and complete with the usual assortment of children's rides, bandstands and *buvettes*.

The Palais des Rois de Majorque

Perpignan's most famous sight, and the kernel around which it grew, is the massive **Palais des Rois de Majorque** (daily: June–Sept 10am–6pm; Oct–May 9am–5pm; €3) on the southern fringe of the old city; the entrance is on the west side of the complex in rue des Archers, around fifteen minutes' walk from place de la Loge, and slightly longer from the church of St-Jacques.

The history of Perpignan is more or less synonymous with that of the palace, originally built in the late thirteenth century as a residence for Jaume II of Mallorca, son of Jaume I ("The Conqueror"), Count of Barcelona and King of Aragón and Valencia, who captured Mallorca from the Muslims. At his death "The Conqueror" divided his kingdom between his two sons: to the elder, Pere II, went the titles of King of Aragón and Valencia and Count of Barcelona, but only a portion of the actual kingdom; the remainder, including Roussillon and Mallorca, went to the younger Jaume. The two branches of the family were immediately at each other's throats, and stayed that way until Roussillon was reunited with Aragón and Catalonia in the early fourteenth century by the powerful Pere III. Having passed to the French, then back to the Catalans, Perpignan changed hands for the last time in 1642, a couple of years after France had occupied Roussillon in the wake of the Catalans' revolt against the Hapsburg rulers of Madrid; in September, after a siege that was at times commanded personally by Louis XIII and Richelieu, Perpignan fell. Vauban, military engineer to Louis XIV, constructed the imposing outer walls in the fit of over-enthusiastic fortification that followed consolidation of French sovereignty accorded by the 1659 Treaty of the Pyrenees.

After ascending an impressive zigzagging ramp, large enough for several cavalry to ride abreast, you enter a grassy park, with the square thirteenth-century **castle** ahead of you, standing incongruously with its curious stone and mortar construction. Passing into the splendid two-storey **courtyard**, whose upper level opens into graceful Gothic galleries on the east and west sides, you ascend the stairs to the former kings' apartments, now a boutique for Roussillon vintages. Across from these you'll find the unsullied but sparsely furnished queens' apartments, which have delicately vaulted period ceilings and windows. Between the two sets of royal apartments are the so-called king's and queen's **chapels**, one on the upper floor and one on the lower, and both with interesting details in Gothic style, from carved corbels to fading frescoes. The palace frequently holds temporary exhibitions on local history and culture (included in admission).

The new town

Although the far bank of the Basse opposite place d'Arago fell within the boundaries of the medieval ramparts, its character resembles more that of the new town which grew up around it. There's little in the way of specific sights here, but a stroll through the series of attractive nineteenth-century *places* – Gabrielle Péri, Bardou-Job and Jean-Payra – is pleasant. The last of these leads into the large place de Catalogne, dominated on its east side by the beautiful and derelict Aux Dames de France department store. From here, avenue du Général-de-Gaulle heads due west to the *gare*, the main artery of a surprisingly lively neighbourhood, with workaday shops, grungy bars and tattoo salons, as well as many good hotels and restaurants. Running north from the place de Catalogne, the busy cours Lazare-Escarguel leads to avenue de Grand Bretagne, where, at no. 42, you'll find the **Musée Numismatique Joseph-Puig** (Tues–Sat 10am–6pm; €4), an impressive early twentieth-century mansion, with some 1500 coins on display, ranging from ancient small change to monies of medieval France, Aragon and the Catalan lands. Prize of the collection is the "treasure of Bompas", a Gallo-Roman coin hoard found by a local farmer.

Eating, drinking and nightlife

Don't dally when pondering **dinner**: most of Perpignan's restaurant shutters seem to roll down at 10pm sharp, though you can get served later at several brasseries which stay open till midnight, including the popular *Arago* and *Café Vienne* in the palm-shaded place Arago – this and avenue Général-de-Gaulle are the places to head for if you don't feel like spending a lot of time looking around. For a fix of Asian or North African food, head for the eastern side of the old town, particularly rue Llucia, where modest establishments serve up stir-fries and couscous/*tajine* dishes – you'll find food like this in very few other places along the Pyrenees.

Perpignan is not great for nightlife, but it has plenty of **cafés**. Start on place de la Loge – call in at *Brasserie de la Loge* or *Grande Café de la Bourse* – and place de Verdun, where the *Grande Café de la Poste*, shaded by huge plane trees, is the best. *Café la Paix* in place Arago is another popular choice, but best of all is the huge, airy *Palmarium*, on the opposite side overlooking the River Basse, a low-key, self-service place, where you can linger for hours over a coffee. All of these serve reasonably priced *menus* at mealtimes.

In July and August the town comes alive on Thursday nights with a **street festival** featuring markets and music. Otherwise there are **bars** scattered throughout town: *Casa Nova*, at 8 rue de la Fusterie, features Afro-Cuban sounds; the Spanish *bar musical*, *La Movida*, at 45 avenue Général-Leclerc; and

O'Shannon, at 3 rue de l'Incindie, which is the local headquarters for stout. Most of Perpignan's **discos** are on the fringes of town, but in the centre you can dance at *Napoli*, 3bis place Catalogne (Wed–Sat 11pm–3am; €8), and the *L'Uba*, 5 boulevard Mercader (Wed–Sat 11pm–3am; closed mid-July to mid-Aug; €10). *La Baratina* is a large disco in 5bis place de la Sardane (Thurs–Sun), which caters to crowds from 18–70 depending on the night and what floor you're on (Tues–Sun 11pm–3am; free–€10).

Restaurants

Casa Sansa 2 rue Fabriques-Nadal ☎04.68.34.21.84. Catalan cuisine served up in this comfortable establishment, founded in 1846, in one of the old town's most beautiful streets. Wheelchair accessible. Closed Sun. *Menus* €24–38 (children's *menu* available).

Le Divil 9 rue Fabriques-Nebot ☎04.68.34.57.73. A swish, designer-ish restaurant tucked away in a little alley near the Loge. The speciality is wood-grilled meats, including succulent shoulder of lamb. *Menus* €12–29. Closed Sun & Mon.

des Expéditeurs 19 av Général-Leclerc. *Bo i barat* – "good and cheap" – if unsophisticated, local cuisine, in the hotel of the same name. *Menus* from €11. Closed Mon & Sat eve & all Sun.

La Fontaine 12 rue du Théâtre ☎04.68.51.09,39. Quaint and homely little place deep in the old town. Home-cooked Franco-Catalan *menus* with a range of salads and tempting desserts. Open till 1am. Closed Sun & Mon eve. *Menu* €12.

Au Père Pernot 16 av Général-de-Gaulle ☎04.68.51.33.25. Locally respected Catalan cooking featuring a variety of meat and fish dishes, as well as a tempting array of home-made soups. *Menus* €12–30. There is also an all-you-can-eat pancake brunch Sat noon–4pm. Closed Sun.

Le Perroquet 1 av Général-de-Gaulle ☎04.68.34.34.36. Very close to the station on the north side of the street, with a good choice of Catalan specialities; *menus* from €20. Closed Wed Sept–April.

Le Poissonerie 12 rue Lazare Escarguel ☎04.68.34.02.01. Cheery seafood place not far

from the Loge, and just opposite *El Triquet.* Snack on a plate of a dozen oysters (€12.50) or splurge on the "Super Neptune" platter that feeds four or five people for €120.

Le Route de Tanger 1 rue du Four St-Jean ☎04.68.51.07.57. Welcoming Moroccan restaurant with the traditional *tajines* and couscous, as well as more adventurous fusion recipes. *Menu* €12. Closed Sun & Mon lunch.

Le Sud 12 rue Bausil ☎04.68.34.55.71. Eclectic and delicious Mediterranean cuisine served up in the heart of Perpignan's Romany quarter. No *menu*, and à la carte for about €30. Closed Jan–March.

Tarteline 10 rue Petite la Monnaie. Good stop for delicious home-made quiches and tarts, to eat in or take away. Open lunchtime only Mon–Fri (except hols). *Menu* for €8 (also children's *menu*).

Le Tire Bouchon 20 av Général-de-Gaulle ☎04.68.34.31.91. A small family-run brasserie, the best of those in the vicinity of the station. *Menu* at €13, although an à la carte meal for two can easily run over €50. Closed all Sun, Mon & Wed eve.

El Triquet 9 rue Lazare ☎04.68.35.19.18. Friendly Spanish-run eatery specializing in Catalan cuisine as well as tapas. *Plats* from €8. Closed Sun & Mon.

Les Trois Soeurs 2 rue Fontfroide ☎04.68.51.22.33. Off pl Gambetta, this campy Spanish-flavoured features free jazz concerts (Wed 7.30pm Oct–June) and a "women only" male revue and dinner theatre on Saturdays (Sat 7.30pm Oct–June). In addition to the *carte,* there are tapas and a lunch *menu* from €15. Closed Sun.

Listings

Airlines Ryanair ☎08.92.55.56.66, ⊛www.ryanair.com.

Airport Aéroport de Perpignan Rivesaltes ☎04.68.52.60.70, ⓔaeroport@perpignan.cci.fr.

Banks and exchange All major French and some Spanish banks have offices in the centre, many along bd Clemenceau, and quai Vauban – most have ATMs.

Bike rental Véloland, 95 av Mal Juín ☎04.68.08.19.99; Cycles Mercier, 20 av Gilbert Brutus ☎04.68.85.02.71.

Bus departures On Wednesdays at the *gare routière* (☎04.68.35.29.02) you can get a tourist pass (€22.88) giving eight days' unlimited bus travel around the Pyrénées-Orientales *département* – take a passport-sized photo and your passport.

Car rental Avis, 13 bd du Conflent ☎04.68.34.26.71; Budget, 9 av Général-de-Gaulle ☎04.68.56.95.95; Europcar, 28 av Général-de-Gaulle ☎04.68.34.65.03; Leclerc, 27 av Général-de-Gaulle ☎04.68.34.77.74; Sixt, 48 av Général-de-Gaulle ☎04.68.35.62.84. Europcar, Budget and

Avis also have offices at the airport.
Cinemas Rive Gauche, 29 quai Vauban
⌾04.68.51.13.84 has four screens, with some VO.
Internet access La G@re, 62bis av Général-de-
Gaulle, or Arena Games, 9 rue de Docteur Pous
(daily 3pm–midnight).
Laundry Laverie Foch, 23 rue Maréchal Foch
(daily 9am–7pm); Laverie St-Jean, 3 rue Cité E.
Bartisol, near Campo Santo (daily 7.30am–7pm).
Markets General market in pl de la République
(Mon 7am–1pm, Tues–Sat 7am–12.30pm &
4.30–7.30pm), plus antiques in Allées Maillol (Sat
8am–6pm) and organic food in pl Rigaud (Sat
8am–noon). The most colourful market takes place
on Saturday and Sunday mornings in the tree-
shaded place Cassanyes, with a mixture of French,
Arab and African traders selling cheap clothes,
crafts and all sorts of local produce.
Medical Centre Hospitalier, av du Languedoc
⌾04.68.61.66.33, on the north side of the city,
reached via av Maréchal-Joffre.
Police av de Gran Bretagne ⌾04.68.35.70.00,

and allée Marc Pierre ⌾04.68.66.30.70.
Rugby Perpignan's Rugby à XV team, USAP, has
long held a place in France's First Division, and
has won the championship four times. It plays at
Stade Aimé Giral on allées Aimé-Giral; for ticket
information call ⌾04.68.61.18.18, or go to
Ⓦwww.usap.fr. The rugby à XIII team, XIII Catalan,
plays at stade Jean-Laffon, on av des Sports
⌾04.68.55.13.13.
Swimming Champs de Mars, rue Paul Valéry (Mon
& Sat 12.15–1.30pm, Tues, Thurs & Fri 6.30–8pm;
€3).
Taxis ⌾04.68.35.15.15 or 046.09.36.96.86.
There are also taxi stands at pl de Verdun, at the
gare SNCF and on pl Arago.
Train information ⌾08.36.35.35.35,
Ⓦwww.sncf.fr.
Travel agency Nouvelles Frontières, 40 bd
Clemenceau ⌾04.68.35.50.55.
Youth information Bureau d'Information
Jeunesse, 35 quai Vauban ⌾04.68.34.56.56.

Around Perpignan: Salses and the coast

The main attraction heading north from Perpignan towards Narbonne along
the N9 is the enormous stronghold of **Salses-le-Château**, built to dominate
the strategic strip of land between the Étang de Leucate and the uplands of the
Corbières. The **fortress** (daily: June–Sept 9.30am–7pm; Oct–May
10am–12.15pm & 2–5pm; €5.50), constructed by the Spanish in the fifteenth
century to guard the northern border of Roussillon from French attack, is a
curious structure – set low within a deep moat, like a cannon-age fortress, but
with the basic design and overall squareness of a medieval castle, it represents
an intermediary stage in the evolution from early to modern fort. Salses withstood four sieges before it was taken by the French in 1642; with the shift of
the frontier south to the mountains, the fortress was first abandoned and then
later used as a prison until being declared a monument in 1886. Back in the
village, which lies to the east of the castle, you can also visit the **Musée
Catalan d'Histoire** (Tues–Sat 9.30am–12.30pm & 2.30–7.30pm; free), which
has a small collection of arms as well as archaeological relics going back to the
Roman period, when the Via Domitia passed through town.

The narrow strip of sand which hedges in the Étang de Leucate to the northeast of Salses is buried under a holiday conurbation but **wind-surfers** may be
attracted to this part of the coast for the relentless winds which pelt the lagoon.
The northern end of the *étang* has parking along the spit and is the best place
to get in the water.

At only 15km from Perpignan, Salses is a fairly easy **bike** ride (wind permitting), but it also has a **gare SNCF**, just west of the fortress, while **buses** stop
at the place de la République, where you will find a small **tourist office** (July
& Aug daily 9am–7pm; Sept–June Mon–Fri 9am–6pm, Sat 10am–5pm;
⌾04.68.38.66.13, Ⓔot.salses@libertysurf.fr). The only accommodation is the
chambres d'hôtes *La Salsepareille* (⌾04.68.38.61.70,
Ⓦwww.salsepareille.com; ❸; English spoken) set in a century-old house in the
village centre. Otherwise, you'll find the **campsite** *Le Bois des Pins*

(☎04.68.38.68.44; July–Sept), on the far side of the *autoroute* (follow rue Jean-Jaurés, and then route d'Opoule). The **restaurant** situation is pretty grim here too, with the only good choice the twelfth-century farmhouse and bakery *Auberge de Vespeille*, also on route d'Opoule (☎04.68.64.19.51; weekends only in spring and autumn, Sun only in winter), which has an open-hearthed fire in its rustic dining room. Alternatively, stock up on supplies at the Wednesday-morning **market**.

You might also want to join the locals at Perpignan's own beach resort, **Canet-la-Plage**, 12km to the south (Perpignan bus #1, departures every 20min). The only sight here is the **aquarium** (May & June Tues–Sun 10am–noon & 2–6pm; July & Aug daily 10am–8pm; €5), home to over three thousand species, including shark, piranha and coral. Otherwise, Canet has everything that you would expect from a beach-town: sun, fun, bars and music. The town's **tourist office** (July & Aug daily 9am–7pm; Sept–May Mon–Sat 9am–noon & 2–5pm, Sun 10am–noon & 2–5pm, ☎04.68.86.72.00, ⓦwww.ot-canet.fr), is in the central Espace Mediterranée. Their website has complete **accommodation** listings, but one option is the economical *Clair-Soleil* (☎04.68.80.32.06, ⓦwww.hotel-clair-soleil.com; ❷) at 26 av de Catalogne, just 150m from the beach. Among the wide range of **restaurants**, a good choice is *Le Don Quichotte* at 22 av de Catalogne (☎04.68.80.35.17; closed Sun & Mon out of season), a *gastronomique* with *menus* at €21–43. There are several **campsites**, including the year-round *Le Domino* (☎04.68.80.27.25) in rue des Palmiers, which also rents trailers. The local morning **market** is held in the village (Wed) and at the beach (Tues & Sun).

Fans of medieval art and sculpture will also want to make a pilgrimage to **Cabestany**, 5km southeast of downtown Perpignan, where the eleventh- to fourteenth-century church of Notre-Dame-des-Anges is home to a remarkably vividly carved tympanum, the discovery of which in 1930 led to the identification of the "Master of Cabestany" (see box on p.111). At time of writing, the **Centre of Romanesque Sculpture "Maître de Cabestany"** is still very much under construction, but is slated to open in 2004 (Mon–Sat 9am–5pm & Sun 1–5.30pm; free).

The Fenouillèdes

Stretching out to the northwest of Perpignan, the **Fenouillèdes** is the range of scrubby limestone hills that marked the inland border between France and Spain until the Treaty of the Pyrenees gave Roussillon to France in 1659. It is a rich area to discover, with highlights including the caves at **Tautavel**, where some of Europe's earliest hominids have been discovered, and several Cathar castles, the most famous being **Quéribus** and **Peyrepertuse**. Further west, you can explore the dramatic **Gorges de Galamus** and continue to another Cathar stronghold at **Puilaurens**. The main artery through the Fenouillèdes is the D117, running westward from Perpignan to Quillan (see p.137); all the sights can be accessed from various points along this road, whether you're driving or reliant on the bus. If you have time to take the hills in by foot, however, head out on the **Sentier Cathare**, which leads west into the Pays de Sault (see p.141), or the **Tour du Fenouillèdes**, a seven-day circuit that links the main sights of the region (for information on this see the tourist office in Perpignan, or visit their website – see p.345).

Tautavel

In 1971, archaeologists working at the Caune de l'Arago, a cave near the village of **TAUTAVEL**, 20km northwest of Perpignan on the edge of the Fenouillèdes, discovered the front part of a skull of *Homo erectus* – an evolutionary midpoint between the African *Homo habilis* and modern *Homo sapiens* – dating back to half a million years ago, a period from which scarcely any other human remains have been found in Europe. The reconstructed skull, with its enormous cranial ridge and low eye sockets, is displayed in Tautavel's **Musée de la Préhistoire** (Jan & Dec Mon, Sun & public hols 1.30–5.30pm; Feb–March & Oct–Nov daily 1.30–5.30pm; April–June & Sept daily 10am–12.30pm & 1.30–7pm; July & Aug daily 10am–8pm; €7), the centrepiece of a small but extremely moving exhibition which includes stone tools, animal bones and casts from the floor of the cave. The cave itself (July & Aug daily 10am–noon & 12.30–5.30pm; otherwise visits by arrangement with the museum) is situated in a low hill on the opposite side of the Verdouble valley. All of the finds – some 250,000 objects – have been removed, but it's exciting to stand where primordial hunters dwelt half a million years ago.

Nearby **Estagel**, 7km south on the main road and bus route, makes the best base in the Tautavel area. The *Charmotel les Graves*, 9 boulevard Jean Jaurès (℡04.68.29.00.84, ℻04.68.29.30.26; ❷) is the best place to stay; the municipal **campsite** is on avenue du Docteur Cortade, on the west side of town. Local **markets** are held at Tautavel in front of the town hall (Tues & Thurs mornings) and at Estagel's allée des Tilleuls (Mon & Fri mornings). Local information can be obtained from the *mairie* of either Tautavel (℡04.68.29.44.29, ✉tautavel.mairie@wanadoo.fr) or Estagel (℡04.68.29.10.42, ✉aglyverdouble@wanadoo.fr).

Quéribus and Peyrepertuse

The Cathar stronghold of **Quéribus**, the easternmost of "mother" Carcassonne's five "sons", is a short detour off the D117, from the turn-off at Maury, 10km beyond Estagel. If you don't have transport of your own, take the Perpignan–Quillan bus to Maury, from where it's a steep two-hour uphill walk. Visible on its turret of bare rock long before you reach it, the **castle** turns

The Fenouillèdes railway

The best and most relaxed way to appreciate the rugged landscape of the Fenouillèdes is the *Train du Pays Cathares*, a narrow-gauge line refurbished as a tourist route. Starting from the station at Rivesaltes, 7km north of central Perpignan, it climbs along the vine-clad route of the Agly river before turning up the valley of La Boulzane. Climbing through forests of fir, it arrives at **St-Paul-de-Fenouillet** (see p.356) and threads the **Gorges de Galamus**, before stopping at Caudies-des-Fenouillèdes. From here it continues to **Lapradelle** (see p.356), from where a stiff three-kilometre walk leads up to the castle of **Puilaurens**, before the final seven-kilometre leg takes it to **Axat** (see p.138) – the end of the line.

The train functions from April through September, with afternoon departures daily (except Mon) in July and August, and weekend departures (by reservation only) during the other months. The fare varies from €8 to €13 per adult, with a €2 reduction for children under 12. For **information** on departures and to make reservations, call or visit the office: Train du Pays Cathares et du Fenouillèdes, 7 av de la Gare, in Caudies-de-Fenouillèdes (℡ & ℻04.68.59.96.18).

out to be much bigger than it looks, since much of the **interior** (Jan Sat, Sun & school hols 10am–5pm; otherwise daily: Feb 10am–5.30pm; March, Nov & Dec 10am–6pm; April–June & Sept 10am–8pm; July & Aug 10am–9pm; Oct 10am–7.30pm; €4) is below ground level. A single stairway links all the various structures, including the so-called **salle de palmier** in the polygonal keep, where the vaulted ceiling is supported by a graceful pillar sprouting a canopy of intersecting ribs.

Quéribus was constructed at the end of the tenth century, and belonged successively to the count-kings of Barcelona and Aragón and the counts of Fenouillèdes. After the fall of Montségur in 1244 it became the refuge of some of the last surviving Cathars (see p.350), an affront that King Louis IX decided to erase. His opportunity came in 1255, when the local lord who sponsored the Cathars, Chabert de Barbaira, was captured by royal forces and forced to cede this and other castles as his ransom. But, unlike at Montségur, the Cathar garrison here had time to escape, probably south across the mountains.

Another of the five "sons" of Carcassonne, **Peyrepertuse** (daily: Feb–March & Nov–Dec 10am–5pm; April, May & Oct 9am–7pm; June–Sept 8.30am–8.30pm; €4), 4km northwest of Cucugnan, is the largest and one of the best preserved of the so-called **Cathar castles**. Its age and history are nearly identical to those of Quéribus, with Paris assuming definitive control here by treaty with Catalonia-Aragon in 1258. As well as the ten-minute drive along the D14 from Cucagnan, you can approach the *château* on **foot** via the Sentier Cathare, or along the GR36 from Rouffiac (see below). The setting of the castle, draped the length of a jagged ridge with sheer drops at most points, is its most impressive feature. No single architectural feature amongst various cisterns, chapels and towers claims attention, but from the highest chamber, the **Chapelle San Jordi**, there are sweeping views east to the Mediterranean and Perpignan, with Quéribus perched on its rock stalk in between.

Practicalities

Both of the castles are isolated. The closest amenities to Quéribus are 3km west, in **Cucugnan**, which has crumbled vestiges of its own castle and vineyards all around. You can **stay** at the *Auberge du Vigneron* (☎04.68.45.03.00, Ⓔauberge.vigneron@ataraxie.fr; ❷), or at the *Auberge de Cucugnan* (☎04.68.45.40.84, Ⓕ04.68.45.01.52; closed Jan & Feb; ❸), both in the centre of the village. Each has a **restaurant**, but the *Vigneron* (€19–28; closed Sun eve & Mon), is outshone by the *Cucugnan* (closed Wed out of season), where you can enjoy abundant four-course *menus* that range from €16 to €40 (including house wine) and *cargolades* (Catalan barbecues) in an interior garden.

Near Peyrepertuse, the village of **Duilhac** coils picturesquely at the eastern foot of the castle ridge. Here you'll find a shop and bakery, plus both a *gîte d'étape* (☎04.68.45.01.74; closed Jan; ❶) in the centre and the comfortable, stone-clad *Auberge du Vieux Moulin* (☎04.68.45.02.17; ❷), on the northerly through road; you can get meals here as well (*menu* from €12.50; closed Wed). But better accommodation can be found in **Rouffiac des Corbières**, 3km north, where the *Auberge de Peyrepertuse* on the main through road (☎04.68.45.40.40; ❷) serves hearty food and offers excellent en-suite rooms. Otherwise there's a **gîte** (☎04.68.45.01.74; ❶) and a **campsite** in the hamlet.

The Gorges de Galamus and Puilaurens

From Rouffiac, the D14 winds westwards to the **Gorges de Galamus**, a short but impressive limestone *défilé* worn through the ridge by the River La Boulzane, although most visitors enter the gorge at its downstream end, 3km out of St-Paul-de-Fenouillet. At this end there's a free car park and the start of a path to the exquisitely sited **Ermitage de St-Antoine**, about halfway down the gorge's east flank (daily 10am–6pm) – a huge, sanctified grotto thrusting deep into the cliff, from which a steep path, culminating in a rock ladder, drops down to pools below. The river is deep enough for swimming, and the gorge also a popular **rafting** venue (see below). Some 18km west of St-Paul along the D117, at Lapradelle, you'll find the turn-off for the **castle** at **Puilaurens** (Feb, March & early Nov Sat, Sun & hols 10am–5pm; otherwise daily: April–June & Sept–Oct 10am–6pm; July & Aug 9am–8pm; Dec–Jan Christmas hols 10am–5pm; €3.50), another of Carcassonne's "sons", perched majestically on a 700-metre-high ridge. Built originally by the Visigoths, Puilaurens was enlarged not long before its captured lord, the Cathar Chabert de Barbaira, turned it over to Crusader forces as a condition of his release. You enter from the west, via a stepped maze of *chicanes* or staggered low walls; much of the interior is dilapidated, but make sure you catch the view east over pined hills from outside the southeastern gate, and the point on the **western donjon** complex where you're allowed briefly on the curtain wall to take in the vista in the opposite direction.

St-Paul-de-Fenouillet has little to offer aside from its role as staging point for **buses** west, and two **hotels**: *Le Châtelet*, on the main road (☎04.68.59.01.20, ✉chatelet.rauss@wanadoo.fr; ❷), and the more upmarket *Relais des Corbières* (☎04.68.59.23.89, ✉relais.corbieresfrance.fr; ❸), which has a restaurant. A more economical option is Didier Pons' **chambres d'hôtes**, *Le Pastedou* (☎04.68.59.25.21; ❷), at 42 av Jean Mouin, or the **campsite**, which is open year-round (☎04.68.59.09.09). You may also want to stock up on local produce at the twice-weekly morning **market** (Wed & Sat) in place du Foyer Rural. In Caudies, there is a **chambres d'hôtes** (☎04.68.59.91.97; ❷). At **Lapradelle**, you can stay at the *Le Grilladou* (☎04.58.20.53.01; ❷) on 29 av Languedoc, which also has a restaurant. If you're interested in taking a **rafting** trip down the gorges de Galamus, contact Sud Rafting (call ahead; ☎04.68.20.53.73, ✉esudrafting@libertysurf.fr), whose office is situated 16km west of St-Paul at the crossroads near Axat. It also offers canyoning through Galamus, as well as rafting and hydrospeed trips through the Aude gorges. There's no **tourist office** but the local *mairie* (☎04.68.59.07.57, ⊛www.st-paul66.com) can provide current information on accommodation and on outdoor activities.

The lower Têt valley

From Perpignan, the Têt valley (also known as the Conflent), provides a fast if initially not very scenic route southwest into the Pyrenees. The **lower Têt valley** is that stretch running up to the peak of Canigou, and its most interesting parts are found some 30km west of Perpignan, where **Ille-sur-Têt** provides a jumping-off point for the spectacular rock formations of **Les Orgues** to the north and, just west, the narrow Boulès gorge climbs south to the region of Les Aspres, within whose wooded isolation you'll find the magnificent Romanesque **priory of Serrabone**. Further west along the Têt valley, you'll come to **Prades**, a good access point for the Canigou mountain and, skirting the north side of the famous massif, you reach **Villefranche-de-Conflent**, which marks the transition to the upper valley, covered on p.363. Both regular trains and buses run along this part of the valley.

Upstream towards Prades

Heading out of Perpignan along the N116, a detour southwards from the river's course at St-Féliu will take you 6km south to **THUIR**, although if you are driving or cycling you can reach it more directly by taking the D612. This town is known chiefly as the main producer of the red aperitif wine called Byrrh (pronounced "beer"), and you can visit the **winery** at 6 boulevard Violet (mid-Jan to March & Nov & Dec Mon, Wed & Thurs 10am–3pm; April & Oct Mon–Sat 9–11.45am & 2.30–5.45pm; May, June & Sept daily 9–11.45am & 2.30–5.45pm; July & Aug daily 10–11.45am & 2–6.45pm; €1.60) and taste the sweet ferment, which is aged in a cathedral-like gallery of enormous oak vats. From Thuir you can head directly to Ille-sur-Têt along the D615 or go via **CASTELNOU**, a lovely stone village capping a hill-top 4km west from Thuir, where you'll find a tenth-century **castle** (Jan Sat & Sun 11am–5pm; Feb–March & Dec daily 11am–5pm; April–June daily 10am–7pm; July & Aug daily 10am–8pm; Sept–Nov 11am–6pm; €4.50), with good views and a restaurant (noon–2pm & 7–10pm; roughly €15, closed Wed off-season). The hamlet is strong on medieval ambience, and has a well-preserved gate and walls. The best day to come is Tuesday, when a local **market** breathes extra life into the little village (June–Sept). Back at the riverside, and 12km beyond Castelnou, **ILLE-SUR-TÊT** has an attractive medieval quarter of narrow alleys, within which a well-run **Centre d'Art Sacré** (mid-June to Sept daily 10am–noon & 2–7pm; Oct to mid-June Mon & Wed–Fri 10am–noon & 3–6pm, Sat & Sun 3–6pm; €3.20) is housed in the seventeenth-century Hospice d'Illà – the local headquarters of the medieval Hospitaller Knights – and hosts temporary exhibitions of local religious art. More remarkable are the clay cliffs just across the River Têt, a kilometre or so on the road north towards Sournia, and which the elements have eroded into extraordinary figures known as **Les Orgues**, so called because of their resemblance to organ pipes. Rising dramatically up from a deep tributary of the Têt, they can be explored by a series of **footpaths** laid out within the gorge (July & Aug daily 9.30am–8pm; April–June & Sept daily 10am–6.30pm; Oct to March Mon–Fri 10am–12.30pm & 2–5pm, Sat & Sun 10am–5pm; €3.20).

The priory of Serrabone

The most compelling stop en route to Prades involves a detour south from Bouleternère, 5km after Ille-sur-Têt, up a perilous eight-kilometre track to Roussillon's celebrated **priory of Serrabone** (mid-Jan to Oct daily except public holidays 10am–6pm; €3). The location of the simple church, set as it is on a high hill-top, against a precipitous and wooded drop, is impressive; in the grounds around the priory, a botanical garden has been set up to showcase the region's diverse flora. The building's modest facade conceals a strange cloistered gallery, which looks out on the hills, and leads inside to the church's equally curious interior. Here, the almost windowless nave is dominated by an exquisitely decorated tribune of rose marble – an unusual "indoor" cloister, reminiscent of some Spanish Mozarab churches and perhaps a faint echo of Córdoba's great mosque. Excavated columns found here suggest that much of the original priory – founded in the twelfth century – was as elaborate as the tribune. From the foot of the hill on which the priory sits, the road continues 5km south to the village of Boulès d'Amont. From here a harrowing nine-kilometre drive brings you to the chapel of **La Trinité**, just before the Col Xatard (752m). Superb ironwork adorns the outside of the door, and inside there's a *Christ en Majesté* – a Gothic sculpture in which a regally robed Christ reposes impassively on the Cross. If you're **hiking**, you can get to Serrabonne and La Trinité by taking a trail from Vinça, 6km beyond Bouletenère on the N116.

Practicalities

Ille's gare SNCF is a five-minute walk south of the town centre, which is where you will find the town's **tourist office** (July & Aug Mon–Fri 9am–noon & 2–7pm, Sat & Sun 9am–noon & 2–6pm; Sept–June Mon–Fri 9am–noon & 2–6pm, Sat 9am–noon; ☎04.68.84.02.62, ⓦwww.ille-sur-tet.com) in square de la Poste. There's little by way of services in this neck of the woods, and if you decide to stay in Ille, the only **hotel** is the noisy and uninviting *Hôtel du Midi* on the main avenue Pasteur (☎ & ⓕ04.68.84.19.60; ❷). Other options include several **chambres d'hôtes**: the palatial *Les Buis* (☎04.68.84.27.67, ⓦwww.lesbuis.com; ❺; English spoken) at 37 rue Carnot in Ille, the humbler *Les Mandariniers* (☎04.68.53.25.64, ⓕ04.68.53.55.49; ❸; English spoken), in 8 rue des Mésanges in Castelnou, and Maire de Clauzier's home (☎04.68.53.25.64; ❸) at 8 rue de Mesanges in Thuir. The best **restaurant** hereabouts is *Le Patio* (☎04.68.53.23.30; closed part Oct & part Jan), just up the street from Castelnou's old gate, which offers Catalan cuisine in a relaxed, intimate atmosphere from €15. In Thuir, the best accommodation are the deluxe **chambre d'hôtes** of *Casa del Arte* (☎04.68.53.44.78, ⓦwww.casadelarte.fr; ❺; English spoken) set in a renovated eleventh-century farmhouse.

Prades and around

Midway along the Têt valley, **PRADES** is by far its biggest town. Distinctively pink with its marble masonry and pavements, it is the birthplace of Thomas Merton, the twentieth-century Catholic mystic who eventually settled in a Trappist monastery in Kentucky. But it is best known for hosting the annual summer music festival founded in 1950 by the Catalan cellist **Pablo Casals** (or Pau Casals in Catalan). In exile from Franco's Spain, Casals spent the second half of his life here, composing such works as the oratorio *The Crib* and the popular *Song of the Birds*. A one-room **Musée Pablo Casals** (July & Aug Mon–Fri 9am–noon & 2–6pm; rest of year Mon–Fri 9am–noon & 2–5pm; free), housed in the same building as the municipal tourist office (see opposite), commemorates the virtuoso, who died in 1973, two years before the Spanish dictator. In the main place de la République, you'll find the **church of St-Pierre**, which contains a huge and sumptuous seventeenth-century retable, a masterpiece by the Catalan sculptor Joseph Sunyer. Prades is in fact conspicuously Catalan in feel, hosting a summertime Catalan university course (ten days in August; ☎04.68.96.10.84) and having established the first Catalan-language primary school in France. On Tuesday and Saturday mornings there is an excellent produce **market** in the square and surrounding streets.

Much of the music festival takes place at the restored ninth-century Benedictine monastery of **St-Michel-de-Cuxà** (May–Sept Mon–Sat 9.30–11.50am & 2–6pm; Oct–April Mon–Sat 9.30–11.50am & 2–5pm, Sun 2–5pm; €3.80), whose single, ponderous square tower suddenly appears above a copse of poplars 3km south of the town, on the orchard-lined road to Taurinya. St-Michel reached its peak in the eleventh century and then went into slow decline: closed and abandoned in 1790, much of its stone was pillaged during the Revolution, some of it eventually finding its way – like many other Romanesque fragments from the region – to the Cloisters Museum in New York. Today the highlights of a visit include a subterranean crypt consisting of a circular chapel dating back to the monastery's foundation, and the remains of the broad cloister, whose columns are capped by fine twelfth-century detailings. The church, accessed from a tiny door off the cloister, contains a puzzling mishmash of features, superimposed on each other during the long series of renovations which followed the building's construction.

Practicalities

The **gare SNCF** is at the southern edge of Prades, about ten minutes' walk from the centre; **buses** set you down on avenue Général de Gaulle (RN116), which is the main road through the centre of town. The **tourist office** (July & Aug Mon–Sat 9am–12.30pm & 2–7pm, Sun 9am–noon; Sept–June Mon–Fri 9am–noon & 2–5pm; ☎04.68.05.41.02, ℱ04.68.05.21.79, ⓦwww.prades-tourisme.com), at 4 rue Victor-Hugo, is a mine of information about everything from *chambres d'hôtes* and changing money to walking trails, biking trails and climbing the Pic du Canigou. The **music festival office** is next door (☎04.68.96.33.07). You can **rent bikes** at Cycles Flament at 8 rue Arago and Cycles Cerda on chemin de las Bouchères (near the "Super U" supermarket).

For cheap and reasonable **accommodation** you can't beat the faded elegance of the white-painted, simply furnished *Hostalrich*, at 156 av Général de Gaulle (☎04.68.96.05.38, ℱ04.68.96.00.73; ❶), still run by a family who were friends of Casals; its spacious restaurant, with a €12 *menu*, also offers the best value in town. The best alternative is *Les Glycines* at no. 129 on the same street (☎04.68.96.51.65, ⓦwww.glycines.com; ❷) – slightly more expensive, but spotlessly clean and friendly. The beautifully sited municipal **campsite** (April–Sept ☎04.68.96.29.83) in the valley just east of the town centre, off chemin du Gaz, also has chalets for rent (❷). For **eating** out in Prades, apart from the reliable *Hostalrich*, you could try *El Patio*, at 19 place de la République (closed Wed), which serves both traditional and Andalucian-style food for about €20 per person. **Café** life is centred on the place de la République, where the *Café de France* has a reputation for the best *plats du jour*.

Villefranche-de-Conflent and around

Beyond Prades, the Têt valley narrows dramatically, becoming a gorge 6km further on, where the high walls of **VILLEFRANCHE-DE-CONFLENT** almost block the way. As there's almost no construction outside the walls, externally at least the town looks much as it did three hundred years ago: an elongated, two-street place squeezed between the palisade just to the south and the river. Within the ramparts, the most evocative area is along the bank of the Têt, by the thirteenth-century church of **St-Pierre**; the best view is from the far side, from where the weathered red-tiled roofs and the tower of the twelfth-century church of **St-Jacques** peer over the ramparts. But more satisfying, perhaps, than any man-made constructions are the vast **cave** complexes (see p.360) which riddle the strata below and around the town.

Villefranche dates from 1092, when Guillaume Raymond, Count of Cerdagne, granted the charter for the town, meant as a strategic bulwark against the counts of Roussillon. Some remnants from that period still stand, notably the **Tour d'en Solenell** on the little square known as the **Placette**. In 1654 Villefranche – then controlled by Spain – was besieged by Louis XIV's troops, and fell after eight days' fighting. After the Treaty of the Pyrenees confirmed their annexation of Roussillon, the French rebuilt the Spanish fortifications according to plans drawn up by Vauban.

As you walk the immense and maze-like **ramparts** (daily: Feb–May & Oct–Dec 10am–12.30 & 2–6pm; June & Sept 10am–7pm; July & Aug

10am–8pm; €3.50), their vulnerability to attack from the surrounding heights is obvious – a defensive weakness that Vauban remedied by adding various bastions and building the upper fort now known as **Fort Libéria** (daily: June–Sept 9am–8pm; Oct–May 10am–6pm; €5.50), rising high above the main town on the steep northern bank of the Têt. The castle has seen more service as a prison than as a fortress; its interns have included a group of seventeenth-century noble-women of the court of Versailles, locked up in isolation and silence for over thirty years, on allegations of witchcraft and poisoning. You can reach the fort by hiking up the winding dirt road which starts just outside the eastern gates, or by catching the complimentary minibus, either from outside the Porte de France or at the insipid new **museum** opposite the ticket office for the ramparts.

The caves

The most celebrated incident in Villefranche's history was the 1674 revolt against French rule, which culminated in the betrayal of the rebellion's leader, Charles de Llar, and his co-conspirators by Llar's own daughter, Inès. His hiding place was the Cova Bastéra, now known as the **Grottes de la Préhistoire** (daily: July & Aug 10am–8pm; Sept–June 10am–noon & 2–6pm; €6), a cave which he could enter and exit from within the walls of the town – today the entrance is just west of the town walls on the N116. If you plan on visiting the cave, consider buying a combined ticket, also good for the limestone formations of the **Grottes des Canalettes** (April–Sept 10am–6.30pm, off-season call ☎04.68.05.20.76; 45min guided tour; €6), 1km along the road south towards Vernet-les-Bains. The most spectacular caves, however, are the adjoining **Grottes des Grandes Canalettes**, which require a separate ticket (April to mid-June & mid-Sept to Oct daily 10am–6pm; mid-June to mid-Sept daily 10am–6.30pm; Nov–March Sun & school hols 2–5pm; by appointment ☎04.68.96.23.11, ⓦwww.grottes-grandes-canalettes.com; 1hr guided tour; €7; €10 for entry and *son et lumière*). Entry is via a 160-metre passageway, hollowed out by water over the past four hundred million years; the water dripping down the sides is now directed over moulds to create limestone images for sale at the shop. Beyond a door you then enter a succession of huge chambers crammed with stalactites, stalagmites, pillars and tiny, feathery formations.

Practicalities

Main-line trains from Perpignan terminate in Villefranche, at the **gare SNCF** (☎04.68.96.56.62), 400m north of the town; for onward *Train Jaune* services (see box on p.364), simply change platforms. The **tourist office** (Feb–Dec daily 10am–12.30pm & 2–5.30pm; ☎04.68.96.22.96, ⓕ04.68.96.23.93) runs a booth at the entrance to the ramparts, where they sell local hiking and biking guides (€5–9); you can also enquire here about jeep excursions up the Canigou, which depart from outside the train station (call M. Bouzan ☎04.68.05.62.28). The only **hotel** here is the magnificent old *Auberge du Cédre* (closed Nov–April; ☎ & ⓕ04.68.96.05.05; ❷) situated just east of the old walls, near the *gare*, and there is a welcoming **chambre d'hôtes**, *Mireille Pena* (☎04.68.96.52.35, ⓔmpebafain@aol.com; ❹), with a swimming pool, located off the same lane. There is also **gîte** accommodation (contact the *mairie* ☎04.68.96.10.78) and a **campsite**, *Mas de Lastourg* (April–Nov). Of the **restaurants**, the most interesting is *Le Menestrel* (some vegetarian dishes) in rue St-Pierre, the alley leading down to the Pont St-Pierre (and on to Fort Libéria); if you visit the **Grottes des Grandes Canalettes** with an €22 ticket, an all-you-can-eat Catalan-food buffet is included. **Market**-day is Saturday, with vendors gathered around the place de l'Église.

The Pic du Canigou and around

Rising to a height of 2785m between the Tech and Têt valleys, **Pic du Canigou** (*Canigó* in Catalan) is the great landmark of Catalonia, dominating the whole of the Roussillon lowlands. Situated well inside French territory, the mountain became a symbol for Catalonia's lost independence in the course of the nineteenth-century literary renaissance, and came to signify Catalan cultural unity, endorsed today by the small flags and other patriotic paraphernalia festooned from its summit cross. Before modern geographic surveys had covered the whole of the Pyrenees, the Canigou was thought erroneously to be the range's highest peak – it does, however, overshadow the rest of the **Canigou Massif**, wedged between the two rivers. The massif has been protected as a nature reserve and the peak (when not clouded) affords breathtaking views; if you're intent on reaching the summit, you must **hike**, and the most direct route is from the **Chalet des Cortalets** (2150m) on the peak's northeastern slopes – you can get to this by vehicle or on foot. There are, however, other, more challenging hikes up to the peak either from the Tech valley to the south or from the amenable village of **Vernet-les-Bains** on its northwestern slopes; if you choose to take on these trails or explore the massif further you should purchase either the 1:50,000 "Canigou/Vallespir/Fenouillèdes" *carte de randonnée* published by IGN, or the TOP 25 1:25,000 **map** (no. 2349ET "Massif du Canigou"), readily available at shops in the area. Vernet is also the place from which to access the key sight around Canigou – the **monastery of St-Martin-du-Canigou**, easily reachable by car. For all route information, contact the regional tourist office in Perpignan (see p.345), or visit their website. Before setting out to the summit, either by car or foot, be sure to check the weather conditions. In general, the best time of year to hike up is the autumn, when there is no snow on the summit (as in late spring); summer is not the best of times to make the ascent, as the heat can be uncomfortable and humidity reduces visibility from the top.

To the summit via the Chalet des Cortalets

Most hikers tackle Canigou from the *Chalet des Cortalets*, a busy refuge a couple of hours from the summit. You can get to the chalet from either the east or the north. The easternmost route is the quiet and impressively steep (but not difficult) approach from **Valmanya**, which you can drive or **hike** to (along the GR36) from Vinça – some 20km to the north. From the village, a narrow road climbs a further 5km west, before petering out – you must then use the GR36 to complete the remaining 8km to the chalet. Approaching from the north, there is a jeep track from near **Prades**. A scenic but busy alternative, this route provides the gentlest ascent to the chalet and is the one used by **jeep-taxis** (roughly €25 per person) from Prades; booking offices in the town include Ria (☎04.68.05.27.08) and Corbières Grand Riad (☎04.68.05.24.24). If you're **driving**, take the D35 out of the south side of Prades to Villerach (8km; signposted as "Clara-Villerach"), from where an unpaved *route forestière* dirt track rises to the chalet – an hour's drive. This is a superb approach, often running close to the River Llech, each turn revealing a new arrangement of rock, water, sky and forest. An ordinary car can easily get as far as the ruined hut at Prat Cabrera (1650m), an hour's walk from the *Chalet des Cortalets*, and – with extra care and ideal conditions – all the way to Cortalets itself.

A maquisard hideout in the last war, and consequently heavily shelled by occupation forces, the restored **Chalet des Cortalets** (May–Oct; other times emergency shelter only; ☎04.68.96.36.19; ❷) is run by the Club Alpin Français (www.clubalpin.com). There are double rooms as well as dorm beds (€17), while **meals** in the bar-restaurant cost about €12. The smaller shelter adjacent, with no bunk linen provided, costs half as much as the dorms. Be warned that the main lodge can get overcrowded, and the tracks bring up jeeps full of revellers (as opposed to walkers) at weekends to picnic at the tables around the little lake, ten minutes' walk west of the refuge. **Tents** are tolerated on the lakeshore, and next to another smaller pond closer to *Cortalets*.

The summit

The well-marked **hike to the summit** goes past the larger lake, with its fine view up into the summit cirque, then climbs south along the ridge connecting with the **Pic Joffre**, which often teems with lizards at sunset. It takes about ninety minutes and provides only a slight sense of exposure as you reach the wrought-iron summit cross and *table d'orientation*. Even though it's the process of getting to the top that makes Canigou so memorable – rather than the experience of standing on the peak – the views encompassing everything from Andorra to the sea are wonderful.

At midsummer (technically June 21 but in Catalonia observed on the eve of June 23–24, the Festa de Sant Joan), the refuge and the peak are a frenzy of activity as seemingly half the population of Catalonia congregates for merrymaking and the kindling of the traditional bonfire, which is then relayed to light numerous others in Catalan villages on both sides of the frontier. Even at other times there is often a patriotic Catalan or two prepared to bivouac the night beside the peak's highest cairn.

Vernet-les-Bains and St-Martin-du-Canigou

The biggest village on the Canigou's slopes and the major stop en route to the famous abbey of St-Martin is the pleasant if slightly stuffy spa town of **VERNET-LES-BAINS**, whose easiest approach is via the D116 for 10km south from Villefranche. English visitors such as Rudyard Kipling made the place fashionable during the last century and a waterfall, 3km out of town on a well-marked track, is even called the **Cascade des Anglaises**. Along with the thermal paraphernalia of plunge-pools and institutional adjoining therapy wings – first installed in 1377 – a range of more contemporary pastimes is now offered (mountain-biking, canyoning, hydrospeed and caving), though the baths are still the focus of activity. Often overlooked, the old quarter's warren of alleys is capped by the ninth-century but much-restored double church of **Notre Dame del Puig/St-Saturnin**, which incorporates remaining bits of a castle. You can also visit the town's **geological museum** (daily 9.30am–noon & 2–6pm; €3) in Parc du Casino, which has a collection of local silex and other fossils.

From Vernet-les-Bains, a paved road and a footpath lead 2.5km south to **Casteil**, an appealing, quiet hamlet, close to the **monastery of St-Martin-du-Canigou**, a ubiquitous sight on local book covers, postcards and posters. Access to the monastery is only by a thirty-minute climb up the continuation of the footpath, or by jeep transport from Casteil along a steep, narrow road. Inaccessibility helps protect the place from becoming over-commercialized – as does its continuing use by an active religious community. Built

The Train Jaune

The best way to move up the Têt valley and on into the Cerdagne is on the **Train Jaune**, once an essential local service, but now more of a fun ride – during summer some carriages are open-air. Built in the early twentieth century, the railway climbs for 63km from Villefranche (427m) up to Latour-de-Carol (1231m), where it connects with the Transpyrenean railway (Toulouse–Barcelona). Tourism saved the scenic narrow-gauge line from closure early in the 1970s, but its future remains uncertain. As it is, return tickets are valid for only 24 hours, with **fares** double those of French main-line services; as an example, Villefranche to Mont-Louis and back (the most popular stretch) will cost at least €16.

From late May through to September there are four to six **departures** a day in each direction; the first train of the day leaves Latour-de-Carol soon after 8am, and takes two and a half hours to reach Villefranche. For the rest of the year service is cut to two round trips. Since most of the line is single track, there are often delays caused by long halts at Mont-Louis or Font-Romeu to allow the uphill train to pass, the first of these leaving Villefranche well before 8am. The train is scheduled to stop only at certain stations, and if you want to alight at one of the smaller, unstaffed stations (designated *arrêts facultatifs* on carriage placards) you have to notify the driver in advance. Similarly, to get on at such stations, you have to flag the train down. Beware when walking near the line, as the electrified "third rail" which provides power for the train is exposed and is a potential safety hazard.

For **information** on timetables and prices contact the following stations: Villefranche-Vernet-Fuilla (☎04.68.96.56.62); Mont-Louis (☎04.68.04.23.27); Font-Romeu (☎04.68.30.03.12); Bourg-Madame (☎04.68.04.53.29); or Latour-de-Carol (☎04.68.04.80.62). You can also call the main information number (☎08.92.35.35.35) or go to ⓦwww.ter-sncf.com/trains_touristiques/train_jaune.htm.

from tan stone and roofed with grey slates, the monastery ranks as one of the most gorgeous monuments in the eastern Pyrenees, and the surrounding woods of sweet chestnut, beech and aspen form an unbeatable backdrop to the pinnacle of rock on which it stands. Founded in 1001 by Count Guifred de Cerdagne, it was severely damaged by an earthquake in the fifteenth century and thoroughly pillaged after abandonment in 1782. Restored through the twentieth century, the glory of the place resides in its **cloister capitals**, reassembled in unity by a bishop of Perpignan. The monastery is now occupied by an unusual mixed order of monks and nuns, called the "Beatitudes", with a sprinkling of lay workers. Ordinarily, visitors are allowed only on silent **guided tours** (hourly departures: Feb to Easter Mon & Wed–Sat 10am, noon & 2.30–4.30pm, Sun 10am, 12.30pm & 2.30–4.30pm; Easter to mid-June & late Sept Mon–Sat 10am, noon & 2.30–4.30pm, Sun 10am, 12.30pm & 2.30–4.30pm; mid-June to mid-Sept Mon–Sat 10am, noon & 2–5pm, Sun 10am, 12.30pm & 2–5pm; €3.85). Descending from the rear of the complex, you can take an alternative marked footpath for half an hour back to Casteil via the entrance to the **Gorges du Cady**, where the river falls 500m over a distance of 3km, making this a popular spot for **canyoning**.

Practicalities

The **tourist office** is quite central, on place de la Mairie, near the corner of boulevard Lambert-Violet and rue du Canigou (Mon–Fri 9am–noon & 2–6pm; ☎04.68.05.55.35, ⓦwww.ot-vernet-les-bains.fr), close to where buses will drop you. **Jeep–taxis** up Canigou (same price as from Prades) and to the monastery can be arranged through Garage Villaceque (☎04.68.05.66.58).

Vernet has three two-star **hotels**, each offering a range of amenities and all good value: *Eden*, 2 promenade du Cady (☎04.68.05.54.09, Ⓦwww.logis–de–france.fr; ❷), the *Moderne le Colibri*, 7 av des Thermes (☎04.68.05.52.17, Ⓕ04.68.05.66.64; ❸), and the *Princess*, rue de Lavandiers (☎04.68.05.56.22, Ⓦwww.hotel-princess.com; ❸). A better choice than any of these is the cosy *Le Molière* (☎04.68.05.50.97, Ⓦwww.lemoliere.com; ❷) in Casteil, also worth stopping in for its fine country **restaurant** in the apple orchard (*menus* from €17). There's also a *gîte d'étape* (☎04.68.05.51.30; ❶) and a **campsite**, *Camping St-Martin* (April–Sept; ☎04.68.05.52.09), with a swimming pool. In Vernet, you'll also find a *gîte d'étape* in chemin St-Saturnin, on the left bank of the Cady next to the municipal pool (☎04.68.05.51.30; ❶). There are plenty of **campsites** too: the nearest are *Les Cerisiers* (open mid-May to Sept; ☎04.68.05.66.38), on the same side of the river as the *gîte*, and *Dels Bosc*, 1km north on the Villefranche road (open April–Sept; ☎04.68.05.54.54).

For **eating**, you can easily spend a fortune in the elegant surroundings of *Le Cortal* (closed Mon and in Oct & Nov), up in the old quarter behind the church at rue de Château. On Mondays, Thursdays and Saturdays the place de la République is home to a bustling morning **market**.

The upper Têt and the Capcir

The lower Têt valley finishes at Villefranche-de-Conflent, above which the shaggy flanks of the **upper Têt** close dramatically around the narrow-gauge *Train Jaune* rail line and N116, which forge their separate ways along the river up to **Mont-Louis**, at the top of the Têt. En route, interspersed with abandoned villages colonized by hippies and New Age travellers, are a number of small hamlets, on the valley floor or perched just above, which make serviceable bases for excursions into the hills. Of these, the hot springs and the splendour of **Carança gorge** near **Thuès** make it one of the most accessible and rewarding. North of Mont-Louis, a sedimentary plateau called the **Capcir** spreads towards the gorges of the upper Aude. Bare and extremely flat, dominated in the centre by the large artificial lakes of Matemale and Puyvalador, it is cradled by densely wooded slopes that sweep up to Pic Madrès and the Carlit Massif, with only the pistes of the **ski resorts** Les Angles, Formiguères and Puyvalador interrupting the trees. One of the harshest winter climates in southern France also makes this excellent **cross-country skiing** terrain. The Capcir woodlands, with their sprinkling of *gîtes* and hotels, provide ample opportunities for **hiking** during warmer months, well within the capabilities of a novice walker; for information on the area's more challenging trails or longer circuits like the four-day **La Tour du Capcir**, which winds around the bleak Capcir plateau (see p.366), contact local tourist offices. In July and August, and during ski season, all the main Capcir villages and resorts are served by a taxi-bus, which departs from the Mont-Louis/La Cabanasse train station.

The Carança gorge area

At **NYER**, less than an hour from Villefranche on the *Train Jaune*, the road south from the station to the village climbs on into the impressive Gorges de Nyer, but you're probably better off staying on the train until **THUÈS-**

CARANÇA, four minutes above the small spa of Thuès-les-Bains and the gateway for the even more spectacular **Gorges de Carança**. The gorge is clearly signposted from the train station and from Thuès village, and more notices at its mouth (over which the *Train Jaune* clatters across a bridge) advise you of entry at your own risk. After a short walk from the car park, the path divides: the left-hand path (signposted for Roc Madrieu) climbs steeply up the wooded side of the valley, while the right-hand path (over a small bridge) follows the more spectacular corniche route; the two paths converge at the *pont des singes* (suspension bridge). The first ninety minutes of corniche walkway are the most amazing, poised over sheer four hundred-metre drops – not for the vertigo-prone. Next is a series of nerve-wracking catwalks, ladders and wobbly, metal suspension bridges, these last not advisable for heavily laden walkers. If you want to **hike** further, beyond the narrows the route becomes a shady streamside trail on the west bank; soon the countryside opens out, and you should reach **Ras de Carança** (1830m), with its summer-staffed refuge, in about four to five hours – here you can join up with the GR10-36 (see below).

As you would expect, there is little by way of services in this rugged and under-populated stretch, but you'll find enough **accommodation** to make even an overnight visit possible. At Nyer, you'll find a **campsite**, *La Catalane* (℡04.68.97.07.63), but more enticing is Thuès-entre-Valls' delightful **gîte-campsite**, *Mas de Bordes* (℡04.68.97.05.00, ℻04.68.97.11.51), with self-catering suites (❷), next to the church. This restored farm is part of a substantial property which includes its own outdoor hot springs, a remote log cabin and a meadow for pitching tents. The place is always mobbed during July and August, when you must ring ahead, but it's worth trying to fit into your plans for a night or two. Good *table d'hôte* suppers are provided for overnight guests for about €14, a blessing, since the village itself is not up to much at all. Information on local excursions can be obtained from the local Maison de la Réserve in Nyer (℡04.6897.05.56, ✉reserve.nyer@libertysurf.fr). The **nature reserve** itself (open year round; free) consists of over 22 square kilometres of mountain wilderness between 700 and 2663m in altitude, and is home to rare and varied Pyrenean flora and fauna, including the Pyrenees lily, bearded vulture and royal eagle, as well as wildcats.

Mont-Louis and around

Approaching Mont-Louis, the *Train Jaune* passes over the 150-metre-long **Pont Gisclard** suspension bridge, which carries the track 80m above the river; it was designed early last century by the mathematician and engineer Albert Gisclard, who was tragically killed by a runaway train on the very day of the official bridge trials in 1909. Soon afterwards you'll find the turn-off for **PLANÈS**, whose peculiar triangular church was once thought to be an adapted Muslim structure. To get to Mont-Louis from here you can get back on the train (stop at La Cabanasse) or **hike** 4km down the GR10-36, which passes through the hamlet. At 1600m, the garrison town of **MONT-LOUIS** is the highest on the Têt, only 14km southeast of the river's source, the Lac des Bouillouses. Known as the gateway to the Cerdagne, Mont-Louis is the quintessential work of Louis XIV's military engineer Vauban, and its massive moat-ringed **ramparts** (Tues–Sat 10am–noon & 2–6pm; €2), built between 1679 and 1682, represent a glorious but failed effort to close off the Spanish frontier. Though promoted as a resort, Mont-Louis is still essentially a military town (now a commando training centre), and apart from the walls, its only other attraction is the world's first **solar oven** (*four solaire*), built in 1949 and now open for one-hour **guided tours** (mid-June to mid-Sept daily

10am–12.30pm & 2–7pm; rest of year Mon–Sat 10am–12.30pm & 2–6.30pm; €5); the huge mirror for the *four* stands in the moat, just to the left of the main gate (Porte de France).

In Mont-Louis, there's a **tourist office** in rue du Marché (July & Aug daily 9.30am–noon & 2–7pm; Sept–June Tues–Sat 10am–noon & 2–6pm; ℡04.68.04.21.97, 🖳www.mont-louis.net), while the best deal for **accommodation** is *La Volute* (℡ & 🖷 04.68.04.27.21; ❸; English spoken), a B&B set in the seventeenth-century former governor's mansion. Otherwise, the top **hotel** is the attractively furnished *La Taverne*, in 10 rue Victor Hugo (℡04.68.04.23.67, 🖳www.logis-de-france.fr; closed part March, part Nov & part Dec; ❸), which has excellent-value *menus* (€15–41) and delicious pizzas from a wood-fired oven. If this is full, try the *Bernagie*, 10 rue Victor (℡04.68.04.23.67, 🖳www.bernagie.fr; ❸), whose restaurant does Catalan cuisine (from €15; closed Sun eve & Mon, part Nov & Dec). The closest **campsite**, *Pla de Barres* (℡04.68.04.26.04; mid-June to mid-Sept), lies 3km west along the road towards Lac des Bouillouses. *Lou Roubaillou*, a celebrated **restaurant** in rue des Écoles Laïques, offers mushrooms, boar and duck among other local delicacies (*menus* from €20). Near Planès, there's a *gîte d'étape* (℡04.68.04.21.40; ❶) at *La Cassagne* farm, along the GR10-36 towards Mont-Louis. Mont-Louis' **market** days are Tuesday and Thursday.

The Capcir ski resorts

All of the Capcir **ski resorts** lie on, or just off, the D118 road served by the taxi-bus. Nearest to Mont-Louis, **LES ANGLES** is also the area's largest, with 40km of pistes – half of them red, with the top run at 2100m. Chalets predominate rather than high-rises, but the old village has still been almost completely swamped. **FORMIGUÈRES**, 6km further north, is far more attractive with its shops (some selling outdoor gear), cafés and crêperies giving it the feel of a county town. Its **church of Ste-Marie** features an unusual triangular facade culminating in the belfry; inside is a masterful, seventeenth-century *majestat*, or clothed figure of Christ, typical of the Catalan regions. The pistes here total just 20km, with no really tough runs, but a good-value seasonal pass is available through the local tourist office (see below). Moreover, standing at the heart of 100km of marked trails, Formiguères is the perfect place to start your **cross-country skiing** career; this sort of skiing requires no lessons – experience teaches you how to avoid falling over – and equipment rental can cost less than half downhill piste rates. The ski station at **PUYVALADOR**, at the north end of the Capcir plateau, is 5km west of its namesake reservoir and village (which has no amenities). It was created in 1982, with 20km of pistes, and has a top station at 2380m.

There is **tourist office** at Les Angles (℡04.68.04.32.76, 🖳www.les-angles.com) and at Formiguères (July & Aug 8.30am–12.30pm & 2.30–6.30pm; Sept–June 9am–noon & 3–6pm; ℡04.68.04.47.35, 🖳www.formigueres.net), which also has two **hotels**: the one-star *Picheyre* behind the church (℡04.68.04.40.07, 🖂hotel-picheyre@wanadoo.fr; closed mid-April to early June & Nov to early Dec; ❷) and the fancier *Auberge de la Tutte*, on the road out of town by the junction for Les Angles (℡04.68.04.40.21, 🖂latutte@laposte.net; ❸). The *Picheyre's* **restaurant** is old-fashioned if dull, but good value for about €15. In Les Angles you can choose between five hotels, with the *Lloret Hôtel*, 12 avenue de Balcère (℡04.68.30.90.90, 🖳www.logis-de-france.com; closed May–June & mid-Sept to Nov; ❸; English spoken) providing good value. In nearby Rieutort, the comfortable **gîte** *Le Moulin* (℡04.68.30.97.37, 🖳www.gitecariolettes.com; ❶; English spoken) offers five pleasant rooms. The Bureau Montagne in Angles (℡04.68.04.34.30) is a multidisciplinary sports outfitter for summertime **activities** such as horse-riding, mountain-biking and canyoning. Close to Puyvalador (which has no independent services) you'll find the excellent *Al Cortal* **restaurant** (℡04.68.04.45.00; eve only during ski season; also lunch time in summer; otherwise, weekends only), with slightly pricey four-course *menus* from €28. **Market** days are Saturday for Formiguères and Tuesday for Les Angles. For additional information on this region see Ⓦwww.capcir-pyrénées.com.

The Cerdagne and the Carlit Massif

The French **Cerdagne** is half of the ancient Catalan county of La Cerdanya, chopped in two by the Treaty of the Pyrenees. It is the highest point of the Segre watershed which descends south to Catalan Lleida, and the sunniest area in the French Pyrenees, the ripe colours of summer grain and hay on its tree-less, rolling hills reinforcing this impression. Due to a technicality in the treaty, the Cerdagne consists of the hamlets and countryside surrounding the sizeable Spanish enclave of Llívia. To its northeast, the ski-centre of **Font-Romeu** is the biggest town in the region. To the south, **Saillagouse**, **Err** and **Bourg-Madame** ring the island of Spanish territory and can be traced west to **Latour-de-Carol**, which marks the terminus and frontier-crossing of the railway which ascends the Ariège valley from Toulouse; north of Latour is the excellent ski-station of **Porté-Puymorens**. The granite ridges of the lake-spangled **Carlit Massif**, the last truly alpine region of the Pyrenees, occupy a compact area just north of the Cerdagne and offer one of the most challenging regions for serious **hiking**. As with the upper Têt valley, the *Train Jaune* provides the best access to the entire area.

Font-Romeu and around

Sprawling at the foot of Roc de la Calme, at the southeast corner of the Carlit Massif, **FONT-ROMEU** is one of the most famous ski resorts in the Pyrenees. Its reputation though, is somewhat unjustified – a triumph of marketing over reality – since the much-touted Cité Préolympique was nothing more than an altitude training camp for the 1968 Mexico summer games. Its top station is a mere 2200m, with a maximum vertical descent of just 500m, and out of thirty pistes only five are challenging to the good skier; it does, however, have good cross-country skiing – more than 80km of marked trails. The nearby Superbolquère, better known as **Pyrénées 2000**, is no higher than Font-Romeu and of an ugliness exceeded only by other purpose-built French winter resorts.

Aside from the nightlife, the town is known for its famous Virgin statue, a source of devotion and the origin of Font-Romeu's name, meaning "pilgrim's spring" in Catalan. The legend tells of a cowherd uncovering a buried figure of the Virgin – a recurring motif throughout upland Catalonia – having been led to the spot by a bull. The statue is now housed in the **Ermitage**, just a stroll from the main town, off avenue Emmanuel Brousse (early July to early Sept daily 10am–noon & 3–6pm; free), much altered since its fourteenth-century construction. The Catalan artist Joseph Sunyer sculpted the retable in 1707, and five years later created a flamboyantly Baroque "bedroom" for the Virgin, known as the *camaril*. On September 8 the Virgin is taken down the hill to **ODEILLO**, returning on Trinity Sunday the following year. Odeillo has the only other "sight" of the immediate area – the **Four Solaire**, or solar power station (daily: July & Aug 10am–7.30pm; Sept–June 10am–12.30pm & 2–6pm; €5). It no longer functions as a generator, but rather as a museum and PR exercise, with occasional full-moon-powered demonstrations on summer evenings.

Practicalities

The *Train Jaune* **station** is at Via, from where it's a fairly steep two-kilometre walk north to Font-Romeu, passing Odeillo about halfway. **Accommodation** in Font-Romeu tends to be expensive, but with eighteen thousand beds you should be able to find something. For a list of holiday apartments ask at the **tourist office** (daily 9am–12.30pm & 2–6.30pm; ☎04.68.30.68.30, Ⓦwww.font-romeu.fr) near the top of avenue Emmanuel Brousse. The cheapest **hotel** is *L'Oustalet* (☎04.68.30.11.32, Ⓕ04.68.30.11.32; ❷) in rue des Viollettes, which has an outdoor swimming pool. The two-star *Le Regina*, on avenue Emmanuel Brousse (☎04.68.30.03.81, Ⓔhotel.regina@laposte.net; ❸), is also open year round, while west of town the *Hôtel Y Sem Bé* (☎04.68.30.00.54, Ⓕ04.68.30.25.42; ❹) enjoys views over much of the Cerdagne. A good **restaurant** here is *La Chaumière* (☎04.68.30.04.40; closed Sun & Mon, part June & July) at 96 av Emmanuel Brousse, while *L'Equirol* is an excellent option for regional food (*menus* from €14). For those on a budget, the **gîte** *Les Cariolettes* (☎04.68.30.25.48, Ⓦwww.gite-cariolettes.com; English spoken; ❶) on 1 rue de Fontanilles is the place to head for. This renovated old house offers both private rooms and dorms, plus a common room and a patio with barbeque; they will even prepare picnic lunches. **Market** day is Wednesday.

West to Porté-Puymorens

Beyond Odeillo, the *Train Jaune* winds its way across the wide open plain to the south side of the Cerdagne, to depopulated **SAILLAGOUSE** (1320m), also along the N116, and a base for the glorious twelve-kilometre round-trip **hike** through the **Gorges du Sègre**. The road snakes southeast from the village, passing through the extremely picturesque hamlet of **LLÓ**, before continuing up the gorge as a *route forestière*. The next *Train Jaune* stop is on the north edge of **ERR**, a tiny village at the foot of heavily wooded Puigmal – and another place with a "found Virgin" legend. The twelfth-century effigy is housed in the **Chapelle de la Vierge**, considerably enlarged in the eighteenth century. Separated from it by the cemetery is the church of **St-Genis**, which an almost indecipherable inscription says is the burial place of Bishop Radulf of Urgell, a close relative of Guifré el Pelós of Ripoll (known in English as "Wilfred the Hairy" and hailed as the first of the line of the great Catalan count-kings). Skirting the Spanish enclave of Llívia, the *Train Jaune* reaches the frontier at **BOURG-MADAME**, which in 1815 changed its name from Les Guinguettes d'Hix in honour of the wife of the Duc d'Angoulême, bearer of the title "Madame Royale". It had grown from insignificance to a major bazaar over the course of the eighteenth century, both as a smuggler's entrepôt and legitimate competitor to Puigcerdà across the Spanish border. But since the renaming it hasn't amounted to much, and is visibly depressed and fading, its vitality sapped by its more favoured neighbour. It is the best place, however, to buy souvenirs such as earthenware. From Bourg-Madame, the *Train Jaune* continues for fifteen minutes to the end of the line, the Gare Internationale of **LATOUR-DE-CAROL/ENVEITG**, the interchange for trains south towards Barcelona and north towards Toulouse. The *gare* lies between the two villages, though it's actually much closer (700m) to Enveitg, the larger place. Finally, north of Latour-de-Carol on the N20 or by train, on the western slopes of the Carlit Massif, the ski station above the village of **PORTÉ-PUYMORENS** is probably the best the French Catalan Pyrenees has to offer. For although the nearby Col de Puymorens marks the shift from the arid Cerdagne to the damp Ariège, a lot of snow often falls on the Cerdan side and stays there, protected from the worst of the wind. The seventeen runs here are fairly evenly distributed amongst all difficulties, with the highest points at a respectable 2400m and 2500m. There are also 25km of trails for *ski de fond*, a snowboarders' "board park" and a whole gamut of non-ski leisure facilities (including horse-riding, bike trails and fitness). The village itself has a pleasant valley setting, off the main road.

Practicalities

Saillagouse's *Train Jaune* station is actually across the river, about a fifteen-minute walk from the town's *mairie*, where you'll find a small **tourist office** (July & Aug daily 10am–noon & 3–7pm: ☎04.68.04.55.35, ✉mairie-saillagouse@wanadoo.fr). Local produce can be found at the open **market** (Tues & Fri). You can stay at the **youth hostel**, on the edge of the village (☎04.68.04.71.69; ❶), or the *Hôtel Planes*, place de Cerdagne (☎04.68 .04.72.08, ⓦwww.planotel.fr; ❸), at the **chambres d'hôtes** *Mas Rondole* (☎04.68.04.00.51; ❸), or one of two **campsites**, *Le Sègre* (☎04.68.04.74.72) and *Le Cerdan* (☎04.68.04.70.46). In Lló, the only option is the three-star *Auberge Atalaya* (☎04.68.04.70.04, ✉atalaya@francimel.com; ❻), providing expensive accommodation and more affordable high-quality meals, and in **Err**, you can stay the night at a *gîte d'étape* (☎04.68.04.74.20; ❶).

Bourg-Madame's cheapest option is the two-star *Celisol* (☎04.68.04.53.70; ❷), though you've a choice of **campsites**, both open year round: *Le Sègre* on route de Toulouse (☎04.68.04.65.87), and the *Caravaneige Mas Piques* (☎04.68.04.62.11). The **market** is held on Saturdays. Because it's on the main road between Spain and Ariège, **Latour-de-Carol/Enveitg** has some very tacky **hotels** which can get away with charging too much. It's best to stay at Enveitg's *Hôtel Transpyrénéen* (☎04.68.04.81.05, ✉hotel.transpyreneen @wanadoo.fr; closed mid-Jan to mid-Feb & late Oct to Dec; ❸), between the Enveitg village centre and the station. You can **camp** at either the riverside *Municipal de l'Oratoire* in Latour-de-Carol (☎04.68.04.83.70) or *Caravaneige Le Sègre* (☎04.68.04.65.87) in Bourg-Madame. At **Porté-Puymorens** (ⓦwww.porte-puymorens.net), which has a small gare SNCF, accommodation can be found at *Hôtel Restaurant du Col* (☎04.68.04.82.06, ☏04.68.04.87.22; ❸) down in the village. The valley-bottom **campsite** – *La Rivière* (☎04.68.04.82.20) – is open all year, but you'd have to be a polar bear to stay in winter.

The Carlit Massif

Being easy of access, the mountains of the **Carlit Massif** are popular, and the lakes – even where not dammed – are sometimes a little overly manicured, but still provide opportunities for several days of **trekking**. Three major walking routes which range in difficulty from moderate to extreme – the **HRP**, the north–south **GR7** and the trans-Pyrenean **GR10** – as well as marked secondary trails, cross the massif, while parts of the GR7 and GR10 comprise sections of the less demanding **Tour du Carlit**, aimed at hikers of medium experience. For all of these explorations you'll want the IGN 1:50,000 *Carte de Randonnées no. 7*, "Cerdagne-Capcir"; the IGN TOP 25 no. 2249 ET is also well worth having. The ascent of **Pic Carlit** (2921m) itself is within the capabilities of any reasonably fit person, especially from Lac des Bouillouses, accessible either by car or foot, on its eastern slopes.

Climbing Pic Carlit

A quick approach to the summit can be made from Mont-Louis on the **east** side, up the very narrow but paved D60 road. On a fine summer day, expect hundreds of cars at the **Lac des Bouillouses** parking area 13km along, with an even greater number of trippers milling about – definitely not virgin wilderness, and with family groups crammed four to a vehicle, you've little chance of hitching a lift. For purist hikers who don't mind a long slog, the **GR10** out of Bolquère, two stops west of Mont-Louis on the *Train Jaune*, climbs gently through woods to the **Col del Pam** (2005m), where it links with the HRP coming from Font-Romeu, both continuing past ski lifts and pistes to Lac des Bouillouses (5hr from either town).

There's plenty of **accommodation** and **food** at the Bouillouses lake, actually a huge reservoir dating from the early 1900s. The CAF-run *Refuge des Bouillouses* (formerly *Combaleran*; ☎04.68.04.20.76; dorm beds from €10, doubles with half-pension ❹), the cheapest option, stands east of the dam wall at just below 2000m. Tucked inconspicuously behind this is the smallish, privately managed *Auberge du Carlit* (☎04.68.04.22.23) which has rooms (❷) and a half-pension plan (❺), as well as a **gîte** (❶). Just above the west end of the dam at 2050m looms the gigantic *Refuge Le Bones Hores* (☎04.68.04.24.22, ⒻＯ4.68.04.13.63; obligatory half-board ❺), which is popular with families.

From next to *Le Bones Hores*, where a placard informs fishermen which lakes are legally open, you get on the **HRP**, whose course is scantily marked with faded paint splodges but deeply grooved into the terrain. You arc up gently through the woods, between **Étang Noir** and **Étang Vive**, reached twenty minutes along; the next natural lake, **Dougues**, is a mere 45 minutes above the dam, and thus a hugely popular outing. However, the crowds do thin somewhat as you press on past the necklace of smaller lakes – Casteilla, Trébens and Soubirans – under the shadow of **Touzal Colomé** (2804m), and finally up the ridge that leads to the summit from the east. This is a superb climb, with the tarns glinting in the sun, the grass green in June but usually a faded ochre by August, and the scree-strewn pyramid of Carlit overhead. There and back from Lac des Bouillouses is at most six-and-a-half hours, a day's walk in good conditions – though rather ominously there are green sheds by most of the lakes, for sheltering from the foul weather which is often not long in appearing. If – as so many do – you just want to take in the lakes, it's only a three-hour round trip from the dam to the highest one, Soubirans, at 2320m.

The Tech valley and the Albères

Running more or less parallel to the Têt valley, but roughly 30km further south, the **Tech valley** (or Vallespir) is the southernmost in France, endowed with exceptional sunshine (300 days a year) and relatively low rainfall which nurtures a flora that includes oranges, cacti and bougainvillea – as well as dense forest on the higher, wetter slopes. Heading up the valley will take you through the Hispanified art-centre, **Céret**, and on to **Arles-sur-Tech**, the gateway to the exciting **Gorges de la Fou**. Further upstream, the upper Tech is dominated by **Prats-de-Molló**, where the main road departs from the river to reach the Spanish frontier. The northern face of the Pyrenees, rising out of the sea at the rugged Côte Vermeille and bordered by the Tech to the north, is known as the **Albères**. Here, a myriad of paths – a traditional route of shepherds, refugees and smugglers – cross the frontier into Spain, which is officially marked by the village of **Le Perthus**. Access into both regions from

Perpignan by car or bus is via **Le Boulou**, where the N9 splits to head straight south for Le Perthus, and west to shadow the Tech valley as the D115.

South to Le Perthus

Aside from being the cork capital of France, **LE BOULOU**, 20km south of Perpignan, is a fairly nondescript little spa town, although it is worth stopping at the **Église Ste-Marie,** the doorway of which features a fine frieze by the "Master of Cabestany" (see box on p.111).There is also a small **history museum**, the *Espace des Arts* (Mon–Fri 9am–noon & 2–6pm, Sun 9am–noon; free), with more works by the master. Die-hard fans should drive or cycle 14km north to the outskirts of Passa, where the cloister, **Monastir del Camp Prieuré** (tours on the hour Fri–Wed 10am July–Sept 10am–noon & 3–6pm; €4), features more of the anonymous sculptor's work. To further tempt, the monastery is now a wine *domaine*, where you can taste local vintages.

Heading east from Le Boulou will take you past a number of other Romanesque monuments (see box on p.378), or head a few minutes south, where the Tech cuts by on its way to the sea, to visit the remarkable **chapel of St-Martin-de-Fenollar** (mid-June to mid-Sept daily 10.30am–noon & 3.30–7pm; mid-Sept to mid-June Mon & Wed–Sun 2–5pm; €3) in Maureillas-las-Illas. Its twelfth-century frescoes are the best Romanesque wall-paintings in Roussillon, and their clarity and simplicity of line may well have been influential on Picasso, who sometimes stayed in nearby Céret. Nine kilometres further south, **LE PERTHUS** was marked in history on the night of February 5, 1939, when a column of twenty thousand Spanish Republicans arrived at the border post to seek sanctuary in France. Nowadays consumer armies descend here every day, disgorging from coaches to spend their money on foodstuffs, booze and perfume, or to cross the border to fill up their tanks in Spain. The main landmark is **Fort de Bellegarde** (July–Sept daily 10.30am–6.30pm; €3), which looms on a peak above the town. Built in the sixteenth century and later reinforced by Vauban, it comprises two rows of dilapidated buildings and the deepest well in Europe (63m) within an enclosure of mighty walls, and gives superb views south into Spain and north across Roussillon. In Roman times the Via Domitia crossed the Albères 2km to the west at the **Col de Panissars**, accessible by the narrow road which continues past Fort Bellegarde, and is probably the way that Hannibal came in 218 BC. When Pompey returned to Rome fresh from putting down a rebellion in Spain a century and a half later, he ordered a triumphal monument to be built at the col, and the excavated base of this edifice is now visible through a cordon of barbed wire.

Le Boulou's **tourist office** (Mon–Fri 9am–noon & 2–6pm, Sun 9am–noon; ☎04.68.87.50.95, ⓦwww.ot-leboulou.fr) is in the central place de la Mairie. With its proximity to Perpignan, the coast and Céret, spending the night in the Albères may not seem an obvious choice. But if you are looking for a cheap alternative in high season or are making the rounds of the local Romanesque churches, you could do worse. There are a few **hotels** here, including *Chez Grand-Mère* in Le Perthus, at the summit of the main road (☎04.68.83.60.96. Ⓕ04.68.8363.72; ❹ with obligatory half-pension), and *Le Grillon* (☎04.68.83.03.60, Ⓔle-grillon@wanadoo.fr, ❸) in 40 rue de la République at Le Boulou (*menus* €15–35).The deluxe option is the elegantly rustic *Le Relais des Chartreuses* (mid-March to Oct; ☎04.68.83.15.88; ❸–❻), set in an old Catalan *masia* (farmhouse) on 106 av d'En Carbouner in Le Boulou, while at the bottom end of the budget scale there's a *gîte* (☎04.68.83.62.20; ❶) 5km east of Le Perthus in l'Albère. If you do go to Le Perthus, the best option for a meal is to hop across the border into Spain, where any of La Jonquera's many bustling **roadside eateries** will lay out an all-you-can-eat buffet, or a hefty four-course meal for €8–12. If you do nip into Spain, taking the toll *autoroute* (less than €1) will probably save you hours of delay in bottle-necked Le Perthus.

Céret

Just 10km or so upstream along the Tech from Le Boulou lies the cherry capital of southern France, **CÉRET**, a friendly and bustling place with a shady old town of narrow and winding streets, still dominated by its much built-into medieval fortifications. The best time to visit is during any of the town's famous **festivals** (see box on pp.242–3), which have a markedly Catalan and Spanish flavour, including *sardanas* and *corridas* held in the arena to the north of town – but you'll have to plan ahead, as accommodation sells out well in advance. At the entrance to the town, the single-arched **Pont du Diable** was said to have been built by the Devil in 1321 in return for the soul of the first Cérétan to cross. The engineer who made the bargain duly sent a cat over first, but the trick backfired as none of the locals would then risk the Devil's vengeance by using the bridge themselves. Like Prades on the Têt, Céret was a place of refuge for escapees from Franco's fascist regime, with many artists passing through or staying here. At that point, the town was already a creative colony, having been a temporary home to luminaries such as Pablo Picasso, Marc Chagall and a clutch of Catalan and French artists, including Pierre Brune, who in 1950 opened the **Musée d'Art Moderne** at 8 bd Maréchal Joffre (mid-June to mid-Sept daily 10am–7pm; rest of year Wed–Mon 10am–6pm; **W**www.musee-ceret.com; €5.50). This museum's small but varied collection includes works by the Fauvists, Cubists and Surrealists, as well as pieces by recent artists such as Tàpies, but the highlight is a series of painted bowls with bull motifs by Picasso. Other sights in the town include the small **archeological museum** (daily 10am–noon & 2–6pm; €1.50) tucked behind one of the old gates, the **war memorial** by Aristide Maillol in the old town and the **monument** to the composer Déodat de Sévérac by the Catalan sculptor Manolo in avenue Clemenceau. If you head north 100m from the town centre on avenue d'Espagne, you'll come upon **Le Capelleta** (Sat 10.30am–12.30pm & 3.30–7pm; free), a tiny church with a well-executed Romanesque lintel over the entrance, which houses temporary art exhibits.

Practicalities

The **tourist office** (July & Aug Mon–Sat 9am–12.30pm & 2–7pm; Sept–May Mon–Fri 10am–noon & 2–5pm, Sat 10am–noon; **T**04.68.87.00.53, **W**www.ot-ceret.fr) is at the top of avenue Clemenceau, on the corner of boulevard Maréchal Joffre. The most central **accommodation** is provided by the atmospheric one-star *Vidal*, housed in the old bishop's palace, off place Soutine (**T**04.68.87.00.85, **W**www.hotelvidalceret.com; ➋). Opposite stands the two-star *Arcades* (**T**04.68.87.12.30, **F**04.68.87.49.44; ➌), and you might also try the *Pyrénées* on rue de la République (**T**04.68.87.11.02, **E**ericlegentil@wanadoo.fr; ➌). All these places have a variety of rooms available, with and without bath. The best option, however, is *Le Mas Trilles* (**T**04.68.87.38.37, **F**04.68.87.42.62; ➎) at Le Pont de Reynes, a small hotel set in a seventeenth-century *mas* overlooking the Tech. There are several local **campsites**, two of them on route de Maureillas: *Les Cerisiers* (**T**04.68.87.00.08; closed Nov–Feb) and *Saint-Géorges* (**T**04.68.87.03.73). If you are interested in guided **hikes**, contact Céret Les Sentiers de Pyrène (**T**04.68.87.06.93, **E**leyaouanq@aol.com; English spoken), or VTT 66 (**T**04.68.87.44.16) for **biking** excursions.

When it comes to **eating**, you should perhaps forgo the hotel kitchens in favour of the good bistro-crêperie, *Le Pied dans le Plat* (closed Sun; from €11.20), and an adjacent pizzeria, both on place des Neuf-Jets, with outdoor seating. Social life at the *Grand Café* in boulevard Maréchal Joffre is perhaps not what it was when the "made Picasso" hung out there, but it's still a good place to sit outside with a glass of wine and a plate of *frites*; there are more **cafés** around the corner by the Porte de France. Finer dining can be found at *Les Feuillants* (☎04.68.87.37.88), set in a grand old house at 1 boulevard La Fayette (*menus* €30 and €46). Saturdays see a morning farmers' **market** along the old walls, the street stalls groaning with local produce.

Arles-sur-Tech and around

Continuing upstream from Céret, the next town which merits a visit is **ARLES-SUR-TECH**, which is known for having preserved the curious folk traditions of the eastern Pyrenees – if you can manage it, try to make it for one of the several festivals that are celebrated throughout the year (see box on pp.343–4). The heart of the town is formed by its compact medieval quarter, centred on the eleventh-century **abbey-church of Ste-Marie** (Mon–Sat 9am–noon & 2–6pm; €3.40). Before passing through the main door built into its impressive facade, check out the grilled-off marble block just to the left. This is the *saint tombe*, a fourth-century sarcophagus, revered for the pure water which it miraculously issues, and which plays a key part in the town's ancient religious rituals. The interior of the church has a number of good **chapels**, as well as an elegant thirteenth-century **cloister**. The cloister itself leads to the **Musée du Fer**, which recreates the town's medieval iron-smelting and mining industries (April–June & Sept–Oct Mon–Fri 2–7pm; July & Aug Mon–Fri 10am–noon & 3–7pm, Sat 3–7pm; €2).

From Arles, you can **hike** up the northbound GR10 towards the Canigou, but a less ambitious and more spectacular option is the nearby **Gorges de la Fou** (☎04.68.39.16.21; April–Nov daily 10am–6pm, weather permitting; €5), one of the great – if touristy – spectacles of the eastern Pyrenees. It can be reached by taking the Corsavy road from Arles, or by ascending the trail leading off the D115, 3km west of Arles. You need at least an hour to cover the 1500m of metal walkway to the end and back, squeezing between 200-metre-high walls, so close together that they have trapped falling rocks. In places, water erosion has made the walls as smooth as plaster, and the force of the torrent during storms in 1988 was sufficient to sweep part of the walk away – when storms threaten, the route is closed. If you have your own transport, you should consider leaving the main road at Arles, and continuing past the top end of the Gorges de Fou trail to Corsavy and on to **MONTFERRER**, which, with its ruined castle and Romanesque church, is one of the most attractive settlements in the upper Tech. Set amongst dense forest and crags, with sweeping views east to the opposite side of the valley, it enjoys its status as the truffle capital of Roussillon.

South of the main road a tortuous side road ascends through forests of sweet chestnut to the village of **ST-LAURENT-DE-CERDANS**, an important junction on the World War II refugee route to Spain. Here the local history museum, **Musée d'Arts et Traditions Populaire** (May, June & Sept daily 10am–noon & 3–6pm; July & Aug 10am–noon & 2–7pm; Oct–April Mon–Fri 10am–noon & 3–6pm; €2), preserves rural arts such as the manufacture of espadrilles, the traditional esparto woven shoes favoured by refugee guides (*passeurs*). The **market** is held on Saturday. Further on at tiny **COUS-TOUGES**, the spine of the Albères rises northeastwards to the highest point of the chain at **Roc de France** (1450m).

Practicalities

Buses stop in Arles a short walk from the **tourist office** (Mon–Sat 9am–noon & 2–6pm; ☎ & ℻ 04.68.39.11.99, ⓦ www.villes-arles-sur-tech.fr), in rue Barjou at the top of the town, which has suggestions for walks and trails around Arles, and also stocks a list of *chambres d'hôtes*, invaluable in hotel-poor Arles. The place to **stay** in town is the comfortable two-star *Les Glycines*, 7 rue du Jeu-de-Paume (☎ 04.68.39.10.09, ✉ hotelglycines@wanadoo.fr; ❸), which also has the best **restaurant**, with a shaded terrace and Catalan specialities (*menus* from €18). Among **campsites**, the scenic *Riuferrer* (☎ 04.68.39.11.06), is on the west side of town, near the mouth of the Freixe stream; *Le Vallespir* (☎ 04.68.39.90.00; closed Nov–March) lies on the road to Amélie-les-Bains; or there's the naturist camp *Le Ventous* (☎ 04.68.87.83.38, ⓦ www.perso.club-internet.fr/le vento; June–Sept) on the road to Prats-de-Molló. Between St-Laurent and Coustouges you can stay at the very comfortable but pricey *Domaine de Falgos* (closed Jan & Feb; ☎ 04.68.39.51.42, ⓦ www.silencehotel.com; ❼), converted from an old barn. Arles' alternatives for **eating** – other than *Les Glycines* – are *La Treille* (closed Mon Sept–May ☎ 04.68.39.89.59) at the beginning of boulevard Riuferrer, with a pleasant vine-shaded terrace (€12 *menu*) or the grill-bar at the Musée Jean Cordomi (€15 and up; March–Dec 10am–10pm), opposite the *mairie*.

Prats-de-Molló

From Arles, the road climbs 19km to the medieval city of **PRATS-DE-MOLLÓ**, and its sister town of **La Preste**, famous as a spa since 1302. The present road follows the path of a former railway (the station houses can be seen along the way), since the old road, along with houses and bridges, was washed away in the disastrous floods of October 1940. In the seventeenth century, when the Treaty of the Pyrenees subjected this area to the outrageous tax policies of Louis XIV, Prats-de-Molló and a number of other towns and villages revolted against the French Crown. Living at the far end of what was then a densely wooded valley, the rebels probably felt themselves invulnerable when they murdered the king's tax collectors. And indeed, they held off two battalions before the forces of Maréchal de Noailles made a surprise attack over the western flanks of Canigou to put down the insurrection.

Fort Lagarde (daily: April–June 2–6pm; July & Aug 10am–6pm; Sept–March 2–5pm; €3.50), which dominates the town from above, was built in 1680 under the direction of Vauban, as much to subdue the local population as to keep the Spanish at bay; the town walls, raised on fourteenth-century foundations, are another Vauban relic from this period. To make the 25-minute climb up to the fort, head for Porte de la Fabrique on the north side of town, then either follow the footpath which winds up the hill from behind the church or take the covered walk which starts in a ruined building to the right of the cemetery entrance. The fort itself has been beautifully restored, and there are superb views all around from the ramparts. An extra attraction here is the **Visite-Spectacle** on summer afternoons, when horsemen dressed as cavaliers recreate eighteenth-century cavalry training, with trick riding, sword fights and the firing of muskets and cannons (Mon–Fri & Sun: July & Aug 2.30pm & 4pm; June 3.30pm; €7).

With Canigou at its back and the River Tech in front, picturesque Prats-de-Molló has now become a tourist attraction but is still surprisingly unspoilt – particularly the old *ville haute* within the city wall, with its steep, cobbled streets and ancient fortified church. In summer, the pedestrianized streets buzz with activity; the rest of the year the hotels are locked up, and the locals pass the time playing *boules* under the plane trees of El Firal, the huge square outside the walls, where markets and fairs have been held since 1308.

Practicalities

The **tourist office** in place du Foiral (July & Aug daily 9am–12.30pm & 1.30–6.30pm; April–June, Sept & Oct Mon–Sat 9am–noon & 2–6pm; Jan–March, Nov & Dec Mon–Fri 9am–noon & 2–6pm; ☎04.68.39.70.83, Ⓦwww.pratsdemollolapreste.com) has a wealth of information, including maps and advice for walking in the Haut-Vallespir. Nearby, the Maison de la Réserve in La Preste (☎04.68.39.74.49, Ⓔresnatprats@wanadoo.fr) can arrange guides for one to five day hikes into the upper Tech. There is a good selection of **hotels** here. The best deal is the *Hotel des Touristes* (☎04.68.39.72.12; Ⓕ04.68.39.79.22; ❷) at 3 av Haut-Vallespir, decorated with original antique furniture. Otherwise, the family-orientated *Le Relais*, no. 3 on place Joseph Trinxeria (☎04.68.39.71.30, Ⓦwww.lerelaishotel.com; ❷) and the friendly *Bellevue* overlooking place le Foiral (☎04.68.39.72.48, Ⓕ04.68.39.78.04, Ⓦwww.logis-de-france.fr; closed Nov–March; ❸) are good, and serve reasonable meals. A better choice of **restaurant**, however, is *Costabonne* (☎04.68.39.70.24) at 6 place du Foiral, renown for its home-made *foie gras* (*menus* from €12.50). You can also stay at the **gîtes** *Chalet de Conques* (☎04.68.39.23.49; ❶) or *Notre Dame de Coral* (☎ & Ⓕ04.68.39.75.00; ❶), and there's plenty of local **camping**, too. The two sites with the longest seasons are *St Martin* (☎04.68.39.77.40; closed Dec) and *Can Nadal* (☎04.68.39.70.89; April–Nov) about 1km along the road towards La Preste. Stock up on supplies at the local **market**, held Wednesday and Friday mornings.

The Côte Vermeille

When the nineteenth-century Fauvists discovered the **Côte Vermeille**, which extends southeast from Argelès-sur-Mer to the Spanish border, they found natural inspiration for their revolutionary use of colour: the sunsets (from which the coast earned its name) are a gentle red, the sea is turquoise and, as Matisse wrote, "no sky is more blue than that at Collioure." **Elne**, inland, and once Roussillon's main town, is the gateway to the coast, and proceeding south you'll pass the broad beaches of **Argelès**, before reaching the characteristically rocky coves of **Collioure**, **Banyuls** and **Cerbère**. The beauty of this stretch of coastline has inevitably been exploited, but cut up along the trails into the hills at the back of the resorts and you'll often be on your own. Public transport along the coast is good, with a regular train and bus service connecting all the major points of call.

Elne

Standing on a hill just 6km from the sea, the first stop on the coastal transport line is **ELNE**, an ancient fortified town which was once the capital of Roussillon. Despite the heavy beach-bound traffic whizzing past on the main road, the old town, inside the sixteenth-century ramparts, is eerily quiet after dark. Its one great attraction is the former **cathedral of Ste-Eulalie** (daily: April & May 9.30am–6pm; June–Sept 9.30am–7pm; Oct 9.30am–12.30pm & 2–6pm; Nov–March 9.30am–12.30pm & 2–5pm; €5), the seat of Roussillon's bishops until their transfer to Perpignan in 1602. The **cloister**, built from Céret marble, is the highlight: one intact side of twelfth-century Romanesque pillars and capitals, immaculately carved with motifs such as foliage, lions, goats and biblical figures, is complemented on the other sides by fourteenth-century Gothic work. A small museum in the twelfth-century St-Laurent chapel, which you access from the cloister, is mainly given over to exhibits found in the excavations of Roman villas around Elne. Opposite the cathedral, at 3 rue Balaguer, is the **Musée Terrus** (same times and ticket as the cathedral), dedicated to the landscape painter Étienne Terrus (1857–1922), a contemporary of the Fauvists and friend of sculptor Aristide Maillol (whose bust of Terrus stands on the plateau des Garaffes, nearby); the *salon de thé*, on the first floor, has a panoramic view.

Practicalities

The **gare SNCF** (℡04.68.22.06.15), on the main line from Perpignan to the Côte Vermeille, lies about ten minutes' walk west of the old town; **buses** stop at the parking area in the centre, near the cathedral. The **tourist office** is at 2 rue du Docteur Bolte (June & Sept Mon–Fri 9.30am–noon & 2–5pm, Sat 9.30am–noon; July & Aug Mon–Fri 9.30am–noon & 2–6pm, Sat 9.30am–noon; Oct–May Mon–Fri 9.30am–noon & 2–5pm; ℡04.68.22.05.07, Ⓦwww.ot-elne.fr), between the post office and Hôtel de Ville. Of the three **hotels**, the modest *Cara Sol*, in boulevard Illibéris on the edge of the old town (℡04.68.22.10.42, Ⓦwww.hotelcarasol.com; ❷), offers the best value and location, with great views from the front rooms over the Tech valley, the Albères and Canigou. For slightly more luxury in the same price bracket, the two-star *Le Weekend*, 31 av Paul Reig (℡04.68.22.06.68, Ⓔhotel.weekend@libertysurf.fr; ❷), just off centre on the Argelès road, has a celebrated garden **restaurant** (*menus* from €16). There are two municipal **campsites** (June to late Sept): *Les Padraguets* (℡04.68.22.21.59) on the Argelès road and *Al Mouly* (℡04.68.22.08.46) on boulevard d'Archimède, in the direction of St-Cyprien. The local **market** is held on the place de la République (Mon, Wed & Fri).

Argelès-sur-Mer and around

Poised on the northern edge of the Côte Vermeille, **ARGELÈS-SUR-MER** has the last wide, sandy beach on the coast. At the end of the Spanish Civil War thousands of refugees lived in camps here, their numbers including the Republican poet Antonio Machado, who failed to survive the first harsh winter. Not surprisingly, given camp conditions, nearly ten thousand of the inmates volunteered to serve in the French army upon the 1939 outbreak of hostilities. Nowadays, more than any other resort on this section of coast, this is a mass-tourist town, wooing its visitors with holiday essentials like mini-golf, gambling tables and beauty contests.

The town itself is divided in two: the old **Argelès–Ville**, a little inland, and the new **Argelès–Plage**, which receives an annual inundation of up to 300,000 French, Belgian, Dutch and English visitors. Plage Nord and Plage des Pins are **beaches** of the smooth, sandy and potentially windblown variety, whereas **Le Racou** – the first bay of the Côte Vermeille – is more intimate and

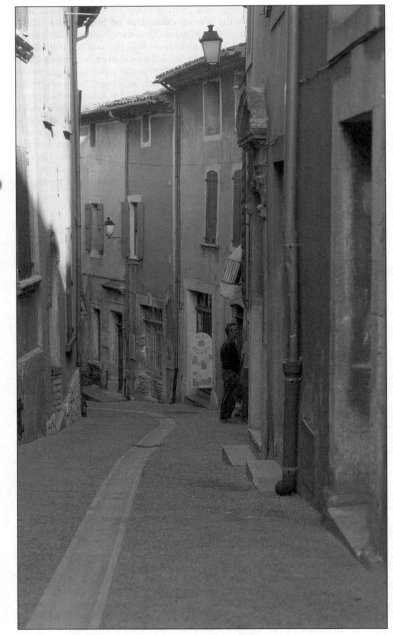

▲ Roussillon street

Romanesque in the Albères

The northern slopes of the Pyrenees and the plains which spill out below them were heavily populated in the Middle Ages, a fact attested to by the numerous churches and monasteries which were built here a millennium ago. This was not the wealthiest area, and these humble foundations cannot compete with the grandeur of Toulouse or the North of France, but the very fact that they were relatively isolated and poor means that many of their original features, which would have been remodeled and effaced elsewhere, have been left intact. **Romanesque churches** here are typically compact and squat, with few windows and single-naved chapels capped by primitive barrel-vaulting. The surviving artwork from this period is chiefly in sculpture and painting. Romanesque sculptors, the most famous of whom is the "Master of Cabestany" (see box on p.111), devoted their attention to capitals and corbels, which they shaped into complex vegetal and geometric patterns or carved into biblical scenes peopled by bulbous-featured human figures; their best work is often found on the lintel above a church's main door. Rarer, and more striking, are the magnificent frescos which once fully covered the interiors of many of these buildings. Fresco painting lends itself well to the bold and colourful (and surprisingly modern-looking) designs favoured by these artists. These frescos served to dramatically illustrate biblical scenes for the illiterate parishioners; Old Testament patriarchs, apostles, God and the angels were brought to life in vivid, kinetic scenes.

In addition to the better-known sites, such as Elne, St-Génis and St-Martin-de-Fenollar, several other churches can be taken in on a circuit of the area. Touring by bicycle, scooter or car will take a day, or you can walk, if you don't mind taking longer – either way, it's a stimulating break from the easy beach-side hedonism of Argelès and Collioure. Heading west out of Argelès, you'll pass the N114, after which a minor road leads 3km to **St-André** (non-suicidal cyclists should avoid the busy D618). Here an old abbey-church in allée de la Liberté houses the **Musée Transfrontalier d'Art Roman** (June–Sept Mon–Sat 9am–noon & 2–6.30pm; Oct–May Wed–Sat 10am–noon & 2–5.30pm; €2), which is visited on an hour-long guided tour. A further 5km takes you to St-Génis (see p.380), where another former abbey holds a rich sculpture collection. From here the D11 leads 3.5km south to Laroque, where it continues west to Villelongue-des-Monts. Here a steep and winding road, intermittently sign-posted for the "Église", leads up to the former Augustine convent and pilgrims' hostel of **Santa Maria Vilar** (daily 3–6pm; 1hr guided tour; €4). Originally founded in 1089, the present church dates to 1149, although sections, such as the impressive Carolingian hall, are older. The main attractions here are the beautiful eleventh- and twelfth-century fresco murals, featuring both geometric and human motifs. Santa Maria is home to a renowned Festival Lyrique, featuring Gregorian chant and troubadours (July & Aug Sat 9pm; €16; see box on p.344) – an event well worth planning for. A further 2km along the road brings you to the ancient chapel of **Santa Coloma de Cabanes** (irregular hours). From here you can follow the D2 back east to Argelès, or continue on the D11 to Montesquieu-des-Albères (3km), before descending to Le Boulou.

offers a taste of mountain coastline. The only cultural attraction is the old town's **Casa de les Albères**, in place des Castellans, a small museum of local art and traditions, mostly agricultural tools and implements (June–Sept Mon–Fri 9am–noon & 3–6pm, Sat 9am–noon; €2). Otherwise, a great attraction for children and adults alike is **Les Aigles du Château de Valmy** (March–June & Sept Tues–Sun 1.30–6.30pm; July & Aug daily 1.30–6.30pm; €7.50–9), which puts on exhibits of birds of prey and sheepdogs at Valmy castle, just over the RN112 from Argelès (exit 12).

Some 10km due west of Argelès, **ST-GÉNIS-DES-FONTAINES** was once home to an ancient Benedictine abbey. Most of this has disappeared, but the two-metre lintel over the doorway of the church, dating from 1020, is one of the earliest examples of Romanesque sculpture in France – a disarmingly archaic array of apostles and angels. When the church is open (June–Sept Mon–Fri 10am–noon & 3–7pm, Sat & Sun 9am–noon & 3–7pm; Oct–May daily 9.30am–noon & 2–5pm; €2) you can visit its fine thirteenth-century Romanesque cloister, whose single row of short columns supports semicircular arches of multicoloured marble (white from Céret, pink from Villefranche, black from Baixas), and has capitals carved with engaging primitive figures: half-human and half-beasts, fantastic creatures, and Christ crucified. St-Génis is only one in a constellation of beautiful Romanesque churches, spreading down from the Pyrenees onto the Roussillon littoral; for more on this subject see the box on p.378.

Practicalities

The **gare SNCF** is a few minutes' walk west of the centre of the Argelès-Ville, while **buses** stop opposite the Hôtel de Ville. An hourly bus service (€2) runs in summer between the station, the old town and Plage-Nord. There is a summer-only **tourist office** in the old town (July & Aug Mon–Sat 9.30am–12.30pm & 2.30–6.30pm; ☎04.68.95.81.55, ☏04.68.95.16.01), by the Hôtel de Ville on allée Ferdinand-Buisson; Argelès-Plage has its own office (summer daily 8.30am–8pm; winter Mon–Fri 9am–noon & 2–6pm, Sat 9am–noon; ☎04.68.81.15.85, ⊛www.argeles-sur-mer.com), in place de l'Europe, on the corner of avenue des Platanes and avenue des Mimosas. Holiday Bikes (☎04.68.95.86.34, ✉argeles@holidaybikes.com) on avenue Charles-de-Gaulle, rents out **bikes** and **motorbikes**.

    Accommodation can be difficult to find in midsummer, especially for a short stay. The best choice for a hotel in Argelès-Ville is *La Belle Demeure* (☎04.68.95.85.85, ✉belle.demeure@little-france.com; ➌), a renovated Catalan *masia* on Chemin du Roua. For those on a budget, the two-star *Clair Logis*, 78 route de Collioure (☎04.68.81.03.27, ☏04.68.95.93.01; ➋) is a good choice. Among dozens of hotels in Argelès-Plage, the two-star *Les Mimosas*, 51 avenue des Mimosas (☎04.68.81.14.77, ✉hotellesmimosasm@minitel.net; ➌), and *Al Pescadou*, rue des Aloes (☎04.68.81.31.12, ✉franckfrexinos@wanadoo.fr; ➌), are reasonably priced and well situated. There should never be a problem finding a spot for your tent, as there are more than fifty **campsites** in the neighbourhood. Two with good beach access are the three-star *Beauséjour* (☎04.68.81.10.63; April to mid-Oct) near Centre Plage and *Les Pins* (☎04.68.81.10.46; mid-May to late Sept) on avenue du Tech. The **food** situation in Argelès is a little on the bleak side, rarely rising above mediocre beach-town fare. One of the few places that manages to stand out is *Amadeus* (closed Mon April–Nov & all Jan; ☎04.68.81.12.38) on avenue des Platanes (by Argelès-Plage's tourist office), which offers reasonable Catalan dishes, with *menus* from €20. A regular **market** (Wed & Sat) is held year-round in Argelès-Ville, and from mid-June to mid-September markets convene daily in Argelès-plage.

Collioure

Eleven kilometres down the coast from Argelès-sur-Mer, **COLLIOURE**, a true Côte Vermeille town, which to a certain extent still banks on its maritime and artistic past, sits nestled in a picturesque cove. Established as a trading port by the Phoenicians and ancient Greeks, Collioure was later occupied by Romans, Visigoths and Arabs. Altogether, the place has been the focus of nearly a dozen territorial squabbles, including four invasions by the French and two by the Spanish. The sixteenth-century **Fort St Elme** overlooking the town from the south (now privately owned), and the seventeenth-century **Fort Miradou** to the north (still used by the military), are reminders of this turbulent past. In the early 1900s, invaders of a different sort came; the group of painters – including Matisse and Derain – known as the **Fauvists** (*les Fauves*) made Collioure their summer base. Some of their original work adorns the bar at *Les Templiers* (see opposite); you can also follow the "Chemin du Fauvisme" around the town, a trail of twenty reproductions of paintings by Matisse and Derain placed on the sites where they were painted (a map is available from the tourist office; regular guided tours; €6). Collioure's **Musée d'Art Moderne** (July & Aug daily 10am–noon & 2–6pm; Sept–June Mon & Wed–Sun same times; €3), housed in the beautiful Villa Pams on the edge of the town in route de Port-Vendres, has a small permanent collection, which includes Picasso's poster *Hommage à Antonio Machado*, remembering the Spanish Republican poet and martyr, who is buried in the town, and temporary exhibitions by artists associated with the region.

The artistic tradition of Collioure survives today, albeit with less distinction; the forest of easels that occupies the promenade in summer produces mainly tourist souvenirs, but there are also a few serious commercial galleries. Many of these are in the old quarter of the town, the **Mouré**, whose steep, narrow streets are lined by pastel-tinted houses and assorted shops and cafés. Lateen-rigged fishing boats might be moored in the **harbour** itself, or drawn up on the palm-lined beach; those no longer used by fishermen are now beautifully restored and sailed as pleasure vessels by their new owners. The **château-royal** (daily: June–Sept 10am–6pm; Oct–May 9am–5pm; €4), the imposing fortress which dominates the harbour, was founded by the Templars in the twelfth century, rebuilt and used as a sometime residence by the kings of Mallorca and Aragón two hundred years later, and modernized by Vauban after the Treaty of the Pyrenees. Impressive as it may be from the inside, the fortress is hardly worth going into unless you are going to attend one of the concerts hosted in the ramshackle courtyard; the bare rooms hold a few mediocre exhibitions that lack explanatory information (a French-only pamphlet is available for €2). On the other hand, the two **beaches** which bookend the castle are worth the time, although they become hopelessly crowded in summer months. One is sandy and the other stony, so you can take your pick, or head up to the **nude beach** just around the cape at the town's north end.

At the opposite end of the harbour, the **church of Notre-Dame-des-Anges** was erected in the seventeenth century, replacing the ancient Ste-Marie, razed on the orders of Vauban. The distinctive round bell tower – once doubling as the lighthouse – onto which it was grafted has been damaged many times by storm and war: the base dates from the thirteenth century, the middle from the fourteenth to seventeenth centuries, and the bell chamber from the nineteenth. It's worth taking a look inside (daily 8am–noon & 2–5.30pm) to see the magnificent gilt retable, carved and painted in three tiers, another work by Joseph Sunyer. Beyond the church, the tiny **Chapelle-St-Vincent** stands above the sea on a rocky peninsula, with the south-facing St Vincent beach on one side and the Plage Nord on the other.

Practicalities

Collioure's **gare SNCF** is less than ten minutes' walk west of the centre, along avenue Aristide Maillol; **buses** stop at the central car park, off avenue Général de Gaulle. **Parking** on the street is usually a nightmare here; unless you luck out, head for the large and reasonably priced parking lot on the hill which rises over the sea behind the castle. The very helpful **tourist office** is just behind the har-

ROUSSILLON | The Côte Vermeille

bour in place du 18 Juin (July & Aug daily 9am–8pm; Sept–June Mon–Sat 9am–noon & 2–6.30pm; ☎04.68.82.15.47, ℻04.68.82.46.29, ⓦwww.collioure.com) and there is also an information kiosk (July–Sept Mon–Sat 9am–5pm) in the small tower by the beach on the other side of the castle.

The quieter Plage Boutigue, southeast of the harbour, has some desirable seaview **hotels**, the best of which is *Triton*, 1 rue Jean-Bart (☎04.68.98.39.39, ⓔhoteltriton@wanadoo.fr; ❸).The most unusual accommodation is *Hostellerie des Templiers*, 12 quai de l'Amirauté (☎04.68.98.31.10, ⓦwww.hotel-templiers.com; ❸), in which the individually decorated rooms, staircases and dining rooms are filled with original artworks; reservations here are essential, and if you do call ahead, make sure your reservation is for the main building, and not one of the less-attractive annexes. For something quieter, try the very attractive *La Casa Païral*, in impasse des Palmiers (☎04.68.82.05.81, ⓔcontact@hotel-casa-pairal.com; closed Nov & Dec; ❺).There are two seasonal (April–Sept) **campsites** to the north of the town, near the coast: *Les Amandiers* (☎04.68.81.14.69), in the sheltered bay known as L'Ouille, and, better, *La Girelle*, plage d'Ouille (☎04.68.81.25.56).

For **eating**, there's a great choice of very reasonable crêperies, sandwich bars and pizza-pasta places around the old Mouré quarter, but it's worth paying the premium to sit at a table on the fashionable rue Camille Pelletan, by the harbour, to watch the world go by – the most atmospheric is *Les Templiers*, a café-bar well known to the Fauvists, and now filled with drawings and paintings donated by Matisse, Maillol, Picasso and Dufy, among many other artists. While in town, try to sample the famous salted anchovies, a local standby and an important component in Roussillonaise cookery. **Markets** (Wed & Sun morning) are held in place du Maréchal Leclerc. *Collioure Location* (☎04.68.82.24.59) at 7 av Général du Gaulle rents **bikes** and **scooters** by the day or week.

Port-Vendres

The next settlement southeast, **PORT-VENDRES**, a five-minute ride from Collioure, is marred by the busy main road, but for a genuine, unsophisticated fishing port, this is your best (indeed only) choice on the Côte Vermeille – though you probably won't want to stay longer than it takes to have a look around the port and tuck into a fish lunch, or to watch the fish auctions which take place at the far end of the port every weekday evening (usually 5–7pm). A huge fish-processing factory dominates one side of the harbour, while sardine- and tuna-fishing boats are moored under the Maillol-designed war memorial opposite, with nets and other paraphernalia piled along the harbour wall. Salt has taken its toll on Maillol's work, and the uncharacteristically draped figures have lost limbs, noses and various other features.

To the Romans, the town was Portus Veneris (Port of Venus), a place of strategic trading importance. By the Middle Ages its significance was diminishing in direct relation to the rising star of neighbouring Collioure, but by the eighteenth century it had recovered somewhat through the business of shipping Roussillon wines. In 1830 it became the primary port for dispatching soldiers and supplies to the French colony in Algeria, a link that lasted for more than a century. There is a regular Saturday **market** in town, as well as a Thursday-morning "Peasants' market" (mid-June to mid-Sept), but it's worth stopping in for lunch or dinner at the numerous quay-side fish **restaurants** on any day of the week.

Banyuls-sur-Mer to the Spanish border

As the road crosses the Col du Père Carnère and drops down towards the Plage des Elmes, the once-elegant wine town of **BANYULS-SUR-MER**, 6km south of Port-Vendres, comes into view, with dry-stone walls and orderly rows of vines stretching into the hills behind it. Banyuls is famous for its dessert wine, which the French tend to drink as an aperitif; if you fancy a tipple, try a 45-minute **guided tour** of one of the larger cellars, such as the Cellier des Templiers in route du Mas-Reig (April–Oct daily 10am–7.30pm; Nov–March Mon–Sat 10am–1pm & 2.30–6.30pm; free). Less fashionable than Collioure, Banyuls is still a lively and popular seaside resort. The busy road which runs along the seafront spoils it, and the wide, stony main beach is less attractive than some of the smaller bays to the north and south, but the whole town comes alive in the evenings when everyone gets together to promenade along the seafront, play *boules* or eat out at one of the many beach cafés and seafood restaurants.

You shouldn't leave Banyuls without visiting the **Laboratoire Arago**, the large white building overlooking the port. Run by the marine biology and land ecology department of the Sorbonne, its **aquarium** (daily: July & Aug 9am–noon & 2–10pm; Sept–June 9am–noon & 2–6.30pm; €4) comprises over forty tanks of fascinating local specimens, including seahorses, bright red starfish and wicked-looking eels, and is supplemented by a comprehensive display of local birds. The coastal waters of this area, rich in marine life due to the Pyrenees' steep underwater descent, were the first *réserve marine* to be declared in France, indeed throughout the Mediterranean. If you have the necessary qualifications you can **dive** within the reserve area by contacting Plongez Rederis Club, operating from the port (℡04.68.88.31.66 or 04.68.92.02.01).

Practicalities

The **gare SNCF** lies at the very western edge of town, while **buses** stop on the coastal boulevard. The **tourist office** is on the seafront, opposite the *mairie* (July & Aug daily 9.30am–12.30pm & 2.30–7pm; Sept–June Tues–Sat 9.30am–12.30pm & 2–6.30pm; ℡04.68.88.31.58, Ⓦwww.banyuls-sur-mer.com). Recommendable one-star **hotels**, open all year, include the quaint and unpretentious *Hôtel Canal*, 9 rue Dugommier (℡04.68.88.00.75, Ⓔhotelcanal@aol.com; ❶), and the slightly smarter *Le Manoir*, 20 rue de Maréchal-Joffre (℡04.68.88.32.98; closed Nov & Dec; ❷), both in the quieter back streets. For a reasonably priced hotel on the seafront, try *El Llagut*, 18 avenue du Fontaulé (℡04.68.88.00.81, Ⓦwww.al-fanal.com; closed Nov & Dec; ❷), near the port, where many of the rooms have a balcony and sea view. Another good option is *Les Elmes* (℡04.68.88.03.12, Ⓦwww.hotel-des-elmes.com; ❸) perched on the cliffs at the north end of town; not only is it comfortable and well-equipped, but it also has a private beach. **Camping** is at the *Camping du Stade*, rue Jean Boin (℡04.68.88.35.66; mid-June to early Sept), or the cheaper *Camping Municipal La Pinede* nearby, on route du Mas-Reig (℡04.68.88.32.13; late March to early Nov).

Banyuls has a good choice of **restaurants** specializing in fresh seafood. The most expensive, with starched tablecloths and live lobster tanks – among which *Le Sardinal*, 4bis place Paul Reig, is reckoned the best – are lined up opposite the seafront, but there are several less expensive choices: the best of these is *Les Canadells*, just off the main boulevard at 4 avenue du Général de Gaulle, with delicious *menus* (from €10 at lunch, €16 at dinner; closed Sun eve & Mon Oct–March) and specializing in *zarzuela* and other fishy dishes. Nearby rue St-Pierre is home to a number of restaurants, including *Chez Rosa* at no. 22, *Casa Miguel*, which has Spanish and Catalan specialities, at no. 3 and the livelier *La Paillotte* at no. 14, which features eclectic world cuisine. The best choice here, however, is *La Littorine* (℡04.68.88.03.12) at the Plage les Elmes, where you can savour roast lobster, fire-grilled bass or squid in its own ink (from €26). The local morning **market** is held year-round on Sundays and Thursdays.

Maillol's tomb

The four-kilometre **hike** from Banyuls to **Maillol's tomb** and house makes a pleasant excursion up into the vine-clad Albères. Sculptor **Aristide Maillol** (1861–1944) was a Banyuls native famous for fleshy nude sculptures. He is buried at his farm, La Baillaurie, now restored as the **Musée Maillol** (daily: May–Sept 10am–noon & 4–7pm; Oct–April 10am–noon & 2–5pm; ⓦwww.museemaillol.com; €3.10), which contains his personal art collection, featuring works by Duchamp, Bonnard and Picasso. The artist's tomb is topped by his *La Pensée*. To get here, walk the length of avenue Général de Gaulle, until you pass under a bridge. Shortly afterwards, where the road curves around to the right, take the left-hand road, following the line of a river: signs from here point to the "Musée et Tombeau de Maillol". The round trip takes about two-and-a-half hours.

Cerbère

The Côte Vermeille comes to an end at **CERBÈRE**. The harbour is quite pretty and the mountain backdrop is impressive, but the beach is negligible. Depending on the service, train passengers have to change either here or on the Spanish side of the border, at the much nicer **Port Bou**, where the rail line changes track size. In Cerbère, you can **stay** and **eat** at *La Dorade* on the harbour (☎04.68.88.41.93, Ⓕ04.68.88.41.93; ➌) or tent down at the municipal *Camping Cap Peyrefite* (☎04.68.88.41.17).

Travel details

Trains

SNCF buses may run in lieu of trains on these lines; services are reduced on Sundays and holidays.
Note that the *Train Jaune* (see p.364) also runs a service up the Tech valley, and the *Train du Pays Cathares et du Fenouillèdes* (p.355) serves the Fenouillèdes.
Perpignan to: Argelès (26 daily; 20min); Banyuls-sur-Mer (26 daily; 30min); Carcassonne (24 daily; 1hr 15min–2hr); Cerbère (26 daily; 40min); Collioure (24 daily; 25min); Elne (24 daily; 10min); Ille-sur-Têt (8 daily; 22–35min); Montpellier (12 daily; 2hr 15min); Narbonne (24 daily; 36–45min); Nîmes (12 daily; 2hr 45min); Prades (9 daily; 45min); Salses (12 daily; 15min); Toulouse (15 daily; 2hr 30min–3hr 45min); Villefranche-de-Conflent (12 daily; 50min).
Villefranche-de-Conflent to: Font-Romeu (6–8 daily; 1hr 15min); Ille-sur-Têt (18 daily; 30min); Latour-de-Carol (5 daily; 2hr 45min); Mont-Louis (6–8 daily; 1hr); Perpignan (12 daily; 50min); Prades/Molitg (14 daily; 10min).

Buses

Many lines have no or reduced service on Saturdays, Sundays and holidays, and in summer months. The shuttle Roussillon Interplages runs

frequently from Port-Bacarès to Collioure and back (July & Aug only), connecting the beach towns inbetween.
Argelès to: Céret (1–2 daily; 1hr); St-Génis (Tues & Thurs daily; 22min).
Arles-sur-Tech to: Coustouges (3 daily; 40min); Prats-de-Mollό (6 daily; 15min); St-Laurent-de-Cerdans (2–4 daily; 30min).
Mont-Louis to: Formiguères (2–4 daily; 30min).
Perpignan to: Argelès (3 daily; 30min); Arles-sur-Tech (7 daily; 1hr 15min); Axat (2 daily, 1hr 40min); Banyuls-sur-Mer (3 daily; 1hr 10min); Cerbère (3 daily; 1hr 15min); Céret (14 daily; 55min); Collioure (3 daily; 45min); Elne (3 daily; 35min); Font-Romeu (2–3 daily; 2hr 30min); Ille-sur-Tet (11 daily; 35min); Latour-de-Carol (2–3 daily; 3hr); Le Perthus (6 daily; 45min); Mont-Louis (4 daily; 2hr 15min); Narbonne (daily; 2hr 30min); Prades (7 daily; 1hr); Prats-de-Mollό (7 daily; 1hr 40min); Quillan (2 daily; 1hr 30min); St-Génis (4 daily; 45min); St-Paul-le-Fenouillet (7 daily; 50min); Salses (4 daily; 15min); Tautavel (1–3 daily; 30–40min); Thuir (3–5 daily; 25min); Vernet (4 daily; 1hr 25min); Villefranche-de-Conflent (7 daily; 1hr 15min); Vinca (8 daily; 55min).
Prades to: Casteil (3 daily; 20min); Vernet (8 daily; 20min).
Villefranche-de-Conflent to: Casteil (3 daily; 20min); Prades (14 daily; 10min); Vernet-les-Bains (12 daily; 10min).

Contexts

Contexts

History 387–405

Books 405–410

History

T he two areas of Occitan Languedoc and Catalan Roussillon, in addition
to their own cultural particularities, have strong historical differences.
Languedoc was traditionally ruled by a native aristocracy, while
Roussillon fell into the ambit of Catalonia, fated to become part of
modern Spain. Even before they were integrated into the nation-state of
France, though, their geographical proximity meant there were parallels and
connections; each enjoyed its "golden age" in the Middle Ages, which may
account for the nostalgia with which the inhabitants regard the period, and
their shared borders saw considerable movement and contact.

Prehistory

The earliest traces of the human occupation of Languedoc and Roussillon date
back to the early **Paleolithic era** (Stone Age): the cranial remains of the slight
but upright *Homo erectus*, discovered in the 1970s at Tautavel, near Perpignan,
date back nearly half a million years. These early ancestors, who do not appear
to have harnessed fire, hunted with the aid of simple stone weapons and tools
and lived off the abundant (and dangerous) fauna of the region, which included wolves, hippos, rhinos, wild sheep and goats and the ferocious cave bear,
whose claw marks are still visible on cave walls in the region (for example at
Limousis, in the Montagne Noire). As the evolutionary tree branched off, taller
and smarter **Neanderthal** humans appeared, dominating the local scene during the mid-Paleolithic era (approximately 150,000–35,000 BC). With a better
tool-making capability than *Homo erectus*, the Neanderthals were able to pursue
the mammoths and elephants of the Languedocian plain, and the remains of
burial places scattered about the Pyrenean foothills dating from this time point
to the beginnings of culture and religion.

It was not until the late Paleolithic era that **modern humans** (*Homo sapiens*)
came to monopolize the area, thriving especially in the Magdalenian period,
some 14,000 years ago, which followed the last retreat of the glaciers. The earliest **cave paintings** of the Ariège valley (at Niaux and Mas d'Azil) date from
this period and show the preoccupation of this early people with the hunt. In
addition to cave art, they fashioned the small corpulent "Venus" statuettes,
which are generally considered to relate to fertility rites.

With the invention of the harpoon, the development of fishing began to
draw people towards the coasts of modern Roussillon. Nevertheless, the mid-
altitude caves remained the favoured habitat into the Mesolothic and Neolithic
(middle and new Stone Age) periods, which lasted here until about 1500 BC.
Several important innovations occurred in the Neolithic era: **agriculture** and
animal husbandry came into being in the fifth millennium BC, as did the use
of grain-storage facilities. **Mining** and smelting were developed for the crude
utilization of metals, such as copper, and better management of fire also permitted the manufacture of ceramics. Technical improvements encouraged spe-
cialization and this, in turn, trade, which seems to have first arisen among the
lowland settlements of the Narbonnais plain. It was also in the last millennium
of the Stone Age that the **dolmens** (megalithic henges) and **tumuli** (burial
mounds) which dot the mid-level Pyrenees and Haut Languedoc appeared.

The Bronze Age

The Bronze Age in Languedoc and Roussillon was an era of great movement and change. Around 800 BC, the **Celts** arrived and began displacing the indigenous peoples, and an area roughly analogous with modern Languedoc – stretching from Nîmes in the east past Toulouse in the west – came under the hegemony of the Volcae, one of several large Celtic tribal groups who dominated the South of France. Meanwhile, **Phoenicians** and **Greeks** began to arrive on the region's shores. They set up outposts (such as Maguelone and Port-Vendres) and began to trade with natives, who lived for the most part in fortified hill-top towns now known as **oppida** (plural of the Latin *oppidum*, or "town"), like the settlement of Ensérune. As archeological finds have confirmed, the native tribes were not uncivilized "barbarians" as Romans were later wont to claim, but participants in complex, technologically capable societies linked to extensive trade networks. Their rich culture is evinced by the objects which have survived them: skilfully worked bronze weapons and jewellery. Although perhaps not comparable with contemporary civilizations of the eastern Mediterranean, they had their own diversified agricultural and craft-based economies and stratified social structures. Their one weakness was that they were not oriented towards the sea and so needed intermediaries like the Phoenicians to reach foreign markets.

The Romans

In the fourth century BC, the **Romans** embarked on a series of campaigns of conquest which brought the whole Iberian peninsula and the bulk of Greek possessions under its power and set it against the **Carthaginians**, heirs of Phoenicia in the western Mediterranean. The Romans were the ultimate victors, and the futile rumble of **Hannibal**'s elephants across the length of Languedoc in 218 BC presaged the beginning of a long colonial period in southern France. A few decades later the **Via Domitia**, the Rome–Cadiz superhighway, was built along the Languedoc coast, facilitating Roman military and economic expansion, and the Roman city of Narbo was founded. By about 70 BC all of what is now France south of Lyon and Toulouse constituted Narbonensian Gaul. With the completion of the conquest by **Julius Caesar** and his successor, the Emperor **Augustus**, the zone was elevated to the rank of an imperial province, and subdivided (in 27 BC), so that Narbonne became the capital of the lands from the Rhône to the Pyrenees.

Enjoying the benefits of *pax Romana*, the region enjoyed an easy prosperity under the first emperors. Trade flourished (wine was a big export item) and there were major settlements at Baeterra (Béziers) and Nemausus (Nîmes). Nîmes became the region's most important city under in the mid-second -century Antoninus Pius – an emperor who lavished favours on his home town. During this period, Roman organizational infrastructure and slave labour permitted the elaboration of architectural projects of a scale and complexity which were not to be duplicated for fifteen hundred years. This is particularly true in the case of public civic architecture, such as Nîmes' huge amphitheatre, **Les Arènes**, the nearby aqueduct, the **Pont du Gard**, and the **bridges** at Sommières and Ambrussum. Religious buildings, the finest surviving example of which is Nîmes' **Maison Carrée**, were based on Greek styles – temples usually consisting of a *cella* or inner sanctum (the abode of the god), ringed by a colonnade of columns which were topped by decorative capitals. Less grandiose remains of civic and residential structures can be found at Mèze and Ensérune, along the length of the Via Domitia. The cities and settlements of Roman Languedoc-Roussillon have yielded a wealth of intricate mosaics and Roman-style civic and religious statuary.

But there were rocky times ahead for the empire, as the expansion on which its prosperity had depended slowed. Domestic economic crises were compounded by the growing threat of neighbouring powers: Persia in the east, and "barbarians" in North Africa and northwest Europe. While the frontiers under attack by **Franks** and **Goths** were far from Languedoc, the disruption of the empire's stability had economic repercussions which reached Gallia-Narbonensis. The growing dissatisfaction and malaise in the empire encouraged a certain trend towards new religions such as the Mithras cult and **Christianity**, which spread rapidly through urban Languedoc. The latter was seen as a threat to the imperial order and a series of emperors set about trying to quash it. The fiercest persecutions, which saw Christians submitted to all manner of brutal public tortures and executions, were carried out under Valerian and Diocletian between 257 and 311 – many of the area's martyred saints date from this era.

When **Constantine the Great** became sole emperor in 324, he proclaimed Christianity a tolerated religion and it quickly took hold in the towns and cities of Languedoc. With the capital of the empire now in far-off Constantinople, the bishops, who were appointed in each Roman town after 391, helped hold together the decaying fabric of administration. In the new, contracting Christianized empire, Nîmes and Narbonne waned, as Roman cities in Provence, like Arles, came to the forefront. But great changes were afoot, and as central power declined, people left the cities, taking refuge in smaller fortified towns and villas, and frequently trading off their liberty for the protection of a powerful patron. Imperial policy in the east was to deflect the waves of semi-nomadic steppe peoples westward, a tactic which saved the core of the empire, but brought about its disappearance in the west.

After the Romans

In the fifth century wave after wave of these small but aggressive invading bands passed through Languedoc and Roussillon: first the Suevi, then the Vandals and finally the **Visigoths**. It was the last of these who set up a durable kingdom, which in its greatest extent covered the southwest of France and most of Iberia. Their first capital was **Tolosa** – modern Toulouse – and they initially ruled, in name, as Roman imperial governors. At this time, however, a rival group, the **Franks**, had coalesced in the Low Countries and, led by King Clovis (482–511), drove southwards, incorporating Toulouse into their Kingdom of Aquitaine. Most of Languedoc and Roussillon, however, known then as **Septimania** (after its seven great cities: Narbonne, Agde, Béziers, Maguelone, Lodève, Nîmes and Uzès), remained under the Visigoths.

The weak and conflictive Visigothic kingdom was dealt a deathblow by **Muslim armies**, which arrived in Iberia around 711. Wiping out the Spanish Visigothic nobility in a single battle, they quickly conquered most of modern Spain and Portugal, and small raiding parties crossed the Pyrenees, taking

Toulouse and Septimania in the 720s. The most northern of these groups was turned back near Poitiers by Charles Martel in 732. Numerically too few to hang onto such an extensive area, the Muslims occupied the towns, exacting tribute and using them as raiding bases. In the years that followed the battle of Poitiers, the Muslims were turned out of Toulouse, Carcassonne and eventually their coastal enclaves as one by one these fell to the Franks; it was to prevent their return that Martel destroyed the town of Maguelone (see p.279). This long campaign was carried out under the leadership of **Pepin the Short**, the first Carolingian king (751–68), and it was his successor, **Charlemagne** (Charles the Great), who pushed Muslim power back over the Pyrenees. Languedoc was absorbed into the **Frankish Empire** and Roussillon became part of the semi-autonomous frontier region known as the **Spanish Marches**. After the decline of Roman power in the west, the empire continued in the east, but despite the fact that Constantinople was now its capital, its rulers continued to bear the title "Emperor of Rome". During Charlemagne's era, it so happened that it was a woman, Irene, who was in power in Constantinople; seeing an opportunity to enhance his prestige – given that no one actually held the title of "Emperor" – Charlemagne journeyed to Rome and had the pope crown him as "Holy Roman Emperor" in 800. Thus, his dominions, which covered almost all of western Europe, came to be known as the **Holy Roman Empire**, and the papacy, which up till then had been little more than an ordinary bishopric, gained justification for its later claims to be the power which could (or not) crown emperors.

The counts and feudalism

Despite his centralizing policies, Charlemagne followed Germanic custom, separating his kingdom among his heirs, and Languedoc fell into the **Kingdom of the Western Franks**, more or less contiguous with modern France. When its second king, Louis the Stammerer, died heirless in 879, the kingdom rapidly disintegrated, leaving power in the hands of local **counts**, although nominally Charlemagne's other descendants held the highest authority. Among the local nobility, one family, the "**Raymonds**" or "dynasty of St-Gilles", eventually came to dominate. They had ruled Toulouse since 840, thanks to a grant by Pepin II, and by the late 900s, they were to all intents and purposes independent rulers. As such, they began to expand, absorbing neighbouring territories, such as Albi, or co-opting other, lesser noble lines, such as the **Trencavels** of Carcassonne, as vassals. **Raymond IV** ruled a realm which stretched from Toulouse to the banks of the Rhône; it was he who adopted the surname of "St-Gilles", in honour of his favourite possession. Meanwhile, the most powerful lord of the Spanish March, **Guifré el Pelós** ("Wilfred the Hairy"), Count of the Cerdagne, Girona and Barcelona, was granted independence from the empire. Roussillon, then dominated by Elne, came under his power; it is at this point that Languedoc and Roussillon's histories as separate regions begin, and over the course of the centuries that followed their paths would be linked, but not united again until Louis XIV's formal annexation of Roussillon in the 1600s.

In these early medieval centuries, what little industry and urban life existed under the Romans all but disappeared. Western Europe became overwhelmingly agrarian, developing an economy of near subsistence in which the noble class siphoned off the meagre surplus and provided military protection to the masses. Local magnates depended on military strength to maintain their power and protect their subjects, obtaining warriors by granting lands in exchange for loyalty, and **feudal** structures developed. Religion too was a largely private and local affair: the nobles built churches and monasteries and put them under the charge of their friends and relatives, who lived comfortably off the income from these posts. The common folk continued to depend as much on traditional pre-Christian beliefs and magic – just as well, since most local priests knew no more than a smattering of Church Latin and were not particularly exemplary in their moral life. Learned culture too all but vanished with the disappearance of towns, and was maintained only by the monks who lived in isolated and introspective communities – fortresses of faith, hidden in isolated valleys and on remote mountainsides.

Twelfth-century revival

In the twelfth century the picture began to change rapidly. A shift away from subsistence, possibly as the result of climatic change and aided by improvements in agricultural technology, allowed the population to grow, while under the counts the region began to enjoy a stability which stimulated **trade** and **industry**. People started to move around Europe looking for better opportunities; towns expanded, shaking Toulouse and the cities of Septimania back to life. The agrarian social structures which had developed in the previous period were not suitable to town life, and the counts, anxious to promote economic growth, recognized that by extending liberties and privileges to the townsfolk, their own position could be improved. Oligarchic **town councils**, such as the **Capitolo** in Toulouse, were formed, sharing in or taking over urban administration and further stimulating growth.

Changes were afoot in the Church as well: the papacy was in the process of becoming a geopolitical power, initiating a level of bureaucracy and organization which would give it control of the resources and policies of local churches – traditionally the turf of the nobles. Some efforts were made to improve the priesthood too, to ensure that priests were educated and lived, at least in appearance, morally upright lives. On the popular level, **pilgrimage** played an important role, carrying ordinary believers across Europe, to Rome or Santiago de Compostela; along the way they visited local churches such as that at St-Gilles and came into contact with a wider Christian world. A wave of reformation also swept over the **monasteries**, where the degenerate and locally independent Benedictines were replaced by new, pious and strict orders, most importantly the Cistercians, who were controlled by a strong central organization.

With all of this new wealth, secular and religious culture began to revive. Great churches were raised in the towns, and old cathedrals were replaced by new, more grandiose and elaborate structures. The courts of the counts' palaces became the focus of a new culture as well, one which sought refinement in the **courtly traditions** of elaborate manners, rich clothes and imported luxuries. The most visible manifestation of this new culture was the tradition of courtly love and the **troubadours**. These singing poets – the first of whom is said to have been Guilhem de Peitieu, count of Poitiers and father of Eleanor of Aquitaine, Queen of France and, later, England – composed odes of yearning, unrequited love to anonymous "dark ladies", and satirical barbs aimed at local nobles. Their language of choice was not Latin, which had previously been the only voice of culture, but the local vernaculars, Occitan and Catalan. It was also in this era that the rites and rituals associated with feudalism, such as heraldry and the tournament, began to be formalized – precisely when the feudal world began to decline.

However, with this period of revival came a greater demand for fulfilment, directed at the Church from just about every corner. The newly wealthy and increasingly literate craftsmen, the **burghers**, who had no role to play in the warrior-aristocratic culture of the court, wanted a level of political power and social prestige which reflected their economic standing and, better educated than before, began to look for more satisfying theological answers than the still feudal-oriented Church could provide. Town life generated new social problems, particularly among the urban poor, which the Church – effectively a social welfare organization in the countryside – was not equipped to address. The peasants too were dissatisfied; although increasingly interested in Christianity, a shortage of priests meant they were frustrated by a lack of pastoral care. In short, the Church was seen as **corrupt** by everyone but the nobility, a situation aggravated by the taxes which people were forced to pay to support it. In addition, Latin, once widely spoken, was the only accepted sacred language – preserving the mystery of the Church, but now acting to cut off the faith and Scripture from the common folk.

Although their religious consciousness was high – local nobles, such as the Crusader Raymond of St-Gilles, distinguished themselves by reclaiming the Holy Land from the Muslim "infidels" – the upper classes in Languedoc began to find themselves turning against the Church too, but for a different reason. The nobility considered it their natural privilege to control local institutions, including bishoprics, parishes and monasteries and, unconcerned by the theological preferences of their subjects as long as they continued to pay their taxes, resented papal expansionism as a threat to their own power.

In the meantime, neighbouring Roussillon, though it went through most of the same social and economic processes as Languedoc, followed a distinctive political and religious course. In the centuries following Guifré el Pelós, his descendants, the **counts of Barcelona**, had been struggling to gain supremacy over their various rival counts in Catalonia, who did not want to recognize them as overlords. They were aided in this campaign in 1142 when Ramon Berenguer IV married the princess of Aragón, obtaining the title of King of Aragón for his heirs. Thus Barcelona became the capital of a multinational monarchy and its rulers, the count-kings, were to govern one of the great powers of the medieval Mediterranean. Linked by ties of marriage to noble houses in Languedoc and further east in Provence, they angled for political expansion, and for a time their holdings included Montpellier and various parts east of the Rhône. Indeed, the counts of Toulouse became their vassals – although this was merely a formality, amounting more to a pact of mutual assistance than a recognition of the count-kings' authority.

Catharism and the Albigensian Crusades

In the climate of dissatisfaction with the Church, popular **heresies** began to spring up, led by men who preached to the people in their own language and led lives of austerity and poverty, in emulation of the Apostles and in contrast to the wealthy and aloof Catholic clergy. The Church tried at first to quash the problem with force, but then, co-opting the impulses which drove the heretics, licensed two new groups, the Dominican and Franciscan preaching friars who – in contrast to the isolated monks – were to minister and preach among the common people. But the damage had already been done, and the most successful of the new heresies, **Catharism** (see box on p.149), had become firmly entrenched. This doctrine was a variant on ancient Middle Eastern beliefs combined with Christianity, a dualistic creed which portrayed the material world as evil and the spiritual world as good. It resonated among the common folk (who appreciated its populism) and nobles (who wanted to set themselves apart from the influence of Rome and its northern French political allies), and a shadow counter-Church began to organize itself, holding its first Council at St-Félix in 1167. In most of the major towns of Languedoc, and the countryside around Toulouse and south of the Aude, this new Church gained a strong presence. Here, the nobility, including the counts of Toulouse, the Trencavels of Carcassonne and a whole array of minor barons, remained Catholic themselves, but gave free reign to Cathar preachers to spread their religious message. As Roussillon did not develop an urban society as quickly as Languedoc and the count-kings had a more favourable political attitude to the papacy, Catharism was discouraged from gaining a strong hold here. Preachers and refugees did arrive in Catalan lands, but they could not live openly in their faith, for fear of persecution.

By the end of the 1100s the Catholic Church had become a powerful corporation, and it was not about to brook the loss of Languedoc to the heretic Cathars – or **Albigensians**, as they are commonly known. When persuasion failed to convert the heretics or influence the Cathar-protecting lords of Languedoc, and excommunication had little effect, the papacy turned to military force. Although it hardly had a formal army, the papacy could count on the support of powerful multinational monastic organizations such as the Cistercian Order, whose headquarters, Cîteaux, was in northern France, and which was dominated by noble families from the north. These same families, which had been united under the Capetian kings of France, began to look with hungry eyes at the extensive but fragmented lands of the counts to the south. Papal efforts to bring the Cathars back into the fold began as early as 1150, and in 1204 **Raymond IV** of Toulouse was excommunicated for refusing to persecute his Cathar subjects. However, the Albigensians and their lords would not cave in – the papal legate Pierre de Castelnau was murdered at a parley in 1208 – and **Pope Innocent III** called a Crusade, providing the northern nobles with the ideological justification to wage war on Languedoc. They were joined by knights from across Christendom, drawn by the allure of religious redemption and loot.

The campaign was led initially by **Arnaud Amaury**, abbot of Cîteaux, whose campaigns carried him rapidly across the littoral from Nîmes, which gave up without a fight, to Béziers. Here, faced by the refusal of the town's Catholics to give up their Cathar neighbours, he ordered the wholesale slaughter of the town's occupants; some 20,000 are said to have perished.

At about this time, the ageing Crusader **Simon de Montfort** set his sights on the Cathar lands and, taking up leadership of military operation, embarked on a campaign marked by its terror and efficiency. Carcassonne was taken, and with it **Count Raymond VI**; thereafter Cathar towns and fortresses were besieged one by one, including Lastours, Minerve, Hautpoul, Lavaur, Termes and Puivert. Almost without exception they fell or surrendered, and the unfortunate defenders were executed or mutilated and sent on as blunt warning to the next victims; the only survivors were those on the inaccessible southern border: Quérigut, Peyrepertuse and Montségur.

After a brief exile in England, **Raymond VII** returned to lead a counter-attack, calling on the aid of various allies, including his liege-lord **Pere el Catòlic**, Count-King of Catalonia-Aragón. Fresh from a decisive victory against Spanish Muslims at Las Navas de Tolosa, Pere went into the field at Muret (14km south of Toulouse) in 1213, but was singled out and killed by de Montfort's men, dealing a grievous blow to Raymond's forces.

It took five more years of fighting to turn the tide against the northern forces, who were deprived of their leader de Montfort (who had assumed the title of Count of Toulouse), when his head was smashed in by a missile outside the walls of Toulouse. His son Arnaud attempted to carry on the campaign, but could not sustain his position and returned to his lands in the north, carrying with him his father's dead body and broken dreams. After this long drawn-out battle, Raymond had no choice but to make **peace** with the papacy in order to recover his lands, reaffirming his Catholicism and recovering his scarred and battered territories. These he began immediately to fortify, founding strategic strongholds such as Cordes-sur-Ciel.

However, despite Raymond's concessions and preparations, **Occitan independence** was not to last. By the mid-1220s the French king, **Louis VIII**, swelled by victories over the English Crown, turned his own sights south, proclaiming a fresh Crusade against the Occitan Cathars, who continued to live discreetly in Raymond's lands, or openly under the defiant and unconquered barons of the south. This time the exhausted forces of the counts and local nobility could not respond, and after a brief campaign much of Languedoc came under the direct power of the king of France. Louis VIII's aggressive policy was followed up by his heir, Louis IX (later St Louis), who came to the throne in 1226 and finished off the job. With the counts out of the way, the papacy sent in the **Inquisition**, led by the Dominican Order. Their job was to investigate and root out heretics, employing torture if necessary, and urging them to recant before turning them over to the king's forces to execute. Needless to say, they were not popular among the local citizenry, and there was some relief when a band of renegade Cathars sallied out of their stronghold at Montségur in 1242 to **massacre** a band of Inquisitors at Avignonet-Lauregais. The royal reaction was immediate: an army of six thousand was assembled and laid siege to the fortress in 1243. Eight months later, when it fell, the garrison of two hundred was burnt alive. Subsequent mopping-up operations finished with the surrenders of Puilaurens and Quéribus in 1256. Catharism had disappeared as a political force and, confined to secrecy and isolation, was hunted into extinction over the next century.

But royal policy was not wholly destructive in Languedoc, as its aim was not to lay waste to the region but to extinguish possible sources of rebellion and resistance. From the time of de Montfort's death, the kings had worked to re-habilitate the area, particularly through the founding of royal **bastides**, such as Revel and Réalmont. These planned and usually fortified towns were set up by royal charter. Ruled by a council, they answered directly to the king rather than to an intermediary noble, and were given privileges such as the right to hold a market. Thus, they strengthened the royal position and, with their liberties and self-determination, helped to boost the economy.

On the fringes of Languedoc, mountainous **Foix**, like Toulouse, had been an independent county since about the time of the Carolingian disintegration. Over the following centuries, it remained isolated, even more than Roussillon, from the modernizing trends which were shaping Languedoc. That said, the counts of Foix were sworn enemies of the French Crown and allied themselves with the Raymonds during the Albigensian Crusade; in the campaigns that followed, the county managed to escape more or less unscathed, and when the French Crown threatened in the 1270s, the ruling house eluded their control by forging a marriage alliance with the neighbouring kingdom of Béarn.

Except for the loss in battle of Count-King Pere, **Roussillon**, too, all but escaped the effects of the Albigensian Crusades. The death of Pere, and the period of uncertainty that followed, when his 5-year-old son, Jaume, was made king, entailed the end of any Catalan-Aragonese pretensions in Provence, so the French Crown had a long breathing period in which to consolidate its power there. Roussillon, however, remained for the moment firmly in the Catalan-Aragonese ambit, and its nobility was drawn towards the campaigns of conquest which the count-kings carried out against their Muslim neighbours (Valencia, Mallorca and Menorca), and Sardinia and Sicily. When **Jaume the Conqueror** died after a 63-year reign, he divided his kingdom between his elder son Pere (who received the mainland holdings south of the Pyrenees) and Jaume, who became **king of Mallorca** and count of Roussillon and Montpellier. Perpignan served as his mainland capital. The kings of Mallorca allied with the French against their Barcelona-based rivals, and in the 1280s Roussillon served as the springboard for the French invasion of Catalonia, launched in retribution for Catalan seizure of French-ruled Sicily.

The Hundred Years' War

Under **Philip le Bel** (1285–1314), France became a superpower. The astute king managed his treasury well, disbanded and appropriated the funds of the wealthy Knights Templar and brought the papacy under his ominous protection in Avignon.

But royal domination of Languedoc brought only short-lived peace and prosperity to the region. Philip died without a male heir, and Edward III of England, who had married Philip's daughter, claimed the throne. Edward's family, the Plantagenets, were French in origin, and the language and culture of their court were northern French, but the prospect of Edward taking the throne was highly undesirable to a large section of the French nobility, who stood to see themselves marginalized by such a turn of events. So they invoked the ancient French Salic Law, which forbade succession to the throne through the female line, and resisted the English claim. These were the circumstances which provoked the series of conflicts which came to be known as the **Hundred Years' War** – essentially a struggle between two French royal houses.

England took the early advantage, defeating the French at Crécy in 1346 and capturing the French king shortly afterwards. Meanwhile, the king's son, Edward, Prince of Wales (known as the **Black Prince**), was unleashed on Aquitaine and ravaged the Aude valley. These military campaigns coincided with a series of disasters, including **crop failures**, the arrival of the **Black Death** and the Jacquerie peasant uprising. In 1360, a **truce** was called and part of western Languedoc remained under English control until nine years later, when **Charles V** began a campaign which all but expelled the English from France.

Unfortunately, Charles' successor, **Charles VI**, was considered mentally unfit to rule, and a struggle ensued between the dukes of Burgundy and Orléans, who had been entrusted with the care of the realm. The English intervened on the side of the Burgundians, against the Duke of Orléans and his Armagnac allies, and began to reconquer the country. After a series of defeats, including Agincourt in 1415, all seemed lost for the French Crown. It was then that the peasant girl **Joan of Arc** appeared on the scene, and helped to turn the tide against the invaders, claiming divine guidance and rallying the French forces in a campaign to push the English off the mainland. Five years later, **Charles VII** entered Toulouse in triumph; a French king was once again master of Languedoc, and although the reconquest of the former royal territories dragged out over the length of the fifteenth century, France emerged from the struggle as a unified, powerful nation-state.

In this protracted period of **crisis**, the people of Languedoc coped as best they could. Population decreased, agriculture suffered and traditional industries, such as leather-working, which accounted for the prosperity of the Tarn region, were almost extinguished. However, in the mid-fifteenth century it was discovered that a local plant, **woad**, could be made to yield a fine blue dye, *pastel*, a high-priced luxury commodity much in demand by the fabric industry of the day, thus provoking an economic renaissance which lasted for over a century. Toulouse, still ruled over by a council of burghers, took the lead in this industry. Fortunes were made, fine palaces were raised, and the city's famous university was founded, turning Toulouse into a centre of culture. On the Occitan coast, Montpellier (which had been bought by the French Crown in 1349) was also driven by the growing textile industry and set up its own prestigious university.

As had happened with the Albigensian Crusade, Catalonia was not involved directly in the Hundred Years' War, but it did have to contend with France's relentless efforts to chip away at its holdings north of the Pyrenees, Cerdanya and Rosilló (the **Cerdagne** and **Roussillon**), and through the fourteenth and fifteenth centuries, they were shifted back and forth between the two powers. In 1462, when **Louis XI** mounted a military campaign against Roussillon – seizing it in response to the Catalan-Aragonese capture of French-dominated Naples – Catalonia was on the verge of a major realignment. The marriage of Ferran (Ferdinand) of Aragon and Isabel of Castile in 1469 laid the foundations for the creation of the Kingdom of Spain, and the ultimate submission of Catalonia and its dependencies to Madrid; it thus became a secondary concern, and Roussillon was set further on the periphery.

The rise of Protestantism and the Wars of Religion

Despite the peace which came with re-establishment of a strong monarchy in France under **François I** (1515–47), there was much dissatisfaction in Languedoc and Roussillon. This resentment took two forms: that towards the Church on the part of the people, and that towards the Crown and the northern nobility on the part of local lords and magnates. As had happened in the Cathar period, the interests of these two groups coincided, and even more so after 1483, when the Crown gained direct control over the Church in France. So social and political discontent was once again voiced on religious terms – this time the revolutionary movement was **Protestantism**.

The new faith first arrived in Haut Languedoc close on the heels of **Martin Luther**'s defiance of Church authority in 1519. However, French Protestantism, or the **Huguenot** movement (named after an obscure Swiss political event), tended to follow the teachings of **John Calvin** (Jean Cauvin), which had a clearer political message. Calvin had studied theology at the conservative University of Paris and had been swept up in the wave of reforming theology which very quickly provoked a clampdown by the religious and royal authorities. He fled into exile in Geneva, which became a hotbed for the Protestant creed that he formulated. His beliefs focused on the omnipotence of God and predestination, denying hierarchies and earthly elites and concentrating on hard work and pastoralism – a recipe for success among the artisanal classes – and it spread like wildfire in Paris and through Occitania.

By 1559, **Calvinism** was established as a religion and organization in France, and had the support of some of the kingdom's greatest noble houses, despite the persecution which had been carried out by François I's son Henri II. When Henri died (in an accident allegedly presaged by Nostradamus), the succession of two weak child-kings gave the rival **noble factions** led by the Protestant Bourbons and the Catholic Guises the opportunity to battle for control of the realm. Forty years of bloody and relentless civil war followed, of which the most notorious episode is the **St Bartholemew's Day massacre** of 1572, in which the Protestant elite, who had come to Paris for a royal wedding, were ambushed. A nationwide campaign against Protestants ensued, during which some 20,000 were killed. The violence was not all one-sided, however: the Calvinists committed atrocities as well, among them the murder of Nîmes' Catholic clergy in the **Michelade massacre** (1567).

The wars were finally concluded by the victory of Henri, King of Béarn (or Navarre, and a successor of Gaston Fébus of Foix), the leader of the Protestant faction. It was, however, politically impossible for him to become king as a Huguenot, so having decided that "Paris is worth a Mass", he converted and was crowned as **Henri IV** of France in 1593. Thanks to his accession, Foix was incorporated into the French realm. Six years later, he proclaimed the **Edict of Nantes**, which granted political and religious freedom to the Hugenots and the right to maintain certain fortified strongholds.

Although most of Languedoc had been ruled by the Catholic Guises, its population was strongly Protestant. Castres became a "protected zone" for Huguenots, and home to one of the four **courts** empowered to mediate legal disputes between Catholics and Protestants. In Nîmes, some three quarters of the population converted to Calvinism, while Montpellier was home to the Protestant Theological Institute. In the east, most of the towns – mainly herding and textile centres – were firmly Huguenot but, despite regional imbalances, the new pluralistic French society seemed to function well.

The Age of Absolutism

The liberal vision of Henri IV was not to last, however. When he was assassinated by a Catholic reactionary, his year-old son **Louis XIII** came to the throne under the strict control of his staunchly Catholic mother, Marie de Medici. In 1624, that supreme Machiavellian **Cardinal Richelieu** managed to wrest control from the queen. Richelieu made it his mission to establish France as an absolutist Catholic state, and for almost two decades he was the sole power behind the Crown. He immediately set about stripping the towns and cities of their defensive walls (to prevent revolt) and then began reducing Protestant strongholds. He also adopted an aggressive foreign policy, attacking France's neighbours and taking Roussillon. But his heavy-handedness provoked reaction at home. In 1622, the Protestant duc de Rohan raised a **revolt** in the Cévennes (just north of Hérault) and although after seven years of fighting he was forced to make a settlement with Richelieu, which stripped the Huguenots of political power, he maintained their freedom to worship.

Heavily Protestant Languedoc was not pacified, however, and shortly thereafter its royal governor, **Henri de Montmorency**, raised a revolt against Richelieu which spanned the region from Nîmes to Toulouse. He was no match for the cardinal, who defeated him in battle at Castelnaudary in 1632 and led him off to be beheaded on the place du Capitoule in Toulouse. The vindictive Richelieu then exacted revenge on Henri's heirs by transferring the title of First Duchy of France from Montmorency to the loyally Catholic dukes of Uzès.

In 1643, the "Sun King" and supreme absolutist **Louis XIV** came to the throne. Continuing the centralizing policies initiated by Richelieu, he hamstrung the French nobility by obliging them to take up residence at his palace in Versailles and to participate in its expensive and regimented court life. His megalomaniac tendencies ("I am the state") led him to embark on a series of costly and ultimately disastrous military adventures, the successful episodes of which are recorded on the Roman-style monuments, such as the equestrian statue and triumphal arch of Montpellier, which he erected to commemorate his grandeur. He waged **war** in Flanders, Germany and Spain, managing to secure the permanent annexation of the Cerdagne and Roussillon with the **Treaty of the Pyrenees** in 1659.

The able management of his successive prime ministers, Mazarin and Colbert, managed to preserve the kingdom from financial ruin, and it was Colbert who gave the green light to Riquet's visionary project of linking the Atlantic and Mediterranean by canal. The main channel of the **Canal du Midi**, which stretched from Toulouse to Agde, was opened in 1666, sparking an economic recovery in the region, which had languished in depression since the wane in demand for the local pastel dye (thanks to the discovery of cheaper alternatives in the Indies); the canal allowed locally grown grain to be shipped to distant markets. But on the whole, Louis' reign was not a happy one for Languedoc and Roussillon. In 1674, the **Catalans** rose up against French rule, which they found even more oppressive than that of the Spanish Hapsburgs, against whom they had risen a generation earlier. The **uprising** was brutally crushed, and its leaders imprisoned and executed in Perpignan.

A decade later, Louis moved against the Protestants by issuing a **Revocation of the Edict of Nantes** (1685), which deprived the Huguenots of their rights and outlawed their religion. Half a million Protestants chose to flee the country, including many merchants and textile workers, dealing a grievous blow to the industry on which the prosperity of eastern Languedoc depended. Those who remained were subjected to **oppression**; they were spied on and hounded, forced to carry on their services in secret and brook the humiliation of having soldiers billeted in their homes. Intransigent Protestants were imprisoned, among them Marie Durand, locked up for over thirty years in a tower in Aigues-Mortes. Some feigned conversion, some were deported to the colonies, and others fled to the "desert" – the wild and isolated hills of the Cévennes. It was here that they rose again in protest, in what is known as the **Camisard revolt**. The spark came in July 1702 when the parish priest of Chayla arrested and detained a small group of fugitive Protestants. A group of villagers stormed the castle to free them and in the course of the struggle the priest was killed. Knowing that retribution would be swift and cruel, Protestants across the Cévennes (mostly refugees from Languedoc proper) began a guerrilla war which pitted their forces, numbering between three and five thousand, against some 30,000 royal troops. The shirts they wore as a sign of recognition earned them the popular name of Camisards (from *chemise*, French for "shirt"). Battles raged across the region, with one of the greatest confrontations taking place at **St-Hippolyte**. The guerrillas and civilian population took refuge where they could, hiding in the remote hills or in caverns, like the Grotte des Demoiselles, south of Ganges.

In the course of the struggle two leaders emerged: the aristocratic **Jean Cavalier**, and the commoner **Roland**. Unable to conclude the struggle militarily, the French commander Villars began to negotiate with Cavalier at Nîmes, offering him the rank of colonel, command of a Protestant legion which would fight for the French abroad, and a hefty annual salary in exchange for submission. Cavalier accepted, greatly undermining the uprising. The former leader left France and served the English, eventually being named governor of Jersey. Roland continued the struggle, but later the same year was killed in battle, bringing an end to the revolt.

In the century or so before the Camisards episode, Languedoc had been tamed into discontented submission by France, ruled by the princes of Conti, members of the ruling Bourbon family, since the defeat of Montmorency. Pézenas, which had been the region's capital since the 1450s, became a paler southern Versailles, especially in the 1650s when **Armand de Bourbon** lavished his patronage on the town, playing host for a time to the playwright Molière and his company.

The absorption of Roussillon, while it aggrandized France, struck a blow against the towns of the Aude valley, which up until then had enjoyed a trade-based prosperity thanks to their position on the Spanish frontier. As part of Madrid's empire, in which Church institutions like the Inquisition kept a very tight lid on any potential sources of dissent or heterodoxy, Protestantism was basically unknown in Roussillon during its efflorescence, and by the time of the region's annexation, it was virtually a spent force.

The Revolution

Languedoc and Roussillon were not the only areas which chafed against the Sun King's absolutism. As the **economic crisis** deepened, taxes were driven up, forcing the masses of the kingdom, the *sans-culottes* ("trouserless"), into an ever more desperate state of poverty. A series of bad harvests compounded the problem, and indebted smallholders had their lands repossessed and were reduced to penury and near servitude. In order to gather the revenue which was necessary to maintain the court, fund expensive military adventures and service the spiralling national debt, the ruling class resorted to **tax-farming**. Speculators paid the Crown a set sum upfront and were then free to extract as much as they could from the area under their control. This excluded most of the nobility, many of whom enjoyed hereditary exemptions, and the largest single land-holder, the Church, which paid no royal taxes and continued to collect its own. At the same time, the Crown's growing obsession with control bred a fear of rebellion, which became self-fulfilling. Law was completely subverted to royal authority, and suspected troublemakers were imprisoned indefinitely without charges, by writ of the feared letters of cachet, or orders of detention.

These **dictatorial** tendencies worsened over the course of the eighteenth century, as Louis XIV's successors continued his absolutist style of ruling and his disastrous policy of foreign intervention. **Louis XV** (1715–74) carried

France into the Polish and Austrian Wars of Succession and the Seven Years' War, as a result of which the kingdom lost all of its colonies. Ironically, the king also encouraged the extraordinary literary and philosophical blossoming, in which Voltaire and Rousseau figured, among others, and which laid the ideological foundations for the Revolution which was shortly to follow.

Poor grain harvests continued after Louis XV's death in 1774, provoking riots and unrest. Royal finance ministers attempted to institute reforms, but to little avail. In Languedoc, the new king Louis XVI's conciliatory policies were chiefly noted in the form of the **Edict of Toleration** (1787), which was aimed at diffusing the rebelliousness of the Protestants by restoring their rights and liberties. The situation was such that the king was forced in 1789 to summon the Estates General (the equivalent of parliament) for the first time in nearly two centuries. The newly constituted Third Estate, made up of commoners, who for the first time joined the nobility and clergy in government, called for the formation of a National Assembly.

When in the months that followed the country rose in **revolution**, Languedoc and Roussillon were solidly Jacobin (revolutionary). Even Montpellier, at that time a wealthy bastion of Catholicism and cotton lords, could not resist. In 1791, the French Republic was declared and as southern troop levies marched towards the capital, a young medical student from Montpellier composed the "War Song of the Army of the Rhine", better known as **La Marseillaise**, which was adopted eventually as the national anthem. The Revolution was a focus for the discontentment of diverse groups in the south: the Protestants, the poor, the Occitans and the local magnates, all of whom had a bone to pick with Paris or the monarchy. But although the monarchy fell, Paris persevered, emerging as the capital of a sharply centralized and thoroughly French state.

The short and bloody revolutionary experiment was centred in Paris, and Languedoc felt its influence chiefly in the administrative novelties which were introduced, the most durable of which was the division of the region (as with the rest of country) into administrative **départements**. The rationalist (and centralist) policies of the new government ensured a break with historical traditions in defining these areas. They were based on geography, for the most part on the major river valleys. Roussillon became the culturally neutral Pyrénées-Orientales.

The Napoleonic era and the nineteenth-century republics

The rise of revolutionary France did not, however, bring about a change in foreign policy, which remained aggressive. The **armies** of the Republic, among whose leaders figured a young **Napoleon Bonaparte**, lashed out against their neighbours on all sides. Back at home, power had devolved to a five-member **Directory**, whose heavy-handed governance was met with growing resentment by the populace. When Bonaparte returned from his defeat by the British in Egypt, he set a coup d'état in motion, which saw him elevated initially, in 1799, to First Consul, and subsequently, to **Emperor**. His campaign of European domination brought him up against practically every other power in Europe and, after initial successes in Germany and Spain, his campaign in Russia brought about the decimation of his Grand Army and his ultimate ruin.

Although most of the Napoleonic Wars took place on foreign soil, Languedoc was to feel the sting of the emperor's defeat. **Wellington**'s British expeditionary force, which had been sent to aid Spain and Portugal, pushed its way across the peninsula and dealt the French a severe defeat at Toulouse in 1814.

For the next forty years France and Languedoc returned to monarchy, with the reigns first of the Bourbon **Louis XVIII** (1814–24) and **Charles X** (1824–30), and then **Louis-Philippe** (1830–48) of the house of Orléan. The Bourbons, who had obviously learnt nothing from previous experience, immediately embarked on a heavy-handed Catholic-oriented policy, and were brought down by popular revolution in 1830. The throne was then taken by Louis-Philippe, the candidate of the middle-class elite, a commercial nobility no less despised than their aristocratic forebears. He was unseated in the **revolution of 1848**, European socialism's *annus mirabilis*, which saw uprisings in capitals across the continent. But the Second Republic quickly gave way to the **Second Empire**, when Bonaparte's crafty nephew gained the throne as **Napoleon III** in 1852. Protests followed his seizure of power, such as the one in Béziers, where troops opened fire on a crowd of republican demonstrators led by the town mayor. As a tactician, Napoleon III proved as unsuccessful as his namesake, first embroiling the country in the bitter Crimean War, and then in 1870 provoking the ignominious **Franco-Prussian War**, which saw his own capture and the subsequent German siege of Paris.

Although Roussillon continued to drift in agrarian poverty, Languedoc weathered all these events with some measure of good fortune. While the bulk of the population suffered in poverty, the **textile industry**, based on wool and cotton and later on silk, boomed. The herds of the uplands of the Cévennes and Haut Languedoc were the chief source of raw material, and the fast-flowing rivers provided the energy to run the newly mechanized factories. All along the fringe of the mountains, towns which had up to then been insignificant villages – Castres, Mazamet, Ganges, St-Hippolyte – enjoyed unprecedented good fortune. As coal was discovered, new industries, such as **mining** and **glassmaking** (at Albi and Carmaux), sprang up, and when the railways arrived in the middle of the century, the towns along their route benefited additionally from better access to distribution networks. Of course, this good fortune tended to remain in the hands of a relative few – the factory owners and merchants – and this fact contributed to the popularity of egalitarian and **socialist ideologies** among the masses of the region.

The era of the **Third Republic**, which followed France's defeat at the hands of the Prussians, was one of introspection, not least because of the massive war indemnities which the state was forced to pay. Socialists were scapegoated, and there were mass executions at the hands of the new reactionary regime: in excess of 20,000 were killed in Paris alone. Nor was all well in Languedoc and Roussillon, as outside the industrial areas the people of the countryside still eked out only the most meagre of livings. Many left, frequently for Paris, compounding the capital's social and economic problems. The new, modern **wine industry** which had developed along the littoral provided a seasonal source of income for many, and stimulated related industries, such as bottle-, cork- and barrel-making, but in 1875 the vineyards were decimated by phylloxera. This was followed by a second epidemic which attacked mulberry trees, the silkworm's staple food, precipitating a crisis in the silk industry.

A marked tendency towards the Left continued to colour local politics, partially fuelled by a resentment towards remote and indifferent Paris. These political trends were personified in **Jean Jaurès**. Born in Castres, he was drawn to

Paris as a brilliant student but later returned to his home region of Tarn. Here he entered politics and embarked on a series of labour-oriented campaigns, helping to organize miners' unions, and setting up co-operative, worker-run factories. He joined other liberals in defending **Alfred Dreyfus**, a Jewish army officer wrongly convicted of espionage in 1898, and founded the communist newspaper *L'Humanité* in 1904 and a new socialist party in 1905. Speaking out against the anti-German nationalist hysteria which gripped the country in the years leading up to World War I, he paid with his life, assassinated by a nationalist in 1914.

However, popular politics in Languedoc and Roussillon were not divided strictly across ideological lines, as the cross-class solidarity of the **wine revolts** would show. As the wine industry recovered in the last years of the nineteenth century from the blow dealt by disease, it received further setbacks. A series of abundant harvests drove down the price of grapes, and the combination of competition from cheap Algerian vintages and a law permitting sugar to be added during fermentation (reducing the amount of grape pulp required) decreased demand. Wages plummeted and unemployment rose. Led by the innkeeper, Marcellin Albert, half a million protesters turned out in Montpellier in 1907, and similar numbers rose up in other wine towns, like Béziers and Narbonne. People across the class spectrum depended on the wine industry, so the uprising had the character of a regional revolt. The interior minister, Georges Clemenceau, responded by sending in the troops, but the locally levied 17th Infantry Regiment sympathized with their countrymen and mutinied. They were packed off to Tunisia in short order, and troops from the north were sent in to quell the "Midi madness". In the confrontations between army and civilians, shots were fired and there were some casualties, but the episode served to instigate the creation of a regional wine board to manage prices and quality and to bring stability to the industry.

The two world wars

In 1914, the diplomatic strain between Europe's uniformly conservative powers finally snapped, and the **assassination** of the Austrian Archduke Ferdinand at the hands of a Serbian nationalist in Sarajevo led to a diplomatic chain reaction which brought about **World War I**. The French were particularly anxious for revenge for their recent defeat at the hands of Prussia, which had deprived them of the Rhenish provinces of Alsace and Lorraine. After an initial German advance, both sides settled in for a long-drawn-out campaign of near-static trench warfare, along a 400km front stretching roughly from the Swiss border to Ostend, which was to last four years.

On the "Western Front" France (with allies Britain and eventually the US) and Germany ground away at each other in the first modern mechanized war; over its course the front shifted almost imperceptibly, but an exhausted Germany surrendered in 1918. France paid a high price for its eventual victory – almost one and half million dead. Although none of the fighting took place in Languedoc and Roussillon, the **cenotaphs** which mark the centre of every hamlet and village bear dramatic testimony to the price which they paid in the struggle.

Languedoc and Roussillon limped through the 1920s and 1930s, suffering along with the rest of Europe in the postwar **flu epidemic** (which claimed more lives than the war) and the **Great Depression**. Weak postwar democracies arose in Italy and Germany and were quickly replaced by dictatorial fascist regimes, and a prelude of the struggle to come took place in Spain, where General Franco's attempted coup set in motion a civil war in 1936. The bitter struggle, from which France – along with the rest of the Allies – remained aloof and uncommitted, lasted until 1939. As fascist troops took over Catalonia and the Basque country, tens of thousands of **refugees** poured over the border, the Catalans arriving initially in Roussillon.

A few months later, German soldiers poured over the Polish border, initiating **World War II**. The following year they circumvented France's defensive white elephant, the Maginot line, and arrived in Paris in June. For the first time in seven hundred years Languedoc and Roussillon found themselves independent of Paris as they were incorporated into the puppet **Vichy Republic**, which enjoyed a fictitious independence under the World War I hero, **Henri Pétain**. He collaborated with the **Nazis**, facilitating the repression of their opponents, the deportation of "undesirable elements" and the wholesale transportation of southern French citizens to labour camps and factories in Germany.

In 1942, the Germans decided to dispense with even the illusion of autonomy in the South and brought the whole region under their direct control. Repression was intensified, but the local guerrilla **Resistance**, the maquis, benefited from a stiffened resolve on the part of the populace. Across France as a whole there were about as many active collaborators with Nazi rule as resisters, but Resistance activity in Languedoc and Roussillon was considerable, the efforts of local companies like the famed Maquis Bir Hakeim of Haut Languedoc, or of individuals like Jean Mance of Béziers, who founded the National Committee for Resistance, proving a significant element in the war. In their mountain redoubts in the Pyrenees and Cévennes and in the hills of Haut Languedoc, they withstood German air attacks and pacification missions, while the civilian population suffered direct reprisals for their collusion with the rebels. In the Cerdagne and Roussillon, clandestine *passeurs*, motivated by either ideals or profit (or a combination of the two), helped to slip people and contraband back and forth over the frontier with neutral Spain.

From 1943 on, the disasters of the Russian campaign focused German manpower in the east, and with the **allied invasions** of Italy in 1943 and Normandy in 1944, the undergunned maquis finally had a chance, and began to mount an open military campaign. The first towns which they managed to recover were mere mountain hamlets, like Mourèze, near Clermont-l'Hérault, but when the Germans sent a column of three thousand troops to retake the upper Hérault, they were fended off after a fierce day-long battle with the local Resistance. Memorial plaques which pepper the streets of Toulouse and other major towns recall the maquis who fell in the widespread **street-fighting** of 1944. By the end of that year, France had been liberated.

Recent history

In the postwar **Fourth Republic** France endeavoured to recover from the damage wrought by four years of occupation and two invasions. The colonial age of Europe was coming to an end and for France this signalled nationalist revolts in Indochina and Algeria. In Languedoc and Roussillon, the wine industry recovered and mining continued, but with the advent of cheaper synthetic fibres, the textile industry all but disappeared. **Poverty** and **depopulation** continued and served to channel political consciousness ever more to the Left.

Former general and self-proclaimed liberator of France **Charles de Gaulle**'s conservative **Fifth Republic**, which came in 1958 on the heels of France's entry into the new European Common Market, gradually became something of a dictatorship. In the South, certain progressive economic policies were embarked upon, including the construction of **reservoirs** and **hydroelectric facilities** and the articulation of a region-wide irrigation plan.

Meanwhile in **Algeria**, native unrest led to open rebellion, and when de Gaulle reacted by announcing the abandonment of the **colony**, the *pieds-noirs* (so-called by the natives for the colour of their shoes) – the French population who had ruled it since 1830 – felt betrayed and carried out a brief armed resistance. With the **Accord of Évian** (1962), they agreed to be settled, along with the **harkis**, their native Algerian allies, in Languedoc. The influx of this population – a largely educated and skilled workforce – gave new life to the cities of the coast (notably Montpellier, Narbonne and Perpignan), although the welcome which the *harkis* received was hardly warm. Forty years later, they continue to protest the official neglect to which they have been subject.

The **Student Revolution** of 1968 presaged the departure of de Gaulle, who resigned in 1969 after a failed attempt to widen his already broad powers by popular referendum. The unrest of that summer also heralded an era of openly **left-wing politics** in Languedoc and Roussillon. In the elections of the years that followed, Languedoc voted massively in favour of the socialists and communists, encouraged by the areas' traditional economic marginalism and an antipathy to the conservative north.

The nation, however, remained under **conservative rule** through the presidencies of Georges Pompidou (1969–74) and Valéry Giscard d'Estaing (1974–81). In this era of baby boom and general prosperity, the infrastructure of Languedoc and Roussillon was improved by the construction of *autoroutes* and the improvement of roads. The **tourist industry** also received stimulus through the revitalization of the abandoned Canal du Midi and the creation of regional parks, such as that of Haut Languedoc. The area still retains a shadow of its former textile industry, but manufacturing has been dominated in the west by the high-profile **aviation industry**, based in Toulouse. The city had been a pioneer of flight since before the days of St-Exupéry, and served as a hub for Africa and South America between the wars. It was here that the Concorde was first put to test, and the European joint-venture Airbus Industries was founded.

Despite these recent successes, the region remains underpopulated and relatively poor, and *départements* like Aude, Ariège and significant parts of Hérault are now actively stimulating tourism as a way of bringing investment and employment. Whether as a result of these efforts, or as a consequence of overcrowding and rising prices in traditional Anglo destinations like the Dordogne, British travellers and property-investors have discovered Languedoc and Roussillon, both as places to take a break in and as somewhere to set up home.

As the French population ages, waves of northern retirees are heading south to the affordable property and agreeable climes of Languedoc and Roussillon – a trend which is seen with a jaundiced eye by many natives, who perceive in it a modern reprise of the invasions of the past. Some also see the massive influx of North African immigrants from France's former colonies and protectorates as an invasion, and this has served to divert part of the traditional extreme Left vote, paradoxically, to the **extreme Right**. The 1995 municipal elections gave a surprisingly high return to the parties of the far Right, dominated then by Jean Le Pen's racist **Front National**. It is not without irony that Roussillon's "Perpignan la Catalane" should be ruled by an extremist French mayor. At the *région* level, the Right scored well in the 1998 elections; the UDF–FDR coalition's (President Chirac's power base) 22 seats added to the FN's thirteen made for a narrow majority over the 31 seats won by the socialists and resurgent communists.

As parties geared up for the 2002 elections, it appeared that the region would return to its traditional socialist orientation, with the FN splintered and the **Chirac government** discredited by an influence-peddling **scandal** involving government contracts which seemed to point at the president's office. Few were prepared for what was to come. The first electoral round was met with record voter apathy and abstention, particularly among socialist voters. This knocked out Jospin's party from the race and catapulted Le Pen into second position. In a typical irony of politics, leftist voters came out for the second round and voted in Chirac, seen as the lesser of two evils.

Unlike some of France's other regions, such as Corsica, Alsace, the Pays Basque and Brittany, the issues of a distinctive language and identity do not seem to have made their way into the political dialogue of either Languedoc or Roussillon. For all the resentment which these regions may feel towards Paris, and despite the survival or revival of their native tongues, there is no doubt among the people of the region that their future lies within France.

Books

Publishers are detailed below in the form of British publisher; American publisher, where both exist. Where books are published in one country only, UK or US follows the publisher's name. Where the publisher is the same in both the UK and US, only one name is given. While we recommend all the books listed below, we do have our favourites: those that are particularly recommended are marked with the ✪ symbol. Abbreviations: o/p (out of print); UP (University Press).

History

General

✪ **Alfred Cobban** *A History of Modern France* (3 vols: 1715–99, 1799–1871 and 1871–1962, Penguin; Viking). Complete and very readable account of the main political, social and economic strands in French history, from the death of Louis XIV to mid–de Gaulle.

Colin Jones *The Cambridge Illustrated History of France* (Cambridge UP, o/p). A political and social history of France from prehistoric times to the mid-1990s, concentrating on issues of regionalism, gender, race and class. Good illustrations and a friendly, non-academic writing style.

The Middle Ages

Richard Barber *Edward, Prince of Wales and Aquitaine* (Boydell Press; University of Rochester Press). A

weighty academic read, but perhaps the best of the biographies on the Black Prince, including much on his campaigns in Languedoc.

Natalie Zemon Davis *The Return of Martin Guerre* (Harvard UP). A vivid account of peasant life in the sixteenth century and a perplexing and titillating hoax in the Pyrenean village of Artigat. Better than the movie and the musical. Not within the strict geographic bounds of this Guide, but culturally very much so.

Emmanuel Le Roy Ladurie *Montaillou* (Penguin; Random House). Village gossip of who's sleeping with whom, tales of trips to Spain and details of work, all extracted by the Inquisition from Cathar peasants of the eastern Pyrenees in the fourteenth century, and stored away until recently in the Vatican archives. Though academic and heavy-going in places, most of this book reads like a novel.

J.R. Maddicott *Simon de Montfort* (Cambridge UP). An academic but readable treatment of this complex and problematic figure – carefully

reflecting de Montfort's combination of piety and ambition.

Stephen O'Shea *The Perfect Heresy* (Walker & Co). Lively but partisan non-academic account of the history of the Cathar Church and faith and the Catholic campaign mounted to wipe it out.

Linda M. Paterson *The World of the Troubadours: Medieval Occitan Society, c.1100-c.1300* (Cambridge UP). Scholarly but clear survey of medieval Occitan culture and society.

Jonathan Sumption *The Albigensian Crusade* (Faber & Faber). Concise but eloquent portrayal of the Albigensian Crusades from the beginnings of the Cathar movement through to the fall of Montségur.

René Weiss *The Yellow Cross: The Story of the Last Cathars, 1290–1329* (Penguin). Lively historical detective work built on the same sources as Montaillou. An energetic, engaging read, not overly academic in tone.

The Wars of Religion

Joseph and Francis Bergin *The Rise of Richelieu* (Manchester UP). An interesting look at Richelieu's rise to power, presenting the cardinal as a complex Machiavellian figure, who was not without his convictions.

Willert Paul Ferdinand *Henry of Navarre and the Huguenots in France* (AMS Press, o/p). Ageing but interesting study of the French Protestant movement, focusing on the figure of Henri IV.

Mack Holt *The French Wars of Religion, 1562–1629* (Cambridge UP). A recent survey of the whole period of the Wars of Religion, available in paperback as part of the New Approaches to European History series.

James Valone *Huguenot Politics, 1601–1622* (Edwin Mellen). Recently published, exacting study of the Huguenot situation during the reign of the former Protestant Henri IV.

Eighteenth and nineteenth centuries

Anthony Crubaugh *Balancing the Scales of Justice: Local Courts and Rural Society in Southwest France, 1750–1800* (Pennsylvania State University, US). Engaging new academic study of local court documents, revealing the subtleties of peasant life in Languedoc in the era of the Revolution.

Norman Hampson *A Social History of the French Revolution* (University of Toronto). An analysis that concentrates on the personalities involved. Its particular interest lies in the attention it gives to the *sans-culottes*, the ordinary poor of Paris.

Christopher Hibbert *The Days of*

the French Revolution (Quill). Well-paced and entertaining narrative treatment by a master historian.

★ **Peter McPhee** *A Social History of France, 1780–1880* (Routledge, o/p). A scholarly work arguing that historians have underestimated the fundamental differences between how people lived and thought in 1880 compared with the time of the 1789 Revolution. He goes into such subjects as relations between men and women, education and reading material, the economy and culture, and changes in the physical environment.

J.M. Thompson *The French Revolution* (Blackwell). A detailed and passionate account, first published in 1943, but still the classic depiction in English.

Twentieth century

H.R. Kedward *In Search of the Maquis: Rural Resistance in South France 1942–44* (Oxford UP). Written in a slightly dry style, but full of fascinating detail about the brave and often mortal struggle of the countless ordinary people across France who fought to drive the Germans from their country.

Barbara Tuchman *The Proud Tower* (Papermac; Ballantine). A portrait of England, France, the US, Germany and Russia in the years 1890–1914. Written in Tuchman's inimitable and readable style, it includes a superb chapter on the extraordinary passions and enmities aroused by the Dreyfus Affair which rocked French society between 1894 and 1899, and on the different currents in the rising socialist movement in the run-up to World War I, centring on the life of Jean Jaurès.

★ **Paul Webster** *Pétain's Crime: The Full Story of French Collaboration in the Holocaust* (Papermac; IR Dee). The fascinating and alarming story of the Vichy regime's more than willing collaboration with the Holocaust, and the bravery of those, especially the communist resistance in occupied France, who attempted to prevent it.

Alexander Worth *France 1940–55* (Beacon Press, US, o/p). Extremely good and emotionally engaged portrayal of the taboo Occupation period in French history, followed by the Cold War and colonial struggle years in which the same political tensions and heart-searching were at play.

Society and politics

David S. Bell *French Politics Today: New Edition* (University of Manchester). Comprehensive yet concise introduction to French politics at the dawn of the twenty-first century.

Jose Bové *The World is Not for Sale: Farmers Against Junkfood* (Verso). A manifesto by the US-born self-proclaimed saviour of French ecology and cuisine.

Bernard Henri-Lévy *Adventures on the Freedom Road: The French Intellectuals in the 20th Century* (Harvill). Huge, clever and complex essays by the contemporary philosopher-celebrity, mercilessly analysing the response of all the great French thinkers, of Left and Right, to the key events of the century. Easy to dip into, surprisingly readable and very provocative.

Ian Ousby *Occupation: The Ordeal of France 1940–1945* (John Murray, UK). Non-academic book which reflects the recent trend to deflate the myth of massive resistance to the Nazis. Examines the development of the Resistance and the counter-weight of collaboration.

David Thomson *Democracy in France Since 1870* (Cassell, UK, o/p). An inquiry into why a country with such a strong socialist tradition should have had so many reactionary governments.

Harold R. Weinstein *Jean Jaurès: A Study of Patriotism in the French Socialist Movement* (Octagon, US, o/p). First published in the 1930s this ageing but eminently eloquent study looks not only at the figure of Jaurès, but locates him in the wider context of late nineteenth-century French socialism.

Art and architecture

John Berger *The Success and Failure of Picasso* (Vintage). Although most strongly associated with Provence, Picasso also was influenced by and influenced Roussillonaise artists. The "success" of the title is self-explanatory; the failure (and the tragedy) lies in Picasso's poverty of subject matter – or so Berger argues in this brief and highly persuasive book. Perhaps the best one-volume study of Picasso in English.

Kenneth J. Conant *Carolingian and Romanesque Architecture, 800–1200* (Yale UP, o/p). Good European study with a focus on Cluny and the St-Jacques pilgrim route, which includes strong coverage of the sections through Languedoc.

Julia Bloch Frey *Toulouse-Lautrec: A Life* (Trafalgar Square, UK). An intimate look at the life of the painter, with special emphasis on his friends, family, and artistic contemporaries.

Walter F. Friedlaender *David to Delacroix* (Harvard UP, o/p).

Respected survey of French art from the late seventeenth to late nineteenth centuries, from Neoclassicism through to Romanticism, and including figures who were influential in Languedoc and Roussillon.

John Golding *Cubism: A History and an Analysis 1907–1914* (Faber & Faber; Harvard UP, o/p). Excellent work on the formative stages of Cubism, particularly relevant for a journey to Céret.

Edward Lucie-Smith *A Concise History of French Painting* (Norton). If you're after an art reference book, this will do as well as any . . . though there are of course hundreds of books on particular French art movements.

Sarah Whitfield *Fauvism* (Thames & Hudson). A survey of the movement, accompanied by colour plates, emphasizing the major figure of Matisse, but with good material on Maillol and lesser-known artists.

Regional literature

Anonymous *Aucassin et Nicolette* (French & European Publications). Dating from the fourteenth century, perhaps the first European musical play. Recounts the impossible love between a prince of Beaucaire and a former Muslim slave-girl in Tarascon.

Michael Baigent, et al. *Holy Blood, Holy Grail* (Dell). Learn what happened to the Holy Grail, how

Jesus didn't die on the cross, how the Knights Templars are a force to be reckoned with and how Rennes-le-Chateau is the key.

★ **Alessandro Barrico** *Silk* (Vintage). Sensual love story set in the aftermath of the silk crisis of nineteenth-century Languedoc.

Sophie Burnham *The Treasure of Montségur: A Novel of Cathars* (Harper San Francisco). A thirteenth-century bodice-ripper in which Cathar Jeanne recounts her sex-tinged heretical past to a Catholic lover.

★ **Julius Caesar** *The Gallic War* (Loeb Classical Library). A highly subjective but majestically written account of the Roman experience in France.

Charmaine Craig *The Good Men: A Novel of Heresy* (Riverhead). Another bodice-ripping tale of heretical lust and unrequited love set in fourteenth-century Montaillou.

Alphonse Daudet *In the Land of Pain* (Knopf). Memoirs and notes which chart the nineteenth-century Beaucaire author's descent into the latter, fatal stages of syphilis.

Lawrence Durrell *Spirit of Place: Letters and Essays on Travel* (Dutton, o/p). A collection of letters to friends and contemporaries, including T.S. Eliot, written during Durrell's retirement in Sommières.

André Gide *If It Die…An Autobiography* (Vintage, US). Gide's spiritual autobiography, sensual and introspective, including his time in Uzès.

Arthur Guirdham *Cathars & Reincarnation* (C.W. Daniel). In this non-fiction study an English schoolgirl is allegedly hypnotically induced to recall her past life as a Cathar.

Christopher Hope *Signs of the Heart: Love and Death in Languedoc* (Macmillan). Award-winning South African-born novelist writes about his life in Languedoc.

Zoe Oldenbourg *Destiny of Fire* (Carrol & Graf). Historical novel set in the age of the Albigensian Crusade, written by a respected French historian.

★ **Gaston Phébus** *The Hunting Book of Gaston Phébus* (PTT). Beautifully illuminated facsimile edition of a 1405 manuscript of the count of Foix's hunting manual.

Antoine de Saint-Exupéry *Night Flight* (Harvest). The Toulousain aviator and author of *The Little Prince* recounts in novel format the dangers and exhilaration of flying the southern Atlantic route in the 1920s and 30s.

★ **Janet Shirley** *Song of the Cathar Wars* (Ashgate). Translation of two contemporary accounts of the Cathar wars of 1204–1218, written by a Crusade-supporter and an Occitan sympathizer.

Robert Louis Stevenson *Travels With a Donkey in the Cévennes* (Marlboro Travel). Traveller, spy and author, Robert Louis Stevenson tours Camisard country in the mid-nineteenth century, reflecting on the land and people of upland Languedoc.

Paul Valéry *Selected Writings* (New Directions). A good introduction for English-speakers to the thoughts and writing of the Sètois Symbolist.

Travel books and guides

Sabine Baring-Gould *In Troubadour-Land: A Ramble in Provence and Languedoc* (W.H. Allen, o/p). A very British, late nineteenth-century aristocratic ramble through the French south, offering an interesting perspective of the region under the Third Republic.

James Bromwich *The Roman Remains of Southern France* (Routledge). The only comprehensive guide on the subject – detailed,

well illustrated and approachable. In addition to accounts of the famous sites, it will lead you off the map to little-known discoveries.

Glynn Christian *Edible France* (Grub Street; Interlink). A guide to food rather than restaurants, concentrating on regional produce, local specialities, markets and the best shops for buying goodies to bring back home.

Cicerone Walking Guides

(Cicerone, UK). Neat, durable guides, with detailed route descriptions. Titles include *The Way of St James* (GR65); *The Pyrenean Trail* (GR10); and *Walks and Climbs in the Pyrénées*.

★ **Henry Cleere** *Southern France* (Oxford, UK). Written by a true expert, this gives detailed information and background on 34 archeological sites, famous and obscure, found within the bounds of this Guide.

Mary Davis *The Green Guide to France* (Green Print, UK, o/p). Definitely not the Michelin version, this is a resource guide to French national parks and wildlife reserves, vegetarian restaurants, communes and the like.

Nina Epton *The Valley of the Pyrene* (Cassell, o/p). Lively Fifties-era memoir of a tour through Ariège, peppered with entertaining anecdotes.

Footpaths of Europe *Walking the Pyrénées* (Robertson McCarta, UK, o/p). Route guide covering the system of GR footpaths, illustrated with 1:50,000 colour survey maps. It is an English version of the Pyrenees *Topoguide des Sentiers de Grande Randonnée* (CNSGR, Paris), which is widely available in France and not hard to follow for anyone with a working knowledge of French.

Peter Gorley *The Wines of Languedoc-Roussillon* (Hamilton John Publishing, UK). Lively, fact-packed guide to wines and *domaines*, with complete information on visiting times, recommended vintages and tips for the aspiring *enologue*.

★ **David Hampshire**, *Living and Working in France* (Survival Books, UK). Now in its fifth edition, this comprehensive book offers everything for the long-term traveller or resident, from house purchasing to signing on.

Rion Klawinski, *Chasing the Heretics: A Modern Journey through Languedoc* (Ruminator, US). A traveller's account of the Cathar heresy and the Albigensian Crusade, arranged in a guidebook format. A good handbook for those who want to make a Cathar-themed trip.

Saskia Reilly and Lorin David Kalisky, *Living, Studying, and Working in France: Everything You Need to Know to Fulfill Your Dreams of Living Abroad* (Owl, US). Two journalists give you a step-by-step rundown on coping with and getting the most out of life in France.

Kev Reynolds, *Walks and Climbs in the Pyrénées* (Cicerone Press, UK). The classic English guide for walking in the Pyrenees.

John Sturrock, *The French Pyrénées* (Faber & Faber, o/p). Well-written travelogue emphasizing the history of the French side of the range. Covers the mountains from coast to coast, but has significant sections covering Ariège and Roussillon.

★ **Topoguide Series** (Féderation Française de Randonnées Pédestres, France). Books featuring detailed hiking instructions (in French) and maps. A volume is published for each *région* (50 routes) and *département* (30 routes) covered in this Guide. Widely available in French bookshops and tourist offices.

Language

Language

Occitan and Catalan 413

French 417

Glossary 430

Occitan and Catalan

B y the time the Roman Empire in the west disintegrated, Latin had become the language of daily speech in nearly all of what is now France. Over the course of the following centuries, spoken Latin began to evolve into local variants and eventually into new Romance languages, from Spanish to Romanian. In the south of France (and in part of modern Italy) Occitan (pronounced ok-si-tan) or the Langue d'Oc developed– so called for its word for "yes", which set it apart from the northern French Langue d'Oïl (oui). Occitan itself had discrete regional variants, chief among them Provençal in the east (including Nîmes), Limousin in the north, Gascon in the west (including Ariège and the Vall d'Aran in Spain) and Languedocien, from the Corbières to the Camargue. In northeast Spain and across the present-day border into southern France emerged the Catalan language, which bears similarities to both Occitan and Castilian Spanish. Ironically, the name Catalan derives from the same root as the name of its chief rival language, Castilian, both terms referring to the castles which covered the landscapes of each region.

Occitan language and culture

Around the turn of the first millennium, a distinct Occitan literary language emerged, thanks to the wealth of the southern counts and their patronage of **troubadours**. These poets composed and performed works which were sung accompanied by music, for which they were also known as *trovadors* or *jongleurs* ("players" [of instruments]). The themes of their works varied from popular or religiously toned epics, like the *Chanson de Roland*, to portrayals of courtly love, considered to be the most elegant of subjects. Across these could be found recurring motifs, including righteous battle (for example, against the infidel), unrequited love and, above all, the glorification of good manners, sophistication and virtues, such as knightly loyalty or pious chastity. The poetry of courtly love was not erotic in nature; the idea was that the poet should be recognized as honourable by the noble woman (or man) who was the object of the work. The genre was so idealized that the great troubadour Jaufré Rudel claimed to have fallen in love with the countess of Tripoli without having ever laid eyes on her. Troubadours were not merely court entertainers, as many were noblemen themselves, and the first is said to have been the powerful duke, William IX of Aquitaine, father of Eleanor of Aquitaine, later Queen of England. But the bulk of them were not wealthy, and they practised their art as a way of ingratiating themselves with a noble house, and entering its service, much as a knight would.

The Albigensian Crusades of the thirteenth century brought about the end of many of the native ruling families in Languedoc and led to an influx of northern nobles. Naturally, these were French in cultural orientation rather than Occitan, and the literature of the language declined as sources of patronage dried up and it waned as an administrative language. Occitan literature persevered in prose, which emphasized secular and narrative themes. The decline

413

of the language was met with some alarm, and in 1323 a group of poets from Toulouse determined to save the poetic tradition of the troubadours by instituting the **jocs florals** ("floral games") – a sort of poetic Olympics in which winners were awarded gilded flowers. The tradition has continued since that time, held annually on May 3, although in 1694, Louis XIV Frenchified it and established in Toulouse a society called the Académie des Jeux Floraux, which administers the games to this day. With the establishment of the Jocs Florals, Occitan survived as a literary language for a time, but with the increasing centralization of the realm, devolved once again into an unwritten language of common speech. In 1539, on the eve of the Wars of Religion, François I declared at Villers-Cotterêts that French – the dialect of the **Langue d'Oïl** which was spoken in the area around Paris – was to be the only language of administration in his realms.

As the language of education and administration, French thus displaced Occitan, which was – and sometimes still is – referred to insultingly by Francophones as *patois* ("the dialect"). It was not until the mid-nineteenth century that it was revived in literature, in an intellectual environment which saw subject peoples across Europe establish or re-establish literatures for their own languages. The major figure in the new Occitan literature was **Frédéric Mistral**, the venerated Provençal poet and cultural messiah. Born in 1830, Mistral spent a lifetime working to revive and modernize Provençal Occitan as a written and spoken language, producing countless works of literature and grammar, and campaiging in favour of Occitan folk practices, such as *tauromachie*. His efforts were recognized on an international level when he received a Nobel Prize in 1904. Meanwhile, philologists strove to standardize the language, which had degenerated into countless local variants as a result of its subjugation to French.

Nevertheless, reform was slow. Although it may have been the common language of the villages and fields through the middle of the twentieth century, the relentlessly centralist policies of the state and the greater diffusion of French-language education and literacy conspired against Occitan's revival. In Toulouse, the **Escola Occitana** (1919) and the **Institut d'Études Occitanes** (1945) were founded to promote and modernize the language, but it was not until 1951 that it was permitted to teach Occitan in schools, and only in 1969 that educational authorities officially ranked it as a language.

Ironically, the only area which has Occitan as an official and dominant language is Spain's **Vall d'Aran**, a tiny valley high in the Pyrenees to the southwest of Toulouse. **Aranese**, as the seven thousand or so inhabitants call the language, is in fact the Gascon dialect of the Langue d'Oc. In Languedoc, proper efforts continue to revive the language, but since the 1920s the number of speakers has decreased from one million to two million – an optimistic estimate which sets the proportion of Occitan speakers as fourteen percent of the whole of Languedoc. (By contrast, in Corsica some fifty percent of the populace speak native Corse.) Nevertheless, there are Occitan-language newspapers (like the weekly *La Setmana*), radio stations (*Ràdio País*) and television broadcasts, and bilingual public schools have been established in Albi, Toulouse, Monestiès and St-Sulpice. As a visitor, you're not likely to encounter Occitan either spoken or written, apart from the Occitan street signs which are frequently set alongside their French counterparts.

Although readership is limited, authors such as **Max Roqueta**, **Bernat Maciet** and **Marcèla Delpastre** have begun to publish novels in Occitan, theatre companies tour performing original and traditional works, and musical groups of the 1970s and 80s, like Massilia and the Fabulous Troubadours, created the modern Occitan musical style called **nòva cançon**, which blends traditional melodies and instruments with modern styles, and still has a hard-core following today. For the most part, however, Occitan musicians have adopted other genres, from jazz, blues and folk, to rap and punk fusions (here known as *ragga-aïoli*), and of course regional and linguistic identity do not necessarily coincide – Toulouse's **Zebda**, a strongly regional-minded group whose mix of politics and music is reminiscent of America's Rage Against the Machine, sings exclusively in French.

Although Languedoc is rich with customs and traditions which set it apart from the rest of France, such as water-jousting and *tauromachie*, it is thoroughly subsumed in the French identity. There is no independence movement here such as exists in Corsica, the Basque Country or Brittany, and regional identity is vague, focusing with romantic nostalgia on episodes of northern French oppression such as the Albigensian Crusades and the Wars of Religion. Bernat Lubat, a renowned Occitan jazz musician, expresses an opinion on the subject of regional independence which is representative of the overwhelming majority of the area's inhabitants: "The desire for independence seems to me neither interesting, nor realistic, nor even poetic."

Catalan language and culture

Most of the world's ten million or so Catalan speakers live in Spain, in a band of territory stretching south from the Pyrenees to Valencia, and in the Balearic Islands. The 120,000 Catalan speakers of France live in the *département* of Pyrénées-Orientales, which incorporates the Catalan cultural regions of **La Cerdanya** and **Rosselló**, and has its capital at Perpignan (Perpinyà in Catalan). Here, they represent 34 percent of the population, although only half of that figure claim a high proficiency level.

The **Cerdagne** and **Roussillon**, traditionally part of the realms of the counts of Barcelona, were long disputed in border wars waged with the French. The French Crown took permanent control of the territory in the 1620s under Richelieu, but the land was not formally ceded by Spain until the Treaty of the Pyrenees (1649), negotiated by Louis XIV. Curiously, a fine reading of the text of the treaty allowed Spain to maintain control of the town of Llívia, which has remained a Spanish enclave, a few kilometres inside the French border, to this day.

Catalan, like Occitan, was a language of troubadours of the Middle Ages, and had a healthy tradition of narrative literature before Spanish or English. One of the most famous early Catalan works is the autobiographical *Llibre de fets* (Book of Deeds), written in the thirteenth century by the great count-king, **Jaume I the Conqueror**, son of Pere el Catòlic, who was killed by Simon de Montfort at Muret. Through the Middle Ages, Catalan culture flourished thanks to the powerful maritime dominion of Barcelona. The count-king Joan I (1387–96) instituted a Catalan version of the **Jocs Florals**, in imitation of the Occitan contest. Winners were given a real, rather than a golden flower though, an early reflection perhaps of the famous Catalan frugality. But as happened to Occitan, the domination of powerful "foreign" administration – in this case, the Hapsburgs of Madrid – contributed to the marginalization of the language, and literary usage declined after the fifteenth century. This process was exacerbated in Roussillon by the French takeover in the seventeenth century. Like Occitan, Catalan was proscribed from official use, and denigrated to the status of a peasant *patois*.

The wave of regional and national consciousness which swept through Europe in the mid-nineteenth century washed over Catalonia as well, where the linguistic renaissance was spearheaded by the philologist **Pompeu Fabra i Poch**, who set about standardizing the Catalan grammar, and writers, such as the poet **Manuel Milà i Fontanals**. In 1859, the Catalan Jocs Florals were revived. With the victory of strongly Castile-centric Franco in the Spanish Civil War, a stream of Catalan refugees spilled over the border into France, giving the native language and culture an additional boost in Roussillon and the Cerdagne. Catalan was proscribed under the fascist dictatorship in Spain, but the postwar period in France signalled a liberalization of language laws and the admission of Catalan to the public school curriculum.

Today, however, while there is a lively literary, television and cinema culture in Catalonia proper, in Roussillon it is almost nonexistent. Some Catalan folkloric customs have survived the centuries of French domination though, and still contribute to the defined flavour of Roussillon. Among these are the distinctive **Christmas customs** (see box on p.349), and the penitents' processions of **Setmana Santa** (Holy Week). A recent addition is the **sardana**, brought to Roussillon by the refugees of 1939, and a symbol of Catalan nationalism. It is a popular dance, in which participants, frequently wearing the traditional woven *espardinya* shoes, form a circle linking hands and do a slow hopping dance to the minor strains of an eleven-piece *colbla* (orchestra). Each dancer places some object (frequently a handbag) in the centre, which is said to symbolize sharing; and the dance is undemanding enough that young and old alike can participate (you'll find information on where and when you can see the *sardana* on p.324).

The sizeable independence movement in Spanish Catalonia advocates the unification of all of the *Països Catalans*, including Roussillon and the Cerdagne, as a separate state. Indeed, the most potent symbol of Catalan identity, towering **Mont Canigou** (*El Canigó* in Catalan), sits in French territory, between Prades and the border. An imposing mountain casting its shadow over all of Roussillon, it had long been venerated by the region's inhabitants when a monastery was founded on its slopes by the grandson of Guifré el Pelós in 1001. Over the centuries its symbolism intensified, and for Catalans it became their sacred mountain, celebrated in literature through to Jacint Verdaguer's epic *Canigó* of the late nineteenth century. To this day it is the site of a yearly midsummer torchlight pilgrimage to celebrate the *día de Sant Joan* (St John's Day) on June 24. The traditional pagan solstice holiday, celebrated here, as in many societies, by raising a great fire, stands as a Catalan "national" holiday, celebrated in both Spanish and French Catalonia. But aside from annoying graffiti on buildings and road signs, there is little evidence of nationalist fervour on the French side of the border. Although Catalan speakers of Roussillon, and even many non-speakers, delight in the distinctiveness which the region's diluted Catalan identity gives them, they tend to recall the revolts against the French merely for their sense of rose-tinted nostalgia. The region is culturally

Studying Catalan

Naturally, the best place to **study Catalan** is in Catalonia proper, but if you are determined to do so in Roussillon, your best option is to take a course at **Prades'** Catalan
summer university (℡04.68.96.10.84 and ℡(34)933.172.411, ⊚www.ucestiu.com).

very much closer to Paris than Barcelona – convincing confirmation of its predominantly French sensibility can be found in the election in 1995 of the
extreme right-wing mayor of Perpignan, Jean-Paul Alduy of the Nouvelle
UDF, who has remained in power since.

French

L

lthough Occitan is still spoken among some older rural folk and by
recent students of the language, it serves little purpose for the visitor.
Catalan, while more current, is nevertheless a second language
throughout Roussillon and the Cerdagne. As a foreigner speaking
French, you will be understood by all and you will not offend anyone's regional sensibilities.

French can be a deceptively familiar language because of the number of
words and structures it shares with English. Despite this, it's far from easy,
though the bare essentials are not difficult to learn and can make all the difference. Even just saying "Bonjour Madame/Monsieur" and then gesticulating
will usually get you a smile and helpful service. People working in tourist
offices, hotels and so on, almost always speak English and tend to use it when
you're struggling to speak French – be grateful, not insulted.

Of the **phrasebooks** and **dictionaries** available, the *Rough Guide French
Dictionary Phrasebook* is a handy and comprehensive companion, with both
English–French and French–English sections, along with cultural tips for tricky
situations and a menu reader. There's also the *French and English Slang Dictionary*
(Harrap/Prentice Hall) and *Dictionary of Modern Colloquial French* (Routledge)
– both volumes are a bit large to carry, but they are the key to all you'll ever
want to know about the French vernacular.

French pronunciation

One easy rule to remember is that **consonants** at the ends of words are usually silent. *Pas plus tard* (not later) is thus pronounced "pa-plu-tarr". But when
the following word begins with a vowel, you run the two together: *pas après*
(not after) becomes "pazaprey".

Vowels are the hardest sounds to get right. Roughly:

a	as in h**a**t		*è*	between g**e**t and g**u**t
e	as in g**e**t		*eu*	like the **u** in h**u**rt
é	between g**e**t and g**a**te		*i*	as in mach**i**ne

o	as in h**o**t	*u*	as in a pursed-lip version of
o, au	as in **o**ver		**u**se
ou	as in f**oo**d		

More awkward are the **combinations** *in/im, en/em, an/am, on/om, un/um* at the ends of words, or followed by consonants other than *n* or *m*. Again, roughly:

in/im like the **an** in **an**xious
an/am, en/em like the **don** in **Don**caster when said with a nasal accent
on/om like the **don** in **Don**caster said by someone with a heavy cold
un/um like the **u** in **u**nderstand

Consonants are much as in English, except that: *ch* is always "sh", *c* is "s", *h* is silent, *th* is the same as "t", *ll* is like the "y" in yes, *w* is "v", and *r* is growled (or rolled).

French words and phrases

Basic vocabulary

French nouns are divided into masculine and feminine. This causes difficulties with adjectives, whose endings have to change to suit the gender of the nouns they qualify. If you know some grammar, you will know what to do. If not, stick to the masculine form, which is the simplest – it's what we have done in this glossary.

today	aujourd'hui	**that one**	celà
yesterday	hier	**open**	ouvert
tomorrow	demain	**closed**	fermé
in the morning	le matin	**big**	grand
in the afternoon	l'après-midi	**small**	petit
in the evening	le soir	**more**	plus
now	maintenant	**less**	moins
later	plus tard	**a little**	un peu
at one o'clock	à une heure	**a lot**	beaucoup
at three o'clock	à trois heures	**cheap**	bon marché
at ten-thirty	à dix heures et	**expensive**	cher
	demie	**good**	bon
at midday	à midi	**bad**	mauvais
man	un homme	**hot**	chaud
woman	une femme	**cold**	froid
here	ici	**with**	avec
there	là	**without**	sans
this one	ceci		

Numbers

1	un	3	trois
2	deux	4	quatre

5	cinq	40	quarante
6	six	50	cinquante
7	sept	60	soixante
8	huit	70	soixante-dix
9	neuf	75	soixante-quinze
10	dix	80	quatre-vingts
11	onze	90	quatre-vingt-dix
12	douze	95	quatre-vingt-quinze
13	treize		
14	quatorze	100	cent
15	quinze	101	cent-et-un
16	seize	200	deux cents
17	dix-sept	300	trois cents
18	dix-huit	500	cinq cents
19	dix-neuf	1000	mille
20	vingt	2000	deux milles
21	vingt-et-un	5000	cinq milles
22	vingt-deux	1,000,000	un million
30	trente		

Days and dates

January	janvier	Sunday	dimanche
February	février	Monday	lundi
March	mars	Tuesday	mardi
April	avril	Wednesday	mercredi
May	mai	Thursday	jeudi
June	juin	Friday	vendredi
July	juillet	Saturday	samedi
August	août	August 1	le premier août
September	septembre	March 2	le deux mars
October	octobre	July 14	le quatorze juillet
November	novembre	November 23	le vingt-trois novembre
December	décembre	2002	deux mille deux

Talking to people

When addressing people, you should always use *Monsieur* for a man, *Madame* for a woman, *Mademoiselle* for a young woman or girl. Plain *bonjour* by itself is not enough. This isn't as formal as it seems, and it has its uses when you've forgotten someone's name or want to attract someone's attention.

excuse me	Pardon	I'm English	Je suis anglais[e]
do you speak English?	Parlez-vous anglais?	Irish	irlandaise[e]
		Scottish	écossais[e]
how do you say it in French?	Comment ça se dit en français?	Welsh	gallois[e]
		American	américain[e]
what's your name?	Comment vous appelez-vous?	Australian	australien[ne]
		Canadian	canadien[ne]
my name is ...	Je m'appelle ...	a New Zealander	néo-zélandais[e]

yes	oui	good night	bonne nuit
no	non	how are you?	Comment allez-vous?/Ça va?
I understand	Je comprends		
I don't understand	Je ne comprends pas	fine, thanks	Très bien, merci
		I don't know	Je ne sais pas
can you speak slower?	S'il vous plaît, parlez moins vite	let's go	Allons-y
		see you tomorrow	Á demain
OK/agreed	d'accord	see you soon	Á bientôt
please	s'il vous plaît	sorry	Pardon, Madame/ Je m'excuse
thank you	merci		
hello	bonjour	leave me alone (aggressive)	Fichez-moi la paix!
goodbye	au revoir		
good morning /afternoon	bonjour	please help me	Aidez-moi, s'il vous plait
good evening	bonsoir		

Finding the way

bus	autobus/bus/car	hitchhiking	autostop
bus station	gare routière	on foot	à pied
bus stop	arrêt	where are you going?	Vous allez où?
car	voiture		
train/taxi/ferry	train/taxi/ferry	I'm going to ...	Je vais à ...
boat	bâteau	I want to get off at ...	Je voudrais descendre à ...
plane	avion		
train station	gare (SNCF)	the road to ...	la route pour ...
platform	quai	near	près/pas loin
what time does it leave?	Il part à quelle heure?	far	loin
		left	à gauche
what time does it arrive?	Il arrive à quelle heure?	right	à droite
		straight on	tout droit
a ticket to ...	un billet pour ...	on the other side of	à l'autre côté de
single ticket	aller simple	on the corner of	à l'angle de
return ticket	aller retour	next to	à côté de
validate your ticket	compostez votre billet	behind	derrière
		in front of	devant
valid for	valable pour	before	avant
ticket office	vente de billets	after	après
how many kilometres?	combien de kilomètres?	under	sous
		to cross	traverser
how many hours?	combien d'heures?	bridge	pont

Questions and requests

The simplest way of asking a question is to start with *s'il vous plaît* (please), then name the thing you want in an interrogative tone of voice. For example:

where is there a bakery?	S'il vous plaît, la boulangerie?	similarly with requests:	
		can we have a room for two?	S'il vous plaît, une chambre pour deux?
which way is it to the Maison Carée?	S'il vous plaît, la route pour la Maison Carée?		
		can I have a kilo of oranges?	S'il vous plaît, un kilo d'oranges?

Question words:		when?	quand?
where?	où?	why?	pourquoi?
how?	comment?	at what time?	à quelle heure?
how many/how much?	combien?	what is/which is?	quel est?

Accommodation

a room for one /two people	une chambre pour une/deux personnes	sheets	draps
a double bed	un lit double	blankets	couvertures
a room with a shower	une chambre avec douche	quiet	calme
		noisy	bruyant
a room with a bath	une chambre avec salle de bain	hot water	eau chaude
		cold water	eau froide
for one/two/three nights	pour une/deux /trois nuits	Is breakfast included?	Est-ce que le petit déjeuner es compris?
can I see it?	Je peux la voir?	I would like breakfast	Je voudrais prendre le petit déjeuner
a room on the courtyard	une chambre sur la cour	I don't want breakfast	Je ne veux pas de petit déjeuner
a room over the street	une chambre sur la rue	can we camp here?	On peut camper ici?
first floor	premier étage	campsite	un camping/ter- rain de camping
second floor	deuxième étage		
with a view	avec vue	tent	une tente
key	clef	tent space	un emplacement
to iron	repasser	youth hostel	auberge de jeunesse
do laundry	faire la lessive		

Cars

service station	garage	air line	ligne à air
service	service	put air in the tyres	gonfler les pneus
to park the car	garer la voiture	battery	batterie
car park	un parking	the battery is dead	la batterie est morte
no parking	défense de stationner/ stationnement interdit	plugs	bougies
		to break down	tomber en panne
		gas can	bidon
		insurance	assurance
gas station	poste d'essence	green card	carte verte
fuel	essence	traffic lights	feux
(to) fill it up	faire le plein	red light	feu rouge
oil	huile	green light	feu vert

Cycling

to adjust	régler	bicycle	le vélo
axle	l'axe	bottom bracket	le logement du pédalier
ball-bearing	le roulement à billes		
battery	la pile	brake cable	le cable
bent	tordu	brakes	les freins

broken	cassé	pedal	le pédale
bulb	l'ampoule	pump	la pompe
chain	la chaîne	puncture	la crevaison
cotter pin	la clavette	rack	le porte-bagages
to deflate	dégonfler	to raise	remonter
derailleur	le dérailleur	to repair	réparer
frame	le cadre	saddle	la selle
gears	les vitesses	to screw	visser/serrer
grease	la graisse	spanner	la clef
handlebars	le guidon	spoke	le rayon
to inflate	gonfler	to straighten	redresser
inner tube	la chambre à air	stuck	coincé
loose	déserré	tight	serré
to lower	baisser	toe clips	les cale-pieds
mudguard	le garde-boue	tyre	le pneu
pannier	le pannier	wheel	la roue

Health matters

doctor	médecin	stomach ache	mal à l'estomac
I don't feel well	Je ne me sens pas bien	period	règles
medicines	médicaments	pain	douleur
prescription	ordonnance	it hurts	ça fait mal
I feel sick	Je suis malade	chemist	pharmacie
I have a headache	J'ai mal à la tête	hospital	hôpital

Other needs

bakery	boulangerie	bank	banque
food shop	alimentation	money	argent
supermarket	supermarché	toilets	toilettes
to eat	manger	police	police
to drink	boire	telephone	téléphone
camping gas	camping gaz	cinema	cinéma
tobacconist	tabac	theatre	théâtre
stamps	timbres	to reserve/book	réserver

Food

Basic terms

l'addition	bill/check	fumé	smoked
beurre	butter	huile	oil
bouteille	bottle	lait	milk
chauffé	heated	moutarde	mustard
couteau	knife	œuf	egg
cru	raw	offert	free
cuillère	spoon	pain	bread
cuit	cooked	poivre	pepper
emballé	wrapped	salé	salted/spicy
à emporter	takeaway	sel	salt
fourchette	fork	sucre	sugar
		sucré	sweet

table	**table**	vinaigre	**vinegar**
verre	**glass**		

Un sandwich/une baguette (a sandwich)

au jambon	**with ham**		**chicken or egg**
au fromage	**with cheese**		**sandwich**
au saucisson	**with sausage**	pain bagnat	**bread roll with egg,**
à l'ail	**with garlic**		**olives, salad,**
au poivre	**with pepper**		**tuna, anchovies**
au pâté	**with pâté (country-**		**and olive oil**
(de campagne)	**style)**	panini	**toasted Italian**
croque-monsieur	**grilled cheese and**		**sandwich**
	ham sandwich	tartine	**buttered bread or**
croque-madame	**grilled cheese and**		**open sandwich**
	bacon, sausage,		

œufs (eggs)

au plat	**fried**	durs	**hard-boiled**
à la coque	**boiled**	brouillés	**scrambled**

omelette (omelette)

nature	**plain**	au fromage	**with cheese**
aux fines herbes	**with herbs**		

Pasta (pâtes), pancakes (crêpes) and flans (tartes)

nouilles	**noodles**		**pancake**
pâtes fraîches	**fresh pasta**	panisse	**thick chickpea flour**
pâte	**pasta or pastry**		**pancake**
raviolis	**pasta parcels of**	pissaladière	**tart of fried onions**
	meat or chard – a		**with anchovies**
	Provençal, not		**and black olives**
	Italian invention	tarte flambée	**thin pizza-like**
crêpe au sucre/	**pancake with**		**pastry topped with**
aux œufs	**sugar/eggs**		**onion, cream and**
galette	**buckwheat pancake**		**bacon or other**
socca	**thin chickpea flour**		**combinations**

Soups (soupes)

baudroie	**fish soup with**	consommé	**clear soup**
	vegetables, garlic	garbure	**potato, cabbage and**
	and herbs		**meat soup**
bisque	**shellfish soup**	pistou	**parmesan, basil and**
bouillabaisse	**soup/stew with**		**garlic paste added**
	chunks of		**to soup**
	assorted fish	potée auvergnate	**cabbage and meat**
bouillon	**broth or stock**		**soup**
bourride	**thick fish soup**	potage	**thick vegetable soup**

rouille	red pepper, garlic and saffron mayonnaise served with fish soup	soupe à l'oignon	onion soup with rich cheese topping
		velouté	thick soup, usually fish or poultry

Starters (hors d'œuvres)

assiette anglaise	plate of cold meats	hors d'œurvres variés	plus smoked or marinated fish
crudités	raw vegetables with dressings		
hors d'œuvres	combination of the above		

Fish (poisson), seafood (fruits de mer) and shellfish (crustaces or coquillages)

aiglefin	small haddock or fresh cod	gambas	king prawns
		hareng	herring
anchois	anchovies	homard	lobster
anguilles	eels	huîtres	oysters
barbue	brill	langouste	spiny lobster
baudroie	monkfish or anglerfish	langoustines	saltwater crayfish (scampi)
bigourneau	periwinkle	limande	lemon sole
brème	bream	lotte de mer	monkfish
bulot	whelk	loup de mer	sea bass
cabillaud	cod	maquereau	mackerel
calmar	squid	merlan	whiting
carrelet	plaice	moules	mussels (with
claire	type of oyster	(marinière)	shallots in white wine sauce)
colin	hake		
congre	conger eel	oursin	sea urchin
coques	cockles	palourdes	clams
coquilles St-Jacques	scallops	poissons de roche	fish from shore-line rocks
crabe	crab	praires	small clams
crevettes grises	shrimp	raie	skate
crevettes roses	prawns	rouget	red mullet
daurade	sea bream	saumon	salmon
éperlan	smelt or whitebait	sole	sole
escargots	snails	thon	tuna
favou(ille)	tiny crab	truite	trout
flétan	halibut	turbot	turbot
friture	assorted fried fish	violet	sea squirt

Fish dishes and terms

aïoli	garlic mayonnaise served with salt cod and other fish	assiette de pêcheur	assorted fish
		beignet	fritter
anchoïade	anchovy paste or sauce	darne	fillet or steak
		la douzaine	a dozen
arête	fish bone	frit	fried

friture	deep-fried small fish	mousse/	mousse
fumé	smoked	mousseline	
fumet	fish stock	pané	breaded
gigot de mer	large fish baked whole	poutargue	mullet roe paste
		raïto	red wine, olive, caper, garlic and shallot sauce
grillé	grilled		
hollandaise	butter and vinegar sauce		
		quenelles	light dumplings
à la meunière	in a butter, lemon and parsley sauce	thermidor	lobster grilled in its shell with cream sauce

Meat (viande) and poultry (volaille)

agneau (de pré-salé)	lamb (grazed on salt marshes)	lard, lardons	bacon, diced bacon
andouille, andouillette	tripe sausage	lièvre	hare
		merguez	spicy, red sausage
bifteck	steak	mouton	mutton
bœuf	beef	museau de veau	calf's muzzle
boudin blanc	sausage of white meats	oie	goose
		onglet	cut of beef
boudin noir	black pudding	os	bone
caille	quail	poitrine	breast
canard	duck	porc	pork
caneton	duckling	poulet	chicken
contrefilet	sirloin roast	poussin	baby chicken
coquelet	cockerel	ris	sweetbreads
dinde, dindon	turkey	rognons	kidneys
entrecôte	rib steak	rognons blancs	testicles
faux filet	sirloin steak	sanglier	wild boar
foie	liver	steak	steak
foie gras	(duck/goose) liver	tête de veau	calf's head (in jelly)
gigot (d'agneau)	leg (of lamb)	tournedos	thick slices of fillet
grenouilles (cuisses de)	frogs (legs)	tripes	tripe
		tripoux	mutton tripe
langue	tongue	veau	veal
lapin, lapereau	rabbit, young rabbit	venaison	venison

Meat and poultry dishes and terms

aïado	roast shoulder of lamb stuffed with garlic and other ingredients	baeckoffe	Alsatian hotpot of pork, mutton and beef baked with potato layers
aile	wing	blanquette, daube, estouffade, hochepôt, navarin, agoût	types of stew
au feu de bois	cooked over wood fire		
au four	baked		

blanquette de veau	veal in cream and mushroom sauce	grillade	grilled meat
bœuf bourguignon	beef stew with Burgundy, onions and mushrooms	garni	with vegetables
		gésier	gizzard
		grillé	grilled
canard à l'orange	roast duck with an orange and wine sauce	hâchis	chopped meat or mince hamburger
		magret de canard	duck breast
canard pâté de périgourdin	roast duck with prunes, foie gras and truffles	marmite	casserole
		médaillon	round piece
		mijoté	stewed
		pavé	thick slice
carré	best end of neck, chop or cutlet	pieds et paques	mutton or pork tripe and trotters
cassoulet	casserole of beans and meat	poêlé	pan-fried
choucroute	pickled cabbage with peppercorns, sausages, bacon and salami	poulet de Bresse	chicken from Bresse – the best
		râble	saddle
		rôti	roast
civit	game stew	sauté	lightly cooked in butter
confit	meat preserve	steak au poivre (vert/rouge)	steak in a black (green/red) peppercorn sauce
côte	chop, cutlet or rib		
cou	neck		
coq au vin	chicken cooked until it falls off the bone, with wine, onions and mushrooms	steak tartare	raw chopped beef, topped with a raw egg yolk
		tagine	North African casserole
cuisse	thigh or leg	tournedos rossini	beef fillet with foie gras and truffles
épaule	shoulder		
en croûte	in pastry	viennoise	fried in egg and breadcrumbs
farci	stuffed		
gigot (d'agneau)	leg (of lamb)		

Terms for steaks

bleu	almost raw	bien cuit	well done
saignant	rare	très bien cuit	very well done
à point	medium	brochette	kebab

Garnishes and sauces

américaine	white wine, cognac and tomato	béarnaise	sauce of egg yolks, white wine, shallots and vinegar
arlésienne	with tomatoes, onions, aubergines, potatoes and rice	beurre blanc	sauce of white wine and shallots, with butter
au porto	in port		
auvergnat	with cabbage, sausage and bacon	bonne femme	with mushrooms, bacon, potatoes and onions

bordelaise	in a red wine, shallot and bone-marrow sauce	forestière	with bacon and mushrooms
boulangère	baked with potatoes and onions	fricassée	rich, creamy sauce
		mornay	cheese sauce
bourgeoise	with carrots, onions, bacon, celery and braised lettuce	pays d'auge	cream and cider
		périgourdine	with foie gras and possibly truffles
chasseur	white wine, mushrooms and shallots	piquante	gherkins or capers, vinegar and shallots
châtelaine	with artichoke hearts and chestnut purée	provençale	tomatoes, garlic, olive oil and herbs
		savoyarde	with gruyère cheese
diable	strong mustard seasoning	véronique	grapes, wine and cream

Vegetables (*légumes*), herbs (*herbes*) and spices (*épices*)   ⓛ

ail	garlic	rouges, beurres)	string, kidney, butter)
anis	aniseed	laurier	bay leaf
artichaut	artichoke	lentilles	lentils
asperge	asparagus	maïs	corn
avocat	avocado	menthe	mint
basilic	basil	moutarde	mustard
betterave	beetroot	oignon	onion
blette/bette	Swiss chard	panais	parsnip
cannelle	cinnamon	pélandron	type of string bean
capre	caper	persil	parsley
cardon	cardoon, closely related to artichoke	petits pois	peas
carotte	carrot	piment	pimento
céleri	celery	pois chiche	chick peas
champignon, cèpe, chanterelle	types of mushrooms	pois mange-tout	mangetout
		pignons	pine nuts
chou (rouge)	(red) cabbage	poireau	leek
choufleur	cauliflower	poivron (vert, rouge)	sweet pepper (green, red)
concombre	cucumber		
cornichon	gherkin	pommes de terre	potatoes
echalotes	shallots		
endive	chicory	primeurs	spring vegetables
épinard	spinach	radis	radish
estragon	tarragon	riz	rice
fenouil	fennel	safran	saffron
férigoule	thyme (in Provençal)	salade verte	green salad
		sarrasin	buckwheat
fèves	broad beans	tomate	tomato
flageolets	white beans	truffes	truffles
gingembre	ginger		
haricots (verts,	beans (French/		

Vegetable dishes and terms

alicot	puréed potato with cheese			cream and eggs
allumettes	very thin chips		à la parisienne	sautéed in butter (potatoes); with white wine sauce and shallots
à l'anglaise	boiled			
beignet	fritter			
biologique	organic		parmentier	with potatoes
duxelles	fried mushrooms and shallots with cream		petits farcis	stuffed tomatoes, aubergines, courgettes and peppers
farci	stuffed			
feuille	leaf		pimenté	peppery hot
fines herbes	mixture of tarragon, parsley and chives		piquant	spicy
			pistou	ground basil, olive oil, garlic and parmesan
gratiné	browned with cheese or butter		râpée	grated or shredded
à la grecque	cooked in oil and lemon		sauté	lightly fried in butter
jardinière	with mixed diced vegetables		à la vapeur	steamed
			en verdure	garnished with green vegetables
mousseline	mashed potato with			

Fruit (*fruit*) and nuts (*noix*)

abricot	apricot		mangue	mango
acajou	cashew nut		marron	chestnut
amande	almond		melon	melon
ananas	pineapple		mirabelle	small yellow plum
banane	banana			
brugnon, nectarine	nectarine		myrtille	bilberry
cacahouète	peanut		noisette	hazelnut
cassis	blackcurrant		noix	nuts
cérise	cherry		orange	orange
citron	lemon		pamplemousse	grapefruit
citron vert	lime		pastèque	watermelon
datte	date		pêche	peach
figue	fig		pistache	pistachio
fraise (de bois)	strawberry (wild)		poire	pear
			pomme	apple
framboise	raspberry		prune	plum
fruit de la passion	passion fruit		pruneau	prune
grenade	pomegranate		raisin	grape
groseille	redcurrant		reine-claude	greengage

Fruit dishes and terms

agrumes	citrus fruits		crème de marrons	chestnut purée
beignet	fritter		flambé	set aflame in alcohol
compôte	stewed fruit			
coulis	sauce of puréed fruit		fougasse	bread flavoured with orange-

		frappé	iced
flower water or			
almonds (can be			
savoury)			

bombe	moulded ice-cream dessert	marrons Mont Banc	chestnut purée and cream on a rum-soaked sponge cake
brioche	sweet, high-yeast breakfast roll		
calisson	almond sweet	mousse au chocolat	chocolate mousse
charlotte	custard and fruit in lining of almond fingers	omelette norvégienne	baked alaska
chichi	doughnut shaped in a stick	palmier	caramelized puff pastry
clafoutis	heavy custard and fruit tart	parfait	frozen mousse, sometimes ice cream
crème Chantilly	vanilla-flavoured and sweetened whipped cream	petit-suisse	a smooth mixture of cream and curds
crème fraîche	sour cream	petits fours	bite-sized cakes/pastries
crème pâtissière	thick, eggy pastry-filling	poires belle hélène	pears and ice cream in chocolate sauce
crêpe suzette	thin pancake with orange juice and liqueur	tarte tatin	upside-down apple tart
fromage blanc	cream cheese	tarte tropezienne	sponge cake filled with custard
gaufre	waffle		
glace	ice cream		cream topped with nuts
Île flottante/ œufs à la neige	soft meringues floating on custard	tiramisu	mascarpone cheese, chocolate and cream
macaron	macaroon		
madeleine	small sponge cake	yaourt, yogourt	yoghurt

Dessert dishes and terms

barquette	small boat-shaped flan	gênoise	rich sponge cake
		pâte	pastry or dough
bavarois	refers to the mould, could be a mousse or custard	sablé	shortbread biscuit
		savarin	a filled, ring-shaped cake
coupe	a serving of ice cream	tarte	tart
		tartelette	small tart
crêpe	pancake		

L

Glossary

French terms

ABBAYE Abbey

AUBERGE DE JEUNESSE Youth hostel

BASILIQUE Basilica

BASSIN Reservoir

BASTIDE Planned, usually fortified town of the thirteenth century, typically laid out on a grid in a square or octagonal area

BOITE Nightclub/discotheque

CANTON District

CHAMBRES D'HÔTES Bed and breakfast

CHÂTEAU Fort, castle, mansion or country house

CITÉ Citadel: the fortified section (usually the oldest and highest part) of a town

CLOCHÉ Bell tower

COL Pass

COLOMBIER Dovecote

DÉCOUVERTE Open-pit mine

DÉFILÉ Narrow gorge, canyon

DÉPARTEMENT Administrative area, similar to an English county, within a *région*

DOMAINE Estate

DONJON Castle keep

ÉCLUSE Canal lock

ÉGLISE Church

ENCEINTE Area falling within the walls of a castle or town, or the defensive enclosure itself

ÉTANG Coastal lagoon, normally salt-water and connected to the sea.

ÉVÊCHÉ Palace or property pertaining to a bishop, or archbishop (archevêché)

FAUBOURG Extramural suburb, usually referring to late medieval town extensions built outside the walls of the original enceinte

FÊTE Festival

GARE Station

GARE ROUTIÈRE Bus station

GROTTE Cave

HALLES Market building

HORLOGE Clock

HÔTEL DE VILLE Town or city hall

HÔTEL PARTICULIER Private mansion or palace

MAIRIE Office of the mayor: town hall

MONASTÈRE Monastery

MUSÉE Museum

NAVETTE Shuttle service

PAYS Country, land

PIC Peak

PLACE Square

PONT Bridge

PONT DU DIABLE Arched medieval bridge

PONT VIEUX Old bridge

PORTE Gateway

PRÉFECTURE Main office, headquarters

PRISE DE L'EAU Dam

RÉGION Administrative region

TERROIR Literally meaning "soil", refers to traditional peasant cooking, using local ingredients

TOUR Tower

USINE Factory, workshop

VILLE BASSE Lower town

Artistic, architectural and archaeological terms

AMBULATORY Passage round the outer edge of a church's choir.

APSE Semicircular termination at the east end of a church.

ART DECO Geometrical style of art and architecture popular in the 1930s.

ART NOUVEAU Ornamental style of art and architecture which developed in the late nineteenth century, emphasizing decorative detail and avoiding straight clean lines.

BAROQUE High Renaissance period of art and architecture, distinguished by extreme ornateness, exuberance and complex spatial arrangement of interiors.

CAROLINGIAN Dynasty founded by Pepin the Short; mid-eighth to early tenth centuries, named after its finest king, Charles the Great (Charlemagne). Also refers to art, sculpture, etc of the time.

CARYATID Sculpted female figure used as a column.

CHAPTERHOUSE Room in a monastery or church where the clergy met daily to discuss business and administrative affairs.

CHEVET East end of a church.

CIRQUE Deep, steep-walled basin on a mountain usually comprising the upper end of a river valley.

CLASSICAL Architectural style incorporating Greek and Roman elements: pillars, domes, colonnades, etc. At its height in France in the seventeenth century and revived in the nineteenth century as Neoclassicism.

CLERESTORY Upper storey of a church, incorporating windows.

CRENELLATION Battlements along the top edge of a wall or tower.

CURTAIN WALL Straight upright medieval defensive wall.

DOLMEN Neolithic stone formation, frequently consisting of a henge.

FAUVISM Artistic school of early twentieth-century France, characterized by vivid colour.

FOLLY Overly ostentatious rural dwellings of seventeenth- to nineteenth-century aristocracy.

FRESCO Wall painting – durable through application to wet plaster.

FRIEZE Sculpted decorative band, typically along the upper or lower limit of a wall, and usually in low relief.

GOTHIC Architectural style of the thirteenth to sixteenth centuries, characterized by pointed arches, rib vaulting, flying buttresses, broad windowed surfaces and a general emphasis on verticality.

IMPRESSIONISM Late nineteenth-century French style of painting which emphasized the perception of objects through the effect of light, rather than shape.

MAJESTÉ Romanesque and early Gothic sculptures of Christ on the Cross (*majestat* in Catalan).

MEROVINGIAN Dynasty ruling France and parts of Germany from the sixth to mid-eighth centuries. Also refers to art, etc of the period.

MOZARAB Arab- and North African-influenced art and architectural style from Spain, brought to France around 900–1100 by Christians.

NARTHEX Entrance hall of a church.

NAVE Main body of a church.

NYMPHAEUM Roman or Greek shrine to a nymph, typically located at a fountainhead or spring.

OPPIDUM Pre-Roman hill-top settlement.

OPUS MIXTUM Roman building technique consisting of interspersed layers of stone and brick.

ORIENTALISM Study of Eastern and, particularly, Middle Eastern peoples from a Western and usually imperialistic and heavily romanticized perspective, from the late seventeenth to nineteenth centuries.

REFECTORY Dining room of a monastery.

RELIEF The three-dimensional quality of a sculpture; its depth.

RENAISSANCE Artistic/architectural movement developed in fifteenth-century Italy and imported to France in the sixteenth century.

RETABLE Altarpiece.

ROMANESQUE Early medieval architectural style distinguished by squat, rounded forms and naive sculpture.

ROOD SCREEN Barrier set in some churches between the area of the altar and choir and the rest of the nave (where the main congregation gathers).

SARCOPHAGUS Latin for "coffin," referring to carved stone tombs.

STUCCO Plaster used to embellish ceilings, etc.

TRANSEPT Transverse arms of a church.

TRIBUNE Apse containing a bishop's throne; a gallery or raised area in a church.

TROMPE L'OEIL Decorative technique popular in the Baroque period, wherein a two-dimensional painting gives the impression of being a three-dimensional object.

TUMULUS Neolithic burial mound, frequently concealing a dolmen.

TYMPANUM A sculpted panel above a church door.

VAULT An arched ceiling or roof.

VOUSSOIR Sculpted wedge-shaped stones in the arch over a church door.

Rough
Guides
advertiser

Rough Guides travel...

...music & reference

Index

and small print

A Rough Guide to Rough Guides

In the summer of 1981, Mark Ellingham, a recent graduate from Bristol University, was travelling round Greece and couldn't find a guidebook that really met his needs. On the one hand there were the student guides, insistent on saving every last cent, and on the other the heavyweight cultural tomes whose authors seemed to have spent more time in a research library than lounging away the afternoon at a taverna or on the beach.

In a bid to avoid getting a job, Mark and a small group of writers set about creating their own guidebook. It was a guide to Greece that aimed to combine a journalistic approach to description with a thoroughly practical approach to travellers' needs – a guide that would incorporate culture, history and contemporary insights with a critical edge, together with up-to-date, value-for-money listings. Back in London, Mark and the team finished their Rough Guide, as they called it, and talked Routledge into publishing the book.

That first *Rough Guide to Greece*, published in 1982, was a student scheme that became a publishing phenomenon. The immediate success of the book – with numerous reprints and a Thomas Cook prize shortlisting – spawned a series that rapidly covered dozens of destinations. Rough Guides had a ready market among low-budget backpackers, but soon also acquired a much broader and older readership that relished Rough Guides' wit and inquisitiveness as much as their enthusiastic, critical approach. Everyone wants value for money, but not at any price.

Rough Guides soon began supplementing the "rougher" information about hostels and low-budget listings with the kind of detail on restaurants and quality hotels that independent-minded visitors on any budget might expect, whether on business in New York or trekking in Thailand.

These days the guides – distributed worldwide by the Penguin group – offer recommendations from shoestring to luxury and cover more than 200 destinations around the globe, including almost every country in the Americas and Europe, more than half of Africa and most of Asia and Australasia. Our ever-growing team of authors and photographers is spread all over the world, particularly in Europe, the US and Australia.

In 1994, we published the *Rough Guide to World Music* and *Rough Guide to Classical Music*; and a year later the *Rough Guide to the Internet*. All three books have become benchmark titles in their fields – which encouraged us to expand into other areas of publishing, mainly around popular culture. Rough Guides now publish:

- Travel guides to more than 200 worldwide destinations
- Dictionary phrasebooks to 22 major languages
- History guides ranging from Ireland to Islam
- Maps printed on rip-proof and waterproof Polyart™ paper
- Music guides running the gamut from Opera to Elvis
- Restaurant guides to London, New York and San Francisco
- Reference books on topics as diverse as the Weather and Shakespeare
- Sports guides from Formula 1 to Man Utd
- Pop culture books from *Lord of the Rings* to Cult TV
- World Music CDs in association with World Music Network

Visit **www.roughguides.com** to see our latest publications.

Rough Guide credits

Text editors: Keith Drew, Helena Smith, Polly Thomas
Layout: Diana Jarvis
Cartography: Sam Kirby
Picture research: Eleanor Hill
Proofreader: Jennifer Speake

....

Editorial: **London** Martin Dunford, Kate Berens, Helena Smith, Claire Saunders, Geoff Howard, Ruth Blackmore, Gavin Thomas, Polly Thomas, Richard Lim, Lucy Ratcliffe, Clifton Wilkinson, Alison Murchie, Fran Sandham, Sally Schafer, Alexander Mark Rogers, Karoline Densley, Andy Turner, Ella O'Donnell, Keith Drew, Andrew Lockett, Joe Staines, Duncan Clark, Peter Buckley, Matthew Milton; **New York** Andrew Rosenberg, Richard Koss, Yuki Takagaki, Hunter Slaton, Chris Barsanti, Thomas Kohnstamm, Steven Horak
Design & Layout: **London** Dan May, Diana Jarvis; **Delhi** Madhulita Mohapatra, Umesh Aggarwal, Ajay Verma

Production: Julia Bovis, John McKay, Sophie Hewat
Cartography: **London** Maxine Repath, Ed Wright, Katie Lloyd-Jones, Miles Irving; **Delhi** Manish Chandra, Rajesh Chhibber, Jai Prakesh Mishra, Ashutosh Bharti, Rajesh Mishra, Animesh Pathak
Cover art direction: Louise Boulton
Picture research: Mark Thomas, Jj Luck
Online: **New York** Jennifer Gold, Cree Lawson, Suzanne Welles, Benjamin Ross; **Delhi** Manik Chauhan, Amarjyoti Dutta, Narender Kumar
Marketing & Publicity: **London** Richard Trillo, Niki Smith, David Wearn, Chloë Roberts, Demelza Dallow, Kristina Pentland; **New York** Geoff Colquitt, David Wechsler, Megan Kennedy
Finance: Gary Singh
Manager India: Punita Singh
Series editor: Mark Ellingham
PA to Managing Director: Julie Sanderson
Managing Director: Kevin Fitzgerald

Publishing information

This second edition published May 2004 by
Rough Guides Ltd,
80 Strand, London WC2R 0RL.
345 Hudson St, 4th Floor,
New York, NY 10014, USA.
Distributed by the Penguin Group
Penguin Books Ltd,
80 Strand, London WC2R 0RL
Penguin Putnam, Inc.
375 Hudson Street, NY 10014, USA
Penguin Books Australia Ltd,
487 Maroondah Highway, PO Box 257,
Ringwood, Victoria 3134, Australia
Penguin Books Canada Ltd,
10 Alcorn Avenue, Toronto, Ontario,
Canada M4V 1E4
Penguin Books (NZ) Ltd,
182–190 Wairau Road, Auckland 10,
New Zealand
Typeset in Bembo and Helvetica to an original design by Henry Iles.

Printed and bound in China

© Brian Catlos

No part of this book may be reproduced in any form without permission from the publisher except for the quotation of brief passages in reviews.

464pp includes index
A catalogue record for this book is available from the British Library

ISBN 1-84353-244-1

The publishers and authors have done their best to ensure the accuracy and currency of all the information in **The Rough Guide to Languedoc and Roussillon**, however, they can accept no responsibility for any loss, injury, or inconvenience sustained by any traveller as a result of information or advice contained in the guide.

3   5   7   9   8   6   4

Help us update

We've gone to a lot of effort to ensure that the second edition of **The Rough Guide to Languedoc and Roussillon** is accurate and up to date. However, things change – places get "discovered", opening hours are notoriously fickle, restaurants and rooms raise prices or lower standards. If you feel we've got it wrong or left something out, we'd like to know, and if you can remember the address, the price, the time, the phone number, so much the better.

We'll credit all contributions, and send a copy of the next edition (or any other Rough Guide if you prefer) for the best letters. Everyone who writes to us and isn't already a subscriber will receive a copy of our full-colour thrice-yearly newsletter. Please mark letters: "**Rough Guide Languedoc and Roussillon Update**" and send to: Rough Guides, 80 Strand, London WC2R 0RL, or Rough Guides, 4th Floor, 345 Hudson St, New York, NY 10014. Or send an email to **mail@roughguides.com**

Have your questions answered and tell others about your trip at **www.roughguides.atinfopop.com**

SMALL PRINT

Acknowledgements

Núria Silleras Fernández; Steve Hart; Claire Hill; Jan Dodd; Hélène Aznar; Gîtes de France; Ian Stewart; Lucy Ridout; Ross Velton (author of *The Naked Truth About Cap d'Agde* [Scarlett, Oh! Publishing]); Stanfords Books; Valèrie Crouineau (CDT Ariège); Myriam Journet-Filiquier (CDT Aude); Lysianne Boissy d'Anglas (CDT Gard); Yolaine Mouaikel (CDT l'Hérault); Christian Rivière (CDT Tarn); Laurence Herlin (CDT Pyrénées-Orientales).

Readers' letters

Thanks to all the readers who have taken the time and trouble to write in with comments and suggestions. Listed below are those who were especially helpful: apologies for any errors, ommissions or misspellings.

Ian and Annette Bowden; Loretta Buckley; Stephen Burke; Mike Burton; Edwin L. Coombes; Jillian Davidson; Mary Evans; Alison Fox & Ian Jones; G. D. K. Fraser; Harry Harrison; Dave Horan; David Hossack; Leslie Kirk; Charlotte and Hannah McCandlish; J. N. McCloskey; Sinead Matine; Sally Nortcliffe; Gail Orton; Graeme Russell; Mark Smith; Patricia and Patrick Stoner; Adrian Taylor; Annalisa Terrizzi; Alys Tomlinson; Ian Pearson; John L. Reid; Mel & Dyana Rodriguez; Mary Wood.

SMALL PRINT

Photo credits

SMALL PRINT

Index

Map entries are in colour

A

absolutism.............397–399
accommodation........36–41
African nature reserve...314
Agde 330
Aigues-Mortes 249–251
airlines
  in Australia and
    New Zealand 14
  in the UK.............................12
  in US and Canada 13
Albères, Les..........373–375
Albi
  accommodation 177
  arrival 177
  Cathédrale Ste-Cécile 178
  festivals............................174
  listings..............................181
  La Madeleine 180
  Musée de
    Toulouse-Lautrec...........178
  old town 179
  Palace de la Berbie..........178
  restaurants.......................180
  tourist office.....................177
Albi................................176
Albi and Haut
  Languedoc.........172–173
Albigensian Crusade
  ....78, 149, 392–395
Alet-les-Bains 134
Amaury, Armand 393
Ambialet.......................182
Anglès 204
Antoninus Pius..............221
Arfons 210
Argèles-Plage................376
Argèles-sur-Mer 376
Ariège valley,
  upper...................161–168
Ariège valley,
  upper...................142–143
Arles-sur-Tech...............373
Arques..........................137
Ascou-Pailhères............165
Aude valley, upper .132–140
Aulus-les-Bains 60
Autorail Touristique de
  Minervois....................323
autoroutes.....................31
autoroutes 16
Auzat............................161
Avignonet-Lauragais.....111
Axat..............................138

Ax-Bonascre 165
Ax-les-Thermes 165
Ayguesvives..................111

B

Balaruc-le-Vieux 284
banks 24
Banyuls-sur-Mer 382
Bassin de Thau..............283
Bassin du Lampy..........210
Bastide de Serou, La 156
bastides 183, 394
beaches 66
Beaucaire...............240–243
bed and breakfast...........38
Bédarieux......................334
beer...............................45
Bélesta..........................144
Bélibaste, Guillaume.....151
Béziers...................325–330
Béziers region 302–303
Béziers..........................326
bike rental 35
bikes 34
Bize-Minervois 323
Black Death 395
Black Prince...121, 319, 395
blanquette....................132
Blayes-les-Mines 184
boat rental....................114
boating...........................35
books 405–410
Bourbon, Armand de 399
Bourg-Madame..............368
Bousquet, Joë 130
Boussagues 335
Bouzigues 284
Bram 113
Brassac.........................203
breakfast 42
Bressens, Georges 281
Bronze Age 368
bullfighting 54, 218, 226,
  230, 305, 325, 342, 372
Burlats...........................197
bus
  in France.............................30
  from the UK and Ireland 17
Byrrh 357

C

Cabestany.....................353
Cabestany, the
  Master of....................111

Cabrières 289
caganer and cagatió.....348
Cagnac 184
Calvin, John.........202, 396
Calvinism 397
Cambous 297
camera film 66
Camino de Santiago.....246
Camisard
  rebellion 221, 398
Camon 150
camping 40
Camurac 145
Canal de la
  Robine 112, 307, 322
Canal de Rhône
  à Sète.........................242
Canal du Midi...35, 74, 111–
  114, 242, 318–325, 398
canal information 114
canals............................35
Canet-la-Plage..............353
Canigou Massif 361
Cap d'Agde 330, 331
Cap Découverte............184
Capcir 366
Capestang 323
Capitolo 391
car rental........................33
Carança gorge 364
Carcassonne
  accommodation 124
  arrival 121
  Cité...........................125–128
  Cité 126
  festivals............................121
  listings..............................131
  nightlife 130
  restaurants 130
  tourist office......................122
  Ville Basse.........................129
  Ville Basse 129
Carcassonne, Upper Aude
  and Ariège 120
Carcassonne: Cité 126
Carcassonne:
  Ville Basse..................129
Carlit Massif..........168, 369
Carmaux 183
Carte Intersite pass 132
Casals, Pau (Pablo) 358
Cascade des
  Anglaises....................362
cassoulet.......................107
Castelnaudary 107–110
Castelnau-de-Guers 287
Castelnau-de-Lévis.......181
Castelnou......................357
Castres 193–197
Castres 193

INDEX

Catalan 415–417
Cathar castles
  Arques.................................138
  Carcassonne.....................126
  Lastours 209
  Minerve..............................320
  Peyrepetuese....................355
  Puilaurens 356
  Quéribus 354
  Termes 316
  Villerouge-Termenès 316
Catharism 102, 146,
    ....149, 392–395
Caunes-Minervois........320
Causse-de-la-Selle 296
cave art 387
cave art, Pyrenean........163
caves
  l'Aguzou 138
  la Baume............................238
  Bédeilhac 164
  Canalettes........................360
  Clamouse...........................297
  Demoiselles 295
  Devèze 205
  Grandes Canalettes 360
  Labouiche 156
  Limousis.............................209
  Lombrives 164
  Mas d'Azil 152
  Niaux..................................164
  Préhistoire.........................360
  Vache 164
Celles 289
Cerbère 383
Cerdagne...............367–370
Céret 372
Cérou Valley..................186
Chagall, Marc.................372
Chalet des Cortalets.....362
chambres d'hôtes...........38
Channel Tunnel, the........17
Charlemagne 124,
    ....150, 296, 390
Château du Bosc...........182
Château du Candiac.....249
Château de Cassan 287
Château de Donezan 140
Châteaux de Lastours 209
Château de
    Roquevidal 104
Château de Soult-Berg..208
Château de St-Privat 238
Château de Villevieille...255
cheese 44
Chemin St-Jacques 246
children 64
circulades......................198
Cirque de Mourèze 289
Cirque de Navacelles....293
Clermont-l'Hérault 289
Col de Panissars...........371

Collias 238
Collioure 379–381
Colombiers 324
Colombiers, route des ..104
communists 290
Comte, Auguste...........271
Comus 145
Constantine the Great ..389
consulates
  in Montpellier 276
  in Toulouse........................99
contraceptives 66
Corbières, the 315–318
Cordes-sur-Ciel 186–188
costs 24
Côte Vermeille......375–383
course
  Camargaise........226, 249
Courtinales....................289
Couserans, the 157–161
Coustouges 374
credit cards....................26
crime 56
Cucagnan 355
cuisine, regional.............43
currency 25
cycling......................34, 55

Dame Carcas,
    legend of 124
Damiette 104
de Montfort, Simon.......393
Défilé de Pierre-Lys 138
denim 221
directory..........................66
disabled travellers..........61
Donezan, the.................140
Donezan, the 142–143
Dougues.......................370
Dourgne 107
Dreyfus, Alfred 195, 402
drinks 45–47
driving
  in France............................31
  from the UK and Ireland 17
  pedestrians 66
drugs..............................56
Dubout, Albert 278
Duilhac 355

Edict of Nantes 202,
    ....397, 400

Edward III......................319
electricity........................66
Elne 375
email 50
embassies abroad,
    French 18
emergencies 57
Enveitg 368
Err 368
Estagel 354
Étang Noir 370
Étang Vive.....................370
euro 25
Eurostar 15

F

Fanjeux 150
Fauvists.........................380
Fébus, Gaston 155
Fenouillèdes, the ..353–356
ferias 230
Ferrières 203
ferries 15
ferry routes.....................16
festivals 53
  in Albi and Haut
    Languedoc 174
  in Carcassonne and
    Ariège 122
  in Montpellier and
    around 264
  in Narbonne, Béziers and
    around 305
  in Nîmes and around 218
  in Roussillon 342
  in Toulouse and around 76
feudalism 390
fishing 66
flights
  from Australia and
    New Zealand 14
  from UK and Ireland 11
  from US and Canada.........12
Foix......................153–156
Foix 153
Fontfroide,
    monastery of 315
Font-Romeu..................367
food............................41–47
food glossary 422–429
football...........................53
Formiguères 366
Fort de Bellegarde 371
Fort de Brescou 331
Fort Lagarde 374
Fort Libéria....................360
Fougax-Barrineuf 144
Fraïsse-sur-Agout 204

François I 396
Franks 389
French Revolution.........399
Front National 404

G

Gaillac 188–190
Ganges 294
garrigues 215
gay travellers...................65
Gide, André..........234, 236
Gijou Valley
  Railway Trail 201
Gijounet 202
Giroussens....................102
gîtes d'étape 38
Gîtes de France
  offices 39
glossary 430
Gorges de l'Aude..........138
Gorges de Carança 364
Gorges de Clamoux......209
Gorges de la Frau 145
Gorges de Galamus......355
Gorges de l'Hérault.......296
Gorges d'Héric.............206
Gorges de Riabouto 159
Gorges du Sègre...........368
Gouffre de Cabrespine ..209
Grand Bassin 110
Grau d'Agde 332
Graulhet 191
Grotte de l'Aguzou........138
Grotte de la Baume 238
Grotte de Bédeilhac......164
Grottes des Canalettes..360
Grotte de Clamouse 297
Grotte des
  Demoiselles................295
Grotte de Devèze..........205
Grottes des Grandes
  Canalettes 360
Grotte de Labouiche.....156
Grottes de Limousis 209
Grotte de Lombrives.....165
Grotte du Mas d'Azil.....152
Grottes de la
  Préhistoire..................360
Grotte de la Vache 164
Gruissan.......................313
Gruissan-Plage 313
Guifré el Pelós 390
Guzet-Neige.................160

H

Haut Languedoc...172–173
Haut Languedoc &
  Montaigne
  Noire 200–201
**Haut Languedoc,
  Parc du** 198–206
Hautpoul 207
Hérault valley 289
Hérépian 334
hiking 35, 55
history 387–405
hitching 33
Homps 320
horse-riding....................55
hostels 39
hotels 36
Huguenots 198, 202, 396
Hundred Years'
  War.............121, 319, 395

I

Ille-sur-Têt....................357
Inquisition 102, 146, 394
insurance 23
Internet...........................50

J

Jaume I ..263, 349, 395, 415
Jaume II 263, 349
Jaurès, Jean ..183, 195, 401
Joan of Arc 396
jocs florals 150, 414

L

L'Hospitalet-près-
  l'Andorre 163
La Grande-Motte ..251, 277
La Preste......................374
La Salvetat-sur-
  Agout 203
Labastides 208
Labouiche 156
Labrugière 198
Lac des Bouillouses 370
Lac de Lauzas 204
Lac de la Ravière 204
Lac de St-Ferreol..........105

Lac des Sts-Peyres 204
Lac du Salagou.............289
Lacaune-les-Bains........199
Lacaze 202
Lagarde.........................150
Lagrasse 317
Lamalou-les-Bains........333
language 411–432
Languedoc Rouge 290
Lapradelle 356
Laroque.........................295
Latour-de-Carol 368
laundry 66
Lauragais 74
Lautrec..........................192
Lavaur 100
Lavelanet 144
Le Boulou......................371
Le-Bousquet 335
Le Grau-du-Roi 251–253
Le Mas de Tourelles......244
Le Pen, Jean-Marie 404
Le Perthus.....................371
Le Somail 321
Les Angles 366
lesbian travellers.............65
Lescure 182
Lézignan-Corbières.......321
Limoux 132–134
Lisle-sur-Tarn 190
Lló 368
Lodève 291–293
Lodève...........................292
Loubens-Lauragais.......104
Louis VIII 394
Louis XI 396
Louis XIV...............272, 398
Louis XV.........................399
Lunas 335
Luther, Martin........202, 396

M

magazines.......................51
Magdalenian period 387
Magrin, Château-
  Musée de 104
Maguelone 279
mail 47
Maillol, Aristide 372, 383
Mallorca
  kingdom of 263, 395
maps 21
maquis 290
Marseillaise, La 400
Martel, Charles 279
Mas d'Azil 152

Massat 159
Mazamet 207
menus 43
Mérens-les-Vals 167
Mèze 284
Michelade massacre 397
Mijanès 140
Minerve 320
Minervois region 320
minitel 50
Mirepoix 148
mobile phones 49
Molière 285
Monestiés 186
money 24
Mont Canigou 416
Mont Caroux 206
Mont St-Clair 280
Montagnac 287
Montagne Noire....207–211
Montaigne Noire....200–201
Montagnes d'Ax,
    Tour des 167
Montagnes de l'Arize ...160
Montaillou 145
Montesquieu-
    Lauragais 111
Montferrer 373
Montfort, Simon de............
    ....78, 149, 154, 329
Montgiscard 111
Mont-Louis 365
Montmorency, Henri
    de 78, 398
Montolieu 210
Montpellier............262–276
    accommodation 265
    airport 263
    Antigone 272
    arrival 263
    cafés, bars and clubs 275
    cathedral 271
    Champs de Mars 270
    festivals 264
    listings 276
    Musée Atger 271
    Musée Fabré 270
    Musée Languedocien 270
    nightlife 274
    old town 270
    place de la Comédie 269
    place du Peyrou 272
    restaurants 274
    tourist office 263
Montpellier 268–269
Montpellier
    and around 262
Monts de
    l'Espinouse 198, 206
Monts de Lacaune 198
Montségur 145, 394
motels 37

motorail 17
motorbike rental 33
Mouthoumet 316
Murat-sur-Vèbre 199
Musée-Parc La Plaine des
    Dinosaures 284

N

Napoleon 400
Narbonne 303–313
    accommodation 306
    archbishop's palace 307
    arrival 306
    Basilique de St-Paul 311
    Cathédral de St-Just et St-
        Pasteur 308
    festivals 305
    listings 313
    medieval neighbourhood ...310
    nightlife 312
    restaurants 311
    tourist office 306
Narbonne 304
Narbonne and
    around................302–303
naturism 331
Naurouze 112
newspapers 51
Niaux 164
Nîmes 219–232
    accommodation 222
    airport 222
    Arènes, Les 226
    arrival 222
    avant-garde architecture....229
    bars and cafés 231
    Carré d'Art 224
    Castellum Divisorum 228
    Cathédrale de Notre-Dame et
        St-Castors 224
    discount passes 224
    entertainment 229
    festivals 219, 230
    listings 232
    Maison Carrée 224
    Musée des Beaux-Arts 228
    Musée des Cultures
        Taurines 228
    Museum of Archeology and
        Natural History 225
    restaurants 230
    Temple of Diana 228
    Tour Magne, La 228
    tourist office....................222
Nîmes 220
Nîmes and
    around 216–217
Nissan-lez-Ensérune 324
Notre-Dame-de-la-
    Drèche 182
Nyer 364

O

Occitan 413–415
Octon 289
Odeillo 367
Olargues 206
Olonzac 320
opening hours 52
oppida 388
Oppidum d'Ensérune ...324
Orb valley..............333–335
Orbiel valley 209
organized tours 10
Orgues, Les 357
Oriège valley 166
Orlu 166

P

Palavas-les-Flots 278
Pamiers 151
**Parc du Haut
    Languedoc**........198–206
Pays de Cocagne 100
Pays de Sault........141–147
Pays de Sault 142–143
Perpignan...............341–352
    accommodation 345
    airport 344
    arrival 344
    Campo Santo 348
    Castillet, Le.....................347
    Cathédrale St-Jean 348
    discount passes 347
    festivals 342
    listings 351
    Loge de Mer 347
    Musée Rigaud 346
    new town 350
    nightlife 350
    Palais des Rois de
        Majorque 349
    place Arago 346
    restaurants 350
    tourist office 344
Perpignan 344
Perrier spring 247
pétanque 54
Petite Camargue ....
    ....247, 249, 253
Petrarch 263
Peyrepertuse 355
Pézenas................285–287
Pézenas........................286
Philip le Bel 395
phones 48–50
Pic Carlit 370
Pic de la Coquillade 334
Pic de Noire 209

Pic du Canigou 361–363
Pic Joffre 362
Pic Rouge de Bassiès ..160
Pic-St-Loup 297
Picasso, Pablo 372
Planès 365
Plateau des Lacs..203–205
police 57
Pont du Gard 237
Pont St-Nicholas 239
Port Bou 383
Port Camargue 251–253
Port-Lauragais 111
Port-Vendes 381
Porté-Puymorens 369
post 47
post offices 47
Pradelles-Cabardés 209
Prades 358
Prats-de-Molló 374
prehistory 387
Prise d'eau d'Alzeau 210
Protestantism 396
public holidays 53
Puichéric 319
Puilaurens 356
Puivert 141
Puylaurens 104
Puyvalador 366
Pyrénées 2000 367
Pyrénées-Orientales 339

Q

Quéribus 354
Quérigut 140
Quillan 137

R

Rabastens 190
Rabelais, François 263
Racine, Jean 234
racism 57
Racou, Le 376
radio 52
rafting 55
Ras de Carança 365
Raymond IV 393
Raymond VII 329
Réalmont 191
refuge huts 38
Remoulins 239
Rennes-le-Château 135
Resistance, the 290, 403

restaurants 42
Revel 105
Revocation of the Edict of
  Nantes 398
Revolution (1848) 401
Rhône–Sète canal 242
Richelieu, Cardinal ...78, 397
Rieux-Minervois 320
Riquet, Pierre-Paul........112
Romanesque 377
Romans, the 388
Roquebrun 333
Roquefixade 147
Rouffiac des Corbières ...55
Roussillon 340–341
rugby 53, 325

S

Saillagouse 363
St Bartholemew's Day
  massacre 397
St-Amans-Soult 208
St-André 377
St-Bauzille....................295
St-Féliu 357
St-Félix-Lauragais 105
St-Génis-des-
  Fontaines 379
St-Gilles.................245–247
St-Girons 157
St-Guilhem-le-Désert ..296
St-Hilaire (Ariège) 133
St-Hilaire (Gard) 299
St-Hippolyte-du-Fort ...256
St-Laurent-de-Cerdans..373
St-Lieux-lès-Lavaur 103
St-Lizier.......................158
St-Martin-de-Fenollar,
  chapel of 371
St-Martin-de-Londres ..297
St-Martin-du-Canigou,
  monastery of 362
St-Maurice-Navacelles 293
St-Michel de Grandmont,
  priory of 293
St-Michel-de-Cuxà 358
St-Papoul, abbey of 110
St-Paul-Cap-de-Joux ...104
St-Paul-de-Fenouillet....356
St-Pierre-de-Rhèdes 334
St-Pons-de-Thomières...205
St-Roman,
  monastery of 243
St-Salvy 197
St-Sulpice 103
Saissac 210

Salasc 289
Sallèles 322
Salses-le-Château 352
sand wine 251
Santa Coloma de
  Cabanes 377
Santa Maria Vilar 377
Saunière,
  Bérenguer de 136
Sauve 256
Seix 160
senior travellers 64
Sentier Cathare 141
Serrabone, priory of 357
Sète 280–283
Sète 281
Seuil de Naurouze 113
Sidorbe 197
Sigean 314
skiing 55, 165
Sommières 254
Sorèze 106
Sorgeat 167
Spanish Marches 390
sports 53–56
Stone Age 387
student accommodation..39
study in France 59
swimming pools 66

T

Tarascon 240, 244
Tarascon-sur-Ariège 161
Tarn 171
tauromachie ...54, 226, 264
Tautavel 354
Tech valley 370–375
telephones 48–50
television 51
Terassac 333
Termes 316
Têt Valley, lower ...356–361
Têt Valley, upper...363–367
Thoré valley 208
Thuès-Carança 364
Thuès-entre-Valls 365
Thuir 357
time zone 66
toilets 66
tolls 31
Toulouse 71–99
  Abattoirs, Les 91
  accommodation 80
  African quarter 83
  airport 78
  arrival 78
  cafés and bars 96

Capitole, the 82
cathedral 89
Cité de l'Espace 92
entertainment 97
festivals 76, 97
Foundation Bemberg 88
Hôtel d'Assézat 86
hôtels particuliers 85
Jacobins, Les 84
listings 98
Musée des Augustins 89
Musée Paul-Dupuy 89
museum passes 82
nightlife 96
Notre-Dame-de-la-
    Daurade.......................... 85
Port St-Saveur 92
restaurants 94
St-Cyprien 90
St-Pierre-des-Cuisines 84
St-Sernin, Basilique de 83
suburbs 92
tourist office 79
Toulouse 75
Toulouse and around 73
Toulouse-Lautrec,
    Henri............................179
tourist information 19
tourist offices abroad 19
Touzal Colomé 370
Train Jaune 364
trains
    Autrorail Touristique
        Minervois 323
    in France 28
    rail passes 29
    steam train 103
    Train Jaune 364
    from the UK and Ireland 15
travel agents
    in Australia and
        New Zealand 14
    in the UK 12
    in US and Canada 13

travellers' cheques 26
Treaty of the
    Pyrenees 344, 398
Trèbes 318
Trencavels 121
troubadours 391, 413

U

Usson 140
Uzès 233–237
Uzès 233

V

Vabre 202
Valéry, Paul ..271, 280, 284
Vallespir 370
Valmagne, abbey of 284
Valmanya 361
Vals 151
Vauban, Sébastian de..349,
    ...360, 365, 371, 374, 380
Vauvert 242, 247
vegetarians 41
Vernet-les-Bains 362
Vers 239
Via Domitia 225, 244,
    ....278, 371
Viane 202
Vicdessos 161
Vidourle valley.......254–257
Villefranche-de-
    Conflent 359
Villelongue, abbey of ...211
Villeneuve-lès-Béziers ..324

Villeneuve-Minervois 209
Villeneuvette 289
Villerouge-Termenès 316
Vindrac 188
Viollet-le-Duc,
    Eugéne 121, 128, 307
Vis valley 293
visas 18
Visigoths 389

W

walking 35
Wars of Religion 202,
    ....221, 254, 396
water 46
water-jousting 264, 282
watersports.....................56
waterways 35
websites 20
wine 45, 46
wine revolts 402
woad 100, 396
working in France 58
World War I 402
World War II 403

Y

youth hostels 39

Z

Zola, Emile 195

LC → WANBONN
10:36 9.55
1 VARL 10.34
17.46

Map symbols

maps are listed in the full index using coloured text

▬▬▬	Motorway	ⓣ	Tram stop
═══	Road	Ⓜ	Metro station
ⅢⅢⅢ	Steps	★	Bus stop
▬▬▬	Railway	⛨	Mountain refuge
▬▬▬	ATM Railway	🗼	Lighthouse
- - - - -	Footpath	⊙	Statue
— —	Ferry route	⊠—⊠	Gate
— — —	Chapter boundary	◠	Cave
—·—·—	International boundary	⚵	Waterfall
⧫	Point of interest	⋔	Spring
▲	Mountain peak	🅿	Parking
⋀	Mountain range	⊞	Hospital
⅔	Gorge/cliff face	ⓘ	Tourist office
✈	Airport	⊠	Post office
∴	Ruins	⛷	Skiing
♔	Castle	)(	Mountain pass
▲	Tower	▬	Building
♜	Fortress	⊞	Church
⌂	Abbey	░	Park
⌂	Monastery	⊞	Cemetery
‡	Church (regional maps)	⊟	Saltpan